VEDIC NUMEROLOGY

A Treatise on Hindu Astronomy

VEDIC NUMEROLOGY

A Treatise on Hindu Astronomy

Part - I

G. V. CHAUDHARY

Foreword to the First Edition
Padmabhushan Dr. N. N. Godbole
M.A., B.Sc., D.Phil., (Berlin), M.I.E.

Foreword to the Second Edition
Prof. Jayantakrishna Harikrishna Dave
Mahamahopadhyaya Vidyavachaspati

1997

Bharatiya Vidya Bhavan

Kulapati K. M. Munshi Marg,
Mumbai-400 007

First Edition : 1968
Second Edition : 1997

Price : Rs. 200/-

PRINTED IN INDIA

Printed at Photo Offset Printers. Ballimaran, Delhi-6

Published by S. Ramakrishnan, Executive Secretary,
Bharatiya Vidya Bhavan, Kulapati K. M. Munshi Marg, Mumbai-400 007

FOREWORD

In a typed volume of 440 pages (half fools'cap sheets) the author has fully explained all about astrology in Ancient Indian and has given a description of the various constellations of stars-on which the Science of Astrology is based. The volume is divided into eight chapters. The first chapter gives an account of the antiquity of the Science of Astrology. Chapters II, III and IV give an account of the movements of the Sun, the Moon and the Earth. Chapter V gives a number of tables pertaining to dates, latitudes and longitudes, etc. From these tables, the necessary calculations are to be made in framing the horoscopes.

Chapters VI and VII, as mentioned in his preface by the author, deal with his special contribution and cover about 200 pages. In these two chapters, the author has examined numerous horoscopes to prove the authenticity of his predictions regarding death and marriage. Chapter VIII is an appendix giving further information to help the calculations.

The Science of Astronomy is an exact science based on the location and movements of planets and stars which can be verified by actual observations. The part played by astrology, on the other hand, is based on certain empirical assumptions giving the influence of distant planets on lives of individuals on this earth which are to be verified by actual happenings in the lives of individuals — as predicted by horoscopes. In this regard, the results are to be confirmed by actual results. In chapters VI and VII the author has given number of cases of marriages and deaths as examined by him. He has based his observations and calculations on old Rig Vedic Mantras and Vedang Jyotish which he has studied carfeully. This part of the volume is of practical values and should be of interest to those who do not have much faith in the practical side of astrology. A critical study of these two chapters shows that in his examination of 37 horoscopes he has predicted the life period of different individuals which have come true. In chapter VII the author has studied the influence of planets on the marriage days of different men and women, 36 in number, which have verified his predictations. It should be remembered that in the life of an individual, marriage and death are events of outstanding importance. It may be observed that even if 50% of these predictions based on mathematical calculations were found to be correct the Science of Astrology deserves a careful study. Very often the correctness of the birth-date and time of birth are in doubt. In such cases, the astrologer cannot be held responsible for the inferences drawn. It is, therefore, necessary that both astronomers and astrologers should come together with an open mind and discuss the scientific aspects of the laws enunciated and the inferences to be drawn. As such, the laborious work done by the present author, single handed, is commendable and deserves encouragement at higher levels, It is obviously beyond the scope of a single individual to handle such a problem of great magnitude and importance.

I am happy to note that the author has consulted a number of specialists in astronomy and astrology and has got their approval and appreciation in writing to enable him to go ahead with his great literary work. These views he has included in the last few pages of his book.

"Udyog",
Purandare Colony, Poona-2   **N.N. Godbole**
3rd March 1966

FOREWORD TO THE SECOND EDITION

The first edition of "Vedic Numerology" by Shri G.V. Chaudhari was published by the Bharatiya Vidya Bhavan in the year 1968. As there is a persistent demand of this book and no copy is available in the market, the Bharatiya Vidya Bhavan is now bringing out its second edition.

Astronomy and Astrology, i.e. — Jyotisha, is a component part of Vedas and being their Anga, Vedic study cannot be complete without its study. Jyotisha is intended to be helpful to the individual in that it shows his limitations and defects and if one profits by its advice, he can be more composed and peaceful, not running after mirage. After reaching a certain height he must know when to get out. It should however be known that Jyotisha warns and inclines but never compels. Lagna is the most important part of the horoscope. It is the imaginary meeting place of heaven and earth in the eastren direction. It symbolizes the meeting point of light and darknoss when the sun rises in the east Lagna which symbolising one's soul is the Ansa of the Divine Infinity and it meets with darkness, i.e., enveloped by ignorance; and malefic planets in the Lagna mean darkness and ignorance and astrologers generally do not like their presence in the Lagna. in order to dispel this darkness, more labour and effort are naturally necessary. This darkness can be in matters worldly and/or spiritual. The situation can improve if the effort is made in the right direction as indicated by other favourite planetary positions and this depends upon how much evolved he is.

The author has made a synthesis of Vedic numerology, astronomy and astrology. Jyotisha is Tri-Skandha, i.e., has three branches - Hora, Ganita and Siddhanta. He has given original and daring interprtations of some of the Vedic mantras. Astronomers andAstrologers may or may not agree with his work, method or interpretations but their is some convincing merit about them and the industry, originality and consistency of the author deserve appreciation.

Jyotisha is a subject of study in M.A. Sanskrit in the universities. The deep knowledge of the Vedic Aryans in this absorbing subject needs further scrutiny. Late Swami Bharatitirthaji Sankaracharya of Puri has worked on the subject of Vedic mathematics. Yajna required the knowlcdge of Astronomy. The author has shown how Vedic numerology can help in predictions and casting of horoscopes. Many of the ideas of modern astronomy and astrology can be traced to the "Asya Vamasya" Sukta of Rigveda 1-164 of Dirghatamas. The Dina-Varsha-paddhati of predicting events from a processed horoscope which is mostly followed in the west - where one day represents one year - "is the same system in Vedanga Jyotisha which lagadha has indicated; and its fundamentals are in the Veda" says the author.

The author points out that Rig Veda 1-164 and certain passages in the Brahamanas need scrutiny and proper interpretation. The author has evolved an elaborate system of predicting the date of marriage and the date of death from the date, time and place of the birth. He has given many illustrations. Even if a sizeable percentage of such predictions came true, there is indeed great merit in this system.

Many of those who know this subject have appreciated the author's work and wish that further work and research in this field be undertaken.

Jayantakrishna Harikrishna Dave

Mahamahopadhyaya Vidyavachaspati

Hon. Director

Bharatiya Vidya Bhavan

Mumbai
Gandhi Jayanti,
October 2, 1996

PREFACE

The object of this book is to give a clear and concise view of the principal results of Astrology, and of the revolution which they have effected in Modern Thought. I do not pretend to discover fresh facts or propound new theories, but simply to discharge the humbler, though still useful, task of presenting what has become the common property of thinking minds, in popular shape, which may interest those who lack time and opportunity for studying the special subject of Astology in more complete and technical treatises.

I have endeavoured also to give unity to the subjects treated of, by connecting them with leading ideas, in the case of Astronomy (Science), that of the gradual progress from human standards to those of almost infinite space and duration, and the prevalence of law throughout the universe to the exclusion of supernatural interference; in the case of Thought, the barings of these discoveris on old Rig Vedic Mantras and Vedang Jyotisha, and on the practical conduct of life. The endeavour to show how much of religion can be saved from the ship wreck of theology has been the main object of the sixth and the seventh chapter.

The sixth and seventh chapters contain more of my own reflections on the important subjects discussed, and must stand or fall on its own merits rather than on authority. I can only say that I have endeavoured to treat these subjects in a reverential spirit, and that the conclusions arrived at are the result of a conscientio1 and dispassionate endeavour to arrive at "the truth the whole truth and nothing but the truth".

It is remarkable that in this country the rigour of original astronomical orientation was never loosened. It is unfortunate that departments of oriental learning in our universities ignored Jyotish-shashtra. But the ancient Hindu view of cosmology was surprisingly modern and was vastly daring in its depth and sweep. It took the great strides made by modern science to realise the comprehensive nature of achievements of the ancient Hindus.

General tendency of the Western scholars and Western-minded Indians is to underestimate the antiquity of Indian culture and to trace every great Indian achievements to ancient Greeks or Chaldeans. The West was baffled by the vast time-scale in which Indian thought and culture had crystallised, restricted as the West was by the Hebrew theoretic world-view and geological time-scale.

The great antiquity of Hindu astronomy was realised by clear thinkers like Viscount Cheiro, Count Bjrostjerne, Mons, Baily, concluded that the Hindu science was co-eval with the Hebrew scriptures.

The famous Western Numerologist late Viscount Cheiro who converted all the verses of Bhishmaparva from Mahabharata and maintained in his famous book "Cheiro's Numerology", for example, he had quoted conversion of the verses for no. 13 as follows :

Rohinim Pidayannesha Sthito Rajan Sanischara

Vyavrittam Lakshma Somasya Bhavishyati mahadbhayam.

Bhishma Parva, Chapter 2, verse 32 :

O King, the planet 'Sani' oppresses Rohini. The sign of the deer in the moon has shifted from its position. A great evil is foreboded by all this.

Alakshe Prabhaya Hinam Paurnamasimch Kartikim.

Chandro Bhudognivarnascha Padmavarne-Nabhastale.

Bhisma Parva, chapter 2 verse 23 :

Even in the night of the Kartika full moon, the moon having lost all its splendour become invisible (or looked like fire), the sky looking like red lotus.

In his first book Cheiro said, "We must not forget that it was the Hindus who discovered what is known as the precession of the Equinoxes, and in their calculation such an occurance takes place every 25,827 years. Our modern science, after labours of hundreds of years has simply proved them to be correct." (Cheiro Book of Numbers" page 19)

Elphinstone held that certain principles underlying the Hindus thought was only comprehended by the West in the last two centuries, contrary to the general European view.

The evolution of Indian astronomy is in three distinct stages—the Vedic period with its astronomical truths and cosmological revelations like Dirghatamasa, the Siddhantic period which crystallised the astronomical knowldge in the form of Siddhantas, and the Post Siddhantic period covering astronomers like Aryabhatta, Varahamihira, Bhaskaracharya.

Aryabhatta, long before Copernicus, held that the Earth moved round the Sun. The 'Aitareya Brahmana' pin-points the fact about the apparent rising and setting of the Sun. Saunaka gave the distance of the Sun from the earth surprisingly close to the modern estimate."Bhoutika

Sutras" speak of Sun's spots and their effects on solar radiation. Bhaskaracharya regards the earth as suspended in the space centuries before Newton. Dirghatamasa who wrote 'Asyavamasya' hymn—discovered the time and space—continuum, was incredibly modern, it is on periodically adjustable luni—solar side-real computation 5000 years before Einstein.

Many learned scholars who have seen the manuscript have welcomed it as an outstanding original contribution to the study of the classical Indian lores deserving the attention of the University students and the patronage of the State. I must mention her that the Government of Maharashtra has been pleased to sanction the sum of Rs. 8000/- (rupees eight thousand) as a grant-in-aid for the publication of the first volume. The Executive Council of the University of Poona has been pleased to sanction a grant of Rs. 500/- from their "Award of Publication Grant" for this book.

G. V. Chaudhary

CONTENTS

CHAPTER I

ANTIQUITY OF THE SCIENCE OF ASTROLOGY

That the antiquity of Indian Astrology is as remote as the Vedas is a fact which it is difficult to disprove. It forms one of the Angas of the Rigveda. The Jyotish-shastra, as mentioned in the Rigveda, consists of 52 verses only (Rigved 1-164—1 to 52). In fact the whole of the Jyotishshastra then consisted of observing the movements of the sun, the moon, the earth and their passage through the Nakshatras and assigning a certain significance to them and then made more applicable to mundane Astrology than to a judicial one.

The ancients wholly depended on the Nakshatras and their qualities. It must not be supposed that no mention is made in regard to signs of the zodiac in Rigveda as the Rashi had no existence then. The division of the Zodiac into twelve parts was known to the Hindus in those times, but then the twelve parts were then known by different names.

द्वादशार न हि तज्जराय वर्वतिचक्र परिद्यामृतस्य ।
आपुत्रा अग्ने मिथुनासो अत्र सप्तशतानि विंशतिश्च तस्थु: ॥

(The wheel of Samvatsara having twelve parts turns round, around the heavens. It knows no discontinuity and it bears 720 children in pairs, day and night). As the time went by, owing to the invasions of the Mohamedans and Greeks and their association with our people, their science got mixed up with ours and the present astrology as it is studied and practised is a combination of Grecian and Egyptian Astrology. I am not entering here into a discussion of claiming priority of the science for the Hindus. It is proved beyond doubt by late Sankar Balkrishna Dikshit in his "Bharatiya Jyotish Sastra". This claim and priority is further supported by "Sepharial" in his book "The Science of foreknowledge" in the chapter on Indian Astrology.

There are a number of methods suggested for the art of interpreting but the following are largely made use of by Indian and European Astrologers:

1. One day for one year (Dina Varsha Paddhati)
2. Solar Revolutions (Tajika Paddhati)
3. Transits (Gochara Paddhati)
4. Planetary Periods (Daśā Paddhati)

In system No. 1 which is exclusively followed by European Astrologers, the number of days after the birth corresponds to the number of years completed and the results are declared from the

positions of the planets on that day and the aspects they form between themselves and the positions of the planets at birth. The
same system is in Vedāṅga Jyotish which Lagadha has formed. But
the fundamentals are in the Rigveda.

In the Rigveda as well as in the Vedang Jyotisha a yuga of
five years

पंच संवत्सरमयं युगाध्यक्षं प्रजापति ।
दिनर्त्वयनमासांगं प्रणम्य शिरसा शुचि: ॥

or a Lustrum has been adopted for convenience of simple calculations. It says that the year begins on the first lunar day of the
bright half of the month Magha and ends by the end of the dark
half of Pausha.

प्रपद्येते श्रविष्ठादौ सूर्याचांद्रमसावुदक् ।
सार्पार्धे दक्षिणार्कस्तु माघश्रावणयो: सदा ॥ ६ ॥

When the sun and the moon are in the beginning of Dhanishtha, the
Uttarayana takes place and when they are in the half part of Sarpa
—Aslesha, the Dakshinayana takes place. Thus a lustrum the
winter and Summer Solstices are in the months of Magha and Shravana. In the clear statement above that the Udak-Ayana or winter
solstice took place in the beginning of the Dhanistha Nakshatra is
sufficient to arrive at the date of the Vedang Jyotisha from the pro-
cession of equinoxes and solstices. But before proceeding to in-
vestigate the implications arising out of these verses, we must first
realise that the Nakshatra system as mentioned here is due to equatorial nakshatra. It means not that the opening nakshatra of the
Zodiac is Dhanishta but at the time of the Lagadha the given nakshatra Dhanishta was near the meridian. The following verse
from the Rik-Recession reads (with reference to my statement)

श्रविष्ठाभ्यां गुणाभ्यस्तान् प्राग्विलग्नान् विनिर्दिशेत् ॥

Barhaspatya translates it as: "The eighth group of stars reckoned
from Shravishtha should be designated as the equatorial nakshatra".
The meaning of the प्राग्विलग्नान् is Lagna, the siderial time, the central portion near the meridian.

It is obvious that the largest difference in time between vernal
equinox and the equator is 23 solar days or in space 19 Lunar Nakshatras. The Barhaspatya said to add eight nakshatras in Dhanishta for the vernal equinox which commenced in Śatapatha Brahmana (vernal equinox was in Krittika nakshatra at the time of
Śatpatha Brahmana).

The Maharshi Lagadha knew the time factor, the difference
between solar time and siderial time. But late Shankar Balkrishna
Dixit said that the Vedang Jyotish did not know the Ayana Cha-

lana or difference in time between equator and vernal equinox per year. It is not true. The Vedang Jyotisha followed double nakshatra system that is one nakshatra for Ayanamasa and the other for the commencement of the Yuga. Jyotishacharya Varahamihira says the same in the following verse (on Shake 427) in regard to the period of Udhishthira

आसन्मवासु मुनयः शासति पृथ्वीं युधिष्ठिरे नृपतौ ।
षट्ब्दिकपंचचब्दि (२५२६) युतः शककालस्तस्य राज्ञश्च ॥

At the time of king Udhishthira the Saptarishi was in Magha nakshatra, 1900 years are gone from his Shake 427.

In old time, they were counting the difference of time from vernal equinox and equator in nakshatra, Saptarshi requires 100 years to go through one nakshatra from Dhruva nakshatra, and the opening nakshatra which they were taking into consideration was Moola nakshatra (Adhana nakshatra) now from Moola to Magha there are 1900 years and 2526 years given in the verse, that is the period of the Pandavas was before 4426 years if the Kaliyuga at the time of Varaha Mihira (Shake 427).

There the Late Shankar Balkrishna Dixit interprets in his book, that there is no motion to Saptarishi, so the whole period given by Varaha Mihira is wrong. No doubt that there is no motion to the Sun, yet we say, and we are counting daily motion of the sun, in the same way Varaha Mihira was counting the motion of the Saptarishi 100 years per nakshatra, that is approximately 20' per year.

The following verse of the Mantreshwara is corroborating the above statement:

रवि: स्फुटं तज्जननं यदासीत् तथाविधश्चेत् प्रतिवर्षमर्कः ।
आवृत्तयाँ सन्ति दशाब्दकानां मागक्रमात् तद्दिवसाः प्रकलह्प्याः ॥

The sun has given birth to the nakshatra and the sun requires 10 years to go through one nakshatra, years can be assumed as days. One day is equivalent to one year or one lunar nakshatra, or 1° of the sum, Saptarishi wants 100 years to go through one nakshatra that is one nakshatra is equivalent to one day or, 1° of the Sun. The verse in Rigveda reads the same पंचपादं पितरं द्वादशाकृति दिव आहुः परे अर्धे पुरीषिणं । अथेमे अन्य उपरे विचक्षणं सप्तचक्रं षळर आहुरर्पितम् ॥ Rik 1-164-12 five pentagon Angles contain 12 forms of the earth, five pentagon Angles of the six seasons contain in one pancha Samvatsara yuga five pentagon Angles of seven days contains one month, one day must be given to each pentagon Angle, and half of the 12 forms possessed rain water; some call him Sun and some call him father; it clearly shows to add one day more to the Angle of 72° that is

$72 \times 5 = 360$ and five days more of each Angle, and the twelve forms are of 365 days, Six seasons into five $= 30$ and one more season, that is 31 seasons means 62 months. Thus Lagadha has formed a yuga of five years which contains 62 Lunar months. We know we have to add $1°$ after 72 years a difference of equator and vernal equinox, when one day is equivalent to one year then 72 days are equivalent to 72 years, when we have to add $1°$ after 72 years naturally we have to add $1°$ in 72 days also.

With the above facts, it clearly shows that Maharishi Lagadha, Garga and Varahamihira were knowing the Ayana Chalana. They were counting Ayanachalana not by Degree but by nakshatra; so at the time of Vedang Jyotisha, Lagadha has shown Dhanishtha nakshatra as equatorial nakshatra as well as Ayanamsa Nakshatra. Here one nakshatra is equivalent to one day, that is, 23rd nakshatra Dhanishtha means 23 days or $23°$, this is what the difference of the equator and vernal equinox. So Lagadha had taken $23°$ Ayanamsa into consideration, not only this but Lagadhacharya fixed the Ayanamsa with motion to some extent. We will see later on how he arranged the fixed ayanamsa with motion to some extent but before that we must know Nakshatra system and their use.

सप्त युंजति रथमेकचक्रं एको अश्वो वहति सप्तनाम ।
त्रिनाभि चक्रं अजरं अनर्व्यं यत्रेमा विश्वाभुवनानि तस्थुः ॥

The seven Rishis or the days are in one, that is, one horse is known by both the names. The one wheeled chariot has three hubs namely Ashwini, Magha, and Moola, it never becomes old and is not loose (Rik 1-64-2).

साकं जानां सप्तथ माहुरेकजं षळिद्यमा ऋषयो देवजा इति ।
तेषामिष्टानि विहितानि धामशः स्थात्रे रेजन्ते विकृतानिरूपशः ॥

The Saptarishi and seven days week, as well as Six (degrees) seasons were born together, but the Saptarishi and Lords of seven days of week are twins and the six seasons were born separate; they move north south and are born of God; sacrifices pertaining to them are performed at the proper periods, (i.e. one day of week is 100 years of Saptarishi) and for him who presides, the auxiliary sacrifices continue in various forms, such as six seasons in one year, four weeks of seven days in a month and 100 years means one day of the Saptarishi. यभा $=$ Both the hemispheres. Rick 1-164-10 and 16

स्त्रियः सतीस्ताँ उमे पुंस आहुः पश्य दक्षणवान् नविचेतदन्धः
कविर्यः पुत्रः सई माचिकेत् यस्ता विजानात् सवितुष्णिपितासत् ॥

They say unto me that they (Ashwini, Magha and Moola) are males although they are females, the one who has eyes sees it (that the northern hemisphere of the sky means female nakshatra and the same nakshatra when they are of the southern hemisphere are males). The blind one does not understand it. A son who is talented understands this thus he who must be educationally old like his grandfather.

तिस्रो मातॄंस्त्रीन् पितॄन् विभ्रदेक: उर्ध्वस्तथौ नेमवग्लापयंति
मंत्रयंन्ते दिवो अमुष्य पृष्ठे विश्वविदं वाचम् विश्वमिन्वाम्। 1-164-10.

One supporting the (three Ashwini, Magha and Moola) mothers (Northern hemisphere) and (three Ashwini, Magha, Moola) fathers (Southern hemisphere) nakshatra stands on high, do not cause fatigue in him, on the surface of the heavens speak of him words being known by all and not reaching all.

चतुर्भि: साकं नवतिं च नामभि: चक्रं न वृत्तं व्यतीरंवीविपत्
बृहच्छरीरो विमिमान ऋक्वभि: युवाऽकुमार: प्रत्येत्याहवम्॥ 1-155-6.

God sets in motion the wheel of Samvatsar with 90 days (Horses) in groups of four in various ways (When one nakshatra means one year, then one part of the nakshatra means three months or 90° (days) four parts of the nakshatra means four groups of 90° (days). That is 21st March, 21st June, 21st September, 21st December, these four groups of 90° (days) make one year of 360° (365 days) and who is young not boy goes to any one who calls him.

With all above verses, we understand that from the period of Rigved our people were knowing the nakshatras, 12 parts of the Zodiac, the motion of the sun and moon, the Ayanachalana. (The retrogression of the vernal equinox), and the male and female nakshatras, the position of the sun on every 90°. Not only this but also they were knowing a fictitious sun, which neither shines nor warms, and were knowing that the earth requires certain period of time to go around the Sun (Rik 1-164-12) the following verse from Aitareya Brahman reads:

सवा एष न कदाचनास्तमेति नौदेति तं यदस्तमेतीति मन्यतेन्ह एव
तदंत मित्वाथात्मानं विपर्यस्यते रात्रीमेवावस्तात् कुरुतेह: परस्तादथ।
यदेव प्रातरूदेतीति मन्यंते रात्रेरेव तदंत मित्वाथात्मानं विपर्यस्यतेऽहरे
वावस्तात् कुरुते रात्रीं परस्तात् सवा एष न कदाचन निम्रोचति॥

The sun neither rises nor sets but the sunset means earth goes downwards from the opposite object sun, and vice versa.

With all these vedic conceptions Maharshi Lagadha has formed Puncha samvatsara yuga system, which gives us correct knowledge of time and the knowledge of numerology too.

वेदाहि यज्ञार्थमभिप्रबृत्ता: कालानुपूर्व्या विहिताश्च यज्ञा:।
तस्मादिदं कालविधानशास्त्रं यो ज्योतिषं वेद स वेदयज्ञान्॥ Ved. Jyo. 36.

He says that nakshatra Ashwni vibrates to the nakshatra Chitra on 180° and the value of the Chitra nakshatra is equal to that of Aswini if the full moon is in the Aswini nakshatra in the month Aswin then the full moon must be in Chitra on 180° of the Aswini in the month Chaitra. The first part of the Aswini nakshatra vibrates to the third part of the Chitra and both the nakshatras are of the Mars; then the value of both the nakshatras is the same but the first one will be a male nakshatra and the other will be a female nakshatra. The first will be in the Southern hemisphere of the sky and the second will be in the northern hemisphere of the sky. The first nakshatra rashi will be Mesha and the other nakshatra Rashi will be Thula? See the following chart for the nakshatra and their Lords as well as their Rashi; the lords of the Aswini, Magha, Moola are same, that is the characteristic value:

Mesha	*Simha*	*Dhanu*
Aswini 13°20'	Magha 13°20'	Moola 13°20' Kethu Mangal
Bharani 13°20'	Purva 13°20'	Purvashadha 13°20' Shukra Rahu
Krittika 3°20'	Uttara 3°20'	Uttarashadha 3°20' Ravi Guru

Vrishabha	*Kanya*	*Makara*
Krittika 10°	Uttara 10°	Uttarashadha 10° Ravi Guru
Rohini 13°20'	Hasta 13°20'	Shravana 13°20' Chandra Shani
Mriga 6° 40'	Chitra 6°40'	Dhanishtha 6°40' Kethu Mars

Mithuna	*Thula*	*Kumbha*
Mriga 6°40'	Chitra 6°40'	Dhanishtha 6°40' Kethu Mars
Aridra 13°20'	Swathi 13°20'	Shatataraka 13°20' Shukra Rahu
Punarvasu 10°	Vishakha 10°	Purva Bhadra 10° Guru Ravi

Karka	*Vrischhika*	*Meena*
Punarvasu 3°20'	Vishakha 3°20'	Purvabhadra 3°20' Guru Ravi
Pushya 13°20'	Anuradha 13°20'	Uttarabhadra 13°20' Shani Moon
Aslesha 13°20'	Jeshtha 13°20'	Revathi 13°20' Budha Chandra or Mars.

of the planet and the nakshatra is equivalent thus the numerical value of the Aswini, Magha and Moola is one. The following group of the nakshatra shows the numerical value:

Aswini	1	Magha	10	Moola 19 is one	
Bharani	2	Purva	11	Purvashadha 20 is two	
Krithika	3	Uttara	12	Uttarashadha 21 is three	
Rohini	4	Hasta	13	Shravana 22 is four	
Mriga	5	Chitra	14	Dhanishtha is five (23)	
Aridra	6	Swathi	15	Shatataraka 24 is six	
Punarvasu	7	Vishakha	16	Purvabhadrapada 25 is seven	
Pushya	8	Anuradha	17	Uttarabhadrapada 26 is Eight	
Aslesha	9	Jeshtha	18	Revathi 27 is nine	

You have seen the difference of 9 digits between the nakshatra but the value is the same. It is not changed, then the following

6

are the numbers in which we will add 9 digit to get numerical value.

1–10–19–28–37–46–55–64–73–82–91–100	= is one
2–11–20–29–38–47–56–65–74–83–92–101	= is two
3–12–21–30–39–48–57–66–75–84–93–102	= is three
4–13–22–31–40–49–58–67–76–85–94–103	= is four
5–14–23–32–41–50–59–68–77–86–95–104	= is five
6–15–24–33–42–51–60–69–78–87–96–105	= is six
7–16–25–34–43–52–61–70–79–88–97–106	= is seven
8–17–26–35–44–53–62–71–80–89–98–107	= is eight
9–18–27–36–45–54–63–72–81–90–99–108	= is nine

We know one nakshatra is equivalent to one year, it means one part of the nakshatra 3°20′ is equivalent to three months (90°, see Rik 1-55-6) and if we assume one nakshatra for one month then naturally one part of the nakshatra is a week, and one day for one nakshatra, then one part of the nakshatra is 6 hours time. It is known that the Indian time is in advance of Greenwich time by 5 hrs. and 30 mts. that is, we are in advance to one part of the nakshatra. Naturally one part of the Nakshatra means three months, seven days and six hours.

The opening star of our year is Aswini and the fullmoon takes place in Aswini nakshatra in the month of Aswin. Naturally the sun will be in Chitra nakshatra on 180° of the Aswini nakshatra. The first part of the Aswini nakshatra vibrates to the third part of the Chitra nakshatra which occurs in Tula Rashi. The commencement of the Sun in Thula according to English month is from the 14th of October. So we will add three months, seven days and six hours to the English month October to get the mutual time, 14th October to 14th of November one month, from 14th of November to 14th December two months, from 14th of December to 14th January three months. 14th day & 7 days=21st day of January.

The commencement of the Sun in Mesha according to English month is 14th of April; so we will go back for three months, seven days and six hours to get mutual time, 14th of April to 14th of March one month, from 14th of March to 14th of February two months, from 14th February to 14th January three months, 14th day + 7 days = 21st day of January. We adjusted the English months and Indian months to get mutual time.

On 14th of January Sun commences Makara Rashi, then put the Makara Rashi in Lagna and see the verse of Lagadha whether we are correct in his statement.

प्रपद्येते श्रविष्ठादौ सूर्या चांद्रमसावुदक् ।
सार्पार्द्धे दक्षिणार्कस्तु माघश्रावणयोः सदा ॥ ६ ॥

7

Northern-Hemisphere

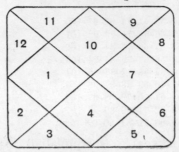

This is what the nature horoscope of the Northern hemisphere of the sky, then what is the nature horoscope of the Southern hemisphere. The following verse of the Rik Recension reads:—

श्रविष्ठाभ्यां गुणाभ्यस्तान्प्राग्विलग्नान् विनिदिशेत् ॥
सूर्यान्मासान् षळभ्यस्तान् विद्याच्चांद्रमसान् ऋतून् ॥

Rik Patha 19

Shravishtha should be designated as the equatorial nakshatra. The meaning of the प्राग्विलग्नान् is Lagna, or the central portion of the meridian, and the month of Makara Lagna should be reckoned as the solar month. Then on 180° of the solar month Karka Lagna should be reckoned as the Lunar month. Thus the nature horoscope of the Southern hemisphere will be like this

Southern -Hemisphere

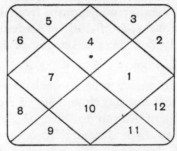

There are three nakshatras in the Karka Rashi, Punarvasu, Pushya, Aslesha which are male nakshatras in day time in lunar month. So also there are three nakshatras in Makara Rashi which are female nakshatras in night time in lunar month.

In northern hemisphere horoscope there are three nakshatras in Makara Rashi, Uttarashadha, Shravana, Dhanishtha which are female nakshatras in day time in the solar month, so also there are three nakshatras in Karka rashi which are male nakshatras in night time in the Solar month (see the verses Rik 1-164-10 and 16).

The Saptarishi requires 100 years to go through one nakshatra from the Dhruva, Aswini nakshatra is in the fourth house of the Solar month horoscope and in the tenth house of the Lunar horoscope; so put up 100, 1000, 1900, 2800, 3700 years in the fourth house of the solar horoscope and the tenth house of the Lunar horoscope. Chitra nakshatra is on 180° of the Aswini; then put the 500, 1400, 2300, 3200 years in the tenth house of the Solar horoscope and in the fourth house of the Lunar horoscope. See the following years in both the horoscopes.

Solar Horoscope   Lunar Horoscope

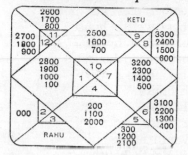
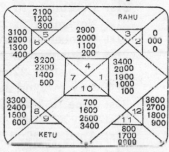

In solar horoscope in the fourth house there are 100, 1000, 1900, 2800, 3700, years, in the third house, 900, 1800, 2700, 3600 years, in the second house 800, 1700, 2600, 3500 years, in the Lagna house 700, 1600, 2500, 3400 and in the twelfth house there is Kethu the descending node of the moon.

In the eleventh house 600, 1500, 2400, 3300 years; in the tenth house 500, 1400, 2300, 3200 years; in the ninth house 400, 1300, 2200, 3100 years; in the eighth house 300, 1200, 2100, 3000 years; in the sixth house there is Rahu the ascending node of the moon. Fifth house is empty to fill up the difference between even and odd years. The fifth house of the Solar horoscope is equivalent to the eleventh house of the Lunar Horoscope. Now put up the years in the twelve houses exactly opposite to the years of Solar horoscope fourth house to Lunar horoscope tenth house.

The motion of the Rahu is anti-clockwise; naturally we will put the months in the houses of the solar horoscope anti-clockwise.

      21st January to 22nd December fourth house
      21st December to 22nd November third house
      21st November to 22nd October second house

21st October to 22nd September first house
21st September to 22nd August twelfth house
21st August to 22nd July eleventh house
21st July to 22nd June tenth house
21st June to 22nd May ninth house
21st May to 22nd April eighth house
21st April to 22nd March seventh house
21st March to 22nd February sixth house
21st February to 22nd January fifth house.

In this way we have set up the months in the Solar horoscope.

The motion of the Kethu is clock-wise; so we will put the months in the houses of the Lunar horoscope clock-wise like this,

21st January to 22nd December tenth house
21st December to 22nd November eleventh house
21st November to 22nd October twelfth house
21st October to 22nd September first house
21st September to 22nd August second house
21st August to 22nd July third house
21st July to 22nd June fourth house
21st June to 22nd May fifth house
21st May to 22nd April sixth house
21st April to 22nd March seventh house
21st March to 22nd February eighth house
21st February to 22nd January 9th house

In this way we have set up the months in the Lunar horoscope.

The nakshatras Krithika, Uttara, Uttarashadha are of the sun; naturally the months in which these nakshatras are commenced are of the sun. From 22nd December to 21st January the sun commences Dhanu Rashi; so from 22nd December to 21st January is a solar period or solar month see as following:

22nd December to 21st January	Solar month
22nd January to 21st February	Lunar month
22nd February to 21st March	Solar month
22nd March to 21st April	Lunar month
22nd April to 21st May	Solar month
22nd May to 21st June	Lunar month
22nd June to 21st July	Solar month
22nd July to 21st August	Lunar month
22nd August to 21st September	Solar month
22nd September to 21st October	Lunar month
22nd October to 21st November	Solar month
22nd November to 21st December	Lunar month

If the birth date of a native falls in the solar month, then give first preference to the sun; birth nakshatra may be any one out of 27 nakshatras. So also if the birth-date of the native falls in the Lunar month then give first preference to the moon; the birth date nakshatra may be any one out of 27 nakshatras. One nakshatra means one year; then one part of the nakshatra is three months, that is 22nd March is first part of the year, 22nd June is second part of the year, 22nd September is third part of the year, 22nd December is the fourth part of the year. The first part of the year vibrates to the third part of the year. The second part of the year vibrates to the fouth part of the year.

तृतीयानवमीं चैव पौर्णमासीं त्रयोदशीं ।
षष्ठीं च विषुवान् प्रोक्तो द्वादश्या च समं भनेत् ॥ ३३ ॥

Any one of the above tithi commences the equator day year-wise in the six groups of puncha samvatsara yuga. The practical application of the above tithis we will see later on.

The same rule is applicable to the date of months. The first part of the year vibrates to the third part of the date of the month. The second part of the year vibrates to the fourth part of the date of the month. The third part of the year vibrates to the first part of the date of the month. The fourth part of the year vibrates to the second part of the date of the month. See the parts of the date of the month as follows:—

1 (first part)		10 (second part)		19 (Third part)		28 (fourth part)	
2	–do–	11	–do–	20	–do–	29	–do–
3	–do–	12	–do–	21	–do–	30	–do–
4	–do–	13	–do–	22	–do–	31	–do–
5	–do–	14	–do–	23	–do–	14	–do–
6	–do–	15	–do–	24	–do–	15	–do–
7	–do–	16	–do–	25	–do–	16	–do–
8	–do–	17	–do–	26	–do–	17	–do–
9	–do–	18	–do–	27	–do–	18	–do–

The group of the above dates are the parts of the month, these parts of the dates are equivalent to the years. Naturally they vibrate one another on 180°. The following verse of the Mantreshwara reads—

रवि स्फुटं तज्जनने यदासीत् तथा विधश्चेत् प्रतिवर्षमर्कः ।
आवृत्तयः सन्ति दशाब्दकानां भागक्रमात् तद्दिवसाः प्रकल्प्या ॥

The years and the dates of the month are equivalent because the sun gave birth to the nakshatra; the cyclic order of the sun to reach each nakshatra is ten years. Ten years mean ten nakshatras and ten nakshatras mean ten days.

If we deduct the Saptarishi period and "the group of eight stars reckoned from Shravishtha, from any century we must get the equatorial nakshatra.

11

Saptarishi requires 100 years to go through one nakshatra from the Dhruva, add eight nakshtras the difference of vernal equinox that is 108 years. Then one nakshtra of the Saptarishi means 108 years. Actually one part of the nakshatra is—27 years. Now we will deduct Saptarishi Kala from the year 1963. Saptarishi has passed 1900 years, 19th nakshatra Moola add eight years, the difference of vernal equinox, that is 1908, 1963-1908=55, Deduct two parts of the Saptarishi nakshatra 55-54=1, that is Saptarishi passed Moola nakshatra, two parts and 1° of the Purvashadha. Aridra is on 180° of the Purvashadha, Aridra is number six nakshatra; that is sixth tithi is equatorial tithi on 22nd of December. From 22nd December to 21st January it is solar month. Naturally the sixth tithi of the equatorial day is in the bright half of the month Pausha. On 180° of the month of December there is March. So on 22nd March the tithi of equatorial day must be the 18th, the dark half of the month Phalgun. Example Number two: Deduct Saptarishi kala and the parts of their nakshatra from the year 1964. 1964-1908=56; 56-54=2. The Saptarishi passed the Moola nakshatra and 2° of Purvashadha. In even nakshatra of the year, Punarvasu nakshatra is on 180° of the Purvashadha. So Punarvasu is the equatorial nakshatra on 21st of the December. Deduct 12° from Purvashadha. Purvashadha (Moola) Jyeshta 18th tithi—15=3rd tithi of the dark half of the Margashirsha that is on 21st December 1964. 3rd tithi of the dark half of the Margashirsha and on 180° of the 3rd tithi of Margashirsha the 9th tithi of the bright half of Chitra on 22nd of the month March of 1964. Thus Vedang Jyothisha verse reads as follows:—

तृतीयां नवमीं चैव पौर्णमासीं त्रयोदशीं ।
षष्ठीं च विषुवान् प्रोक्तो द्वादश्या च समं भवेत् ॥

CHAPTER II

THE MOTION OF THE SUN

(The First Problem of the Three Bodies)

The most obvious classification of the heavenly bodies which we see with the naked eye is that of the Sun, the Moon and the Stars. But there is also this difference among the stars, while great mass of them preserve the same relative position on the celestial sphere year after year and century after century.

If we observe, night after night, the exact hour and minute at which a star passes any point by its diurnal revolution, we shall find that passage to occur some four minutes earlier every morning than it did the morning before. The starry sphere therefore revolves not in 24 hours but in 23 hours 56 minutes. In consequence, if we note its position at the same hour night after night, we shall find it to be farther and farther to the west. Let us take for example the brightest star Magha, the star in Simha rashi. If we watch it on the 22nd of October we shall find that it passes the meridian at 25th O'clock in the night. (1 a.m.) On November 22nd it passes at 23 hours and on 25th it is two hours west of the meridian. On the same day of August it passes at 05 20 before sun rises; so that it cannot be seen on the meridian at all because it will be soon lost entirely in the rays of the sun. This shows that during the months in question the sun has been approaching the star from the west and in August sun has approached so near it and it is no longer visible. In the same way, I have given in the above months the position of the stars which will be the same yearwise and month-wise.

Deduct Saptarishi kala and the parts of the nakshatra from the calendar year and the remainder nakshatra is equatorial year or we call it the siderial hour angle nakshatra. I made 3 groups of 27 nakshatras, that is from Aswini to Aslesha—first series; from Magha to Jyeshtha—second series; and from Moola to Revati—third series. One series of 9 nakshatras divided into three groups, that is, the first group of the first series is 1-2-3, the second group of the first series is 4-5-6, and the third group of the first series is 7-8-9 and so on like this.

The Sun moves in Dhanu from
14th of December to 13th January

The first group of the first series No. 1-2-3 put the nakshatra on the next part of the date of birth. If the birth date of the native is on the fourth part of the date of month then put the nakshatra on the second part of the date of month. The second group of the first series No. 4-5-6. See the nakshatra on 180° of the above nakshatra and put it on the date of birth (see the moon chart for each nakshatra and the nakshatra on 180°) for the sun.

The third group of the first series No. 7-8-9: See the nakshatra on 180° of the above nakshatra and deduct 12° from it and put it on the date of birth for the sun.

The first group of the second series No. 10-11-12: put the nakshatra on the prior part of the date of birth. If the birth date of the native is on the first part of the date of month, then put it on the third part of the date of month. Refer the birth date nakshatra for the Sun and put them on the date of birth for the Sun.

The second group of the second series 13-14-15; see the nakshatra on 180° of the above nakshatra and put them on the next part of the date of birth. See birth date nakshatra for the sun.

The third group of the second series No. 16-17-18: See the nakshatra on 180° of the above nakshatra, deduct 12° from each of the above nakshatra and put them on the next part of the date of birth. If the birth date of the native is on the fourth part of the date of month, then put it on the second part of the date of month. Refer birth date nakshatra for the sun.

The Sun commences Makara from
14th of January to 14th of February

The first group of the first series No. 1-2-3. Add 12° in each nakshatra and put them on the next part of the date of birth. If the birth date of the native is on the fourth part of the date of month then put them on the second part of the date of month. Refer the birth date nakshatra for the sun.

The second group of the first series No. 4-5-6: Put the nakshatra Rohini on the prior part of the date of birth. If the birth date of the native is on the first part then put the Rohini nakshatra on the third part of the date of month. See the nakshatra on 180° of the Mriga and Aridra and add 12° in each nakshatra and put them on the date of birth for the sun (see the moon chart for the above nakshatra). The third group of the first series No. 7-8-9. See the nakshatra on 180° of the above nakshatra and put them on the date of birth for the sun. The first group of the second series No. 10-11-12, add 12° in each of the above nakshatra and put them on the prior part of the date of birth. If the birth date of the native is on the first part of the date of month then put it on the third part of the date of the month. Refer the birth date nakshatra for the Sun.

The second group of the second series No. 13-14-15. See the nakshatra on 180° of the Chitra and Swathi nakshatras and add 12° in each nakshatra and put them on (see the moon chart for the above nakshatra) the next part of the date of birth. Put the Hasta nakshatra on the prior part of the date of birth. If the birth date of the native is on the first part, then put the nakshatra on the third part of the date of month. Refer birth date nakshatra for the Sun.

The third group of the second series No. 16-17-18. See the nakshatra on 180° of the above each nakshatra and put them on the next part of the date of birth. If the birth date of the native is on the fourth part of the date of month, then put the nakshatra on the second part of the date of month. Refer birth date nakshatra for the Sun.

The first group of the third series No. 19-20-21. See the nakshatra on 180° of the Moola and deduct 12° from it and put it on the next part of the date of birth. If the birth date of the native is on the fourth part of the date of month then put it on the second part of the date of month. Add 12° in Purvashadha and Uttarashadha and put them on the date of birth for the sun. The second group of the third series No. 22-23-24. See the nakshatra on 180° of the above nakshatra and add 12° in each nakshatra and put them on the prior part of the date of birth. If the birth date of the native is on the first part of the date of month then put it on the third part of the date of month. Refer the birth date nakshatra for the Sun. (See the Moon chart for the above nakshatra). The third group of the third series 25-26-27; See the nakshatra on 180° of the above nakshatra and add 12° in each nakshatra and put them on the prior part of the date of birth. If the birth date of the native is on the first part of the date of month then put them on the third part of the date of month. Refer birth date nakshatra for the Sun.

The Sun Commences Kumbha from
14th February to 14th of March

The first group of the first series No. 1-2-3. See the nakshatra on 180°of the above nakshatra and put them on the prior part of the date of birth. If the birth date of the native is on the first part of the date of month, then put it on the third part of the date of month. Refer the birth date nakshatra for the Sun.

The second group of the first series No. 4-5-6. Deduct 12° from each of the above nakshatra. See the nakshatra on 180° of the above nakshatra and put them on the prior part of the date of birth. If the birth date of the native is on the first part of the date of month then put it on the third part of the date of month. Refer birth date nakshatra for the Sun.

The third group of the first series No. 7-8-9. See the nakshatra on 180° of the above nakshatra and add 12° in each of the above nakshatra and put them on the date of birth for the Sun. The first group of the second series No. 10-11-12. See the nakshatra on 180° of the above nakshatra and put them on the prior part of the date of birth. Refer birth date nakshatra for the Sun. If the birth date of the native is on the first part of the date of month, then put the nakshatra on the third part of the date of month. The third group of the second series 13-14-15 see the above nakshatra on 180° of the above nakshatra. Deduct 12° from each of the above nakshatra and put them on the date of birth for the Sun.

The third group of the second series No. 16-17-18. Deduct 12° from each of the above nakshatra and put them on the prior part of the date of month. If the birth date of the native is on the first part of the date of month, then put the nakshatra on the third part of the date of month. Refer birth date nakshatra for the sun.

The first group of the third series No. 19-20-21. See the nakshatra on 180° of the above nakshatra and put them on the next part of the date of birth. If the birth date of the native is on the fourth part, then put the nakshatra on the second part of the date of month. Refer birth date nakshatra for the Sun.

The second group of the third series No. 22-23-24. Add 12° in Shravana and Dhanishtha nakshatra and put them on the date of birth for the Sun. See the nakshatra on 180° of the Shatataraka, and 12° in it and put it on the prior part of the date of birth (see the moon chart). Refer the birth date nakshatra for the Sun.

The third group of the first series No. 25-26-27. Deduct 12° from the Uttarabhadrapada and Revathi and put them on the date of birth for the sun.

The Sun commences Meena from
14th March to 14th April

The first group of the first series No. 1-2-3. See the nakshatra on 180° of the above nakshatra and add 12° in each of the above nakshatra and put them on the prior part of the date of birth. If the birth date of the native is on the first part of date of month then put the nakshatra on the third part of the date of month. Refer birth date nakshatra for the Sun.

The second group of the first series No. 4-5-6. See the nakshatra on 180° of the above nakshatra; deduct 12° from each of the above nakshatra and put them on the prior part of the date of birth. If the birth date of the native is on the first part of the date of month then put them on the third part of the date of month. Refer birth date nakshatra for the Sun.

The third group of the first series No. 7-8-9. Put the above nakshatra on the next part of the date of birth. If the birth date of the native is on the fourth part of the date of month then put the nakshatra on the second part of the date of month. Refer birth date nakshatra for the Sun.

The first group of the second series No. 10-11-12. See the nakshatra on 180° of the Uttara and put it on the date of birth for the Sun. Deduct 12° from Magha and Purva and put them on the next part of the date of birth. If the birth date of the native is on the fourth part of the date of month, then put the nakshatra on the second part of the date of month. Refer birth date nakshatra for the Sun.

The second group of the second series No. 13-14-15. See the nakshatra on 180° of the above nakshatra. Deduct 12° from each nakshatra and put them on date of birth for the Sun.

The third group of the second series No. 16-17-18. Put the above nakshatra on the prior part of the date of birth. If the birth date of the native is on the first part of the date of month then put the nakshatra on the third part of the date of month. Refer birth date nakshatra for the Sun.

The first group of the third series No. 19-20-21. Deduct 12° from the nakshatra Moola and Purvashadha and put them on the prior part of the date of birth. If the birth date of the native is on the first part of the date of month then put the nakshatra on the third part of the date of month. Refer birth date nakshatra for the Sun. See the nakshatra on 180° of the nakshatra Uttara-shadha and put it on the next part of the date of birth. Refer birth date nakshatra for the Sun.

The second group of the third series No. 22-23-24. Add 12° in Dhanishtha and Shatataraka nakshatra and put them on the date of birth for the Sun. Deduct 12° from Shravana nakshatra. See the nakshatra on 180° of the Purvashadha and put it on the next part of the date of birth. If the birth date of the native is on the fourth part of the date of month, then put the nakshatra on the second part of the date of month. Refer birth date nakshatra for the Sun.

The third group of the first series No. 25-26-27. Put the above nakshatra on the date of birth for the Sun.

17

The Sun commences Mesha from
14th April to 14th May

The first group of the first series No. 1-2-3. Put the above nakshatra on the date of birth for the Sun. The second group of the first series 4-5-6. See the nakshatra on 180° of the above nakshatra and put them on the prior part of the date of birth. If the birth date of the native is on the first part, then put the nakshatra on the third part of the date of month. Refer birth date for the Sun. The third group of the first series 7-8-9. See the nakshatra on 180° of the above nakshatra and deduct 12° from each of the above nakshatra and put them on the next part of the date of birth. (Refer Moon chart for the above nakshatra). If the birth date of the native is on the fourth part of the date of month, then put the nakshatra on the second part of the date of month. Refer birth date nakshatra for the Sun.

The first group of the second series No. 10-11-12. Put the above nakshatra on the next part of the date of birth. Refer the birth date nakshatra for the Sun.

The second group of the second series No. 13-14-15. (Refer moon chart). See the nakshatra on 180° of the above nakshatra and put them on the birth date for the Sun.

The third group of the second series No. 16-17-18. See the nakshatra on 180° of the above nakshatra and deduct 12° from each of the above nakshatra and put them on the date of birth for the Sun.

The first group of the third series No. 19-20-21. Put the above nakshatra on the next part of the date of birth. If the birth date of the native is on the fourth part then put the nakshatra on the second part of the date of month. Refer birth date nakshatra for the Sun.

The second group of the third series No. 22-23-24. (Refer moon chart). See the nakshatra on 180° of the above nakshatra and put them on the next part of the date of birth. If the birth date of the native is on the fourth part of the date of month, then put the nakshatra on the second part of the date of month. Refer birth date nakshatra for the Sun.

The third group of the first series No. 25-26-27. See the nakshatra on 180° of the above nakshatra. Deduct 12° from each of the above nakshatra and put them on the next part of the date of birth. If the birthdate of the native is on the fourth part of the date of month, then put the nakshatra on the second part of the date of month. Refer birth date nakshatra for the Sun.

The Sun commences Vrishabha from
14th of May to 14th June

The first group of the first series No. 1-2-3. Add 12° in each of the above nakshatra and put them on the date of birth for the Sun.

The second group of the first series No. 4-5-6. (Refer moon chart). See the nakshatra on 180° of the above nakshatra. Add 12° in each of the above nakshatra and put them on the prior part of the date of birth. If the birth date of the native is on the first part of the date of month, then put the nakshatra on the third part of the date of month. Refer birth date nakshatra for the Sun.

The third group of the first series No. 7-8-9. See the nakshatra on 180° of the above nakshatra and put them on the prior part of the date of birth. If the birth date of the native is on the first part of the date of month, then put the nakshatra on the third part of the date of month. Refer birth date nakshatra for the Sun.

The first group of the second series No. 10-11-12. Add 12° in each of the above nakshatra and put them on the next part of the date of birth. If the birth date of the native is on the fourth part of the date of month, then put the nakshatra on the second part of the date of month. Refer the birth date nakshatra for the Sun.

The second group of the second series No. 13-14-15. (Refer the moon chart). See the nakshatra on 180° of the above nakshatra. Add 12° in each nakshatra and put them on the date of birth for the Sun.

The third group of the second series No. 16-17-18. See the nakshatra on 180° of the above nakshatra. Deduct 12° from each nakshatra and put them on the date of birth for the Sun.

The first group of the third series No. 19-20-21. Add 12° in each of the above nakshatra and put them on the prior part of the date of birth. If the birth date of the native is on the first part of the date of month, then put them on the third part of the date of month. Refer the birth date nakshatra for the Sun.

The second group of the third series No. 22-23-24. (Refer the moon chart). See the nakshatra on 180° of the above nakshatra and add 12° in each nakshatra and put them on the next part of the date of birth. If the birth date of the native is on the fourth part of the date of month, then put the nakshatra on the second part of the date of month. Refer birth date nakshatra for the Sun.

The third group of the third series No. 25-26-27. See the nakshatra on 180° of the above nakshatra and put them on the next part of the date of birth. If the birth date of the native is on the fourth part of the date of month, then put the nakshatra

19

on the second part of the date of month. Refer the birth date nakshatra for the sun.

The Sun commences Mithuna from
14th June to 14th July

The first group of the first series No. 1-2-3. See the nakshatra on 180° of the above nakshatra and put them on the next part of the date of birth. If the birth date of the native is on the fourth part of the date of month, then put the nakshatra on the second part of the date of month. Refer the birth date nakshatra for the Sun.

The second group of the first series No. 4-5-6. Add 12° in Rohini and Mrig nakshatra and put them on the date of birth for the sun. See the nakshatra on 180° of the Aridra nakshatra and add 12° to it. Put it on the prior part of date of birth. If the birth date of the native is on the first part of the date of the month then put the nakshatra on the third part of the date of the month. Refer birth date nakshatra for the Sun.

The third group of the first series No. 7-8-9. Deduct 12° from each of the above nakshatra and put them on the date of birth for the sun. The first group of the second series No. 10-11-12. See the nakshatra on 180° of the above nakshatra and put them on the prior part of the date of birth. If the birth date of the native is on the first part of the date of month, then put the nakshatra on the third part of the date of month. Refer the birth date nakshatra for the Sun.

The second group of the second series No. 13-14-15. Add 12° in Hasta and Chitra nakshatra and put them on the next part of the date of birth. If the birth date of the native is on the fourth part of the date of month, then put the nakshatra on the second part of the date of month. See the nakshatra on 180° of the Swathi nakshatra and add 12° to it and put it on the date of birth for the Sun. (See the moon chart for Swathi).

The third group of the second series No. 16-17-18. See the nakshatra on 180° of the above nakshatra and add 12° in each of the above nakshatra and put them on the date of birth for the Sun.

The first group of the third series No. 19-20-21. See the nakshatra on 180° of the above nakshatra and put them on the date of birth for the sun.

The second group of the third series No. 22-23-24. Add 12° in Shravana and Dhanishta nakshatra and put them on the first part of the date of birth. If the birth date of the native is on the first part of the date of month, then put the nakshatra on

20

the third part of the date of month. Refer the birth date nakshatra for the Sun. See the nakshatra on 180° of the Shatataraka. Add 12° in it and put it on the next part of the date of birth. If the birth date of the native is on the fourth part of the date of month then put the nakshatra on the second part of the date of month. Refer birth date nakshatra for the Sun. (See the moon chart for the Shatataraka).

The third group of the third series No. 25-26-27. Deduct 12° from the above nakshatra and put them on the prior part of the date of birth. If the birth date of the native is on the first part of date of month, then put the nakshatra on the third part of the date of month. Refer birth date nakshatra for the Sun.

The Sun commences Karka from
14th July to 14 August

The first group of the first series No. 1-2-3. See the nakshatra on 180° of the above nakshatra and add 12° in each of the above nakshatra and put them on the next part of the date of birth. If the birth date of the native is on the fourth part of the date of month then put the nakshatra on the second part of the date of month. Refer the birth date nakshatra for the Sun.

The second group of the first series No. 4-5-6. See the nakshatra on 180° of the above nakshatra and put them on the next part of the date of birth. If the birth date of the native is on the fourth part of the date of month, then put the nakshatra on the second part of the date of month. Refer birth date nakshatra for the Sun (See the moon chart).

The third group of the first series No. 7-8-9. Put the above nakshatra on the date of birth for the Sun.

The first group of the second series No. 10-11-12. Deduct 12° from Magha and Purva nakshatra and put them on the date of birth for the Sun. See the nakshatra on 180° of the Uttara and put them on the date of birth for the sun. See the nakshatra on 180°. Put on the prior part of the date of birth. If the birth date is on the first part of the date of month, then put the nakshatra on the third part of the date of month. Refer birth date nakshatra for the Sun.

The second group of the second series No. 13-14-15. (Refer moon chart). See the nakshatra on 180° of the above nakshatra and put them on the prior part of the date of birth. If the birth date of the native is on the first part of the date of month, then put the nakshatra on the third part of the date of month. Refer birth date nakshatra for the Sun.

21

The third group of the second series No. 16-17-18. Put the above nakshatra on the next part of the date of birth. If the birth date of the native is on the fourth part, then put the nakshatra on the second part of the date of month. Refer birth date nakshatra for the Sun.

The first group of the third series No. 19-20-21. Deduct 12° from Moola and Purvashadha nakshatra and put them on the next part of the date of month. If the birth date of the native is on the fourth part of the date of month, then put the nakshatra on the second part of the date of month. See the nakshatra on 180° of Uttarashadha and put it on the date of birth for the Sun.

The second group of the third series No. 22-23-24. (Refer the moon chart). See the nakshatra on 180° of the above nakshatra and put them on the date of birth for the Sun.

The third group of the third series No. 25-26-27. Put the above nakshatra on the prior part of the date of birth. If the birth date of the native is on the first part of the date of month then put the nakshatra on the third part of the date of month. Refer birth date nakshatra for the Sun.

The Sun commences Simha from
14th of August to 14th of September

The first group of the first series No. 1-2-3. Put the above nakshatra on the prior part of the date of birth. If the birth date of the native is on the first part of the date of month, then put the nakshatra on the third part of the date of month. (Refer birth date nakshatra for the Sun).

The second group of the first series No. 4-5-6. (Refer the moon chart). See the nakshatra on 180° of the above nakshatra and put them on the next part of the date of birth. If the birth date of the native is on the fourth part of the date of month, then put the nakshatra on the second part of the date of month. (Refer birth date nakshatra for the Sun.)

The third group of the first series No. 7-8-9. See the nakshatra on 180° of the above nakshatra. Deduct 12° from each of the above nakshatra and put them on the next part of the date of birth. If the birth date of the native is on the fourth part of the date of month, then put them on the second part of the date of month. (Refer birth date nakshatra for the Sun).

The first group of the second series No. 10-11-12. Put the above nakshatra on the birth date for the Sun.

The second group of the second series No. 13-14-15. (Refer moon chart). See the nakshatra on 180° of the above nakshatra and put

22

them on the prior part of the date of birth. If the birth date of the native is on the first part of the date of month, then put the nakshatra on the third part of the date of month. (Refer birth date nakshatra for the Sun).

The third group of the second series No. 16-17-18. See the nakshatra on 180° of the above nakshatra. Deduct 12° from each of the above nakshatra and put them on the prior part of the date of birth. If the birth date of the native is on the first part of date of month. then put the nakshatra on the third part of the date of month. (Refer birth date nakshatra for the Sun).

The first group of the third series No. 19-20-21. Put the above nakshatra on the next part of the date of birth. If the birth date of the native is on the fourth part of the date of month, then put the nakshatra on the second part of the date of month. (Refer birth date nakshatra for the Sun).

The second group of the third series 22-23-24. (Refer the moon chart). See the nakshatra on 180° of the above nakshatra and put them on the date of birth for the sun.

The third group of the third series No. 25-26-27. See the nakshatra on the 180° of the above nakshatra. Deduct 12° from each of the above nakshatra and put them on the date of birth for the Sun.

The Sun commences Kanya from
14th September to 14th October

The first group of the first series No. 1-2-3. Add 12° in each of the above nakshatra. Put them on the prior part of the date of birth. If the birth date of the native is on the first part of the date of month, then put the nakshatra on the third part of the date of month. (Refer birth date nakshatra for the Sun).

The second group of the first series No. 4-5-6. (Refer moon chart). See the nakshatra on 180° of the above nakshatra and add 12° in each of the above nakshatra and put them on the next part of the date of birth. If the birth date of the native is on the fourth part of the date of month, then put the nakshatra on the second part of the date of month. Refer birth date nakshatra for the Sun.

The third group of the first series No. 7-8-9. See the nakshatra on 180° of the above nakshatra and put them on the next part of the date of birth. If the birth date of the native is on the fourth part of the date of month, then put the nakshatra on the second part of the date of month. Refer birth date nakshatra for the Sun.

23

The first group of the second series No. 10-11-12. Add 12° in each of the above nakshatra and put them on the date of birth for the Sun.

The second group of the second series No. 13-14-15. (Refer moon chart). See the nakshatra on 180° of the above nakshatra. Add 12° in each of the above nakshatra and put them on the prior part of the date of birth. If the birth date of the native is on the first part of the date of month, then put the nakshatra on the third part of the date of month. Refer birth date nakshatra for the Sun.

The third group of the second series No. 16-17-18. See the nakshatra on 180° of the above nakshatra. Put them on the prior part of the date of birth; if the birth date of the native is on the first part of the date of month, then put the nakshatra on the third part of the date of month. Refer birth date nakshatra for the Sun.

The first group of the third series No. 19-20-21. Add 12° in each nakshatra and put them on the next part of the date of birth. If the birth date of the native is on the fourth part, then put the nakshatra on the second part of the date of month. Refer birth date nakshatra for the Sun.

The second group of the third series No. 22-23-24. (Refer the Moon chart). See the nakshatra on 180° of the above nakshatra and add 12° in the each of the above nakshatra and put them on the date of birth for the Sun.

The third group of the third series No. 25-26-27. See the nakshatra on 180° of the above nakshatra and put them on the date of birth for the Sun.

The Sun commences in Thula from
14th October to 14th November

The first group of the first series No. 1-2-3. See the nakshatra on 180° of the above nakshatra and put them on the date of birth for the Sun.

The second group of the first series 4-5-6. (Refer moon chart) Deduct 12° from each of the above nakshatra. See the nakshatra on 180° of the above nakshatra and put them on the date of birth for the Sun.

The third group of the first series No. 7-8-9. Deduct 12° from each of the above nakshatra and put them on the prior part of the date of birth. If the date birth of the native is on the first part of the date of month, then put the nakshatra on the third part of the date of month. Refer birth date nakshatra for the Sun.

The first group of the second series No. 10-11-12. See the nakshatra on 180° of the above nakshatra and put them on the next part of the date of birth. If the birth date of the native is on the fourth part of the date of month, then put the nakshatra on the second part of the date of month. Refer the birth date nakshatra for the Sun.

The second group of the second series No. 13-14-15. (Refer Moon chart). Deduct 12° from each of the above nakshatra. See the nakshatra on 180° of the above nakshatra and put them on the next part of the date of birth. If the birth date of the native is on the fourth part of the date of month, then put the nakshatrra on the second part of the date of month. Refer birth date nakshatra for the Sun.

The third group of the third series No. 16-17-18. Deduct 12° from each of the above nakshatra and put them on the date of birth for the Sun.

The first group of the third series 19-20-21. See the nakshatra on 180° of the above nakshatra and put them on the prior part of the date of birth. If the birth date of the native is on the first part of the date of month, then put the nakshatra on the third part of the date of month. Refer birth date nakshatra for the Sun.

The second group of the third series No. 22-23-24. (Refer Moon chart). Deduct 12° from each of the above nakshatras. See the nakshatra on 180° of the above nakshatra and put them on the prior part of the date of birth. If the date of birth of the native is on the first part of the date of month, then put the nakshatra on the third part of the date of month. Refer birth date nakshatra for the Sun.

The third group of the third series No. 25-26-27. Deduct 12° from each of the above nakshatras. Put them on the next part of the date of birth. If the birth date of the native is on the fourth part of the date of month, then put the nakshatra on the second part of the date of month. Refer birth date nakshatra for the Sun.

The Sun commences in Vrischika from 14th of November to 14th of December

The first group of the first series No. 1-2-3. See the nakshatra on 180° of the above nakshatra and add 12° in each of the above nakshatras and put them on the date of birth for the Sun.

The second group of the first series No. 4-5-6. (Refer Moon chart). See the nakshatra on 180° of the above nakshatras and put them on the date of birth for the Sun.

The third group of the first series No. 7-8-9. Put the above nakshatra on the prior part of the date of birth. If the birth date of the native is on the first part of the date of month then put them on the third part of the date of month. Refer birth date nakshatra for the Sun.

The first group of the second series No. 10-11-12. See the nakshatra on 180° of the above nakshatra. Add 12° in each of the above nakshatra and put them on the next part of the date of birth. If the birth date of the native is on the fourth part, then put the nakshatra on the second part of the date of month. Refer the birth date nakshatra for the Sun.

The second group of the second series No. 13-14-15. (Refer Moon chart). Deduct 12° from each of the above nakshatras. See the nakshatra on 180° of the above nakshatra and put them on the next part of the date of birth. If the birth date of the native is on the fourth part of the date of month, then put the nakshatra on the second part of the date of month. Refer the birth date nakshatra for the Sun.

The third group of the second series No. 16-17-18. Put the above nakshatra on the date of birth for the Sun.

The first group of the third series No. 19-20-21. See the nakshatra on 180°of the above nakshatras. Add 12°in each of the above nakshatras and put them on the prior part of the date of birth. If the birth date of the native is on the first part of the date of month, then put the nakshatra on the third part of the date of month. Refer birth date nakshatra for the Sun.

The second group of the third series No. 22-23-24. (Refer the moon chart). See the nakshatra on 180° of the above nakshatra and put them on the prior part of the date of birth. If the date of birth of the native is on the first part of the date of month then put the nakshatra on the third part of the date of month. Refer the birth date nakshatra for the Sun.

The third group of the third series No. 25-26-27. Put the above nakshatra on the next part of the date of birth. If the birth date of the native is on the fourth part of the date of month, then put the nakshatra on the second part of the date of month. Refer the birth date nakshatra for the Sun.

NOTE: *Addition or subtraction of 12° in nakshatra means addition or subtraction of the difference between the star of equinoxes and the star of months.*

CHAPTER III

THE MOTION OF THE MOON

(The Second Problem of the Three Bodies)

Every one knows that the moon makes a revolution in the celestial sphere in about a month and during its revolution it presents a number of different phases known as 'New Moon', pratipada, dwitiya, tritiya and so on depending on its position relative to the Sun. A study of these phases during a single revolution will make it clear that the Moon is a globular dark body illuminated by the light of the Sun.

As the Sun makes a revolution around the celestial sphere in a year, so the moon makes a similar revolution among the stars in little more than 27 days. This motion can be seen on any clear night between first quarter and full moon, if the moon happens to be near a bright star. If the position of the moon in relation to the star be noted from hour to hour it will be found that she is constantly moving towards the east by a distance equal to her own diameter in an hour. The following night she will be found from 12° to 14° east of the star and will rise, cross the meridian and set from half an hour to an hour later than she did the preceding night. At the end of 27 days 8 hours she will be back in the same position among the stars in which she was first seen.

If, however, starting from one new-moon, we count forwards this period we shall find that the moon although she has returned to the same position among the stars, has not got back to new-moon again. The reason is that the Sun has moved forwards, in virtue of his apparent annual motion, so far that it will require more than two days for the Moon to overtake him. So although the moon really revolves around the earth in 27 days, the average interval between one new-moon and the next is 29½ days. The following verse reads the same:

तदर्धं दिनमागानां सदा पर्वणि पर्वणि ।
ऋतुशेषं तु तद्विद्यात् संख्याय सहपर्वणाम् ॥ २३ ॥

1830 solar days are in the yuga of five years; 60 solar months are in the yuga of five years; that is 120 fortnights, and in 120 fortnights there are 124 parvas. Then the fortnight of the moon will be $(\frac{1830}{124}) = 14\frac{94}{124}$ of solar days. 1830 solar days mean 120 solar fortnights i.e. $\frac{1830}{120} = 15\frac{1}{4}$ solar days, $15\frac{1}{4} - 14\frac{94}{124} = \frac{61}{124}$ is the diffe-

27

rence of the moon per parva to overtake the Sun. It clearly shows that there is a relation between the motions of the Sun and Moon which materially assisted the old astronomers in the prediction of the eclipses. We have said that the moon makes one revolution among the stars in about 27 1/3 days. Since the node of the orbit is constantly moving back to meet the moon, as it were, the sun after passing any node of the orbit, will reach the same node again in 346.6201 days. The relation between sun and moon is this: 242 returns of the moon to a node take very nearly the same time with 19 returns of the sun, the intervals being

> 242 returns of the moon to her node 6585.357

> 19 returns of the sun to moon's node 6585.780.

Consequently, if at any time the sun and the moon should start out together from a node, they would, at the end of 6585 days or 18 years and 11 days, be again found together very near the same node. During the interval, there would have been 223 new and full moons but none so near the node as this. The following verse reads the same:

रवि स्फुटं तज्जनने यदासीत् तथाविधश्चेत् प्रतिवर्षमर्कः ।
आवृत्तयः संति दशाब्दकानां भागक्रमात् तद्दिवसाः प्रकल्प्याः ॥

The sun gave birth to the nakshatra and the cycle of the sun is ten years to reach each number of the nakshatra. The ten years of the sun can be valued as ten days, then ten days of the sun are equal to nakshatras of the moon in number of days. The following verse from Aitereya Brahmana reads the position of the sun and moon on equinoxes or the equatorial day:

एकर्विंशमेतदहरूपर्यंति विषुवंतं मध्ये संवत्सरस्थैतेन वै देवा एकर्विंशेनादित्यं स्वर्गीय लोकायोदयछंत्स एष इत एकर्विंशस्तस्य दशावस्तादहानि दिवाकीर्त्यस्य भवंति दशपरस्तान् मध्य एष एकर्विंश उमयतो विराजि प्रतिष्ठितस्तस्मा देवांतरेमां लोकान्यन् न व्यथते तस्य वै देवा आदितस्य स्वर्गलिलोकादवपाताः दवि मयूस्तं त्रिमिः स्वर्गलोकैंखस्तात्प्रस्तात्प्रत्युत भ्नुवन् स्तोमा वैंत्रयः स्वर्गलोकास्तस्य पराचोतिपातादविभयूस्तं त्रिमिः स्वर्गलोकैं परस्तात्प्रत्यस्तभ्नुव स्तोमा वै त्रयः स्वर्गलोकास्तत्र योऽवस्तस्प्तदशा भवंति त्रयः परस्तान्मव्य एष एकर्विंशः Aitereya Brahmana 18-18

The central portion of the samvatsara on equatorial day, the celebration of the Ekvinshah takes place with the help of this Ekvinshah God placed the sun on heaven. This Ekvinshah is on the middle of the nakshatra (or day). This Ekvinshah stands on 19th nakshatra in between the Aswini and the Magha nakshatra, that is ten days difference back and forth of the 19th nakshatra. God has given support to this Ekvinshah by both sides (back and forth) by which the sun may not come down. The support of three Swargaloka (Aswini Magha, Moola means the stoma and the swargaloka);

among these three swargaloka 17 are at the first side and three
are at the second side. The Ekvinshah is in between. Add 17 in
19 nakshatras 19 plus $17 = 36 - 27 = 9$ the Aslesha nakshatra
which is of moon. Add 3 in 19th nakshatras 19 plus $3 = 22$ is the
swarga nakshatra which is of the moon. Thus Ekvinshah means
19 returns of the sun to moon's node Ketu. The following verses
from Atharva Jyotish strengthen the above statement of Ekvinshah:

जन्मसंपद्विपत्क्षेम्यः प्रत्वरः साधकस्तया ॥ १०३ ॥ नैधनोमित्रवर्गश्च परमो मैत्र
एवच ॥ दशमं जन्मनक्षत्रात्कर्मनक्षत्रमुच्यते एकोनविंशति चैव गर्भाधानकमुच्यते ॥ १०४ ॥
द्वितीयमेकादशं विशमेष संपत्करो गणः ॥ तृतीयमेकर्विश तु द्वादशंतु विपत्क रं ॥ १०५ ॥ क्षेम्यं
चतुर्थं द्वाविंशं तथा यच्च त्रयोदश प्रत्वर पंचमं विद्यालयोदिशं चतुर्वंश ॥ १०६ ॥ साधकं तु
चतुर्विशं षष्ठं पंचदशंच यत् नैधनं पंचर्विशंतु षोडशं सप्तमं तथा ॥ १०७ ॥ मैत्रे सप्तदशं
विद्यात्खड्विशमिति चाष्टमं सप्तविंशं परं मैत्रं नवमष्टादशं च यत् ॥ १०८ ॥

If we divide the whole circle of $360°$ into three divisions, we get a
division of $120°$. We shall take up for convenience the fixed rashis
for consideration. The first division of $120°$ commences with Aswini,
the second with Magha and the third with Moola. The beginning
of each division is a janma-naksatra i.e. the nakshatra in which
the moon is found at the time of birth. We shall suppose that
the moon is either in Aswini, Magha or Moola nakshatra. The
second nakshatra from the Janma-nakshatra is sampat, the third
part is vipat, the fourth kshemya, the fifth pratiwara, the sixth
sadhaka, the seventh naidhana, the eighth maitra and the ninth
parama maitra; thus the cycle repeats itself with the remaining two
divisions of $120°$ each; but, when the whole life cycle of $120°$ is
spread over $360°$ twentyseven nakshatras are to be included in it;
then the ninteenth nakshatra is Adhana, tenth is karma and first
is janma nakshatra. The nineteenth nakshatra is Adhana that is
the nakshatra of the conception of the earth. The tenth nakshatra
is Karma, the nakshatra of the Sun and the first nakshatra is Janma
nakshatra of the Moon. It clearly shows that the Adhana nakshatra
No. 19 gives us Janma nakshatra or the nakshatra of the Moon.

19th number is in the third part of the date, that is, the third
part of the Adhana year vibrates to the first part of the date and it
shows the position of the moon.

Assume that first day is first year or first date of the month.
Second day is tenth year or tenth date of the month. Third day
is nineteenth year or nineteenth date of the month. These are
what the three days of the celebration of Ekvinshah and this is
the meaning of the third eye of the Lord Shankara and Chakra

of the God or there are what the three brothers Brahman, Vishnu and Maheshwara.

अस्य वामस्य पलितस्य होतुः तस्य भ्राता मध्यमो अस्त्यश्नः ।
तृतीयो भ्राता घृतपृष्ठः अस्यात्रापश्यम् विश्पति सप्तपुत्रम् ॥

On the left hand of Vishnu (Adhana nakshatra) there is God Sun with his seven sons (Saptarishi); the middle brother of Vishnu is moon. Third brother is Brahma (Brahmanda means earth which is greater).

The uttrayana or the Northern hemisphere is on the left hand of Brahma (the four faces of Brahma means four equinoxes). The first equinox of the northern hemisphere is on the 22nd of December; naturally the sun is on the left hand in short Brahma the face of the earth. The sun and the moon are brothers and seven sons of sun are saptarishi which shows equator day position. Thus we can find the position of moon on Adhan year nakshatra. See the position of the moon, year and month-daywise.

No. 18   The second part of the Saptarishikal
West No. 0   The third part of the Saptarishikal

January October	Add 12° in Jyeshtha nakshatra; put Purvashadha on the first day of the month.
February November	Add 12° in Jyeshtha nakshatra. See Aridra nakshatra 180° of the Purvashadha and put it on the second day of the month.
March December	Deduct 12° from the Jyeshtha nakshatra and put the Vishakha on the first day of the month.
April	Add 12° in Jyeshtha and put Purvashadha on the third day of the month.
June	Add 12° in Jyeshtha nakshatra. See the nakshatra on 180° of the Purvashadha, put it on the first day of the month.
July	Add 12° in Jyeshtha nakshatra and put the Purvashadha on the second day of the month.
August	See the Rohini nakshatra on 180° of Jyeshtha and put it on the third day of the month.
September	Put the Jyeshtha nakshatra on the first day of the month.

West No. 1 Third part of the Saptarishikal.
No. 19 Second part of the Saptarishikal

January October	Add 12° in Aswini and put the Krittika nakshatra on the first day of the month.

February November	See the nakshatra Swati on 180° of the Aswini nakshatra and put it on the second day of the month.
March December	Add 12° in Aswini and see the nakshatra Vishakha on 180° of the Krittika, put it on the second day of the month.
April	Add 12° in Aswini and put the Krittika on the third day of the month.
May	Deduct 12° from Aswini. See nakshatra Hasta on 180° of the Uttarabhadrapada. Put it on the second day.
June	Deduct 12° from Aswini, put the Uttarabhadrapada on the second day of the month.
July	Add 12° in Aswini and put the Krittika on the second day of the month.
August	See the nakshatra Chitra on 180° of the Aswini and put it on the third day of the month.
September	Put the Aswini on the first day of the month.

East No. 2 The Third part of the Saptarishikal
No. 20 The second part of the Saptarishikal

January October	Deduct 12° of the Bharani. See the nakshatra Uttara on 180° of the Uttarabhadrapada, put it on the first day of the month.
February November	See the nakshatra Vishakha on 180° of Bharani and put it on the first day of the month.
March December	Add 12° in Bharani. See the nakshatra Jyeshtha on 180° of the Rohini and put it on the first day of the month.
April	Add 12° in Bharani and put the Rohini on the second day of the month.
May	Deduct 12° from Bharani. See the nakshatra Chitra on 180° of Revathi and put it on the third day of the month.
June	Put the nakshatra Bharani on the first day.
July	Add 12° in Bharani and put the Rohini on the first day.
August	See the nakshatra Vishakha on 180° of Bharani and put it on the second day of the month.
September	Put the Bharani nakshatra on the third day of the month.

East No. 4 The third part of the Saptarishikal
No. 22 The second part of the Saptarishikal

January October	Add 12° in Rohini and put Aridra on the first day of the month.
February November	Add 12° in Rohini. See the nakshatra Moola on 180° of Aridra and put it on the second day of the month.
March December	Add 12° in Rohini and put Moola on 180° of Aridra on the second day of the month.
April	Add 12° in Rohini and put Aridra on the first day of the month.
May	See the nakshatra Anuradha on 180° of Rohini and put it on the first day of the month.
April June	Deduct 12° from Rohini and put Bharani on the second day of the month.
July	Add 12° in Rohini and put Aridra on the second day of the month.
August	See the nakshatra Anuradha on 180° of Rohini and put it on the third day of the month.
September	Put Rohini on the first day of the month.

East No. 5 The third part of the Saptarishikal
No. 23 The second part of the Saptarishikal.

January October	Deduct 12° from Mriga. See the nakshatra Vishakha on 180° of Krittika and put it on first day of the month.
February November	See the nakshatra Moola on 180° of Mriga and put it on the first day of the month.
March December	Deduct 12° from Mriga and put Krittika on the second day of the month.
April	Add 12° in the Mriga nakshatra and put the Punarvasu nakshatra on first day of the month.
May	See the nakshatra Moola on 180° of Mriga and put it on the second day of the month.
June	Put Mriga nakshatra on the third day of the month.
July	Add 12° in Mriga nakshatra and put the Punarvasu nakshatra on the third day of the month.
August	Add 12° in Mriga nakshatra. See the Poorvashadha nakshatra on 180° of the Punarvasu

32

| | nakshatra and put it on the first day of the month. |
| September | Put the Mriga nakshatra on the second day of the month. |

East No. 6 The third part of the Saptarishikal
No. 24 The second part of the Saptarishikal

January October	Put the Aridra nakshatra on the first day of the month.
February November	Deduct 12° from Aridra and put Rohini on the third day of the month.
March December	Deduct 12° from Aridra and put the Rohini nakshatra on the third day of the month.
April	Add 12° in Aridra and put the Pushya nakshatra on the third day of the month.
May	See Poorvashadha on 180° of Aridra and put it on the first day of the month.
June	Put Aridra nakshatra on the second day of the month.
July	Add 12° in Aridra and put Pusya on the second day of the month.
August	Add 12° in Aridra nakshatra. See the Uttarashadha on 180° of Pushya and put it on the third day of the month.
September	Put Aridra on the first day of the month.

No. 7 The third part of the Saptarishikal
No. 25 The second part of the Saptarishikal

January October	Add 12° in Punarvasu nakshatra and put Aslesha on the first day of the month.
February November	Add 12° in Punarvasu. See the nakshatra Shravana on 180° of Aslesha and put it on the second day of the month.
March December	Add 12° in Punarvasu. See the nakshatra Shravana on the second day of the month.
April	Put the Punarvasu on the third day of the month.
May	See the nakshatra Purvashadha on 180° of Punarvasu and put it on the first day of the month.
June	Deduct 12° from the Punarvasu and put the Mriga nakshatra on the second day of the month.
July	Put the Punarvasu nakshatra on the second day of the month.

33

August	See the nakshatra Uttarashadha on 180° of Punarvasu and put it on the third day of the month.
September	Put the nakshatra Punarvasu on the first day of the month.

No. 8   The third part of the Saptarishikal
No. 26   The second part of the Saptarishikal

January October	Add 12° in Pushya nakshatra and put Magha on the third day of the month.
February November	Add 12° in Pushya nakshatra. See the nakshatra Dhanishtha on 180° of Magha and put it on the first day.
March December	Add 12° in Pushya nakshatra. See the nakshatra Dhanishtha on 180° of Magha and put it on the first day.
April	Put Pushya on the second day of the month.
May	Deduct 12° from Pushya nakshatra. See the nakshatra Purvashadha on 180° of Aridra and put it on the third day of the month.
June	Deduct 12° from Pushya and put Aridra on the first day of the month.
July	Put Pushya nakshatra on the first day of the month.
August	See the nakshatra Shravana on 180° of Pushya and put it on the second day of the month.
September	Deduct 12° from Pushya and put Aridra on the third day of the month.

No. 9   The third part of the Saptarishikal
No. 27   The second part of the Saptarishikal

January October	Add 12° in Aslesha and put Poorva nakshatra on the second day of the month.
February November	See the nakshatra Dhanishtha on 180° of Aslesha and put it on the third day of the month.
March December	Add 12° in Aslesha. See the nakshatra Shataraka on 180° of the Purva nakshatra and put it on the third day of the month.
April	Put Aslesha on the first day of the month.
May	Deduct 12° from Aslesha. See the nakshatra Uttarashadha on 180° of Punarvasu and put it on the second day of the month.

34

June	Deduct 12° from Aslesha. Put Punarvasu on the third day of the month.
July	Put Aslesha on the third day of the month.
August	See the nakshatra Shravana on 180° of the Aslesha nakshatra and put it on the first day of the month.
September	Deduct 12° from Aslesha and put Punarvasu on the second day of the month.

West Nô. 10 The third part of the Saptarishikal
No. 1 The first part of the Saptarishikal

January October	Add 12° in Magha nakshatra and put the Uttara nakshatra on the first day of the month.
February November	See the nakshatra Shatataraka on 180° of the Magha nakshatra and put it on the second day of the month.
March December	Add 12° in Magha. See the nakshatra Uttarabhadrapada on 180° of the Uttara and put it on the seond day.
April	Put the Magha nakshatra on the third day of the month.
May	See the nakshatra Dhanishtha on 180° of the Magha nakshatra and put it on the first day of the month.
June	Deduct 12° from Magha and put Pushya nakshatra on the second day of the month.
July	Put the Magha nakshatra on the second day of the month.
August	See the nakshatra on 180° of Magha and put it on the third day of the month.
September	Put the Magha nakshatra on the first day of the month.

East No. 11 The third part of the Saptarishikal
No. 2 The first part of the Saptarishikal

January October	Add 12° in Poorva nakshatra and put the Hasta nakshatra on the third day of the month.
February November	Add 12° in Poorva. See the Uttarabhadrapada on 180° of Hasta and put it on the first day of the month.
March December	Add 12° in Poorva. See Uttarabhadrapada on 180° of the Hasta nakshatra and put it on the first day of the month.

April	Put Poorva nakshatra on the second day of the month.
May	Deduct 12° from Poorva. See the nakshatra Dhanistha on 180° of the Aslesha and put it on the third day of the month.
June	Deduct 12° from Poorva and put Aslesha on the first day of the month.
July	Add 12° in Poorva and put it on the first day of the month.
August	See the nakshatra Shatataraka on 180° of Poorva and put it on the second day of the month.
September	Put the Poorva nakshatra on the third day of the month.

East No. 12 The third part of the Saptarishikal
No. 3 The first part of the saptarishikal

January October	Add 12° in Uttara nakshatra and put it on the second day of the month.
February November	See the nakshatra Uttarabhadrapada on 180° of the Uttara and put it on the third day of the month.
March December	Deduct 12° from Uttara and put the Magha nakshatra on the first day of the month.
April	Put Uttara nakshatra on the first day of the month.
May	Deduct 12° from Uttara. See the nakshatra Shatatarka on 180° of Magha and put it on the second day of the month.
June	Add 12° in Uttara. See the nakshatra Aswini 180° of Chitra and put it on the second day of the month.
July	Put the nakshatra Uttara on the third day of the month.
August	See the nakshatra Poorvabhadrapada on 180° of the Uttara nakshatra and put it on the first day of the month.
September	Put Uttara nakshatra on the second day of the month.

East No. 13 The third part of the Saptarishikal
No. 4 The first part of the Saptarishikal

| January October | Add 12° in Hasta nakshatra and put Swathi on the first day of the month. |

36

February November	See the nakshatra Revati on 180° of Hasta and put it on the second day of the month.
March December	put it on the second day of the month. See the nakshatra Revati on 180° of Hasta and
April	Put the Hasta nakshatra on the third day of the month.
May	Deduct 12° from Hasta. See the nakshatra Poorvabhadrapada on 180° of Poorva and put it on the first day of the month.
June	Deduct 12° from the Hasta nakshatra and put the Poorva on the second day of the month.
July	Put the Hasta nakshatra on the second day of the month.
August	Deduct 12° from Hasta. See the Poorvabhadrapada on 180° of Poorva and put it on the third day of the month.
September	Deduct 12° from Hasta and put the Poorva nakshatra on the first day of the month.

East No. 14 The Third part of the Saptarishikal
No. 5 The first part of the Saptarishikal

January October	Put the Chitra nakshatra on the third day of the month.
February November	See the nakshatra Revati on 180° of Chitra and put it on the first day of the month.
March December	Deduct 12° from Chitra. See the nakshatra Uttarabhadrapada on 180° of the Uttara nakshatra and put it on the first day of the month.
April	Add 12° in Chitra, put the Vishakha nakshatra on the second day of the month.
May	Deduct 12° from Citra. See the Uttarabhadrapada on 180° of Uttara and put it on the third day of the month.
June	Deduct 12° from Chitra and put the Uttara nakshatra on the first day of the month.
July	Add 12° in Chitra and put the Vishakha nakshatra on the first day of the month.
August	See the nakshatra Revati on 180° of Chitra and put it on the second day of the month.
September	Deduct 12° from Chitra and put the Uttara

37

West No. 15 The third part of the Saptarishikal
No. 6 The first part of the Saptarishikal

January October	Add 12° in Swati and put the Anuradha Nakshatra on the second day of the month.
February November	See the nakshatra Bharani on 180° of Swati and put it on the third day of the month.
March December	Deduct 12° from Swati and put the Hasta nakshatra on the first day of the month.
April	Add 12° to Swati and put the Anuradha nakshatra on the first day of the month.
May	Deduct 12° from Swati. See the nakshatra Revati on 180° of the Hasta and put it on the second day of the month.
June	Deduct 12° from Swati and put Hasta on the third day of the month.
July	Add 12° in Swati and put the Anuradha Nakshatra on the third day of the month.
August	See the nakshatra Aswini on 180° of the Swati Nakshatra and put it on the first day of the month.
September	Put the nakshatra Swati on the second day of the month.

West No. 16 The third part of the Saptarishikal
No. 7 The first part of the Saptarishikal

January October	Add 12° in Vishakha and put Jyeshtha on the first day of the month.
February November	See the nakshatra Bharani on 180° of Vishakha and put it on the second day of the month.
March December	See the nakshatra Krittika on 180° of Vishakha and put it on the second day of the month.
April	Put the Vishakha nakshatra on the third day of the month.
May	Deduct 12° from Vishakha. See Aswini on 180° of Chitra and put it on the first day of the month.
June	Deduct 12° from Vishakha and put Chitra on the second day of the month.
July	Put Vishakha on the second day of the month.
August	Deduct 12° from Vishakha. See Aswini on 180° of Chitra and put it on the third day of the month.

September	Deduct 12° from Vishakha and put Chitra on the first day of the month.
	West No. 17 The third part of the Saptarishikal No. 8 The first part of the Saptarishikal
January October	Add 12° in Anuradha and put Moola on the third day of the month.
February November	See the nakshatra Krittika on 180° of the Anuradha nakshatra and put it on the first day of the month.
March December	See the nakshatra Rohini on 180° of Anuradha and put it on the first day of the month.
April	Put Anuradha nakshatra on the second day of the month.
May	Add 12° in Anuradha and put the Moola nakshatra on the second day of the month.
June	Deduct 12° from Anuradha and put Swati on the first day of the month.
July	Put Anuradha on the first day of the month.
August	See the nakshatra Krittika on 180° of Anuradha and put it on the second day of the month.
September	Deduct 12° from Anuradha and put Swati on the third day of the month.
	West No. 18 The third part of the Saptarishikal No. 9 The first part of the Saptarishikal
January October	Add 12" in Jyeshtha and put the Poorvashadha nakshatra on the second day of the month.
February November	See the nakshatra Rohini on 180° of Jyeshtha and put it on the third day of the month.
March December	See the nakshatra Rohini on 180° of the Jyeshtha nakshatra. Add 12° in Rohini and put Aridra on the third day of the month.
April	Add 12° in Jyeshtha and put Purvashadha on the first day of the month.
May	See the nakshatra Rohini on 180° of Jeshtha and put it on the second day of the month.
June	Deduct 12° from Jyeshtha and put Vishakha on the third day of the month.
July	Put the Jyeshtha nakshatra on the third day of the month.

39

August	See the nakshatra Rohini on 180° of the Jyeshtha nakshatra and put it on the first day of the month.
September	Deduct 12° from Jyeshtha and put Vishakha nakshatra on the third day of the month.

West No. 19 The third part of the Saptarishikal
No. 10 The first part of the Saptarishikal

January October	Add 12° in Moola nakshatra and put the Uttarashadha nakshatra on the first day of the month.
February November	See the nakshatra Aridra on 180° of Moola and put it on the second day of the month.
March December	Add 12° in Moola. See the nakshatra Punarvasu on 180° of Uttarashadha and put it on the second day of the month.
April	Put the Moola nakshatra on the third day of the month.
May	See the Mriga nakshatra on 180° of Moola and put it on the first day of the month.
June	Deduct 12° from Moola and put Anuradha on the second day of the month.
July	Put Moola nakshatra on the second day of the month.
August	See the nakshatra Mriga on 180° of Moola and put it on the third day of the month.
September	Deduct 12° from Moola and put Anuradha on the first day of the month.

East No. 20 The third part of the Saptarishikal
No. 11 The first part of the Saptarishikal

January October	Add 12° in Purvashadha and put Shravana nakshatra on the third day of the month.
February November	See the nakshatra Punarvasu on 180° of Purvashadha and put it on the first day of the month.
March December	Add 12° in Purvashadha. See the nakshatra Pushya on 180° of Shravana and put it on the first day of the month.
April	Put the Purvashadha nakshatra on the second day of the month.
May	Add 12° in Purvashadha and put Shravana on the second day of the month.
June	Deduct 12° from Purvashadha and put Jyeshtha on the first day of the month.

July	Put the Purvashadha nakshatra on the first day of the month.
August	See Aridra on 180° of the Purvashadha nakshatra and put it on the second day of the month.
September	Deduct 12° from Purvashadha and put Jyeshtha on the third day of the month.

East No. 21 The third part of the Saptarishikal
No. 12 The first part of the Saptarishikal

January October	Put Uttarashadha on the second day of the month.
February November	See the nakshatra Punarvasu on 180° of the Uttarashadha and put it on the third day of the month.
March December	See the nakshatra Pushya on 180° of Uttarashadha and put it on the third day of the month.
April	Put Uttarashadha on the first day of the month.
May	Add 12° in Uttarashadha and put the Dhanishtha nakshatra on the first day of the month.
June	Add 12° in Uttarashadha. See the nakshatra Aslesha on 180° of Dhanishtha and put it on the second day of the month.
July	Put Uttarashadha on the second day of the month.
August	See the Punarvasu nakshatra on 180° of the Uttarashadha and put it on the first day of the month.
September	Deduct 12° from Uttarashadha and put Moola nakshatra on the second day of the month.

East No. 22 The third part of the Saptarishikal
No. 13 The first part of the Saptarishikal

January October	Put the Shravana nakshatra on the first day of the month.
February November	See the nakshatra Pushya on 180° of Shravana and put it on the second day of the month.
March December	Add 12° in Shravana. See the Magha nakshatra on 180° of Shatataraka and put it on the second day of the month.
April	Put the Shravana nakshatra on the third day.

May	Add 12° in Shravana and put Shatataraka on the third day of the month.
June	Deduct 12° from Shravana and put Purvashadha on the second day of the month.
July	Put Shravana on the second day of the month.
August	See the nakshatra Pushya on 180° of Shravana and put it on the third day of the month.
September	Deduct 12° from Shravana and put the Purvabhadrapada nakshatra on the first day of the month.

East No. 23 The third part of the Saptarishikal
No. 14 The first part of the Saptarishikal

January October	Add 12° in Dhanishtha and put Purvabhadrapada on the third day of the month.
February November	See the nakshatra Magha on 180° of Dhanishtha and put it on the first day of the month.
March December	Add 12° in Dhanishtha. See the Purva nakshatra on 180° of Purvabhadrapada and put it on the first day of the month.
April	Put Dhanishtha on the second day of the month.
May	Add 12° in Dhanishtha and put Purvabhadrapada on the second day of the month.
June	Add 12° in Dhanishtha. See the nakshatra Uttara on 180° of Purvabhadrapada and put it on the first day of the month.
July	Put Dhanishtha on the first day of the month.
August	See the Aslesha nakshatra on 180° of Dhanishtha and put it on the second day of the month.
September	Add 12° in Dhanishtha. See the nakshatra Uttara on 180° of Purvabhadrapada and put in the second day.

West No. 24 The third part of the Saptarishikal
No. 15 The first part of the Saptarishikal

January October	Put the nakshatra Shatataraka on the first day of the month.
February November	See the nakshatra Magha on 180° of Shatataraka and put it on the third day of the month.

March December	See the nakshatra Purva on 180° of Shatataraka and put it on the third day of the month.
April	Put Shatataraka on the first day of the month.
May	Add 12° in Shatataraka. See the nakshatra Uttarabhadrapada and put it on the first day of the month.
June	Add 12° to Shatataraka. See the nakshatra Uttara on 180° of Uttarabhadrapada and put it on the second day of the month.
July	Put Shatataraka on the third day of the month.
August	See the nakshatra Magha on 180° of Shatataraka and put it on the first day of the month.
September	Deduct 12° from the Shatataraka nakshatra and put it on the second day of the month.

West No. 25 The third part of the Saptarishikal
No. 16 The first part of the Saptarishikal

January October	Put the Purvabhadrapada on the first day of the month.
February November	See the nakshatra Purva on 180° of Purvabhadra and put it on the second day of the month.
March December	See the nakshatra Uttara on 180° of Purvabhadrapada and put it on the second day of the month.
April	Put Purvabhadrapada on the third day of the month.
May	Add 12° in Purvabhadrapada and put it on the third day of the month.
June	Add 12° in Purvabhadrapada. See the nakshatra Hasta on 180° of Revati and put it on the first day of the month.
July	Put Purvabhadrapada on the second day of the month.
August	Deduct 12° from Purvabhadrapada and put Dhanishtha on the first day of the month.
September	Deduct 12° from Uttarabhadrapada and put Shatataraka on the third day of the month.

West No. 26 The third part of the Saptarishikal
No. 17 The first part of the Saptarishikal

January October	Put Uttarabhadrapada on the third day of the month.
February November	See the nakshatra Uttara on 180° of Uttarabhadrapada and put it on the first day of the month.
March December	See the nakshatra Hasta on 180° of Uttarabhadrapada and put it on the first day of the month.
April	Put Uttarabhadrapada on the second day of the month.
May	Add 12° in Uttarabhadrapada and put Aswini on the second day of the month.
June	Deduct 12° from Uttarabhadrapada and put Shatataraka on the first day of the month.
July	Put Uttarabhadrapada on the first day of the month.
August	See the nakshatra Uttara on 180° of Uttarabhadrapada and put it on the second day of the month.
September	Deduct 12° from Uttarabhadrapada and put the Shatataraka on the third day of the month.

West No. 27 The third part of the Saptarishikal
No. 18 The first part of the Saptarishikal

January October	Add 12° in Revati and put Bharani on the second day of the month.
February November	See the nakshatra Hasta on 180° of Revati and put it on the third day of the month.
March December	See the nakshatra Chitra on 180° of Revati and put on the third day of the month.
April	Put the Revati nakshatra on the first day of the month.
May	Deduct 12° from Revati. See the nakshatra Poorva on 180° of the Purvabhadrapada nakshatra and put it on the second day of the month.
June	Deduct 12° from Revati and put Uttarabhadrapada on the third day of the month.
July	Put Revati on the third day of the month.

August	Deduct 12° from the Revati nakshatra. See the nakshatra Uttara on 180° of Purvabhadrapada and put it on the first day of the month.
September	Deduct 12° from Revati and put Purvabhadrapada on the second day of the month.

West No. 1 The fourth part of the Saptarishikal
No. 19 The third part of the Saptarishikal

January October	Add 12° in Aswini and put Krittika on the first day of the month.
February November	See the nakshatra Chitra on 180° of Aswini and put it on the second day of the month.
March December	See the nakshatra Swati on 180° of Aswini and put it on the second day of the month.
April	Put Aswini on the third day of the month.
May	Add 12° in Aswini and put Krittika on the third day of the month.
June	See Swati on 180° of Aswini and put it on the first day of the month.
July	Put Aswini on the second day of the month.
August	Deduct 12° from Aswini. See the nakshatra Hasta on 180° of Uttarabhadrapada and put it on the third day of the month.
September	Deduct 12° from Aswini and put Uttarabhadrapada on the first day of the month.

East No. 2 The fourth part of the Saptarishikal
No. 20 The third part of the Saptarishikal

January October	Put Bharani nakshatra on the third day of the month.
February November	See the nakshatra Swati on 180° of Bharani and put it on the first day of the month.
March December	See the nakshatra Vishakha on 180° of Bharani and put it on the first day of the month.
April	Put the nakshatra Bharani on the second day of the month.
May	Add 12° in Bharani and put the Rohini nakshatra on the second day of the month.
June	See the nakshatra Vishakha on 180° of Bharani and put it on the third day of the month.
July	Put Bharani on the first day of the month.

August	Deduct 12° from Bharani. See the nakshatra Chitra on 180° of Revathi and put it on the second day of the month.
September	Deduct 12° from Bharani and put Revati on the third day of the month.

East No. 3 The fourth part of the Saptarishikal
No. 21 The third part of the Saptarishikal

January October	Put Krittika nakshatra on the second day of the month. Refer birth date for the moon.
February November	See the nakshatra Vishakha on 180° of Krittika and put it on the third day of the month.
March December	See the nakshatra on 180° of Krittika and put it on the third day of the month.
April	Put Krittika nakshatra on the first day of the month.
May	Deduct 12° from Krittika. See the nakshatra Swati on 180° of Aswini and put it on the second day of the month. Refer birth-date nakshatra to moon.
June	Add 12° in Krittika. See the nakshatra Jyeshtha on 180° of Mriga and put it on the second day of the month.
July	Put Krittika on the third day of the month.
August	See the nakshtra Vishakha on 180° of Krittika and put it on the first day of the month.
September	Deduct 12° from Krittika and put Aswini on the second day of the month.

East No. 4 The fourth part of the Saptarishikal
No. 22 The third part of the Saptarishikal

January October	Add 12° in Rohini and put Aridra on the first day of the month.
February November	See the nakshatra Anuradha on 180° of Rohini and put it on the second day of the month.
March December	See the nakshatra Jyeshtha on 180° of Rohini and put it on the second day of the month.
April	Put Rohini nakshatra on the third day of the month.
May	Add 12° in Rohini and put Aridra on the third day of the month.
June	Add 12° in Rohini. See the nakshatra Moola on 180° of Aridra and put it on the first day.
July	Put the Rohini nakshatra on the second day of the month.

46

August	Put the nakshatra Anuradha on the 180° of Rohini on the third day of the month.
September	Deduct 12° from the Rohini nakshatra and put Bharani on the first day of the month.

East No. 5 The fourth part of the Saptarishikal No. 23 The third part of the Saptarishikal

January October	Put Mriga nakshatra on the third day of the month.
February November	See the nakshatra Moola on 180° of Mriga and put it on the first day of the month.
March December	See the nakshatra Moola on 180° of Mriga and put on the first day of the month.
April	Put Mriga nakshatra on the second day of the month.
May	Deduct 12° from Mriga. See the nakshatra Vishakha on 180° of Krittika and put it on the third day of the month.
June	Add 12° in Mriga. See the Purvashadha on 180° of Punarvasu and put it on the third day of the month.
July	Put Mriga, on the first day of the month.
August	Deduct 12° from Mriga. See nakshatra Anuradha on 180° of Krittika and put it on the second day of the month.
September	Deduct 12° from Mriga and put Krittika on the third day of the month.

West No. 6 The fourth part of the Saptarishikal No. 24 The third part of the Saptarishikal

January October	Put Aridra on the second day of the month.
February November	See the nakshatra Moola on the 180° of Aridra and put it on the third day of the month.
March December	See the nakshatra Purvashadha on 180° of Aridra and put it on the third day of the month.
April	Put Aridra on the first day of the month.
May	Add 12° in Aridra and put Pushya on the first day of the month.
June	Add 12° to Aridra. See the nakshatra Uttarashadha on 180° of Pushya and put it on the second day.
July	Deduct 12° from Aridra and put Rohini on the third day of the month.

August	See the nakshatra Moola on 180° of Aridra and put it on the first day of the month.
September	Deduct 12° from Aridra and put Rohini on the second day of the month.

West No. 7 The fourth part of the Saptarishikal
No. 25 The third part of the Saptarishikal

January October	Put Punarvasu on the first day of the month.
February November	See the nakshatra Purvashadha on 180° of Punarvasu and put it on the second day of the month.
March December	See the nakshatra Uttarashadha on 180° of Punarvasu and put it on the second day of the month.
April	Put Punarvasu on the third day of the month.
May	Deduct 12° from Punarvasu. See the nakshatra Moola on 180° of Mriga.
June	Add 12° in Punarvasu. See the nakshatra Shravana on 180° of Aslesha and put it on the first day of the month.
July	Put Punarvasu on the second day of the month.
August	See the nakshatra Purvashadha on 180° of Punarvasu and put it on the third day of the month.
September	Deduct 12° from Punarvasu and put Mriga nakshatra on the first day of the month.

West No. 8 The fourth part of the Saptarishikal
No. 26 The third part of the Saptarishikal

January October	Put Pushya on the third day of the month.
February November	See the nakshatra Shravana on 180° of Pushya and put it on the first day of the month.
March December	See the nakshatra Shravana on 180° of Pushya and put it on the first day of the month.
April	Put Pushya nakshatra on the second day of the month.
May	Add 12° in Pushya. See the nakshatra Shatataraka on 180° of Magha and put it on the third day of the month.
June	Add 12° in Pushya. See the nakshatra Shatataraka on 180° of Magha and put it on the third day of the month.

July	Put Pushya on the first day of the month.
August	See the nakshatra Uttarashadha on 180° of the Pushya nakshatra and put it on the second day of the month.
September	Deduct 12° from Pushya and put Aridra on the third day of the month.
	West No. 9 The fourth part of the Saptarishi-kal
	No. 27 The third part of the Saptarishikal
January October	Put Aslesha on the second day of the month.
February November	See the nakshatra Dhanishtha on 180° of the Aslesha nakshatra and put it on the third day of the month.
March December	See the nakshatra Dhanishtha on 180° of Aslesha and put it on the third day of the month.
April	Put the nakshatra Aslesha on the first day of the month.
May	Add 12° in Aslesha. See the nakshatra Shatataraka on 180° of Purva and put it on the second day.
June	Add 12° in Aslesha and put Purva on the first day of the month.
July	Deduct 12° from Aslesha and put Punarvasu on the third day of the month.
August	Deduct 12° from Aslesha. See the nakshatra Uttarashadha on 180° of Punarvasu and put it on the first day of the month.
September	Deduct 12° from Aslesha and put Punarvasu on the second day of the month.
	East No. 10 The fourth part of Saptarishikal
	No. 0 The first part of Saptarishikal
January October	Put Magha nakshatra on the first day of the month.
February November	See the nakshatra Dhanishtha on 180° of Magha and put it on the second day of the month.
March December	See the nakshatra Shatataraka on 180° of Magha and put it on the second day of the month.
April	Put Aslesha nakshatra on the third day of the month.

May	Add 12° in Magha nakshatra and put the Uttara nakshatra on the third day of the month.
June	Add 12° in Magha nakshatra. See Purvabhadrapada on 180° of Uttara and put it on the first day of the month.
July	Put Aslesha on the second day of the month.
August	Add 12° in Magha and put Uttara on the second day of the month.
September	Add 12° in Magha. See Purvabhadrapada on 180° of Uttara and put it on the third day of the month.

East No. 11 The fourth part of the Saptarishikal

No. 10 The first part of the Saptarishikal

January October	Put Purva nakshatra on the third day of the month.
February November	See the nakshatra Shatataraka on 180° of Purva and put it on the first day of the month.
March December	See the nakshatra Purvabhadrapada on 180° of Purva and put it on the first day of the month.
April	Put Magha nakshatra on the second day of the month.
May	Add 12° in Magha and put Uttara on the second day of the month.
June	See the nakshatra Shatataraka on 180° of Purva and put it on the first day of the month.
July	Put Magha on the first day of the month.
August	Add 12° in Purva and put Hasta on the first day of the month.
September	Add 12° in Purva. See the nakshatra Uttarabhadrapada on 180° of the Hasta nakshatra and put it on the second day of the month.

East No. 12 The fourth part of Saptarishikal

No. 11 The first part of the Saptarishikal

January October	Put the nakshatra Uttara on the second day of the month.
February November	Deduct 12° from Uttara. See the nakshatra Dhanishtha on 180° of Magha and put it on the third day of the month.

March December	Deduct 12° from Uttara. See the nakshatra Shatataraka on 180° of Magha and put it on the third day of the month.
April	Put Purva on the first day of the month.
May	Add 12° in Uttara and put the Chitra nakshatra on the first day.
June	See the nakshatra Purvabhadrapada on 180° of the Uttara nakshatra and put it on the second day of the month.
July	Deduct 12° from Uttara and put Magha on the third day of the month.
August	Deduct 12° from Uttara. See the nakshatra Dhanishtha on 180° of Magha and put it on the first day of the month.
September	Add 12° in Uttara. See the nakshatra Revati on 180° of Chitra and put it on the first day of the month.
	East No. 13 The fourth part of the Saptarishikal
	No. 12 The first part of the Saptarishikal
January October	Put the nakshatra Hasta on the first day of the month.
February November	Deduct 12° from Hasta. See the nakshatra Shatataraka on 180° of Purva and put it on the second day of the month.
March December	Deduct 12° from Hasta. See the nakshatra Purvabhadrapada on 180° of Purva and put it on the second day of the month.
April	Deduct 12° from Hasta and put Purva on the third day of the month.
May	Add 12° in Uttara and put Chitra on the third day of the month.
June	See the nakshatra Uttarabhadrapada on180° of Uttara and put it on the first day of the month.
July	Deduct 12° from Hasta and put Purva on the second day of the month.
August	Deduct 12° from Hasta. See the nakshatra Shatataraka on 180° of Purva and put it on the third day of the month.
September	See the nakshatra Revati on 180° of Hasta and put it on the third day of the month.

West No. 14 The fourth part of Saptarishikal
No. 13 The first part of the Saptarishikal

January October	Put Hasta nakshatra on the third day of the month.
February November	Add 12° in Chitra and put Vishaka on the third day of the month.
March December	Add 12° in Chitra and put Vishaka on the third day of the month.
April	Deduct 12° from Chitra and put Uttara on the second day of the month.
May	Add 12° in Hasta and put Swati on the second day of the month.
June	See nakshatra Revati on 180° of Chitra and put it on the third day of the month.
July	Deduct 12° from Chitra and put Uttara on the first day of the month.
August	Add 12° in Hasta and put Swati on the first day of the month.
September	See the nakshatra Revati on 180° of Chitra and put it on the second day of the month.

West No. 15 The fourth part of Saptarishikal
No. 14 The first part of Saptarishikal

January October	Put Chitra on the second day of the month.
February November	Add 12° in Swati and put Anuradha on the second day of the month.
March December	See the nakshatra Revati on 180° of Chitra and put it on the third day of the month.
April	Put Chitra on the first day of the month.
May	Add 12° in Chitra and put the Vishakha nakshatra on the first day of the month.
June	See the nakshatra Aswini on 180° of Swati and put it on the second day of the month.
July	Deduct 12° from Swati and put Hasta on the third day of the month.
August	Deduct 12° from Swati. See the nakshatra Uttarabhadrapada on 180° of Hasta and put it on the first day of the month.
September	See the nakshatra Bharani on 180° of Swati and put it on the first day of the month.

West No. 16 The fourth part of Saptarishikal
No. 15 The first part of Saptarishikal

January October	Put the Vishakha nakshatra on the first day of the month.

February November	See the nakshatra Aswini on 180° of Swati and put it on the second day of the month.
March December	See the nakshatra Aswini on 180° of Swati and put it on the second day of the month.
April	Deduct 12° from Vishakha and put Chitra on the third day of the month.
May	Add 12° in Swati and put Anuradha on the third day of the month.
June	See the nakshatra Krittika on 180° of Vishakha and put it on the first day of the month.
July	Deduct 12° from Vishakha and put Chitra on the second day of the month.
August	Add 12° in Vishakha and put Jyeshtha on the second day of the month.
September	See the nakshatra Krittika on 180° of Vishakha and put it on the third day of the month.

West No. 17 The fourth part of Saptarishikal
No. 16 The first part of Saptarishikal

January October	Put the nakshatra Vishakha on the third day of the month.
February November	See the nakshatra Bharani on 180° of Vishakha and put it on the first day of the month.
March December	Deduct 12° from Anuradha. See the nakshatra Bharani on 180° of Swati and put it on the first day of the month.
April	Deduct 12° from Anuradha and put Swati on the second day of the month.
May	Put Anuradha on the second day of the month.
June	See the nakshatra Krittika on 180° of Anuradha and put it on the third day of the month.
July	Deduct 12° from Anuradha and put Swati on the first day of the month.
August	Add 12° in Anuradha and put Moola on the first day of the month.
September	See the nakshatra Rohini on 180° of Anuradha and put it on the second day of the month.

West No. 18 The fourth part of Saptarishikal
No. 17 The first part of Saptarishikal

January October	Deduct 12° from Jyeshtha and put Vishakha on the second day of the month.

February November	Add 12° in Jyeshtha and put Purvashadha on the second day of the month.
March December	Deduct 12° from Jyeshtha. See the nakshatra Krittika on 180° of Vishakha and put it on the third day of the month.
April	Deduct 12° from Jyeshtha and put Vishakha on the first day of the month.
May	Put Jyeshtha on the first day of the month.
June	See Rohini on 180° of Jyeshtha and put it on the second day of the month.
July	Deduct 12° from Jyeshtha and put Vishakha on the third day of the month.
August	Add 12° in Anuradha and put Moola on the third day of the month.
September	See the nakshatra Mriga on 180° of Jyeshtha and put it on the first day of the month.

East No. 19 The fourth part of Saptarishikal
No. 18 The first part of Saptarishikal

January October	Deduct 12° from Moola and put Anuradha on the first day of the month.
February November	Add 12° in Moola and put Uttarashadha on the first day of the month.
March December	See the nakshatra Mriga on 180° of Moola and put it on the second day of the month.
April	Add 12° in Moola nakshatra. See Pushya on 180° of Uttarashadha and put it on the second day of the month.
May	Put Moola nakshatra on the third day of the month.
June	See the nakshatra Aridra on 180° of Moola and put it on the first day of the month.
July	Add 12° in Moola nakshatra. See Pushya on 180° of Uttarashadha and put it on the first day.
August	Add 12° in Moola nakshatra and put Uttarashadha on the second day of the month.
September	See the nakshatra Aridra on 180° of Moola and put it on the third day of the month.

East No. 20 The fourth part of Saptarishikal
No. 19 The first part of Saptarishikal

| January October | Deduct 12° from Purvashadha and put Jyeshtha on the third day of the month. |

54

February November	Deduct 12° from Purvashadha. See the nakshatra Mriga on 180° of Jyeshtha and put it on the first day of the month.
March December	See the nakshatra Aridra on 180° of Purvashadha and put it on the first day of the month.
April	Deduct 12° from Purvashadha and put Jyesh tha on the second day of the month.
May	Put Purvashadha on the second day of the month.
June	See the nakshatra Punarvasu on 180° of Purvashadha and put it on the third day of the month.
July	Deduct 12° from Purvashadha and put Jyeshtha on the first day of the month.
August	Add 12° in Purvashadha and put Shravana on the first day of the month.
September	See Punarvasu on 180° of Purvashadha and put it on the second day of the month.
	East No. 21 The fourth part of Saptarishikal No. 20 The first part of Saptarishikal
January October	Deduct 12° from Uttarashadha and put Moola on the second day of the month.
February November	Deduct 12° from Uttarashadha. See the nakshatra Mriga on 180° of Moola and put it on the third day of the month.
March December	Deduct 12° from Uttarashadha. See the nakshatra Aridra on 180° of Moola and put it on the third day of the month.
April	Deduct 12° from Uttarashadha and put Moola on the first day of the month.
May	Put Uttarashadha on the first day of the month.
June	See Punarvasu on 180° of Uttarashadha and put it on the second day of the month.
July	Deduct 12° from Uttarashadha and put Moola on the third day of the month.
August	Add 12° in Purvashadha and put Shravana on the third day of the month.
September	See the nakshatra Pushya on 180° of Uttarashadha and put it on the first day of the month.

	East No. 22 The fourth part of Saptarishikal No. 21 The first part of Saptarishikal
January October	Deduct 12° from Shravana and put Purvashadha on the first day of the month.
February November	Add 12° in Shravana and put Shatataraka on the first day of the month.
March December	Add 12° in Shravana and put Shatataraka on the first day of the month.
April	Add 12° in Shravana nakshatra. See Purva nakshatra on 180° of Shatataraka and put it on the second day.
May	Put the Shravana nakshatra on the third day of the month.
June	See the nakshatra Pushya on 180° of Shravana and put it on the first day of the month.
July	Add 12° in Shravana. See the nakshatra Magha on 180° of Shatataraka and put it on the first day.
August	Put Shravana nakshatra on the second day of the month.
September	See nakshatra Aslesha on 180° of Shravana and put it on the third day of the month.
	East No. 23 The fourth part of Saptarishikal No. 22 The first part of Saptarishikal
January October	Deduct 12° from Dhanishtha and put Uttarashadha on the third day of the month.
February November	Add 12° in Dhanishtha and put Purvabhadrapada on the third day of the month.
March December	Deduct 12° from Dahnishtha. See the nakshatra Pushya on 180° of Uttarashadha and put it on the first day of the month.
April	Deduct 12° from Dhanishtha and put Uttarashadha on the second day of the month.
May	Put Dhanishtha on the second day of the month.
June	See the nakshatra Aslesha on 180° of Dhanistha and put it on the third day of the month.
July	Deduct 12° from Dhanishtha and put the Uttarashadha nakshatra on the first day of the month.
August	Add 12° in Dhanishtha and put Purvabhadrapada on the first day of the month.

September	See the nakshatra Magha on 180° of Dhanistha and put it on the second day of the month.
	West No. 24 The fourth part of Saptarishikal. No. 23 The first part of Saptarishikal.
January October	Put Dhanishtha on the second day of the month.
February November	Add 12° in Shatataraka and put Uttarabhadrapada on the second day of the month.
March December	Deduct 12° from Shatataraka. See the nakshatra Aslesha on 180° of Shravana and put it on the second day of the month.
April	Deduct 12° from Shatataraka and put Shravana on the first day of the month.
May	Put Shatataraka on the first day of the month.
June	See Magha nakshatra on 180° of Shatataraka and put it on the second day of the month.
July	Add 12° to Shatataraka. See nakshatra Hasta on 180° of Uttarabhadrapada and put it on the second day of the month.
August	Add 12° in Shatataraka and put Uttarabhadrapada on the third day of the month.
September	See the nakshatra Purva on 180° of Shataraka and put it on the first day of the month.
	West No. 25 The fourth part of Saptarishikal. No. 24 The first part of Saptarishikal.
January October	Put the Shatataraka on the first day of the month.
February November	Add 12° in Purvabhadrapada and put Revati on the first day of the month.
March December	See the nakshatra Magha on 180° of Shatataraka and put it on the second day of the month.
April	Add 12° in Purvabhadrapada. See the Nakshatra Hasta on 180° of Revati and put it on the second day of the month.
May	Put Purvabhadrapada on the third day of the month.
June	See the nakshatra Purva on 180° of Purvabhadrapada and put it on the first day of the month.

July	Add 12° in Purvabhadrapada. See the nakshatra Hasta on 180° of Revati and put it on the first day of the month.
August	Add 12° in Purvabhadrapada and put Revati on the second day of the month.
September	See the nakshatra Uttara on 180° of Purvabhadrapada and put it on the first day of the month.

West No. 26 The fourth part of Saptarishikal.
No. 25 The first part of Saptarishikal.

January October	Deduct 12° from Uttarabhadrapada and put the Dhanishtha nakshatra on the third day of the month.
February November	Add 12° in Uttarabhadrapada and put Aswini on the third day of the month.
March December	Add 12° in Uttarabhadrapada and put Aswini on the third day of the month.
April	Add 12° in Uttarabhadrapada. See the nakshatra Chitra on 180° of Aswini and put it on the first day of the month.
May	Put Uttarabhadrapada on the second day of the month.
June	See the nakshatra Purva on 180° of Purvabhadrapada and put it on the third day of the month.
July	Deduct 12° from Uttarabhadrapada and put Shatataraka on the first day of the month.
August	Add 12° in Purvabhadrapada and put Revati on the first day of the month.
September	See the nakshatra Uttara on 180° of Uttarabhadrapada and put it on the second day of the month.

West No. 27 The fourth part of Saptarishikal.
No. 26 The first part of Saptarishikal.

January October	Deduct 12° from Revati and put Purvabhadrapada on the second day of the month.
February November	Deduct 12° from Revati. See the nakshatra Purva on 180° of Purvabhadrapada and put it on the first day of the month.
March December	Deduct 12° from Revati. See the nakshatra Uttara on 180° of Purvabhadrapada and and put it on the third day of the month.

April	Deduct 12° from Revati and put Purvabhadrapada on the first day of the month.
May	Add 12° in Revati and put Bharani on the first day of the month.
June	See the nakshatra Hasta on 180° of Revati and put it on the second day of the month.
July	Deduct 12° from Revati and put Purvabhadrapada on the third day of the month.
August	Add 12° in Revati and put Bharani on the third day of the month.
September	See the nakshatra Chitra on 180° of Revati and put it on the first day of the month.

No. 27 The first part of Saptarishikal.
No. 8 The second part to Saptarishikal.

January October	Put Aslesha on the second day of the month.
February November	See the nakshatra Shravana on 180° of Aslesha and put it on the third day of the month.
March December	See the nakshatra Shravana on 180° of Aslesha and put it on the third day of the month.
April	Put the nakshatra Pushya on the first day of the month.
May	Add 12" in Pushya and put Magha on the first day.
June	See the nakshatra Revati on the first day of the month.
July	Deduct 12° from Revati and put Purvabhadrapada on the second day of the month.
August	Add 12° in Revati and put Bharani on the second day of the month.
September	Add 12° in Pushya. See the nakshatra Shatataraka on 180° of Magha and put it on the first day of the month.

No. 10 The first part of the Saptarishikal.
No. 9 The second part of the Saptarishikal.

January October	Put Magha nakshatra on the first day of the month.
February November	See the nakshatra Shravana on 180° of Aslesha and put it on the second day of the month.
March December	See the nakshatra Shravana on 180° of Aslesha and put it on the second day of the month.

April	Deduct 12° from Magha. See the nakshatra Uttarashadha on 180° of Pushya and put it on the second day of the month.
May	Add 12° in Magha and put Uttara on the third day.
June	See the nakshatra Dhanishtha on 180° of Aslesha and put it on the first day of the month.
July	Put Aslesha on the second day of the month.
August	Deduct 12° from Magha. See the nakshatra Uttarashadha on 180° of Pushya and put it on the third day of the month.
September	Deduct 12° from Magha and put Pushya on the first day of the month.

No. 11 The first part of Saptarishikal.
No. 10 The second part of Saptarishikal.

January October	Put Purva nakshatra on the third day of the month.
February November	Deduct 12° from Purva. See the nakshatra Shravana on 180° of Aslesha and put it on the first day of the month.
March December	See the nakshatra Shatataraka on 180° of Purva and put it on the first day of the month.
April	Deduct 12° from Purva and put Aslesha on the second day of the month.
May	Add 12° in Purva and put Hasta on the second day.
June	See the nakshatra Shatataraka on 180° of Purva and put it on the third day of the month.
July	Deduct 12° from Purva and put Aslehsa on the first day of the month.
August	Add 12° in Purva and put Hasta on the first day of the month.
September	See the nakshatra Purvabhadrapada on 180° of Purva and put it on the second day of the month.

No. 12 The first part of Saptarishikal.
No. 11 The second part of Saptarishikal.

January October	Put Uttara on the second day of the month.
February November	Deduct 12° from Uttara. See the nakshatra Dhanistha on 180° of Magha and put it on the second day of the month.

March December	See the nakshatra Shatataraka on 180° of Purva and put it on the third day of the month.
April	Put Uttara nakshatra on the first day of the month.
May	Add 12° in Uttara and put Chitra on the first day.
June	See the nakshatra Uttarabhadrapada on 180° of Uttara and put it on the second day of the month.
July	Add 12° in Uttara. See the nakshatra Ashwini on 180° of Chitra and put it on the second day of the month.
August	Add 12° in Uttara and put Chitra on the third day of the month.
September	See the nakshatra Uttarabhadrapada on 180° of Uttara and put it on the first day of the month.

No. 13 The first part of Saptarishikal
No. 12. The second part of Saptarishikal

January October	Put the nakshatra Hasta on the first day of the month.
February November	See the nakshatra Purvabhadrapada on 180° of Uttara and put it on the second day of the month.
March December	Deduct 12° from Hasta. See the nakshatra Purvabhadrapada on 180° of Purva and put it on the second day of the month.
April	Deduct 12° from Hasta and put Purva on the third day of the month.
May	Add 12° in Hasta and put Swati on the third day.
June	See the nakshatra Revati on 180° of Hasta and put it on the first day of the month.
July	Deduct 12° from Hasta and put Purva on the second day of the month.
August	Deduct 12° from Hasta. See the Shatataraka on 180° of Purva and put it on the third day of the month.
September	See Revati on 180° of Hasta and put on the third day of the month.

No. 14 The first part of Saptarishikal
No. 13 The second part of Saptarishikal

January October	Put Chitra nakshatra on the third day of the month.
February November	Deduct 12° from Chitra. See the nakshatra Uttarabhadrapada on 180° of Uttara and put it on the first day of the month.
March December	See the nakshatra Uttarabhadrapada on 180° of Hasta and put it on the first day of the month.
April	Deduct 12° from Chitra and put Uttara on the second day of the month.
May	Add 12° in Chitra and put Vishakha on the second day of the month.
June	See the nakshatra Revati on 180° of Chitra and put it on the third day of the month.
July	Deduct 12° from Chitra and put Uttara on the first day of the month.
August	Add 12° in Chitra and put Vishakha on the first day of the month.
September	Put nakshatra Ashwini on 180° of Chitra on the second day of the month.

No. 15 The first part of Saptarishikal
No. 14 The second part of Saptarishikal

January October	Put Chitra on the second day of the month.
February November	Deduct 12° from Swati. See the nakshatra Uttarabhadrapada on 180° of Hasta and put it on the third day of the month.
March December	See nakshatra Revati on 180° of Chitra and put it on the third day of the month.
April	Deduct 12° from Swati and put Hasta on the first day of the month.
May	Put Swati on the first day of the month.
June	See the nakshatra Aswini on 180° of Chitra and put it on the second day of the month.
July	Add 12° in Swati. See the nakshatra Rohini on 180° of Anuradha and put it on the second day of the month.
August	Add 12° in Swati and put Anuradha on the third day of the month.
September	See nakshatra Bharani on 180° of Swati and put it on the first day of the month.

No. 16 The first part of the Saptarishikal
No. 15 The second part of the Saptarishikal

January October	Deduct 12° from Vishakha and put Chitra on the first day of the month.
February November	Add 12° in Vishakha and put the Jyeshtha nakshatra on the first day of the month.
March December	See the nakshatra Bharani on 180° of Vishakha and put it on the second day of the month.
April	Deduct 12° from Vishakha and put Chitra on the third day of the month.
May	Add 12° in Vishakha and put Jyeshtha on the third day of the month.
June	See the nakshatra Krittika on 180° of Vishakha and put it on first day of the month.
July	Deduct 12° from Vishakha and put Chitra on the second day of the month.
August	Add 12° in Vishakha and put Jyeshtha on the second day of the month.
September	Add 12° in Vishakha. See the nakshatra Rohini on 180° of Jyeshtha and put it on the third day of the month.

No. 17 The first part of Saptarishikal
No. 16 The second part of Saptarishikal

January October	Deduct 12° from Anuradha and put Swati on the third day of the month.
February November	See the nakshatra Krittika on 180° of Anuradha and put it on the first day of the month.
March December	See the nakshatra Krittika on 180° of Anuradha on the third day of the month.
April	Deduct 12° from Anuradha and put Swati on the second day of the month.
May	Put Anuradha on the second day of the month.
June	See the nakshatra Krittika on 180° of Anuradha and put it on the third day of the month.
July	Deduct 12° from Anuradha and put Swati on the first day of the month.
August	Add 12° in Anuradha and put Swati on the first day of the month.
September	Add 12° in Anuradha. See the nakshatra Mriga on 180° of Moola and put it on the second day of the month.

No. 18 The first part of Saptarishikal
No. 17 The second part of Saptarishikal

January October	Deduct 12° from Jyeshtha and put Vishakha on the second day of the month.
February November	See the nakshatra Krittika on 180° of Anuradha and put it on the third day of the month.
March December	See the nakshatra Rohini on 180° of Jyeshtha and put it on the third day of the month.
April	Deduct 12° from Jyeshtha and put Vishakha on the first day of the month.
May	Put Jyeshtha nakshatra on the first day of the month.
June	See the nakshatra Rohini on 180° of Jyeshtha and put it on the second day of the month.
July	Deduct 12° from Jyeshtha and put Vishakha on the third day of the month.
August	Add 12° in Jyeshtha and put Purvashadha on the third day of the month.
September	Add 12° Jyeshtha. See the nakshatra Aridra on 180° of Purvashadha and put it on the first day of the month.

No. 19 The first part Saptarishikal
No. 18 The second part of Saptarishikal

January October	Deduct 12° from Moola and put Anuradha on the first day of the month.
February November	Add 12° in Moola nakshatra and put Uttarashadha on the first day of the month.
March December	Add 12° in Moola nakshatra and put Uttarashadha on the first day of the month.
April	Deduct 12° from Moola and put Anuradha on the third day of the month.
May	Put Moola nakshatra on the third day of the month.
June	See the nakshatra Mriga on 180° of Moola and put it on the first day of the month.
July	Deduct 12° from Moola and put Anuradha on the second day of the month.
August	Put Moola nakshatra on the first day of the month.
September	See the nakshatra Aridra on 180° of Moola and put it on the third day of the month.

No. 20 The first part of Saptarishikal
No. 19 The second part of Saptarishikal

January October	Deduct 12° from Purvashadha and put Jyeshtha on the third day of the month.
February November	Add 12° in Purvashadha and put Shravana on the third day of the month.
March December	See the nakshatra Aridra on 180° of Moola and put on the first day of the month.
April	Deduct 12° from Purvashadha and put Jyeshtha on the second day of the month.
May	Put purvashadha on the first day of the month.
June	See the nakshatra Punarvasu on 180° of Purvashadha and put it on the third day of the month.
July	Deduct 12° from Purvashadha and put Jyeshtha on the first day of the month.
August	Add 12° in Purvashadha and put Shravana on the first day of the month.
September	Add 12° in Purvashadha. See the nakshatra Pushya on 180° of Shravana and put it on the first day of the month.

No. 21 The first part of Saptarishikal
No. 20 The second part of Saptarishikal

January October	Deduct 12° from Uttarashadha and put Moola on the second day of the month.
February November	Add 12° in Uttarashadha and put Dhanishtha on the second day of the month.
March December	Deduct 12° from Uttarashadha. See the nakshatra Aridra on 180° of Moola and put it on the third day of the month.
April	Deduct 12° from Uttarashadha and put Moola on the first day of the month.
May	Put Uttarashadha on the First day of the month.
June	See Pushya nakshatra on 180° of Uttarashadha and put it on the second day of the month.
July	Add 12° in Uttarashadha. See the nakshatra Magha on 180° of Dhanishtha and put it on the second day of the month.
August	Add 12° in Uttarashadha and put Dhanishtha on the third day of the month.

September	See the nakshatra Pushya on 180° of Uttara-shadha and put it on the first day of the month.
	No. 22 The first part of Saptarishikal
	No. 21 The second part of Saptarishikal
January October	Deduct 12° from Shravana and put Purva-shadha on the first day of the month.
February November	Add 12° in Shravana and put Shatataraka on the first day of the month.
March December	Deduct 12° from Shravana. See Punarvasu on the 180° of Purvashadha and put it on the second day of the month.
April	Add 12° in Shravana. See the nakshatra Purva on 180° of Shatataraka and put it on the second day.
May	Put Shravana nakshatra on the third day of the month.
June	See the nakshatra Pushya on 180° of Shra-vana and put it on the first day of the month.
July	Add 12° in Shravana. See the nakshatra Pur-va on 180° of Shatataraka and put it on the first day.
August	Add 12° in Shravana and put Shatataraka on the second day of the month.
September	See the nakshatra Aslesha on 180° of Shra-vana and put it on the third day of the month.
	No. 23 The first part of Saptarishikal
	No. 22 The second part of Saptarishikal
January October	Deduct 12° from Dhanishtha and put Uttara-shadha on the third day of the month.
February November	Add 12° in Dhanishtha and put Purvabhadra-pada on the third day of the month.
March December	Add 12° in Dhanishtha and put Purvabhadra-pada on the third day of the month.
April	Add 12° in Dhanishtha. See the nakshatra Purva on 180° of Purvabhadra and put it on on the first day of the month.
May	Put Dhanishtha on the second day of the month.

66

June	Deduct 12° from Dhanishtha. See the nakshatra Pushya on 180° of Uttarashadha and put it on the third day.
July	Deduct 12° from Dhanishtha and put Uttarashadha on the first day of the month.
August	Add 12° in Dhanishtha and put Purvabhadrapada on the first day of the month.
September	See the nakshatra Aslesha on 180° of Dhanishtha and put it on the second day of the month.

No. 24 The first part of Saptarishikal
No. 23 The second part of Saptarishikal

January October	Deduct 12° from Shatataraka and put Shravana on the second day of the month.
February November	Add 12° in Shatataraka and put Uttarabhadrapada on the second day of the month.
March December	Put Aslesha nakshatra on 180° of Dhanishtha and put it on the third day of the month.
April	Deduct 12° from Shatataraka and put Shravana on the first day of the month.
May	Add 12° in Shatataraka and put Uttarabhadrapada on the first day of the month.
June	See the nakshatra Magha on 180° of Shatataraka on the second day of the month.
July	Deduct 12° from Shatataraka and put Shravana on the third day of the month.
August	Add 12° in Shatataraka and put Uttarabhadrapada on the third day of the month.
September	See the nakshatra Purva on 180° of Shatataraka and put it on the first day of the month.

No. 25 The first part of Saptarishikal
No. 24 The second part of Saptarishikal

January October	Put the Purvabhadrapada nakshatra on the first day.
February November	Add 12° in Purvabhadrapada and put Revati on the first day of the month.
March December	See the nakshatra Magha on 180° of Shatataraka and put it on the second day of the month.
April	Add 12° in Purvabhadrapada. See Hasta on 180° of Revati and put it on the second day of the month.

May	Put Purvabhadrapada on the third day of the month.
June	See the nakshatra Magha on 180° of Shatataraka and put it on first day of the month.
July	Add 12° in Purvabhadrapada. See the nakshatra Hasta on 180° of Revati and put it on the first day of the month.
August	Add 12° in Purvabhadrapada and put Revati on the Second day of the month.
September	See the nakshatra Purva on 180° of Purvabhadrapada and put it on the third day of the month.

No. 26 The first part of Saptarishikal
No. 25 The second part of Saptarishikal

January October	Put Uttarabhadrapada on the third day of the month.
February November	Add 12° in Uttarabhadrapada and put Aswini on the third day of the month.
March December	Add 12° in Uttarabhadrapada. See the nakshatra Chitra on 180° of Aswini and put it on the first day of the month.
May	Put Uttarabhadrapada on the second day of the month.
June	Deduct 12° from Uttarabhadrapada. See Purva on 180° of Shatataraka and put it on the third day.
July	Deduct 12° from Uttarabhadrapada and put Shatataraka on the first day of the month.
August	Add 12° in Uttarabhadrapada and put Aswini on the third day of the month.
September	See the nakshatra Uttara on 180° of Uttarabhadrapada and put it on the second day of the month.

No. 27 The first part of Saptarishikal
No. 26 The second part of Saptarishikal

January October	Deduct 12° from Revati and put Purvabhadrapada on the second day of the month.
February November	Add 12° in Revati and put Bharani on the second day.
March December	Deduct 12° from Revati. See the nakshatra Purva on 180° of Purvabhadrapada and put it on the third day of the month.

68

April	Add 12° in Revati. See Swati on 180° of Bharani and put it on the third day of the month.
May	Put Revati on the first day of the month.
June	Deduct 12° from Revati. See Uttara on 180° of Purvabhadrapada and put it on the second day.
July	See the nakshatra Chitra on 180° of Revati and put it on the second day of the month.
August	Add 12° in Revati and put Bharani on the third day of the month.
September	See the nakshatra Hasta on 180° of Uttarabhadrapada and put it on the first day of the month.

No. 1 The second part of Saptarishikal
No. 0 The second part of Saptarishikal

January October	Deduct 12° from Aswini and put Uttarabhadrapada on the first day of the month.
February November	Add 12° in Aswini and put Krittika on the first day.
March December	See the nakshatra Hasta on 180° of Revati and put it on the second day of the month.
April	Deduct 12° from Aswini and put Uttarabhadra-pada on the third day of the month.
May	Put Aswini nakshatra on the third day of the month.
June	See the nakshatra Chitra on 180° of Revati and put it on the first day of the month.
July	Deduct 12° from Aswini and put Uttarabhadrapada on the second day of the month.
August	Add 12° in Aswini and put Krittika on the second day of the month.
September	See Swati on 180° of Aswini and put it on the third day of the month.

No. 2 The Second part of Saptarishikal
No. 9 The third part of Saptarishikal

January October	Deduct 12° from Bharani and put Revati on the third day of the month.
February November	Add 12° in Bharani and put Rohini on the third day of the month.

69

March December	Deduct 12° from Bharani. See the nakshatra Chitra on 180° of Revati and put it on the first day of the month.
April	Add 12° in Bharani. See the nakshatra Anuradha on 180° of Rohini and put it on the first day of the month.
May	Put Bharani on the second day of the month.
June	See the nakshatra Swati on 180° of Bharani and put it on the third day of the month.
July	Add 12° in Bharani. See the nakshatra Anuradha on 180° of Rohini and put it on the third day of the month.
August	See the nakshatra Shravana on 180° of Aslesha and put it on the third day of the month.
September	See the nakshatra Vishakha on 180° of Bharani and put it on the second day of the month.

No. 3 The second part of Saptarishikal
No. 10 The third part of Saptarishikal

January October	Deduct 12° from Krittika and put Aswini on the second day of the month.
February November	Add 12° in Krittika and put Mriga on the second day of the month.
March December	Add 12° in Krittika and put Mriga on the second day of the month.
April	Deduct 12° from Magha and put Pushya on the first day of the month.
May	Put Krittika on the first day of the month.
June	See the nakshatra Vishakha on 180° of Krittika and put it on the second day of the month.
July	Add 12° in Krittika. See the nakshatra Jyeshtha on 180° of Mriga and put it on the second day.
August	Put Krittika nakshatra on the third day of the month.
September	See the nakshatra Anuradha on 180° of Krittika and put it on the first day of the month.

No. 4 The second part of Saptarishikal
No. 11 The third part of Saptarishikal

| January October | Put Purva nakshatra in the second day of the month. |

70

February November	Add 12° in Rohini and put Aridra on the first day.
March December	Add 12° in Rohini and put Aridra on the first day.
April	Add 12° in Rohini. See the nakshatra Moola on 180° of Aridra and put it on the second day of the month.
May	Put Rohini on the third day of the month.
June	See the nakshatra Anuradha on 180° of Rohini and put it on the first day of the month.
July	Add 12° in Rohini. See the nakshatra Moola on 180° of Aridra and put it on the first day of the month.
August	Put Rohini on the second day of the month.
September	Deduct 12° from Rohini and put Bharani on the first day of the month.

No. 5 The second part of Saptarishikal
No. 12 The third part of Saptarishikal

January October	Put Uttara on the first day of the month.
February November	Deduct 12° from Mriga and put Krittika on the third day of the month.
March December	Deduct 12° from Mriga and put Krittika on the second day of the month.
April	Deduct 12° from Mriga nakshatra and put Krittika on the second day of the month.
May	Put Mriga nakshatra on the second day of the month.
June	See Jyeshtha nakshatra on 180° of Mriga and put it on the third day of the month.
July	Deduct 12° from Mriga and put Krittika on the first day of the month.
August	Add 12° in Mriga and put Punarvasu on the first day.
September	Add 12° in Mriga. See the nakshatra Purvashadha on 180° of Punarvasu and put it on the second day of the month.

No. 6 The second part of Saptarishikal
No. 13 The third part of Saptarishikal

January October	Put Hasta on the third day of the month.
February November	Add 12° in Aridra and put Pushya on the second day of the month.
March December	Add 12° in Aridra and put Pushya on the second day of the month.

71

April	Put Hasta on the second day of the month.
May	Put Aridra on the first day of the month.
June	See the nakshatra Moola on 180° of Aridra and put it on the second day of the month.
July	Put the nakshatra Hasta on the first day of the month.
August	Put Aridra on the third day of the month.
September	See the nakshatra Purvashadha on 180° of Aridra and put it on the first day of the month.

No. 7 The second part of Saptarishikal
No. 14 The third part of Saptarishikal

January October	Put Chitra on the second day of the month.
February November	See the nakshatra Revati on 180° of Chitra and put it on the third day of the month.
March December	See the nakshatra Revati on 180° of Chitra and put it on the third day of the month.
April	Add 12° in Punarvasu. See the nakshatra Shravana on 180° of Aslesha and put it on the second day.
May	Put Punarvasu on the third day of the month.
June	See the nakshatra Aswini on 180° of Chitra and put it on the second day of the month.
July	Add 12° in Punarvasu. See the nakshatra Shravana on 180° of Aslesha and put it on the first day.
August	Put Punarvasu on the second day of the month.
September	See the nakshatra Purvashadha on 180° of Punarvasu and put it on the third day of the month.

No. 8 The second part of Saptarishikal
No. 15 The third part of the Saptarishikal.

January October	Put Swati on the first day of the month.
February November	Add 12° in Pushya and put Magha on the third day.
March December	Add 12° in Pushya and put Magha on the third day.
April	Add 12° in Pushya. See Dhanishtha on 180° of Magha and put it on the first day of the month.
May	Put Pushya on the second day of the month.
June	See the nakshatra Bharani on 180° of Swati and put it on the first day of the month.

72

July	See the nakshatra Shravana on 180° of Pushya and put it on the third day of the month.
August	Put Pushya on the first day of the month.
September	See the nakshatra Uttarashadha on 180° of Pushya and put it on the second day of the month.

No. 9 The second part of Saptarishikal
No. 16 The third part of Saptarishikal

January October	See the nakshatra Dhanishtha on 180° of Aslesha and put it on the first day of the month.
February November	See the nakshatra Bharani on 180° of Vishakha and put it on the first day of the month.
March December	See the nakshatra Krittika on 180° of Vishakha and put it on the third day of the month.
April	Put Vishakha on the second day of the month.
May	Put Aslesha on the first day of the month.
June	See the nakshatra Shravana on 180° of Aslesha and put it on the second day of the month.
July	Put Vishakha on the first day of the month.
August September	Add 12° in Aslesha and put Purva on the second day. See the nakshatra Shravana on 180° of Aslesha and put it on the first day of the month.

No. 10 The second part of Saptarishikal
No. 17 The third part of Saptarishikal

January October	Put the Anuradha nakshatra on the second day of the month.
February November	Add 12° in Magha and put Uttara on the first day of the month.
March December	Add 12° in Magha and put Uttara on the first day of the month.
April	Add 12° in Magha. See the nakshatra Purvabhadrapada on 180° of Uttara and put it on the second day of the month.
May	Put the Magha nakshatra on the third day of the month.
June	See the nakshatra Dhanishtha on 180 of Magha and put it on the first day of the month.
July	Add 12° in Magha. See Purvabhadrapada on 180° of Uttara and put it on the first day of the month.

73

August	Add 12° in Magha and put Uttara on the second day of the month.
September	See the nakshatra Dhanishtha on 180° of Magha and put it on the third day of the month.
	No. 11 The second part of Saptarishikal No. 18 The third part of Saptarishikal
January October	Put Jyeshtha on the first day of the month.
February November	Add 12° in Purva and put Hasta on the third day of the month.
March December	Add 12° in Purva and put Hasta on the third day.
April	Add 12° in Purva nakshatra. See Uttarabhadrapada on 180° of Hasta and put it on the first day of the month.
May	Put Purva nakshatra on the second day of the month.
June	See the nakshatra Mriga on 180° of Jyeshtha and put it on the first day of the month.
July	See the nakshatra Purvabhadrapada on 180° of Purva and put it on the third day of the month.
August	Add 12° in Purva and put Hasta on the first day.
September	See the nakshatra Shatataraka on 180° of Purva and put it on the first day of the month.
	No. 12 The second part of Saptarishikal No. 19 The third part of Saptarishikal
January October	Put Moola nakshatra on the third day of the month.
February November	Add 12° in Uttara and put Chitra on the second day.
March December	Add 12° in Uttara and put Chitra on the second day.
April	See nakshatra Uttarabhadrapada on 180° of Uttara and put it on the third day of the month.
May	Put Uttara on the first day of the month.
June	See the nakshatra Mriga on 180° of Moola and put it on the third day of the month.

74

July	See the nakshatra Uttarabhadrapada on 180° of Uttara and put it on the second day of the month.
August	Put Uttara on the third day of the month.
September	See nakshatra Aridra on 180° of Moola and put it on the second day of the month.
	No. 13 The second part of Saptarishikal No. 20 The third part of Saptarishikal.
January October	Put Purvashadha on the second day of the month.
February November	See Punarvasu on 180° of Purvashadha and put it on the third day of the month.
March December	See Punarvasu on 180° of Purvashadha and put it on the third day of the month.
April	Add 12° in Hasta. See the nakshatra Aswini on 180° of Swati and put it on the second day of the month.
May	Put Hasta on the third day of the month.
June	See the nakshatra Punarvasu on 180° of Purvashadha and put it on the second day of the month.
July	Add 12° in Hasta. See the nakshatra Aswini on 180° of Swati and put it on the first day of the month.
August	Add 12° in Hasta and put Swati on the second day of the month.
September	See the nakshatra Uttarabhadrapada on 180° of Hasta and put it on the third day of the month.
	No. 14 The second part of Saptarishikal No. 21 The third part of Saptarishikal
January October	Put Uttarashadha on the first day of the month.
February November	Add 12° in Chitra and put Vishika on the third day of the month.
March December	Add 12° in Chitra and put Vishika on the third day of the month.
April	Add 12° in Chitra. See the nakshatra Bharani on 180° of Vishakha and put it on the first day of the month.
May	Put Chitra nakshatra on the second day.

June	See the nakshatra Pushya on 180° of Uttara-shadha and put it on the first day of the month.
July	See the nakshatra Aswini on 180° of Chitra and put it on the third day of the month.
August	Add 12° in Chitra and put Vishakha on the first day.
September	See the nakshatra Revati on 180° of Chitra and put it on the second day of the month.

No. 15 The second part of Saptarishikal
No. 22 The third part of Saptarishikal

January October	Add 12° in Swati. See the nakshatra Rohini on 180° of Anuradha and put it on the first day.
February November	Add 12 in Swati and put Anuradha on the second day of the month.
March December	Add 12° in Swati and put Anuradha on the second day of the month.
April	See the Bharani nakshatra on 180° of Swati and put it on the third day of the month.
May	Put Swati on the first day of the month.
June	Deduct 12° from Swati. See the nakshatra Revati on 180° of Hasta and put it on the second day.
July	See Bharani on 180° of Swati and put it on the second day of the month.
August	Put Swati on the third day of the month.
September	See the nakshatra Bharani on 180° of Swati and put it on the first day of the month.

No. 16 The second part of Saptarishikal
No. 23 The third part of Saptarishikal

January October	Add 12° in Vishakha and see Mriga on 180° of Moola and put it on the third day of the month.
February November	Add 12° in Vishakha and put Jyeshtha on the first day of the month.
March December	Add 12° in Vishakha and put Jyeshtha on the first day of the month.
April	Add 12° in Vishakha and see Rohini on 180° of Jyeshtha and put it on the second day of the month.
May	Deduct 12° from Vishakha and put Chitra on the third day of the month.

76

June	Deduct 12° from Vishakha and see Aswini on 180° of Chitra and put it on the first day.
July	Add 12° in Vishakha and see Rohini on 180° of Jyeshtha and put it on the first day of the month.
August	Put Vishakha on the second day of the month.
September	See the nakshatra Bharani on 180° of Vishakha and put it on the third day of the month.

No. 17 The second part of Saptarishikal
No. 24 The third part of Saptarishikal

January October	Add 12° in Anuradha. See the nakshatra Mriga on 180° of Moola and put it on the second day.
February November	Put Anuradha on the third day of the month.
March December	Add 12° in Anuradha and put Moola on the third day.
April	Put Shatataraka on the third day of the month.
May	Put Anuradha on the second day of the month
June	See the nakshatra Purva on 180° of Shatataraka and put it on the first day of the month.
July	Add 12° in Anuradha. See the nakshatra Mriga on 180° of Moola and put it on the third day of the month.
August	Put Anuradha on the first day of the month.
September	See Rohini nakshatra on 180° of Anuradha and put it on the second day of the month.

No. 18 The second part of the Saptarishikal
No. 25 The third part of Saptarishikal

January October	Put Purvabhadrapada on the third day of the month.
February November	Add 12° in Jyeshtha and put Purvashadha on the second day of the month.
March December	Add 12° in Jyeshtha and put Purvashadha on the second day of the month.
April	Add 12° in Jyeshtha. See nakshatra Aridra on 180° of Purvashadha and put it on the third day of the month.

May	Put Jyeshtha nakshatra on the first day of the month.
June	See nakshatra Uttara on 180° of Purvabhadrapada and put it on the third day of the month.
July	Add 12° in Jyeshtha. See nakshatra Aridra on 180° of Purvashadha and put on the second day of the month.
August	Put Jyeshtha nakshatra on the third day of the month.
September	See nakshatra Mriga on 180° of Jyeshtha and put it on the first day of the month.

No. 19 The second part of the Saptarishikal
No. 26 The third part of the Saptarishikal

January October	Put Uttarabhadrapada on the second day of the month.
February November	Add 12° in Moola and put Uttarashadha on the first day of the month.
March December	Add 12° in Moola and put Uttarashadha on the first day of the month.
April	Add 12° in Moola nakshatra. See Punarvasu on 180° of Uttarashadha and put it on the second day of the month.
May	Put Jyeshtha nakshatra on the third day of the month.
June	See nakshatra Hasta on 180° of Uttarabhadrapada and put it on the second day of the month.
July	Add 12° in Moola nakshatra. See Punarvasu on 180° of the Uttarashadha and put it on the first day.
August	Put Moola nakshatra on the second day of the month.
September	See Mriga nakshatra on 180° of Moola and put it on the third day of the month.

No. 20 The second part Saptarishikal
No. 27 The third part of Saptarishikal

January October	Put Revati on the first day of the month.
February November	Put Purvashadha on the third day of the month.
March December	Add 12° in Purvashadha and put Shravana on the third day of the month.

April	Add 12° in Purvashadha and see nakshatra Pushya on 180° of Shravana and put it on the first day.
May	Put Revati on the third day of the month.
June	Add 12° in Purvashadha and put Shravana on the second day of the month.
July	See nakshatra Punarvasu on 180° of Purvashadha and put it on the third day of the month.
August	Put Purvashadha on the first day of the month.
September	See nakshatra Chitra on 180° of Revati and put it on the third day of the month.

No. 21 The second part of the Saptarishikal
No. 1 The third part of the Saptarishikal

January October	See nakshatra Chitra on 180° of Aswini and put it on the third day of the month.
February November	Put Uttarashadha on the second day of the month.
March December	See nakshatra Chitra on 180° of Aswini and put it on the first day of the month.
April	Add 12° in Uttarashadha. See nakshatra Aslesha on 180° of Dhanishtha and put it on the third day.
May	Put Uttarashadha on the first day of the month.
June	Deduct 12° from Uttarashadha. See nakshatra Aridra on 180° of Moola and put it on the second day of the month.
July	Add 12° in Uttarashadha. See nakshatra Aslesha on 180° of Dhanishtha and put it on the second day.
August	Put Uttarashadha on the third day of the month.
September	See nakshatra Punarvasu on 180° of Uttarashadha and put it on the first day of the month.

No. 22 The second part of Saptarishikal
No. 2 The third part of Saptarishikal

January October	Put Bharani on the second day of the month.
February November	Add 12° in Shravana and put Shatataraka on the first day of the month.
March December	Add 12° in Shravana and put Shatataraka on the first day of the month.

79

April	See nakshatra Aslesha un 180° of Shravana and put it on the second day of the month.
May	Put Shravana on the third day of the month.
June	See nakshatra Vishakha on 180° of Bharani and put it on the second day of the month.
July	See nakshatra Aslesha on 180° of Shravana and put it on the first day of the month.
August	Put Shravana nakshatra on the second day of the month.
September	See nakshatra Vishakha on 180° of the·Bharani and put it on the first day of the month.

No. 23 The second part of Saptarishikal
No. 3 The third part of Saptarishikal

January October	Put Krittika nakshatra on the third day of the month.
February November	Add 12° in Dhanishtha and put Purvabhadrapada on the third day of the month.
March December	Add 12° in Dhanishtha and put Purvabhadrapada on the third day of the month.
April	See nakshatra Magha on 180° of Dhanishtha and put it on the first day of the month.
May	Put nakshatra Dhanishtha on the second day of the month.
June	See nakshatra Vishakha on 180° of Krittika and put it on the first day of the month.
July	See nakshatra Magha on 180° of Dhanishtha and put it on the third day of the month.
August	Put nakshatra Dhanishtha on the first day of the month.
September	See nakshatra Anuradha on 180° of Krittika and put it on the third day of the month.

No. 24 The second part of Saptarishikal
No. 4 The third part of Saptarishikal

January October	Put Rohini on the third day of the month.
February November	Add 12° in Shatataraka and put Uttarabhadrapada on the second day of the month.
March December	Add 12° in Shatataraka and put Uttarabhadrapada on the second day of the month.
April	See nakshatra Purva on 180° of Shatataraka and put it on the third day of the month.
May	Put Shatataraka on the first day of the month.
June	See nakshatra Anuradha on 180° of Rohini and put it on the third day of the month.

July	See nakshatra Purva on 180° of Shatataraka and put it on the second day of the month.
August	Put Shatataraka nakshatra on the third day of the month.
September	See nakshatra Jyeshtha on 180° of Rohini and put it on the first day of the month.

No. 25 The second part of Saptarishikal
No. 5 The third part of Saptarishikal

January October	See nakshatra Uttara on 180° of Purvabhadrapada and put it on the third day of the month.
February November	See nakshatra Jyeshtha on 180° of Mriga and put it on the third day of the month.
March December	See nakshatra Jyeshtha on 180° of Mriga and put it on the third day of the month.
April	Add 12° in Purvabhadrapada and see nakshatra Hasta on 180° of Revati and put it on the second day.
May	Put Purvabhadrapada on the third day of the month.
June	See nakshatra Jyeshtha on 180° of Mriga and put it on the second day of the month.
July	See nakshatra Uttara on 180° of Purvabhadrapada and put it on the first day of the month.
August	See nakshatra Jyeshtha on 180° of Mriga and put it on the first day of the month.
September	See nakshatra Moola 180° of Mriga and put it on the first day of the month.

No. 26 The second part of Saptarishikal
No. 6 The third part of Saptarishikal

January October	Add 12° in Uttarabhadrapada. See nakshatra Chitra on 180° of Aswini and put it on the second day of the month.
February November	See nakshatra Moola on 180° of Aridra and put it on the second day of the month.
March December	See nakshatra Moola on 180° of the Aridra and put it on the second day of the month.
April	See nakshatra Hasta on 180° of Uttarabhadrapada and put it on the first day of the month.
May	Put Uttarabhadrapada on the second day of the month.
June	See nakshatra Moola on 180° of Aridra and put it on the first day of the month.

81

July	See nakshatra Hasta 180° of Uttarabhadrapada and put it on the second day of the month.
August	Put Uttarabhadrapada on the first day of the month.
September	Put nakshatra Aridra on the third day of the month.

No. 27 The second part of the Saptarishikal
No. 7 The third part of Saptarishikal

January October	Add 12° in Revati. See nakshatra Swati on 180° of Bharani and put it on the first day of the month.
February November	Add 12° in Revati and put Bharani on the second day of the month.
March December	Add 12° in Revati and put Bharani on the second day of the month.
April	See nakshatra Chitra on 180° of Revati and put it on the third day of the month.
May	Put Punarvasu on the second day of the month.
June	Add 12° in Revati and put Bharani on the first day of the month.
July	See nakshatra Chitra on 180° of Revati and put it on the second day of the month.
August	Put Revati on the third day of the month.
September	See nakshatra Hasta on 180° of Revati and put it on the first day of the month.

In the first pages of the preceding Chapter we described the apparent diurnal motion of the Moon. We have seen the verses of Mantreshwara, as well as the verses from Atharvajyotish, it clearly shows that the difference of the parva between two days are years; it means one part of the nakshatra; naturally on opening day the nakshatra which we have taken into consideration will not be the same on the next day or year, but less than the first by one part of the nakshatra such of on 1.1.1962—1908—54—54=0 that is Revati nakshatra is in the second part. So we will see No. 27 the second part of the Saptarishikal; it shows Swati nakshatra on 1.1.1962 but the commencement of Swati is 6 hours before Sunrise, then on 28th the commencement of the Swati will be 6 hours after Sunrise, that is there will be a difference of 6 hours on every tenth day of the month. In this way we can find out the position of the nakshatra on the part of the dates.

Note: *Addition or subtraction of 12° in nakshatra means, addition or subtraction of the difference between the star of equinoxes and the star of months.*

CHAPTER IV

THE MOTION OF THE EARTH
(The Third Problem of the Three Bodies)

In the opening chapter of Lagna, or the Earth position it is shown that all the heavenly bodies seem to be and move on the surface of a sphere, in the interior of which the earth and the observer are placed. The operations of practical Astronomy consist largely in determining the apparent positions of the heavenly bodies on this sphere. These positions are defined in a way analogous to that in which the position of a city is defined on the earth, namely, by a system of celestial latitudes and longitudes. That measure which, in the heavens, corresponds most nearly to terrestrial longitude is called Right Ascension, and that which corresponds to terrestrial latitude is called Declination.

The meridian lines radiate from the north pole in every direction, cross the equator at right angles, and meet again at the south pole. Just like meridians on the earth the meridian from which right ascensions are counted, corresponding in this respect to the meridian of Ujjaini on the surface of the earth, is that which passes through the vernal equinox or point of crossing of the equator and ecliptic. It is called the first meridian. Three bright stars near which this meridian now passes may be seen during the vernal equinox; they are Aswini, Bharani, Krittika. The right ascension of any star on this meridian is zero, and right ascension of any other star is measured by the angle which the meridian passing through it makes with first meridian, this angle being always counted towards east. Right ascension is generally reckoned, not in degrees, but in hours, minutes and seconds of time. The ecliptic, crossing the equator at its point of intersection with the first meridian, and making an angle of $23\frac{1}{2}°$ with it. The declination of a star is its distance from the celestial equator, whether north or south, exactly as latitude on the earth is distance from the earth's equator. Thus, when the right ascension and declination of a heavenly body are given, the astronomer knows its position in the celestial sphere, just as we know the position of a city on the earth when its longitude and latitude are given.

It must be observed that the declinations of the heavenly bodies are, in a certain sense, referred to the earth. In astronomy the equator is regarded as a plane passing through the centre of the earth, at right angles to its axes, and dividing it into two hemispheres. The line where this plane intersects the surface of the earth is our terrestrial, or geographical, equator. If an observer standing on the geographical equator imagines this plane running east and west, and cutting into and through the earth, where he stands he will have the astronomical equator, which differs from the geographical equator. The following verses from Rigved reads:—

पंचपादं पितरं द्वादशाकृतिं दिवं आहुः परे अर्वेपुरोषिणं ।
अथेमे अन्य उपरे विचक्षणं सप्तचक्रं षळर आहुर्रपितम् ॥

Rig. 1-164-12.

सनेमिचक्रं अजरं विवावृते उत्तानायां दशयुक्ता वहंति ।
सूर्यस्य चक्षू रजसैत्यावृत्तं तस्मिन्नर्रापिता भुवनानि विश्वा ॥

Rig. 1-164-14.

रवि स्फुटं तज्जनने यदासीत् तथाविधश्चेत् प्रतिवर्षमर्कः ।
आवृत्तयः सन्ति दशाब्दकानां भागक्रमात् तद्दिवसाः प्रकल्प्याः ॥

Mantreshwara.

Add one day more in each of the five pentagon angles of 72° and half of it possesses rain. This wheel of twelve forms and ten months does not get old; turns round and round on its single axle and it holds all the (Bhuvana) nakshatras. The Sun gave birth to all nakshatras and cycle of the Sun to reach nakshatra is of nine years.

Now we know that on every day each star crosses the meridian about 4 minutes earlier than on the preceding day, that is, roughly about 2 hours earlier per month. Stars, therefore, which are near the meridian on any date, will occupy the same position about 2 hours earlier on the same day of the next month and so on. In this way we can find out the position of the stars per month, but we must know the opening day of the year. The natural year is that measured by the return of the seasons. All the operations of agriculture are so intimately dependent on this recurrence, that man must have begun to make use of it for measuring time long before he had fully studied the astronomical cause on which it depends. The verse from Rigveda says the same; the Maharishi Lagadha has formed his year according to the same verse, and the calendar made by Gregory is a simulacrum of Lagadha.

त्रिशत्यन्हां सषट् षष्टिरब्द: पडऋतवोयने ।
मासाद्वादश सूर्या: स्युरेतत्पंचगुणं युगम् ॥

Vedang Jyotish

366 days, six seasons, twelve months, into five is punch samvatsara yugam.

प्रपद्येते श्रविष्ठादौ सूर्याचांद्रमसा बुदक ।
सार्पाद्धे दक्षिणार्कस्तु माघ श्रावणयो: सदा ॥

Vedang Jyotish

On the half of the Aslesha nakshatra the Sun turns to the Southern hemisphere, and on the half of the Dhanishtha nakshatra the Sun turns to the Northern hemisphere, that is on the 22nd ot September Dakshinayana takes place. So we will start our punch samvatsara yug from 22nd September.

Now we know that one nakshatra means one day and one day means one year, naturally one part of the nakshatra vibtrates to the third part of the nakshatra on 180° of the first nakshatra, the second part of the first nakshatra vibrates to the fourth part of the nakshatra on 180° of the first nakshatra and vice versa.

One year means 12 Rashis, then one part of the year means three Rashis, but we have to see two types of years, the first is Solar year, and the second is Lunar year.

श्रविष्ठाभ्यां गुणाभ्यस्तान्प्राग्विलग्नान् विनिर्दिशेत्
सूर्यान्मासान् षळभ्यस्तान् विद्याच्चांद्रमसान् ऋतून्

Rigpatha 19

Dhanishtha nakshatra is a meridian nakshatra in the Solar month, and on 180° of Dhanishtha nakshatra is Aslesha nakshatra which is the meridian nakshatra of the Lunar month. So in solar year first part will be of Makara, Kumbha, Meena rashi; second part will be Mesha, Vrishabha, Mithuna, the third part will be of Karka, Simha, Kanya and the last part of the year will be Thula, Vrischika, Dhanu. The first part of the Lunar year will be, Karka, Simha, Kanya; the second part will be, Thula, Vrischika, Dhanu, the third will be Makara, Kumbha, Meena, and the last part of the year will be Mesha, Vrishabha and Mithuna. Thus there are eight parts of the year out of it four will be of the Sun, and four will be of the Moon.

About March 22nd of every year, sidereal 0 hour occurs very nearly at Sunrise. On each successive day it occurs about 3 minutes, 56 seconds earlier, which in the course of a year brings it back to Sunrise again. Since the sidereal time gives the position of the celestial sphere relatively to the meridian of any place, it is convenient to know it in order to find what stars are on the meridian. The following table shows the sidereal time of mean, or ordinary civil, Sunrise at the beginning of each month of the English year:

January	..	18h 45m	July	..	6h 38m
February	.	20h 47m	August	..	8h 40m
March	..	22h 37m	September	..	10h 43m
April	..	0h 40m	October	..	12h 41m
May	..	2h 38m	November	..	14h 43m
June	..	4h 40m	December	..	16h 42m

THE SOUTHERN HEMISPHERE OF THE SKY

22nd of August to 21st of September.
Dec. 14-30, 13-30, 12-30, 11-30, 10-30   Dhanu, Vrischika.
Thus., Wed., Tue., Mon., Sun.,   First Part.

Year	Part	East Year No.	West Year No.	Part	Year	Part	East Year No.	West Year No.	Part
1953	2	18,19,20,21	22,23,24,25,26	4	2025	1	17,18,19,20	21,22,23,24,25	3
1809	1	1, 2, 3, 4	5, 6, 7, 8, 9	3	2097	4	8, 9,10,11	12,13,14,15,16	3
1881	3	19,20,21,22	23,24,25,26,27	1	2169	3	7, 8, 9,10	11,12,13,14,15	1
1737	2	2, 3, 4, 5	6, 7, 8, 9,10	4	2241	2	6, 7, 8, 9	10,11,12,13,14	4
1665	3	3, 4, 5, 6	7, 8, 9,10,11	1	2313	1	5, 6, 7, 8	9,10,11,12,13	3

Dec. 11-30, 10-30, 9-30, 8-30 7-30   Vrishabha, Thula.
Mon., Sun., Sat., Fri., Thur.,   Second Part.

Year	Part	East Year No.	West Year No.	Part	Year	Part	East Year No.	West Year No.	Part
1944	2	9,10,11,12	13,14,15,16,17	1	2016	2	8, 9,10,11	12,13,14,15,16	1
1872	3	10,11,12,13	14,15,16,17,18	1	2088	3	26,27, 1, 2	3, 4, 5, 6, 7	4/3
1800	4	11,12,13,14	15,16,17,18,19	2	2160	4	25,26,27, 1	2, 3, 4, 5, 6	3/2
1728	1	20,21,22,23	24,25,25,27, 1	3/4	2232	1	24,25,26,27	1, 2, 3, 4, 5	1
1656	2	21,22,23,24	25,26,27, 1, 2	4/1	2304	2	15,16,17,18	19,20,21,22,23	4

Dec., 8-30, 7-30, 6-30, 5-30, 4-30,   Kanya, Simha.
Fri., Thur., Wed., Tue., Mon.,   Third Part.

Year	Part	East Year No.	West Year No.	Part	Year	Part	East Year No.	West Year No.	Part
1935	1/2	27, 1, 2, 3	4, 5, 6, 7, 8	4	2007	4	18,19,20,21	22,23,24,25,26	4
1863	3	1, 2, 3, 4	5, 6, 7, 8, 9	1	2079	3	17,18,19,20	21,22,23,24,25	3
1791	4	2, 3, 4, 5	6, 7, 8, 9,10	2	2157	2	16,17,18,19	20,21,22,23,24	2
1719	1	11,12,13,14	15,16,17,18,19	3	2223	3	15,16,17,18	19,20,21,22,23	4
1647	2	12,13,14,15	16,17,18,19,20	4	2295	4	6, 7, 8, 9	10,11,12,13,14	2

Dec., 5-30,4-30, 3-30, 2-30, 1-30,   Simha, Karka.
Tue., Mon., Sun., Sat., Fri.,   Fourth Part.

Year	Part	East Year No.	West Year No.	Part	Year	Part	East Year No.	West Year No.	Part
1926	1	18,19,20,21	22,23,24,25,26	4	1998	4	9,10,11,12	13,14,15,16,17	2
1854	4	19,20,21,22	23,24,25,26,27	3	2070	3	8, 9,10,11	12,13,14,15,16	1
1782	3	20,21,22,23	24,25,26,27, 1	1/2	2142	2	7, 8, 9,10	11,12,13,14,15	4
1710	1	2, 3, 4, 5	6, 7, 8, 9,10	3	2214	1	6, 7, 8, 9	10,11,12,13,14	3
1638	2	3, 4, 5, 6	7, 8, 9,10,11	4	2286	3	24,25,26,27	1, 2, 3, 4, 5	1

THE NORTHEN HEMISPHERE OF THE SKY

22nd of August to 21st of September.

First Part

Dec. 2-30, 1-30, 24-30, 23-30, 22-30   Mithuna, Vrishabha.   Sat., Fri., Thur., Wed., Tue.,

Year	Part	East Year No.	Part	West Year No.	Part	Year	East Year No.	West Year No.	Part
1917	1	9,10,11,12	2	13,14,15,16,17	4	1989	0, 1, 2, 3	4, 5, 6, 7, 8	2
1845	2	10,11,12,13	4	14,15,16,17,18	3/2	2061	25,27, 1, 2	3, 4, 5, 6, 7	1
1773	3	11,12,13,14	1	15,16,17,18,19	2/1	2133	25,26,27, 1	2, 3, 4, 5, 6	4
1701	4	12,13,14,15	2	16,17,18,19,20	4	2205	16,17,18,19	20,21,22,23,24	2
1629	1	21,22,23,24	3/4	25,26,27, 1, 2	3	2277	15,16,17,18	19,20,21,22,23	1

Second Part

Dec. 23-30, 22-30, 21-30, 20-30, 19-30   Vrishabha, Mesha.   Wed., Tue., Mon., Sun., Sat.,

Year	Part	East Year No.	Part	West Year No.	Part	Year	East Year No.	West Year No.	Part
1908	1	0, 1, 2, 3	3	4, 5, 6, 7, 8	3	1980	18,19,20,21	22,23,24,25,26	1
1836	2	1, 2, 3, 4	4	5, 6, 7, 8, 9	2	2052	17,18,19,20	21,22,23,24,25	1
1764	3	2, 3, 4, 5	1	6, 7, 8, 9,10	1	2124	16,17,18,19	20,21,22,23,24	3
1692	4	3, 4, 5, 6	2	7, 8, 9,10,11	4	2196	7, 8, 9,10	11,12,13,14,15	2
1620	1	12,13,14,15	3	16,17,18,19,20	3	2268	6, 7, 8, 9	10,11,12,13,14	1

Third Part

Dec. 20-30, 19-30, 18-30, 17-30, 16-30   Meena Kumbha.   Sun., Sat., Fri., Thur., Wed.,

Year	Part	East Year No.	Part	West Year No.	Part	Year	East Year No.	West Year No.	Part
1899	4	10,11,12,13	4	14,15,16,17,18	3	1971	9,10,11,12	13,14,15,16,17	1
1827	2	19,20,21,22	3	23,24,25,26,27	3	2043	8, 9,10,11	12,13,14,15,16	4
1755	1	20,21,22,23	4/2	24,25,26,27, 1	1	2115	7, 8, 9,10	11,12,13,14,15	3
1683	3	21,22,23,24	1/2	25,26,27, 1, 2	4/3	2187	25,26,27, 1	2, 3, 4, 5, 6	2
1611	1	3, 4, 5, 6	3	7, 8, 9,10,11	2	2259	24,25,26,27	1, 2, 3, 4, 5	1

Fourth Part

Dec. 17-30, 16-30, 15-30, 14-30, 13-30   Makara, Dhanu.   Thur., Wed., Tue., Mon., Sun.,

Year	Part	East Year No.	Part	West Year No.	Part	Year	East Year No.	West Year No.	Part
1890	4	1, 2, 3, 4	2	5, 6, 7, 8, 9	3	1962	0, 1, 2, 3	4, 5, 6, 7, 8	4
1818	1	10,11,12,13	3	14,15,16,17,18	2/1	2034	26,27, 1, 2	3, 4, 5, 6, 7	4
1746	2	11,12,13,14	4	15,16,17,18,19	4	2016	17,18,19,20	21,22,23,24,25	2
1674	3	12,13,14,15	1	16,17,18,19,20	3	2178	16,17,18,19	20,21,22,23,24	1
1602	4	13,14,15,16	2	17,18,19,20,21	3	2250	15,16,17,18	19,20,21,22,23	4

One part of the nakshatra means 6 hours, then 18 hours means three parts of the nakshatra, thus the first part of the year vibrates the third part of the sidereal time.

The sidereal time at any hour of the year may be found from the following table:

Example No. 1 (Second part of the Northern Hemisphere) Birth date: 22.8.1915. Deduct the Saptarishikal from the year 1915 1915-1808=7. Punarvasu Nakshatra from the first division, Saptarishikal is in the first part, Birth date is in the fourth part, Birth date is 22=No. 4 birth month is No. 8, it is a spherical triangle. See the year 1915 in the column 1908 west year 7 the second part of the Northern Hemisphere but due to spherical triangle it is a negative part. Then the second part of the northern hemisphere vibrates to fourth part of the Northern hemisphere internal third part of the west year No. 7 vibrates to internal first part of the east year No. 12 (Punarvasu is negative nakshatra because of the spherical triangle Purvabhadrapada is a greater nakshatra, Uttara nakshatra is on 180° of the Purvabhadrapada. Uttara is No. 12). No. 12 means 12-30 hours; add two hours the difference of the west 12-30 plus 2=14-30 hours; it shows Dhanu rashi. The second part of the northern hemisphere vibrates to fourth part of the southern hemisphere internal third part of the west year. 7 vibrates to internal first part of the east year No. 3 (Punarvasu is negative nakshatra, Vishakha is greater nakshatra, Krittika No. 3 is on 180° of Vishakha) No. 3 means 3-30 hours; add two hours the difference of the west 3-30 plus 2=5-30 hours; it shows Simha Lagna that is on 22.8.1951 at 5-30 hours (3-30 is R.A. of the Simha and 5-30 is Dece) there is Simha Lagna and Dhanu Rashi on the meridian of Ujjain.

Example No. 2 (First part of the Northern hemisphere) Birth date 22.8.1921. Deduct the saptarishikal from the year 1921. 1921-1908=13=Hasta nakshatra from second division, saptarishikal is in the first part, Birth date is in the fourth part, Birth month is No. 8, saptarishikal nakshatra is 13=4, it is a spherical triangle. See the year 1921 in the column 1917 west year No. 13, the first part of the northern hemisphere but due to spherical triangle it is negative part, No. 13 is Hasta nakshatra it, is, negative. Shravana nakshatra is a greater nakshatra). Shravana is No. 22; add two hours the difference of the negative part 22-30 plus 2=24-30 hours; it shows Mithuna Rashi. The first part of the northern hemisphere vibrates to third part of the northern hemisphere internal third part of the west year 13 vibrates to internal third part of the east year No. 22, deduct two hours the

88

difference of the west 22-30 minus 2=20-30 hours; it shows Meena Lagna that is on 22.8.1921 at 20-30 hours there is Mithuna rashi and Meena Lagna on the Meridian of Ujjain, birth place Lat. 6° N. Long 80° 10′ east, Birth time 20-30 hours.

Example No. 3 (Third part of the Southern hemisphere) Birth date 28.6.1863. Deduct the saptarishikal from the year 1863. 1863-1808=55-54=1=Aswini nakshatra from the first division saptarishikal is in the third part, birth date is in the fourth part. Birth date is 28=No. 1 saptarishikal nakshatra is No. 1; it is a spherical triangle. See the year 1863 in the column 1863 east year No. 1 the third part of the Southern hemisphere but due to spherical triangle it is a negative part. Then the third part of the Southern hemisphere vibrates to third part of the Northern hemisphere internal third part of the east year No. 1 vibrates to internal third part of the west year No. 14 (Aswini is on 180° of the Chitra No. 14) No. 14 means 14-30 hours add 2 hours the difference of the east 14-30 plus 2=16-30 hours it shows Kumbha rashi. The third part of the Southern hemisphere vibrates to first part of the northern hemisphere internal third part of the east year No. 1 vibrates to internal fourth part of west year No. 1. No. 1 means 1-30 hours add two hours the difference of the east 1-30 plus 2—3-30 hours it shows Mithuna Lagna that is on 28.6.1863 at 1-30 hours (R.A of the Mithuna Lagna is 24-30 hours and 2-30 is Dece) there is Mithuna Lagna and Kumbha rashi on the meridian of Ujjain Birth place Lat. 13° North, Long. 5h. 10m. 20s. east.

Example No. 4 (Fourth part of the southern hemisphere) Birth date 30.8.1927. Deduct the saptarishikal from the year 1927. 1927-1908=19=Moola nakshatra from the third division. Saptarishikal is in first part, birth date is in the fourth part. Birth date is 30=No. 3 birth month is No. 8, it is a spherical triangle. See the year 1927 in the column 1926 east year No. 19 the fourth part of the Southern hemisphere but due to spherical triangle it is a negative part. Then the fourth part of the Southern hemisphere vibrates to the first part of the southern hemisphere, internal first part of the east year 19 vibrates to internal first part of the west year No. 10 (Moola nakshatra is negative because of the spherical triangle Magha is greater nakshatra) No. 10 means 10-30 hours add two hours the difference of the east, 10-30 plus 2=12-30 hours it shows Vrischika Lagna. The fourth part of the Southern hemisphere vibrates to the Third part of the Southern hemisphere. Internal first part of the east year No. 19 vibrates to internal first part of the west year No. 5. No. 5 means 5-30 hours add two hours the difference of the east 5-30 plus 2=7-30 hours it shows Kanya Rashi that is on 30.8.1927 at 12-30 hours there is Vrischika Lagna and Kanya Rashi on the meridian of Ujjain Birth place Lat. 21° N. Long 72° 50′ east Birth time 12-30 hours.

Example No. 5 (Third part of the Southern hemisphere) Birth date 1.9.1868. Deduct the saptarishikal from the year 1868, 1868-1808=60-54=6=Aridra nakshatra from the first division, Saptarishikal is in the third part, Birth date is in the first part, Birth date is No. 1 Saptarishikal Nakshatra is No. 6, it is a spherical triangle. See the year 1868 in the column 1863 west year No. 6 the third part of the Southern hemisphere, but due to spherical triangle it is a nagative part. Then the third part of the southern hemisphere vibrates to the third part of the northern hemisphere the internal first part of the west year 6 virbates to internal second part of the east year 15 (Aridra nakshatra is negative because of the spherical triangle Swati is greater nakshatra No. 15) No. 15 means 15-30 hours add two hours the difference of the east. 15-30 hours plus 2=17-30 hours it shows Kumbha rashi. The third part of the Southern hemisphere vibrates to first part of the northern hemisphere. The internal first part of the west year No. 6 vibrates to the internal first part of the east year No. 24 Aridra nakshatra is negative, Shatataraka nakshatra is greater. No. 24 means 24-30 hours. Deduct two hours the difference of the west, 24-30—2=22-30 hours, it shows Vrishabha Lagna. That is on 1.9.1868 at 22-30 hours there is Vrishabha Lagna and Kumbha rashi on the meridian of Ujjain Birth place Lat. 12° N. Long. 5h, 10m, 20s, east. Birth time 23-58 hours.

Example No. 6 (Fourth part of the northern hemisphere) Birth date 1.9.1897. Deduct the Saptarishikal from the year 1897, 1897-1808=89-81=8=Pushya nakshatra from the first division saptarishikal is in the fourth part, Saptarishikal Nakshatra is No. 8, Birth month is No. 9 it is spherical triangle. See the year 1897 in the column, 1890 west year No. 8 the fourth part of the northern hemisphere but due to spherical triangle it is a negative part; then the fourth part of the northern hemisphere vibrates to second part of the northern hemisphere Internal second part of the west year 8 vibrates to internal third part of the east year 21 (Uttarashadha is on 180° of the Pushya, Uttarashadha is No. 21 it is a greater nakshatra). No. 21 means 21-30 hours. Deduct 2 hours the difference of the west 21-30—2=19-30 hours, it shows Mesha Lagna. The fourth part of the Northern hemisphere vibrates to second part of the southern hemisphere Internal second part of the west year 8 vibrates to the Internal first part of the east year No. 8. No. 8 means 8-30 hours it shows Thula rashi. That is on 1.9.1897 at 19-30 hours there is Mesha Langna and Thula rashi on the Meridian of

Ujjain Birth place Lat. 11° N, Long 78° 40′ east Birth time 20-15 hours.

Example No. 7 (Third part of the Southern hemisphere) Birth date 6.9.1943. Deduct the Saptarishikal from the year 1943. 1943-1908=35-27=8=Pushya nakshtra from the first division. Saptarishikal is in the second part. Saptarishikal nakshatra is No. 8, birth month is No. 9, it is a spherical triangle. See the year 1943 in the column 1935 west year No. 8. The third part of the Southern hemisphere, but due to spherical triangle it is a negative part. Then the third part of the southern hemisphere vibrates to the first part of the Southern hemisphere. The internal fourth part of the west year No. 8 vibrates to the internal second part of the east year No. 12 (Pushya nakshatra is negative Uttara Bhadrapada is greater nakshatra. Uttara is on 180° of the Uttara bhadrapada) No. 12 means 12-30 hours, deduct two hours, the difference of the west, 12-30—2=10-30 hours, it shows Vrischika Rashi. The third part of the southern hemisphere vibrates to the fourth part of the Northern hemisphere. The internal fourth part of the west year 8 vibrates to the internal second part of the west year 17. Pushya nakshatra is negative and Anuradha is greater Nakshatra (Anuradha is No. 17). No. 17 means 17-30 hours deduct two hours the difference of the Southern hemisphere 17-30—2=15-30 hours, it shows Makara Lagna that is on 6.9.1943 at 15-30 hours there is Makara Lagna and Vrischika rashi on the meridian of Ujjain Birth place Bombay Birth time 14-15 hours.

Example No. 8 (Third part of the Northern hemisphere) Birth date 7.9.1904. Deduct the Saptarishikal from the year 1904. 1904-1808=96—81=15=Swathi Nakshatra from the second division, Saptarishikal is in the fourth part. Birth date is in the first part, Saptarishikal nakshatra is 15=No. 6, Birth date is No. 7, it is a spherical triangle. See the year 1904 in the column 1899 west year 15 the third part of the Northern hemisphere but due to spherical triangle it is a negative part. Then the third part of the northern hemisphere vibrates to the first part of the Southern hemisphere. The internal second part of the west year 15 vibrates to the internal second part of the west year 15. No. 15 means 15-30 hours, deduct 2 hours the difference of the northern hemisphere 15-30—2=13-30 hours, it shows Dhanu Lagna. The third part of the northern hemisphere vibrates to the fourth part of the Southern hemisphere. The internal second part of the west year 15 vibrates to the internal first part of the east year No. 2 (Swati nakshatra is on 180° of the Bharani). No. 2 means 2-30 hours; it shows Karka Rashi that is on 7.9.1943 at 13-30 hours there is Dhanu lagna and Karka—rashi on the meridian of Ujjain, birth place lat. 180° 54' N. Long. 4 hrs 11m 6s, east, birth time 13-55 hours.

Example No. 9 (Third part of the northern hemisphere). Birth date 5.9.1906. Deduct the spatarishikal from the year 1906. 1906—1808=98-81=17=Anuradha Nakshatra from the second division. Saptarishikal is in the fourth part, birth date is in the first part. Birth date is No. 5, birth month is No. 9, it is a spherical triangle. See the year 1906 in the column 1899 west year 17 the third part of the northern hemisphere but due to spherical traingle it is a negative part, then add 2 hours the difference of the negative part 17-30 hours plus 2=19-30 hours it shows Meena Rashi. The third part of the Northern hemisphere vibrates to the second part of the Southern hemisphere. The Internal second part of the west year No. 17 vibrates to the internal first part of the east year 8 (Anuradha is negative nakshatra; Pushya nakshatra is greater) No. 8 means 8-30 hours; it shows Thula Lagna that is on 5.9.1906 at 8-30 hours there is Thula Lagna and Meena rashi on the meridian of Ujjain, Birth place Lat. 25° N, Long. 84° 45' east. Birth time 9-16 hours.

Example No. 10 (Fourth part of the Southern hemisphere) Birth date 15.9.1861. Deduct the Saptarishikal from the year 1861. 1861—1808=53-27=26=Uttarabhadrapada nakshatra from the third division. Saptarishikal is in the second part. Birth date is in the second part Saptarishikal nakshatra is No. 8. Birth month is No. 9, it is the spherical triangle. See the year 1861 in the column 1854 west year 26 the fourth part of the Southern hemisphere but due to spherical triangle it is a negative part. Then the fourth part of the Southern hemisphere vibrates to the fourth part of the northern hemisphere. Internal fourth part of the west year No. 26 vibrates to the internal fourth part of the west year 17 (Uttarabhadrapada is negative nakshatra because of the spherical triangle, Anuradha is greater nakshatra No. 17). Deduct two hours the difference of the Southern hemisphere 17-30—2=15-30 hours; it shows Makara Lagna. The fourth part of the Southern hemisphere vibrates to the fourth part of the northern hemisphere. Internal fourth part of the west year 26 vibrates to the internal second part of the east year No. 13 (Hasta nakshatra is on 180° of the Uttarabhadrapada). No. 13 means 13-30 hours; add two hours the difference of the west 13-30 plus 2=15-30 hours; it shows Makara Rashi that is on 15.9.1861 at 15-30 hours there is Makara Lagna and Makara Rashi on the meridian of Ujjain. Birth time 14-10 hours.

THE SOUTHERN HEMISPHERE OF THE SKY.

22nd of September to 21 of October.

Dec. 10-30, 9-30, 8-30, 7-30, 6-30 Vrischika, Thula.

Tue, Mon, Sun, Sat., Fri. First Part.

Year	Part	East Year No.	Part	West Year No.
1917	1	9,10,11,12	3	13,14,15,16,17
1845	2	10,11,12,13	4	14,15,16,17,18
1773	3	11,12,13,14	1	15,16,17,18,19
1701	4	12,13,14,15	2	16,17,18,19,20
1629	1	21,22,23,24	3/4	25,26,27, 1, 2

Dec. 7-30, 6-30, 5-30, 4-30, 3-30, Thula. Kanya

Sat., Fri., Thurs., Wed., Tues. Second Part.

Year	Part	East Year No.	Part	West Year No.
1908	1	0, 1, 2, 3	3	4, 5, 6, 7, 8
1836	2	1, 2, 3, 4	4	5, 6, 7, 8, 9
1764	3	2, 3, 4, 5	1	6, 7, 8, 9,10
1692	4	3, 4, 5, 6	2	7, 8, 9,10,11
1620	1	12,13,14,15	3	16,17,18,19,20

Dec., 4-30, 3-30, 2-30, 1-30, 24-30 Kanya, Simha

Wed., Tue., Mon., Sun., Sat. Third Part.

Year	Part	East Year No.	Part	West Year No.
1899	4	10 11,12,13	2	14,15,16,17,18
1827	1	19,20,21,22	3	23,24,25,26,27
1755	2	20,21,22,23	4/1	24,25,26,27, 1
1683	3	21,22,23,24	1/2	25,26,27, 1, 2
1611	1	3, 4, 5, 6	3	7, 8, 9,10,11

Dec., 1-30, 24-30, 23-30, 22-30, 21-30 Karka, Mithuna

Sun., Sat., Fri., Thurs., Wed. Fourth Part.

Year	Part	East Year No.	Part	West Year No.
1890	4	1, 2, 3, 4	2	5, 6, 7, 8, 9
1818	1	10,11,12,13	3	14,15,16,17,18
1746	2	11,12,13,14	1	15,16,17,18,19
1674	3	12,13,14,15	1	16,17,18,19,20
1602	4	13,14,15,16	2	17,18,19,20,21

Year	Part	East Year No.	West Year No.	Part
1889	4	0, 1, 2, 3	4, 5, 6, 7, 8	2
2061	3/2	26,27, 1, 2	3, 4, 5, 6, 7	1
2133	3/1	25,26,27, 1	2, 3, 4, 5, 6	4
2205	4	16,17,18,19	20,21,22,23,24	2
2277	3	15,16,17,18	19,20,21,22,23	1
1980	3	18,19,20,21	22,23,24,25,26	1
2052	2	17,18,19,20	21,22,23,24,25	4
2124	1	16,17,18,19	20,21,22,23,24	3
2196	4	7, 8, 9,10	11,12,13,14,15	3
2268	3	6, 7, 8, 9	10,11,12,13,14	2/1
1971	3	9,10,11,12	13,14,15,16,17	1
2043	2	8, 9,10,11	12,13,14,15,16	4
2115	1	7, 8, 9,10	11,12,13,14,15	3
2187	4/3	25,26,27, 1	2, 3, 4, 5, 6	2/1
2259	3/2	24,25,26,27	1, 2, 3, 4, 5	1
1962	3	0, 1, 2, 3	4, 5, 6, 7, 8	1
2034	1/2	26,27, 1, 2	3, 4, 5, 6, 7	4
2106	4	17,18,19,20	21,22,23,24,25	2
2178	3	16,17,18,19	20,21,22,23,24	1
2250	2	15,16,17,18	19,20,21,22,23	4

THE NORTHERN HEMISPHERE OF THE SKY

22nd of September to 21st of October.

Dec. 22-30, 21,30, 20-30, 19-30, 18-30 Mithuna, Vrishabha.
Sun., Sat., Fri., Thurs., Wed.   First Part.

Year	Part	East Year No.	Part	West Year No.
1953	2	18,19,20,21	4	22,23,24,25,26
1809	1	1, 2, 3, 4	3	5, 6, 7, 8, 9
1881	3	19,20,21,22	1	23,24,25,26,27
1737	2	2, 3, 4, 5	4	6, 7, 8, 9,10
1665	3	3, 4, 5, 6	1	7, 8, 9,10,11

Dec. 19-30, 18-30, 17-30, 16-30, 15-30 Thurs., Wed., Tue., Mon., Sun. Second Part.

Year	Part	East Year No.	Part	West Year No.
1944	2	9,10,11,12	4	13,14,15,16,17
1872	3	10·11,12,13	1	14,15,16,17,18
1800	4	11,12,13,14	2/3	15,16,17,18,19
1728	1	20,21,22,23	3/4	24,25,26,27, 1
1656	2	21,22,23,24	4/1	25,26,27, 1, 2

Dec. 16-30, 15-30, 14-30, 13-30, 12-30 Mon., Sun., Sat., Fri., Thurs. Third Part.

Year	Part	East Year No.	Part	West Year No.
1935	1/2	27, 1, 2, 3	4	4, 5, 6, 7, 8
1863	3	1, 2, 3, 4	1	5, 6, 7, 8, 9
1791	4	2, 3, 4, 5	2	6, 7, 8, 9,10
1719	1	11,12,13,14	3	15,16,17,18,19
1647	2	12,13,14,15	4	16,17,18,19,20

Dec. 13-30, 12-30,11-30, 10-30, 9-30 Fri., Thurs., Wed., Tue., Mon. Fourth Part.

Year	Part	East Year No.	Part	West Year No.
1926	1	18,19,20,21	3	22,23,24,25,26
1864	2	19,20,21,22	4	23,24,25,26,27
1782	3	20,21,22,23	1/2	24,25,26,27, 1
1710	1	2, 3, 4, 5	3	6, 7, 8, 9,10
1638	2	3, 4, 5, 6	4	7, 8, 9,10,11

Year	Part	East Year No.	West Year No.	Part
2025	1	17,18,19,20	21,22,23,24,25	3
2029	4	8, 9,10,11	12,13,14,15,16	2
2169	3	7, 8, 9,10	11,12,13,14,15	1
2241	2	6, 7, 8, 9	10,11,12,13,14	4
2313	1	5, 6, 7, 8	9,10,11,12,13	3

Mesha Meena Second Part.

Year	Part	East Year No.	West Year No.	Part
2016	1	8, 9,10,11	12,13,14,15,16	3
2088	3/1	26,27, 1, 2	3, 4, 5, 6, 7	2
2160	4/1	25,26,27, 1	2, 3, 4, 5, 6	1
2232	1	24,25,26,27	1, 2, 3, 4, 5	4
2304	4	15,16,17,18	19,20,21,22,23	2

Kumbha, Makara Third Part.

Year	Part	East Year No.	West Year No.	Part
2007	4	18,19,20,21	22,23,24,25,26	2
2079	3	17,18,19,20	21,22,23,24,25	1
2157	2	16,17,18,19	20,21,22,23,24	4
2223	1	15,16,17,18	19,20,21,22,23	3
2295	4	6, 7, 8, 9	10,11,12,13,14	2

Makara, Dhanu Fourth Part.

Year	Part	East Year No.	West Year No.	Part
1998	4	9,10,11,12	13,14,15,16,17	2
2070	3	8, 9,10,11	12,13,14,15,16	1
2142	2	7, 8, 9,10	11,12,13,14,15	4
2214	1	6, 7, 8, 9	10,11,12,13,14	3
2286	4	24,25,26,27	1, 2, 3, 4, 5	2

Example No. 1. Birth date 24.9.1871. Deduct the Saptarishikal from the year 1871. 1871-1808—63-54=9=Aslesha nakshatra from the first division. Saptarishikal is in the third part. Birth date is in the third part. Birth date is 24=2 plus 4=6. Birth month is No. 9, Saptarishikal is No. 9. it is a spherical triangle. See the year 1871 in the column 1863 west year No. 9 in the third part of the southern hemisphere but due to spherical triangle it is a negative part. No. 9 is Aslesha nakshatra; it vibrates to nakshatra No. 22. But due to spherical triangle Aslesha is negative nakshatra. Then Revati is the positive nakshatra. Hasta No. 13 is on 180° of the Revati. Hasta nakshatra is No. 13. No. 13 means 13-30 hours; it shows Makara Rashi. The third part of the Southern hemisphere vibrates to the Second part of the Northern hemisphere. The Internal first part of the west year No. 9 vibrates to the internal first part of the east year No. 4. No. 4 means 4-30 hours; add the difference of two hours of the Southern hemisphere 4-30 plus 2=6-30 hours; it shows Thula Lagna. That is on 24.9.1871 at 6-30 hours there is Thula lagna and Makara Rashi on the meridian of Ujjain, Birth place Lat. 10° N. Long. 5h. 10m 20s east.

Example No. 2. Birth date 26.9.1874. Deduct the Saptarishikal from the year 1874. 1874-1808=66—54=12=Uttara nakshatra from the second division, saptarishikal is in the third part. Birth date is in the third part. Birth date is 26—2 plus 6=0. Saptarishikal is 12=1 plus 2=3. It is a spherical triangle. See the year 1874 in the column 1872 east year No. 12 in the second part of the Southern hemisphere but due to spherical triangle it is a negative part. Then add 2 hours, the difference of the negative part in the Saptarishikal No. 12. No. 12 means 12-30 hours plus 2 hours=14-30 hours; it shows Meena Rashi. The second part of the Southern hemisphere vibrates to the first part of the Southern hemisphere. The internal third part of the east year No. 12 vibrates to the internal third part of the east year No. 21. No. 21 means 21-30 hours; it shows Vrishabha Lagna that is on 26.9.1874 there is Vrishabha Lagna and Meena Rashi at 21-30 hours on the meridian of Ujjain. Birth place Lat. 13° N. Long. 5h 10m 20s east. Birth time 22 hours.

Example No. 3 (Fourth part of the Northern hemisphere) Birth date 29.9.1890. Deduct the Saptarishikal from the year 1890. 1890—1808=82—81=1=Aswini nakshatra from the first division. Saptarishikal is in the fourth part. Birth date is in the third part. Birth date is 6, Saptarishikal is 1, it is a spherical triangle. See the year 1890 in the column 1890 east year No. 1 in the fourth part of the northern hemisphere. But due to spherical triangle it is a negative part. Then the fourth part of the Northern hemisphere vibrates to Second part of the Southern hemisphere. Internal fourth part of the east year No. 1 vibrates to internal second part of the west year 15. No. 15 means 15-30 hours it shows Meena Lagna. (add 2 hours the difference of the west 15-30 plus 2=17-30 that is 15-30 is R.A. and 17-30 Dec. of the Meena Rashi). The fourth part of the northern hemisphere vibrates to first part of the Northern hemisphere. Internal fourth part of the east year No. 1 vibrates to internal second part of the east year 10. No. 10 means 10-30—2=8-30 hours. It shows Vrischika Rashi (8-30 hours is R.A. and 10-30 Dece). That is on 24.9.1890 at 15-30 hours there is Meena Lagna and Vrischika Rashi on the meridian of Ujjain. Birth place Lat. 13 N. Long. 77° 35′ east.

Example No. 4 (Second part of the Southern hemisphere) Birth date 30.9.1946. Deduct the Saptarishikal from the year 1946. 1946-1908=38—27=11=Purvanakshatra from the second division. Saptarishikal is in the second part. Birth date is 30= No. 3 Saptarishikal nakshatra is 11=No. 2. It is a spherical triangle. See the year 1946 in the column 1944 east year No. 11 the second part of the Southern hemisphere but due to a spherical triangle it is a negative part. Then the second part of the Southern hemisphere vibrates to the first part of the northern hemisphere. The internal second part of the east year No. 11 vibrates to the internal second part of the west year No. 7. No. 7 means 7-30 hours; add two hours the difference of the west 7-30 plus 2=9-30 hours; it shows Vrischika Rashi. The second part of the southern hemisphere vibrates to the third part of the Northern hemisphere. The internal second part of the west year—11 Vibrates to the internal second part of the west year No. 2. No. 2 means 2-30 plus 2=4-30 hours; that is on 30.9.1946 at 4-30 hours there is Kanya Lagna and Vrischika Rashi on the meridian of Ujjain. Birth place Lat. 25° N. Long. 82° 30′ east. Birth time 5-30 hours.

Example No. 5. Birth date 22.9.1933. Deduct the Saptarishikal from the year 1933. 1933—1908=25=Purvabharapada nakshatra from the third division. Saptarishikal is in the first part. Birth date is in the third part. Birth date is 22=2 plus 2=4. Birth month is No. 9; it is spherical triangle. See the year 1933 in the column, 1926 west year No. 25 in the fourth part of the Southern hemisphere but due to spherical triangle it is a negative part. The fourth part of the Southern hemisphere vibrates to the first part of the northern hemisphere. The internal third part of the west year No. 25 vibrates to the internal first part of the west year No. 7. No. 7 means 7-30 hours; it shows Thula

Rashi. The fourth part of the Southern hemisphere vibrates to the third part of the northern hemisphere. The internal third part of the west year No. 25 vibrates to the internal first part of the west year No. 25. No. 25 means 25-30 hours; it shows Simha Lagna, add 2 hours the difference of the Southern hemisphere 1-30 plus 2=3-30 hours; that is on 22.9.1933 at 3-30 hours there is Simha Lagna and Thula Rashi on the meridian of Ujjain, Birth place Bombay.

Example No. 6. Birth date 1.10.1901. Deduct the Saptarishikal from the year 1901. 1901-1808=93-81=12=Uttara Nakshatra from the second division. Saptarishikal is in the fourth part. Birth date is in the first part. Birth date is No. 1. Birth month is 10=1 plus 0=1 it is a spherical triangle. See the year 1901 in the column 1899 east year No. 12 in the third part of the Northern hemisphere. But due to a spherical triangle it is a negative part. No. 12 means 3-30 hours it shows Kanya Lagna. Add 2 hours, the difference of the negative part. 3-30 plus 2=5-30 hours. The third part of the Northern hemisphere vibrates to the second part of the Southern hemisphere. Internal fourth part of the east year No. 12 vibrates to the internal first part of the west year No. 26. No. 26 means 17-30 hours; it shows Mesha Rashi; that is on 1.10.1901 at 5-30 hours there is Kanya Lagna and Mesha Rashi on the meridian of Ujjain. Birth place Bangalore. Birth time 6-48 hours.

Example No. 7. Birth date 1.10.1945. Deduct the Saptarishikal from the year 1945. 1945-1908=37—27=10—Magha nakshatra from the second division. Saptarishikal is in the second part. Birth date is in the first part. Birth date is No. 1. Birth month is No. 1 (1 plus 0=1) Saptarishikal No. 1 (1 plus 0=1) it is a spherical triangle. See the year 1945 in the column 1944 east year 10 in the second part of the Southern hemisphere but due to a spherical triangle it is a negative part. Then the second part of the southern hemisphere vibrates to the first part of the Southern hemisphere. The internal second part of the east year vibrates to the internal second part of the east year 10. No. 19 means 19-30 hours; add 2 hours the difference of the negative part 19-30 plus 2=21-30 hours; it shows Mithuna Lagna. The second part of the Southern hemisphere vibrates to the fourth part of the Northern hemisphere. The internal second part of the east year No. 10 vibrates to the internal fourth part of the east year No. 1. No. 1 means 1-30 hours; it shows Karka Rashi; that is on 1.10.1945 at 1-30 hours there is Karka Rashi and Mithuna Lagna on the meri-

97

dian of Ujjain. Birth place Lat. 78° 52′ N. Long. 72° 35′ east. Birth time 2 hours.

Example No. 8. Birth date 11.10.1916. Deduct the saptarishikal from the year 1916. 1916-1908=8=Pushya nakshatra from the first division. Spatarishikal is in the first part. Birth date is in the second part. Birth date is 11=2. Birth month is No. 10=1. It is a spherical triangle. See the year 1916 in the column 1908 west year, No. 8 in the second part of the Northern hemisphere. But due to the spherical triangle it is a negative part, then deduct 2 hours, the difference of the negative part, 8-30—2= 6-30 hours it shows Kanya Lagna. The second part of the Northern hemisphere vibrates to the second part of the Southern hemisphere. The internal third part of the west year 8 vibrates to the internal first part of the west year 17. No. 17 means 17-30 hours; deduct 2 hours the difference of the Northern hemisphere 17-30—2=15-30 hours; it shows Meena Rashi. That is on 11.10. 1916 at 6-30 hours there is Kanya Lagna and Meena Rashi on the Meridian of Ujjain. Birth place Lat. 13° 35′ N. Long, 77° 35′ east. Birth time 5-35 hours.

Example No. 9. Birth date 9.10.1923. Deduct the Saptarishikal from the year 1923. 1923-1908=15=Swati Nakshatra from the second division. Saptarishikal is in the first part. Birth date is in the first part. Birth date is No. 9. Birth month is No. 1, Saptarishikal is 15=1 plus 5=6, it is a spherical triangle. See the year 1923 in the column 1917 west year No. 15 in first part of the Northern hemisphere, but due to spherical triangle it is a negative part. Then the first part of the Northern hemisphere vibrates to the second part of the Southern hemisphere. The internal third part of the west year 15 vibrates to the internal second part of the west year 19. No. 19 means 19-30 hours, it shows Mesha Lagna. The first part of the Northern hemisphere vibrates to the second part of the Northern hemisphere. The internal third part of the west year 15 vibrates to the internal first part of the east year 15. No. 15 means 6-30 hours, deduct 2 hours, the difference of the negative part. 6-30—2=4-30 hours, it shows Kanya Rashi, that is on 9.10.1923 at 19-30 hours there is Mesha Lagna and Kanya rashi on the meridian of Ujjain. Birth place Lat. 10° 58′ N. Long. 79° 25′ East. Birth time 18-30 hours.

Example 10. Birth date 16.10.1918. Deduct the saptarishikal from the year 1918. 1918-1908=10=Magha nakshatra from the second division. Saptarishikal is in the first part, birth date in in the second part. Birth month is No. 10=1. Saptarishikal is No. 10=1, it is a spherical triangle. See the year 1918 in the column 1917 east year 10 in the first part of the northern hemisphere, but due to a spherical triangle it is a negative part. Then the first part of the northern hemisphere vibrates to the third part of the Southern hemisphere. The internal first part of the east year 10 vibrates to the internal third part of the west year 23. No. 23 means 23-30 hours, that is 14-30 hours, it shows Makara Lagna. The first part of the Northern hemisphere vibrates to the third part of the Southern hemisphere. Internal first part of the east year 10 vibrates to the internal third part of the west year 23. No. 23 is Dhanishtha nakshatra on 180° of the Magha. Magha is in the Simha Rashi, then Dhanishtha is in the Kumbha, that is on 16.10.1918 at 14-30 hours there is Makara Lagna and Kumbha Rashi on the meridian of Ujjain. Birth place, Lat. 13° N. Long. 5h 10m 20s east. Birth time 14-20 hours.

Example No. 11. Birth date 20.10.1883. Deduct the Saptarishikal from the year 1883. 1883—1808=95-54=21=Uttarashadha nakshatra from the third division. Saptarishikal is in the third part. Birth date is in the third part. Birth date 20=2. Saptarishikal is 21=3. Birth month is 10=1 No. 1-2-3 shows spherical triangle. See the year 1883 in the column 1881 east year 21 in the first part of the Southern hemisphere, but due to the spherical triangle it is a negative part, then the first part of the Southern hemisphere vibrates to the fourth part of the Southern hemisphere. The internal third part of the east year 21 virbrates to the internal first part of the west year No. 12. No. 12 means 12-30 hours, deduct 2 hours, the difference of the negative part, 12-30—2=10-30 hours, it shows Dhanu Lagna. The first part of the Southern hemisphere vibrates to the fourth part of the Northern hemisphere. The internal third part of the east year 21 vibrates to the internal first part of the west year 21. No. 21 means 21-30 hours. Add the 2 hours, the difference of the negative part. 21-30 plus 2=23-30 hours, it shows Karka Rashi, that is on 20.10.1883 at 10-30 hours there is Dhanu Lagna and Karka Rashi on the meridian of Ujjain. Birth place Lat. 12° N. Long 76° 38′ East. Birth time 10 hours.

Example No. 12. Birth date 1.10.1913. Deduct the Saptarishikal from the year 1913. 1913-1908=5=Mriga nakshatra from the first division. Saptarishikal is in the first part. Birth date is in the first part. Birth date is No. 1 Saptarishikal is No. 5. It is a spherical triangle. See the year 1913 in the column 1908 west year No. 5 in the second part of the Northern hemisphere, but due to a spherical triangle it is a negative part. Then instead of the Lagna we will see Rashi No. 5 means 5-30 hours, it shows Thula rashi. The second part of the Northern hemisphere vibrates to

99

the first part of the Northern hemisphere. The internal third part of the west year No. 5 vibrates to the internal first part of the east year No. 10. No. 10 means 10-30 hours, it shows Vrischika Lagna, that is on 1.10.1913 at 10-30 hours there is Thula Rashi and Vrischika Lagna on the meridian of Ujjain. Birth place Lat. 25° N. Long 67° 3′ east. Birth time 10-49 hours.

Example No. 13. Birth date 10.10.1871. Deduct the Saptarishikal from the year 1871. 1871-1808=63-54=9=Aslesha Nakshatra from the first division. Saptarishikal is in the third part. Birth date is in the second part. Birth date is No. 1. Birth month is 10=1, it is a spherical triangle. See the year 1871 in the column 1863 west year No. 9, in the third part of the Southern hemisphere, but due to spherical triangle it is a negative part. No. 9 vibrates to No. 5. No. 5 means 14-30 hours, it shows Kumbha rashi but it is negative, then the third part of the Southern hemisphere vibrates to the third part of the Northern hemisphere. The internal first part of the west year No. 5 vibrates to the internal third part of the west year 10. No. 10 means 1-30 hours, it shows Simha rashi. The third part of the southern hemisphere vibrates to the fourth part of the Southern hemisphere. Internal first part of the west year No. 9 vibrates to the internal third part of the east year No. 9 means 9-30 hours, it shows Dhanu Lagna, that is on 10.10.1871 at 14-30 hours there is Dhanu Lagna and Simha rashi on the meridian of Ujjain. Birth place Lat. 57° 26′ N. Long. 2°.35′ west. Birth time 14 hours.

Example No. 14. Birth date 15.10.1916. Deduct the Saptarishikal from the year 1916. 1916-1908=8=Pushya Nakshatra from the first division. Saptarishikal is in the first part. Birth date is in the second part. Birth date is 15=6. Birth month is 10=1, it is a spherical triangle. See the year 1916 in the column 1908 west year 8 in the second part of the Northern hemisphere. But due to spherical triangle it is a negative part. Then the second part of the Northern hemisphere vibrates to the first part of the Southern hemisphere. The internal third part of the west year No. 8 vibrates to the internal first part of the east year No. 17. No. 17 means 17-30 hours, add the difference of the negative part 17-30 plus 2=19-30 hours, it shows Vrishabha rashi. The second part of the Northern hemisphere vibrates to the fourth part of the Southern hemisphere. The internal third part of the west year No. 8 vibrates to the internal first part of the west year No. 12. No. 12 means 12-30 hours, it shows Dhanu Lagna (Deduct 2 hours the difference of the negative part) that is on 15.10.1916 at 12-30 hours there is Dhanu Lagna and Vrishabha rashi on the meridian of Ujjain. Birth place lat. 13° N. Long. 77° 35′ east. Birth time 12 -26 hrs.

*The spherical triangle means: the sum of the three angles of a triangle is 180° no more holds on curvature surface. It is always greater; so saptarishikal nakshatra is to be negative and the greater nakshatra is positive. If any of the three, birth date, birth month, saptarishikal vibrates to each other on 180° the greater nakshatra should be taken into consideration. The following pairs show the greater Angle Nakshatra:

1-5, 2-6, 3-7, 4-8, 5-9, 6-1, 7-2, 8-3, 9-4,
1-1, 2-2, 3-3, 4-4, 5-5, 6-6, 7-7, 8-8, 9-9.

1-2-3, 2-3-4, 3-4-5, 4-5-6, 5-6-7, 6-7-8,
7-8-9, 8-9-1, 1-4-7, 2-5-8, 3-6-9

*अस्य वामस्य पलितस्य होतुः तस्य भ्राता मध्यमो अस्तश्न
तृतीयो भ्राता घृतपृष्ठः अस्या त्रापश्यम् विश्पति सप्तपुत्रम्

On the left hand of vishnu (Adhananakshatra) there is God Sun with his seven Sons (Saptarishi). The middle brother of Vishnu is Moon, third brother is greater one who is Brahma; in short Aswini is first angle, Magha is second angle, and Moola is third angle which is greater one. घृतपृष्ठः means greater. (The egg of Brahma is earth which is greater). "भूतेन पृथिवी व्युबाी" अस्य—ध्रुवस्य=विष्णु.

Example No. 1. (Second part of the Northern hemisphere) Birth date 31.10.1915. Deduct the Saptarishikal from the year 1915. 1915-1908=7=Punarvasu nakshatra from the first division. Birth date in the fourth part. Saptarishikal is in the first part. See the year 1915 in the column 1908 west year 7 in the second part of the Northern Hemisphere but due to the spherical triangle is a negative part. No. 7 nakshatra is Punarvasu, it is in the west, then see the nakshatra Purvashadha on 180° of the Punarvasu. Purvashadha nakshatra is in the east. Purvashadha nakshatra is No. 20 means 20-30 hours, it shows Karka rashi. The second part of the northern hemisphere vibrates to the second part of the Southern hemisphere. The internal third part of the west year 7 vibrates to the internal first part of the east year 20. Second part of the southern hemisphere vibrates to third part of the Southern hemisphere. The internal first part of the east year 20 vibrates to the internal fourth part of the east year and deduct 2 hours the difference of the Northern hemisphere 20-30—2=18-30. That is on 31.10.1915 at 18-30 hours there is Karka Rashi and Vrishabha Lagna on the Meridian of Ujjain. Birth place Lat. 31° 27' N. Long. 74° 26' east. Birth time 19 hours.

THE SOUTHERN HEMISPHERE OF THE SKY

22nd of October to 21st of November.

FIRST PART — Dec. 2-30, 1-30, 24-30, 23-30, 22-30 Kanya, Simha. Mon., Sun., Sat., Fri., Thurs.

Year	Part	East Year No.	Part	West Year No.	Year	Part	East Year No.	Part	West Year No.	Part
1953	2	18,19,20,21	4	22,23,24,25,26	2025	1	17,18,19,20	4	21,22,23,24,25	3
1809	1	1, 2, 3, 4	3	5, 6, 7, 8, 9	2097	4	8, 9,10,11	3	12,13,14,15,16	2
1881	3	19,20,21,22	1	23,24,25,26,27	2169	3	7, 8,9,10	1	11,12,13,14,15	1
1737	2	2, 3, 4, 5	4	6, 7, 8, 9,10	2241	3	6, 7, 8, 9	2	10,11,12,13,14	4
1665	3	3, 4, 5, 6	1	7, 8, 9,10,11	2313	1	5, 6, 7, 8	1	9,10,11,12,13	3

SECOND PART — Dec. 23-30, 22-30, 21-30, 20-30, 19-30 Simha, Karka. Fri., Thus., Wed., Tue., Mon.

Year	Part	East Year No.	Part	West Year No.	Year	Part	East Year No.	Part	West Year No.	Part
1944	2	9,10,11,12	4	13,14,15,16,17	2016	1	8, 9,10,11	1	12,13,14,15,16	3
1872	3	10,11,12,13	1	14,15,16,17,18	2088	4/3	26,27, 1, 2	4	3, 4, 5, 6, 7	2
1800	4	11,12,13,14	2	15,16,17,18,19	2160	3/2	25,26,27, 1	3	2, 3, 4, 5, 6	1
1728	1	20,21,22,23	3/4	24,25,25,27, 1	2232	2	24,25,26,27	2	1, 2, 3, 4, 5	4
1656	2	21,22,23,24	4/1	25,26,27, 1, 2	2304	4	15,16,17,18	4	19,20,21,22,23	2

THIRD PART — Dec. 20-30, 19-30, 18-30, 17-30, 16-30 Mithuna, Vrishabha. Tues., Mon., Sun., Sat., Fri.

Year	Part	East Year No.	Part	West Year No.	Year	Part	East Year No.	Part	West Year No.	Part
1935	1/2	27, 1, 2, 3	4	4, 5, 6, 7, 8	2007	4	18,19,20,21	2	22,23,24,25,26	2
1863	3	1, 2, 3, 4	1	5, 6, 7, 8, 9	2079	3	17,18,19,20	1	21,22,23,24,25	1
1791	4	2, 3, 4, 5	2	6, 7, 8, 9,10	2157	2	16,17,18,19	4	20,21,22,23,24	4
1719	1	11,12,13,14	3	15,16,17,18,19	2223	2	15,16,17,18	3	19,20,21,22,23	3
1647	2	12,13,14,15	4	16,17,18,19,20	2295	4	6, 7, 8, 9	2	10,11,12,13,14	2

FOURTH PART — Dec. 17-30, 16-30, 15-30, 14-30, 13-30 Vrishabha, Mesha. Sat., Fri., Thus., Wed., Tue.

Year	Part	East Year No.	Part	West Year No.	Year	Part	East Year No.	Part	West Year No.	Part
1926	1	18,19,20,21	3	22,23,24,25,26	1998	4	9,10,11,12	2	13,14,15,16,17	2
1854	2	19,20,21,22	4	23,24,25,26,27	2070	3	8, 9,10,11	1	12,13,14,15,16	1
1782	3	20,21,22,23	1/2	24,25,26,27, 1	2142	2	7, 8, 9,10	4	11,12,13,14,15	4
1710	1	2, 3, 4, 5	3	6, 7, 8, 9,10	2214	1	6, 7, 8, 9	3	10,11,12,13,14	3
1638	2	3, 4, 5, 6	4	7, 8, 9,10,11	2286	2	24,25,26,27	2	1, 2, 3, 4, 5	4

THE NORTHERN HEMISPHERE OF THE SKY

22nd of October to 21st of November.

Dec. 14-30, 13-30, 12-30, 11-30, 10-30 Meena, Kumbha. Wed., Tue., Mon., Sun., Sat. FIRST PART.

Year	Part	East Year No.	Part	West Year No.	Year	Part	East Year No.	West Year No.	Part
1917	1	9,10,11,12	3	13,14,15,16,17	1889	4	0, 1, 2, 3	4, 5, 6, 7, 8	2
1845	2	10,11,12,13	4	14,15,16,17,18	2061	3/2	26,27, 1, 2	3, 4, 5, 6, 7	1
1773	3	11,12,13,14	1	15,16,17,18,19	2133	2/1	25,26,27, 1	2, 3, 4, 5, 6	4
1701	4	12,13,14,15	2	16,17,18,19,20	2205	4	16,17,18,19	20,21,22,23,24	2
1629	1	21,22,23,24	3/4	25,26,27, 1, 2	2277	3	15,16,17,18	19,20,21,22,23	1

Dec. 11-30, 10-30, 9-30, 8-30, 7-30, Makara, Dhanu. Sun., Sat., Fri., Thus., Wed. SECOND PART.

Year	Part	East Year No.	Part	West Year No.	Year	Part	East Year No.	West Year No.	Part
1908	1	0, 1, 2, 3	3	4, 5, 6, 7, 8	1980	3	18,19,20,21	22,23,24,25,26	1
1836	2	1, 2, 3, 4	4	5, 6, 7, 8, 9	2052	2	17,18,19,20	21,22,23,24,25	4
1764	3	2, 3, 4, 5	1	6, 7, 8, 9,10	2124	1	16,17,18,19	20,21,22,23,24	3
1692	4	3, 4, 5, 6	2	7, 8, 9,10,11	2196	4	7, 8, 9,10	11,12,13,14,15	2
1620	1	12,13,14,15	3	16,17,18,19,20	2268	3	6, 7, 8, 9	10,11,12,13,14	1

Dec. 8-30, 7-30, 6-30, 5-30, 4-30 Dhanu, Vrischika. Thus., Wed., Tue., Mon., Sun. THIRD PART.

Year	Part	East Year No.	Part	West Year No.	Year	Part	East Year No.	West Year No.	Part
1899	4	10,11,12,13	2	14,15,16,17,18	1971	3	9,10,11,12	13,14,15,16,17	1
1827	1	19,20,21,22	3	23,24,25,26,27	2043	2	8, 9,10,11	12,13,14,15,16	4
1755	2	20,21,22,23	4/1	25,26,27, 1	2115	1	7, 8, 9,10	11,12,13,14,15	3
1683	3	21,22,23,24	1/2	25,26,27, 1, 2	2187	4/3	25,26,27, 1	2, 3, 4, 5, 6	2
1611	1	3, 4, 5, 6	3	7, 8, 9,10,11	2259	3/2	24,25,26,27	1, 2, 3, 4, 5	4

Dec. 5-30, 4-30, 3-30, 2-30, 1-30 Thula, Kanya. Mon., Sun., Sat., Fri., Thus. FOURTH PART.

Year	Part	East Year No.	Part	West Year No.	Year	Part	East Year No.	West Year No.	Part
1890	4	1, 2, 3, 4	2	5, 6, 7, 8, 9	1962	3	0, 1, 2, 3	4, 5, 6, 7, 8	1
1818	1	10,11,12,13	3	14,15,16,17,18	2034	2/1	26,27, 1, 2	3, 4, 5, 6, 7	4/3
1746	2	11,12,13,14	4	15,16,17,18,19	2106	4	17,18,19,20	21,22,23,24,25	2
1674	3	12,13,14,15	1	16,17,18,19,20	2178	3	16,17,18,19	20,21,22,23,24	1
1602	4	13,14,15,16	2	17,18,19,20,21	2250	2	15,16,17,18	19,20,21,22,23	4

Example No. 2. (Second part of the Northern hemisphere) Birth date 23.10.1910. Deduct the Saptarishikal from the year 1910. 1910-1908=2=Bharani nakshatra from the first division. Saptarishikal is in the first part. Birth date is in the third part. Birth date is No. 23=5. Birth month is No. 10=1, it is a spherical triangle. See the year 1910 in the column 1908 east year No. 2 in the second part of the Northern hemisphere. Nakshatra Bharani is No. 2 but due to the spherical triangle it is greater. The greater Nakshatra in the west is 11. Purva nakshatra means 11-30 hours, it shows Makara Lagna. The second part of the northern hemisphere vibrates to fourth part of the northern hemisphere. The internal second part of the west year No. 11 vibrates to the internal fourth part of the east year No. 2. No. 2 means 2-30 hours, it shows Kanya Rashi. That is on 23.10.1910 at 11-30 hours there is Makara Lagna and Kanya Rashi on the meridian of Ujjain. Birth place lat 13° N. Long, 5 hrs. 10m 20s East.

Example No. 3 (Second part of the Northern hemisphere) Birth date 1.11.1910. Deduct the saptarishikal from the year 1910. 1910-1908=2=Bharani nakshatra from the first division. Saptarishikal is in the first part. Birth date is in the first part. Birth month is No. 2. Saptarishikal nakshatra is No. 2, it is a spherical triangle No. 2 is Bharani nakshatra, but due to spherical triangle it is greater. The greater nakshatra is No. 11. Purva Nakshatra means 11-30 hours, it shows Makara Lagna. The second part of the Northern hemisphere vibrates to the fourth part of the northern hemisphere. The internal first part of the east year No. 2 vibrates to the internal third part of the west year No. 6. No. 6 means 6-30 hours, deduct 2 hours, the difference of the negative part 6-30 hours—2=4-30 hours, it shows Thula Rashi. No. 6 is Aridra nakshatra but due to the spherical triangle it is greater. The greater nakshatra is Swati, deduct 2 hours the difference of the east (day) 15—2=13=Hasta nakshatra shows 13-30 hours. That is on 1-11-1910 at 13-30 hours there is Makara Lagna and Thula Rashi on the Meridian of Ujjain. Birth place lat 13° N. Long 77° 55′ east. Birth time is 13 hours.

Example No. 4 (Third part of the Southern hemisphere) Birth date 5.11.1937. Deduct the Saptarishikal from the year 1937. 1937-1908=29-27=2=Bharani nakshatra from the first division. Saptarishikal is in the second part. Birth date is in the first part. Saptarishikal is No. 2. Birth month is No. 2. It is a spherical triangle. See the year 1937 in the column 1935, east year No. 2. The third part of the southern hemisphere but due to spherical triangle it is a negative part. Then the third part of the southern hemisphere vibrates to the first part of the northern hemisphere. The internal second part of the east year No. 2 vibrates to the internal second part of the west year No. 16 (Bharani vibrates to Vishakha No. 16) No. 16 means 16-30 hours. Deduct 2 hours, the difference of the east (day) 16-30—2=14-30 hours, it shows Meena Lagna. The third part of the southern hemisphere vibrates to the third part of the southern hemisphere. No. 2 vibrates to No. 16. 16 means 16-30 hours, it shows Vrishabha Rashi. That is on 5.11.1937 at 16-30 hours there is Meena Lagna and Vrishabha Rashi on the meridian of Ujjain. Birth place Lat. 13° N. Long. 77° 35′ east. Birth time 16-24 hours.

Example No. 5 (Third part of the Northern hemisphere) Birth date 18.11.1900. Deduct the Saptarishikal from the year 1900. 1900-1808=92-81=11=Purva nakshatra from the second division. Saptarishikal is in the fourth part. Birth date is in the second part. Birth month is No. 2. Saptarishikal is No. 2, it is a spherical triangle. See the year 1900 in the column 1899 east year No. 11. The third part of the northern hemisphere, but due to the spherical triangle it is a negative part. Then the third part of the northern hemisphere vibrates to the fourth part of the southern hemisphere. The internal fourth part of the year 11 vibrates to the internal second part of the west year No. 25. No. 25 means Purvabhadrapada. It is a greater Nakshatra. Vishakha is original nakshatra. Vishakha is No. 16. No. 16 means 16-30 hours, it shows Mesha Lagna. The third part of the northern hemisphere vibrates to the fourth part of the northern hemisphere. The internal fourth part of the east year No. 11 vibrates to the internal second part of the west year 2. No. 2 means 2-30 hours, it shows Kanya Rashi, that is on 18.11.1900 at 16-30 hours there is Mesha Lagna and Kanya Rashi on the meridian of Ujjain. Birth place Lat. 13° N. Long. 77° 35′ east. Birth time 16-17 hours.

Example No. 6 (The first part of the Southern hemisphere). Birth date 8.11.1888. Deduct the saptarishikal from the year 1888. 1888—1808=80-54=26=Uttara Bhadrapada nakshatra from the third division. Saptarishikal is in the third part, birth date is in the first part, birth date is No. 8. Saptarishikal is No. 26=8, it is a spherical triangle. See the year 1888 in the column 1881 west year 26 the first part of the southern hemisphere, but due to the spherical triangle it is the negative part. Then the first part of the southern hemisphere vibrates to the second part of the northern hemisphere. The internal first part of the west year 26 vibrates to the internal third part of the west year 8. No. 8 means 8-30 hours, it shows Dhanu Rashi. The first part of the southern hemisphere vibrates to the fourth part of the northern hemisphere. The internal first part of the west year 26 vibrates to the internal third part of the year 12. No. 12 means Uttara nakshatra, it is a greater nakshatra due to spherical triangle, Krittika Nakshatra No. 3 is original nakshatra. No. 3 means 3-30 hours, add two hours the difference of the east 3-30 plus 2=5-30 hours, it shows Thula Lagna, that is on 8.11.1888 at 5-30 hours there is Thula Lagna and Dhanu Rashi on the meridian of Ujjain. Birth place Lat. 10° 47′ N. Long. 79° 10′ east. Birth time 5-47 hours.

Example No. 7 (The third part of the Northern hemisphere) Birth date 2.11.1903. Deduct the saptarishikal from the year 1903. 1903-1808=95-81=14=Chitra nakshatra from the second division Saptarishikal is in the fourth part. Birth date is in the first part. Birth date is No. 8. Birth month is No. 2 Saptarishikal is No. 5, it is a spherical triangle. See the year 1903 in the column 1899 west year No. 14 the third part of the Northern hemisphere but due to the spherical triangle it is a negative part. Then the third part of the northern hemisphere vibrates to the first part of the northern hemisphere. The internal second part of the west year 14 vibrates to the internal fourth part of the east year 14. No. 14 means 14-30 hours, it shows Meena Lagna. The third part of the northern hemisphere vibrates to the third part of the Southern hemisphere. The internal second part of the west year 14 vibrates to the internal fourth part of the west year 19. No. 19 means 19-30 hours, it shows Mithuna Rashi (14 is a greater nakshatra) No. 5 is original Mriga. Moola nakshatra is on 180° of Mriga That is on 8.11.1903 at 14-30 hours there is Meena Lagna and Mithuna Rashi on the meridian of Ujjain. Birth place Lat. 17° 30′ Long. 78° 40′ east. Birth time 14-30 hours.

Example No. 8. (The second part of the Northern hemisphere). Birth date 5.11.1915. Deduct the saptarishikal from the year 1915. 1915-1908=7=Punarvasu Nakshatra from the first division. Saptarishikal is in the first part. Birth date in the first part. Birth month is No. 2. Saptarishikal is No. 7. It is a spherical triangle. See the year 1915 in the column 1908 west year 7, the second part of the northern hemisphere. No. 7 Punarvasu is on 180° of Purvashadha. Purvashadha is greater nakshatra. Purva No. 11 is original No. 11 means 11-30 hours, it shows Makara Lagna. The second part of the northern hemisphere vibrates to the fourth part of the northern hemisphere. The internal third part of the west year 7 vibrates to the internal third part of the east year 2. No. 2 means 2-30 hours, it shows Kanva rashi. that is on 5.11.1915 at 11-30 hours there is Makara Lagna and Kanya rashi on the meridian of Ujjain. Birth place Lat. 15° N. Long. 77° East. **Birth** time 11-30 hours.

Example No. 9 (Second part of the sourthern hemisphere) Birth date 17.11.1944. Deduct the saptarishikal from the year 1944. 1944-1908=36—27=9=Aslesha nakshatra from the first division. Saptarishikal is in the second part, Birth date is in the second part. Birth date is 17=8. Saptarishikal is No. 9, it is a spherical triangle. See the year 1944 east year No. 9 in the second part of the southern hemisphere but due to spherical triangle it is a negative part. Then the second part of the southern hemisphere vibrates to the fourth part of the northern hemisphere. The internal second part of the east year No. 9 vibrates to the internal fourth part of the west year 5. No. 5 means 5-30 hours, deduct two hours the difference of the east 5-30—2=3-30 hours, it shows Kanya Lagna. Second part of the southern hemisphere vibrates to the third part of the northern hemisphere. The internal second part of the east year 9 vibrates to the internal fourth part of the west year 5. No. 5 means 5-30 hours, it shows Vrischika Rashi, that is on 17.11.1944 at 3-30 hours there is Kanya Lagna and Vrishchika Rashi on the meridian of Ujjain. Birth place Lat. 33° N. Long. 44° 15' East. Birth time 3-17 hours.

Example No. 10 (The first part of the southern hemisphere). Birth date 14.11.1889. Deduct the saptarishikal from the year 1889. 1889-1808=81=0 Revati nakshatra No. 27 from the third division. Saptarishikal is in the third part. Birth date is in the second part. Birth date is No. 5. Saptarishikal nakshatra is No. 9, it is a spherical triangle. See the year 1889 in the column 1881 west year 27 the first part of the southern hemisphere but due to the spherical triangle it is a negative part. Aslesha is a greater nakshatra than the Revati No. 27. Aslesha is No. 9. Shravana nakshatra is on 180° of the Aslesha. Aslesha is in the west. Shravana nakshatra is in the east. Shravana is No. 22. No. 22 means 22-30 hours, it shows Simha Lagna. The first part of the southern hemipshere vibrates to the second part of the southern hemisphere. The internal first part of the west year No. 27 vibrates to the internal first part of the west year No. 22. No. 22 means 22-30 hours, deduct 2 hours the difference of the west year 22-30—2=20-30 hours, it shows Karka Rashi, that is on 14-11-1889 at 22-30 hours there is Simha Lagna and Karka Rashi on meridian of Ujjain. Birth place Allahabad. Birth time 22-30 hours.

THE SOUTHERN HEMISPHERE OF THE SKY

22nd of November to 21st of December.

Dec. 6-30, 5-30, 4-30, 3-30, 2-30 Dhanu, Vriscika

Tue., Mon., Sun., Sat., Fri. First Part.

Year	Part	East Year No.	Part	West Year No.	Year	Part	East Year No.	West Year No.	Part
1953	2	18,19,20,21	4	22,23,24,25,26	2025	1	17,18,19,20	21,22,23,24,25	3
1809	1	1, 2, 3, 4	3	5, 6, 7, 8, 9	2097	4	8, 9,10,11	12,13,14,15,16	2
1881	3	19,20,21,22	1	23,24,25,26,27	2169	3	7, 8,9,10	11,12,13,14,15	1
1737	2	2, 3, 4, 5	4	6, 7, 8, 9,10	2241	2	6, 7, 8, 9	10,11,12,13,14	4
1665	3	3, 4, 5, 6	1	7, 8, 9,10,11	2313	1	5, 6, 7, 8	9,10,11,12,13	3

Dec. 3-30, 2-30, 1-30, 20-30, 23-30 Thula, Kanya.

Sat., Fri., Thus., Wed., Tues. Second Part.

Year	Part	East Year No.	Part	West Year No.	Year	Part	East Year No.	West Year No.	Part
1944	2	9,10,11,12	4	13,14,15,16,17	2016	1	8, 9,10,11	12,13,14,15,16	3
1872	3	10,11,12,13	1	14,15,16,17,18	2088	4/3	26,27, 1, 2	3, 4, 5, 6, 7	2
1800	4	11,12,13,14	2	15,16,17,18,19	2160	3/2	25,26,27, 1	2, 3, 4, 5, 6	1
1728	1	20,21,22,23	3/4	24,25,26,27, 1	2232	1	24,25,26,27	1, 2, 3, 4, 5	3
1656	2	21,22,23,24	4/1	25,26,27, 1, 2	2304	4	15,16,17,18	19,20,21,22,23	2

Dec. 24-30, 23-30, 22-30, 21-30, 20-30 Kanya, Simha.

Wed., Tue., Mon., Sun., Sat. Third Part.

Year	Part	East Year No.	Part	West Year No.	Year	Part	East Year No.	West Year No.	Part
1935	1/2	27, 1, 2, 3	4	4, 5, 6, 7, 8	2007	4	18,19,20,21	22,23,24,25,26	2
1863	3	1, 2, 3, 4	1	5, 6, 7, 8, 9	2079	3	17,18,19,20	21,22,23,24,25	1
1791	4	2, 3, 4, 5	2	6, 7, 8, 9,10	2157	2	16,17,18,19	20,21,22,23,24	4
1719	1	11,12,13,14	3	15,16,17,18,19	2223	1	15,16,17,18	19,20,21,22,23	3
1647	2	12,13,14,15	4	16,17,18,19,20	2295	4	6, 7, 8, 9	10,11,12,13,14	2

Dec. 21-30, 20-30, 19-30, 18-30, 17-30 Karka, Mithuna.

Sun., Sat., Fri., Thus., Wed. Fourth Part.

Year	Part	East Year No.	Part	West Year No.	Year	Part	East Year No.	West Year No.	Part
1926	1	18,19,20,21	3	22,23,24,25,26	1998	4	9,10,11,12	13,14,15,16,17	2
1854	2	19,20,21,22	4	23,24,25,26,27	2070	3	8, 9,10,11	12,13,14,15,16	1
1782	3	20,21,22,23	1/2	24,25,26,27, 1	2142	2	7, 8, 9,10	11,12,13,14,15	4
1710	1	2, 3, 4, 5	3	6, 7, 8, 9,10	2214	1	6, 7, 8, 9	10,11,12,13,14	3
1638	2	3, 4, 5, 6	4	7, 8, 9,10,11	2286	4	24,25,26,27	1, 2, 3, 4, 5	2

THE NORTHERN HEMISPHERE OF THE SKY

22nd of November to 21st of December.

Dec. 18-30, 17-30, 16-30, 15-30, 14-30 Mithuna, Vrishabha. Thurs., Wed., Tue., Mon., Sun. FIRST PART.

Year	Part	East Year No.	Part	West Year No.	Year	Part	East Year No.	West Year No.	Part
1917	1	9,10,11,12	3	13,14,15,16,17	1989	4	0, 1, 2, 3	4, 5, 6, 7, 8	2
1845	2	10,11,12,13	4	14,15,16,17,18	2061	3/2	26,27, 1, 2	3, 4, 5, 6, 7	1
1773	3	11,12,13,14	1	15,16,17,18,19	2133	2/1	25,26,27, 1	2, 3, 4, 5, 6	4
1701	4	12,13,14,15	2	16,17,18,19,20	2205	4	16,17,18,19	20,21,22,23,24	2
1629	1	21,22,23,24	3/4	25,26,27, 1, 2	2277	3	15,16,17,18	19,20,21,22,23	1

Dec. 15-30, 14-30, 13-30, 12-30, 11-30 Mesha, Meena. Mon., Sun., Sat., Fri., Thurs., SECOND PART.

Year	Part	East Year No.	Part	West Year No.	Year	Part	East Year No.	West Year No.	Part
1908	1	0, 1, 2, 3	3	4, 5, 6, 7, 8	1980	3	18,19,20,21	22,23,24,25,26	1
1836	2	1, 2, 3, 4	4	5, 6, 7, 8, 9	2052	2	17,18,19,20	21,22,23,24,25	4
1764	3	2, 3, 4, 5	1	6, 7, 8, 9,10	2124	1	16,17,18,19	20,21,22,23,24	3
1692	4	3, 4, 5, 6	2	7, 8, 9,10,11	2196	4	7, 8, 9,10	11,12,13,14,15	2
1620	1	12,13,14,15	3	16,17,18,19,20	2268	3	6, 7, 8, 9	10,11,12,13,14	1

Dec. 12-30, 11-30, 10-30, 9-30, 8-30 Kumbha, Makara. Fri., Thurs., Wed., Tue., Mon., THIRD PART.

Year	Part	East Year No.	Part	West Year No.	Year	Part	East Year No.	West Year No.	Part
1899	4	10,11,12,13	2	14,15,16,17,18	1971	3	9,10,11,12	13,14,15,16,17	1
1827	1	19,20,21,22	3	23,24,25,26,27	2043	2	8, 9,10,11	12,13,14,15,16	4
1755	3	20,21,22,23	4/1	24,25,26,27, 1	2115	1	7, 8, 9,10	11,12,13,14,15	3
1663	4	21,22,23,24	1/2	25,26,27, 1, 2	2187	4/3	25,26,27, 1	2, 3, 4, 5, 6	2
1611	1	3, 4, 5, 6	3	7, 8, 9,10,11	2259	3/2	24,25,26,27	1, 2, 3, 4, 5	1

Dec. 9-30, 8-30, 7-30, 6-3, 5-30 Makara, Dhanu. Tue., Mon., Sun., Sat., Fri., FOURTH PART.

Year	Part	East Year No.	Part	West Year No.	Year	Part	East Year No.	West Year No.	Part
1890	4	1, 2, 3, 4	2	5, 6, 7, 8, 9	1962	3	0, 1, 2, 3	4, 5, 6, 7, 8	1
1818	1	10,11,12,13	3	14,15,16,17,18	2034	2/1	26,27, 1, 2	3, 4, 5, 6, 7	3
1746	2	11,12,13,14	4	15,16,17,18,19	2106	4	17,18,19,20	21,22,23,24,25	2
1674	3	12,13,14,15	1	16,17,18,19,20	2178	3	16,17,18,19	20,21,22,23,24	1
1602	4	13,14,15,16	2	17,18,19,20,21	2250	2	15,16,17,18	19,20,21,22,23	4

Example No. 1. (Third part of the southern hemisphere). Birth date 26.11.1935. Deduct the saptarishikal from the year 1935. 1935-1908=27=Revati nakshatra from the third division. Saptarishikal is in the first part. Birth date is in the third part. Birth date is 26=8. Saptarishikal is 27=9, it is spherical triangle. See the year 1935 in the column 1935 east year No. 27 the third part of the southern hemisphere, but due to spherical triangle it is a negative part; then the third part of the Southern hemisphere vibrates to the second part of the southern hemisphere. The internal first part of the east year No. 27 vibrates to the internal third part of the west year 27. No. 27 means 3-30 hours (27-24= 3 hours), it shows Thula Lagna. The third part of the southern hemisphere vibrates to the first part of the southern hemisphere. The internal first part of the east year No. 27 vibrates to the internal third part of the west year No. 5 (Revati is a negative nakshatra, due to a spherical triangle. Jyeshtha is greater nakshatra, Mriga nakshatra No. 5 is on 180° of the Jyeshtha. No. 5 means 5-30 hours, deduct two hours, the difference of the east, 5-30—2=3-30 hours, it shows Vrischika Rashi, that is on 26.11.1935 at 3-30 hours there is Thula Lagna and Vrischika Rashi on the meridian of Ujjain. Birth place Ahmednagar, Maharashtra State.

Example No. 2 (Fourth part of the Southern hemisphere). Birth date is 28=No. 1. Saptarishikal nakshatra is 19=No. 1, it 1927. 1927—1908=19=Moola nakshatra from the third division. Saptarishikal is in the first part. Birth date is in the fourth part. Birth date is 28=No. 1. Saptarishikal nakshatra is 19=No. 1, it is a spherical triangle. See the year 1927 in the column 1926 east year 19 the fourth part of the southern hemisphere, but due to the spherical triangle it is a negative part. (Moola No. 19 is a negative nakshatra. Magha is greater nakshatra, Dhanishtha nakshatra is on 180° of the Magha). Then the fourth part of the southern hemisphere vibrates to the third part of the southern hemisphere. The internal first part of west year No. 19 vibrates to the internal first part of the west year No. 23. No. 23 means 23-30 hours. Deduct two hours, the difference of the east 23-30—2=hours, it shows Simha Lagna. The fourth part of the southern hemisphere vibrates to the fourth part of the northern hemisphere. The internal first part of the east year No. 19 vibrates to the internal |first part of the west year No. 5 (Moola nakshatra is on 180° |of Mriga) No. 5 means 5-30 hours, add two hours the difference of the west of the southern hemisphere 5-30 plus 2=7-30 hours, it shows Makara rashi, that is on 28.11.1927 at 21.30 hours there is Simha Lagna and Makara Rashi on the meridian of Ujjain. Birth place Ahmednagar, Maharashtra State.

Example No. 3 (Fourth part of the northern hemisphere) Birth date 14.12.1895. Deduct the saptarishikal from the year 1895. 1895-1808=87—81=6=Aridra nakshatra from the first division. Saptarishikal is in the fourth part. Birth date is in the second part. Birth date is 14=No. 5. Saptarishikal nakshatra is No. 6. It is a spherical triangle. See the year 1895 in the column 1890 west year No. 6 the fourth part of the northern hemisphere, but due to the spherical triangle it is a negative part. Then the fourth part of the northern hemisphere vibrates to the first part of the southern hemisphere. The internal second part of the west year No. 6 vibrates to the internal first part of the east year. No. 1 (Moola nakshatra is on 180° of the Aridra. Moola nakshatra is negative because of the spherical triangle. Aswini is a greater nakshatra). No. 1 means 1-30 hours, add two hours the difference of the west 1-30 plus 2=3-30 hours, it shows Vrischika Rashi. The fourth part of the northern hemisphere vibrates to the second part of the southern hemisphere. The internal second part of the west year 6 vibrates to the internal fourth part of the west year No. 1. No. 1 means 1-30 hours, add two hours, the difference of the southern hemisphere. 1-30 plus 2=3-30 hours, it shows Thula Lagna, that is on 14.12.1895 at 3-30 hours there is Thula Lagna and Vrishchika rashi on the meridian of Ujjain. Birth time 3-30 hours.

Example No. 4 (First part of the Northern hemisphere) Birth date 8.12.1921. Deduct the Saptarishikal from the year 1921. 1921-1908=13. Hasta nakshatra from the second division. Saptarishikal is in the first part. Birth date is in the first part. Birth date is No. 8. Saptarishikal is 13=4, it is a spherical triangle. See the year 1921 in the column 1917 west year No. 17 the first part of the northern hemisphere, but due to the spherical triangle it is a negative part. Then the first part of the northern hemisphere vibrates to the third part of the southern hemisphere. The internal third part of the west year No. 13 vibrates to the internal first part of the west year 22. No. 22 means 22-30 hours, add 2 hours, the difference of the northern hemisphere 22-30 plus 2=24-30 hours, it shows Kanya Lagna. First part of the northern hemisphere vibrates to the third part of the northern hemisphere. The internal third part of the west year 13 vibrates to the internal fourth part of the east year 13. No. 13 means 13-30 hours, deduct two hours, the difference of the southern hemisphere 13-30—2= 11-30 hours, it shows Kumbha rashi. That is on 8.12.1921 at 24-30 hours there is Kanya Lagna and Kumbha rashi on the meridian of Ujjain.

Example No. 5 (Second part of the southern hemisphere). Birth date 2.2.1948. Deduct the saptarishikal from the year 1948. 1948-1908=40, 40-27=13=Hasta nakshatra from the second division, Saptarishikal is in the second part. Birth date is in the first part. Birth date is No. 2. Birth month is 12=No. 3. Saptarishikal nakshatra is 13=4, it is a spherical triangle. See the year 1948 in the column 1944 west year 13, second part of the southern hemisphere, but due to the spherical triangle it is a negative part. Then the second part of the southern hemisphere vibrates to the second part of the northern hemisphere. The internal fourth part of the west year 13 vibrates to the internal first part of the east year 13. Add two hours, the difference of the east, 13 plus 2=15. No. 15 means 15-30 hours, it shows Mesha Lagna. Second part of the southern hemisphere vibrates to the fourth part of the northern hemisphere. (Hasta Nakshatra is a negative. Rohini is greater nakshatra. The internal fourth part of the west year 13 vibrates to the internal fourth part of the east year 4. No. 4 means 4-30 hours, add two hours, the difference of the east, 4-30 plus 2=6-30 hours, it shows Dhanu Rashi, that is on 2.12.1948 at 15-30 hours there is Mesha Lagna and Dhanu rashi on the Meridian of Ujjain. Birth time 14-28 hours.

Example No. 6 (Fourth part of the Northern hemisphere). Birth date 18.12.1898. Deduct the saptarishikal from the year 1898. 1898-1808=90. 90-81=9=Aslesha nakshatra from the first division. Saptarishikal is in the fourth part. Birth date is in the second part. Birth date 18=9 Saptarishikal Nakshatra is No. 9. It is a spherical triangle. See the year 1898 in the column 1890 west year No. 9 fourth part of the northern hemisphere but due to the spherical triangle it is a negative part. Then the fourth part of the northern hemisphere vibrates to the third part of the northern hemisphere. The internal second part of the west year No. 9 vibrates to the internal third part of the east year No. 9. Add two hours, the difference of the west No. 9, it means 9-30 hours plus 2=11—30 hours, it shows Kumbha Rashi. Fourth part of the northern hemisphere vibrates to the second part of the southern hemisphere. The internal second part of the west year No. 9 vibrates to the internal third part of the west year No. 4 (Shravana nakshatra is on 180° of the Aslesha, Shravana is a negative nakshatra because of the spherical triangle. Rohini is greater nakshatra) No. 4 means 4-30 hours, deduct two hours, the difference of the Northern hemisphere 4-30—2=2-30 hours, it shows Thula Lagna, that is on 18.12.1898 at 2-30 hours there is Thula Lagna and Kumbha Rashi on the meridian of Ujjain. Birth time 2-30 hours.

THE NORTHERN HEMISPHERE OF THE SKY

22nd of December to 21st of January.

Dec. 10-30, 9-30, 8-30, 7-30, 6-30 Meena, Kumbha.
Wed., Tue., Mon., Sun., Sat. First Part.

Year	Part	East Year No.	Part	West Year No.	Year	Part	East Year No.	West Year No.	Part
1953	2	18,19,20,21	4	22,23,24,25,26	2025	1	17,18,19,20	21,22,23,24,25	3
1809	1	1, 2, 3, 4	3	5, 6, 7, 8, 9	2097	4	8, 9,10,11	12,13,14,15,16	2
1881	3	19,20,21,22	1	23,24,25,26,27	2169	3	7, 8, 9,10	11,12,13,14,15	1
1737	2	2, 3, 4, 5	4	6, 7, 8, 9,10	2241	2	6, 7, 8, 9	10,11,12,13,14	4
1665	3	3, 4, 5, 6	1	7, 8, 9,10,11	2313	1	5, 6, 7, 8	9,10,11,12,13	3
Dec. 7-30, 6-30, 5-30, 4-30, 3-30 Makara, Dhanu. Sun., Sat., Fri., Thur., Wed. Second Part.									
1944	2	9,10,11,12	4	13,14,15,16,17	2016	1	8, 9,10,11	12,13,14,15,16	3
1872	3	10,11,12,13	1	14,15,16,17,18	2088	4/3	26,27, 1, 2	3, 4, 5, 6, 7	2
1800	4	11,12,13,14	2	15,16,17,18,19	2160	3/2	25,26,27, 1	2, 3, 4, 5, 6	1
1728	1	20,21,22,23	3/4	24,25,25,27, 1	2232	2/1	24,25,26,27	1, 2, 3, 4, 5	3
1656	2	21,22,23,24	4/1	25,26,27, 1, 2	2304	4	15,16,17,18	19,20,21,22,23	2
Dec. 4-30, 3-30, 2-30, 1-30, 24-30 Dhanu, Vrischika. Thur., Wed., Tue., Mon., Sun. Third Part.									
1935	1/2	27, 1, 2, 3	4	4, 5, 6, 7, 8	2007	4	18,19,20,21	22,23,24,25,26	2
1863	3	1, 2, 3, 4	1	5, 6, 7, 8, 9	2079	3	17,18,19,20	21,22,23,24,25	1
1791	4	2, 3, 4, 5	2	6, 7, 8, 9,10	2157	2	16,17,18,19	20,21,22,23,24	4
1719	1	11,12,13,14	3	15,16,17,18,19	2223	1	15,16,17,18	19,20,21,22,23	3
1647	2	12,13,14,15,	4	16,17,18,19,20	2295	4	6, 7, 8, 9	10,11,12,13,14	2
Dec. 1-30, 24-30, 23-30, 22-30, 21-30 Thula, Kanya. Mon., Sun., Sat., Fri., Thur. Fourth Part.									
1926	1	18,19,20,21	3	22,23,24,25,26	1998	4	9,10,11,12	13,14,15,16,17	2
1854	2	19,20,21,22	4	23,24,25,26,27	2070	3	8, 9,10,11	12,13,14,15,16	1
1782	3	20,21,22,23	1/2	24,25,26,27, 1	2142	2	7, 8, 9,10	11,12,13,14,15	4
1710	1	2, 3, 4, 5	3	6, 7, 8, 9,10	2214	1	6, 7, 8, 9	10,11,12,13,14	3
1638	2	3, 4, 5, 6	4	7, 8, 9,10,11	2286	2	24,25,26,27	1, 2, 3, 4, 5	2

THE SOUTHERN HEMISPHERE OF THE SKY

22nd of December to 21st of January.

Dec. 22-30, 21-30, 20-30, 19-30, 18-30 Kanya, Simha.
Fri., Thur., Wed., Tue., Mon. FIRST PART

Year	Part	East Year No.	Part	West Year No.	Year	Part	East Year No.	West Year No.	Part
1917	1	9,10,11,12	3	13,14,15,16,17	1989	4	0,1,2,3	4,5,6,7,8	2
1845	2	10,11,12,13	4	14,15,16,17,18	2061	3/2	26,27,1,2	3,4,5,6,7	1
1773	3	11,12,13,14	1	15,16,17,18,19	2133	2/1	25,26,27,1	2,3,4,5,6	4
1701	4	12,13,14,15	2	16,17,18,19,20	2205	4	16,17,18,19	20,21,22,23,24	2
1629	1	21,22,23,24	3/4	25,26,27,1,2	2277	3	15,16,17,18	19,20,21,22,23	1

Dec. 19-30, 18-30, 17-30, 16-30, 15-30 Karka, Mithuna. SECOND PART.
Tue., Mon., Sun., Sat., Fri.

Year	Part	East Year No.	Part	West Year No.	Year	Part	East Year No.	West Year No.	Part
1908	1	0,1,2,3	3	4,5,6,7,8	1980	3	18,19,20,21	22,23,24,25,26	1
1836	2	1,2,3,4	4	5,6,7,8,9	2052	2	17,18,19,20	21,22,23,24,25	4
1764	3	2,3,4,5	1	6,7,8,9,10	2124	1	16,17,18,19	20,21,22,23,24	3
1692	4	3,4,5,6	2	7,8,9,10,11	2196	4	7,8,9,10	11,12,13,14,15	2
1620	1	12,13,14,15	3	16,17,18,19,20	2268	3	6,7,8,9	10,11,12,13,14	1

Dec. 16-30, 15-30, 14-30, 13-20, 12-30 Mithuna, Vrishabha THIRD PART.
Sat., Fri., Thur., Wed., Tue.

Year	Part	East Year No.	Part	West Year No.	Year	Part	East Year No.	West Year No.	Part
1899	4	10,11,12,13	2	14,15,16,17,18	1971	3	9,10,11,12	13,14,15,16,17	1
1827	1	19,20,21,22	3	23,24,25,26,27	2042	2	8,9,10,11	12,13,14,15,16	4
1755	2	20,21,22,23	4/1	24,25,26,27,1	2115	1	7,8,9,10	11,12,13,14,15	3
1683	3	21,22,23,24	1/2	25,26,27,1,2	2187	4/3	25,26,27,1	2,3,4,5,6	2
1611	1	3,4,5,6	3	7,8,9,10,11	2259	3/2	24,25,26,27	1,2,3,4,5	1

Dec. 13-30, 12-30, 11-30, 10-30, 9-30 Mesha, Meena. FOURTH PART.
Wed., Tue., Mon., Sun., Sat.

Year	Part	East Year No.	Part	West Year No.	Year	Part	East Year No.	West Year No.	Part
1890	4	1,2,3,4	2	5,6,7,8,9	1962	3	0,1,2,3	4,5,6,7,8	1
1818	1	10,11,12,13	3	14,15,16,17,18	2034	2/1	26,27,1,2	3,4,5,6,7	4
1746	2	11,12,13,14	4	15,16,17,18,19	2106	4	17,18,19,20	21,22,23,24,25	2
1674	3	12,13,14,15	1	16,17,18,19,20	2178	3	16,17,18,19	20,21,22,23,24	1
1602	4	13,14,15,16	2	17,18,19,20,21	2250	2	15,16,17,18	19,20,21,22,23	4

Example No. 1 (Fourth part of the southern hemisphere) Birth date 29.12.1893. Deduct the saptarishikal from the year 1893. 1893-1808=85-81=4=Rohini nakshatra from the first division. Saptarishikal is in the fourth part. Birth date is in the fourth part. Birth date is 29=No. 2. Birth month is No. 3. Saptarishikal is No. 4. No. 2-3-4 are in series, it is a spherical triangle. See the year 1893 in the column 1890 east year No. 4. The fourth part of the southern hemisphere, but due to spherical triangle it is a negative part. Then the fourth part of the Southern hemisphere vibrates to second part of the southern hemisphere. The internal fourth part of the east year 4 vibrates to the internal second part of the east year 18. No. 18 means 18-30 hours, it shows Karka Lagna. The fourth part of the Southern hemisphere vibrates to first part of the southern hemisphere. Internal fourth part of the east year No. 4 vibrates to the internal second part of the west year No. 22. No. 22 means 22-30 hours, it shows Kanya Rashi, that is on 29.12.1893 at 18-30 hours there is Karka Lagna and Kanya Rashi on the Meridian of Ujjain.

Example No. 2. (Third part of the Southern hemisphere) Birth date 29.1.1901. Deduct the saptarishikal from the year 1901. 1901-1808=93-81=12=Uttara nakshatra from the second division. Saptarishikal is in the fourth part. Birth date is in the fourth part. Birth month is No. 1. Birth date is No. 2. Saptarishikal nakshatra is No. 3, it is a spherical triangle. See the year 1901 in the column 1899 east year 12 the third part of the southern hemisphere, but due to the spherical triangle it is a negative part for the Lagna No. 12, it means 12-30 hours, it shows Vrishabha Rashi. The third part of the Southern hemisphere vibrates to the second part of the southern hemisphere. The internal fourth part of the east year 12 vibrates to the internal third part of the West year 17. No. 17 means 17-30 hours. Add two hours, the difference of east. 17-30 hours plus 2=19-30 hours. It shows Karka Lagna. That is on 29.1.1901 at 19-30 hours there is Karka Lagna and Vrishabha rashi on the Meridian of Ujjain.

Example No. 3 (Second part of the Southern hemisphere) Birth date 19.1.1913. Deduct the Saptarishikal from the year 1913. 1913-1908=5=Mriga nakshatra from the first division. Saptarishikal is in the first part. Birth date is in the third part. Birth date is 19=No. 1, Birth month is No. 1 saptarishikal is No. 5, it is spherical triangle. See the year 1913 in the column 1908 west year 5, the second part of the Southern hemisphere: but due to spherical triangle it is a negative part. Then the second part of the Southern hemisphere vibrates to the third part of the southern hemisphere. Internal third part of the west year No. 5 vibrates to the internal first of the east year No. 5. No. 5 means 5-30 hours greater nakshatra is 14, it means 14-30 hours, it shows Vrishabha Rashi. The third part of the Southern hemisphere vibrates to first part of the northern hemisphere. The internal first part of the west year 5 vibrates to the internal third part of the west year 5. No. 5 means 5-30 hours, add two hours the difference of the southern hemisphere 5-30 plus 2=7-30 hours. 7-30 hours means Punarvasu nakshsatra. Purvashadha is on 180° of the Punarvasu that is No. 20. No. 20 means 20-30 hours. On 19.1.1913 at 20-30 hours there is Kumbha Lagna and Vrishabha Rashi on the meridian of Ujjain (Moola nakshatra=Birth date which is on 180° of the Mriga Nakshatra=Saptarishikal nakshatra, add 2 hours in Mriga nakshatra. Mriga plus 2=Punarvasu) Birth time 20 hours.

Example No. 4 (Fourth part of the Southern hemisphere). Birth date 2.1.1895. Deduct the saptarishikal from the year 1895. 1895-1808=87-81=6=Aridra nakshatra from the first division. Saptarishikal is in the fourth part, Birth date is in the first part. Birth date is No. 2. Saptarishikal is No. 6, it is a spherical triangle. See the year 1895 in the column 1890 west year 6 the fourth part of the Southern hemisphere. Shatataraka is a greater nakshatra in the southern hemisphere. Shatataraka is No. 24. Magha nakshatra is on 180° of the Shatataraka Magha nakshatra is no. 10. No. 10 means 10-30 hours, it shows Meena Lagna. Birth date is no. 2. No. 2 Bharani nakshatra. Greater nakshatra is Purva No. 11. No. 11 means 11-30 hours it shows Meena Rashi, that is on 2.1.1895 at 11-30 hours there is Meena Rashi and Meena Lagna on the Meridian of Ujjain.

Example No. 1 (Second part of the Southern hemisphere). Birth date 22.1.1914. Deduct the saptarishikal from the year 1914. 1914-1908=6=Aridra nakshatra from the first division. Birth date is in the third part. Saptarishikal is in the first part. Saptarishikal is No. 6. Birth date is No. 4. Birth month is No. 1. No. 1 birth month and No. 6 Saptarishikal, it is a spherical triangle. See the year 1914 in the column 1908 west year 6, Second part of the southern hemisphere, but due to spherical triangle No. 6 is a negative nakshatra. Shatataraka is greater nakshatra. Shatataraka is No. 24. No. 24 means 24-30 hours, it shows Vrischika Rashi. The second part of the southern hemisphere vibrates to the first part of the southern hemisphere. The internal third part of the west year No. 6 vibrates to the internal first part of the west year 6. No. 6 means 6-30 hours, it shows Makara Lagna, that is on 22.1.1914

116

THE NORTHERN HEMISPHERE OF THE SKY

22nd of January to 21st of February

Dec. 18-30, 17-30, 16-30, 15-30 14-30, Simha, Karka, Thur., Wed., Tue., Mon., Sun. FIRST PART.

Year	Part	East Year No.	Part	West Year No.	Year	Part	East Year No.	West Year No.	Part
1953	2	18,19,20,21	4	22,23,24,25,26	2025	1	17,18,19,20	21,22,23,24,25	3
1809	1	1, 2, 3, 4	3	5, 6, 7, 8, 9	2097	4	8,9,10,11	12 13 14,15,16	2
1881	3	19,20,21,22	1	23,24,25,26,27	2169	3	7,8, 9,10	11,12,13,14,15	1
1737	2	2, 3, 4, 5	4	6, 7, 8, 9,10	2241	2	6, 7, 8, 9	10,11,12,13,14	4
1665	3	3, 4, 5, 6	1	7, 8, 9,10,11	2313	1	5, 6, 7, 8	9,10,11,12,13	3

Dec. 15-30, 14-30, 13-30, 12-30, 11-30 Karke, Mithuna, Mon., Sun., Sat., Fri., Thur. SECOND PART.

Year	Part	East Year No.	Part	West Year No.	Year	Part	East Year No.	West Year No.	Part
1944	2	9,10,11,12	4	13,14,15,16,17	2016	1	8, 9,10,11	12,13,14,15,16	3
1872	3	10,11,12,13	1	14,15,16,17,18	2038	4/3	26,27, 1, 2	3, 4, 5, 6, 7	2
1800	4	11,12,13,14	2	15,16,17,18,19	2160	3/2	25,26,27, 1	2, 3, 4, 5, 6	1
1728	1	20,21,22,23	3/4	24,25,26,27, 1	2232	1/2	24,25,26,27	1, 2, 3, 4, 5	4
1656	2	21,22,23,24	4/1	25,26,27, 1, 2	2304	4	15,16,17,18	19,20,21,22,23	2

Dec. 12-30, 11-30, 10-30, 9-30, 8-30, Vrishabha, Mesha Fri., Thur., Wed., Tue., Mon. THIRD PART.

Year	Part	East Year No.	Part	West Year No.	Year	Part	East Year No.	West Year No.	Part
1935	1/2	27, 1, 2, 3	4	4, 5, 6, 7, 8	2007	4	18,19,20,21	22,23,24,25,26	2
1863	3	1, 2, 3, 4	1	5, 6, 7, 8, 9	2079	3	17,18,19,20	21,22,23,24,25	1
1791	4	2, 3, 4, 5	2	6, 7, 8, 9,10	2157	2	16,17,18,19	20,21,22,23,24	4
1719	1	11,12,13,14	3	15,16,17,18,19	2223	1	15,16,17,18	19,20,21,22,23	3
1647	2	12,13,14,15,	4	16,17,18,19,20	2295	4	6, 7, 8, 9	10,11,12,13,14	2

Dec. 9-30, 8-30, 7-30, 6-30, 5-30 Meena, Kumbha Tue., Mon., Sun., Sat., Fri. FOURTH PART.

Year	Part	East Year No.	Part	West Year No.	Year	Part	East Year No.	West Year No.	Part
1926	1	18,19,20,21	3	22,23,24,25,26	1998	4	9,10,11,12	13,14,15,16,17	2
1854	2	19,20,21,22	4	23,24,25,26,27	2070	3	8, 9,10,11	12,13,14,15,16	1
1782	3	20,21,22,23	1/2	24,25,26,27, 1	2142	2	7, 8, 9,10	11,12,13,14,15	4
1710	1	2, 3, 4, 5	3	6, 7, 8, 9,10	2214	1	6, 7, 8, 9	10,11,12,13,14	3
1638	2	3, 4, 5, 6	4	7, 8, 9,10,11	2286	2	24,25,26,27	1, 2, 3, 4, 5	2

117

THE SOUTHERN HEMISPHERE OF THE SKY

22nd of January to 21st of February.

Dec. 6-30, 5-30, 4-30, 3-30, 2-30 Makara, Dhanu,
Sat., Fri., Thurs., Wed., Tue. FIRST PART.

Year	Part	East Year No.	Part	West Year No.	Year	Part	East Year No.	West Year No.	Part
1917	1	9,10,11,12	3	13,14,15,16,17	1889	4	0, 1, 2, 3	4, 5, 6, 7, 8	2
1845	2	10,11,12,13	4	14,15,16,17,18	2061	3/2	26,27, 1, 2	3, 4, 5, 6, 7	1
1773	3	11,12,13,14	1	15,16,17,18,19	2133	2/1	25,26,27, 1	2, 3, 4, 5, 6	4
1701	4	12,13,14,15	2	16,17,18,19,20	2205	4	16,17,18,19	20,21,22,23,24	2
1629	1	21,22,23,24	3/4	25,26,27, 1, 2	2277	3	15,16,17,18,	19,20,21,22,23	1

Dec. 3-30, 2-30, 1-30, 24-30, 23-30 Dhanu. Vrischika
Wed., Tue., Mon., Sun., Sat. SECOND PART.

Year	Part	East Year No.	Part	West Year No.	Year	Part	East Year No.	West Year No.	Part
1908	1	0, 1, 2, 3	3	4, 5, 6, 7, 8	1980	3	18,19,20,21	22,23,24,25,26	1
1836	2	1, 2, 3, 4	4	5, 6, 7, 8, 9	2052	2	17,18,19,20	21,22,23,24,25	4
1764	3	2, 3, 4, 5	1	6, 7, 8, 9,10	2124	1	16,17,18,19	20,21,22,23,24	3
1692	4	3, 4, 5, 6	2	7, 8, 9,10,11	2296	4	7, 8, 9,10	11,12,13,14,15	2
1620	1	12,13,14,15	3	16,17,18,19,20	2268	3	6, 7, 8, 9	10,11,12,13,14	1

Dec. 24-30, 23-30, 22-30, 21-30, 20-30 Thula, Kanya.
Sun., Sat., Fri., Thurs., Wed. THIRD PART.

Year	Part	East Year No.	Part	West Year No.	Year	Part	East Year No.	West Year No.	Part
1899	4	10,11,12,13	2	14,15,16,17,18	1971	3	9,10,11,12	13,14,15,16,17	1
1827	1	19,20,21,22	3	23,24,25,26,27	2043	2	8, 9,10,11	12,13,14,15,16	4
1755	2	20,21,22,23	4/1	24,25,26,27, 1	2115	1	7, 8, 9,10	11,12,13,14,15	3
1683	3	21,22,23,24	1/2	25,26,27, 1, 2	2187	4/3	25 26 27, 1	2, 3, 4, 5, 6	2
1611	1	3, 4, 5, 6	3	7, 8, 9,10,11	2259	2/4	24,25,26,27	1, 2, 3, 4, 5	4

Dec. 21-30, 20-30, 19-30, 18-30, 17-30 Kanya Simha.
Thurs., Wed., Tue., Mon., Sun. FOURTH PART.

Year	Part	East Year No.	Part	West Year No.	Year	Part	East Year No.	West Year No.	Part
1890	4	1, 2, 3, 4	2	5, 6, 7, 8, 9	1962	3	0, 1, 2, 3	4, 5, 6, 7, 8	1
1888	1	10,11,12,13	3	14,15,16,17,18	2034	2/1	26,27, 1, 2	3, 4, 5, 6, 7	4
1746	2	11,12,13,14	4	15,16,17,18,19	2106	4	17,18,19,20	21,22,23,24,25	1
1674	3	12,13,14,15	1	16,17,18,19,20	2178	3	16,17,18 19	20,21,22,23,24	
1602	4	13,14,15,16	2	17,18,19,20,21	2250	2	15,16,17,18	19,20,21,22,23	4

at 6-30 hours there is Makara Lagna and Vrischika Rashi on the meridian of Ujjain. Birth time 6-40 hours.

Example No. 2 (Fourth part of the southern hemisphere) Birth date 31.1.1896. Deduct the saptarishikal from the year 1896. 1896-1808=88-81=7=Punarvasu Nakshatra from the first division. Saptarishikal is in the fourth part. Birth date is in the fourth part. Birth date is 31=No. 4. Birth month is No. 1. Saptarishikal is No. 7, it is a spherical triangle. See the year 1896 in the column 1890 west year No. 7. The fourth part of the southern hemisphere, but due the spherical triangle it is a negative part. Then the fourth part of the southern hemisphere vibrates to the first part of the northern hemisphere. The internal second part of the west year 7 vibrates to the internal second part of the west year 16. No. 16 means 16-30 hours, it shows Karka rashi. The fourth part of the southern hemisphere vibrates to the first part of the southern hemisphere. The internal second part of the west year 7 vibrates to the internal fourth part of the east year 2. No. 2 means 2-30 hours. Add 2 hours the difference of the Northern hemisphere of west year 7. 2-30 plus 2=4-30 hours, it shows Dhanu Lagna, that is on 31.1.1896 at 4-30 hours there is Dhanu Lagna and Karka Rashi on the Meridian of Ujjain.

Example No. 3. (First part of the Northern hemisphere) Birth date is 31.1.1884. Deduct the Saptarishikal from the year 1884. 1884-1808=76. 76-54=22=Shravana nakshatra from the third division. Saptarishikal is in the third part. Saptarishikal is 22=No. 4. Birth date is 31=4, it is a spherical triangle. See the year 1884 in the column 1881 east year 22 the first part of the northern hemisphere. But due to the spherical triangle it is a negative part. No. 22 Shravana nakshatra is a negative, greater nakshatra is Rohini. Then the first part of the Northern hemisphere vibrates to the fourth part of the Southern hemisphere. The internal third part of the east year No. 22 vibrates to the internal first part of the west year 18. No. 18 means 18-30 hours, it shows Simha Lagna. The first part of the Northern hemisphere vibrates to the fourth part of the Northern hemisphere. The internal third part of the east year No. 22 vibrates to the internal third part of the west year 9. No. 9 means 9-30 hours, it shows Meena Rashi, that is on 31.1.1884 at 18.30 hours there is Simha Lagna and Meena Rashi on the Meridian of Ujjain. Birth place Poona, Maharashtra State, Birth time 19 hours.

Example No. 4 (Fourth part of the Northern hemisphere) Birth date 12.2.1856. Deduct the Saptarishikal from the year 1856. 1856-1808=48. 48-27=21=Uttarashadha nakshatra from the third

119

division. Saptarishikal is in the second part. Birth date is in the second part. Birth date is 12=No. 3. Saptarishikal is 21=No. 3, it is a spherical triangle. See the year 1856 in the column 1854 east year No.. 21, the fourth part of the northern hemisphere, but due to the spherical triangle it is a negative part. Then the fourth part of the northern hemisphere vibrates to the third part of the northern hemisphere. The internal second part of the east year No. 21 vibrates to the internal second part of the east year No. 12 means 12-30 hours, it shows Vrishabha Lagna. The fourth part of the northern hemisphere east year No. 21 Uttarashadha is on 180° of the Pushya No. 8. No. 8 means 8.30 hours, it shows Mesha Rashi, that is on 12.2.1856 at 12-30 hours there is Vrishabha Lagna and Mesha Rashi on the Meridian of Ujjain. Birth place Lat. 18° N. Long. 84° East Birth time 12-27 hours.

Example No. 5 (Second part of the Northern hemisphere). Birth date 21.2.1879. Deduct the Saptarishikal from the year 1879. 1879-1808=71-54=17=Anuradha nakshatra from the second division. Saptarishikal is in the third part. Birth date is in the third part. Birth date is 21=No. 3. Saptarishikal is 17=No. 8, it is a spherical triangle. See the year 1879 in the column 1872 west year 17 the second part of the northern hemisphere. (No. 17 is Anuradha nakshatra on 180° of the Rohini but due to spherical triangle Rohini is a negative nakshatra. Hasta nakshatra is greater nakshatra. Hasta is No. 13 means 13-30 hours, it shows Karka Lagna), but due to the spherical triangle it is a negative part. The second part of the northern hemisphere vibrates to the first part of the Southern hemisphere. The internal first part of the west year 17 vibrates to the internal first part of the west year No. 4. No. 4 means 4-30 hours, it shows Makara Lagna. Second part of the northern hemisphere vibrates to fourth part of the northern hemisphere. The internal first part of the west year 17 vibrates to the internal first part of the east year 4. No. 4 means 4-30 hours. Add two hours the difference of the west 4-30 hours plus 2=6-30 hours, it shows Kumbha Rashi, that is on 21.2.1879 at 4-30 hours there is Makara Lagna and Kumbha Rashi on the meridian of Ujjain. Birth place Lat. 10° 43' N. Long. 76° 48' east. Birth time 4-50 hours.

Example No. 6 (First part of the southern hemisphere) Birth date 19.2.1630. Deduct the Saptarishikal from the year 1630. 1630-1608=22=Shravana nakshatra from the third division. Saptarishikal is in the first part. Birth date is in the third part. Birth date is 19=1. Birth month is 2, it is a spherical triangle. See the year 1630 in the column 1629 east year 22 the first part of the

THE NORTHERN HEMISPHERE OF THE SKY

22nd of February to 21st of March.

Dec. 14-30, 13-30, 12-30, 11-30, 10-30 Karka, Mithuna.
Fri., Thurs., Wed., Tue., Mon., FIRST PART.

Year	Part	East Year No.	Part	West Year No.	Year	Part	East Year No.	West Year No.	Part
1953	2	18,19,20,21	4	22,23,24,25,26	2025	1	17,18,19,20	21,22,23,24,25	3
1809	1	1, 2, 3, 4	3	5, 6, 7, 8, 9	2097	4	8, 9,10,11	12,13,14,15,16	2
1881	3	19,20,21,22	1	23,24,25,26,27	2169	3	7, 8, 9,10	11,12,13,14,15	1
1737	2	2, 3, 4, 5	4	6, 7, 8, 9,10	2241	2	6, 7, 8, 9	10,11,12,13,14	4
1665	3	3, 4, 5, 6	1	7, 8, 9,10,11	2313	1	5, 6, 7, 8	9,10,11,12,13	3

Dec. 11-30, 10-30, 9-30, 8-30, 7-30 Mithuna, Vrishabha.
Tue., Mon., Sun., Sat., Fri. SECOND PART.

Year	Part	East Year No.	Part	West Year No.	Year	Part	East Year No.	West Year No.	Part
1944	2	9,10,11,12	2	13,14,15,16,17	2016	1	8, 9,10,11	12,13,14,15,16	3
1872	3	10,11,12,13	1	14,15,16,17,18	2088	3/4	26,27, 1, 2	3, 4, 5, 6, 7	2
1800	4	11,12,13,14	2	15,16,17,18,19	2160	3/2	25,26,27, 1	2, 3, 4, 5, 6	1
1728	1	20,21,22,23	3/4	24,25,26,27, 1	2232	1	24,25,26,27	1, 2, 3, 4, 5	3
1656	2	21,22,23,24	4/1	25,26,27, 1, 2	2304	4	15,16,17,18	19,20,21,22,23	2

Dec. 8-30, 7-30, 6-30, 5-30, 4-30 Mesha, Meena.
Sat., Fri., Thurs., Wed., Tue. THIRD PART.

Year	Part	East Year No.	Part	West Year No.	Year	Part	East Year No.	West Year No.	Part
1935	1/2	27, 1, 2, 3	4	4, 5, 6, 7, 8	2007	4	18,19,20,21	22,23,24,25,26	2
1863	3	1, 2, 3, 4	1	5, 6, 7, 8, 9	2079	3	17,18,19,20	21,22,23,24,25	1
1791	4	2, 3, 4, 5	2	6, 7, 8, 9,10	2157	2	16,17,18,19	20,21,22,23,24	4
1719	1	11,12,13,14	3	15,16,17,18,19	2223	1	15,16,17,18	19,20,21,22,23	3
1647	2	12,13,14,15	4	16,17,18,19,20	2295	4	6, 7, 8, 9	10,11,12,13,14	2

Dec. 5-30, 4-30, 3-30, 2-30, 1-30 Kumbha, Makara.
Wed., Tue., Mon., Sun., Sat. FOURTH PART.

Year	Part	East Year No.	Part	West Year No.	Year	Part	East Year No.	West Year No.	Part
1926	1	18,19,20,21	3	22,23,24,25,26	1998	4	9,10,11,12	13,14,15,16,17	2
1854	2	19,20,21,22	4	23,24,25,26,27	2170	3	8, 9,10,11	12,13,14,15,16	1
1772	3	20,21,22,23	1/2	24,25,26,27, 1	2142	2	7, 8, 9,10	11,12,13,14,15	4
1710	1	2, 3, 4, 5	3	6, 7, 8, 9,10	2214	1	6, 7, 8, 9	10,11,12,13,14	3
1638	2	3, 4, 5, 6	4	7, 8, 9,10,11	2286	3	24,25,26,27	1, 2, 3, 4, 5	1

THE SOUTHERN HEMISPHERE OF THE SKY

22nd of February to 21st of March.

FIRST PART.

Dec. 2-30, 1-30, 24-30, 23-30, 22-30 Dhanu, Vrischika.
Sun., Sat., Fri., Thurs., Wed.

Year	Part	East Year No.	Part	West Year No.	Year	Part	East Year No.	Part	West Year No.
1917	1	9,10,11,12	4	13,14,15,16,17	1989	4	0, 1, 2, 3	2	4, 5, 6, 7, 8
1845	2	10,11,12,13	3/2	14,15,16,17,18	2061	3/2	26,27, 1, 2	1	3, 4, 5, 6, 7
1773	3	11,12,13,14	2/1	15,16,17,18,19	2133	2/1	25,26,27, 1	4	2, 3, 4, 5, 6
1701	4	12,13,14,15	4	16,17,18,19,20	2205	4	16,17,18,19	2	20,21,22,23,24
1629	1	21,22,23,24	3	25,26,27, 1, 2	2277	3	15,16,17,18	1	19,20,21,22,23

SECOND PART.

Dec. 23-30, 22-30, 21-30, 20-30, 19-30 Vrischika, Thula.
Thurs., Wed., Tue., Mon., Sun.

Year	Part	East Year No.	Part	West Year No.	Year	Part	East Year No.	Part	West Year No.
1908	1	0, 1, 2, 3	3	4, 5, 6, 7, 8	1980	3	18,19,20,21	1	22,23,24,25,26
1836	2	1, 2, 3, 4	4	5, 6, 7, 8, 9	2052	2	17,18,19,20	4	21,22,23,24,25
1764	3	2, 3, 4, 5	1	6, 7, 8, 9,10	2124	1	16,17,18,19	3	20,21,22,23,24
1692	4	3, 4, 5, 6	2	7, 8, 9,10,11	2196	4	7, 8, 9,10	2	11,12,13,14,15
1620	1	12,13,14,15	3	16,17,18,19,20	2268	3	6, 7, 8, 9	1	10,11,12,13,14

THIRD PART.

Dec. 20-30, 19-30, 18-30, 17-30, 16-30 Kanya, Simha.
Mon., Sun., Sat., Fri., Thurs.

Year	Part	East Year No.	Part	West Year No.	Year	Part	East Year No.	Part	West Year No.
1899	4	10,11,12,13	2	14,15,16,17,18	1971	3	9,10,11,12	1	13,14,15,16,17
1827	1	19,20,21,22	3	23,24,25,26,27	2043	2	8, 9,10,11	4	12,13,14,15,16
1755	2	20,21,22,23	4/1	24,25,26,27, 1	2115	1	7, 8, 9,10	3	11,12,13,14,15
1683	3	21,22,23,24	1/2	25,26,27, 1, 2	2187	4/3	25,26,27, 1	2	2, 3, 4, 5, 6
1611	1	3, 4, 5, 6	3	7, 8, 9,10,11	2259	2	24,25,26,27	1	1, 2, 3, 4, 5

FOURTH PART.

Dec. 17-30, 16-30, 15-30, 14-30, 13-30 Simha, Karka.
Fri., Thurs., Wed., Tue., Mon.

Year	Part	East Year No.	Part	West Year No.	Year	Part	East Year No.	Part	West Year No.
1890	4	1, 2, 3, 4	2	5, 6, 7, 8, 9	1962	3	0, 1, 2, 3	1	4, 5, 6, 7, 8
1818	1	10,11,12,13	3	14,15,16,17,18	2034	2/1	26,27, 1, 2	4	3, 4, 5, 6, 7
1746	2	11,12,13,14	4	15,16,17,18,19	2106	4	17,18,19,20	2	21,22,23,24,25
1674	3	12,13,14,15	1	16,17,18,19,20	2178	3	16,17,18,19	1	20,21,22,23,24
1602	4	13,14,15,16	2	17,18,19,20,21	2250	2	15,16,17,18	4	19,20,21,22,23

Southern hemisphere, but due to the spherical triangle it is a negative part. Then the first part of the Southern hemisphere vibtrates to the first part of the northern hemisphere. The internal first part of the east year No. 22 vibrates to the internal first part of the east year 18 (Shravana is negative.. Rohini is greater nakshatra. Jyeshtha nakshatra is on 180° of the Rohini) No. 18 means 18-30 hours, it shows Simha Lagna. The first part of the southern hemisphere vibrates to the fourth part of the southern hemisphere. The internal first part of the east year No. 22 vibrates to the internal third part of the west year 18. No. 18 means 18-30 hours, add two hours, the difference of the east year 18-30 plus 2=20-30 hours, it shows Kanya Rashi, that is on 19.2.1630 at 18-30 hours there is Simha Lagna and Kanya Rashi on the meridian of Ujjain. Birth place Lat. 18° 32' N. Long. 73° 53' east. Birth time 18-26 hours.

Example No. 1 (Third part of the Northern hemisphere). Birth date is 22.2.1863. Deduct the Saptarishikal from the year 1863. 1863-1808=55. 55-54=1=Aswini nakshatra from the first division. Saptarishikal is in the third part. Birth month is No. 2. Saptarishikal is No. 1, it is a spherical triangle. See the year 1863 east year No. 1 in the third part of the northern hemisphere: but due to the spherical triangle No. 1 is a negative part. Moola nakshatra is greater in the third part of the Saptarishikal. Aridra nakshatra is on 180° of the Moola, Aridra is No. 6. No. 6 means 6-30 hours, it shows Mesha Rashi. The third part of the northern hemisphere vibrates to the second part of the southern hemisphere. The internal third part of the east year No. 1 vibrates to the internal third part of the east year 19. No. 19 means 19-30 hours, it shows Thula Lagna, that is on 22.2.1863 at 19-30 hours there is Mesha Rashi and Thula Lagna on the meridian of Ujjain. Birth place Lat. 13° N. Long 5h 10m 20s east.

Example No. 2 (Fourth part of the Southern hemisphere) Birth date 23.2.1896. Deduct the Saptarishikal from the year 1896. 1896-1808=88-81=7=Punarvasu nakshatra from the first division. Saptarishikal is in the fourth part. Birth date is in the third part. Birth month is No. 2. Saptarishikal is No. 7, it is a spherical triangle. See the year 1896 in the column 1890 west year No. 7 the fourth part of the Southern hemisphere but due to the spherical triangle it is negative part. Then the fourth part of the Southern hemisphere vibrates to the second part of the southern hemisphere. The internal second part of the west year 7 vibrates to the internal third part of the west year 20 (Purvashadha nakshatra is on 180° of the Punarvasu) No. 20 means 20-30 hours, it shows Thula Lagna. The fourth part of the southern hemisphere vibrates to the first part of the Northern hemisphere. The internal second part of the west year 7 vibrates to the internal second part of the west year 11. No. 11 means 11-30 hours, it shows Mithuna Rashi, that is on 23.2.1896 at 20-30 hours there is Thula Lagna and Mithuna Rashi on the meridian of Ujjain.

Example No. 3 (Fourth part of the southern hemisphere) Birth date 25.2.1894. Deduct the Saptarishikal from the year 1894. 1894-1808=86-81=5=Mriga nakshatra from first division Saptarishikal is in the fourth part. Birth date is in the third part. Birth date is 25=No. 7. Birth month is No. 2, it is a spherical triangle. See the year 1894 in the column 1890 west year No. 5 the fourth part of the southern hemisphere, but due to the spherical triangle it is a negative part. Then the fourth part of the southern hemisphere vibrates to the third part of the northern hemisphere. The internal second part of the west year No. 5 vibrates to the internal second part of the west year No. 10. 10 means 10-30 hours, it shows Mesha Lagna. The fourth part of the southern hemisphere vibrates to the second part of the southern hemisphere, the internal second part of the west year No. 5 vibrates to the internal first part of the east year 19 (Moola nakshatra is on 180° of the Mriga) No. 19 means 19-30 hours, it shows Thula rashi, that is on 25.2.1894 at 8-30 hours there is Mesha Lagna and Thula rashi on the meridian of Ujjain. Birth place Lat. 18° 32′ N. Long. 73° 53′ east. Birth time 8-55 hours.

Example No. 4 (Fourth part of the Northern hemisphere). Birth date 29.2.1932. Deduct the Saptarishikal from the year 1932. 1932—1908=24=Shatataraka nakshatra from the third division. Saptarishikal is in the first part. Birth date is in the fourth part. Birth date is 29=No. 2 Saptarishikal is 24=6, it is a spherical triangle. See the year 1932 in the column 1926 west year 24 the fourth part of the Northern hemisphere: but due to a spherical triangle Shatataraka is negative nakshatra. Aridra is a greater nakshatra. Aridra is No. 6. No. 6 means 6-30 hours, deduct 2 hours, the difference of the negative nakshatra 6-30-2=4-30 hours, it shows Kumbha Lagna. The fourth part of the northern hemisphere vibrates to the second part of the southern hemisphere. The internal third part of the west year No. 24 vibrates to the internal first part of the east year 24. No. 24 means 24-30 hours, deduct 2 hours the difference of the northern hemisphere. 24-30—2=22-30 hours, it shows Vrischika rashi, that is on 20.2.1932 at 4-30 hours there is Kumbha lagna and Vrischika rashi on the meridian of Ujjain. (Birth month as well as birth date vibrates to Saptarishikal, that is, in both ways Shatataraka nakshatra is negative, Aridra nakshatra is greater for the moon and sidereal time, deduct the difference of two

124

hours from both the hemispheres because of the Mula Trikona, nakshatra day 1. Birth place Lat. 13° N. Long. 77° 35′ East. Birth time 5-39 hours.

Example No. 5 (Fourth part of the southern hemisphere) Birth date 3.3.1894. Deduct the saptarsihikal from the year 1894. 1894-1808-86-81=5=Mriga nakshatra from the fourth part. Birth date is No. 3. Birth month is No. 3, it is a spherical triangle. See the year 1894 in the column 1890 west year No. 5, due to the spherical triangle Mriga nakshatra is negative. Chitra No. 14 is a greater nakshatra. Chitra No. 14 means 14-30 hours minus 2, it shows Karka Lagna. The fourth part of the southern hemisphere vibrates to the fourth part of the northern hemisphere. The internal second part of the west year No. 5 vibrates to the internal first part of the east year 19 (Moola nakshatra is on 180° of the Mriga) due to spherical triangle Moola nakshatra No. 19 is negative. Aswini No. 1 is a greater nakshatra. No. 1 means 1-30 hours, there is Karka Lagna and Makara rashi on the meridian of Ujjain. Birth place Lat. 12° 52′ N. Long 74° 54′ east. Birth time 15-16 hours.

Example No. 6 (first part of the northern hemisphere) Birth date 4.3.1886. Deduct the Saptarishikal from the year 1886. 1886-1808=78-54=24=Shatataraka nakshatra from the third division. Saptarishikal is in the third part. Birth date is in the first part. Birth date is No. 4. Birth month is No. 3, it is a spherical triangle. See the year 1886 in the column 1881 west year No. 24 the first part of the northern hemisphere: but due to the spherical triangle it is a negative part. Then the first part of the northern hemisphere vibrates to the first part of the southern hemisphere. The internal third part of the west year No. 24 vibrates to the internal first part of the west year No. 24. No. 24 means 24-30 hours, it shows Vrischika Lagna. The first part of the Southern hemisphere vibrates to the fourth part of northern hemisphere. The internal third part of the west year 24 vibrates to the internal first part of the east year No. 6. No. 6 means 6-30 hours, deduct two hours the difference of the west. 6-30 hours minus 2=4-30 hours, it shows Kumbha rashi, that is on 4.3.1886 at 24-30 hours there is Kumbha rashi and Vrischika Lagna on the Meridian of Ujjain. Birth place Lat. 16° 40′ N. Long. 81° east. Birth time 23-30 hours.

Example No. 7 (Fourth part of the northern hemisphere) Birth date 11.3.1858. Deduct the saptarishikal from the year 1858. 1958-1808=50-27=23=Dhanistha nakshatra from the third division. Saptarishikal is in the second part. Birth date is in the second part, birth date is 11=No. 2. Birth month is No. 3, it is a spherical triangle. See the year 1858 in the column 1854 west year 23, the fourth part of the northern hemisphere: but due to a spherical triangle Dhanistha No. 23 is a negative nakshatra. Chitra No. 14 is a greater nakshatra. Chitra is on 180° of the Aswini. Aswini is No. 1. No. 1 means 1-30 hours, it shows Makara rashi. The fourth part of the northern hemisphere vibrates to the second part of the southern hemisphere. The internal fourth part of the west year No. 23 vibrates to the internal first part of the east year No. 19. No. 19 means 19-30 hours, add two hours, the difference of the west. 19-30 hours plus 2=21-30 hours, it shows Thula Lagna. That is on 11.3.1858 at 21-30 hours there is Thula Lagna and Makara Rashi on the meridian of Ujjain. Birth place Lat. 13° N. Long. 5h. 10 20s. east. Birth time 21 hours.

Example No. 8 (First part of the southern hemisphere) Birth date 21.3.1921. Deduct the saptarishikal from the year 1921. 1921-1908=13=Hasta nakshatra from the second division. Saptarishikal is in the first part. Birth date is in the third part. Birth date is 21=3. Birth month is No. 3. Saptarishikal nakshatra is 13=No. 4, it is a spherical triangle. See the year 1921 in the column 1917 west year No. 13 the first part of the southern hemisphere, but due to the spherical triangle (No. 13 Hasta nakshatra is negative, Shravana nakshatra No. 22 is a greater nakshatra, Aslesha nakshatra is on 180° of the Shravana) it is a negative part, then the first part of the southern hemisphere vibrates to the second part of the northern hemisphere. The internal third part of the west year 13 vibrates to the internal first part of the east year No. 9 means 9-30 hours, add two hours the difference of the west. 9-30 plus 2=11-30 hours, it shows Mithuna Lagna. The first part of the southern hemisphere vibrates to the third part of the Southern hemisphere. The internal third part of the west year 13 vibrates to the internal second part of the west year No. 18, due to the spherical triangle Hasta nakshatra is a negative and the greater nakshatra is Rohini for the moon. Jyeshtha nakshatra is on 180° of the Rohini). No. 18 means 18-30 hours, it shows Simha rashi. That is on 21.3.1921 there is Mithuna Lagna and Simha rashi at 11-30 hours on the meridian of Ujjain. Birth place Lat. 10° N. Long. 5 h. 10m. 20s. East. Birth time 12 hours.

Example No. 1 (Fourth part of the Northern Hemisphere). Birth date 23.3.1929. Deduct the Saptarishikal from the year 1929. 1929-1908=21=Uttarashadha nakshatra from the third division. Saptarishikal is in the first part. Birth month is No. 3. Saptarishikal is 21=3, it is a spherical triangle. See the year 1929 in the column 1926 east year No. 21 the fourth part of the northern hemisphere, but due to spherical triangle it is negative

THE NORTHERN HEMISPHERE OF THE SKY

22nd of March to 21st of April.

Dec. 10-30, 9-30, 8-30, 7-30, 6-30 Mithuna, Vrishabha.
Sat., Fri., Thurs., Wed., Tue. FIRST PART.

Year	Part	East Year No.	Part	West Year No.	Part	Year	Part	East Year No.	West Year No.	Part
1953	2	18,19,20,21	4	22,23,24,25,26	1	2025	1	17,18,19,20	21,22,23,24,25	3
1809	1	1, 2, 3, 4	3	5, 6, 7, 8, 9	4	2097	4	8, 9,10,11	12,13,14,15	2
1881	3	19,20,21,22	1	23,24,25,26,27	3	2169	3	7, 8, 9,10	11,12,13,14	1
1737	2	2, 3, 4, 5	4	6, 7, 8, 9,10	2	2241	2	6, 7, 8	10,11,12,13,14	4
1665	3	3, 4, 5, 6	1	7, 8, 9,10,11	1	2313	1	5, 6, 7, 8	9,10,11,12,13	3

Dec. 7-30, 6-30, 5-30, 4-30, 3-30 Mesha, Meena.
Wed., Tue., Mon., Sun., Sat. SECOND PART.

Year	Part	East Year No.	Part	West Year No.	Part	Year	Part	East Year No.	West Year No.	Part
1944	2	9,10,11,12	4	13,14,15,16,17	1	2016	1	8, 9,10,11	12,13,14,15,16	3
1872	3	10,11,12,13	1	14,15,16,17,18	4/3	2088	4/3	26,27, 1, 2	3, 4, 5, 6, 7	2
1800	4	11,12,13,14	2	15,16,17,18,19	3/2	2160	3/2	25,26,27, 1	2, 3, 4, 5, 6	1
1728	1	20,21,22,23	3/4	24,25,25,27, 1	1	2232	1	24,25,26,27	1, 2, 3, 4, 5	3
1656	2	21,22,23,24	4/1	25,26,27, 1, 2	4	2304	4	15,16,17,18	19,20,21,22,23	2

Dec. 4-30, 3-30, 2-30, 1-30, 24-30 Meena, Kumbha.
Sun., Sat., Fri., Thurs., Wed. THIRD PART.

Year	Part	East Year No.	Part	West Year No.	Part	Year	Part	East Year No.	West Year No.	Part
1935	1/2	27, 1, 2, 3	4	4, 5, 3, 7, 8	4	2007	4	18,19,20,21	22,23,24,25,26	2
1863	3	1, 2, 3, 4	1	5, 6, 7, 8, 9	3	2079	3	17,18,19,20	21,22,23,24,25	1
1791	4	2, 3, 4, 5	2	6, 7, 8, 9,10	2	2151	2	16,17,18,19	20,21,22,23,24	4
1719	1	11,12,13,14	3	15,16,17,18,19	1	2223	1	15,16,17,18	19,20,21,22,23	3
1647	2	12,13,14,15	4	16,17,18,19,20	4	2295	4	6, 7, 8, 9	10,11,12,13,14	2

Dec. 1-30, 24-30, 23-30, 22-30, 21-30 Makara, Dhanu.
Thurs., Wed., Tue., Mon., Sun. FOURTH PART.

Year	Part	East Year No.	Part	West Year No.	Part	Year	Part	East Year No.	West Year No.	Part
1926	1	18,19,20,21	3	22,23,24,25,26	4	1998	4	9,10,11,12	13,14,15 16,17	2
1854	2	19,20,21,22	4	23,24,25,26,27	3	2070	3	8, 9,10,11	12,13,14 15,16	1
1782	3	20,21,22,23	1/2	24,25,25,27, 1	2	2142	2	7, 8, 9,10	11,12,13,14,15	4
1710	1	2, 3, 4, 5	3	6, 7, 3, 9,10	1	2214	1	6, 7, 8, 9	10,11,12,13,14	3
1638	2	3, 4, 5, 6	4	7, 8, 9,10,11	3	2286	3	24,25,26,27	1, 2, 3, 4, 5	2

THE SOUTHERN HEMISPHERE OF THE SKY

22nd of March to 21st of April.

Dec., 22-30, 21-30, 20-30, 19-30, 18-30 Dhanu, Vrischika.

Mon., Sun., Sat., Fri., Thurs., FIRST PART.

Year	Part	East Year No.	Part	West Year No.	Year	Part	East Year No.	West Year No.	Part.
1917	1	9,10,11,12	3	13,14,15,16,17	1998	4	0, 1, 2, 3	4, 5, 6, 7, 8	2
1845	2	10,11,12,13	4	14,15,16,17,18	2061	3/2	26,27, 1, 2	3, 4, 5, 6, 7	1
1773	3	11,12,13,14	1	15,16,17,18,19	2133	2/1	25,26,27, 1	2, 3, 4, 5, 6	4
1701	4	12,13,14,15	2	16,17,18,19,20	2205	4	16,17,18,19	20,21,22,23,24	2
1629	1	21,22,23,24	3/4	25,26,27, 1, 2	2277	3	15,16,17,18	19,20,21,22,23	1

Dec. 19-30, 18-30, 17-30, 16-30, 15-30 Thula, Kanya.

Fri., Thurs., Wed., Tue., Mon., SECOND PART.

Year	Part	East Year No.	Part	West Year No.	Year	Part	East Year No.	West Year No.	Part.
1908	1	0, 1, 2, 3	3	4, 5, 6, 7, 8	1980	3	18,19,20,21	22,23,24,25,26	1
1836	2	1, 2, 3, 4	4	5, 6, 7, 8, 9	2052	2	17,18,19,20	21,22,23,24,25	4
1764	3	2, 3, 4, 5	1	6, 7, 8, 9,10	2124	1	16,17,18,19	20,21,22,23,24	3
1692	4	3, 4, 5, 6	2	7, 8, 9,10,11	2196	4	7, 8, 9,10	11,12,13,14,15	2
1620	1	12,13,14,15	3	16,17,18,19,20	2268	3	6, 7, 8, 9	10,11,12,13,14	1

Dec. 16-30, 15-30, 14-30, 13-30, 12-30, Kanya, Simha.

Tue., Mon., Sun., Sat., Fri., THIRD PART.

Year	Part	East Year No.	Part	West Year No.	Year	Part	East Year No.	West Year No.	Part.
1899	4	10,11,12,13	2	14,15,16,17,18	1971	3	9,10,11,12	13,14,15,16,1	1
1827	1	19,20,21,22	3	23,24,25,26,27	2042	2	8, 9,10,11	12,13,14,15,1	4
1755	2	20,21,22,23	4/1	24,25,26,27, 1	2115	1	7, 8, 9,10	11,12,13,14	3
1683	3	21,22,23,24	1/2	25,26,27, 1, 2	2187	4/3	25,26,27, 1	2, 3, 4, 5, 6	3
1611	1	3, 4, 5, 6	3	7, 8, 9,10,11	2259	3/2	24,25,26,27	1, 2, 3, 4, 5	4

Dec. 13-30, 12-30, 11-30, 10-30, 9-30 Karka, Mithuna.

Sat., Fri., Thurs., Wed., Tue., FOURTH PART.

Year	Part	East Year No.	Part	West Year No.	Year	Part	East Year No.	West Year No.	Part.
1890	4	1, 2, 3, 4	2	5, 6, 7, 8, 9	1962	3	0, 1, 2, 3	4, 5, 6, 7, 8	1
1818	1	10,11,12,13	3	14,15,16,17,18	2034	2/1	26,27, 1, 2	3, 4, 5, 6, 7	4
1746	2	11,12,13,14	4	15,16,17,18,19	2106	4	17,18,19,20	21,22,23,24,25	2
1674	3	12,13,14,15	1	16,17,18,19,20	2178	3	16,17,18,19	20,21,22,23,24	1
1602	4	13,14,15,16	2	17,18,19,20,21	2250	2	15,16,17,18	19,20,21,22,23	4

part. Then the fourth part of the northern hemisphere vibrates to the third part of the southern hemisphere. The internal first part of the east year 21 vibrates to the internal third part of the east year No. 12. No. 12 means 12-30 hours, it shows Simha Rashi. The fourth part of the northern hemisphere vibrates to the second part of the southern hemisphere. The internal first part of the east year No. 21 vibrates to the internal third part of the west year 16 (Uttarashada is a negative nakshatra, Krittika is a greater nakshatra, Vishakha nakshatra is on 180° of the Krittika. Vishakha nakshatra is No. 16) No. 16 means 16-30 hours, it shows Kanya Rashi, that is on 23.3.1929 at 16-30 hours there is Kanya Lagna and Simha Rashi on the meridian of Ujjain. Birth place Lat. 20° N. Long. 77° 30′ east. Birth time 17-10 hours.

Example No. 2 (Third part of the southern hemisphere) Birth date 27.3.1902. Deduct the Saptarishikal from the year 1902. 1902—1808=94—81=13=Hasta nakshatra from the second division. Saptarishikal is in the fourth part. Birth date is 27=No. 9. Birth month is No. 3, Saptarishikal is No. 4. It is a spherical triangle. See the year 1902 in the column 1899 east year No. 13 the third part of the southern hemisphere, but due to the spherical triangle Hasta nakshatra No. 13 is a negative. Shravana nakshatra is a greater nakshatra. Aslesha nakshatra No. 9 is on 180° of the shravana. Aslesha nakshatra is No. 9. No. 9 means 9-30 hours, it shows Vrishabha Lagna. The third part of the southern hemisphere vibrates to the second part of the southern hemisphere. Internal fourth part of the east year 13 vibrates to the internal third part of the west year 18. No. 18 means 18-30 hours. Add two hours the difference of the east. 18-30 plus 2 hours, it shows Thula rashi, that is on 27.3.1902 at 9-30 hours there is Vrishabha Lagna and Thula rashi on the meridian of Ujjain. Birth place Lat 13° N. Long 77° 35′ east. Birth time 10-15 hours.

Example No. 3 (First part of the southern hemisphere) Birth date 3.4.1920. Deduct the Saptarishikal from the year 1920. 1920—1908=12=Uttara nakshatra from the second division. Saptarishikal is in the first part. Birth date is No. 3. Birth month is No. 4. Saptarishikal nakshatra is 12=No. 3 it is a spherical triangle. See the year 1920 in the column 1917 east year No. 12 the first part of the southern hemisphere, but due to the spherical triangle Uttara Nakshatra is negative. Krittika nakshatra is greater. Anuradha is on 180° of Krittika. Anuradha is No. 17. No. 17 means 17-30 hours, it shows Kanya Rashi. Birth month is No. 3, that is Krittika nakshatra. Anuradha is on 180° of the Krittika. Anuradha is No. 17. No. 17 means 17-30 hours, it shows Kanya Rashi. That is on 3.4.1920 at 17.30 hours there is Kanya Lagna and Kanya rashi on the meridian of Ujjain. Birth place Lat. 17° N. Long. 78° 15′ east. Birth time 17-13 hours.

Example No. 4 (Second part of the northern hemisphere) Birth date 4.4.1949. Deduct the saptarishikal from the year 1949. 1949—1908=41-27=14=Chitra nakshatra from the second division. Birth date is No. 4. Birth month is No. 4. Saptarishikal is No. 14=5. Saptarishikal is in the second part, it is a spherical triangle. See the year 1949 in the column 1944 west year 14 the second part of the Northern hemisphere, but due to spherical triangle (Chitra nakshatra No. 14 is negative. Dhanishtha nakshatra is greater nakshatra. Aslesha nakshatra is on 180° of Dhanishtha. Aslesha is No. 9. No. 9 means 9-30 hours), it is a negative part, then the second part of the northern hemisphere vibrates to the first part of the northern hemisphere. The internal fourth part of the west year 14 vibrates to the internal fourth part of the west year 9. No. 9 means 9-30 hours, it shows Mithuna rashi. The second part of the Northern hemisphere vibrates to the fourth part of the southern hemisphere. The internal fourth part of the west year 14 vibrates to the internal second part of the west year No. 9. No. 9 means 9-30 hours, add two hours the difference of the northern hemisphere 9-30 plus 2=11-30 hours, it shows Karka Lagna, that is on 4.4.1949 at 11-30 hours there is Karka Lagna and Mithuna rashi on the meridian of Ujjain. Birth place Lat. 38° N. Long. 77° 3′ west.

Example No. 5 (First part of the Northern hemisphere) Birth date 6.4.1886. Deduct the saptarishikal from the year 1886. 1886-1808=78—54=24=Shatataraka nakshatra from the third division. Saptarishikal is in the third part. Birth date is in the first part. Birth date is No. 6. Saptarishikal nakshatra is 24=6, it is a spherical triangle. See the year 1886 in the column 1881 west year No. 24. The first part of the northern hemisphere, but due to the spherical triangle it is a negative part. Then the first part of the northern hemisphere vibrates to the second part of the southern hemisphere. The internal first part of the west year No. 24 vibrates to the internal third part of the west year No. 19 (due to spherical triangle Shatataraka is a negative nakshatra. Aridra nakshatra is greater. Moola nakshatra is on 180° of the Aridra). No. 19 means 19-30 hours, it shows Thula Lagna. The first part of the northern hemisphere vibrates to the second part of the northern hemisphere. The internal first part of the west year No. 24 vibrates to the internal first part of the west year 6. No. 6 means

6-30 hours, it shows Mesha rashi, that is on 6.4.1886 at 19-30 hours there is Thula Lagna and Mesh Rashi on the meridian of Ujjain. Birth place Lat. 17° 30' N. Long. 78° 30' east. Birth time 18-30 hrs.

Example No. 6 (Second part of the northern hemisphere) Birth date 11.4.1880. Deduct the saptarishikal from the year 1880. 1880—1808=72-54=18=Jyeshtha nakshatra from the second division. Birth date is in the second part. Birth month is No. 4. Samptarishikal is 18=9, it is a spherical tringle. See the year 1880 in the column 1872 west year 18. But due to spherical triangle Jyeshtha nakshatra is negative. Mriga nakshatra is on 180° of the Jyeshtha. Mirga nakshatra is No. 5. No. 5 means 5-30 hours, it shows Mesha rashi. The second part of the northern hemisphere vibrates to first part of the northern hemisphere. Internal first part of the west year No. 18 vibrates to internal third part of the west year No. 9 (Jyeshtha is negative nakshatra. Aslesha is greater nakshatra) No. 9 means 9-30 hours, it shows Mithuna Lagna, that is on 11.4.1880 there is Mithuna Lagna and Mesha rashi at 9-30 hours on the Meridian of Ujjain, Birth Place Lat 17° 30' N. Long. 78° 30' east.

Example No. 7 (first part of the southern hemisphere) Birth date 14.4.1924. Deduct the saptarishikal from the year 1924. 1924—1908=16=Vishkha nakshatra from the second division. Saptarishikal is in the first part. Birth date is in the second part. Birth date is 14=No. 5. Birth month is No. 4, it is a spherical triangle. See the year 1924 in the column 1917 west year 16 but due to spherical triangle it is a negative part (Vishakha nakshatra No. 16 is negative, Purvabhadrapada is greater nakshatra. Uttara No. 12 is on 180° of the Purvabhadrapada). The first part of the Southern hemisphere vibrates to fourth part of the southern hemisphere. The internal third part of the west year 16 vibrates to the internal first part of the east year. No. 12. No. 12 means 12-30 hours, it shows Karka rashi. The first part of the southern hemisphere vibrates to the third part of the northern hemisphere. The internal third part of the west year 16 vibrates to the internal third part of the east year No. 3 (Vishakha nakshatra is on 180° of the Krittika) No. 3 means 3-30 hours, deduct 2 hours the difference of the west. 3-30—2=1-30 hours, it shows Kumbha Lagna. That is on 14.4.1924 at 1-30 hours there is Kumbha Lagna and Karka rashi on the meridian of Ujjain. Birth place Lat. 13° N. Long. 5h 10m 20s. Birth time 2-34 hours.

Example No. 8. (Third part of the Southern hemisphere) Birth date 20.4.1899. Deduct the saptarishikal from the year 1899. 1899-1808=91-81=10=Magha nakshatra from the second division. Saptarishikal is in the fourth part. Birth date is in the third part. Birth date is 20=2, Saptarishikal is 10=1, it is a spherical triangle. See the year 1899 in the column 1899 east year No. 10. Third part of the southern hemisphere, but due to spherical triangle it is a negative part. (Magha nakshatra is negative, Moola is a greater nakshatra). Then the third part of the southern hemisphere vibrates to the first part of the southern hemisphere. The internal fourth part of the east year No. 10 vibrates to the internal second part of the west year No. 19, add two hours the difference of the east. 19-30 hours plus 2=21-30, it shows Dhanu Rashi. The third part of the southern hemisphere vibrates to second part of the southern hemisphere. Internal fourth part of the east year 10 vibrates to the internal second part of the west year No. 19. No. 19 means 19-30 hours, it shows Thula Lagna, that is on 20.4. 1899 at 19-30 hours there is Thula Lagna and Dhanu rashi on the meridian of Ujjain, Birth place Lat. 48° N. Long. 13° east. Birth time 18-30 hours.

Example No. 9 (Third part of the northern hemisphere) Birth date 21.4.1867. Deduct the saptarishikal from the year 1867. 1867-1808=59-54=5=Mriga nakshatra from the first division. Saptarishikal is in the third part. Birth date is in the third part. Birth date is 21=No. 3. Birth month is No. 4, Saptarishikal nakshatra is No. 5, it is a spherical triangle. See the year 1867 in the column 1863 west year No. 5 the third part of the northern hemisphere, but due to the spherical triangle (it is negative nakshatra, Chitra is greater nakshatra) it is a negative part. Then the third part of the northern hemisphere vibrates to first part of the southern hemisphere. The internal first part of the west year No. 5 vibrates to the internal first part of the west year No. 18 (No. 18 Jyeshtha nakshatra is on 180° of the Mriga No. 5) No. 18 means 18-30 hours, it shows Vrischik rashi. The third part of the northern hemisphere vibrates to the first part of the southern hemisphere. The internal first part of the west year No. 5 vibrates to the internal fourth part of the east year No. 19. No. 19 means 19-30 hours, add two hours, the difference of the west 19-30 plus 2=21-30 hours, it shows Vrischik Lagna. That is on 21.4.1867 at 21-30 hours there is Vrischika Lagna and Vrischika Rashi on the meridian of Ujjain Birth place Lat. 13° N. Long. 5th 10m 20s. Birth time 21-30 hour

THE NORTHERN HEMISPHERE OF THE SKY

22nd of April To 21st of May.

Dec. 18-30, 17-30, 16-30, 15-30, 14-30 Vrischika, Thula.
Sun, Sat, Fri, Thurs, Wed. FIRST PART.

Year	Part	East Year No.	Part	West Year No.	Year	Part	East Year No.	West Year No.	Part
1953	2	18,19,20,21	4	22,23,24,25,26	2025	1	17,18,19,20	21,22,23,24,25	3
1809	1	1, 2, 3, 4	3	5, 6, 7, 8, 9	2097	4	8, 9,10,11	12,13,14,15,16	2
1881	3	19,20,21,22	1	23,24,25,26,27	2169	3	7, 8, 9,10	11,12,13,14,15	1
1737	2	2, 3, 4, 5	4	6, 7, 8, 9,10	2241	2	6, 7, 8, 9	10,11,12,13,14	4
1665	1	3, 4, 5, 6	1	7, 8, 9,10,11	2313	1	5, 6, 7, 8	9,10,11,12,13	3

Dec. 15-30, 14-30, 13-30, 12-30, 11-30 Kanya, Simha. SECOND PART.
Thurs., Wed., Tue., Mon., Sun.

Year	Part	East Year No.	Part	West Year No.	Year	Part	East Year No.	West Year No.	Part
1944	2	9,10,11,12	4	13,14,15,16,17	2016	1	8, 9,10,11	12,13,14,15,16	3
1872	3	10,11,12,13	1	14,15,16,17,18	2088	4/3	26,27, 1, 2	3, 4, 5, 6, 7	2
1800	4	11,12,13,14	2	15,16,17,18,19	2160	3/2	25,26,27, 1	2, 3, 4, 5, 6	1
1728	1	20,21,22,23	3/4	24,25,25,27, 1	2232	1	24,25,26,27	1, 2, 3, 4, 5	3
1656	2	21,22,23,24	4/1	25,26,27, 1, 2	2304	4	15,16,17,18	19,20,21,22,23	2

Dec. 12-30, 11-30, 10-30; 9-30; 8-30 Simha, Karka. THIRD PART.
Mon, Sun, Sat, Fri, Thurs.

Year	Part	East Year No.	Part	West Year No.	Year	Part	East Year No.	West Year No.	Part
1935	1/2	27, 1, 2, 3	4	4, 5, 6, 7, 8	2007	4	9,10,11,12	13,14,15,16,17	2
1863	3	1, 2, 3, 4	1	5, 6, 7, 8, 9	2079	3	8, 9,10,11	12 13 14 15 16	1
1791	4	2, 3, 4, 5	2	6, 7, 8, 9,10	2151	2	7, 8, 9,10	11,12,13,14,15	4
1719	1	11,12,13,14	3	15,16,17,18,19	2223	1	6, 7, 8, 9	10,11,12,13,14	3
1647	2	12,13,14,15	4	16,17,18,19,20	2295	4	24,25,26,27	1, 2, 3, 4, 5	1

Dec. 9-30, 8-30, 7-30, 6-30, 5-30 Mithuna, Vrishabha. FOURTH PART.
Fri., Thurs., Wed., Tue., Mon.

Year	Part	East Year No.	Part	West Year No.	Year	Part	East Year No.	West Year No.	Part
1926	1	18,19,20,21	3	22,23,24,25,26	1998	4	9,10,11,12	13,14,15,16,17	2
1854	2	19,20,21,22	4	23,24,25,26,27	2061	2/3	8, 9,10,11	12,13,14,15,16	1
1782	3	20,21,22,23	1/2	24,25,26,27, 1	2133	2/1	7, 8, 9,10	11,12,13,14,15	4
1710	1	2, 3, 4, 5	3	6, 7, 8, 9,10	2205	4	6, 7, 8, 9	10,11,12,13,14	2
1638	2	3, 4, 5, 6	4	7, 8, 9,10,11	2277	3	24,25,26,27	1, 2, 3, 4, 5	1

THE SOUTHERN HEMISPHERE OF THE SKY

22nd of April to 21st of May.

Dec. 6-30, 5-30, 4-30, 3-30, 2-30 Vrishabha, Mesha.
Tue., Mon., Sun., Sat., Fri. FIRST PART.

Year	Part	East Year No.	Part	West Year No.	Year	Part	East Year No.	West Year No.	Part
1917	1	9,10,11,12	3	13,14,15,16,17	1889	4	0, 1, 2, 3	4, 5, 6, 7, 8	2
1845	2	10,11,12,13	4	14,15,16,17,18	2061	3/2	26,27, 1, 2	3, 4, 5, 6, 7	1
1773	3	11,12,13,14	1	15,16,17,18,19	2133	2'1	25,26,27	2, 3, 4, 5, 6	4
1701	4	12,13,14,15	2	16,17,18,19,20	2205	4	16,17,18,19	20,21,22,23,24	2
1629	1	21,22,23,24	3/4	25,26,27, 1, 2	2277	3	15,16,17,18,	19,20,21,22,23	1

Meena, Kumbha. SECOND PART.

Dec. 3-3, 2-30, 1-30, 24-30, 23-30
Sat., Fri., Thurs., Wed., Tue.

Year	Part	East Year No.	Part	West Year No.	Year	Part	East Year No.	West Year No.	Part
1908	1	0, 1, 2, 3	3	4, 5, 6, 7, 8	1980	3	18,19,20,21	22,23,24,25,26	1
1836	2	1, 2, 3, 4	4	5, 6, 7, 8, 9	2052	2	17,18,19,20	21,22,23,24,25	4
1764	3	2, 3, 4, 5	1	6, 7, 8, 9,10	2124	1	16,17,18,19	20,21,22,23,24	3
1692	4	3, 4, 5, 6	2	7, 8, 9,10,11	2196	4	7, 8, 9,10	11,12,13,14,15	2
1620	1	12,13,14,15	3	16,17,18,19,20	2268	4	6, 7, 8, 9	10,11,12,13,14	1

Makara, Dhanu. THIRD PART.

Dec. 24-30, 23-30, 22-30, 21-30, 20-30
Wed., Tue., Mon., Sun., Sat.

Year	Part	East Year No.	Part	West Year No.	Year	Part	East Year No.	West Year No.	Part
1899	4	10,11,12.13	2	14,15 16,17,18	1971	3	9,10,11,12	13,14,15,16,17	1
1827	1	19,20,21,22	3	23,24,25,26,27	2043	2	8, 9,10,11	12,13,14,15,16	4
1755	2	20,21,22,23	4/1	24,25,26,27. 1	2115	1	7, 8, 9,10	11,12,13,14,15	3
1683	3	21,22,23,24	1/2	25,26,27 1, 2	2187	4/3	25,26,27, 1	2, 3, 4, 5, 6	2
1611	1	3, 4, 5, 6	3	7, 8, 9,10,11	2259	3/2	24,25,26,27	1, 2, 3, 4, 5	1

Dhanu, Vrischika. FOURTH PART.

Dec. 21-30, 20-30, 19-30, 18-30, 17-30
Sun., Sat., Fri., Thurs., Wed.

Year	Part	East Year No.	Part	West Year No.	Year	Part	East Year No.	West Year No.	Part
1890	4	1, 2, 3, 4	2	5, 6, 7, 8, 9	1962	3	0, 1, 2, 3	4, 5, 6, 7, 8	1
1818	1	10,11,12,13	3	14,15,16,17,18	2034	2/1	26,27, 1, 2	3, 4, 5, 6, 7	4/3
1746	2	11,12,13,14	4	15,16,17,18,19	2106	4	17,18,19,20	21,22,23,24,25	2
1674	3	12,13,14,15	1	16,17,18,19,20	2178	3	16,17,18,19	20,21,22,23,24	1
1602	4	13,14,15,16	2	17,18,19,20,21	2250	2	15,16,17,18	19,20,21,22,23	4

Example No. 1 (Second part of the northern hemisphere) Birth date 25.4.1945. Deduct the saptarishikal from the year 1945. 1945-1908=37-27=10=Magha nakshatra from the second division. Saptarishikal is in the second part, Birth date is in the third part. Birth date is 25=No. 7. Saptarishikal is 10'=1. Birth month is No. 4. No. 1-4-7 shows the spherical triangle. See the year 1945 in the column 1944 east year. No. 10 the second part of the northern hemisphere, but due to the spherical triangle it is a negative part. (Magha nakshatra is negative and Aswini nakshatra is greater nakshatra in the northern hemisphere. Chitra nakshatra is on 180° of Aswini. Chitra nakshatra No. 14. No. 14 means 14-30 hours, add two hours the difference of the east of northern hemisphere 14-30 plus 2 = 16-30 hours, it shows Kanya rashi and Kanya Lagna. That is on 25.4.1945 at 16-30 hours there is Kanya Lagna and Kanya rashi on the meridian of Ujjain. Birth place Lat. 18° 52' N. Long. 72° 35' east. Birth time 16h. 7m.

Example No. 2 (Third part of the southern hemisphere) Birth date 29.4.1901. Deduct the saptarishikal from the year 1901. 1901-1808 = 93-81 = 12 = Uttara nakshatra from the second division. Saptarishikal is in the fourth part. Birth date is in the fourth part. Birth date is 29=2 Saptarishikal is No. 3. Birth month is No. 4. No. 2-3-4 show the spherical triangle. See the year 1901 in the column 1899 east year 12 the third part of the southern hemisphere, but due to the spherical triangle it is a negative part (Uttara nakshatra is negative, Krittika nakshatra is a greater nakshtra). Then the third part of the southern hemisphere vibrates to the first part of the southern hemisphere. The internal fourth part of the east year 12 vibrates to the internal fourth part of the west year No. 3. No. 3 means 3-30 hours, it shows Mesha Lagna. Add two hours the difference of the east 3-30 hours plus 2=5-30 hours. The third part of the Southern hemisphere vibrates to the second part of the northern hemisphere. The internal fourth part of the east year No. 12 vibrates to the internal fourth part of the east year No. 12. No. 12 means 12-30 hours, it shows Simha rashi. That is on 29.4.1901 at 5-30 hours there is Mesha Lagna and Simha Rashi on the meridian of Ujjain. Birth place Lat. 32° 10' N. Long. 74° 15' East. Birth time 4-47 hours.

Example No. 3 (Third part of the northern hemisphere) Birth date 5.5.1871. Deduct the saptarishikal from the year 1871. 1871-1808=63-54=9=Aslesha nakshatra from the first division. Saptarishikal is in the third part. Birth date is in the first part. Birth date is No. 5. Birth month is No. 5. Saptarishikal nakshatra is No. 9, it is a spherical triangle. See the year 1871 in the column 1863 west year No. 9. the third part of the northern hemisphere but due to the spherical triangle it is a negative part. (Aslesha nakshatra is negative. Greater nakshatra is Jyeshtha). Then the third part of the northern hemisphere vibrates to the fourth part of the southern hemisphere. The internal first part of the west year 9 vibrates to the internal third part of the west year 18. No. 18 means 18-30 hours, it shows Vrischika Rashi. The third part of the northern hemisphere vibrates to the third part of the southern hemisphere. The internal first part of the west year No. 9 vibrates to the internal third part of the east year No. 23 (Aslesha nakshatra is on 180° of the Dhanishtha No. 23) No. 23 means 23-30 hours, it shows Makara Lagna, that is on 5.5.1871 at 23-30 hours there is Makara Lagna and Vrischika rashi on the meridian of Ujjain. Birth place Lat. 13° N. Long. 76° 9' east. Birth time 23-14 hours.

Example No. 4 (Fourth part of the northern hemisphere) Birth date 7.5.1861. Deduct the saptarishikal from the year 1861. 1861-1808=53-27=26=Uttarbhadrapada nakshatra from the third division. Saptarishikal is in the second part. Birth date is in the first part. Birth date is No. 7. Saptarishikal nakshatra is 26=No. 8, it is a spherical triangle. See the year 1861 in the column 1854 west year 26 the fourth part of the northern hemisphere but due to spherical triangle it is a negative part. (Uttara Bhadhapada is a negative nakshatra and Anuradha No. 17 is a greater nakshatra. Krittika is on 180° of Anuradha) then the fourth part of the Northern hemisphere vibrates to the second part of the southern hemisphere. The internal fourth part of the west year 26 vibrates to the internal fourth part of the east year No. 4. No. 4 means 4-30 hours, deduct two hours, the difference of the west 4-30—2=2-30 hours, it shows Meena Rashi. The fourth part of the northern hemisphere vibrates to the second part of the southern hemisphere. The internal fourth part of the west year 26 vibrates to the internal fourth part of the east year No. 3. No. 3 means 3-30 hours, it shows Meena Lagna. That is on 7.5.1861 at 4-30 hours there is Meena Lagna and Meena rashi on the meridian of Ujjain. Birth place Lat. 22° 40' N. Long. 88° 30' East Birth time 4 hrs. 2m.

Example No. 5 (Third part of the northern hemisphere) Birth date 7.5.1886. Deduct the saptarishikal from the year 1886. 1886-1808=78.54=24 Shatataraka nakshatra from the third division Saptarishikal is in the third part. Birth date is in the first part. Birth month is No. 5. Saptarishikal nakshatra is 24=6. Birth date is No. 7. No. 5-6-7 show spherical triangle. See the year 1886 in the column 1881 west year 24 the first part of the northern hemisphere, but due

136

to the spherical triangle, it is a negative part, then the first part of the northern hemisphere vibrates to the second part of the northern hemisphere. The internal first part of the west year No. 24 vibrates to the internal first part of the west year 15. No. 15 means 15-30 hours, it shows Kanya Lagna. The first part of the northern hemisphere vibrates to the fourth part of the northern hemisphere. The internal first part of the west year No. 24 vibrates to the first part of the east year No. 6. No. 6 means 6-30 hours. Add two hours the difference of the west. 6-30 plus 2=8-30 hours, it shows Mithuna Rashi. That is on 7.5.1886 at 15-30 hours there is Kanya Lagna and Mithuna rashi on the meridian of Ujjain. Birth place Lat. 40° 24' N. Long. 3h 45m west. Birth time 14-20 hours.

Example No. 6 (First part of the Southern hemisphere) Birth date 13.5.1917. Deduct the saptarishikal from the year 1917. 1917-1908=9=Aslesha nakshatra from the first division. Saptarishikal is in the first part. Birth date is in the second part. Birth date is 13=No. 4. Birth month is No. 5. Saptarishikal is No. 9. It is a spherical triangle. See the year 1917 in the column 1917 east year of the first part of the southern hemisphere, but due to spherical triangle Aslesha is a negative nakshatra. Jyeshtha is greatar nakshatra. Mriga nakshatra is on 180° of the Jyeshtha. Mriga nakshatra is No. 5. No. 5 means 5-30 hours, it shows Vrishabha Lagna. The first part of the southern hemisphere vibrates to the third part of the southern hemisphere. The internal first part of the east year No. 9 vibrates to the internal third part of the west year 23 (Dhanishtha No. 23 is on 180° of Aslesha) No. 23 means 23-30 hours, it shows Makara Rashi, that is on 13.5.1917 at 5-30 hours there is Vrischika Lagna and Makara Rashi on the meridian of Ujjain. Birth place Lat. 20° 53' N. Long. 75° 39' east. Birth time 6-25 hours.

Example No. 7 (fourth part of the Southern hemisphere) Birth date 14.5.1896. Deduct the saptarishikal from the year 1896. 1896-1808=88-81=7=Punarvasu nakshatras from the first division. Saptarishikal is in the fourth part. Birth date is in the second part. Birth dat is 14=No. 5. Birth month is No. 5, it is a spherical triangle. See the year 1896 in the column 1890 west year No. 7 the fourth part of the southern hemisphere, but due to spherical triangle it is a negative part. Then the fourth part of the southern hemisphere vibrates to the fourth part of the northern hemisphere. The internal second part of the west year No. 7 vibrates to the internal second part of the west year No. 7. No. 7 means 7-30 hours, deduct two hours the difference of the southern hemisphere. 7-30 —2=5-30 hours, it shows Vrishabha rashi. The fourth part of the

137

southern hemisphere vibrates to the second part of the northern hemisphere. The internal second part of the west year vibrates to the internal first part of the east year No. 11 (Punarvasu is negative nakshatra. Purvabhadrapada is a greater nakshatra. Purva is on 180° of Purvabhadrapada). No. 11 means 11-30 hours, it shows Simha Lagna. That is on 14-5-1896 at 11-30 hours there is Simha Lagna and Vrishabha rashi on the meridian of Ujjain. Birth place Lat. 13° N. Long. 77° 35′ East.

Example No. 8 (Second part of the southern hemisphere) Birth date 15.5.1909. Deduct the saptarishikal from the year 1909. 1909=1908=1=Aswini nakshatra from the first division. Saptarishikal is in the first part. Birth date is in the second part. Birth date is 15=No. 6 Birth month is No. 5. Saptarishikal nakshatra is No. 1, it is a spherical triangle. See the year 1909 in the column 1908 east year 1 the second part of the southern hemisphere, but due to the spherical triangle it is a negative part. Because of the birth month No. 5 and saptarishikal No. 1, it is a positive part because of the birth date No. 6 and saptarishikal No. 1. No. 1 means 1-30 hours, it shows Meena Rashi. The second part of the southern hemisphere vibrates to the first part of the southern hemisphere. The internal first part of the east year No. 1 vibrates to the internal first part of the west year No. 5 (Aswini nakshatra is a negative nakshatra. Moola is a greater nakshatra. Mriga No. 5 is on 180° of Moola). No. 5 means 5-30 hours, it shows Vrishabha Lagna. That is on 15.5.1909 at 5-30 hours there is Vrishabha Lagna and Meena Rashi on the meridian of Ujjain. Birth place Lat. 13° N. Long. 77° 35′ east. Birth time 6 hours.

Example No. 9 (Fourth part of Southern hemisphere) Birth date 15.5.1895. Deduct the saptarishikal from the year 1895. 1895-1808=87-81=6 Aridra nakshatra from the first division. Saptarishikal is in the fourth part. Birth date is in the second part. Birth date is 15=No. 6. Birth month is No. 5, saptarishikal is No. 6, it is a spherical triangle. See the year 1895 in the column 1890 west year No. 6 the fourth part of the southern hemisphere, but due to the spherical triangle it is a negative part, then the fouth part of the southern hemisphere vibrates to the fourth part of the northern hemisphere. The internal second part of the west year No. 6 vibrates to the internal second part of the east year No. 6. No. 6 means 6-30 hours, add two hours the difference of the west. 6-30 hours plus 2=8-30 hours, it shows Mithuna Lagna. The fourth part of the southern hemisphere vibrates to the third part. Internal second part of the west year 6 vibrates to the internal fourth part of the west year 24. No. 24 means 24-30 hours, it shows Makara Rashi. That is on 15.5.1895 at 8-30 hours there is Mithuna Lagna

THE NORTHERN HEMISPHERE OF THE SKY

22nd of May to 21st of June.

Dec. 14-30, 13-30, 12-30, 11-30, 10-30 Kanya, Simha.
Mon., Sun., Sat., Fr., Thurs. FIRST PART.

Year	Part	East Year No.	Part	West Year No.	Year	Part	East Year No.	Part	West Year No.	East Year No.	Part
1953	2	18,19,20,21	4	22,23,24,25,26	2025	1	17,18,19,20	3	21,22,23,24,25	17,18,19,20	1
1809	1	1, 2, 3, 4	3	5, 6, 7, 8, 9	2007	4	8, 9,10,11	21	12,13,14,15,16	8, 9,10,11	4
1881	3	19,20,21,22	1	23,24,25,26,27	2169	3	7, 8, 9,10	1	11,12,13,14,15	7, 8, 9,10	3
1737	2	2, 3, 4, 5	4	6, 7, 8, 9,10	2241	2	6, 7, 8, 9	4	10,11,12,13,14	6, 7, 8, 9	2
1665	3	3, 4, 5, 6	1	7, 8, 9,10,11	2313	1	5, 6, 7, 8	3	9,10,11,12,13	5, 6, 7, 8	1

Dec. 11-30, 10-30, 9-30, 8-30, 7-30 Simha, Karka.
Fri., Thurs., Wed., Tue., Mon. SECOND PART.

Year	Part	East Year No.	Part	West Year No.	Year	Part	East Year No.	Part	West Year No.	East Year No.	Part
1944	21	9,10,11,12	4	13,14,15,16,17	2016	4	8, 9,10,11	3	12,13,14,15,16	8, 9,10,11	1
1872	3	10,11,12,13	1	14,15,16,17,18	2088	43	26,27, 1, 2	21	3, 4, 5, 6, 7	26,27, 1, 2	43
1800	4	11,12,13,14	2	15,16,17,18,19	2160	32	25,26,27, 1	1	2, 3, 4, 5, 6	25,26,27, 1	32
1728	1	20,21,22,23	34	24,25,25,27, 1	2232	1	24,25,26,27	4	1, 2, 3, 4, 5	24,25,26,27	1
1656	2	21,22,23,24	41	25,26,27, 1, 2	2304	4	15,16,17,18	21	19,20,21,22,23	15,16,17,18	4

Dec. 8-30, 7-30, 6-30, 5-30, 4-30 Karka Mithuna.
Tue., Mon., Sun., Sat., Fri. THIRD PART.

Year	Part	East Year No.	Part	West Year No.	Year	Part	East Year No.	Part	West Year No.	East Year No.	Part
1935	12	27, 1, 2, 3	4	4, 5, 6, 7, 8	2007	4	18,19,20,21	21	22,23,24,25,26	18,19,20,21	4
1863	3	1, 2, 3, 4	1	5, 6, 7, 8, 9	2079	3	17,18,19,20	1	21,22,23,24,25	17,18,19,20	3
1791	4	2, 3, 4, 5	2	6, 7, 8, 9,10	2157	2	16,17,18,19	4	20,21,22,23,24	16,17,18,19	2
1719	1	11,12,13,14	3	15,16,17,18,19	2223	1	15,16,17,18	3	19,20,21,22,23	15,16,17,18	1
1647	2	12,13,14,15,	4	16,17,18,19,20	2295	4	6, 7, 8, 9	21	10,11,12,13,14	6, 7, 8, 9	4

Dec. 5-30, 40-30, 3-30, 2-30, 1-30 Vrishabha, Mesha.
Sat., Fri., Thurs., Wed., Tue. FOURTH PART.

Year	Part	East Year No.	Part	West Year No.	Year	Part	East Year No.	Part	West Year No.	East Year No.	Part
1926	1	18,19,20,21	3	22,23,24,25,26	1998	4	9,10,11,12	21	13,14,15,16,17	9,10,11,12	4
1854	2	19,20,21,22	4	23,24,25,26,27	2070	3	8, 9,10,11	1	12,13,14,15,16	8, 9,10,11	3
1782	3	20,21,22,23	12	24,25,26,27, 1	2142	21	7, 8, 9,10	4	11,12,13,14,15	7, 8, 9,10	21
1710	1	2, 3, 4, 5	3	6, 7, 8, 9,10	2214	2	6, 7, 8, 9	3	10,11,12,13,14	6, 7, 8, 9	2
1638	2	3, 4, 5, 6	4	7, 8, 9,10,11	2286	2	24,25,26,27	4	1, 2, 3, 4, 5	24,25,26,27	2

THE SOUTHERN HEMISPHERE OF THE SKY

22nd of May To 21st of June.

Dec. 2-30, 1-30, 24-30, 23-30, 22-30 Meena, Kumbha.
Wed., Tue., Mon., Sun., Sat. FIRST PART.

Year	Part	East Year No.	Part	West Year No.	Year	Part	East Year No.	West Year No.	Part
1917	1	9,10,11,12	3	13,14,15,16,17	1889	4	0, 1, 2, 3	4, 5, 6, 7, 8	2
1845	2	10,11,12,13	4	14,15,16,17,18	2061	3^{72}	26,27, 1, 2	3, 4, 5, 6, 7	1
1773	3	11,12,13,14	1	15,16,17,18,19	2133	2^{71}	25,26,27, 1	2, 3, 4, 5, 6	4
1701	4	12,13,14,15	2	16,17,18,19,20	2205	4	16,17,18,19	20,21,22,23,24	2
1629	1	21,22,23,24	3^{74}	25,26,27, 1, 2	2277	3	15,16,17,18,	19,20,21,22,23	1

Dec. 23-30, 22-30, 21-30, 20-30, 19-30 Kumbha, Makara.
Sun., Sat., Fri., Thurs., Wed. SECOND PART.

Year	Part	East Year No.	Part	West Year No.	Year	Part	East Year No.	West Year No.	Part
1908	1	0, 1, 2, 3	3	4, 5, 6, 7, 8	1980	3	18,19,20,21	22,23 24,25,26	1
1836	2	1, 2, 3, 4	4	5, 6, 7, 8, 9	2052	2	17,18,19,20	21,22,23,24,25	4
1764	3	2, 3, 4, 5	1	6, 7, 8, 9,10	2124	1	16,17,18,19	20,21,22,23,24	3
1692	4	3, 4, 5, 6	2	7, 8, 9,10,11	2196	4	7, 8, 9,10	11,12,13,14,15	2
1620	1	12,13,14,15	3	16,17,18,19,20	2268	4	6, 7, 8, 9	10,11,12,13,14	1

Dec. 20-30, 19-30, 18-30, 17-30, 16-30 Dhanu, Vrischika.
Thurs., Wed., Tue., Mon., Sun. THIRD PART.

Year	Part	East Year No.	Part	West Year No.	Year	Part	East Year No.	West Year No.	Part
1899	4	10,11,12,13	2	14,15,16,17,18	1971	3	9,10,11,12	13,14,15,16,17	1
1827	1	19,20,21,22	3	23,24,25,26,27	2043	2	8, 9,10,11	12,13,14,15,16	4
1755	2	20,21,22,23	4^{71}	24,25,26,27, 1	2115	1	7, 8, 9,10	11,12,13,14,15	3
1683	3	21,22,23,24	1^{72}	25,26,27 1, 2	2187	4^{73}	25,26,27, 1	2, 3, 4, 5, 6	2
1611	1	3, 4, 5, 6	3	7, 8, 9,10,11	2259	3^{72}	24,25,26,27	1, 2, 3, 4, 5	4

Dec. 17-30, 16-30, 15-30, 14-30, 13-30 Thula, Kanya.
Mon., Sun., Sat., Fri., Thurs. FOURTH PART.

Year	Part	East Year No.	Part	West Year No.	Year	Part	East Year No.	West Year No.	Part
1890	4	1, 2, 3, 4	2	5, 6, 7, 8, 9	1962	3	0, 1, 2, 3	4, 5, 6, 7, 8	1
1818	1	10,11,12,13	3	14,15,16,17,18	2034	2^{71}	26,27, 1, 2	3, 4, 5, 6, 7	4^{73}
1746	2	11,12,13,14	4	15,16,17,18,19	2106	4	17,18,19,20	21,22,23,24,25	2
1674	3	12,13,14,15	1	16,17,18,19,20	2178	3	16,17,18,19	20,21,22,23,24	1
1602	4	13,14,15,16	2	17,18,19,20,21	2250	2	15,16,17,18	19,20,21,22,23	4

140

and Makara Rashi on the meridian of Ujjain. Birth place Lat. 22° 25′ N. Long. 87° 21′ east. Birth time 9-17 hours.

Example No. 1 (First part of the southern hemisphere) Birth date 22.5.1921. Deduct the saptarishikal from the year 1921. 1921—1908=13=Hasta nakshatra from the second division. Saptarishikal is in the first part. Birth date is in the third part. Birth date is 22=4. Saptarishikal is 13=No. 4, it is a spherical triangle. See the year 1921 in the column 1917 west year 13, the first part of the Southern hemisphere, but due to the spherical triangle it is a negative part. Then the first part of the southern hemisphere vibrates to the first part of the northern hemisphere. The internal third part of the west year 13 vibrates to the internal first part of the west year 13. No. 13 means 13-30 hours, deduct two hours the difference of the southern hemisphere. 13-30—2=11-30 hours, it shows Simha Lagna. The first part of the southern hemisphere vibrates to the third part of the southern hemisphere. The internal third part of the west year 13 vibrates to the internal first part of the west year 17 (Hasta No. 13 is negative nakshatra, Rohini No. 4 is a greater nakshatra. Anuradha No. 17 is on 180° of the Rohini). No. 17 means 17-30 hours, it shows Vrischika Rashi. That is on 22.5.1921 at 13-30 hours there is Simha Lagna and Vrischika Rashi is on he meridian of Ujjain. Birth place Lat. 18° 52′ N. Long. 72° 35′ east. Birth time 14-5 hours.

Example No. 2 (Third part of the southern hemisphere) Birth date 28.5.1903. Deduct the Saptarishikal from the year 1903. 1903—1808=95-81=14=Chitra nakshatra from the second division. Saptarishikal is in the fourth part. Birth date is in the fourth part. Birth date is 28=No. 1. Birth month is No. 5. Saptarishikal is No. 5, it is a spherical triangle. See the year 1903 in the column 1899 west year 14, the third part of the southern hemisphere, but due to the spherical triangle it is a negative part. Then the third part of the southern hemisphere vibrates to the first part of the Southern hemisphere. The internal second part of the west year 14 vibrates to the internal second part of the west year 23. No. 23 means 23-30 hours, it shows Kumbha Lagna. The third part of the southern hemisphere vibrates to the fourth part of the northern hemisphere. The internal second part of the west year 14 vibrates to the internal second part of the west year No. 1 (Chitra is on 180° of the Aswini) No. 1 means 1-30 hours, add two hours the difference of the southern hemisphere. 1-30 hours plus 2=3-30 hours, it shows Vrishabha rashi, that is on 28.5.1903 at 1-30 hours there is Kumbha Lagna and Vrishabha rashi on the meridian of Ujjain. Birth place Lat. 9° N. Long. 5h 10m 48s east. Birth time 1-19 hours.

Example No. 3 (Fourth part of the southern hemisphere) Birth date 2.6.1892. Deduct the saptarishikal from the year 1892. 1892 —1808=84. 84-81=3=Krittika nakshatra from the first division. Saptarishikal is in the fourth part. Birth date is in the first part. Birth date is No. 2. Birth month is No. 6, it is a spherical triangle. See the year 1892 in the column 1890 west year No. 3 the fourth part of the southern hemisphere, but due to spherical triangle it is a negative part. Then the fourth part of the southern hemisphere vibrates to the second part of the Northern hemisphere. The internal fourth part of the east year No. 3 vibrates to the internal second part of the west year No. 7. No. 7 means 7-30 hours, add two hours the difference of the east year. 7-30 hours plus 2=9.30 hours, it shows Karka Lagna (Krittika nakshatra is negative. Uttarashadha nakshatra is greater nakshatra. Punarvasu nakshatra is on 180° of the Uttarashadha. Punarvasu is No. 7) The fourth part of the southern hemisphere vibrates to the first part of the northern hemisphere. The internal fourth part of the east year 3 vibrates to the internal second part of the east year No. 12. No. 12 means 12-30 hours. Deduct two hours the difference of the southern hemisphere 12-30 hours—2=10-30 hours, it shows Simha rashi (Kritika nakshatra is negative, Uttara is greater nakshatra, Uttara is No. 12). That is on 2.6.1892 at 9-30 hours, there is Karka Lagna and Simha Rashi on the meridian of Ujjain. Birth place Lat. 13° N. Long. 77° 35′ East. Birth time 10-16 hours.

Example No. 4 (First part of the northern hemisphere) Birth date 4.6.1884. Deduct the saptarishikal from the year 1884. 1884-1808=76-54=22=Shravana Nakshatra from the third division. Saptarishikal is in the third part. Birth date is in the first part. Birth date is No. 4. Saptarishikal is 22=No. 4. it is a spherical triangle. See the year 1884 in the column 1881 east year 22, the first part of the northern hemisphere, but due to spherical triangle it is a negative part, then the first part of the northern hemisphere vibrates to the second part of the northern hemisphere. The internal third part of the east year 22 vibrates to the internal fourth part of the east year No. 9 No. 9 means 9-30 hours, it shows Karka Lagna. The first part of the northern hemisphere vibrates to the fourth part of the southern hemisphere. The internal third part of the east year No. 22 vibrates to the internal third part of the east year 13. No. 13 means 13-30 hours, add two hours the difference of the northern hemisphere. 13-30 plus 2=15-30 hours, it shows Thula Rashi. That is on 4.6.1884 at 9-30 hours there is Karka Lagna and Thula rashi on the meridian of Ujjain. Birth place Lat. 12° N. Long. 76° 38′ east. Birth time 10-18 hours.

Example No. 5 (Second part of the southern hemisphere) Birth date 6.6.1913. Deduct the saptarishikal from the year 1913. 1913-1908=5= Mriga nakshatra from the first division. Saptarishikal is in the first part. Birth date is in the first part. Saptarishikal nakshatra is No. 5. Birth date is No. 6. Birth month is No. 6, it is a spherical triangle. See the year 1913 in the column 1908 west year No. 5, the second part of the southern hemisphere, but due to the spherical triangle it is a negative part, then the second part of the southern hemisphere vibrates to the second part of the northern hemisphere. The internal third part of the west year No. 5 vibrates to the internal third part of the east year No. 9. No. 9 means 9-30 hours, add two hours the difference of the west. 9-30 hours plus 2=11-30 hours, it shows Simha Lagna. The second part of the southern hemisphere vibrates to the third part of the northern hemisphere. The internal third part of the west year No. 5 vibrates to the internal first part of the west year No. 5. No. 5 means 5-30 hours, it shows Mithuna Rashi. That is on 6.6.1913 at 11-30 hours there is Simha Lagna and Mithuna rashi on the meridian of Ujjain. Birth place Lat. 57° N. Long. 1° west. Birth time 11-59 hours.

Example No. 6 (Second part of the southern hemisphere) Birth date 10.6.1910. Deduct the saptarishikal from the year 1910. 1910-1908=2=Bharani nakshatra from the first division. Saptarishikal is in the first part. Birth date is in the second part. Birth date is No. 1. Saptarishikal is No. 2, it is a spherical triangle. See the year 1910 in the column 1908 east year No. 2, the second part of the southern hemisphere, but due to the spherical triangle it is a negative part. Then the second part of the southern hemisphere vibrates to the fourth part of the southern hemisphere. The internal first part of the east year No. 2 vibrates to the internal third part of the east year 15 (Swati nakshatra is on 180° of the Bharani) No. 15 means 15-30 hours, it shows Thula Lagna, the second part of the southern hemisphere vibrates to the second part of the northern hemisphere. The internal first part of the west year No. 2 vibrates to the internal second part of the west year No. 7. (Bharani nakshatra is negative. Purvashadha is a greater nakshatra. Punarvasu No. 7 is on the 180° of the Purvashadha. Punarvasu is No. 7) No. 7 means 7-30 hours, it shows Karka Lagna and Karka rashi on the meridian of Ujjain. Birth place Lat. 13° N. Long. 77° 35' east. Birth time 15-20 hours.

Example No. 7 (Second part of the southern hemisphere). Birth date 12.6.1909. Deduct the saptarishikal from the year 1909. 1909-1908=1=Aswini nakshatra from the first division. Saptarishikal

143

is in the first part. Birth date is in the third part. Saptarishikal is No. 1. Birth month is No. 6, it is a spherical triangle. See the year 1909 in the column 1908 east year No. 1 second part of the southern hemisphere, but due to the spherical triangle it is a negative part. Then the second part of the southern hemisphere vibrates to the fourth part of the northern hemisphere. The internal first part of the west year No. 1 vibrates to the internal third part of the west year No. 6. No. 6 means 6-30 hours, deduct two hours the difference of the east. 6-30-2=4-30 hours, it shows Vrishabha Lagna. The second part of the southern hemisphere vibrates to the first part of the southern hemisphere. The internal first part of the east year No. 1 vibrates to the internal fourth part of the east year No. 1. No. 1 means 1-30 hours, it shows Meena Rashi (No. 1 means 25-30 hours, it is a greater hour nakshatra, Vishakha No. 16 is original. No. 16 means 16-30 hours), that is on 12.6.1909 at 16-30 hours there is Vrishabha Lagna and Meena Rashi on the meridian of Ujjain. Birth place Lat. 13° N. Long. 77° 25′ east. Birth time 16-25 hours.

Example No. 8 (Second part of the northern hemisphere) Birth date 13.6.1873. Deduct the Saptarishikal from the year 1873. 1873-1808=65-54=11=Purva nakshatra from the second division. Saptarishikal is in the third part. Birth date is in the second part. Saptarishikal nakshatra is 11=2. Birth month is No. 6, it is spherical triangle. See the 1873 in the column 1872 east year 11, the second part of the northern hemisphere, but due to the spherical triangle it is a negative part, then second part of the northern hemisphere vibrates to the second part of the southern hemisphere. The internal third part of the east year No. 11 vibrates to the internal third part of the west year No. 24 (Shatataraka No. 24 is on 180° of Purva). No. 24 means 24-30 hours, deduct two hours the difference of the east 24-30—2=22-30 hours, it shows Kumbha Lagna. The second part of the northern hemisphere vibrates to the second part of the southern hemisphere. The internal third part of the east year No. 11 vibrates to the internal third part of the west year 20 (Purva nakshatra is negative due to the spherical triangle, Purvashadha No. 20 is a greater nakshatra) No. 20 means 20-30 hours, it shows Makara Rashi, that is on 13.6.1873 at 22-30 hours there is Kumbha Lagna and Makara rashi on the meridian of Ujjain. Birth place Lat. 42° N. Long. 75°. Birth time 23-55 hours.

Example No. 9 (Third part of the southern hemisphere) Birth date 19.6.1904. Deduct the saptarishikal from the year 1904. 1904-1808=96-81=15=Swati nakshatra from the second division. Saptarishikal is in the fourth part. Birth date is in the third part.

144

Birth date is 19=No. 1 Saptarishikal nakshatra is Swati No. 15=6, it is a spherical triangle. See the year 1904 in the column 1899 west year No. 15 the third part of the southern hemisphere, but due to the spherical triangle it is a negative part. Then the third part of the southern hemisphere vibrates to the second part of the northern hemisphere. The internal second part of the west year 15 vibrates to the internal second part of the west year 11 (Swati nakshatra is negative. Shatataraka nakshatra is greater. Purva No. 11 is on 180° of the Shatataraka) No. 11 means 11-30 hours, it shows Simha Rashi. The third part of the southern hemisphere vibrates to the third part of the northern hemisphere. The internal second part of the west year No. 15 vibrates to the internal second part of the west No. 6. No. 6 means 6-30 hours, it shows Karka Lagna, that is on 19.6.1904 at 6-30 hours there is Simha Rashi and Karka Lagna on the meridian of Ujjain. Birth place Lat. 13° N. Long. 76° 9' east. Birth time 7-30 hours.

Example No. 1 (First part of the northern hemisphere). Birth date 26.6.1920. Deduct the saptarishikal from the year 1920. 1920—1908=12=Uttara nakshatra from the second division. Saptarishikal is in the first part. Birth date is in the third part. Birth date is 26=No. 8, saptarishikal is 12=No. 3, it is a spherical triangle. See the year 1920 in the column 1917 east year No. 12 the first part of the northern hemisphere, but due to a spherical triangle it is a negative part, then the first part of the northern hemisphere vibrates to the fourth part of the southern hemisphere. The internal first part of the east year No. 12 vibrates to the internal fourth part of the east year No. 21. Uttara nakshatra is negative because of the spherical triangle. Uttarashadha nakshatra is greater. No. 21 means 21-30 hours, it shows Meena rashi. The first part of the northern hemisphere vibrates to the third part of the southern hemisphere. The internal first part of the east year No. 12 vibrates to the internal third part of the east year No. 3 (Uttara nakshatra is negative, Krittika nakshatra is a greater nakshatra) No. 3 means 3-30 hours, it shows Vrishabha Lagna, that is on 26.6.1920 at 3-30 hours there is Vrishabha Lagna and Meena rashi on the meridian of Ujjain (Vrishabha R.A. 2-30 Dec. 4-30) Birth place Lat. 24° 54' N. Long. 4h 28m east. Birth time 2-6 (deduct two hours the difference of the northern hemisphere 3-30 hours—2=1-30 hours).

Example No. 2 (Fourth part of the northern hemisphere) Birth date 28.6.1897. Deduct the saptarishikal from the year 1897. 1897—1808=89-81=8=Pushya nakshatra from the first division. Saptarishikal is in the fourth part. Birth date is in the fourth part.

THE SOUTHERN HEMISPHERE OF THE SKY

22nd of June to 21st of July.

Dec. 10-30, 9-30, 8-30, 7-30, 6-30   Kanya Simha.
Tue., Mon., Sun., Sat., Fri.,   FIRST PART.

Year	Part	East Year No.	Part	West Year No.	Year	Part	East Year No.	Part	West Year No.
1953	2	18,19,20,21	4	22,23,24,25,26	2025	1	17,18,19,20	3	21,22,23,24,25
1809	1	1,2,3,4	3	5,6,7,8,9	2097	4	8,9,10,11	2	12,13,14,15,16
1881	3	19,20,21,22	1	23,24,25,26,27	2169	3	7,8,9,10	1	11,12,13,14,15
1737	2	2,3,4,5	4	6,7,8,9,10	2241	2	6,7,8,9	4	10,11,12,13,14
1665	3	3,4,5,6	1	7,8,9,10,11	2313	1	5,6,7,8	3	9,10,11,12,13

Dec. 7-30, 6-30, 5-30, 4-30, 3-30   Karka, Mithuna.
Sat., Fri., Thurs., Wed., Tue.,   SECOND PART.

Year	Part	East Year No.	Part	West Year No.	Year	Part	East Year No.	Part	West Year No.
1944	2	9,10,11,12	4	13,14,15,16,17	2016	1	8,9,10,11	3	12,13,14,15,16
1872	3	10,11,12,13	1	14,15,16,17,18	2088	4/3	26,27,1,2	2	3,4,5,6,7
1800	4	11,12,13,14	2	15,16,17,18,19	2160	3/2	25,26,27,1	1	2,3,4,5
1728	1	20,21,22,23	3/4	24,25,25,27,1	2232	4	24,25,26,27	3	1,2,3,4,5
1656	2	21,22,23,24	4/1	25,26,27,1,2	2304	4	15,16,17,18	2	19,20,21,22,23

Dec. 4-30, 3-30, 2-30, 1-30, 24-30   Vrishabha, Mesha.
Wed., Tue., Mon., Sun., Sat.,   THIRD PART.

Year	Part	East Year No.	Part	West Year No.	Year	Part	East Year No.	Part	West Year No.
1935	1/2	27,1,2,3	4	4,5,6,7,8	2007	4	18,19,20,21	2	22,23,24,25,26
1863	3	1,2,3,4	1	5,6,7,8,9,10	2079	3	17,18,19,20	1	21,22,23,24,25
1791	4	2,3,4,5	2	6,7,8,9,10	2157	2	16,17,18,19	4	20,21,22,23,24
1719	1	11,12,13,14	3	15,16,17,18,19	2223	1	15,16,17,18	3	19,20,21,22,23
1647	2	12,13,14,15,	4	16,17,18,19,20	2295	4	6,7,8,9	2	10,11,12,13,14

Dec. 1-30, 24-30, 23-30, 22-30, 21-30   Mesha, Meena.
Sun., Sat., Fri., Thurs., Wed.,   FOURTH PART.

Year	Part	East Year No.	Part	West Year No.	Year	Part	East Year No.	Part	West Year No.
1926	1	18,19,20,21	3	22,23,24,25,26	1998	4	9,10,11,12	2	13,14,15,16,17
1854	2	19,20,21,22	4	23,24,25,26,27	2070	3	8,9,10,11	1	12,13,14,15,16
1782	3	20,21,22,23	1/2	24,25,26,27,1	2142	2	7,8,9,10	4	11,12,13,14,15
1710	1	2,3,4,5	3	6,7,8,9,10	2214	1	6,7,8,9	3	10,11,12,13,14
1638	2	3,4,5,6	4	7,8,9,10,11	2286	3	24,25,26,27	1	1,2,3,4,5

THE NORTHERN HEMISPHERE OF THE SKY

22nd of June to 21st of July.

FIRST PART — Kumbha Makara.
Dec. 22-30, 21-30, 20-30, 19-30, 18-30 — Thurs., Wed., Tue., Mon., Sun.

Year	Part	East Year No.	West Year No.	Part
1917	1	9,10,11,12	13,14,15,16,17	3
1845	2	10,11,12,13	14,15,16,17,18	4
1773	3	11,12,13,14	15,16,17,18,19	1
1701	4	12,13,14,15	16,17,18,19,20	2
1629	1	21,22,23,24	25,26,27,1,2	3/4
1889	4	0,1,2,3	4,5,6,7,8	1
2061	3/2	26,27,1,2	3,4,5,6,7	2
2133	2/1	25,26,27,1	2,3,4,5,6	4
2025	4	16,17,18,19	20,21,22,23,24	2
2277	3	15,16,17,18	19,20,21,22,23	1

SECOND PART — Makara, Dhanu.
Dec. 19-30, 18-30, 17-30, 16-30, 15-30 — Mon., Sun., Sat., Fri., Thurs.

Year	Part	East Year No.	West Year No.	Part
1908	1	0,1,2,3	4,5,6,7,8	3
1836	2	1,2,3,4	5,6,7,8,9	4
1764	3	2,3,4,5	6,7,8,9,10	1
1696	4	3,4,5,6	7,8,9,10,11	2
1620	1	12,13,14,15	16,17,18,19,20	3
1980	3	18,19,20,21	22,23,24,25,26	1
2052	2	17,18,19,20	21,22,23,24,25	4
2124	1	16,17,18,19	20,21,22,23,24	3
2196	4	7,8,9,10	11,12,13,14,15	2
2263	4	6,7,8,9	10,11,12,13,14	1

THIRD PART — Vrischika, Tula.
Dec. 16-30, 15-30, 14-30, 13-30, 12-30 — Fri., Thurs., Wed., Tue., Mon.

Year	Part	East Year No.	West Year No.	Part
1899	4	10,11,12,13	14,15,16,17,18	2
1827	1	19,20,21,22	23,24,25,26,27	3
1755	2	20,21,22,23	24,25,26,27,1	4/1
1683	3	21,22,23,24	25,26,27,1,2	1/2
1611	1	3,4,5,6	7,8,9,10,11	3
1971	3	9,10,11,12	13,14,15,16,17	1
2042	2	8,9,10,11	12,13,14,15,16	4
2115	1	7,8,9,10	11,12,13,14,15	3
2187	4/3	25,26,27,1	2,3,4,5,6	2
2259	3/2	24,25,26,27	1,2,3,4,5	1

FOURTH PART — Thula, Kanya.
Dec. 13-30, 12-30, 11-30, 10-30, 9-30 — Tue., Mon., Sun., Sat., Fri.

Year	Part	East Year No.	West Year No.	Part
1890	4	1,2,3,4	5,6,7,8,9	2
1818	1	10,11,12,13	14,15,16,17,18	3
1746	2	11,12,13,14	15,16,17,18,19	4
1674	3	12,13,14,15	16,17,18,19,20	1
1602	4	13,14,15,16	17,18,19,20,21	2
1962	3	0,1,2,3	4,5,6,7,8	1
2034	2	26,27,1,2	3,4,5,6,7	2
2106	4	17,18,19,20	21,22,23,24,25	4
2178	1	16,17,18,19	20,21,22,23,24	3
2250	2	15,16,17,18	19,20,21,22,23	4

Birth date is 28=No. 1. Birth month is No. 6, it is a spherical triangle. See the year 1897 in the column 1890 west year No. 8, the fourth part of the northern hemisphere, but due to a spherical triangle it is a negative part. Then the fourth part of the northern hemisphere vibrates to the second part of the northern hemisphere. The internal second part of the west year 8 vibrates to the internal second part of the east year 17 (Pushya nakshatra is negative because of the spherical triangle, Anuradha is a greater nakshatra) No. 17 means 17-30 hours, add two hours the difference of the west 17-30 plus 2=19-30 hours (that is 17-30 R.A. of the Dhanu Lagna) it shows Dhanu Lagna. The fourth part of the northern hemisphere vibrates to the third part of the southern hemisphere. The internal second part of the west year No. 8 vibrates to the internal fourth part of the east year No. 4 (Pushya nakshatra is negative because of the spherical triangle Anuradha is a greater nakshatra. Rohini nakshatra is on 180° of the Anuradha. Rohini is No. 4) No. 4 means 4-30 hours, deduct two hours the difference of the west 4-30—2=2-30 hours, it shows the R.A. of the Vrishabha Rashi, that is on 28.6.1897 at 19-30 hours there is Dhanu Lagna and Vrishabha Rashi on the meridian of Ujjain. Birth place Lat. 13° N. Long. 77° 35′ east. Birth time 18-50 hours.

Example No. 3 (fourth part of the southern hemisphere) Birth date 14.7.1926. Deduct the saptarishikal from the year 1926. 1926—1908=18=Jyeshtha nakshatra from the second division. Saptarishikal is in the first part. Birth date is 14=No. 5. Saptarishikal nakshatra is 18=No. 9, it is a spherical triangle. See the year 1926 in the column 1926 east year No. 18 the fourth part of the Southern hemisphere, but due to the spherical triangle it is a negative part. Then the fourth part of the Southern hemisphere vibrates to the first part of the southern hemisphere. The internal first part of the east year 18 vibrates to the internal first part of the west year No. 9 (Jyeshtha nakshatra is negative, Aslesha nakshatra is greater). No. 9 means 9-30 hours, deduct two hours the difference of the east 9-30—2=7-30 hours, it shows Simha Rashi. The fourth part of the southern hemisphere vibrates to the third part of the northern hemisphere. The internal first part of the east year 18 vibrates to the internal second part of the west year No. 18. No. 18 means 18-30 hours, Deduct two hours the difference of the east 18-30—2=16-30 hours it shows Vrischika Lagna. That is on 14.7.1926 at 16-30 hours there is Vrischika Lagna and Simha Rashi on the meridian of Ujjain. Birth place Lat. 13° N. Long 77° 35′ east. Birth time 15-21 hours.

Example No. 4 (Second part of the Northern hemisphere) Birth date 28.6.1914. Deduct the saptarishikal from the year

1914. 1914-1908=6=Aridra nakshatra from the first division. Saptarishikal is in the first part. Birth date is in the fourth part. Birth date is 28=1 saptarishikal is No. 6. Birth month is No. 6, it is a spherical triangle. See the year 1914 in the column 1908 west year No. 6, the second part of the northern hemisphere, but due to a spherical triangle it is a negative part. Then the second part of the northern hemisphere vibrates to the first part of the southern hemisphere. The internal third part of the west year No. 6 vibrates to the internal third part of the east year 6, add two hours the difference of the west 6-30 hours plus 2=8-30 hours. 6-30 hours shows the R.A. of the Simha Rashi. The second part of the northern hemisphere vibrates to the first part of the northern hemisphere. The internal third part of the west 6 vibrates to the internal first part of the west year No. 24 (Aridra Nakshatra is negative because of the spherical triangle Shatataraka is a greater nakshatra, shatataraka is No. 24) No. 24 means 24-30 hours, deduct two hours the difference of the east, 24-30—2=22-30 hours, it shows Kumbha Lagna, that is on 28.6.1914 at 22-30 hours there is Kumbha Lagna and Simha Rashi on the meridian of Ujjain. Birth place Lat. 13° N. Long 77°35′ east. Birth time 21-57 hours.

Example No. 5 (First part of the southern hemisphere) Birth date 14.7.1887. Deduct the saptarishikal from the year 1887. 1887—1808=79-54=25=Purvabhadrapada nakshatra from the third division. Saptarishikal is in the third part. Birth date is in the second part. Birth month is No. 7. Saptarishikal nakshatra is 25=7 it is a spherical triangle. See the year 1887 in the column 1881 west year 25 the first part of the southern hemisphere, but due to spherical triangle it is a negative part. That is Purvabhadrapada nakshatra is negative. Punarvasu nakshatra is a greater nakshatra. Punarvasu is No. 7. No. 7 means 7-30 hours, it shows Simha Lagna. The first part of the southern hemisphere vibrates to the third part of the southern hemisphere. The internal first part of the west year No. 25 vibrates to the internal first part of the west year 25. No. 25 means 25-30 hours, it shows Mesha rashi. That is on 14.7.1887 at 9-30 hours (7-30 is the R.A. of the Simha Lagna and 9-30 is Dec). There is Simha Lagna and Mesha rashi on the meridian of Ujjain. Birth place Lat. 13° N. Long. 5h. 10m. 20s. east. Birth time 9-57 hours.

Example No. 6 (fourth part of the northern hemisphere) Birth date is 14.7.1897. Deduct the saptarishikal from the year 1897. 1897—1808=89-81=8= means Pushya nakshatra from the first division. Saptarishikal is in the fourth part. Birth date is in the second part. Birth month is No. 7. Saptarishikal nakshatra is No. 8. it is a spherical triangle. See the year 1897 in the column 1890 west

149

year 7 the fourth part of the northern hemisphere, but due to a spherical triangle it is a negative part. Then the fourth part of the northern hemisphere vibrates to the first part of the northern hemisphere. The internal second part of the west year No. 8 vibrates to the internal fourth part of the east year 17 (Pushya nakshatra is negative because of the spherical triangle Anuradha nakshatra is a greater nakshatra. Anuradha is No. 17) No. 17 means 17-30 hours, add two hours the difference of the west 17-30 hours plus 2=19-30 hours, it shows Makara Rashi. The fourth part of the northern hemisphere vibrates to the third part of the northern hemisphere. The internal second part of the west year 8 vibrates to the internal first part of the east year No. 17 means 17-30 hours. Deduct two hours the difference of the west 17-30—2=15-30 hours, it shows Vrischika Lagna. That is on 14.7.1897 at 15-30 hours there is Vrischika Lagna and Makara Rashi on the meridian of Ujjain. Birth place Lat. 41° 15′ N. Long. 0° east. Birth time 16 hours.

Example No. 7 (first part of the southern hemisphere) Birth date 19.7.1816. Deduct the saptarishikal from the year 1816. 1816—1808=8=Pushya nakshatra from the first division. Saptarishikal is in the first part. Birth month is No. 7. Saptarishikal is No. 8. it is a spherical triangle. See the year 1816 in the column 1809 west year 8, the first part of the southern hemisphere. But due to spherical triangle it is a negative part. Then the first part of the southern hemisphere vibrates to the third part of the southern hemisphere. The internal third part of the west year No. 8 vibrates to the internal second part of the east year No. 26 (Pushya nakshatra is negative, Uttarabhadrapada nakshatra is a greater nakshatra) No. 26 means 26-30 hours. Deduct two hours the difference of the west 26-30 hours—2=24-30 hours, it shows Mesha Rashi. The first part of the southern hemisphere vibrates to the third part of the northern hemisphere. The internal third part of the west year 8 vibrates to the internal third part of the east year 12. (Uttara nakshatra is on 180° of the Uttarabhadrapada). No. 12 means 12-30 hours, it shows Thula Lagna, that is on 19.7.1816 at 12-30 hours there is Thula Lagna and Mesha Rashi on the meridian of Ujjain. Birth place Lat. 17° N. Long. 5h. 10m. 20s. east.

Example No. 1 (Second part of the northern hemisphere) Birth date 22.7.1916. Deduct the Saptarishikal from the year 1916. 1916—1908=8=Pushya nakshatra from the first division. Saptarishikal is in the first part. Birth date is in the third part. Birth date is 22=No. 4. Birth month is No. 7, saptarishikal nakshatra is No. 8, it is spherical triangle. See the year 1916 in the column

THE SOUTHERN HEMISPHERE OF THE SKY

22nd of July to 21st of August.

Dec. 18-30, 17-30, 16-30, 15-30, 14-30 Makara, Dhanu.
Wed., Tue., Mon., Sun., Sat. FIRST PART.

Year	Part	East Year No.	Part	West Year No.	Year	Part	East Year No.	West Year No.	Part
1953	2	18,19,20,21	4	22,23,24,25,26	2025	1	17,18,19,20	21,22,23,24,25	3
1809	1	1, 2, 3, 4	3	5, 6, 7, 8, 9	2097	4	8, 9,10,11	12,13,14,15,16	2
1881	3	19,20,21,22	1	23,24,25,26,27	2169	3	7, 8, 9,10	11,12,13,14,15	1
1737	2	2, 3, 4, 5	4	6, 7, 8, 9,10	2241	2	6, 7, 8, 9	10,11,12,13,14	4
1665	3	3, 4, 5, 6	1	7, 8, 9,10,11	2313	1	5, 6, 7, 8	9,10,11,12,13	3

Dec. 15-30, 14-30, 13-30, 12-30, 11-30 Dhanu, Vrischika.
Sun., Sat., Fri., Thurs., Wed. SECOND PART.

Year	Part	East Year No.	Part	West Year No.	Year	Part	East Year No.	West Year No.	Part
1944	2	9,10,11,12	4	13,14,15,16,17	2016	1	8, 9,10,11	12,13,14,15,16	3
1872	3	10,11,12,13	1	14,15,16,17,18	2088	4/3	26,27, 1, 2	3, 4, 5, 6, 7	2
1800	4	11,12,13,14	2	15,16,17,18,19	2160	3/2	25,26,27, 1	2, 3, 4, 5, 6	1
1728	1	20,21,22,23	3/4	24,25,25,27, 1	2232	1	24,25,26,27	1, 2, 3, 4, 5	3
1656	2	21,22,23,24	4/1	25,26,27, 1, 2	2304	4	15,16,17,18	19,20,21,22,23	2

Dec. 12-30, 11-30, 10-30, 9-30, 8-30, Thula, Kanya.
Thur., Wed., Tue., Mon., Sun. THIRD PART.

Year	Part	East Year No.	Part	West Year No.	Year	Part	East Year No.	West Year No.	Part
1935	1/2	27, 1, 2, 3	4	4, 5, 6, 7, 8	2007	4	18,19,20,21	22,23,24,25,26	2/1
1863	3	1, 2, 3, 4	1	5, 6, 7, 8, 9	2079	3	17,18,19,20	21,22,23,24,25	1
1791	4	2, 3, 4, 5	2	6, 7, 8, 9,10	2157	2	16,17,18,19	20,21,22,23,24	4
1719	1	11,12,13,14	3	15,16,17,18,19	2223	1	15,16,17,18	19,20,21,22,23	3
1647	2	12,13,14,15	4	16,17,18,19,20	2295	4	6, 7, 8, 9	10,11,12,13,14	2

Dec. 9-30, 8-30, 7-30, 6-30, 5-30 Kanya, Simha.
Mon., Sun., Sat., Fri., Thurs. FOURTH PART.

Year	Part	East Year No.	Part	West Year No.	Year	Part	East Year No.	West Year No.	Part
1926	1	18,19,20,21	3	22,23,24,25,26	1998	4	9,10,11,12	13,14,15,16,17	2
1854	2	19,20,21,22	4	23,24,25,26,27	2090	3	8, 9,10,11	12,13,14,15,16	1
1782	3	20,21,22,23	1/2	24,25,26,27, 1	2142	2	7, 8, 9,10	11,12,13,14,15	4
1710	1	2, 3, 4, 5	3	6, 7, 8, 9,10	2214	1	6, 7, 8, 9	10,11,12,13,14	3
1638	2	3, 4, 5, 6	4	7, 8, 9,10,11	2286	3	24,25,26,27	1, 2, 3, 4, 5	1

THE NORTHERN HEMISPHERE OF THE SKY

22nd of July to 21st of August.

Dec. 6-30, 5-30, 4-30, 3-30, 2-30, Karka Mithuna.
Fri., Thurs., Wed., Tue., Mon., First Part.

Year	Part	East Year No.	Part	West Year No.	Year	Part	East Year No.	West Year No.	Part
1917	1	9,10,11,12	3	13,14,15,16,17	1989	4	0,1,2,3	4,5,6,7,8	2
1845	2	10,11,12,13	4	14,15,16,17,18	2061	3/2	26,27,1,2	3,4,5,6,7	1
1773	3	11,12,13,14	1	15,16,17,18,19	2133	2/1	25,26,27,1	2,3,4,5,6	4
1701	4	12,13,14,15	2	16,17,18,19,20	2205	4	16,17,18,19	20,21,22,23,24	2
1629	1	21,22,23,24	3/4	25,26,27,1,2	2277	3	15,16,17,18	19,20,21,22,23	1
				Dec. 3-30, 2-30, 1-30, 24-30, 23-30 Mithuna, Vrishabha. Tue., Mon., Sun., Sat., Fri., Second Part.					
1908	1	0,1,2,3	3	4,5,6,7,8	1980	3	18,19,20,21	22,23,24,25,26	1
1836	2	1,2,3,4	4	5,6,7,8,9	2052	2	17,18,19,20	21,22,23,24,25	4
1764	3	2,3,4,5	1	6,7,8,9,10	2124	1	16,17,18,19	20,21,22,23,24	3
1692	4	3,4,5,6	2	7,8,9,10,11	2196	4	7,8,9,10	11,12,13,14,15	2
1620	1	12,13,14,15	3	16,17,18,19,20	2268	4	6,7,8,9	10,11,12,13,14	1
				Dec. 24-30, 23-30, 22-30, 21-30, 20-30, Vrishabha, Mesha. Sat., Fri., Thurs., Wed., Tue., Third Part.					
1899	4	10,11,12,13	2	14,15,16,17,18	1971	3	9,10,11,12	13,14,15,16,17	1
1827	1	19,20,21,22	3	23,24,25,26,27	2043	2	8,9,10,11	12,13,14,15,16	4
1755	2	20,21,22,23	4/1	24,25,26,27,1	2115	1	7,8,9,10	11,12,13,14,15	3
1683	3	21,22,23,24	1/2	25,26,27,1,2	2187	4/3	25,26,27,1	2,3,4,5,6	2
1611	1	3,4,5,6	3	7,8,9,10,11	2259	2	24,25,26,27	1,2,3,4,5	4
				Dec. 21-30, 20-30, 19-30, 18-30, 17-30 Meena, Kumbha. Wed., Tue., Mon., Sun., Sat., Fourth Part.					
1890	4	1,2,3,4	2	5,6,7,8,9	1962	3	0,1,2,3	4,5,6,7,8	1
1818	1	10,11,12,13	3	14,15,16,17,18	2034	2/1	26,27,1,2	3,4,5,6,7	4
1746	2	11,12,13,14	4	15,16,17,18,19	2106	4	25,26,27,1	21,22,23,24,25	2
1674	3	12,13,14,15	1	16,17,18,19,20	2178	3	16,17,18,19	20,21,22,23,24	1
1602	4	13,14,15,16	2	17,18,19,20,21	2250	2	15,16,17,18	19,20,21,22,23	4

1908 west year 8, the second part of the northern hemisphere, but due to the spherical triangle it is a negative part. Then the second part of the northern hemisphere vibrates to the fourth part of the northern hemisphere. The internal third part of the west year No. 8 vibrates to the internal third part of the west year No. 17 (Pushya nakshatra is negative. Anuradha nakshatra is greater) No. 17 means 17-30 hours it shows Kumbha Lagna. The second part of the northern hemisphere vibrates to the third part of the northern hemisphere. The internal third part of the west year No. 8 vibrates to the internal first part of the east year No. 22 (Shravana nakshatra is on 180° of Pushya). No. 22 means 22-30 hours. Deduct two hours the difference of the west 22-30—2=20-30 hours, it shows Mesha Rashi. That is on 22.7.1916 at 20-30 hours there is Kumbha Lagna and Mesha Rashi on the meridian of Ujjain. Birth place Lat. 9° 30′ N. Long. 76° 13′ each. Birth time 20-34 hours.

Example No. 2 (Fourth part of the northern hemisphere) Birth date 25.7.1896. Deduct the saptarishikal from the year 1896. 1896—1808=88-81=7=Punarvasu nakshatra from the first division. Saptarishikal is in the fourth part. Birth date is in the third part. Birth date is 25=No 7. Birth month is No. 7, saptarishikal nakshatra is No. 7, it is a spherical triangle. See the year 1896 in the column 1890 west year No 7, the fourth part of the northern hemisphere, but due to the spherical triangle it is a negative part. Then the fourth part of the northern hemisphere vibrates to the fourth part of the southern hemisphere. The internal second part of the west year No. 7 vibrates to the internal fourth part of the west year No. 7, add two hours the difference of the northern hemisphere. No. 7 means 7-30 hours plus 2=9-30 hours, it shows Kanya Lagna. The fourth part of the northern hemisphere vibrates to the first part of the southern hemisphere. The internal second part of the west year No. 8 vibrates to the internal first part of the east year No. 17 (Pushya nakshatra is negative. Anuradha is greater nakshatra) No. 17 means 17-30 hours it shows Makara Rashi, that is on 25.7.1896 at 9-30 hours there is Kanya Lagna and Makara Rashi on the meridian of Ujjain. Birth place Lat. 18° 15′ N. Long 72° 54′ east. Birth time 10-52 hours.

Example No. 3 (Fourth part of the northern hemisphere) Birth date 28.7.1896. Deduct the saptarishikal from the year 1896. 1896—1808=88-81=7=Punarvasu nakshatra from the first division. Saptarishikal is in the fourth part. Birth date is in the fourth part. Birth month is No. 7. Saptarishikal nakshatra is No. 7; it is a spherical triangle. See the year 1896 in the column 1890 west year No. 7 the fourth part of the northern hemisphere, but due to the spherical triangle it is a negative part. Punarvasu is a negative nakshatra, Vishakha is greater nakshatra. Vishakha is No. 16. No. 16 means 16-30 hours, add two hours the difference of the negative part. 16-30 plus 2=18-30 hours, it shows Kumbha Rashi. The fourth part of the northern hemisphere vibrates to the fourth part of the southern hemisphere. The internal second part of the west year 7 vibrates to the internal fourth part of the west year No. 7. No. 7 means 7-30 hours, add two hours the difference of the northern hemisphere. 7-30 plus 2=9-30 hours, it shows Kanya Lagna. That is on 28.7.1896 at 7-30 hours there is Kanya Lagna and Kumbha rashi on the meridian of Ujjain. Birth place Lat. 13° N. Long. 5h 10m 20s. East.

Example No. 4 (First part of the southern hemisphere). Birth date 29.7.1883. Deduct the saptarishikal from the year 1883. 1883—1808=75-54=21=Uttarashadha nakshatra from the third division. Saptarishikal is in the third part. Birth date is in the fourth part. Birth date is 29=No. 2. Saptarishikal nakshatra is 21=No. 3. Birth month is No. 7, it is a spherical triangle. See the year 1883 in the column 1881 east year No. 21 the first part of the southern hemisphere, but due to a spherical triangle it is a negative part. Then the first part of the southern hemisphere vibrates to the second part of the northern hemisphere.. The internal third part of the east year No. 21 vibrates to the internal third part of the east year No. 21. No. 21 means 21-30 hours add two hours, the difference of the east. 21-30 plus 2=23-30 hours, it shows Vrishabha Rashi. The first part of the southern hemisphere vibrates to the second part of the southern hemisphere. The internal third part of the east year No. 12. No. 12 means 12-30 hours, it shows Vrischika Lagna (add two hours the difference of the east 12-30 plus 2=14-30 hours). That is on 29.7.1883 at 12-30 hours there is Vrischika Lagna and Vrishabha rashi on the meridian of Ujjain. Birth place Lat. 45° 26′ N. Long 11° east. Birth time 14 hours.

Example No. 5 (second part of the northern hemisphere) Birth date 29.7.1909. Deduct the Saptarishikal from the year 1909. 1909—1908=1=Aswini nakshatra from the first division. Sapta-rishikal is in the first part. Birth date is in the fourth part. Birth date is 29=2, saptarishikal nakshatra is No. 1, it is a spherical triangle. See the year 1909 in the column 1908 east year No. 1, the second part of the northern hemisphere, but due to a spherical triangle it is a negative part. Then the second part of the northern hemisphere vibrates to the second part of the southern hemisphere. The internal first part of the east year No. 1 vibrates to the internal third part of the east year No. 10. No. 10 means 10-30 hours, add two hours the difference of the northern hemisphere. 10-30 plus 2=12-30 hours, it shows Vrischika Rashi (Aswini nakshatra is negative. Magha nakshatra is a greater nakshatra). The second part of the northern hemisphere vibrates to first part of the northern hemisphere. The internal first part of the year No. 1 vibrates to the internal second part of the west year No. 5 (Aswini nakshatra is negative. Moola nakshatra is a greater nakshatra. Mriga nak-shatra is on 180° of Moola) No. 5 means 5-30 hours. Add two hours the difference of the west 5-30 hours, plus 2=7-30 hours it shows Karka Lagna that is on 29.7.1909 at 5-30 hours there is Karka Lagna and Vrischika Rashi on the meridian of Ujjain. Birth place Lat. 17° N. Long. 5h 10m 20s.

Example No. 6 (Third part of the southern hemisphere). Birth date 30.7.1863. Deduct the saptarishikal from the year 1863. 1863—1808=55. 55-54=1=Aswini nakshatra from the first division. Saptarishikal is in the third part. Birth date is in the third part. Birth date is 30=3. Birth month is No. 7, it is a spherical triangle. See the year 1863 in the column 1863 east year No. 1, the third part of the southern hemisphere, but due to a spherical triangle it is negative part. Then the third part of the southern hemisphere vibrates to the first part of the southern Hemisphere. The internal third part of the east year No. 1 vibrates to the internal first part of the west year No. 14 (Aswini nakshatra is on 180° of Chitra No. 14) No. 14 means 14-30 hours, add two hours the difference of the east. 14-30 plus 2=16-30 hours, it shows Makara Rashi. The third part of the southern hemisphere vibrates to the second part of the southern hemisphere. The internal third part of the east year No. 1 vibrates to the internal first part of the west year No. 14. No. 14 means 14-30 hours deduct two hours the difference of the west 14-30—2=12-30 hours, it shows Vrischika Lagna that is on 30.7.1863 at 12-30 hours there is Makara Rashi and Vrischika Lagna on the meridian of Ujjain. Birth place Lat. 42° 5' north Long 83°.5' west Birth time 14-9 hours.

Example No. 7 (Second part of the northern hemisphere) Birth date 31.7.1910. Deduct the saptarishikal from the year 1910. 1910—1908=2=Bharani nakshatra from the first division. Saptarishikal is in the first part. Birth date is in the fourth part. Saptarishikal nakshatra is No. 2. Birth month is No. 7, it is a spherical triangle. See the year 1910 in the column 1908 east year No. 2, the second part of the northern hemisphere, but due to a spherical triangle it is a negative part. Bharani nakshatra No. 2 is negative. Purva No. 11 is a greater nakshatra. Purva No. 11 is on 180° of the Purvabhadrapada No. 25. No. 25 means 25-30 hours, deduct two hours the difference of the negative part. 25-30—2=23-30 hours, it shows Vrishabha Rashi. The second part of the northern hemisphere vibrates to the first part of the southern hemisphere. Internal first part of the east year No. 2 vibrates to the internal second part of the west year No. 16 (Vishakha nakshatra is on 180° of Bharani) No. 16 means 16-30 hours. add two hours the difference of the northern hemisphere 16-30 plus 2=18-30 hours, it shows Makara Lagna that is on 31.7.1910 at 16-30 hours there is Makara Lagna and Vrishabha rashi on the meridian of Ujjain. Birth place Lat. 8° 44′ N. Long. 77° 44′ East.

Example No. 8 (First part of the southern hemisphere) Birth date 7.8.1887. Deduct the saptarishikal from the year 1887. 1887— 1808=79. 79-54=25=Purvabhadrapada from the third division. Saptarishikal is in the third part. Birth date is in the first part. Birth date is No. 7. Birth month is No. 8. Saptarishikal nakshatra is No. 7 it is a spherical triangle. See the year 1887 in the column 1881 west year No. 25 the first part of the southern hemisphere, but due to the spherical triangle it is a negative part. Then the first part of the southern hemisphere vibrates to the fourth part of the northern hemisphere. The internal first part of the west year No. 25 vibrates to the first part of the west year No. 20 (Purvabhadrapada is negative nakshatra. Punarvasu is greater nakshatra. Punarvasu is on 180° of the Purvashadha No. 20) No. 20 means 20-30 hours, it shows Meena Rashi. The first part of the southern hemisphere vibrates to the second part of the southern hemisphere. The internal first part of the west year 25 vibrates to the internal first part of the east year No. 11 (Purva nakshatra is on 180° of the Purvabhadrapada) No. 11 means 11-30 hours, add two hours the difference of the west 11-30 plus 2=13-30 hours, it shows Vrischika Lagna, that is on 7.8.1887 at 13-30 hours there is Vrischika Lagna and Meena Rashi on the meridian of Ujjain. Birth place Lat. 11° N. Long 5h. 8m. 8s. east. Birth time 13-30 hours.

Example No. 9 (second part of the northern hemisphere) Birth date 8.8.1912. Deduct the saptarishikal from the year 1912. 1912— 1908=4=Rohini nakshatra from the first division. Saptarishikal is in the first part. Birth date is in the first part. Birth date is No. 8. Birth month is No. 8. Saptarishikal nakshatra is No. 4, it is a spherical triangle. See the year 1912 in the column 1908 west year No. 4 the second part of the northern hemisphere but due to a spherical triangle it is a negative part. Then the second part of the northern hemisphere vibrates to the fourth part of the northern hemisphere. The internal third part of the west year No. 4 vibrates

156

to the internal third part of the west year 17 (Rohini is on 180° of the Anuradha No. 17) No. 17 means 17-30 hours it shows Kumbha Langna. The second part of the northern hemisphere vibrates to the third part of the northern hemisphere. The internal third part of the west year No. 4, vibrates to the internal first part of the east year No. 22 (Rohini nakshatra is negative. Shravana Nakshatra is greater nakshatra. Shravana is No. 22) No. 22 means 22-30 hours deduct two hours the difference of the east 22-30—2= 20-30 hours, it shows Vrishabha Rashi, that is on 8.8.1912 at 17-30 hours there is Kumbha Lagna and Vrishabha Rashi on the meridian of Ujjain. Birth place Lat. 13° N. Long. 5h. 10m. 20s. east.

Example No. 10 (Second part of the northern hemisphere). Birth date 9.8.1911. Deduct the saptarishikal from the year 1911. 1911—1908=3=Krittika nakshatra from the first division. Saptarishikal is in the first part. Birth date is in the first part. Birth date is No. 9. Birth month is No. 8. saptarishikal nakshatra is No. 3, it is a spherical triangle. See the year 1911 in the column 1908 east year No. 3 second part of the northern hemisphere, but due to a spherical triangle it is a negative part. Then the second part of the northern hemisphere vibrates to the first part of the southern hemisphere. The internal first part of the east year No. 3 vibrates to the internal second part of the west year 16 (Vishakha nakshatra is on 180° of the Krittika. Vishakha is No. 16) No. 16 means 16-30 hours, add two hours the difference of the east 16-30 plus 2=18-30 it shows Makara Rashi. The internal first part of the east year No. 3 vibrates to the internal fourth part of the west year No. 3. No. 3 means 3-30 hours add two hours the difference of the east 3- 30 plus 2=5-30 hours it shows Karka Lagna. That is on 9.8.1911 at 5-30 hours there is Karka Lagna and Makara Rashi on the Meridian of Ujjain. Birth place Lat. 29° 11' N. Long. 77° 41' east. Birth time 6h. 7m.

Example No. 11 (fourth part of the southern hemisphere). Birth date 10.8.1928. Deduct the saptarishikal from the year 1928. 1928-1908=20=Purvashadha nakshatra from the third division. Saptarishikal is in the first part. Birth date is in the second part. Birth date is 10=1. Saptarishikal nakshatra is 20=No. 2 it is a spherical triangle. See the year 1928 in the column 1926 east year No. 2 the fourth part of the southern hemisphere, but due to a spherical triangle it is a negative part. Then the fourth part of the southern hemisphere vibrates to the second part of the northern hemisphere. The internal first part of the east year 20 vibrates to the internal first part of the west year No. 24 (Purvashadha No. 20 nakshatra is negative because of the spherical triangle. Purva is greater nakshatra. Shatataraka is on 180° of the Purva) No. 24 means 24-30 hours it shows Vrishabha Rashi. The fourth part of the southern hemisphere vibrates to the first part of the northern hemisphere. The internal first part of the east year No. 20 vibrates to the internal first part of the west year No. 6 (Aridra No. 6 nakshatra is on 180° of the Purvashadha). No. 6 means 6-30 hours, deduct two hours the difference of the west. 6-30—2=4-30, it shows Karka Lagna. That is on 10.8.1928 at 4-30 hours there is Karka Lagna and Vrishabha Rashi on the meridian of Ujjain. Birth place Lat. 25° 22′ N. Long 68° 20′ east. Birth time 4-46 hours.

Example No. 12. (Third part of the Southern hemisphere) Birth date 10.8.1937. Deduct the saptarishikal from the year 1937. 1937-1908=29-27=2=Bharani nakshatra from the first division. Saptarishikal is in the second part. Birth date is in the second part. Birth date is 10=1 saptarishikal nakshatra is No. 2, it is a spherical triangle. See the year 1937 in the column 1935 east year No. 2. The third part of the southern hemisphere, but due to a spherical triangle it is a negative part. Then the third part of the southern hemisphere vibrates to the first part of the southern hemisphere. The internal second part of the east year No. 2 vibrates to the internal second part of the west year 16 (Bharani nakshatra is on 180° of the Vishakha No. 16) No. 16 means 16-30 hours it shows Makara Lagna (add two hours the difference of the east 16-30 plus 2=18-30 hours that is 16-30 is R.A. and 18-30 is Dec. of Makara). The third part of the southern hemisphere vibrates to the fourth part of the southern hemisphere. The internal second part the east year 20 vibrates to the internal fourth part of the west year 7. No. 7 means 7-30 hours (add two hours the difference of the east. 7-30 plus 2=9-30 hours that is 7-30 is R.A. and 9-30 is Dec. of Kanya) it shows Kanya Rashi. That is on 10.8.1937 at 16-30 hours there is Makara Lagna and Kanya Rashi on the meridian of Ujjain. Birth place Lat. 7° N. Long. 79° 45′ east. Birth time 16-57 hours.

Example No. 13 (Fourth part of the northern hemisphere) Birth date 13.8.1894. Deduct the saptarishikal from the year 1894. 1894-1808=86—81=5=Mriga nakshatra from the first division. Saptarishikal is in the fourth part. Birth date is in the second part. Birth date is 13=No. 4. Birth month is No. 8, it is a spherical triangle. See the year 1894 in the column 1890 west year No. 5 in the fourth part of the northern hemisphere, but due to a spherical triangle it is a negative part. Then the fourth part of the northern hemisphere vibrates to the first part of the southern hemisphere. The internal second part of the west year No. 5 vibrates to the internal second part of the west year No. 14. Mriga nakshatra is negative because of the spherical triangle. Chitra nakshatra is a greater nakshatra No. 14 means 14-30 hours, add two hours the difference of the Northern hemisphere. 14-30 hours plus 2=16-30 (14-30 is R.A. and 16-30 is Dec. of the Dhanu Rashi) it shows Dhanu Rashi. The fourth part of the northern hemisphere vibrates to second part of the southern hemisphere. The internal second part of the west year No. 5 vibrates to the internal second part of the east year No. 9 (Mriga nakshatra is negative. Dhanishtha nakshatra is greater. Dhanishtha is on 180° of the Aslesha No. 9). No. 9 means 9-30 hours, add two hours the difference of the east 9-30 plus 2=11-30 hours, it shows Vrischika Lagna, that is on 13.8.1894 at 11-30 hours there is Vrischika Lagna and Dhanu Rashi on the meridian of Ujjain. Birth place Lat. 23° N. Long 5h. east. Birth time 11-50 hours.

Example No. 14 (Second part of the Northern hemisphere) Birth date 14.8.1912. Deduct the Saptarishikal from the year 1912. 1912-1908—4=Rohini nakshatra from the first division. Saptarishikal is in the first part. Birth date is in the second part. Birth month is No. 8. Saptarishikal nakshatra is No. 4, it is a spherical triangle. See the year 1912 in the column 1908 west year No. 4 vibrates to the internal third part of the east year No. 13 (Rohini nakshatra is negative due to spherical triangle Hasta nakshatra is a greater nakshatra) (No. 13 means 13-30 hours, deduct two hours the difference of the west. 13-30—2=11-30 hours, it shows Vrishika Lagna. The second part of the Northern hemisphere vibrates to the fourth part of the southern hemisphere. The internal third part of the west year No. 4 vibrates to the internal 3rd part of the west year (Rohini nakshatra is negative because of the spherical triangle Shravana nakshatra is greater nakshatra. Shravana nakshatra is on 180° of the Pushya No. 8). No. 8 means 8-30 hours, deduct two hours the difference of the northern hemisphere 8-30—2=6-30 hours, it shows Simha Rashi. That is on 14.8.1912 at 11-30 hours there is Vrischika Lagna and Simha Rashi on the meridian of Ujjain. Birth place Lat. 13° N. Long. 5h 10m 20s East. Birth time 13-7 hours.

Example No. 15 (Third part of the northern hemisphere) Birth date 20.8.1902. Deduct the saptarishikal from the year 1902. 1902-1808=94-81=13=Hasta nakshatra from the second division. Saptarishikal is in the fourth part. Birth date is in the fourth part. Birth month is No. 8 Saptarishikal nakshatra is 13=No. 4, it is a spherical triangle. See the year 1902 in the column 1899 east year 13 the third part of the Northern hemisphere, but due to a spherical triangle it is a negative part. Then the third part of the northern hemisphere vibrates to the third part of the southern hemisphere. The internal fourth part of the east year 13 vibrates to the internal second part of the west year 13. No. 13 means 13-30 hours. Deduct two hours the difference of the northern hemisphere. 13-30—2=11-30 hours, it shows Thula Lagna. The third part of the northern hemisphere vibrates to the fourth part of the northern hemisphere. The internal fourth part of east year 13 vibrates to the internal fourth part of the west year 17. (Hasta nakshatra is negative because of the spherical triangle. Rohini nakshatra is a greater nakshatra. Anuradha No. 17 is on 180° of the Rohini). No. 17 means 17-30 hours add two hours the difference of the east 17-30 plus 2=19-30 hours, it shows Kumbha rashi, that is on 20.8.1902 at 11.30 hours there is Tula Lagna and Kumbha Rashi on the meridian of Ujjain. Birth place Lat. 9° 58′ N. Long. 78° 10′ east. Birth time 11-33 hours.

Example No. 16 (second part of the southern hemisphere) Birth date 20.8.1944. Deduct the saptarishikal from the year 1944. 1944—1908=36-27=9=Aslesha nakshatra is from the first division. Saptarishikal is in the second part. Birth date is in the third part. Birth month is No. 8. Saptarishikal nakshatra is No. 9, it is a spherical triangle. See the year 1944 in column 1944 east year No. 9. The second part of the southern hemisphere, but due to the spherical triangle it is a negative part. Then the second part of the southern hemisphere vibrates to the fourth part of the southern hemisphere. The internal second part of the east year No. 9 vibrates to the internal second part of the east year No. 5 (Aslesha is on 180° of the Dhanistha No. 23 but because of the spherical triangle Dhanishtha is negative. Mriga nakshatra is a greater nakshatra) No. 5 means 5-30 hours, it shows Simha Rashi, add two hours, the difference of the northern hemisphere, 5-30 hours plus 2=7-30 hours (5-30 is R. A. and 7-30 is Dec. of the Simha Rashi.) The second part of the northern hemisphere vibrates to fourth part of the southern hemisphere). The internal second part of the east year 9 vibrates to the internal second part of the west year 18. (Aslesha nakshatra is negative because of the spherical triangle Jyeshtha No. 18 is a greater nakshatra. No. 18 means 18-30 hours, add 2 hours the difference of the east 18-30 plus 2=20-30 hours. 7-30 hours of the Rashi vibrates to 20-30 hours of the Lagna that is on 20.8.1944 at 20-30 hours there is Simha Lagna and Simha Rashi on the meridian of Ujjain. Birth place Lat. 31° 33′ N. Long. 74° 16′ east. Birth time 20 hours.

Example No. 17 (Fourth part of the northern hemisphere) Birth date 20.8.1891. Deduct the saptarishikal from the year 1891. 1891 —1808=83-81=2=Bharani nakshatra from the first division. Saptarishikal is in the fourth part. Birth date is in the third part. Birth date is 20=No. 2. Saptarishikal nakshatra is No. 2, it is a spherical triangle. See the year 1891 in the column 1890 east year No. 2 the fourth part of the northern hemisphere, but due to the spherical triangle it is negative. Add two hours the difference of the negative part. No. 2 means 2-30 hours. 2-30 plus 2=4-30 hours, 4-30 hours means Rohini nakshatra. Rohini is on 180° of the Anuradha No. 17. No. 17 means 17-30 hours, it shows Kumbha Rashi. The fourth part of the northern hemisphere vibrates to the third part of the northern hemisphere. The internal fourth part of the east year No. 2 vibrates to the internal second part of the east year No. 20 (Bharani is a negative nakshatra because of the spherical triangle Purvashadha is a greater nakshatra). 20 means 20-30 hours, it shows Mesha Lagna (add two hours the difference of the negative nakshatra, 20-30 hours plus 2=22-30 that is 20-30 is R.A. and 22-30 is Dec. That is on 20.8.1891 at 20-30 hours there is Mesha Lagna and Kumba Rashi on the meridian of Ujjain. Birth place Lat. 19° N. 72° 35′ long. east. Birth time 22 hours.

CHAPTER V

RULES TO FIND THE LAGNA (SIDEREAL TIME) AND RASHI

चत्वारि श्रृंगास्त्रयो अस्य पादा द्वे शीर्षे सप्तहस्तासो अस्य ।
त्रिधा बद्धो वृषभो रोरवीति महोदेवो मर्त्यां आविवेश ॥ २ ॥

The sun who is Yadnya Purusha has got two heads. One is Dakshinayana and the other is Uttarayana. In Dakshinayana the Sun
moves in four parts and he moves in fourth parts of the Uttarayana.
His constant journey is within three stations Aswini, Magha, and
Moola. The third station is a great one for the mortals. The days
of the week are his hands to show the stations.

त्रिधाहित पणिभिर्गुह्य मानंगविदेवासो धृतमन्वविदन् ।
इंद्रंएकँ सूर्य एकँ जनानवेनदि कंस्वधयानिष्ट तक्षुः ॥

There are three station masters on three stations. One is Indra
Aswini; The second is Surya-Magha and the third is Yama-Moola.
The person who is talented understands the Parmatma Vishwa,
Tejasa, and Pradnya. Thus the nakshatra, the days of the week,
the Southern and the Northern hemisphere and their parts were
known to the Rishis and according to this knowledge they made a
chart.

पंचपादं पितरं द्वादशाकृति दिव आहुः परेअर्वे पुरीषिणं ।
अर्थेमे अन्य उपरे विचक्षणं सप्तचक्रं शळर आहुर्रपितम् ॥

The twelve forms (Rashis) of Pancha Samvatsara Yuga (Pentagon
Angle) makes one circle, half of it (one half of the Circle 180°) possesses Rain water (Southern hemisphere)—six forms (Six Rashis)
and the other half (Northern hemisphere) has got six forms (Six
Rashis). The wheel revolves along with seven days. Add one day
more per pentagon and we will get the cycle continuous.

According to Vedic conception I prepared the charts of 12
months. One month is taken as one year; naturally Bright half
has got four parts and Dark half has got four parts. Saptarishikal
nakshatra is taken as Nakshatra of a day. According to Rikpatha
I made two groups of one series of nine nakshatras, one group is
for the day and the other for the night. Rules to find Lagna (Sidereal time), Latitude and Longitude.

जौद्राग: खेश्वेहीरोषाचितमूषण्य: ।
रे मृघास्वापोज: कृष्योह जेष्ठाइत्यृक्षा लिंगै: ॥

These are the names of the nakshatra given in Rikpatha. The names are as follows:

1. जौ=अश्वयुजौ Aswini; 2. द्रा=आर्द्रां Aridra; 3. ग: भग: Purva; 4. =खे =विशाखे Vishakha; 5. =श्वे=विश्वे Uttarashadha; 6. हि=उ. भाद्रपदा Uttarabhadrapada; 7. रो=रोहिणी Rohini; 8. षा=आश्लेषा Aslesha; 9. चित्=चित्रा Chitra; 10. मू=मूल Moola; 11. षक्=शतभिषक् Shatataraka; 12. ण्य=भरण्य Bharani; 13. सू=पुनर्वसू Punarvasu; 14. मा:=अर्यमा Uttara; 15. घा=अनुराधा Anuradha; 16. न:=श्रवण: Shravana; 17. रे=रेवती Revati; 18. मृ—मृगशीर्ष Mriga; 19. घा=मघा Magha; 20. स्वा=स्वाती Swati; 21. प:=आप:=पूर्वाषाढा Purvashadha; 22. अ.नं:=पू.भाद्रपदा Purvabhadrapada; 23. कृ=कृत्तिका Krittika; 24 ण्य—पुष्य Pushya; 25. ह=हस्त Hasta; 26. ज्ये—ज्येष्ठा Jyestha: 27. ष्ठा=श्रविष्ठा Dhanistha.

Rigpatha has not shown nakshatra by serial order of the nakshatra but first and sixth, that is 1 vibrates to 6, 2-7, 3-8, 4-9, 5-1, 2-6, 3-7, 4-8, 5-9, 6-1 because the knowledge of the planets and their movements in the North or in the South was known to them and they knew that the planet goes to 6 degrees, which is the utmost motion of the planet either in the North Latitude or in the South. सप्तचक्रं पळरआहुरर्पितम् means the group of the seven planets goes to 6 degrees in two hemispheres, north and south. Not only this but they knew also the position or phases of the planets. The following verse reads the same (7 days means 7 planets):

शुक्राकौं प्राङ्गमुखौ ज्ञेयोगुरू सौम्यावुदङमुखी ।
प्रत्यङमुख: शनि: सोम: शेषा दक्षिणतो मुखा: ॥

We know one Solar degree means one Lunar Nakshatra or one Degree of the Sun means one nakshatra of the Moon, one hour means one Degree of the Sun, and one Nakshatra of the Moon.

We will see how to find out Latitudes from the given examples in Chapter IV.

Example No. 1. Birth date; 24.9.1871. We will find out the Birth Day. 1800=4, 71=4; September 4, birth date 24=24 plus 4 plus 4 plus 4=36 divided by 7=1 is remainder=Sunday is Birth day. See the year 1871 in the column 1863. Sunday shows 15 hours, means 15° of the Sun or 15 Nakshatra Swati of the Moon but due to spherical triangle it is a negative nakshatra. Shatataraka is a positive nakshatra in the Kumbha Rashi. Purva nakshatra is on 180° of the Shatataraka. Purva nakshatra is in Simha

Rashi. Birth day is Sunday. Wednesday is on 180° of the Birth day. Buddha is Lord of the Wednesday, that is, Buddha is in Simha Rashi. 15 nakshatra means 15° of Budha. See the Wednesday in the Chart of the Latitude for 15°. 15° Wednesday shows 10° Latitude North. 15 hours × 15=225 divided by 30=15° of Vrischika Rashi. Mangal is the lord of the Vrischika, in Lagna part Tuesday shows 5-30 hours, deduct 20′ of Ayanachalana=5 hours 10 m=5 hrs. 30 m. 20 s. is Longitude.

Put the birth date on the birth day in second group of the moon

8	1	3	5
Sun	Tues	Thurs	Sat
9	2	4	6
Mon	Wed	Fri	Sun

Birth date is 24=2 plus 4=6, Sun 6, Sat 5, Fri 4, Thurs 3, Wed 2, Tues 1, Mon 9, Sun 8. We put the birth date on the second Sunday because first Sunday is negative due to spherical triangle.

Example No. 2. Birth date: 26.9.1874; 1800=4, 74=1, September=4, Date 26=26 plus 4 plus 1 plus 4=35 divided by 7=Remainder is 0. Birth day is Saturday. See the year 1874 in the column 1872 the second part of the northern hemisphere. There is no Saturday in the second part, because birth date is 26=Uttarabhadrapada nakshatra, Saptarishikal nakshatra is Uttara No. 12. Birth date nakshatra is on 180° of the year nakshatra; it shows full moon day or New Moon day. Then Tuesday is on 180° of the Saturday. Thuesday shows 17 hours but due to spherical triangle it is a negative; 26 Uttarabhadrapada is a positive nakshatra in Meena Rashi. That is Moon is in the Uttarabhadrapada; from 14 September to 14 October Sun is in Kanya that is the Sun is in Uttara nakshatra and it is Full Moon day. Uttarabhadrapada nakshatra means 26° of the Sun. See the chart of Latitude for 26°= 13° North. See the second part of the Southern hemisphere for Sunday 15 hours; it shows 15, add 2 hours=17 hours of Tuesday, it shows 5 hours and 8m, add 2′. The difference of the Sun and Mars 5h 8m plus 2′=5h 10m is the Longitude. Put the Birth day on the Birth date in the second group of Saturday. Birth date is 26=2 plus 6=Saturday 8, Friday 7.

1	3	5	7
Sat	Mon	Wed	Fri
2	4	6	8
Sun	Tues	Thurs	Sat

Thursday 6, Wednesday 5, Thuesday 4, Monday 3, Sunday 2 and Saturday 1.

Note the full moon day shows the opposition between the Lords of the days. New Moon day shows the conjunction or angle of 120° between the Lords of the days.

Example No. 3. Birth date: 24.9.1890. 1800=4, 90=0 September=4 date 24=24 plus 4 plus 4=32 divided by 7=Remainder is 4=Wednesday. See the year 1890 in the fourth part of the northern hemisphere. Wednesday shows 21-30 hours. it is a negative part. Budha is Lord of Wednesday. Mithuna Rashi is negative, then second Rashi is positive. Wednesday in Kanya Rashi shows 4-30 hours, add two hours the difference of the negative part. 4-30 plus 2=6-30, deduct 20″ of Ayanachalana, 6-30′—20′=6-10′. See 6° of the Budha in the Latitude chart. Wednesday 6° shows 13′ Latitude North. Sunday is on 180° of Wednesday from 14th of the September to 14th of October. Sun is in Kanya. Deduct 10 hours the difference of the southern hemisphere 15-30—10=5.30 hours. See the Longitude chart for 5-30 hours, 5-30′—20′ of Ayanachalana 5-10 hours, 77′ Longitude. Put the birth date on the birth day 24=2 plus 4=6 Wednesday, 7 Thursday.

6	8	1	3
Wed	Fri	Sun	Tues
7	9	2	4
Thur	Sat	Mon	Wed

8 Friday, 9 Saturday, 1 Sunday, 2 Monday, 3 Tuesday, 4 Wednesday.

Example No. 4. Birth date: 30.9.1946. 1900=2, 46=1, September=4, Date 30=30 plus 1 plus 2 plus 4=37 divided by 7=Remainder is 2, Monday is Birth day. See the year in the column 1944 the second part of the southern hemisphere. Monday shows 16-30 hours. But due to the spherical triangle Monday is in Meena Rashi, it is negative. Thursday is on 180° of the Monday, as well as Kanya Rashi is on 180° of the Meena Rashi. So see the Meena Rashi in the second part of the Northern hemisphere. Thursday shows 5-30 hours. See Longitude chart for 5-30 hours. 82°-30′ Longitude east. 16 hours of Meena Rashi means 16×15=240 divided by 30=0 Degrees of Vrishcika Rashi in the southern part. Convert it in the Northern part Vrishabha Rashi 0 Degree. Refer Latitude chart for Thursday, Vrishabha Rashi 0 Degree, it shows

25° Latitude North. Put the birth date on the birth day. Birth date is 30=3 plus 0=3

5	7	9	2
Mon	Wed	Fri	Sun
6	8	1	3
Tue	Thurs	Sat	Mon

Example No. 5. Birth date: 22.9.1933. 1900=2 33=6, September=4. Date 22=22 plus 4 plus 6 plus 2=34 divided by 7 =Remainder is 6=Friday is the birth day. Shukra is the Lord of the Friday as well as he is Lord of the Vrishabha and Thula Rashi. See the year 1933 in the column 1926 the fourth part of the Southern hemisphere. Friday shows 13-30 hours and Makara Rashi. 22nd September is the day of equinox for Southern hemisphere, Tuesday is on 180° of Friday. Birth date is 22=4. Birth month is 9, it shows the conjunction of the planets Mangal and Shukra, as well as new Moon day on the positive day Tuesday. Tuesday is in Dhanu Rashi, it is also a negative rashi. Mithuna is on 180° of Dhanu rashi. Spherical triangle shows the difference of 120°. So Thula rashi is positive and there is conjunction of Mangal and Shukra because Shukra is the Lord of Thula Rashi. Friday shows 6-30 hours,, deduct 20' of Ayanachalana 6-30'—20' =6-10'. See the Longitude chart for 6-10'=92°, deduct 13° of Mangal, 92°—13°=79° Longitude East. Monday is on 180° of the Friday. Simha rashi is on 120° of Dhanu. Monday shows 2-30 hours, deduct 2 hours the difference of the southern hemisphere, 2-30—2=30'. Monday—Sunday—Saturday=Friday. See Friday in Latitude chart for 0° of Mithuna rashi. Mriga No. 5=0.0° of Mithuna means Mriga nakshatra. Jyeshtha is on 180° of Mriga. Jyeshtha is No. 18. See 18° of Mithuna 18°=109°-25'—90°=19°-25' Lat. North. Put the birth date on the Birth day; Friday 4, Saturday 3, Sunday 2, Monday 1, Tuesday 9, Wednesday 8, Thursday 7, Friday 6.

Example No. 6. Birth date: 31.10.1915. 1900=2, 15=4, October=6, Date 31=31 plus 6 plus 4 plus 2=43 divided by 7=Remainder is 1=Sunday is Birth day. See the year 1915 in the column 1908 the second part of the Northern hemisphere. Sunday shows 11-30 hours and Makara rashi, but due to the spherical triangle Makara rashi is negative. Sun is the Lord of Sunday, it is negative, then Wednesday is on 180° of Sunday. Karka Rashi is on 180° of the Makara. See Wednesday and Karka rashi in the second part of the southern hemisphere. Wednesday shows 21-30 hours in Karka Rashi. The Sun is not the Lord of Makara rashi or Budha is not the Lord of the Karka Rashi. Both the planets and their nakshatras are negative. 11-30 hours means Purva, it is negative. Bharani nakshatra is greater nakshatra. Bharani means 2-30 hours. 2-30×15=30 plus 2=32° Latitude North. Add two hours the difference of the Northern hemisphere in 21-30 hours. 21-30 plus 2=23-30 hours means Dhanishtha nakshatra, it is negative. Mriga nakshatra is greater. Mriga nakshatra means 5-30 hours, deduct 20' of Ayanachalana 5h 10m shows 75° Longitude East. (Birth date is 31=4, birth month is 10=1, Saptarishikal nakshatra is 7, it shows conjunction of the planets in Moon's Rashi and conjunction of the planets in Sun's Rashi Thula. Mriga Nakshatra is of Mangal and Kethu. Bharani nakshatra is of Rahu and Shukra, that is Moon is with Kethu and Mangal, and Sun is with Shukra, Rahu is on 120° of the Sun and Shukra.

Example No. 7. Birth date 23.10.1910. 1900=2, 10=5, October=6, Date 23=23+2+5+6=36 divided by 7=Remainder is 1=Sunday is Birth day. See the year 1910 in the second part of the Northern hemisphere. Sunday shows 11-30 hours of Makara Rashi but due to spherical triangle Makara Rashi is negative. Wednesday is on 180° of the Sunday. Karka Rashi is on 180° of Makara. Wednesday in Karka Rashi shows 21-30 hours. The Sun is not the Lord of the Makara Rashi and Budha is not the Lord of Karka Rashi. 11-30 hours means Purva nakshatra, it is negative nakshatra. Bharani is greater nakshatra. 21-30 hours means Uttarashadha nakshatra. Uttarashadha is negative. Uttara is greater nakshatra. Bharani nakshatra means 2 solar degrees of Mesha Rashi in north and Uttara means 12-30 hours, deduct 10 hours the difference of northern hemisphere day, 12-30—10=2-30 hours. Wednesday—Tuesday= Monday. Wednesday in second part of the northern hemisphere shows 7-30 hours and Monday in first part of the southern hemisphere shows 2-30 hours. 7-30—2-30=5 hours is Longitude of the Budha in the east 2° of the Mesha is the Latitude on Monday. See Latitude chart for Mesha, 2° on Monday, it shows 13° Latitude North.

Example No. 8. Birth date: 1.11.1910. 1900=2, 10=5, November=2, Date 1=1 plus 2 plus 5 plus 2=10 divided by 7=Remainder is 3=Tuesday is Birth day. See the year 1910 in the second part of the northern hemisphere. There is no Tuesday in the second part. Mangal is the Lord of Tuesday as well as he is the Lord of

Vrischika Rashi and Mesha Rashi. Saturday is on 180° of Tuesday. Shani is the Lord of Saturday as well as he is the Lord of Makara and Kumbha Rashi. Saturday shows 10-30 hours. 10-30 hours means Magha nakshatra. Magha nakshatra is in Simha Rashi. Shatataraka nakshatra is on 180° of Magha. Shatataraka is 24 nakshatra or 24° Solar degrees. See 24° on Saturday in Simha Rashi for Latitude, it shows 13° Latitude North. Mangal is the Lord of Vrischika Rashi. So see the Third part of the northern hemisphere. Tuesday shows 6-30 hours, deduct one hour the difference because Mriga nakshatra is of Mangal and deduct 20' of the Ayanachalana. 6-30—1-20'=5h 10m is the Longitude of Mangal in east. See the chart of Longitude for 5-10, it shows 77° 30' east.

Example No. 9. Birth date 5.11.1937. 1900=2, 37=4. November=2. Date 5=5 plus 2 plus 4 plus 2=13 divided by 7=Remainder is 6=Friday is the birth day. See the year 1937 in the third part of the Southern hemisphere. Friday shows 16-30, Shukra is the Lord of Friday as well as he is the Lord of Vrishabha and Thula Rashi. Bharani and Aridra are his nakshatras. 16-30 hours are negative, due to the spherical triangle 16-30 hours means Vishakha nakshatra, it is negative. Punarvasu nakshatra is greater nakshatra. Punarvasu nakshatra means 7-30 hours, deduct 2 hours of the negative part. 7-30 minus 2=5-30 hours, deduct 20' of the Ayanachalana, 5-30—20'=5h 10m. See the Longitude chart for 5h 10m, 77° 30' east. Monday is on 180° of Friday. Moon is the Lord of Monday and Karka Rashi, Rohini, Hasta, Shravana are the nakshatras of the Moon. Makara rashi is on 180° of Karka, but there is no Monday in the second part of the northern hemisphere. Then see the first part of the northern hemisphere. Meena Rashi is on 120° of Karka. Monday shows 12-30 hours, deduct 12 hours the difference of the southern hemisphere day. 12-30—12=30'—20'=10' of Kanya rashi in the northern hemisphere. See Latitude chart for 1° on Monday, it shows 13° Latitude North.

Example No. 10. Birth date 18.11.1900. 1900=2, November =2, Date 18=18 plus 2 plus 2=22 divided by 7=Remainder is 1=Sunday is the birth day. See the year 1900 in the third part of the Northern hemisphere. Sunday shows 4-30 hours, but due to the spherical triangle Sunday is negative. 4-30 hours means Rohini nakshatra, it is negative. Shravana nakshatra is greater nakshatra. Thursday is on 180° of the Sunday. The Sun is the Lord of Sunday and Simha Rashi. Thursday is on 180° of Sunday. Guru is the Lord of Thursday and Dhanu Rashi, but Dhanu rashi is negative here, then Guru is Lord of Meena Rashi, but there is no Thursday in the first part of the Northern hemisphere. Guru and Sun both the planets are negative for Dhanu and Meena Rashi. it is typical horo-scope. So we will put the Date on the Birth day and we will see nakshatra of the Sun in Moon's chart

1	3	5	7
Sun	Tues	Thurs	Sat
2	4	6	9
Mon	Wed	Fri	Sun

2-5, 3-9, 4-7, 1-6. That is instead of the Sun see Mangal and see the Moon on behalf of Guru. Mangal is the Lord of Vrischika and Mesha. Moon is the Lord of Karka. Sun shows 4-30 hours means Rohini nakshatra. $4 \times 15 = 60° = 0°$ of Declination Mesha. See Monday 0 Degree of Mesha rashi, it shows 13° Latitude. Thursday shows 8-30 hours, deduct it from the hours of Tuesday. 13-30—8-30 hours, it shows 75° Longitude. There will be difference of 2° because of the (conjunction of Guru, Rahu, Budha and Ravi in the second Rashi of Mangal.) Tuesday 1° Wednesday 2°.

Example No. 11. Birth date 14.11.1889. 1800=4, 89=6, November=2, Date 14=14 plus 2 plus 6 plus 4=26, divided by 7=Remain-der is 5=Thursday. See the year 1889 in the first part of the Southern hemisphere. No. Thursday. There is Sunday on 180° of Thursday. The Sun is the Lord of the Simha Rashi and Sunday. Sunday shows 21-30 hours, add two hours the difference of the negative part. 21-30 plus 2=23-30. 23-30' deduct 20' of the Ayana-chalana. 23-30'—20'=23-10'. 23 hours means 23 nakshatra. Magha nakshatra is on 180° of the Dhanistha. Magha nakshatra is 0° Degree of Simha. See Thursday 0° of Simha in Latitude chart. 25° Latitude North. See the Mithuna Rashi on 180° of the Dhanu Rashi which is negative first part of Southern hemisphere. Sunday shows 21-30 hours, deduct 18-10 of Thursday, 20' of Ayanacha-lana 18-30'—20'=18-10', 21-30—18-10'=3-20' add 2 hours the differ-ence of the negative part 3-30 plus 2=5-20=80° the Longitude of Guru. See Longitude chart for 5-20 hours, 80° Longitude east (deduct 6° of the Sun and 3° of Ketu). Put the Birth date on the Birth day;

7	9	2	4
Thurs	Sat	Mon	Wed
8	1	3	5
Fri	Sun	Tue	Thur

Example No. 12. Birth date 26.11.1935. 1900=2, 35=1. November=2, Date 26=26 plus 2 plus 1 plus 2=31 divided by

7=Remainder is 3=Tuesday is birth day. **See the year 1935 in** third part of the southern hemisphere. **Tuesday shows 23-30 hours,** but due to the spherical triangle it is a negative part. **Mangal is** the Lord of Tuesday as well as he is the Lord of the Mesha and Vrischika rashis. Saturday is on 180° of Tuesday. **See first part** of the southern hemisphere for Vrischika Rashi. **Saturday shows** 3-30 hours. 3-30 hours means Krittika nakshatra, Vishakha nakshatra is on 180° of Krittika. 23-30 hours of Tuesday means Dhanishtha nakshatra. Magha nakshatra is on 180° of Dhanishtha. Magha nakshatra means 1-30 hours. Dhanishtha nakshatra means 5-30 hours or 5 solar degrees of Simha Rashi. Then see 5 degrees of Simha rashi on Saturday. 19° Latitude North. 3-30 hours plus 2 hours of the difference of the negative part. 3-30 plus 2 =5-30 hours. See Longitude chart for 5-30 hours, it shows 82° Longitude. Deduct 5° of Saturday 82°—5°=77° Longitude East. Difference of 2° Longitude shows the conjunction of Sun and Moon on Tuesday, that is Tuesday is new Moon day. On the otherway 3-30 hours deduct 20' of Ayanachalana. 3-30×15=45 divided by 30=15° of Vrishabha rashi shows the Lord of the Vrishabha on 180° of Mesha, the rashi of Mangal. Angle of 120° between Shani and Shukra, Shani is in Dhanishtha and Shukra is in Chitra. Both the nakshatras are of Mangal. Put the Birth date on the Birth day.

1	3	5	7
Tues	Thur	Sat	Mon
2	4	6	8
Wed	Fri	Sun	Tues

Example No. 13. Birth date 28.11.1927. 1900=2, 27=5, November=2, date 28=28 plus 2 plus 5 plus 2=37 divided by 7=Remainder is 2=Monday is the Birth day. See the year 1927 in the fourth part of the Southern hemisphere. No Monday is there to see the hours. Then Friday is on 180° of Monday. Friday shows 19-30 hours, but due to the spherical triangle it is a negative part. 19-30 hours means Moola nakshatra, it is a negative nakshatra. Aswini is a greater nakshatra. Shukra is the Lord of the Friday as well as he is the lord of Vrishabha and Thula Rashi. Chitra nakshatra, is 180° of Aswini and Chitra nakshatra is in Thula Rashi, but the fourth part of Southern hemisphere shows Mithuna Rashi. Mriga nakshatra is in Mithuna Rasi. Mriga nakshatra means 5-30 hours. See the Longitude chart for 5-30 hours. It shows 83° Longitude. Deduct 6° for the negative part and Angle of 120°. 83°—6°=77° is the Longitude east. Moon is the Lord of the Karka Rashi but there is no Monday in Karka Rashi. Makara Rashi is 180° of the

Karka Rashi. So see the third part of the northern hemisphere. Monday shows 8-30 hours. 8-30 hours means Pushya nakshatra. It is negative in Makara Rashi. Uttarashadha is on 180° of Pushya, it is the nakshatra of the Sun. The Sun is the Lord of Simha rashi. The Moon is negative, so Uttarashadha nakshatra is nega- tive. Krittika nakshatra is the greater nakshatra. Krittika nak- shatra means 3 Solar Degrees, add 2 hours or 2° the difference of the Southern hemisphere, 3 plus 2=5° of Simha rashi. See the Latitude chart for 5° on Sunday, it shows 19° Latitude North. Put the birth day on the birth date.

3	5	7	9
Mon	Wed	Fri	Sun
4	6	8	1
Tues	Thur	Sat	Mon

Example No. 14. Birth date 31.1.1884. 1800=4, 84=0 Janu- ary=5, Date 31=31 plus 5 plus 4=40 divided by 7 Remainder is 5. Thursday is Birth day. See the year 1884 in the first part of the northern hemisphere. Thursday shows 18-30 hours but due to the spherical triangle it is a negative day. Guru is the Lord of Thurs- day as well as he is the Lord of Dhanu and Meena Rashi. Sunday is on 180° of Thursday. See the Sunday on 180° of the Simha Rashi. The fourth part of the northern hemisphere Sunday shows 7-30 hours. 7-30 hours means Punarvasu nakshatra, it is negative. Purvabhadrapada is the greater nakshatra which is of Guru. 7-30 hours means Punarvasu nakshatra, add two hours the difference of the negative part. 7-30 plus 2=9-30 hours. Deduct 20' of Aya- nachalana 9-30—20'=9-10'. See the Latitude chart for 9 hours on Sunday. 9 hours means 9 nakshatra or 9 Solar Degrees of Simha Rashi or 22° of Kumbha Rashi (Aslesha nakshatra vibrates to Shravana nakshatra) it shows 18° Latitude North. On Sunday Guru shows 18-30 hours. 18-30 hours means Jyeshtha nakshatra, Mriga nakshatra is on 180° of the Jyeshtha, (but due to the spherical triangle it is a negative nakshatra, Aslesha is the greater naksha- tra. Dhanistha nakshatra is on 180° of Aslesha. From 14th of January to 14th February the Sun is in Makara Rashi, that is he is in Dhanistha nakshatra). Mriga nakshatra means 5-30 hours. See 5-30 hours in Longitude chart, it shows 82°, it is of Mangal. Deduct 4° more degrees for Guru, 82°—4°=78° Longitude east. (352° will be of the west for Kumbha Lagna). Put the birth date on the birth day

6	8	1	3
Thur	Sat	Mon	Wed
7	9	2	4
Fri	Sun	Tue	Thur

Example No. 15. Birth date 12.2.1856. 1800=4. 56=0, February=2. Date 12=12 plus 2 plus 4=20 divided by 7=Remainder is 6=Friday is Birth day. See the year 1856 in the fourth part of the northern hemisphere. Friday shows 5-30 hours, but due to the spherical triangle it is a negative day. Shukra is the lord of Vrishabha and Thula Rashi as well as he is the Lord of Friday. See the third part of the northern hemisphere for Vrishabha Rashi. Friday shows 12-30 hours. Monday is on 180° of the Friday, it shows 8-30 hours. Deduct the difference 12-30—8-30=4 hours deduct 20' of the Ayanachalana. 4 hours—20'=3-40' means Krittika nakshatra or 3 Solar Degrees. See 3° of the Vrishabha rashi on Friday in the Latitude chart, it shows 18° North. Friday shows 12-30 hours, add two hours the difference of the negative part. 12-30 hours plus 2=14-30 hours. 14-30 means Chitra nakshatra which is in Thula Rashi which we have seen for the Latitude. Then 5-30 hours of Friday is Longitude. See the Longitude chart for 5-30 hours, it shows 82°. Add 2° the difference of the Moon. 82° plus 2°=84° is Longitude of East.

Example No. 16. Birth date 22.2.1863. 1800=4, 63=1, February =2, Date 22=22 plus 2 plus 1 plus 4=29 divided by 7=Remainder is 1=Sunday is the Birth day. See the year 1863 in the third part of the northern hemisphere for Sunday. No Sunday seems in the third part of the Northern hemisphere. Tuesday is on 180° of the Sunday, Mangal is the Lord of Tuesday as well as he is the Lord of Vrischika and Mesha Rashis. Then see the second part of the Scuthern hemisphere for Vrischika Rashi. Sunday shows 19-30 hours and Tuesday shows 21-30 hours. The Sun shows the nakshatra of Mangal and Mangal shows the nakshatra of the Sun. Deduct Sunday hours from Tuesday 21-30—19-30=2 hours of Vrischika rashi in South and 0 hour of Vrishabha in north. So see the Latitude chart for 0° of Monday, of Vrishabha, it shows 13° Latitude north. See the Longitude of Mriga nakshatra. Mriga nakshatra means 5-30 hours, deduct 20' of Ayanachalana 5-30—20'=5-10 is Longitude east.

Example No. 17. Birth date. 25.2.1894. 1800=4 94=5, February=2, Date 22=22 plus 2 plus 5 plus 4=33 divided by 7=Remainder is 5=Thursday is birth day. See the year 1894 in the fourth part of the Southern hemisphere. Thursday shows 16-30 hours but due to spherical triangle it is a negative day. Guru is the Lord of Thursday as well as he is the Lord of Dhanu and Meena Rashis. So see the first part of the southern hemisphere for Dhanu Rashi. Thursday shows 23-30 hours. Sunday is on 180° of Thursday. The Sun is the Lord of the Simha rashi. See the third part of the southern hemisphere for Sunday. Sunday shows 19-30 hours. Both the days show the nakshatra of Mangal. So deduct the difference from 23-30 hours—19-30=5 hours. See the Longitude chart for 5 hours, it shows 75°—2° the difference of the Mangal. 75°—2°=73° Longitude east. Sunday shows 19-30 hours. add 2 hours the difference of the negative part, where Thursday shows 16-30 hours. 19-30 plus 2=21-30 hours of the Sun, it is a negative nakshatra in Kumbha Rashi. Punarvasu is on 180° of the Uttarashadha. Punarvasu is Seventh nakshatra or 7° Solar degrees. See the Latitude chart for Sunday 7° in Simha rashi, it shows 18° North.

Example No. 18. Birth date 21.3.1921. 1900=2. 21=5, March=2; Date 21=21 plus 2 plus 5 plus 2=30 divided by 7=Remainder is 2=Monday is Birth day. See the year 1921 in the first part of the southern hemisphere. No Monday seems in the first part. The Moon is the Lord of Monday as well as she is the Lord of Karka rashi. Thursday is on 180° of the Monday. Guru is the Lord of Thursday as well as he is the Lord of Dhanu and Meena Rashi. Thursday shows 23-30 hours but due to the spherical triangle it is a negative part. See the Karka rashi in the fourth part of the southern hemisphere. Monday shows 13-30 hours. Thursday shows 16-30 hours. Deduct 20′ of Ayanachalana 16-30—20′=16-10 hours means Vishakha nakshatra or 16 solar degrees. See 16° on Thursday in Kanya rashi. It shows 10° Latitude. Add 2 hours the difference of the negative part. 13-30 plus 2=15-30 hours. 15-30 hours shows Swati nakshatra. Bharani nakshatra is on 180° of Swati. Bharani nakshatra is in Mesha Rashi. Mangal is the Lord of the Mesha rashi. Mriga nakshatra is of Mangal. Mriga nakshatra shows 5-30 hours (The other way is Thursday shows 23-30 hours and Thursday shows 16-30 hours. The difference is of 7 hours. Deduct the difference of the negative part, 7-2=5 hours means Mriga nakshatra. Mriga nakshatra is of Mangal. 5 hours shows 75°, add 3° for the Moon, 78° Longitude east.

Example No. 19. Birth date 23.3.1929. 1900=2 29=1. March =2. Date 23=23 plus 2 plus 1 plus 2=28 divided by 7=Remainder is 0=Saturday is Birth day. See the year 1929 in the fourth part of the Northern hemisphere. No Saturday seems in the fourth part of the Northern hemisphere. Shani is the Lord of Saturday as well as he is the Lord of Makara and Kumbha rashi. So see the Kumbha rashi in the third part of the northern hemisphere. Saturday shows 3-30 hours. Budha is the Lord of Wednesday as well as he is the Lord of Mithuna and Kanya Rashis. Wednesday shows 24-30 hours. 24-30 means Shatataraka Nakshatra. It is a nega-

173

tive nakshatra. Swati is the greater nakshatra. Swati means 15-30 hours. Deduct 20′ of Ayanachalana 15-30—20′=15-10. See 15° of Kumbha Rashi on Wednesday for Latitude 15° on Wednesday shows 20° North. Saturday shows 3-30 hours, add 2 hours the difference of the negative part. 3-30 plus 2=5-30 hours. It shows 82°, deduct the Longitude of Buddha 82—2=80° East.

Example No. 20. Birth date 4.4.1949. 1900=2, 49=5, April =5. Date 4=4 plus 5 plus 5 plus 2=16 divided by 7=Remainder is 2=Monday is the Birth day. See the year 1949 in the second part of the Northern hemisphere. Monday shows 5-30 hours but due to spherical triangle it is a negative day. Moon is the Lord of Monday as well as she is the lord of Karka Rashi. Then see Karka rashi in the fourth part of the Southern hemisphere. There is no Monday in Karka Rashi. Thursday is on 180° of the Monday. Guru is the Lord of Thursday as well as he is the Lord of Dhanu and Meena rashis. Thursday shows 11-30 hours. 11-30 hours means 11 nakshatra or 11 solar degrees of the Mesha. See the Latitude chart of the R.A. for 11 degress on Monday it shows 37° 54′ North. Monday shows 5-30 hours. See the Longitude chart for 5-30 hours. 82° deduct the Longitude of Guru 82°-5°=77° West, because Mesha Rashi is negative in the east and positive in the west.

Example No. 21. Birth date 20.4.1899. 1800=4 99=3, April=5. Date 20=20 plus 5 plus 3 plus 4=32 divided by 7= Remainder is 4=Wednesday is the Birth day. See the year 1899 in the third part of the Southern hemisphere, but there is no Wednesday in the third part of the southern hemisphere. Saturday is on 180° of the Wednesday. Saturday shows 13-30 hours, but due to the spherical triangle it is a negative part. Budha is the Lord of Wednesday as well as he is the Lord of Mithuna and Kanya rashi. Shani is the Lord of the Saturday as well as he is the lord of Makara and Kumbha rashis. See the Kumbha rashi on 180° of Simha which is a negative rashi in the third part of the Southern hemisphere. Kumbha rashi is in the second part of the Northern hemisphere. Wednesday shows 24-30 hours. Deduct 2 hours the difference of the Southern hemisphere. 24-30—2=22-30 hours. Deduct 20′ of the Ayanachalana. 22-30—20′=22-10′ hours. 22-10 hours means 22 nakshatra or 22 Solar degrees. See the Latitude chart for 22° on Wednesday in Mithuna rashi, 48° north. Saturday shows 13-30 hours in Northern hemisphere and Saturday in Southern hemisphere shows 3-30 hours. 13-30 hours are negative due to the Spherical triangle. 13-30 hours means Hasta nakshatra, it is negative. Rohini is the greater nakshatra. Rohini means 4-30

hours. Deduct the difference of the both Saturdays. 4-30—3-30=
1 hour is the Longitude of the Shani. See the chart of the Longitude for one hour. It shows 15°. Deduct 2 degrees of Budha
(Wednesday 0°, Thursday 1°, Friday 2°) 15°—2°=13° Longitude east.

Example No. 22. Birth date 25.4.1945. 1900=2, 45=0, April=5.
Date is 25=25 plus 5 plus 2—32 divided by 7=Remainder is 4=
Wednesday is the Birth day. See the year 1945 in the second
part of the Northern hemisphere. Wednesday shows 14-30 hours,
but due to the spherical triangle it is a negative part. Budha is
the lord of Kanya rashi and he is the Lord of Wednesday. Kanya
rashi is there with Wednesday still it is a negative part. It means
Budha shows Longitude. 14-30 hours means Chitra nakshatra, it
is negative. Mriga nakshatra is the greater nakshatra. Mriga
nakshatra means 5-30 hours, Saturday is on 180° of the Wednesday.
Shani is the lord of Saturday as well as he is the lord of Makara
and Kumbha rashi. Then see the second part of the southern hemisphere for Kumbha rashi. Saturday shows 3-30 hours. Wednesday
shows 24-30 hours. Deduct 3-30 hours from the hours of Wednesday, 24-30—3-30=21 hours. Deduct 20' of Ayanachalana 21 hours—
20'=20-40 hours. 20-40 hours means 20 nakshatra or 20 Solar degrees.
See the Latitude chart for 20° on Wednesday, it shows 18° 35' Latitude north. See the Longitude of Mriga nakshatra or 5-30 hours, it
shows 82°. Deduct 5° of the Shani. (82°—5°=77° Longitude east
—Saturday 1, Sunday 2, Monday 3, Tuesday 4, Wednesday 5).

Example No. 23. Birth date 29.4.1901. 1900=2, 1=1, April 5,
Date 29=29 plus 5 plus 1 plus 2=37 divided by 7=Remainder is
2=Monday is the Birth day. See the year 1901 in the third part
of the southern hemisphere. Monday shows 22-30 hours, but due
to the spherical triangle it is a negative part. Moon is the Lord
of Monday as well as she is the Lord of Karka rashi. Friday is
on 180° of Monday. See Karka rashi of the Moon in the third
part of the northern hemisphere. Friday shows 9-30 hours, and
Monday shows 12-30 hours. Deduct the hours of Friday from the
hours of Monday 12-30—9-30=3 hours. Deduct 20' of the Ayanachalana 3 hours—20'=2-40'. Deduct 2 hours the difference of
the southern hemisphere. 2-40'—2=40' that is 0 degree of Karka
rashi on Monday. See the Latitude chart for Monday, Karka
rashi 0 degree 122°—39' deduct 90°=32°—39' North. The third
part of the southern hemisphere Monday shows 22-30 hours but
due to the spherical triangle it is a negative part. 22-30 hours
means Shravana nakshatra, it is negative. Rohini is a greater nakshatra. Rohini means 4-30 hours, it shows 68°-30' Longitude. Add

5° of the shukra (Monday 1, Tuesday 2, Wednesday 3, Thursday 4 Friday 5) 68° plus 5°=73° 30' East.

Example No. 24. Birth date 6.6.1913. 1900=2, 13=2, June =3, Date 6=6 plus 3 plus 2 plus 2=13 divided by 7=Remainder is 6=Friday is the Birth day. See the year 1913 in the second part of the Southern hemisphere. Friday shows 21-30 hours, but due to the spherical triangle it is a negative part (21-30 hours means Uttarashadha nakshatra; it is a negative nakshatra. Krittika is the greater nakshatra). Shukra is the Lord of Friday as well as he is the Lord of Vrishabha and Thula rashi. Tuesday is on 180° of Friday. See Vrishabha rashi of Shukra in the fourth part of the northern hemisphere. Friday shows 4-30 hours and Tuesday shows 1-30 hours. Deduct Tuesday hours from the Friday hours of greater nakshatra Krittika. Krittika means 3-30 hours, 3-30—1-30=2 hours, now deduct 2 hours the difference of the Southern hemisphere, 2—2=0 hours of Friday. Friday itself has got 4° 1' east. Friday shows 4-30 hours. 4-30 hours means Rohini nakshatra. Jyeshtha nakshatra is on 180° of Rohini. Jyeshtha is 18th nakshatra or 18° Solar degrees. Then see 18° of the Kumbha rashi on Friday. It shows 351° Latitude. Deduct 300° of Makara, 351°-300°=51° Latitude North.

Example No. 25. Birth date 28.6.1897. 1800=4, 97=1, June =3, Date 28=28 plus 3 plus 1 plus 4=36 divided by 7=Remainder is 1=Sunday is the Birth day. See the year 1897 in the fourth part of the northern hemisphere. Sunday shows 11-30 hours but due to the spherical triangle it is a negative part. Wednesday is on 180° of Sunday, Budha is the Lord of Wednesday as well as he is the Lord of Mithuna and Kanya rashis. Kanya rashi is negative, then see the other rashi in the second part of the Southern hemisphere. Wednesday shows 4-30 hours in Mithuna rashi, add two hours the difference of the northern hemisphere. 4-30 plus 2=6-30 hours, deduct 20' of Ayanachalana. 6-30—20' =6-10' hours. Deduct 6-10' hours of Wednesday from the hours of Sunday 11-30—6-10=5-20 hours. See the Longitude chart for 5-20' hours, it shows 80°. Deduct Longitude of the Sun (Sunday 0, Monday 1, Thuesday 2, Wednesday 3) 80°—3°=77° Longitude East. Sunday shows 11-30 hours, he is the Lord of the Simha rashi. Uttara is his nakshatra in Simha rashi. Uttara is No. 12. 12 nakshatra means 12° solar degrees. See 12° of Sunday in Mithuna rashi, it shows, 103°—90°=13° Latitude North.

Example No. 26. Birth date 14.7.1897. 1800=4, 97=1. July =5, Date 14=14 plus 5 plus 1 plus 4=24 divided by 7=Remainder is 3=Tuesday is the Birth day. See the year 1897 in the fourth part of the northern hemisphere. Tuesday shows 13-30 hours, but due to the spherical triangle it is a negative part. Friday is on 180° of Tuesday. Friday shows 9-30 hours. Mangal is the Lord of Tuesday as well as he is the Lord of Mesha and Vrischika rashi. Shukra is the Lord of Friday as well as he is the Lord of Vrishabha and Thula rashis. Thula rashi of Shukra is negative here, then see the other rashi of Shukra in the third part of the southern hemisphere. Tuesday shows 3-30 hours. Add 2 hours the difference of the northern hemisphere 3-30 plus 2=5-30. 5-30 hours means 0 hours or the other way deduct 3-30 hours of southern hemisphere Tuesday, 13-30 hours of northern hemisphere Tuesday and deduct 10 hours difference of the night, 13-30—3-30 =10-10=0 hours. See the longitude chart for 0 hours, it shows 0° East. Friday shows 9-30 hours. Deduct 20′ of Ayanachalana 9-30—20′=9-10′ hours. 9-10 hours are negative. 9-10 hours means Aslesha Nakshatra, it is negative. Revati nakshatra is the greater nakshatra. Hasta nakshatra is on 180° of the Revati nakshatra. Hasta nakshatra is No. 13, it means 13 solar degrees. See latitude chart for 13 Solar degrees on Tuesday in Vrischika rashi. It shows 251°-58′. Deduct the degrees of Thula Rashi. 251°-58′-210°=41°-58′ North.

Example No. 27. Birth date 23.7.1856. 1800=4, 56=0, July= 5, Date 23=23 plus 5 plus 4=32 divided by 7=Remainder is 4= Wednesday is the Birth day. See the year 1856 in the fourth part of the southern hemisphere, but here is no Wednesday. Then Saturday is on 180° of Wednesday. Saturday shows 7-30 hours. Budha is the Lord of Wednesday as well as he is the Lord of Kanya and Mithuna Rashis. Kanya rashi is negative here. Then see the other rashi in the first part of the northern hemisphere. Wednes- day shows 4-30 hours, add two hours the difference of the southern hemisphere 4-30 plus 2=6-30 hours, deduct 20′ of Ayanachalana. 6-30—20′=6-10 hours. See the Longitude chart for 6-10 hours, it shows 92°, deduct 13° of Wednesday which was not in the fourth part of the southern hemisphere. 92°-13°=77° Longitude East. Saturday of southern hemisphere shows 7-30 hours. add 2 hours the difference of the nothern hemisphere. 7-30 plus 2=9-30 hours. 9-30 hours means Aslesha nakshatra. Shravana nakshatra No. 22 is on 180° of Aslesha. 22 nakshatra means 22 Solar Degrees. 22-30 hours shows the declination of Aslesha. Then see 22 solar degrees of Tuesday declination in Karka Rashi, it shows 17° Latitude N. or see 7° of Mesharashi on Wednesday.

Example No. 28. Birth date 25.7.1896. 1800=4, 96=0, July =5, Date 25=25 plus 5 plus 4=34 divided by 7=Remainder is

177

6=Friday is the Birth day. See the year 1896 in the fourth part of the northern hemisphere. There is no Friday. Then Monday is on 180° of Friday. Monday shows 19-30 hours, but due to the spherical triangle it is a negative part. Moon is the Lord of Monday as well as she is the Lord of Karka rashi. Then see Karka rashi in the first part of the Northern hemisphere. Monday shows 2-30 hours, and Friday shows 6-30 hours. Northern hemisphere Monday shows 19-30 hours. 19-30 hours means Moola nakshatra. It is negative. Aswini nakshatra is the greater nakshatra. Aswini means 1-30 hours. Deduct it from hours of Friday, 6-30—1-30= 5 hours. See the Longitude chart for 5 hours. It shows 75° Longitude. Aswini and Moola nakshatras are of Mangal. add 3° of Mangal in Monday Longitude, 75° plus 3°=78°. Aswini is the declination nakshatra of the Mesha rashi, then see 19° Monday in declination Latitude chart. 17°-1' Latitude 17° 1' Latitude north.

Example No. 29. Birth date 28.8.1921. 1900=2, 21=5, August=1, Date 28=28 plus 1 plus 5 plus 2=36 divided by 7= Remainder is 1=Sunday is the Birth day. See the year 1921 in the first part of the Northern hemisphere. No Sunday is there, then see Wednesday on 180° of Sunday. Wednesday shows 23-30 hours, but due to the spherical triangle it is the negative part. Buddha is Lord of Wednesday as well as he is the Lord of Mithuna and Kanya rashis. Mithuna rashi is negative here, then see the other rashi of Budha in the third part of the southern hemisphere. Wednesday shows 6-30 hours, deduct 6-30 hours and difference of the night in northern hemisphere from 23-30 hours of Wednesday. 23-30—6-30=17-00—11=6 hours means Aridra nakshatra or 6 solar degrees. See 6° solar degrees on Wednesday in declination Latitude chart for Vrishabha rashi, it shows 6° Latitude North. 23-30 hours of Friday in the first part of the northern hemisphere is negative. 23-30 hours means Dhanistha nakshatra, it is negative. Mriga nakshatra is greater nakshatra. Mriga nakshatra means 5-30 hours. Deduct 20' of Ayanachalana. 5-30'—20'=5-10. See the Longitude chart for 5-10 hours, it shows 78°. Add 2° of Shukra because he is the Lord of the declination rashi Vrishabha (Wednesday 0, Thursday 1, Friday 2) 78° plus 2°=80° Longitude east.

I have shown 29 examples in which you will find the Birth dates of the Leaders and other Nativities. Readers will understand the mistake of Great Astrologers who prepared the wrong horoscopes of the Late Lokamanya Tilak and the Late Jagatmanya Nehru. I do not understand how these people are getting titles after titles when their Ephemeries and Almanacs are absolutely wrong. This shows the absolute ignorance of the so called astrologers as well as of the title givers! The most important thing is that the Ephemeries of 19 Ayanamasa will never give Latitude and Longitude chart, because their Latitude and Longitude will be different, which will not tally with the Map of the World. Simple rule of spherical geometry "The sum of the three angles of the triangle is 180° no more holds on curveture surface". It is always greater upto 4° is not known to them and that is why they are showing the mistake of other ephemeries but our examples will show them their own mistake. (In their opinion other Ephemeries are mistaken by 4° which is absolutely wrong).

TABLE TO FIND THE DAY OF BIRTH

1600	1900	—	1800	—	1700	—
2000	2300	—	2200	—	2100	—
2400	2700	—	2600	—	2500	—
2800	3100	—	3000	—	2900	—
1	2	3	4	5	6	7—0

1	2	3	4	5	6	7 or 0
SUNDAY	MONDAY	TUESDAY	WEDNESDAY	THURSDAY	FRIDAY	SATURDAY
1	2	3	—	4	5	6
7	—	8	9	10	11	—
12	13	14	15	—	16	17
18	19	—	20	21	22	23
—	24	25	26	27	—	28
29	30	31	—	32	33	34
35	—	36	37	38	39	—
40	41	42	43	—	44	45
46	47	—	48	49	50	51
—	52	53	54	55	—	56
57	58	59	—	60	61	62
63	—	64	65	66	67	—
68	69	70	71	—	72	73
74	75	—	76	77	78	79
—	80	81	82	83	—	84
85	86	87	—	88	89	90
91	—	92	93	94	95	96
97	98	99	—	—	—	—

Months of Odd Years

1	2	3	4	5	6	7
AUGUST	FEBRUARY	JUNE	SEPTEMBER	APRIL	JANUARY	MAY
—	MARCH	—	DECEMBER	JULY	OCTOBER	—
—	NOVEMBER	—	—	—	—	—

Months of Even Years

1	2	3	4	5	6	7
AUGUST	MARCH	JUNE	SEPTEMBER	JANUARY	OCTOBER	MAY
—	FEBRUARY	—	DECEMBER	APRIL	—	—
—	NOVEMBER	—	—	JULY	—	—

179

Table of Right Ascension

Vrishabha, Mithuna, Taurus and Gemini ... North Latitude

VRISHABHA	SATURDAY	SUNDAY	MONDAY	TUESDAY	WEDNESDAY	THURSDAY	FRIDAY
0	57 48	57 35	57 21	57 7	56 53	56 38	56 23
1	58 57	58 38	58 24	58 10	57 57	57 42	57 28
2	59 53	59 41	59 27	59 14	59 1	58 47	58 33
3	60 56	60 44	60 31	60 18	60 5	59 52	59 38
4	61 59	61 47	61 35	61 22	61 10	60 57	60 44
5	63 3	62 57	62 39	62 27	62 15	62 2	61 50
6	64 6	63 55	63 43	63 32	63 20	63 8	62 56
7	65 9	64 59	64 47	64 37	64 25	64 13	64 2
8	66 13	65 3	65 52	65 42	65 30	65 19	65 8
9	67 17	67 7	66 57	66 47	66 36	66 25	66 14
10	68 21	68 11	68 2	67 52	67 42	67 31	67 21
11	69 25	69 16	69 7	68 57	68 48	68 38	68 28
12	70 29	70 21	70 12	70 3	70 54	69 45	69 25
13	71 34	71 26	71 17	71 9	71 0	70 51	70 42
14	72 38	72 31	72 22	72 15	72 6	71 58	71 49
15	73 43	73 36	73 28	73 21	73 13	73 5	72 57
16	74 47	74 41	74 33	74 27	74 19	74 12	74 4
17	75 52	75 46	75 39	75 33	75 26	75 19	75 12
18	76 57	76 51	76 45	76 39	76 33	76 27	76 20
19	78 2	77 56	77 51	77 45	77 40	77 34	77 28
20	79 7	79 2	78 57	78 52	78 47	78 41	78 36
21	80 12	80 8	80 3	79 59	79 54	79 49	79 44
22	81 17	81 13	81 9	81 5	81 1	80 56	80 52
23	82 22	82 18	82 15	82 11	82 8	82 4	82 0
24	83 28	83 24	83 21	83 18	83 15	83 11	83 9
25	84 33	84 30	84 27	84 25	84 22	84 20	84 17
26	85 38	85 36	85 33	85 32	85 29	85 28	85 25
27	86 44	86 42	86 40	86 39	86 37	86 36	86 34
28	87 49	87 48	87 46	87 46	87 44	87 44	87 42
29	88 55	88 54	88 53	88 53	88 52	88 52	88 51
MITHUNA							
0	90 0	90 0	90 0	90 0	90 0	90 0	90 0
1	91 5	91 6	91 7	91 7	91 7	91 8	91 9
2	92 11	92 12	92 14	92 14	92 15	92 16	92 18
3	93 16	93 18	93 20	93 21	93 23	93 24	93 26
4	94 22	94 24	94 27	94 28	94 30	94 32	94 35
5	95 27	95 30	95 33	95 35	95 38	95 40	95 43
6	96 32	96 36	96 39	96 42	96 45	96 48	96 51
7	97 38	97 42	97 35	97 49	97 52	97 56	98 0
8	98 43	98 47	98 51	98 55	99 0	99 4	99 8
9	99 48	99 52	99 57	100 1	100 7	100 12	100 16
10	100 53	100 58	101 3	101 8	101 14	101 19	101 24
11	101 58	102 4	102 9	102 15	102 21	102 22	102 32
12	103 3	103 9	103 15	103 21	103 27	103 33	103 40
13	104 8	104 14	104 21	104 27	104 34	104 41	104 48
14	105 13	105 19	105 27	105 33	105 41	105 48	105 56
15	106 17	106 24	106 33	106 39	106 47	106 55	107 3
16	107 22	107 29	107 38	107 45	107 53	108 2	108 11
17	108 26	108 34	108 43	108 53	108 59	109 9	109 18
18	109 31	109 39	109 48	109 57	110 5	110 15	110 25
19	110 35	110 44	110 53	111 3	111 12	111 22	111 32
20	111 39	111 49	111 58	112 8	112 18	112 29	112 35
21	112 43	112 54	113 8	113 13	113 24	113 35	113 46
22	113 47	113 57	114 8	114 18	114 30	114 41	114 52
23	114 51	115 1	115 13	115 23	115 35	115 47	115 58
24	115 54	116 5	116 17	116 28	116 41	116 52	117 4
25	116 57	117 9	117 21	117 33	117 46	117 58	118 10
26	118 1	118 13	118 25	118 38	118 51	119 3	119 16
27	119 4	119 16	119 29	119 42	119 55	120 8	120 22
28	120 7	120 19	120 33	120 46	120 59	121 13	121 27
29	121 9	121 22	122 36	121 50	122 3	122 18	122 32
°	° ′	° ′	° ′	° ′	° ′	° ′	° ′

Table of Right Ascension

Karka, Simha, Cancer and Leo ... North Latitude

KARKA	SATURDAY		SUNDAY		MONDAY		TUESDAY		WEDNESDAY		THURSDAY		FRIDAY	
0	122	12	122	25	122	39	122	53	123	7	123	22	123	37
1	123	14	123	28	123	42	123	57	124	11	124	36	124	42
2	124	16	124	31	124	45	125	0	125	15	125	30	125	46
3	125	18	125	33	125	47	126	3	126	18	126	34	126	50
4	126	20	126	36	126	51	127	6	127	22	127	38	127	54
5	127	22	127	38	127	54	128	9	128	25	128	42	128	58
6	128	24	128	40	128	56	129	12	129	28	129	45	130	2
7	129	25	129	42	129	58	130	14	130	31	130	47	131	5
8	130	26	130	43	131	0	141	16	131	33	131	51	132	8
9	131	27	131	44	132	1	132	18	132	35	132	53	133	11
10	132	28	132	45	133	2	133	20	133	37	133	55	134	14
11	133	28	133	46	134	3	134	21	134	39	134	57	135	16
12	134	29	134	47	135	4	135	22	135	40	135	59	136	18
13	135	29	135	47	136	5	136	25	136	42	137	0	137	20
14	136	29	136	47	137	6	137	24	137	42	138	1	138	21
15	137	29	137	47	138	6	138	24	138	43	139	2	139	22
16	138	29	138	47	139	6	139	25	139	44	140	3	140	24
17	139	28	139	47	140	6	140	25	140	25	141	4	141	25
18	140	28	140	46	141	6	141	25	141	45	142	5	142	26
19	141	27	141	46	142	6	142	25	142	45	143	6	143	26
20	142	26	142	45	143	5	143	25	143	45	144	6	144	27
21	143	25	143	44	144	4	144	24	144	45	145	6	145	27
22	144	23	144	43	145	3	145	24	145	45	146	6	146	27
23	145	22	145	43	146	2	146	23	146	44	147	5	147	27
24	146	20	146	40	147	1	147	22	147	43	148	4	148	26
25	147	18	147	39	148	0	148	21	148	42	149	3	149	25
26	148	16	148	37	148	58	149	19	149	41	150	2	150	24
27	149	14	149	35	149	56	150	17	150	39	151	1	151	23
28	150	11	150	33	150	54	151	15	151	37	151	59	152	22
29	151	9	151	30	151	52	152	13	152	35	152	57	153	20
SIMHA	152	6	152	27	152	49	153	11	153	33	154	55	154	18
1	153	4	153	25	153	47	154	9	154	31	154	53	155	16
2	154	1	154	22	154	44	155	6	155	29	155	51	156	14
3	154	58	155	19	155	41	156	3	156	26	156	49	157	12
4	155	54	156	16	156	39	157	1	157	24	157	47	158	10
5	156	51	157	14	157	36	157	58	158	21	158	44	159	8
6	157	48	158	10	158	33	158	55	159	18	159	41	160	5
7	158	44	159	7	159	30	159	51	160	15	160	38	161	2
8	159	40	160	4	160	27	160	49	161	12	161	35	161	59
9	160	37	161	0	161	23	161	46	172	9	162	32	162	56
10	161	33	161	56	162	19	162	42	163	6	163	29	163	53
11	162	29	162	52	163	15	163	38	164	2	164	25	164	49
12	163	25	163	48	164	11	164	34	164	58	165	21	165	45
13	164	20	164	44	165	7	165	30	164	45	166	18	166	42
14	165	16	166	40	166	3	166	26	166	50	167	14	167	38
15	166	12	166	36	166	59	167	22	167	46	168	10	168	34
16	167	7	167	31	167	55	168	13	168	42	169	6	169	30
17	168	3	168	27	168	31	169	14	169	38	170	2	170	26
18	168	58	169	23	169	46	170	9	170	33	170	57	171	21
19	169	54	170	18	170	42	171	5	171	29	171	53	172	17
20	170	49	172	13	171	37	172	1	172	25	172	49	173	13
21	171	44	172	8	172	32	172	56	173	20	173	44	174	8
22	172	39	173	3	173	27	173	51	174	15	174	39	175	3
23	173	35	173	58	174	22	174	46	175	10	175	34	175	58
24	174	30	174	58	175	17	175	41	176	5	176	29	176	53
25	175	25	175	48	176	12	176	36	177	0	177	24	177	48
26	176	20	176	43	177	7	177	31	177	55	178	19	178	43
27	177	15	177	38	178	2	178	26	178	50	179	14	179	38
28	178	10	178	33	178	57	179	21	179	45	180	9	180	33
29	179	5	179	28	179	52	180	16	180	43	181	4	181	28
°	°	'	°	'	°	'	°	'	°	'	°	'	°	'

Table of Right Ascension

Kanya, Thula, Virgo and Libra ... North Latitude

KANYA	SATURDAY	SUNDAY	MONDAY	TUESDAY	WEDNESDAY	THURSDAY	FRIDAY
0	180 0	180 23	180 47	181 11	181 35	181 59	182 23
1	180 55	181 18	181 42	182 6	182 30	182 55	183 18
2	181 50	182 13	182 37	183 1	183 25	183 49	184 13
3	182 45	183 8	183 32	183 56	184 20	184 44	185 8
4	183 40	184 3	184 27	184 51	185 15	185 39	185 3
5	184 35	184 58	185 22	185 46	186 10	186 34	186 58
6	185 30	185 54	186 18	186 42	187 6	187 30	187 53
7	186 25	186 49	187 13	187 37	188 1	188 25	188 48
8	187 21	187 44	188 8	188 32	188 56	189 20	189 43
9	188 16	188 39	189 3	189 27	189 51	190 15	190 38
10	189 11	189 34	189 58	190 22	190 46	191 10	191 33
11	190 6	190 29	190 53	191 17	191 41	192 5	192 28
12	191 2	191 25	191 48	192 13	192 36	193 0	193 23
13	191 57	192 20	192 43	193 8	193 31	193 55	194 18
14	192 53	193 16	193 39	194 3	194 26	194 50	195 13
15	193 48	194 12	194 35	194 58	195 21	195 45	196 8
16	194 44	195 7	195 30	195 53	196 16	197 40	196 3
17	195 40	196 2	196 25	196 48	197 11	197 35	197 58
18	196 35	196 58	197 21	197 44	198 7	198 30	198 53
19	197 31	197 54	198 17	198 40	199 2	199 25	199 48
20	198 27	198 50	199 13	199 36	199 58	200 21	200 43
21	199 23	199 46	200 9	200 32	200 54	201 16	201 39
22	200 20	200 42	201 5	201 28	201 50	202 12	202 34
23	201 16	201 38	202 1	202 24	202 46	203 8	203 30
24	202 12	202 35	202 57	203 20	203 42	204 2	204 26
25	203 9	203 31	203 53	204 16	204 38	205 0	205 21
26	204 6	204 28	204 50	205 12	205 34	205 56	206 17
27	205 2	205 25	205 47	206 9	206 30	206 52	207 13
28	205 59	206 22	206 43	207 5	207 26	207 48	208 9
29	206 57	207 19	207 0	208 1	208 22	208 44	209 5
THULA	207 54	208 16	208 37	208 58	209 19	209 40	210 1
1	208 51	209 13	209 34	209 55	210 16	210 37	210 57
2	209 49	210 10	210 31	210 52	211 13	211 34	211 54
3	210 46	211 7	211 28	211 49	212 10	212 31	212 51
4	211 44	212 5	212 25	212 46	213 7	213 27	213 47
5	212 42	213 3	213 23	213 43	214 4	214 24	214 44
6	213 40	214 1	214 21	214 41	215 1	215 21	215 41
7	214 38	214 59	215 19	215 39	215 58	216 18	216 38
8	215 37	215 57	216 17	216 37	216 56	217 15	217 35
9	216 36	216 56	217 15	217 35	217 54	218 13	218 32
10	217 34	217 54	218 13	218 33	218 52	219 11	219 29
11	218 33	218 53	219 12	219 31	219 50	220 9	220 27
12	219 33	219 52	220 11	220 30	220 48	221 7	221 25
13	220 32	220 51	221 10	221 28	221 46	222 5	222 23
14	221 31	221 50	222 9	222 27	222 45	223 3	223 21
15	222 31	222 50	223 8	223 26	223 44	224 2	224 19
16	223 31	223 49	224 7	224 25	224 43	225 0	225 17
17	224 31	224 49	225 6	225 24	225 42	225 59	226 15
18	225 31	225 49	326 6	226 23	226 41	226 58	227 14
19	226 32	226 49	227 6	227 23	227 40	227 57	228 13
20	227 32	227 49	228 6	228 23	228 39	228 56	229 12
21	228 33	228 50	229 6	229 23	229 39	229 55	230 11
22	229 34	229 50	230 6	230 23	230 38	230 54	231 10
23	230 35	230 51	231 6	231 23	231 38	231 53	232 9
24	231 36	231 42	232 7	232 23	232 38	232 53	233 8
25	232 38	232 53	233 8	233 24	233 38	233 53	234 8
26	233 40	233 55	234 9	234 24	234 38	234 53	235 7
27	234 41	234 57	235 11	235 25	235 39	235 53	236 7
28	235 43	235 58	236 12	236 26	236 40	236 54	237 7
29	236 46	237 0	237 14	237 28	237 41	237 54	238 7
°	° '	° '	° '	° '	° '	° '	° '

Table of Right Ascension

Vrischika, Dhanu, Scorpio and Sagittarius ... North Latitude

VRISCHIKA	SATURDAY		SUNDAY		MONDAY		TUESDAY		WEDNESDAY		THURSDAY		FRIDAY	
0	237	48	238	2	238	15	238	29	238	42	238	55	239	7
1	238	51	239	4	239	17	239	30	239	43	239	55	240	7
2	239	53	240	6	250	19	240	31	240	44	240	56	241	8
3	240	56	241	9	241	21	241	33	241	45	241	57	242	9
4	241	59	242	11	242	23	242	35	242	46	242	58	243	9
5	243	3	243	14	243	25	243	37	243	48	213	59	244	10
6	244	6	244	17	244	28	244	39	244	50	245	1	245	11
7	245	9	245	20	245	31	245	41	245	52	246	2	246	12
8	246	13	246	23	246	34	246	44	246	54	247	4	247	13
9	247	17	247	27	247	37	257	47	247	56	248	6	248	15
10	248	21	248	30	248	40	248	49	248	58	249	7	249	16
11	249	25	249	34	249	43	249	52	250	0	250	9	250	17
12	250	29	250	38	250	46	250	55	251	3	251	11	251	19
13	251	34	251	42	251	49	251	58	252	5	252	13	252	21
14	252	38	252	46	252	53	253	1	253	8	253	15	253	23
15	253	43	253	50	253	57	254	4	254	11	254	18	254	25
16	254	47	254	54	255	1	255	7	255	14	255	20	255	27
17	255	52	255	58	256	15	256	11	256	17	256	22	256	29
18	256	57	257	3	257	9	257	15	257	20	257	25	257	31
19	258	2	258	7	258	13	258	18	258	23	258	28	258	33
20	259	7	259	12	259	17	259	21	259	26	259	31	259	35
21	260	12	260	17	260	21	260	25	260	29	260	34	260	38
22	261	17	261	21	261	25	261	28	261	32	261	36	261	40
23	262	22	262	25	262	29	262	32	262	35	262	39	262	42
24	263	28	263	30	263	33	263	36	263	39	263	42	263	45
25	264	33	264	35	264	37	264	40	264	42	264	45	264	47
26	265	38	265	40	265	41	265	44	265	45	265	48	265	49
27	266	44	266	45	266	46	266	48	266	49	265	51	266	52
28	267	49	267	50	267	50	267	52	267	52	267	54	267	54
29	268	55	268	55	268	55	268	50	268	56	268	57	268	57
DHANU														
0	270	0	270	0	270	0	270	0	270	0	270	0	270	0
1	271	5	271	5	271	5	271	4	271	4	271	3	271	3
2	272	11	272	10	272	10	272	8	272	8	272	6	272	6
3	273	16	273	15	273	14	273	12	273	11	273	9	273	8
4	274	22	274	20	274	19	274	16	274	12	274	12	274	11
5	275	27	275	25	275	23	275	20	275	18	275	15	275	13
6	276	32	276	30	276	27	276	24	276	21	276	18	276	15
7	277	38	277	38	277	31	278	28	277	25	277	21	277	18
8	278	43	278	39	278	35	278	32	278	28	278	24	278	20
9	279	48	279	43	279	39	279	35	279	31	279	26	279	22
10	280	53	280	48	280	43	280	39	280	34	280	29	280	25
11	281	58	281	53	281	47	281	42	281	37	281	32	281	28
12	283	3	282	57	282	51	282	45	282	40	282	34	282	29
13	284	8	282	2	283	55	283	49	283	43	283	37	283	31
14	285	13	284	6	284	59	284	53	284	46	284	40	284	33
15	286	17	286	10	286	3	285	56	285	49	285	42	285	35
16	287	22	287	14	287	7	287	59	286	52	286	45	286	37
17	288	26	288	18	288	11	288	2	287	55	287	47	287	39
18	289	31	289	22	289	14	289	5	288	57	288	49	288	41
19	290	35	290	26	290	17	290	8	290	0	289	41	289	43
20	291	39	291	30	291	20	291	11	291	2	290	53	290	44
21	292	43	292	33	292	23	292	13	292	4	291	55	291	45
22	293	47	293	37	293	26	293	16	293	6	292	56	292	47
23	294	51	294	40	294	29	294	19	294	8	293	58	293	48
24	295	54	295	43	295	32	295	21	295	10	294	59	294	49
25	296	57	296	46	296	35	296	23	296	12	296	1	295	50
26	298	1	298	49	297	37	297	25	297	14	297	2	296	51
27	299	4	298	51	298	39	298	27	298	15	298	3	297	52
28	300	7	299	54	299	41	299	29	299	16	299	4	298	52
29	301	9	300	56	300	43	300	30	300	17	300	5	299	53
°	°	′	°	′	°	′	°	′	°	′	°	′	°	′

Table of Right Ascension

Makara, Kumbha, Capricon and Aquarius ... North Latitude

MAKARA	SATURDAY		SUNDAY		MONDAY		TUESDAY		WEDNESDAY		THURSDAY		FRIDAY	
0	302	12	301	58	301	45	301	31	301	18	301	5	300	53
1	303	14	303	0	302	47	302	33	302	19	302	6	301	53
2	304	16	304	2	303	38	303	34	303	20	303	6	302	53
3	305	18	305	3	304	50	304	35	304	21	304	7	303	53
4	306	20	306	5	305	57	305	36	305	22	305	7	304	53
5	307	22	307	7	306	52	306	36	306	22	306	7	305	52
6	308	24	308	8	307	53	307	37	307	22	307	7	306	52
7	309	28	309	9	307	54	308	37	308	22	308	7	307	51
8	310	26	310	10	309	54	309	38	309	22	309	6	308	50
9	311	27	311	10	310	54	310	37	310	21	310	5	309	49
10	312	28	312	11	311	54	311	37	311	21	311	4	310	4
11	313	28	313	11	312	54	312	37	312	19	312	3	311	47
12	314	29	314	11	313	54	313	37	313	19	313	2	312	46
13	315	29	315	11	314	54	314	36	314	18	314	1	313	44
14	316	29	316	11	315	53	315	35	315	17	315	0	314	43
15	317	29	317	10	316	52	316	34	316	16	315	48	315	47
16	318	29	318	10	317	51	317	33	317	15	316	57	316	39
17	319	29	319	9	318	50	318	32	318	14	317	55	317	37
18	320	28	320	8	319	49	319	30	319	12	318	53	318	35
19	321	27	321	7	320	48	320	29	320	10	319	57	319	33
20	322	26	322	6	321	47	321	27	321	8	320	49	320	31
21	323	25	323	4	322	45	322	25	322	6	321	47	321	28
22	324	23	324	3	323	43	323	23	323	4	322	45	322	25
23	325	22	325	1	324	41	324	21	224	1	323	42	323	22
24	326	20	325	59	325	39	325	19	324	59	324	39	324	19
25	327	18	326	57	326	37	327	17	225	56	325	36	325	16
26	328	16	327	55	327	35	327	14	326	53	326	33	326	13
27	329	14	328	53	328	32	328	11	327	50	327	30	327	10
28	330	11	329	57	329	29	329	8	328	47	328	27	328	6
29	331	9	330	47	330	26	330	5	329	44	329	25	329	3
KUMBHA														
0	332	6	331	44	331	23	331	2	330	41	330	20	329	59
1	333	4	332	41	332	20	332	59	331	38	331	16	330	55
2	334	1	333	38	333	17	332	55	332	34	332	12	331	57
3	334	58	334	35	334	13	333	57	333	30	333	8	332	47
4	335	55	335	32	335	10	334	48	334	26	334	4	333	43
5	336	57	336	29	336	7	335	44	335	22	335	0	334	39
6	337	48	337	25	337	3	336	40	336	18	335	56	335	34
7	338	44	338	22	337	59	337	36	337	14	336	52	336	30
8	339	40	339	18	338	55	338	32	338	10	337	48	337	26
9	340	37	340	14	339	57	339	28	339	6	338	43	338	21
10	341	33	341	10	340	47	340	24	340	2	339	39	339	17
11	342	29	342	6	341	43	341	20	340	58	340	35	340	12
12	343	25	343	2	342	39	342	16	341	53	341	30	341	7
13	344	20	343	58	343	35	343	12	342	49	342	25	342	2
14	345	16	344	53	344	30	344	7	343	44	343	20	342	57
15	346	12	345	48	345	25	345	2	344	39	344	15	343	52
16	347	7	346	44	346	21	345	57	345	34	345	10	344	47
17	348	3	347	40	347	17	346	52	346	29	346	5	345	42
18	348	58	348	35	348	12	347	49	347	24	347	0	346	37
19	349	54	349	31	349	7	348	43	348	19	347	55	347	32
20	350	49	350	26	350	3	349	38	349	14	348	50	348	27
21	351	44	351	21	351	57	350	33	350	9	349	45	349	22
22	352	39	352	16	351	52	351	28	351	4	350	40	350	17
23	353	35	353	11	352	47	352	23	351	59	351	35	351	12
24	354	30	354	6	353	42	353	18	352	54	352	30	352	7
25	355	25	355	1	354	38	354	14	353	50	353	26	352	2
26	356	20	355	57	355	33	355	9	354	45	354	21	353	27
27	357	15	356	52	356	28	356	4	355	40	355	16	354	52
28	358	10	357	47	357	23	356	59	356	35	356	11	355	47
29	359	5	358	42	358	18	357	54	357	30	357	6	356	42
°	°	′	°	′	°	′	°	′	°	′	°	′	°	′

Table of Right Ascension
Meen, Mesha, Pisces and Aries ... North Latitude

MEENA	SATURDAY		SUNDAY		MONDAY		TUESDAY		WEDNESDAY		THURSDAY		FRIDAY	
	°	′	°	′	°	′	°	′	°	′	°	′	°	′
0	0	0	359	37	359	13	358	49	358	25	358	1	357	37
1	0	55	0	32	0	8	359	44	359	20	358	56	358	32
2	1	50	1	27	1	3	0	39	0	15	359	51	359	27
3	2	45	2	22	1	58	1	34	1	10	0	46	0	22
4	3	40	3	17	2	53	2	9	2	5	1	41	1	17
5	7	35	4	12	3	48	3	24	3	0	2	36	2	12
6	5	30	5	7	4	43	4	19	3	55	3	31	3	7
7	6	25	6	2	5	38	5	14	4	50	4	26	4	2
8	7	21	6	57	6	33	6	9	5	45	5	21	4	57
9	8	16	7	52	7	28	7	4	6	40	6	16	5	52
10	9	11	8	47	8	23	7	59	7	35	7	11	6	47
11	10	6	9	42	9	18	8	55	8	31	8	7	7	43
12	11	2	10	38	10	14	9	57	9	27	9	3	8	39
13	11	57	11	33	11	9	10	46	10	22	9	58	9	34
14	12	53	12	29	12	5	11	42	11	18	10	54	10	30
15	13	48	13	25	13	1	12	38	12	14	11	50	11	26
16	14	44	14	20	13	57	13	34	13	10	12	46	12	22
17	15	40	15	16	14	53	14	30	14	06	13	42	13	18
18	16	35	16	12	15	49	15	26	15	2	14	39	14	15
19	17	31	17	8	16	45	16	22	15	58	15	35	15	11
20	18	37	18	4	17	41	17	18	16	54	16	31	16	7
21	19	23	19	0	18	37	18	14	17	57	17	28	17	4
22	20	20	19	56	19	33	19	11	18	48	18	25	18	1
23	21	16	20	53	20	30	20	8	19	45	19	22	18	58
24	22	12	21	50	21	27	21	5	20	42	20	19	19	55
25	23	9	22	47	22	24	22	2	21	39	21	16	20	52
26	24	6	23	44	23	21	22	59	22	36	22	13	21	50
27	25	2	24	41	24	19	23	57	23	34	23	11	22	48
28	25	50	25	38	25	16	24	54	24	31	24	9	23	46
29	26	57	26	35	26	13	25	57	25	29	25	7	24	44
MESHA	27	54	27	33	27	11	26	49	26	27	26	5	25	42
1	28	57	28	30	28	8	27	47	27	25	27	3	26	40
2	29	49	29	27	29	6	28	45	28	23	28	1	27	38
3	30	46	30	25	30	4	29	43	29	21	28	59	28	37
4	31	44	31	23	31	2	30	41	30	19	29	58	29	36
5	32	42	32	21	32	0	31	39	31	18	30	57	30	35
6	33	40	33	20	32	59	32	38	32	17	31	56	31	34
7	34	38	34	18	33	58	33	37	33	16	32	55	32	33
8	35	37	35	17	34	57	34	16	34	25	33	54	33	33
9	36	36	36	16	35	56	35	36	35	15	34	54	34	33
10	37	34	37	15	36	55	36	35	36	15	35	54	35	33
11	38	33	38	14	37	54	37	35	37	15	36	54	36	33
12	39	33	39	14	38	54	38	35	38	15	37	55	37	34
13	40	32	40	13	39	54	39	35	39	15	38	56	38	35
14	41	31	41	13	40	54	40	35	40	16	39	57	39	36
15	42	31	42	13	41	54	41	36	41	17	40	58	40	38
16	43	31	43	13	42	54	42	36	42	18	41	59	41	39
17	44	31	44	13	43	55	43	37	43	19	43	0	42	40
18	45	31	45	14	44	56	44	38	44	20	44	1	43	42
19	46	32	46	14	45	57	45	39	45	21	45	3	44	44
20	47	32	47	15	46	58	46	40	46	23	46	5	45	46
21	48	33	48	16	47	59	47	42	47	25	47	7	46	49
22	49	34	49	17	49	0	48	44	48	27	48	9	47	52
23	50	35	50	18	50	2	49	46	49	29	49	12	48	55
24	51	56	51	20	51	4	50	48	50	32	50	15	49	58
25	52	58	52	22	52	6	51	51	51	35	51	18	51	2
26	53	40	53	24	53	9	53	54	52	38	52	22	52	6
27	54	42	54	27	54	12	53	57	53	42	53	26	53	10
28	55	44	55	29	55	15	55	0	54	45	54	30	54	14
29	56	46	56	32	56	18	56	3	55	49	55	34	55	18
°	°	′	°	′	°	′	°	′	°	′	°	′	°	′

VEDIC NUMEROLOGY

Table of Right Ascension
Vrishabha, Mithuna, Taurus and Gemini ... South Latitude

VRISHABHA	SATURDAY		SUNDAY		MONDAY		TUESDAY		WEDNESDAY		THURSDAY		FRIDAY	
0	57	48	58	2	58	15	58	28	58	42	58	55	69	7
1	58	57	59	4	59	17	59	30	59	43	59	55	60	7
2	59	53	60	6	60	19	60	31	60	44	60	59	61	8
3	60	56	61	8	61	21	61	33	61	46	61	57	52	9
4	61	59	62	11	62	23	62	35	62	48	62	58	63	9
5	63	3	63	14	63	25	63	37	63	50	63	59	64	10
6	64	6	64	17	64	28	64	39	65	52	65	1	65	11
7	65	9	65	20	65	31	65	41	66	54	66	2	66	12
8	66	13	66	23	66	34	66	44	67	56	67	4	67	13
9	67	17	67	27	67	37	67	46	68	58	68	6	68	15
10	68	21	68	30	68	40	68	49	70	59	69	7	69	16
11	69	25	69	34	69	43	69	52	72	1	70	9	70	17
12	70	29	70	38	70	46	70	55	73	3	71	11	71	19
13	71	34	71	42	71	49	71	58	74	5	72	13	72	21
14	72	38	72	46	72	53	73	1	75	8	73	15	73	23
15	73	43	73	50	73	57	74	4	76	11	74	18	74	25
16	74	49	74	54	75	1	75	7	77	14	75	20	75	27
17	75	52	75	58	76	5	76	11	78	17	76	22	76	29
18	76	57	76	3	77	9	77	15	79	20	77	25	77	31
19	78	2	78	7	78	13	78	18	80	23	78	28	78	33
20	79	7	79	12	79	17	79	21	81	26	79	31	79	35
21	80	12	80	17	80	21	80	25	82	29	80	34	80	38
22	81	17	81	21	81	25	81	28	83	32	81	36	81	40
23	82	22	82	25	82	29	82	32	84	35	82	39	82	42
24	83	28	83	30	83	33	83	36	85	39	83	42	83	45
25	84	33	84	35	84	37	84	40	86	42	84	45	84	47
26	85	38	85	40	85	41	85	44	86	45	85	48	85	49
27	86	44	86	45	86	46	86	48	87	49	86	57	86	52
28	87	49	87	50	87	50	87	52	88	52	87	54	87	54
29	88	55	88	55	88	55	88	56	89	56	88	57	88	57
MITHUNA														
0	90	0	90	0	90	0	90	0	90	0	90	0	90	0
1	91	5	91	5	91	5	91	4	91	4	91	3	91	3
2	92	11	92	10	92	10	92	8	92	8	92	6	92	6
3	93	16	93	15	93	14	93	12	93	11	93	9	93	8
4	94	22	94	20	94	19	94	16	94	15	94	12	94	11
5	95	27	95	25	95	23	95	20	95	18	95	15	95	13
6	96	32	96	20	96	27	96	24	96	21	96	18	96	15
7	97	38	97	35	97	31	97	28	97	25	97	21	97	18
8	98	43	98	39	98	35	98	32	98	28	98	24	98	20
9	99	48	99	43	99	39	99	35	99	31	99	26	99	22
10	100	53	100	48	100	43	100	39	100	34	100	29	100	25
11	101	58	101	53	101	47	101	42	101	37	101	38	101	27
12	103	3	102	57	102	57	102	45	102	40	102	34	102	29
13	104	8	104	2	103	55	103	49	103	43	103	37	103	31
14	105	13	105	6	104	59	104	52	104	46	104	40	104	33
15	106	17	106	10	106	3	105	56	105	49	105	42	105	35
16	107	22	107	14	107	7	106	59	106	52	106	45	106	37
17	108	26	108	18	108	11	108	2	107	55	107	47	107	39
18	109	31	109	22	109	14	109	5	108	57	108	49	108	41
19	100	35	110	26	110	17	110	8	110	0	109	57	109	43
20	111	39	111	30	111	20	111	11	111	2	110	53	110	44
21	112	43	112	33	112	23	112	13	112	4	111	54	111	45
22	113	47	113	37	113	26	113	16	113	6	112	56	112	47
23	114	57	114	40	114	29	114	19	114	8	113	58	113	48
24	115	54	115	43	115	32	115	21	115	10	114	59	114	49
25	116	57	116	46	116	35	116	23	116	12	116	1	115	50
26	118	1	117	49	117	37	117	25	117	14	117	2	116	57
27	119	4	118	57	118	39	118	27	118	15	118	3	117	52
28	120	7	119	54	119	41	119	29	119	16	119	4	118	52
29	121	9	120	56	120	43	120	30	120	17	120	5	119	53
	°	′	°	′	°	′	°	′	°	′	°	′	°	′

RULES TO FIND LAGNA AND RASHI

Table of Right Ascension
Karka, Simha, Cancer and Leo ... South Latitude

KARKA	SATURDAY	SUNDAY	MONDAY	TUESDAY	WEDNESDAY	THURSDAY	FRIDAY
0	112 12	121 58	121 45	121 30	121 18	121 5	120 53
1	123 14	122 47	122 33	122 33	122 19	122 6	121 53
2	124 16	123 2	123 48	123 34	123 20	123 6	122 53
3	125 16	124 3	124 49	124 35	124 21	124 7	123 53
4	126 20	125 5	125 51	125 36	125 22	125 7	124 53
5	127 22	126 7	126 52	126 36	126 22	126 7	125 52
6	128 24	127 8	127 53	127 37	127 22	127 7	126 52
7	129 25	128 9	128 54	128 37	128 22	128 7	127 57
8	130 26	129 10	129 54	129 37	129 22	129 6	128 50
9	131 27	130 10	130 54	130 37	130 21	130 5	129 49
10	132 28	131 11	131 54	131 37	131 21	131 4	130 48
11	133 28	132 11	132 54	132 37	132 20	132 3	131 47
12	134 29	133 11	133 54	133 37	133 19	133 2	132 46
13	135 29	134 11	134 54	134 36	134 18	134 1	133 45
14	136 29	135 11	135 53	135 35	135 17	135 0	134 43
15	137 29	136 10	136 52	136 34	136 16	135 58	135 41
16	138 29	137 10	137 51	137 33	137 15	136 57	136 49
17	139 28	138 9	138 50	138 32	138 14	137 55	137 37
18	140 28	139 8	139 49	139 30	139 13	139 53	138 35
19	141 27	140 7	140 48	140 29	140 10	149 57	139 33
20	142 26	141 6	141 47	141 27	141 8	140 49	140 31
21	143 25	142 4	142 45	142 25	142 6	141 47	141 28
22	144 23	143 3	143 43	143 23	143 4	142 45	142 25
23	145 22	144 1	144 41	144 21	144 2	143 42	143 22
24	146 20	145 59	145 39	145 19	145 59	144 39	144 19
25	147 18	145 57	146 37	146 17	145 56	145 36	145 16
26	148 16	146 55	147 35	147 14	146 53	146 33	146 13
27	149 14	147 53	148 32	148 11	147 50	147 29	147 9
28	150 11	148 50	149 29	149 8	148 47	148 26	148 6
29	157 9	149 47	150 26	150 5	149 44	149 23	149 3
SIMHA							
0	152 6	151 44	151 23	151 2	150 41	150 20	149 59
1	153 4	152 41	152 20	151 59	151 38	151 16	150 55
2	154 1	153 38	153 17	152 55	152 34	152 12	151 57
3	154 58	154 35	154 13	153 57	153 30	153 3	152 47
4	155 54	155 32	155 10	154 58	154 26	154 4	153 43
5	153 57	153 29	156 7	155 54	155 22	155 0	154 39
6	157 48	157 25	157 3	156 40	156 18	155 56	155 34
7	158 44	158 22	157 59	157 36	157 14	156 52	153 30
8	159 40	159 18	158 55	158 32	158 10	157 48	157 26
9	160 37	160 14	159 57	159 28	159 6	158 43	158 21
10	161 33	161 10	160 47	160 24	160 2	159 40	159 17
11	162 29	162 9	161 43	161 20	160 58	160 33	160 12
12	163 25	163 2	162 39	162 16	161 53	161 30	171 7
13	164 20	163 58	163 35	163 12	162 49	162 25	162 2
14	165 16	164 53	164 30	164 7	163 44	163 20	162 57
15	166 12	165 48	165 25	165 2	164 39	164 15	163 52
16	167 7	166 44	166 21	165 57	165 34	165 10	164 47
17	168 3	167 40	167 17	166 52	166 29	166 5	165 42
18	168 58	168 35	168 12	167 47	107 24	167 0	166 37
19	169 54	169 31	168 7	168 43	168 19	167 55	167 32
20	170 49	170 26	170 2	169 38	169 14	168 50	168 27
21	171 44	171 21	170 57	170 33	170 9	169 45	169 22
22	172 39	172 16	171 52	171 28	171 4	170 40	170 17
23	173 35	173 11	172 47	172 23	171 59	171 35	171 12
24	174 30	174 6	173 42	173 18	172 54	172 30	172 7
25	175 25	175 2	174 38	174 14	173 50	173 26	173 2
26	176 20	175 57	175 33	175 9	174 45	174 21	173 57
27	177 15	176 52	176 28	177 4	175 40	175 16	174 52
28	178 10	177 47	177 23	176 59	176 35	176 11	175 74
29	179 5	178 42	178 18	177 54	177 30	177 6	176 42
	° ′	° ′	° ′	° ′	° ′	° ′	° ′

Table of Right Ascension
Kanya, Thula, Virgo and Libra ... South Latitude

KANYA	SATURDAY		SUNDAY		MONDAY		TUESDAY		WEDNESDAY		THURSDAY		FRIDAY	
0	180	0	179	37	179	13	178	49	178	25	178	1	177	37
1	180	55	180	32	180	8	179	44	179	20	178	56	178	32
2	181	50	181	27	181	3	180	39	180	15	179	51	179	37
3	182	45	182	22	181	58	181	34	181	10	180	46	180	22
4	183	40	183	17	182	53	182	29	182	5	181	41	181	17
5	184	35	184	12	183	48	183	24	183	0	182	36	182	12
6	185	30	185	7	184	43	184	19	183	55	183	31	183	7
7	186	25	186	2	185	38	185	14	184	50	184	26	184	2
8	187	21	186	57	186	33	186	9	185	45	185	21	184	57
9	188	16	187	52	187	28	187	4	186	40	186	16	185	52
10	189	11	188	47	188	23	187	59	187	35	187	11	186	47
11	190	6	189	42	189	11	188	55	188	31	188	7	187	39
12	191	2	190	38	190	14	189	51	189	27	189	3	188	34
13	191	57	191	33	191	9	190	46	190	22	189	58	189	30
14	192	53	192	29	192	5	191	42	191	18	190	54	190	26
15	193	48	193	25	193	1	192	38	192	14	191	50	191	22
16	194	44	194	20	193	57	193	34	193	10	192	46	192	18
17	195	40	195	16	194	53	194	30	194	6	193	42	193	15
18	196	35	196	12	195	49	195	26	195	2	194	39	194	11
19	197	31	197	8	196	45	196	22	195	58	195	35	195	7
20	198	27	198	4	197	41	197	18	196	54	196	31	196	4
21	199	23	199	0	198	37	198	14	197	51	197	28	197	1
22	200	20	199	56	199	33	199	11	198	48	198	25	197	58
23	201	16	200	53	200	30	200	8	199	45	199	22	198	55
24	202	12	201	50	201	27	201	5	200	42	200	19	199	52
25	203	9	202	47	202	24	202	2	201	39	201	16	200	50
26	204	6	203	44	203	21	202	59	202	36	202	13	201	48
27	205	2	204	41	204	19	203	57	203	34	203	11	202	46
28	205	59	205	38	205	16	204	54	204	31	204	9	203	46
29	206	57	206	35	206	13	205	51	205	29	205	7	204	44
THULA														
0	207	54	207	33	207	11	206	49	206	27	206	5	205	42
1	208	51	208	30	208	8	207	47	207	25	207	3	206	40
2	209	49	209	27	209	6	208	45	208	23	208	1	207	38
3	210	46	210	25	210	4	209	43	209	21	208	59	208	37
4	211	44	211	23	211	2	210	41	210	18	209	58	209	36
5	212	42	212	21	212	0	211	39	211	19	210	57	210	35
6	213	30	213	20	212	59	212	38	212	17	211	56	211	34
7	214	38	214	18	213	58	213	37	213	16	212	55	212	33
8	215	37	215	17	214	57	214	36	214	15	213	54	213	33
9	216	36	216	16	215	56	216	36	215	15	214	54	214	33
10	217	34	217	15	216	55	216	35	216	15	215	54	215	33
11	218	33	218	14	217	55	217	35	217	15	216	54	226	33
12	219	33	219	14	218	54	218	35	218	15	217	55	217	34
13	220	32	220	13	219	54	219	35	219	15	318	56	218	35
14	221	31	221	13	220	54	220	36	220	16	219	57	219	36
15	222	31	222	13	221	54	221	36	221	17	220	58	220	38
16	223	31	223	13	222	54	222	36	222	18	221	59	221	39
17	224	31	224	13	223	55	223	37	223	19	223	0	222	40
18	225	31	225	14	224	56	224	38	224	20	224	1	223	42
19	226	32	226	14	225	57	225	39	225	51	225	3	224	44
20	227	32	227	15	226	58	226	40	226	23	226	5	225	46
21	228	33	228	16	227	59	227	42	227	25	227	7	226	49
22	229	34	229	17	229	0	228	44	228	27	228	9	227	52
23	230	35	230	18	230	2	229	46	229	29	229	12	228	55
24	231	36	231	20	331	4	230	48	230	32	230	15	229	58
25	232	38	232	22	232	6	231	51	231	35	231	18	231	2
26	233	40	233	24	233	9	232	54	232	38	232	22	232	6
27	234	41	234	27	234	12	233	57	233	42	233	26	233	10
28	235	49	235	29	235	15	235	0	234	45	234	30	234	14
29	236	46	236	32	236	18	236	3	235	49	235	34	235	18
°	°	'	°	'	°	'	°	'	°	'	°	'	°	'

Table of Right Ascension

Vrischika, Dhanu, Scorpio and Sagittarius ... South Latitude

Vrischika	Saturday		Sunday		Monday		Tuesday		Wednesday		Thursday		Friday	
0	237	48	237	35	237	21	237	7	236	53	236	38	236	23
1	238	51	238	38	238	24	238	10	237	57	237	42	237	28
2	239	53	239	41	239	28	239	14	239	1	238	47	238	33
3	240	56	240	44	240	31	240	18	240	5	239	52	239	38
4	241	59	241	47	241	35	241	22	241	10	240	57	240	44
5	243	3	242	51	242	39	242	27	242	15	242	2	241	50
6	244	6	243	55	243	43	243	32	243	20	243	8	242	56
7	245	9	244	59	244	47	244	37	244	25	244	13	244	2
8	246	13	146	3	245	52	245	42	245	30	245	19	245	8
9	247	17	247	7	246	57	246	47	246	36	246	25	246	14
10	248	21	248	11	248	2	247	52	247	42	247	31	247	21
11	249	25	249	10	149	7	248	57	248	48	248	38	248	28
12	250	29	250	21	250	12	250	3	249	54	240	45	249	35
13	251	34	251	26	251	17	251	9	251	0	250	51	250	42
14	252	38	252	31	252	22	252	15	252	6	251	58	251	49
15	253	43	253	36	253	28	253	21	253	13	253	5	252	57
16	254	47	254	41	254	33	254	27	254	19	254	12	254	4
17	255	52	255	46	255	39	255	33	255	26	255	29	255	12
18	256	57	256	51	256	45	256	30	256	33	256	27	256	20
19	258	2	257	56	257	51	257	45	257	40	257	34	257	28
20	259	7	259	2	258	57	258	52	258	47	258	41	258	46
21	260	12	260	8	260	3	259	59	259	54	259	49	259	44
22	261	17	261	13	261	9	261	5	261	1	260	56	260	52
23	262	22	262	18	262	15	262	11	262	8	262	4	262	0
24	263	28	263	24	263	21	263	18	263	15	263	12	263	9
25	264	33	264	30	264	27	264	25	264	22	264	90	264	17
26	265	38	265	36	265	33	265	32	265	29	265	28	265	26
27	266	44	266	42	266	40	266	32	266	37	266	36	266	34
28	267	49	267	48	267	46	267	46	267	11	267	44	267	43
29	268	55	268	54	268	53	268	53	268	52	268	52	208	53
Dhanu														
0	270	0	270	0	270	0	270	0	270	0	270	0	270	0
1	271	5	271	6	271	7	271	7	271	8	271	8	271	9
2	272	11	272	12	272	14	272	14	272	16	272	16	272	18
3	273	16	273	18	273	20	273	21	273	23	273	24	273	16
4	274	22	274	24	274	26	274	28	274	31	274	32	274	54
5	275	27	275	30	275	33	275	35	275	38	275	40	275	43
6	276	32	276	36	276	39	276	42	276	45	276	48	276	51
7	277	38	277	41	277	45	277	50	277	52	277	56	278	0
8	278	43	278	47	278	51	278	55	278	59	279	4	279	8
9	279	48	279	52	279	57	280	1	280	6	280	11	280	11
10	280	53	280	58	281	3	281	8	281	13	281	19	281	24
11	281	58	282	4	282	9	282	15	282	20	282	26	282	32
12	283	3	283	9	283	15	283	21	283	27	283	33	283	40
13	284	8	284	14	284	21	284	27	284	34	284	41	284	48
14	285	13	285	19	185	27	185	33	285	41	185	48	285	56
15	286	17	286	24	286	32	286	39	286	47	286	55	287	3
16	287	22	287	29	287	38	287	45	287	54	288	2	288	11
17	288	26	288	34	288	43	288	51	289	0	289	9	289	18
18	289	31	290	39	289	48	289	57	290	6	290	15	290	25
19	290	35	291	44	299	53	290	3	291	12	291	22	231	32
20	291	39	292	49	291	58	292	8	292	18	292	29	292	39
21	292	43	293	53	293	3	993	13	293	24	293	35	293	46
22	293	47	294	57	294	8	294	18	294	30	294	41	294	52
23	294	51	295	1	295	13	295	23	295	35	295	47	295	58
24	295	54	296	5	296	17	296	28	296	40	296	53	297	4
25	296	57	297	9	297	21	297	33	297	45	297	58	298	10
26	298	1	298	13	298	25	298	38	298	50	299	3	299	16
27	299	4	299	16	299	29	299	41	299	55	300	8	300	12
28	300	7	300	19	300	33	300	46	300	59	301	13	301	27
29	301	9	301	22	301	36	301	50	302	3	302	18	302	32
°	°	'	°	'	°	'	°	'	°	'	°	'	°	'

Table of Right Ascension

Makara, Kumbha, Capricorn and Aquarius ... South Latitude

MAKARA	SATURDAY		SUNDAY		MONDAY		TUESDAY		WEDNESDAY		THURSDAY		FRIDAY	
0	302	12	302	25	302	39	302	53	303	7	303	22	303	37
1	303	14	303	28	303	42	303	57	304	11	304	26	304	42
2	304	16	304	31	304	45	305	3	305	15	305	30	305	46
3	305	18	305	33	305	48	306	3	306	18	306	34	306	50
4	306	20	306	36	306	57	307	6	307	22	307	38	307	54
5	307	22	307	38	307	54	308	9	308	25	308	42	308	58
6	308	24	308	40	308	56	309	12	309	28	309	44	310	2
7	309	25	309	42	309	58	310	14	310	31	310	48	311	5
8	310	26	310	43	311	0	311	16	311	33	311	51	312	8
9	311	27	311	44	312	1	312	18	312	35	312	53	313	11
10	312	28	312	45	313	2	313	20	313	37	313	55	314	14
11	313	28	313	46	314	3	314	21	314	39	314	57	315	16
12	314	29	314	46	315	4	315	22	315	40	315	59	316	18
13	315	29	315	47	316	5	316	23	316	41	317	0	317	20
14	316	29	316	47	317	6	317	24	317	42	318	1	318	21
15	317	29	317	47	318	6	318	24	318	43	319	2	319	22
16	318	29	318	47	319	6	319	25	319	44	320	3	320	24
17	319	28	319	47	320	6	320	25	320	45	321	4	321	25
18	320	27	320	46	321	6	321	25	321	45	322	5	322	26
19	321	27	321	46	322	6	322	25	322	45	323	6	323	27
20	322	26	322	45	323	4	323	25	323	45	324	6	324	27
21	323	25	323	44	324	5	324	24	324	45	325	6	325	27
22	324	23	324	43	325	3	325	24	325	45	326	6	326	27
23	325	22	325	42	326	2	326	23	326	44	327	5	327	27
24	326	20	326	40	327	1	337	22	327	43	328	4	328	26
25	327	18	327	39	328	0	328	21	328	42	329	3	329	25
26	328	16	328	37	329	58	329	19	329	41	330	2	330	24
27	329	14	329	35	329	56	330	17	330	39	331	1	331	23
28	330	11	330	33	330	54	331	15	331	37	331	59	332	22
29	331	9	331	30	331	52	332	13	332	35	332	57	333	20

KUMBHA	SATURDAY		SUNDAY		MONDAY		TUESDAY		WEDNESDAY		THURSDAY		FRIDAY	
0	332	6	332	28	332	49	333	11	333	33	333	55	334	18
1	333	4	333	25	333	47	334	9	334	31	334	53	335	16
2	334	1	334	22	334	44	335	6	335	29	335	57	336	14
3	334	58	335	19	335	41	336	3	336	26	336	49	337	12
4	335	55	336	16	336	39	337	1	337	24	337	47	338	10
5	336	57	437	13	337	36	337	58	338	21	338	44	339	8
6	337	48	338	10	338	33	338	55	339	18	339	41	340	5
7	338	44	339	7	330	30	339	52	340	15	340	38	341	2
8	339	40	340	4	340	27	340	49	341	12	341	35	341	59
9	340	37	341	0	341	23	341	46	342	9	342	32	342	56
10	341	33	341	56	342	19	242	42	343	6	343	29	343	53
11	342	29	342	52	343	15	343	38	344	2	344	25	344	49
12	343	25	343	48	344	11	344	34	344	58	345	21	345	45
13	344	20	344	44	345	7	345	30	345	54	346	18	346	42
14	345	16	345	40	346	3	346	26	346	50	347	14	347	38
15	346	12	346	35	346	59	347	22	347	46	348	10	348	34
16	347	7	347	31	347	55	348	18	348	42	349	6	349	30
17	348	3	348	27	348	57	349	14	349	38	350	2	350	26
18	348	58	349	22	349	46	350	9	350	33	350	57	351	21
19	349	54	350	18	350	42	351	5	351	29	351	53	352	17
20	350	49	351	13	351	37	352	1	352	25	352	49	353	13
21	351	44	352	8	352	36	352	56	353	20	353	48	354	8
22	352	37	353	3	353	27	353	57	354	15	354	30	355	0
23	353	35	353	58	354	22	354	46	355	10	355	34	355	58
24	354	30	354	53	355	17	355	41	356	5	356	29	356	53
25	355	25	355	48	356	12	356	36	357	0	357	24	357	48
26	356	20	256	43	357	7	357	31	357	55	358	19	358	43
27	357	15	357	38	358	2	358	26	358	50	359	14	359	38
28	358	10	358	33	358	57	359	21	359	46	360	9	360	33
29	359	5	359	28	359	52	360	16	360	40	361	4	361	28
	°	′	°	′	°	′	°	′	°	′	°	′	°	′

Table of Right Ascension
Meena, Mesha, Pisces and Aries ... South Latitude

MEENA	SATURDAY	SUNDAY	MONDAY	TUESDAY	WEDNESDAY	THURSDAY	FRIDAY
0	0 0	0 23	0 47	1 11	1 35	1 59	3 23
1	0 55	1 18	1 42	2 6	2 30	2 54	3 18
2	1 50	2 13	2 37	3 1	3 25	3 49	4 13
3	2 45	3 8	3 32	3 56	4 20	4 44	5 8
4	3 40	4 3	4 27	4 57	5 15	5 39	6 3
5	4 35	4 58	5 22	5 46	6 10	6 34	0 58
6	5 30	5 34	6 18	6 42	7 6	7 30	7 53
7	6 25	6 49	7 13	7 37	8 1	8 25	8 48
8	7 21	7 44	8 8	8 32	8 56	9 20	9 43
9	8 16	8 40	9 4	9 28	9 57	10 15	10 38
10	9 11	9 35	9 39	10 25	10 46	11 10	11 33
11	10 6	10 30	10 54	11 18	11 41	12 5	12 28
12	11 2	11 25	11 49	12 13	12 36	13 0	13 23
13	11 57	12 20	12 44	13 8	13 31	13 55	14 18
14	12 53	13 16	13 39	14 3	14 26	14 50	15 13
15	13 48	14 12	14 35	14 58	15 21	15 45	16 8
16	14 44	15 7	15 30	15 53	16 16	16 40	17 3
17	15 40	16 2	16 25	16 48	17 11	17 35	17 58
18	16 35	16 58	17 21	17 44	18 7	18 30	18 53
19	17 31	17 54	18 17	18 40	19 2	19 25	19 48
20	18 27	18 50	19 13	19 36	19 58	20 21	20 43
21	19 23	19 46	20 9	20 23	20 54	21 27	21 39
22	20 20	20 42	21 5	21 28	21 50	22 12	22 34
23	21 16	21 38	22 1	22 24	22 46	23 8	23 30
24	22 12	22 35	22 57	22 20	23 42	24 4	24 26
25	23 9	23 21	23 53	23 16	24 38	25 0	25 21
26	24 6	24 28	24 50	24 12	25 34	25 55	26 17
27	25 2	25 25	25 47	25 9	26 30	26 52	27 13
28	26 59	26 20	26 43	26 5	27 26	27 48	28 9
29	26 57	27 12	27 40	27 1	28 22	28 44	29 5
MESHA							
0	27 54	28 16	28 37	28 58	29 19	29 40	30 1
1	28 57	29 13	29 34	29 55	30 16	30 37	30 57
2	29 49	30 10	30 31	30 52	31 13	31 34	31 54
3	30 46	31 7	31 28	31 49	32 10	32 31	32 57
4	31 44	32 5	32 25	32 46	33 4	33 27	33 47
5	32 42	33 3	33 23	33 43	34 7	34 24	34 44
6	30 40	34 1	34 25	34 41	35 1	35 21	35 41
7	34 38	34 59	35 19	35 39	35 58	36 18	36 38
8	35 37	35 57	36 17	36 37	36 56	37 15	37 35
9	36 36	36 56	37 15	37 35	37 54	38 13	38 32
10	37 34	37 54	38 13	38 33	38 52	39 11	39 29
11	38 33	38 53	39 12	39 31	39 50	40 9	40 27
12	39 33	39 52	40 11	40 30	40 48	41 7	41 25
13	40 22	40 51	41 10	41 28	41 16	42 5	42 23
14	41 31	41 50	42 9	42 27	42 45	43 3	43 21
15	42 31	42 50	43 8	43 26	43 44	44 2	44 19
16	43 31	43 49	44 7	44 25	44 43	45 0	45 17
17	44 31	44 49	45 6	45 24	45 42	45 59	46 15
18	45 31	45 49	46 6	46 23	46 41	46 58	47 14
19	46 32	46 49	47 6	47 23	47 41	47 58	48 13
20	47 32	47 49	48 6	48 23	48 39	48 56	49 12
21	48 33	48 50	49 6	49 23	49 39	49 55	50 11
22	49 34	49 50	50 6	50 23	50 38	50 54	51 10
23	50 35	50 51	51 6	51 23	51 38	51 53	52 9
24	51 36	51 52	52 7	52 23	52 38	52 53	53 8
25	52 38	52 53	53 8	53 24	53 38	53 53	54 8
26	53 38	53 55	54 9	54 24	54 38	54 53	55 7
27	54 42	54 56	55 11	55 25	55 39	55 53	56 7
28	55 44	55 58	56 12	56 26	56 40	56 54	57 7
29	56 46	57 0	57 13	57 27	57 41	57 54	58 7
	° '	° '	° '	° '	° '	° '	° '

Table of Declinations

Mesh, Vrishabha, Mithuna, Karka, Aries, Taurus, Gemini and Cancer ...: North Latitude

MITHUNA	SAT.	SUN.	MON.	TUE.	WED.	THU.	FRIDAY	VRISHABHA
0	23 28	24 28	25 28	26 28	27 28	28 28	29 28	30
1	23 28	24 28	25 28	26 28	27 28	28 28	29 28	29
2	23 27	24 27	25 27	26 27	27 27	28 27	29 27	28
3	23 26	24 26	25 26	26 26	27 26	28 26	29 26	27
4	23 24	24 24	25 24	26 24	27 24	28 24	29 24	26
5	23 22	24 22	25 22	26 22	27 22	28 22	29 22	25
6	23 20	24 20	25 19	26 19	27 19	28 19	29 19	24
7	23 17	24 17	25 16	26 16	27 16	28 16	29 16	23
8	23 14	24 14	25 13	26 13	27 13	28 13	29 13	22
9	23 10	24 10	25 9	26 9	27 9	28 9	29 9	21
10	23 6	24 6	25 5	26 5	27 5	28 5	29 5	20
11	23 1	24 1	25 0	26 0	27 0	28 0	29 0	19
12	22 56	23 56	24 55	25 55	26 55	27 55	28 55	18
13	22 50	23 50	24 49	25 49	26 49	27 49	28 49	17
14	22 44	23 44	24 43	25 43	26 43	27 43	28 42	16
15	22 37	23 37	24 36	25 36	26 36	27 36	28 35	15
16	22 30	23 30	24 29	25 29	26 29	27 28	28 28	14
17	22 23	23 23	24 22	25 22	26 22	27 20	28 19	13
18	22 15	23 15	24 14	25 14	26 14	27 11	28 11	12
19	22 7	23 7	24 6	25 5	26 5	27 3	28 3	11
20	21 58	22 58	23 57	24 56	25 56	26 55	27 53	9
21	21 49	22 49	23 48	24 47	25 46	26 46	27 44	10
22	21 40	22 39	23 38	24 37	25 36	26 36	27 35	8
23	21 30	22 29	23 28	24 27	25 26	26 26	27 25	7
24	21 20	22 18	23 17	24 16	25 15	26 15	27 14	6
25	21 9	22 7	23 6	24 5	25 4	26 4	27 3	5
26	20 58	21 56	22 55	23 54	24 53	25 52	26 51	4
27	20 47	21 44	22 43	23 42	24 41	25 40	26 39	3
28	20 35	21 32	22 31	23 30	24 29	25 18	26 26	2
29	20 23	21 20	22 19	23 18	24 17	25 16	26 14	1
KARKA								**MESHA**
0	20 10	21 8	22 7	23 5	24 5	25 3	26 0	
1	19 57	20 55	21 54	22 52	23 51	24 50	25 48	29
2	19 44	20 42	21 41	22 39	23 37	24 36	25 34	28
3	19 31	20 29	21 27	22 25	23 23	24 22	25 20	27
4	19 17	20 15	21 13	22 11	23 9	24 8	25 6	26
5	19 3	20 1	20 59	21 57	22 55	23 53	24 51	25
6	18 48	19 46	20 44	21 42	22 40	23 38	24 36	24
7	18 33	19 31	20 29	21 27	22 25	23 23	24 21	23
8	18 18	19 15	20 13	21 11	22 9	23 7	24 5	22
9	18 2	18 59	19 57	20 55	21 53	22 51	23 49	21
10	17 46	18 43	19 41	20 38	21 36	22 34	23 31	20
11	17 29	18 26	19 24	20 22	21 19	22 17	23 14	19
12	17 13	18 9	19 7	20 5	21 2	22 0	22 57	18
13	16 56	17 52	18 50	19 48	20 44	21 42	22 39	17
14	16 39	17 35	18 33	19 30	20 27	21 25	22 22	16
15	16 21	17 18	18 15	19 12	20 9	21 7	22 4	15
16	16 3	17 0	17 57	18 54	19 51	20 49	21 46	14
17	15 45	16 42	17 39	18 36	19 33	20 30	21 27	13
18	15 27	16 23	17 20	18 17	19 44	20 11	21 8	12
19	15 9	16 4	17 1	17 58	18 55	19 52	20 49	11
20	14 50	15 45	16 41	17 38	18 35	19 32	20 29	10
21	14 31	15 26	16 22	17 19	18 16	19 13	20 10	9
22	14 11	15 7	16 3	17 0	17 56	19 53	19 50	8
23	13 52	14 47	15 43	16 40	17 36	18 33	19 29	7
24	13 32	14 27	15 23	16 19	17 15	18 12	19 8	6
25	13 12	14 7	15 3	16 0	16 56	17 53	18 49	5
26	12 52	13 47	14 43	15 39	16 36	17 32	18 28	4
27	12 32	13 27	14 23	15 19	16 15	17 12	18 8	3
28	12 11	13 6	14 2	14 58	15 54	16 51	17 47	2
29	11 50	12 45	13 41	14 37	15 33	16 30	17 26	1
30	11 29	12 24	13 20	14 16	15 12	16 8	17 4	0
KARKA	SATURDAY	SUNDAY	MONDAY	TUESDAY	WEDNESDAY	THURSDAY	FRIDAY	MESHA
	o o	/ o	/ o	o /	o /	o /	o /	o

Left margin (upper): Dhanu South Lat. and Mithuna North Lat.
Left margin (lower): Makara South Lat. and Karka North Lat.
Right margin (upper): Vrishabha North and Vrischika South Latitude
Right margin (lower): Mesha North and Thula South Latitude

RULES TO FIND LAGNA AND RASHI

Table of Declinations

Simha, Kanya, Kumbha, Meena, Leo, Virgo, Aquarius and Pisces ... North Latitude

Left margin: Kumbha South Lat. and Simha North Lat. — Meena South Lat. and Kanya North Latitude.
Right margin: Meena North Lat. and Kanya South Lat. — Kumbha South Lat. and Simha North Lat.

SIMHA	SATURDAY	SUNDAY	MONDAY	TUESDAY	WED.	THURSDAY	FRIDAY	MEENA
0	11 29	12 24	13 20	14 16	15 12	16 8	17 4	30
1	11 8	12 4	13 0	13 36	14 51	15 47	16 43	29
2	10 46	11 42	12 38	13 33	14 29	15 25	16 21	28
3	10 25	11 21	12 17	13 12	14 7	15 4	16 0	27
4	10 3	10 59	11 55	12 51	13 46	14 43	15 39	26
5	9 41	10 39	11 35	12 30	13 24	14 22	15 17	25
6	9 19	10 15	11 11	12 6	13 2	13 58	14 54	24
7	8 57	9 53	10 49	11 44	12 40	13 35	14 31	23
8	8 35	9 31	10 27	11 22	12 18	13 13	14 9	22
9	8 12	9 8	10 4	10 59	11 54	12 49	13 45	21
10	7 50	8 46	9 41	10 36	11 31	12 26	13 21	20
11	7 27	8 22	9 17	10 12	11 8	12 3	12 57	19
12	7 4	8 0	8 55	9 50	10 45	11 40	12 34	18
13	6 41	7 37	8 31	9 26	10 21	11 16	12 11	17
14	6 18	7 14	8 8	9 3	9 58	10 53	11 48	16
15	5 55	6 57	7 46	8 41	9 35	10 30	11 26	15
16	5 32	6 28	7 23	8 18	9 13	10 7	11 3	14
17	5 8	6 4	6 59	7 54	8 49	9 44	10 39	13
18	4 45	5 47	6 36	7 31	8 26	9 21	10 16	12
19	4 21	5 17	6 12	7 7	8 2	8 57	9 52	11
20	3 58	4 54	5 49	6 44	7 39	8 34	9 29	10
21	3 34	4 30	5 25	6 20	7 15	8 10	9 5	9
22	3 11	4 7	5 2	5 57	6 52	7 47	8 42	8
23	2 47	3 43	4 38	5 33	6 28	7 23	8 18	7
24	2 23	3 19	4 14	5 9	6 4	6 59	7 54	6
25	2 0	2 55	3 50	4 45	5 40	6 35	7 30	5
26	1 36	2 31	3 26	4 21	5 16	6 11	7 6	4
27	1 12	2 7	3 2	3 57	4 52	5 47	6 42	3
28	0 48	1 43	2 38	3 33	4 28	5 23	6 18	2
29	0 24	1 19	2 14	3 9	4 4	4 59	5 54	1

KANYA	SATURDAY	SUNDAY	MONDAY	TUESDAY	WEDNESDAY	THURSDAY	FRIDAY	KUMBHA
0	0 0	0 55	1 50	2 45	3 40	4 35	5 30	KUMBHA
1	0 24	0 31	1 27	2 21	3 16	4 11	5 6	29
2	0 48	0 7	1 3	1 57	2 52	3 47	4 42	28
3	1 12	0 17	0 39	1 34	2 29	3 24	4 19	27
4	1 36	0 41	0 15	1 10	2 5	3 0	3 55	26
5	2 0	1 5	0 10	0 46	1 41	2 36	3 31	25
6	2 23	1 28	0 33	0 22	1 17	2 12	3 7	24
7	2 47	1 52	0 57	0 2	0 53	1 48	2 43	23
8	3 11	2 16	1 21	0 26	0 29	1 25	2 20	22
9	3 34	2 39	1 44	0 49	0 6	1 2	1 57	21
10	3 58	3 3	2 8	1 13	0 18	0 38	1 33	20
11	4 21	3 26	2 31	1 36	0 41	0 14	1 6	19
12	4 45	3 50	2 55	2 0	1 5	0 10	0 46	18
13	5 8	4 13	3 18	2 23	1 28	0 33	0 24	17
14	5 32	4 37	3 42	2 46	1 52	0 56	0 0	16
15	5 55	5 0	4 5	3 9	2 14	1 18	0 23	15
16	6 18	5 23	4 27	3 32	2 37	1 40	0 45	14
17	6 41	5 45	4 50	3 54	3 0	2 3	1 8	13
18	7 5	6 8	5 14	4 18	3 23	2 27	1 32	12
19	7 27	6 31	5 36	4 40	3 45	2 49	1 54	11
20	7 50	6 54	5 58	5 2	4 6	3 10	2 15	10
21	8 12	7 16	6 20	5 24	4 28	3 32	2 37	9
22	8 35	7 39	6 43	5 47	4 51	3 56	3 0	8
23	8 57	8 1	7 5	6 9	5 13	4 18	3 22	7
24	9 19	8 23	7 27	6 31	5 35	4 40	3 45	6
25	9 41	8 45	7 49	6 53	5 58	5 2	4 6	5
26	10 3	9 7	8 11	7 15	6 19	5 24	4 28	4
27	10 25	9 29	8 34	7 38	6 42	5 46	4 50	3
28	10 46	9 57	8 56	8 1	7 4	6 8	5 12	2
29	11 8	10 13	9 17	8 21	7 24	6 28	5 32	1
30	11 29	10 33	9 37	8 41	7 44	6 48	5 52	0
	° '	° '	° '	° '	° '	° '	° '	°

Table for turning Degrees and Minutes into Time

HM M.S.	HM M.S.	D M	HM M.S.	D M.	HM M.S.	D M	HM M.S.	D M	HM M.S.	D M	HM M.S.	DN M.S.	M SEC
1	0 4	61	4 4	121	8 4	181	12 4	241	16 4	301	20 4	0 15	1
2	0 8	62	4 8	121	8 8	182	12 8	242	16 8	302	20 8	0 30	2
3	0 12	63	4 12	123	8 12	183	12 12	243	16 12	303	20 12	0 45	3
4	0 16	64	4 16	124	8 16	184	12 16	244	16 16	304	20 16	1 0	4
5	0 20	65	4 20	125	8 20	185	12 20	245	16 20	305	20 20	1 15	5
6	0 24	66	4 24	126	8 24	186	12 24	246	16 24	306	20 24	1 30	6
7	0 28	67	4 28	127	8 28	187	12 28	247	16 28	307	20 28	1 45	7
8	0 32	68	4 32	128	8 32	188	12 32	248	16 32	308	20 32	2 0	8
9	0 36	69	4 36	129	8 36	189	12 36	249	16 36	309	20 36	2 15	9
10	0 40	70	4 40	130	8 40	190	12 40	250	16 40	310	20 40	2 30	10
11	0 44	71	4 44	131	8 44	191	12 44	251	16 44	311	20 44	2 45	11
12	0 48	72	4 48	132	8 48	192	12 48	252	16 48	312	20 48	3 0	12
13	0 52	73	4 52	133	8 52	193	12 52	253	16 52	313	20 52	3 15	13
14	0 56	74	4 56	134	8 56	194	12 56	254	16 56	314	20 56	3 30	14
15	1 0	75	5 0	135	9 0	195	13 0	255	17 0	315	21 0	3 45	15
16	1 4	76	5 4	136	9 4	196	13 4	256	17 4	316	21 4	4 10	16
17	1 8	77	5 8	140	9 8	197	13 8	257	17 8	317	21 8	4 15	17
18	1 12	78	5 12	141	9 12	198	13 12	258	17 12	318	21 12	4 30	18
19	1 16	79	5 16	142	9 16	199	13 16	259	17 16	319	21 16	4 45	19
20	1 20	80	5 20	143	9 20	200	13 20	260	17 20	320	21 20	5 0	20
21	1 24	81	5 24	141	9 24	201	13 24	261	17 24	321	21 24	5 15	21
22	1 28	82	5 28	142	9 28	202	13 28	262	17 28	322	21 28	5 30	22
23	1 32	83	5 32	143	9 32	203	13 32	263	17 32	323	21 32	5 45	23
24	1 36	84	5 36	144	9 36	204	13 36	264	17 36	324	21 36	6 0	24
25	1 40	85	5 50	145	9 40	205	13 40	265	17 40	325	21 40	6 15	25
26	1 44	86	5 44	146	9 44	206	13 44	266	17 44	326	21 44	6 30	26
27	1 48	87	5 48	147	8 48	207	13 48	267	17 48	327	21 48	6 45	27
28	1 52	88	5 52	148	9 52	208	13 52	268	17 52	328	21 52	7 0	28
29	1 56	89	6 56	149	9 56	209	13 56	268	17 56	329	21 56	7 15	29
30	2 0	90	6 0	150	10 0	210	14 0	270	18 0	330	22 0	7 30	30
31	2 4	91	6 4	151	10 4	211	14 4	271	18 4	331	22 4	7 45	31
32	2 8	92	6 8	152	10 8	212	14 8	272	18 8	332	22 8	8 0	32
33	2 12	93	7 12	153	10 12	213	14 12	273	18 12	333	22 12	8 15	33
34	2 16	94	6 16	154	10 16	214	14 16	274	19 16	334	22 16	8 30	34
35	2 20	95	6 20	155	10 20	215	14 20	275	18 20	335	22 20	8 45	35
36	2 24	96	6 24	156	10 24	216	14 24	276	18 24	336	22 24	9 0	36
37	2 28	97	6 28	157	10 28	217	14 28	277	18 28	337	22 28	9 15	37
38	2 32	98	6 32	158	10 32	218	14 32	278	18 32	338	22 32	9 30	38
39	2 26	99	6 36	159	10 36	219	14 36	279	18 36	339	22 36	9 45	39
40	2 40	100	6 40	160	10 40	220	14 40	280	18 40	340	22 40	10 0	40
41	2 44	101	6 44	161	10 44	221	14 44	281	18 44	341	22 44	10 15	41
42	2 48	102	6 48	162	10 48	222	14 48	282	18 48	342	22 48	10 30	42
43	2 52	103	6 52	163	10 52	223	14 52	283	18 52	343	22 52	10 45	43
44	2 56	104	6 56	164	10 56	224	14 56	284	18 56	344	22 56	11 0	44
45	3 0	105	7 0	165	11 0	225	15 0	285	19 0	345	23 0	11 15	45
46	3 4	106	7 4	166	11 4	226	15 4	286	19 4	346	23 4	11 30	46
47	3 8	107	7 8	167	11 8	227	15 8	287	19 8	347	23 8	11 45	47
48	2 12	108	7 12	168	11 12	228	15 12	288	19 12	348	23 12	12 0	48
49	3 16	109	7 16	169	11 16	229	15 16	289	19 16	349	23 16	12 15	49
50	3 20	110	7 20	170	11 20	230	15 20	290	19 20	350	23 20	12 30	50
51	3 24	111	7 24	171	11 24	231	15 24	291	19 24	351	23 24	12 45	51
52	3 28	112	7 28	172	11 28	232	15 28	292	19 28	352	23 28	13 0	52
53	3 32	113	7 32	173	11 32	233	15 32	293	19 32	353	23 32	13 15	53
54	3 36	114	7 36	174	11 36	234	15 36	294	19 36	354	23 36	13 30	54
55	3 40	115	7 40	175	11 40	235	15 40	295	19 40	355	23 40	13 45	55
56	3 44	116	7 44	176	11 44	236	16 44	296	19 44	256	23 44	14 0	56
57	3 48	117	7 48	177	11 48	237	15 48	297	19 48	357	23 48	14 15	57
58	3 52	118	7 52	178	11 52	238	15 52	298	19 52	358	23 52	14 30	58
59	3 56	119	7 56	179	11 56	239	15 56	299	19 56	359	23 56	14 45	59
60	4 0	120	8 0	180	12 0	240	16 0	300	20 0	360	24 0	15 0	60
° ′ ″		° ′ ″		° ′ ″		° ′ ″		° ′ ″		° ′ ″		° ′ ″	

RULES TO FIND LAGNA AND RASHI

Table of Opposite Nakshatras
For even years East (Moon Chart)

Nakshtra	Part	Nakshatra	Part	Nakashtara	Part	Nakashatra	Part
1 Aswini	1	4 Hasta	3	9 Aslesha	1	3 U. Shadha	3
1 Aswini	2	4 Hasta	4	9 Aslesha	2	3 U. Shadha	4
1 Aswini	3	5 Chitra	1	9 Aslesha	3	4 Shravana	1
1 Aswini	4	5 Chitra	2	9 Aslesha	4	4 Shravana	2
2 Bharani	1	5 Chitra	3	1 Magha	1	4 Shravana	3
2 Bharani	2	5 Chitra	4	1 Magha	2	4 Shravana	4
2 Bharani	3	6 Swathi	1	1 Magha	3	5 Dhanishtha	1
2 Bharani	4	6 Swathi	2	1 Magha	4	5 Dhanishtha	2
3 Krittika	1	6 Swathi	3	2 Purva	1	5 Dhanishtha	3
3 Krittika	2	6 Swathi	4	2 Purva	2	5 Dhanishtha	4
3 Krittika	3	7 Vishakha	1	2 Purva	3	6 Shatataraka	1
3 Krittika	4	7 Vishakha	2	2 Purva	4	6 Shatararaka	2
4 Rohini	1	7 Vishakha	3	3 Uttara	1	6 Shatararaka	3
4 Rohini	2	7 Vishakha	4	3 Uttara	2	6 Ghatataraka	4
4 Rohini	3	8 Anuradha	1	3 Uttara	3	7 P. Bhadrapada	1
4 Rohoni	4	8 Anuradha	2	3 Uttara	4	7 P. Bhadrapada	2
5 Mriga	1	8 Anuradha	3	4 Hasta	1	7 P. Bhadrapada	3
5 Mriga	2	8 Anuradha	4	4 Hasta	2	7 P. Bhadrapada	4
5 Mriga	3	9 Jeshtha	1	4 Hasta	3	8 U. Bhadrapada	1
5 Mriga	4	9 Jeshtha	2	4 Hasta	4	8 U. Bhadrapada	2
6 Aridra	1	9 Jeshtha	3	5 Chitra	1	8 U. Bhadrapada	3
6 Aridra	2	9 Jeshtha	4	5 Chitra	2	8 U. Bhadrapada	4
6 Aridra	3	1 Moola	1	5 Chitra	3	9 Revathi	1
6 Aridra	4	1 Moola	2	5 Chitra	4	9 Revathi	2
7 Punarvasu	1	1 Moola	3	6 Swathi	1	9 Revathi	3
7 Punarvasu	2	1 Moola	4	6 Swathi	2	9 Revathi	3
7 Punarvasu	3	2 Purvashadha	1	6 Swathi	3	1 Aswini	1
7 Punarvasu	4	2 Purvashadha	2	6 Swathi	4	1 Aswini	2
8 Pushya	1	2 Purvashadha	3	7 Vishakha	1	1 Aswini	3
8 Pushya	2	2 Purvashadha	4	7 Vishakha	2	1 Aswini	4

Table of Opposite Nakshatras
For even years East (Moon Chart)—contd.

Nakshatra	Part	Nakshatra	Part	Nakshatra	Part	Nakshatra	Part
8 Pushya	3	3 U. Shadha	1	7 Vishakha	3	2 Bharani	1
8 Pushya	4	3 U. Shadha	2	7 Vishakha	4	2 Bharani	2
8 Anuradha	1	2 Bharani	3	6 Shatataraka	1	9 Aslesha	3
8 Anuradha	2	2 Bharani	4	6 Shatataraka	2	9 Aslesha	4
8 Anuradha	3	3 Krittika	1	6 Shatataraka	3	1 Megha	1
8 Anuradha	4	3 Krittika	2	6 Shatataraka	4	1 Magha	2
9 Jeshtha	1	3 Krittika	3	7 P.Bhadrapada	1	1 Magha	3
9 Jeshtha	2	3 Krittika	4	7 P.Bhadrapada	2	1 Magha	4
9 Jeshtha	3	4 Rohini	1	7 P.Bhadrapada	3	2 Purva	1
9 Jeshtha	4	4 Rohini	2	7 P.Bhadrapada	4	2 Purva	2
1 Moola	1	4 Rohini	3	8 U.Bhadrapada	1	2 Purva	3
1 Moola	2	4 Rohini	4	8 U.Bhadrapada	2	2 Purva	4
1 Moola	3	5 Mriga	1	8 U.Bhadrapada	3	3 Uttara	1
1 Moola	4	5 Mriga	2	8 U.Bhadrapada	4	3 Uttara	2
2 Purvashadha	1	5 Mriga	3	9 Revathi	9	3 Uttara	3
2 Purvashadha	2	5 Mriga	4	9 Revathi	2	3 Uttara	4
2 Purvashadha	3	6 Aridra	1	9 Revathi	3	4 Hasta	1
2 Purvashadha	4	6 Aridra	2	9 Revathi	4	4 Hasta	2
3 U. Shadha	1	6 Aridra	3				
3 U. Shadha	2	6 Aridra	4				
3 U. Shadha	3	7 Punarvasu	1				
3 U. Shadha	4	7 Punarvasu	2				
4 Shravana	1	7 Punarvasu	3				
4 Shravana	2	7 Punarvasu	4				
4 Shravana	3	8 Pushya	1				
4 Shravana	4	8 Pushya	2				
5 Dhanishtha	1	8 Pushya	3				
5 Dhanishtha	2	8 Pushya	4				
5 Dhanishtha	3	9 Aslesha	1				
5 Dhanishtha	4	9 Aslesha	2				

RULES TO FIND LAGNA AND RASHI

Table of Opposite Nakshatras
For Even years West (Moon chart)

Nakshatra	Part	Nakshatra	Part	Nakshatra	Part	Nakshatra	Part
1 Aswini	1	6 Swathi	3	9 Aslesha	1	5 Dhanishtha	3
1 Aswini	2	6 Swathi	4	9 Aslesha	2	5 Dhanishtha	4
1 Aswini	3	7 Vishakha	1	9 Aslesha	3	6 Shatataraka	1
1 Aswini	4	7 Vishakha	2	9 Aslesha	4	6 Shatataraka	2
2 Bharani	1	7 Vishakha	3	1 Magha	1	6 Shatataraka	3
2 Bharani	2	7 Vishakha	4	1 Magha	2	6 Shatataraka	4
2 Bharani	3	8 Anuradha	1	1 Magha	3	7 P.bhadrapada	1
2 Bharani	4	8 Anuradha	2	1 Magha	4	7 P.bhadrapada	2
3 Krittika	1	8 Anuradha	3	2 Purva	1	7 P.bhadrapada	3
3 Krittika	2	8 Anuradha	4	2 Purva	2	7 P.bhadrapada	4
3 Krittika	3	9 Jeshtha	1	2 Purva	3	8 U.bhadrapada	1
3 Krittika	4	9 Jeshtha	2	2 Purva	4	8 U.bhadrapada	2
4 Rohini	1	9 Jeshtha	3	3 Uttara	1	8 U.bhadrapada	3
4 Rohini	2	9 Jeshtha	4	3 Uttara	2	8 U.bhadrapada	4
4 Rohini	3	1 Moola	1	3 Uttara	3	9 Revathi	1
4 Rohini	4	1 Moola	2	3 Uttara	4	9 Revathi	2
5 Mriga	1	1 Moola	3	4 Hasta	1	9 Revathi	3
5 Mriga	2	1 Moola	4	4 Hasta	2	9 Revathi	4
5 Mriga	3	2 Purvashadha	1	4 Hasta	3	1 Aswini	1
5 Mriga	4	2 Purvashadha	2	4 Hasta	4	1 Aswini	2
6 Aridra	1	2 Purvashadha	3	5 Chitra	1	1 Aswini	3
6 Aridra	2	2 Purvashadha	4	5 Chitra	2	1 Aswini	4
6 Aridra	3	5 U.shadha	1	5 Chitra	3	2 Bharani	1
6 Aridra	4	3 U.shadha	2	5 Chitra	4	2 Bharani	2
7 Punarvasu	1	3 U.shadha	3	6 Swathi	1	2 Bharani	3
7 Punarvasu	2	3 U.shadha	4	6 Swathi	2	2 Bharani	4
7 Punarvasu	3	4 Shravana	1	6 Swathi	3	3 Krittika	1
7 Punarvasu	4	4 Shravana	2	6 Swathi	4	3 Krittika	2
8 Pushya	1	4 Shravana	3	7 Vishakha	1	3 Krittika	3
8 Pushya	2	4 Shravana	4	7 Vishakha	2	2 Krittika	4
8 Pushya	3	5 Dhanishtha	1	7 Vishakha	3	4 Rohini	1

Table of Opposite Nakshatras
For Even years West (Moon chart)—contd.

NAKSHATRA	PART	NAKSHATRA	PART	NAKSHATRA	PART	NAKSHATRA	PART
8 Pushya	4	5 Dhanishtha	2	7 Vishakha	4	4 Rohini	2
8 Anuradha	1	4 Rohini	3	7 P.bhadrapada	1	3 Uttara	3
8 Anuradha	2	4 Rohini	4	7 P.bhadrapada	2	3 Uttara	4
8 Anuradha	3	5 Mriga	1	7 P.bhadrapada	3	4 Hasta	1
8 Anuradha	4	5 Mriga	2	7 P.bhadrapada	4	4 Hasta	2
9 Jeshtha	1	5 Mriga	3	8 U.bhadrapada	1	4 Hasta	3
9 Jeshtha	2	5 Mriga	4	8 U.bhadrapada	2	4 Hasta	4
9 Jeshtha	3	6 Aridra	1	8 U.bhadrapada	3	5 Chitra	1
9 Jeshtha	4	6 Aridra	2	6 Shatatraka	2	5 Purva	4
1 Moola	1	6 Aridra	3	6 Shatataraka	3	3 Uttara	1
1 Moola	2	6 Aridra	4	6 Shatataraka	4	3 Uttara	2
1 Moola	3	7 Punarvasu	1	8 U.bhadrapada	4	5 Chitra	2
1 Moola	4	7 Punarvasu	2	9 Revathi	1	5 Chitra	3
2 Purvashadha	1	7 Punarvasu	3	9 Revathi	2	5 Chitra	4
2 Purvashadha	2	7 Punarvasu	4	9 Revathi	3	6 Swathi	1
2 Purvashadha	3	8 Pushya	1	9 Revathi	4	6 Swathi	2
2 Purvashadha	4	8 Pushya	2				
3 U. shadha	1	8 Pushya	3				
3 U. shadha	2	8 Pushya	4				
3 U. shadha	3	9 Aslesha	1				
3 U. shadha	4	9 Aslesha	2				
4 Shravana	1	9 Aslesha	3				
4 Shravana	2	9 Aslesha	4				
4 Shravana	3	1 Magha	1				
4 Shravana	4	1 Magha	2				
5 Dhanistha	1	1 Magha	3				
5 Dhanishtha	2	1 Magha	4				
5 Dhanishtha	3	2 Purva	1				
5 Dhanishtha	4	2 Purva	2				
6 Shatataraka	1	2 Purva	3				

Table of Opposite Nakashatras
For Odd Years East

Nakshatra	Part	Nakshatra	Part	Nakshatra	Part	Nakshatra	Part
1		5		9		4	
Aswini	1	Chitra	3	Aslesha	1	Shravana	3
1		5		9		4	
Aswini	2	Chitra	4	Aslesha	2	Shravana	4
1		6		9		5	
Aswini	3	Swathi	1	Aslesha	3	Dhanishtha	1
1		6		9		5	
Aswini	4	Swathi	2	Aslesha	4	Dhanishtha	2
2		6		1		5	
Bharani	1	Swathi	3	Magha	1	Dhanishtha	3
2		6		1		5	
Bharani	2	Swathi	4	Magha	2	Dhanishtha	4
2		7		1		6	
Bharani	3	Vishakha	1	Magha	3	Shatataraka	1
3		7		1		6	
Bharani	4	Vishakha	2	Magha	4	Shatararaka	2
3		7		2		6	
Krittika	1	Vishakha	3	Purva	1	Shatataraka	3
3		8		2		6	
Krittika	2	Vishakha	4	Purva	2	Shatataraka	4
3		8		2		7	
Krittika	3	Anuradha	1	Purva	3	P.Bhadrapada	1
4		8		3		7	
Krittika	4	Anuradha	2	Purva	4	P.Bhadrapada	2
4		8		3		7	
Rohini	1	Anuradha	3	Uttara	1	P.Bhadrapada	3
4		9		3		7	
Rohini	2	Anuradha	4	Uttara	2	P.Bhadrapada	4
4		9		3		8	
Rohini	3	Jeshtha	1	Uttara	3	U.Bhadrapada	1
4		9		3		8	
Rohini	4	Jeshtha	2	Uttara	4	U.Bhadrapada	2
5		9		4		8	
Mriga	1	Jeshtha	3	Hasta	1	U.Bhasrapada	3
5		9		4		8	
Mriga	2	Jeshtha	4	Hasta	2	U.Bhadrapada	4
5		1		4		9	
Mriga	3	Moola	1	Hasta	3	Revathi	1
5		1		4		9	
Mriga	4	Moola	2	Hasta	4	Revathi	2
6		1		5		9	
Aridra	1	Moola	3	Chitra	1	Revathi	3
6		1		5		9	
Aridra	2	Moola	4	Chitra	2	Revathi	4
6		2		5		1	
Aridra	3	Purvashadha	1	Chitra	3	Aswini	1
6		2		5		1	
Aridra	4	Purvashadha	2	Chitra	4	Aswini	2
7		2		8		1	
Punarvasu	1	Purvashadha	2	Swathi	1	Aswini	3
7		2		6		1	
Punarvasu	2	Purvashadha	4	Swathi	2	Aswini	4
7		3		6		2	
Punarvasu	3	U.shadha	1	Swathi	3	Bharani	1
7		3		6		2	
Punarvasu	4	U.shadha	2	Swathi	4	Bharani	2
8		3		7		2	
Pushya	1	U.shadha	3	Vishakha	1	Bharani	3
8		3		7		2	
Pushya	2	U.shadha	4	Vishakha	2	Bharani	4

Tables of Opposite Nakshatras
For Odd Years East—contd.

Nakshatra	Part	Nakshatra	Part	Nakshatra	Part	Nakshatra	Part
Pushya 8	3	Shravana 4	1	Vishakha 7	3	Krittika 3	1
Pushya 8	4	Shravana 3	2	Vishakha 7	4	Krittika 2	2
Anuradha 8	1	Krittika 3	3	P.Bhadrapada 7	1	Purva 2	3
Anuradha 8	2	Krittika 4	4	P.Bhadrapada 7	2	Purva 3	4
Anuradha 8	3	Rohini 4	1	P.Bhadrapada 7	3	Uttara 3	1
Anuradha 9	4	Rohini 4	2	P.Bhadrapada 8	4	Uttara 3	2
Jeshtha 9	1	Rohini 4	3	U.Bhadrapada 8	1	Uttara 3	3
Jeshtha 9	2	Rohini 5	4	U.Bhadrapada 8	2	Uttara 4	4
Jeshtha 9	3	Mirga 5	1	U.Bhadrepada 8	3	Hasta 4	1
Jeshtha 1	4	Mirga 5	2	U.Bhadrapada 9	4	Hasta 4	2
Moola 1	1	Mirga 5	3	Revathi 9	1	Hasta 4	3
Moola 1	2	Mirga 6	4	Revathi 9	2	Hasta 5	4
Moola 1	3	Aridra 6	1	Revathi 9	3	Chitra 5	1
Moola 2	4	Aridra 6	2	Revathi 6	4	Chitra 1	2
Purvashadha 2	1	Aridra 6	3	Shatataraka 6	2	Magha 2	4
Purvashadha 2	2	Aridra 7	4	Shatataraka 6	3	Purva 2	1
Purvashadha 2	3	Punarvasu 7	1	Shatataraka	4	Purva	2
Purvashadha 3	4	Punarvasu 7	2				
U.shadha 3	1	Punarvasu 7	3				
U.shadha 3	2	Punarvasu 8	4				
U.shadha 3	2	Pushya 8	1				
U.shadha 4	4	Pushya 8	2				
Shravana 4	1	Pushya 8	3				
Shravana 4	2	Pushya 9	4				
Shravana 4	3	Aslesha 9	1				
Shravana 5	4	Aslesha 9	2				
Dhanishtha 5	1	Aslesha 9	3				
Dhanishtha 5	2	Aslesha 1	4				
Dhanishtha 5	3	Magha 1	1				
Dhanishtha 6	4	Magha 1	2				
Shatataraka 1		Magha	3				

Table of Opposite Nakshatras
For Odd Years West

Nakshatra	Part	Nakshatra	Part	Nakshatra	Part	Nakshatra	Part
2 Bharani	1	6 Swathi	3	1 Magha	1	5 Dhanishtha	3
2 Bharani	2	6 Swathi	4	1 Magha	2	5 Dhanishtha	4
2 Bharani	3	5 Vishakha	1	1 Magha	3	6 Shatataraka	1
2 Bharani	4	7 Vishakha	2	1 Magha	4	6 Shatataraka	2
3 Krittika	1	7 Vishakha	3	2 Purva	1	6 Shatataraka	3
3 Krittika	2	7 Vishakha	4	2 Purva	2	6 Shatataraka	4
3 Krittika	3	8 Anuradha	1	2 Purva	3	7 P.Bhadrapada	1
3 Krittika	4	8 Anuradha	2	2 Purva	4	7 P.Bhadrapada	2
4 Rohini	1	8 Anuradha	3	3 Uttara	1	7 P.Bhadrapada	3
4 Rohini	2	8 Anuradha	4	3 Uttara	2	7 P.Bhadrapada	4
4 Rohini	3	9 Jeshtha	1	3 Uttara	3	8 U.Bhadrapada	1
4 Rohini	4	9 Jeshtha	2	3 Uttara	4	8 U.Bhadrapada	2
5 Mriga	1	9 Jeshtha	3	4 Hasta	1	8 U.Bhadrapada	3
5 Mriga	2	9 Jeshtha	4	4 Hasta	2	8 U.Bhadrapada	4
5 Mriga	3	1 Moola	1	4 Hasta	3	9 Revathi	1
5 Mriga	4	1 Moola	2	4 Hasta	4	9 Revathi	2
6 Aridra	1	1 Moola	3	5 Chitra	1	9 Revathi	3
6 Aridra	2	1 Moola	3	5 Chitra	2	9 Revathi	4
6 Aridra	3	2 Purvashadha	1	5 Chitra	3	1 Aswini	1
6 Aridra	4	2 Purvashadha	2	5 Chitra	4	1 Aswini	2
7 Punarvasu	1	2 Purvashadha	3	6 Swathi	1	1 Aswini	3
7 Punarvasu	2	2 Purvashadha	4	6 Swathi	2	1 Aswini	4
7 Punarvasu	3	3 U.shadha	1	6 Swathi	3	2 Bharani	1
7 Punarvasu	4	3 U.shadha	2	6 Swathi	4	2 Bharani	2
8 Pushya	1	3 U.shadha	3	7 Vishakha	1	2 Bharani	3
8 Pushya	2	3 U.shadha	4	7 Vishakha	2	2 Bharani	4
8 Pushya	3	4 Shravana	1	7 Vishakha	3	3 Krittika	1
8 Pushya	4	4 Shravana	2	7 Vishakha	4	3 Krittika	2
9 Aslesha	1	4 Shravana	3	8 Anuradha	1	3 Krittika	3
9 Aslesha	2	4 Shravana	4	8 Anuradha	2	3 Krittika	4

VEDIC NUMEROLOGY

Tables of Opposite Nakshatras
For Odd Years West—contd.

Nakshatra	Part	Nakshatra	Part	Nakshatra	Part	Nakshatra	Part
9 Aslesha	4	5 Dhanistha	1	8 Anuradha	3	4 Rohini	1
9 Aslesha	4	5 Dhanistha	2	8 Anuradha	4	4 Rohini	2
9 Jeshtha	1	4 Rohini	3	8 U.Bhadrapada	1	3 Uttara	3
9 Jeshtha	2	4 Rohini	4	8 U.Bhadrapada	2	3 Uttara	4
9 Jeshtha	3	5 Mriga	1	8 U.Bhadrapada	3	4 Hasta	1
9 Jeshtha	4	5 Mriga	2	8 U.Bhadrapada	4	4 Hasta	2
1 Moola	1	5 Mriga	3	9 Revathi	1	4 Hasta	3
1 Moola	2	5 Mriga	4	9 Revathi	2	4 Hasta	4
1 Moola	3	6 Aridra	1	9 Revathi	3	5 Chitra	1
1 Moola	4	6 Aridra	2	9 Revathi	4	5 Chitra	2
2 Purvasbadha	1	6 Aridra	3	1 Aswini	1	5 Chitra	3
2 Purvashadha	2	6 Aridra	4	1 Aswini	2	5 Chitra	4
2 Purvashadha	2	7 Punarvasu	1	1 Aswini	3	6 Swathi	1
2 Purvashadha	4	7 Punarvasu	2	1 Aswini	4	6 Swathi	2
3 U.shadha	1	7 Punarvasu	3	5 Dhanishtha	4	1 Magha	2
3 U.shadha	2	7 Punarvasu	4	6 Shatataraka	1	1 Magha	3
3 U.shadha	3	8 Pushya	1	6 Shatataraka	2	1 Magha	4
3 U.shadha	4	8 Pushya	2	6 Shatataraka	3	2 Purva	1
4 Shravana	1	8 Pushya	3	6 Shatataraka	4	2 Purva	2
4 Shravana	2	8 Pushya	4	7 P.bhadrapada	1	2 Purva	3
4 Shravana	3	9 Aslesha	1	7 P.bhadrapada	2	2 Purva	4
4 Shravana	4	9 Aslesha	2	7 P.bhadrapada	3	3 Uttara	1
5 Dhanishtha	1	9 Aslesha	3	7 P.bhadrapada	4	3 Uttara	2
5 Dhanishtha	2	9 Aslesha	4				
5 Dhanishtha	3	1 Magha	1				

Table of Planets and Their houses.

Mangal	Shukra	Budha	Chandra	Ravi	Guru	Shani	Planet
Mars	Venus	Mercury	Moon	Sun	Jupiter	Saturn	Planet
Mesha	Vrishabha	Mithuna	Karka	Simha	Dhanu	Makara	Rashi
Aries	Taurus	Gemini	Cancer	Leo	Sagittarius	Capricorn	Rashi
Vrischika	Thula	Kanya	...	...	Meena	Kumbha	Rashi
Scorpio	Libra	Virgo	...	...	Pisces	Aquarius	Rashi

CHAPTER VI

ILLUSTRATIONS TO FIND LONGEVITY OF THE NATIVES

We have seen nearly hundreds of examples regarding the position of the earth (Sidereal time). The moon, and we can find out the position of the Sun, Moon and earth bcause we know how to find out the Sun from Chapter second.

The Astronomical divisions of time are the day, the month, and the year as well as the week, but almost all astronomers declare that "the week is not such a division because it does not correspond to any astronomical cycle, although as we shall presently see, a certain astronomical signification was said to have been given to it by ancient astrologers". This is the western opinion but Shri Lahiri, the great Indian Astronomer, is also of this opinion 'that the days of the week or the week division does not correspond to any astronomical cycle". Not only this but also he is of the opinion to make a common day for east and west. If it is so, then it will be a very difficult problem to astrologers of India.

I have practically shown that the week days or the week has astronomical division and we can find out the Longitude and Latitude, nearly 30 given examples will prove that we can find out the correct degree of the Right ascension or declination of the Lagna, it is enough to request him to give up the idea of the common day.

My intention to open this chapter is to find out the Longevity of the persons with the help of the given birth date. We know how to find the Rashi, Lagna and the sun, then it is rather easy to find the longevity. We will see some examples.

Example No. 1. Birth date 28.5.1921. We will see the birth day first. 1900=2, 21=5, May=7, Birth date is 28=28 plus 7 plus 5 plus 2=42 divided by 7=Remainder is 0=Saturday is birth day. See the year 1921 in the column 1917 the second part of the southern hemisphere. Saturday shows 22-30 hours, 22-30 hours means Shravana nakshatra but due to spherical triangle it is a negative part. Saturn is the Lord of Saturday as well as he is the Lord of the Kumbha and Makara Rashi, Kumbha rashi is negative here, then see the other rashi of Saturn in the third part of the southern hemisphere. Saturday shows 22-30 hours, it means Shravana nakshatra . and Makara rashi. Wednesday is on 180° of Saturday, Wednesday shows 9-30 hours, 9-30 hours means Aslesha nakshatra. Karka rashi is on 180° of the Makara, Budha, (Mercury) is the lord

203

of Wednesday as well as he is the Lord of Kanya and Mithuna rashi. Shravana nakshatra is nagative and Hasta nakshatra is the greater nakshatra which is in Kanya rashi. Revati is on 180° of Hasta, deduct 12°from Revati or two hours from Revati because of the negative part of Mercury. Revati is No. 27—2=25=Purvabhadrapada. Put the moon in Purvabhadrapada second part, as the birth month is original in the second part of the year, it shows Kumbha rashi, as well as Mercury is in triangle. From 22nd of May to 21st of June Moon is the Lord of the Month. Mercury is working on behalf of the moon. In Lunar horoscope 1900 years are in the tenth house. So we will put the opening month of the year in the tenth house like this:—

22nd of January to 21st of December tenth house, 22nd of December to 21st of November eleventh house, 22nd of November to 21st of October twelfth house, 22nd of October to 21st of September first house, 22nd of September to 21st of August second house, 22nd of August to 21st of July third house, 22nd of July to 21st of June fourth house, 22nd of June to 21st of May fifth house. here is the Birth month of the native and Revati nakshatra of Mercury. Revati nakshatra is in Meena rashi, then put Meena rashi there, it shows Vrischika Lagna. From 14th of May to 14th of June Sun commences Vrishabha rashi, that is the Sun is in Rohini nakshatra, Jyeshtha nakshatra is on 180° of the Rohini, Jyeshtha nakshatra is in Lagna. Jyeshtha nakshatra means 18° Solar degrees, of Vrischika. So we will see 18° of Vrischika for Latitude on Saturday, it shows 256°-57′ deduct 240° of the Vrischika rashi, 256°-57′—240°=16°-57′ Latitude North. Moon is working on behalf of Mercury. The second part of the northern hemisphere Monday shows 7-30 hours, deduct 2 hours the difference of the Southern hemisphere, 7-30—2=5-30 hours, deduct 20′ of the Ayanachalana, 5-30—20′=5-10′ is Longitude. See the Longitude chart for 5-10′ hours, it shows 78°, add the Longitude of Mercury (Monday 1, Tuesday 2, Wednesday 3, 78 plus 3=81 is the Longitude East. Put the birth date 28 on the Birth day, 28=2 plus 8=10=1).

3	5	7	9
Sat	Mon	Wed	Fri
4	6	8	1
Sun	Tue	Thur	Sat

It clearly shows that the sun is working on behalf of Saturn and Moon is working on behalf of Mercury. Group of the Moon shows the years and the group of the Sun shows Months as well as dates. That is in 3-5-7-9 years, 4-6-8-1 months are bad for the native, as well as in 4-6-8-1 months 4-6-8-1 are the dates which are bad for the native. 4-6-8-1 years are good, in these years 3-5-7-9 months are good, and in these months 3-5-7-9 dates are the good dates. Budha is the Lord of the eighth house, Right ascension nakshatra of the Budha in No. 9=Aslesha and declination nakshatra is Punarvasu which is a bad nakshatra in the eighth house. Lagna rashi is of the Mangal. Mriga his original nakshatra, Sun is in Vrishabha that is his right ascension is Mriga and Declination nakshatra is Rohini. So we will count Moon's nakshatra No. 7 upto Suns nakshatra Rohini, Aswini 7, Bharani 16, Krittika 25 Rohini 34 that is the longevity of the native. Now when Sun will come in Vishakha nakshatra at his 34 then the native will pass away, the sun comes in Vishakha nakshatra in the month of October which will be in Thula in the trine of the Moon in Kumbha, or of the Mercury in the eighth house, Mithuna. Opening rashi of the birth month is Meena, Jupiter is the Lord of the Meena rashi, Jupiter shows No. 8, that is Uttarabhadrapada nakshatra in Meena Rashi, that is on 26th of October at his 34 he will pass away, add 34 years in his birth year, 1921 plus 34=1955 that is on 26th October 1955 he died.

Shree D. V. Paluskar

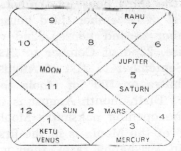

Birth date 20.6.1921
Expiry date 26.10.1955
Latitude 16°-57′ North
Longitude 81° East
Birth time 19-56 hours

Example No. 2. Birth date 25.8.1872. We will find the birth day first, 1800=4, 72=6, August=1, Birth date is 25=25 plus 1 plus 4 plus 6=36 divided by 7=Remainder is 1=Sunday is the birth day. See the month of August and the year 1872 in the second part of the Southern hemisphere. Sunday shows 10-30 hours, but due to the spherical triangle it is negative part. Sun is the Lord of Sunday as well as he is the Lord of Simha rashi, then see the fourth part of the Southern hemisphere for Simha rashi. Sunday shows 3-30 hours, add 2 hours the difference of the negative part. 3-30 plus 2=5-30 hours (5-30 hours shows Tuesday). See the Longitude chart for 5-30 hours, it shows 82°-30′, add three degrees more of Tuesday (Sunday 1°, Monday 2°, Tuesday 3°) 82°-30′ plus 3°=85°-30′ Longitude east. Thursday is on 180° of Sunday, Jupiter is the Lord of Thursday as well as he is the Lord of Dhanu and Meena rashi, then see Dhanu rashi in the first part of the Southern hemisphere, Thursday shows 14-30 hours. add 2 hours the difference of the negative part 14-30 plus 2=16-30 hours, deduct 20′ of Ayanachalana, 16-30—20′=16-10′ hours means Vishakha nakshatra No. 16 or 16 solar degrees, then see 16° of Dhanu rashi on Sunday in Latitude chart, it shows, 287°-14′ deduct 270° of the Dhanu rashi, 287°-14′-270=17°-14′ is the Latitude North. From 14th August to 14th September Sun is in Simha rashi the second part of the southern hemisphere Sunday shows 10-30 hours but it is a negative nakshatra due to the spherical triangle, then Aswini nakshatra is the greater nakshatra, Sun is in Simha, then the Moon must be in the greater nakshatra Ashwini i.e. the Moon is in Mesha, the second rashi of the Mars, the second part of the southern hemisphere Sunday is in Vrischika rashi. It clearly shows that the Moon is working on behalf of Mars, and the Sun is working on behalf of Jupiter. The Sun is in Magha nakshatra and Moon is in Aswini nakshatra, it is a Lunisolar horoscope, we can find the Right ascension by both the ways. Opening rashi of the birth in solar horoscope is Dhanu and Moola nakshatra is the opening nakshatra of the Rashi. Mriga nakshatra is on 180° of the Moola. The opening month of the 1872 year is in the third house of the solar horoscope, then 22nd of January to 21st of December third house, 22nd of December to 21st of November second house, 22nd of November to 21st of October first house, 22nd of October to 21st of September twelfth house, 22nd of September to 21st of August eleventh house, here it is Mriga nakshatra on 180° of Moola the nakshatra of the opening rashi Dhanu. Birth month August is in the third part of the year, naturally the opening nakshatra Moola is in the third part, then Mriga on 180° of the Moola is in the first part, first part of Mriga nakshatra is in Vrishabha rashi, then we will put Vrishabha rashi in the eleventh house. It shows Karka Lagna. Put the birth date 25 on the birth day 25=2 plus 5=7, Birth day Sunday is negative, then No. 3 is on 180° of the No. 7. Then put No. 3 on the birth day.

3	5	7	9
Sun	Tues	Thur	Sat
4	6	8	1
Mon	Wed	Fri	Sun

Right ascension nakshatra of the Sun is Magha and Declination nakshatra is Uttara. Right ascension nakshatra of Jupiter is Vishakha and Declination nakshatra is Jyestha, it shows 3-5-7-9 years are bad for the native and in these years 4-6-8-1 months are bad, Right ascension nakshatra of the Moon is Aswini and declination nakshatra is Krittika, it shows 3-5-7-9 dates of the 4-6-8-1 months are bad. Naturally the good years are 4-6-8-1 and in these good years 3-5-7-9 months are good, in these months 4-6-8-1 are the good dates. We have to see the Longevity of the native. Kumbha rashi is in the eighth house. Purvabhadrapada nakshatra is there which is the right ascension nakshatra of the Jupiter. Revati No. 9 is Declination nakshatra. Aswini nakshatra of the Moon is in the tenth house, it is right ascension nakshatra. Krittika nakshatra is a declination nakshatra of the Moon. Krittika is No. 3, then count the declination nakshatra, Krittika No. 3 upto declination nakshatra Revati No. 9 of the Jupiter, Aswini 3, Bharani 12, Krittika 21, Rohini 30, Mriga 39, Aridra 48, Punarvasu 57, Pushya 66, Aslesha 75. The longevity of the native is 75 years. Opening rashi of the birth month is Dhanu. Moola nakshatra is opening nakshatra, Mriga nakshatra is on 180° of Moola. Mriga nakshatra is No. 5 which is in Vrishabha rashi, Vrishabha rashi is on 180° of Vrishchika. There is Vishakha nakshatra and it commences from 14th of October to 14th of November for the sun. Sun is in Thula, Chitra nakshatra No. 14 is there. Chitra Nakshatra in on 180° of the Moon's Aswini. Magha nakshatra is 5th date Chitra is 14th that is on 14th of October at his 75 he will pass away. Add 75 in his birth year 1872, (1872 plus 75)=1947. That is Tuesday 14th of October 1947 He died on that day.

Shree N. C. Kelkar

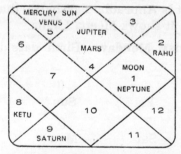

Birth date 25.8.1872

Date of expiry 14.10.1949

Long. 85°-30' East

Lat. 17°-14' North

Birth time 4-46 hours.

Example No. 3. Birth date 26/27.6.1864. We will see first the birth day of the native. 1800=4, 64=3, June=3 birth date is 27=27 plus 3 plus 3 plus 4=37 divided by 7=Remainder is 2=Monday is the Birth day. 26th of June shows Sunday. It seems that the birth time is on the border of both the days. See the month 22nd of June to 21st of July in the year 1864 in the third part of the Southern hemisphere. Monday shows 2-30 hours, it is on the border of Mesha rashi. Deduct 20' of Ayanachalana, 2-30—20' =2-10' means Bharani nakshatra or 2 solar degrees of the declination rashi Mesha. Friday is on 180° of Monday. Shukra is the lord of Friday as well as he is the Lord of Vrishabha and Thula rashi.

See 2 degrees of Mesha declination on Friday, it shows 17°-47′ Latitude North. Moon is the Lord of Monday as well as Karka rashi, then see the second part of the southern hemisphere for Karka rashi, Friday shows 6-30 hours. Deduct one hour the difference of Sunday, 6-30-1=5-30 hours. See the Longitude chart for 5-30 hours, it shows 82°-30′ add 3° more for Monday (Friday 0°, Thursday 1°, Wednesday 2°, Tuesday 3°) 82°-30′ plus 3°=85°-30′ is the Longitude east. From 14th June to 14th July Sun is in Mithuna Rashi. The third part of the Southern hemisphere Monday shows 2-30 hours but due to the spherical triangle it is a negative nakshatra, deduct 2 hours the difference of the negative part. 2-30—2=30′=0° or 27 nakshatra Revati, it shows the Moon is in her negative nakshatra Revati, her positive nakshatra is Hasta, Sun is in Mithuna rashi. Moon is in Meena rashi, Moon is the Lord of Karka rashi and Karka rashi is the opening rashi of the month June, in solar system Vrischika rashi is the opening rashi. In solar system opening Month of the 1864 year is in the third house, in Lunnar system Shravana nakshatra of the Moon is on 180° of Aslesha and in Solar system Rohini nakshatra is on 180° of Anuradha, native is born in the solar month, then 22nd of January to 21st of December third house, 22nd of December to 21st of November second house, 22nd of November to 21st of October first house, 22nd of October to 21st of September Twelfth house, 22nd of September to 21 of August eleventh house, 22nd of August to 21 of July tenth house, 22nd of July to 21st of June nineth house, here it is Anuradha nakshatra, that is Vrischika rashi is in the nineth house, it shows Meena Lagna.

Put the birth date on the birth day Monday. Birth date is 27=2 plus 7=9

2	4	6	8
Mon	Wed	Fri	Sun
3	5	7	9
Tue	Thur	Sat	Mon

It shows 2-4-6-8 years are bad for the native, in these years 3-5-7-9 months are bad and the Moon is in the Revati nakshatra, it means 3-5-7-9 dates are bad in the above months, 3-5-7-9 years are good and in these years 2-4-6-8 months as well as 2-4-6-8 dates are good. The Sun is working on behalf of Saturn and the Moon is working on behalf of Venus. The opening rashi of the Moon in Birth month is Karka. Makara rashi is on 180° of Karka. Makara rashi shows the month September. Aslesha nakshatra No. 9 is the opening nakshatra of the Moon, the Moon is in Revati nakshatra No. 27, that is 27th of September is the date. Moon is in Bharani nakshatra and Bharani nakshatra is negative, it seems that Revati is right ascension of the Moon and Bharani nakshatra is Declination nakshatra of the Moon. Aridra is the right ascension of the Sun and Pushya nakshatra is declination nakshatra of the Sun. So count declination nakshatra Bharani No. 2 of the Moon upto declination nakshatra of the Sun, Pushya No. 8. Aswini 2, Bharani 11, Krittika 20, Rohini 29, Mriga 38, Aridra 47, Punarvasu 56, Pushya 65 this is what the Longevity of the native. Add 65 years in the birth year, 1864 plus 65=1929, that is 27th of September 1929 is the last day of the native.

Shree S. M. Paranjape

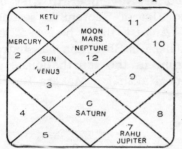

Birth date 26/27.6.1864

Date of expiry 27.9.1929

Birth time 24-20 hours

Long. 85°-30′ East

Lat. 17°-47′ North

Example No. 4. Birth date 1.8.1879. We will see the birth day first, 1800=4, 79=7, August=1, Birth date is 1=1 plus 1 plus 7 plus 4=13 divided by 7=Remainder is 6=Friday is the birth day. See the year 1879 in the month of 22nd of July to 21st of August. The second part of the southern hemisphere Friday shows 13-30 hours, but due to the spherical triangle it is a negative part. Shukra is the Lord of Friday as well as he is the Lord of Vrishabha and Thula rashi. Vrischika rashi is on 180° of Vrishabha. Tuesday is on 180° of Friday, then see second part of the Northern hemisphere for Vrishabha rashi. Tuesday shows 3-30 hours and Friday shows 23-30 hours. Friday of Vrischika rashi shows 13-30 hours, add 2 hours the difference of the Southern hemisphere, 13-30 hours plus 2 hours= 15-30 hours, deduct these hours from the Friday of Vrishabha rashi. 23-30—15.30=8 hours is the Latitude, see the other rashi of the Mangal, Mesha which is the Declination rashi of Shukra, 8 hours means eighth nakshatra or 8 solar degree. See 8° of Declination of the Mesha rashi on Tuesday, it shows 17° Latitude North. Now Tuesday of Vrishabha rashi shows 3-30 hours, add 2 hours the difference of the Southern hemisphere, 3-30 plus 2=5-30 hours. See the Longitude chart for 5-30 hours, it shows 82°-30′ add the Longitude of the Venus. (Tuesday 1°, Wednesday 2°, Thursday 3°, Friday 0°=3°) 82°-30′ plus 3°=85°-30′ Longitude East.

Friday of Vrischika rashi shows 13-30 hours but due to spherical triangle it is negative, 13-30 hours means Hasta nakshatra, it is negative, Shravana nakshatra is the greater nakshatra, it shows that the Moon is in Shravana nakshatra and Venus is in Hasta nakshatra. From 14th of July to 14th of August Sun is in Karka rashi, that is the Sun is in Aslesha nakshatra on 180° of the Shravana. 21st of July to 21st of August shows Lunar month, Shravana nakshatra will be in Lunar month horoscope or Aslesha nakshatra will be in solar month horoscope.

1879 year is in the eleventh house of the Lunar horoscope, then 22nd January to 21st of December eleventh house, 22nd of December to 21 of November twelfth house, 22nd of November to 21st of October first house, 22nd of October to 21st of September second house, 22nd of September to 21st of August third house, 22nd of August to 21st of July fourth house, here is Shravana nakshatra of Makara rashi. Then put Makara rashi in the fourth house, it shows Thula Lagna, Moon is in Shravana Nakshatra Makara Rashi. Sun is in Kara Rashi.

Put the birth date on the birth day.

3	5	7	9
Fri	Sun	Tues	Thur
4	6	8	1
Sat	Mon	Wed	Fri

It shows that the Moon is working on behalf of Venus, and the Sun is working on behalf of Mars, in Lunar horoscope group of the Sun years are bad that is 3-5-7-9 years are bad, moon is in Shravana nakshatra that is group of the moon months are bad in 3-5-7-9 years, and 4-6-8-1 are the dates which are bad in 4-6-8-1 months. The right ascension nakshatra of Mars is Aswini and declination nakshatra is Krittika, Chitra nakshatra is on 180° of the Aswini that is 7th aspect of the Mars. Right ascension is Chitra and Declination is Vishakha No. 7. The right ascension nakshatra of Venus is Hasta and declination nakshatra is Swati No. 6. Venus is the Lord of the eighth house, that is his right ascension nakshatra is Rohini and declination nakshatra is Aridra No. 6. So we will count declination nakshatra of Mars No. 7 upto Venus, declination nakshatra Aridra No. 6, Aswini 7, Bharani 16, Krittika 25, Rohini 34, Mriga 43, Aridra 52 this is what the Longevity of the native. The right ascension nakshatra of the Moon is Shravana and declination nakshatra is Shatataraka, Shatataraka nakshatra is in Kumbha rashi. Kumbha rashi shows the months of June (January is in the eleventh house, count 22nd of January to 21st of December Simha and so upto Kumbha rashi) Aridra is the declination nakshatra 6 Swati is No. 15, add 52 years in the birth year, 1879 plus 52= 1931, that is on 15.6.1931 he died.

Shree A. B. Kolhatkar

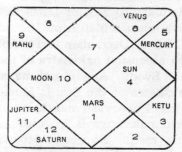

Birth date 1.8.1879

Date of expiry 15.6.1931

Long. 85°-30′ east

Lat. 17° North

Example No. 5. Birth date 29.12.1904. We will see the birth day. 1900=2, 4=5, December=4, Birth date is 29=29 plus 4 plus 5 plus 2=40 divided by 7=Remainder is 5=Thursday is the birth day. See the month 22nd of december to 21st of January in the year 1904 the third part of the Northern hemisphere Thursday shows 11-30 hours, but due to the spherical triangle Makara rashi and Thursday is negative. Monday is on 180° of Thursday. Monday shows 8-30 hours. Jupiter is the Lord of Meena and Dhanu rashi as well as he is the Lord of Thursday. Then see the second part of the northern hemisphere for Meena rashi. Thursday shows 11-30 hours and Monday shows 15-30 hours, add two hours the difference of the negative part. 15-30 plus 2=17-30 hours.

Now deduct 20′ of Ayanachalana 17-30′-20′=17-10′ hours. 17-10 means 17 nakshatra or 17° solar degrees. See 17° of Makara on Thursday in right ascension chart of the north Latitude, it shows, 317°-55′, deduct 300° of Makara, 317°-55′—300°=17°-15′ is North Latitude. Thursday shows 11-30 hours, add 2 hours the difference of the negative part. 11-30 plus 2=13-30 hours, it shows Mesha Lagna, 13-30 hours means Hasta nakshatra, it shows the Moon in Kanya Rashi. Deduct the Monday hours from 13-30 hours, 13-30—8-30=5 hours. See Longitude chart for 5 hours, it shows 75°, add 8° more the difference of the Monday (Monday 1, Tuesday 2, Wednesday 3, Thursday 4, Friday 5, Saturday 6, Sunday 7, Monday 8) 75° plus 8=83° is Longitude East. (The year 1904 is in the West converted into East by adding 8° More).

Put the birth date on the birth day.

4	6	8	1
Thur	Sat	Mon	Wed
5	7	9	2
Fri	Sun	Tues	Thur

It shows that the Moon is working on behalf of Jupiter and the Sun is working on behalf of Mercury, the Lord of the Kanya rashi. From 22nd of December to 21st of January the period is of the Sun, but opening rashi of the month is of the Moon, the beginning of the year 1904 is in the fourth house, 22nd January to 21st of December fourth house, Put Karka rashi in the fourth house which is on 180° of Makara, it shows Mesha Lagna. From 14th of December to 14th of January the Sun is in Dhanu rashi. Right ascension nakshatra of the Moon is Hasta and declination nakshatra is Swati. Aswini nakshatra is on 180° of Swati. Right ascension nakshatra of the Sun is Moola and declination nakshatra is Uttarashadha, Punarvasu nakshatra is on 180° of the Uttarashadha. Punarvasu nakshatra is in Mithuna rashi. Mercury is the Lord of Mithuna rashi. So count Moon's seventh aspect nakshatra Aswini upto Punarvasu nakshatra. Aswini 1, Bharani 10, Krittika 19, Rohini 28, Mriga 37, Aridra 46, Punarvasu 55, this is what the Longevity of the native. Mars is the Lord of the eighth house as well as he is the Lord of the first house, first house shows the month of October.

Moon is on 180° of the Jupiter, that is, the date will be of the Moon and the day will be of the Jupiter. Thursday, that is on 8.10.1959 he died, it shows 4-6-8-1 years, months, and dates were bad, 2-5-7- 9 years, months, and dates were good to him.

Dr. P. L. Deshmukh

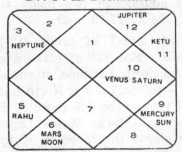

Birth date 29.12.1904

Date of expiry 8.10.1959

Long. 83° East

Lat. 17°-55′ North

Example No. 6. Birth date 2/3.2.1870. We will find the birth day. 1800=4, 70=3, February=2, birth date 2=3 plus 2 plus 3 plus 4=12 divided by 7=Remainder is 5=Thursday is the birth day. Birth date two shows Wednesday, it means the birth time is on the border of Wednesday. See the month 22nd of January to 21st of February in the year 1870, the third part of the Northern hemisphere, Thursday shows 11-30 hours and Vrishabha rashi, but due to the Spherical triangle it is a negative part. Jupiter is the Lord of Thursday as well as he is the Lord of Dhanu and Meena rashi. Then see Meena rashi of Guru. In the fourth part of the Northern hemisphere, Thursday is not there, then see Monday which is on

180° of Thursday. Monday shows 8-30 hours. Moon is the Lord of Monday as well as she is the Lord of Karka rashi. Then see Karka rashi in the first part of the Northern hemisphere. Monday shows 15-30 hours, deduct 20'=15-30—20'=15-10' hours, it means 15th nakshatra or 15 solar degrees. See Latitude chart for 15° on Monday the right ascension of Karka rashi, it shows 138°-6' deduct 120° of the Karka rashi, 138°-6'—120°=18°-6' North Latitude. The first part of the northern hemisphere Monday shows 15-30 hours, and third part as well as fourth part of Northern hemisphere Monday shows 8-30 hours, add 2 hours the difference of the negative part in 8-30 hours. 8-30 plus 2=10-30 hours and deduct these hours from the first part Monday, 15-30—10-30=5 hours.

See the Longitude chart 5 hours, and add 9° of the west Monday. 5 hours shows 75° plus 9°=84° East. The fourth part of the Northern Hemisphere Monday shows 8-30 hours, deduct 2 hours the difference of the negative part 8-30—2=6-30 hours of Kumbha rashi, it means that the Moon is in Shatataraka. The third part of the Northern hemisphere Thursday shows 11-30 hour which is negative due to the spherical triangle, the greater nakshatra is Bharani, it means that the Jupiter is in Bharani nakshatra. From 22nd of January to 21st of February Lunar horoscope works. Beginning of the 1870 January is in the eleventh house, then 22nd of January to 21st of December eleventh house, 22nd of December to 21st of November twelfth house, 22nd of November to 21st of October first house, 22nd of October to 21st of September second house, 22nd of September to 21st of August third house, 22nd of August to 21st of July fourth house, 22nd of July to 21st of June fifth house, 22nd of June to 21st of May sixth house, 22nd of May to 21st of April seventh house, 22nd of April to 21st of March eighth house, 22nd of March to 21st of February nineth house, here is the opening rashi Karka of the birth month, it shows Vrischika Lagna. Birth time is Jupiter's nakshatra Bharani. Bharani means 2-30 hours. From 14th January to 14th February Sun is in Makara rashi. Put the birth date on the birth day.

5	7	9	2
Thur	Sat	Mon	Wed
6	8	1	3
Fri	Sun	Tue	Thur

Sunday shows eighth nakshatra, it is his seventh aspect nakshatra, it means the right ascension nakshatra of the Sun is Shravana and Declination nakshatra is Shatataraka. 7th aspect nakshatra of Shatataraka is Magha, Moon is in Shatataraka, it means 6-8-1-3 years are bad and in these years 5-7-9-2 months are bad and 5-7-9-2 dates are bad for the above months. 5-7-9-2 years are good and in these years 6-8-1-3 months as well as 6-8-1-3 dates are good, we want to see the Longevity of the native.

Sun is working on behalf of Jupiter and Moon is working on behalf of Mars. Both the planets the Sun and the Moon are aspecting the Magha nakshatra. So count Moon's nakshatra No. 1 upto Magha, Aswini 1, Bharani 10, Krittika 19, Rohini 28, Mriga 37, Aridra 46, Punarvasu 55, Pushya 64, Aslesha 73, Magha 82 this is the Longevity of the Native. Mars is the lord of the sixth house and first house Jupiter is in the sixth house, in the house of Mars, sixth house shows the month of May. Bharani nakshatra of Jupiter shows the date. Bharani 2, Purva 11, Purvashadha 20 and Bharani 29, add 82 years in his birth year 1870 plus 82=1952 that is 29th of May 1952 is the last day of the native.

Shree L. R. Gokhale

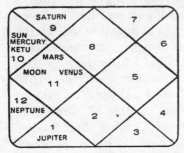

Birth time 2-30 hours
Lat. 18°-6' North
Long. 84° East
Date of expiry 29.5.1952
Birth date 3.2.1870

Example No. 7. Birth date 22.2.1880. We will see the birth day. 1800=4, 80=2, February=2, Birth date 22=22 plus 2 plus 2 plus 4=30 divided by 7=Remainder is 2=Birth day is Monday. See the month 22nd of February to 21 of March in the year 1880 the second part of the northern hemisphere, Monday shows 10-30 hours, but due to the spherical triangle it is negative, Moon is the Lord of Monday as well as she is the Lord of Karka rashi, then see Karka rashi of the Moon in the first part of the northern hemisphere. Add 2 hours the difference of the negative part. 10-30 hours plus 2=12-30 hours. Friday is on 180° · of Monday, Friday shows 14-30 hours, add 2 hours of the negative part, 14-30 plus 2=16-30 hours, deduct 20' of Ayanachalana, 16-30—20'=16-10' hours, it means 16th nakshatra or 16 solar degrees. See the declination chart of the Latitude for 16° on Monday of Karka rashi, it shows 17°-57' Latitude North.

Second part of the northern hemisphere Friday shows 7-30 hours, deduct it from the hours of Monday, 12-30—7-30=5 hours. See the Longitude chart for 5 hours, it shows 75° add 9° more of the West Monday. 75° plus 9°=84° Longitude East. Moon is the Lord of Monday. Monday shows 10-30 hours but due to the spherical triangle it is negative, 10-30 hours means Magha nakshatra is negative. Moola nakshatra is the greater nakshatra, add 2 hours the difference of the negative part 19 plus 2=21 Uttarashadha nakshatra. Punarvasu is on 180° of the Uttarashadha, that is the Moon is in Punarvasu nakshatra and Mithuna rashi, 14th of February to 14th of March Sun is in Kumbha rashi, 22nd of the February to 21st of March shows the Solar horoscope. The beginning of the 1880 year January is in third house, then.

22nd of January to 21st of December third house, 22nd of December to 21st of November second house, 22nd of November to 21st of October first house, 22nd of October to 21st of September twelfth house, 22nd of September to 21st August eleventh house, 22nd of August to 21st of July tenth house, 22nd of July to 21st of June nineth house, 22nd of June 21st of May eighth house, 22nd of May to 21st of April seventh house, 22nd of April to 21st of March sixth house, 22nd of March to 21st of February fifth house, 22nd of February to 21st of January fourth house, here is the opening rashi of the month. Thula it shows Karka Lagna. Put the birth date on the birth day.

4	6	8	1
Mon	Wed	Fri	Sun
5	7	9	2
Tue	Thur	Sat	Mon

It shows the Moon is working on behalf of Saturn and Sun is working on behalf of Venus. The right ascension nakshatra of the Moon is Punarvasu and declination nakshatra is Aslesha. Shravana nakshatra is seventh aspect nakshatra of Mars. Shravana nakshatra is No. 4. Right ascension nakshatra of the Sun is Shatataraka and declination nakshatra is Uttarabhadrapada No. 8, it shows 4-6-8-1 years are bad and in these years 2-5-7-9 months as well as dates are bad. 2-5-7-9 years are good and in these years 4-6-8-1 months as well as dates are good.

We want to see the Longevity of the native, then count Moon's aspecting nakshatra No. 4 upto Sun's declination nakshatra No. 8, opening rashi of this month is Thula and aspecting rashi is Mesha, then start from Aswini; Aswini 4, Bharani 13, Krittika 22, Rohini 31, Mriga 40, Aridra 49, Punarvasu 58, Pushya 67. This is what the Longevity of the native. Moon's declination nakshatra is Aslesha and aspecting nakshatra is Shravana, Makara rashi, it shows month of May. Month of May shows Tuesday and aspecting nakshatra of May is Aslesha No. 9, that is on 9th May at his 67th he died, add 67 years, in the birth year 1880 plus 67=1947, it means 9th May 1947 he died.

Shree N. W. Bhide

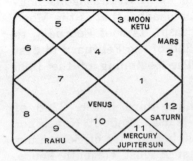

Birth date 22.2.1880
Date of expiry 9.5.1947
Long. 84° East
Lat. 17°-57′ North.

Example No. 8. Birth date 9.5.1866. We will see the birth day, 1800=4, 66=5, May=7, Birth date is 9=9 plus 7 plus 5 plus 4=25 divided by 7=Remainder is 4=Wednesday is the birth day. See the month 22nd April to 21st May in the year 1866 the third part of the Northern hemisphere, but there is no Wednesday in the third part, Budha is the Lord of Wednesday as well as he is the Lord of Mithuna and Kanya rashi, Sunday is on 180° of the Wednesday. Sunday shows 11-30 hours, but due to the spherical triangle it is negative part, then see Mithuna rashi of Budha in the fourth part of the northern hemisphere Wednesday shows 7-30 hours. Deduct 7-30 , hours from the hours of the Sunday 11-30—7-30=4 hours. See the Longitude chart for 4 hours, it shows 60° deduct 6° of the Wednesday (Sun 0°, Monday 1°, Tuesday 2°, Wednesday 3°, Thursday 4°, Friday, 5° and Saturday 6°) 60°—6°=54° Longitude East. See the Latitude chart for 11-30 hours, deduct 20′ of the Ayanachalana, 11-30 —20′=11-10′ hours, 11-10 hours means 11 nakshatra or 11 solar degrees, then see 11° of Mithuna rashi on Sunday the right ascension chart for Latitude North. It shows 24°-1′ Latitude North. From 14th of the April to 14th of May the Sun is in Mesha rashi, Sunday shows 11-30 hours, but it is negative due to the spherical triangle. Bharani nakshatra is greater nakshatra, it means Sun is in Bharani nakshatra and Moon's aspect nakshatra is Purva, it shows the Moon is in Kumbha rashi.

Solar horoscope works from 22nd of April to 21st of May. Opening month January of the year 1866 is in the third house, then 22nd of the January to 21st of December third house, 22nd of December to 21st of November second house, 22nd of November to 21st of October first house, 22nd of October to 21st of September twelfth house, 22nd of September to 21st of August eleventh house.

22nd of August to 21st of July tenth house, 22nd of July to 21st of June nineth house, 22nd of June to 21st of May eighth house, here is the opening Rashi Mithuna of Budha, it shows Vrischika Lagna, Moon is in Kumbha rashi and the Sun is in Mesha. Budha is the Lord of the eighth and eleventh house, his aspect is on Dhanu and Meena rashi. Budha is a neutral planet, his aspect planet or the lord of aspect rashi gives the result. Jupitor is the lord of aspect rashi, then put the birth date on Thursday instead of birth day.

8	1	3	5
Wed	Fri	Sun	Tue
9	2	4	6
Thur	Sat	Mon	Wed

It shows both the planets, the Sun as well as the Moon are working on behalf of Mercury. Right ascension nakshatra of the Sun is Bharani and Declination nakshatra is Rohini. Right ascension nakshatra of the Moon is Shatataraka and declination nakshatra is Uttarabhadrapada, her aspect nakshatra is Hasta, which is on 180° of Uttarabhadrapada. Sun's nakshatra of declination is Rohini, Moon's aspect declination nakshatra is Hasta. Both nakshatras are of No. 4. Then count No. 4 upto No. 6. Right ascension nakshatra of the Moon is No. 6 Shatataraka, because both the nakshatras Hasta and Rohini are originally of the Moon, Aswini 4, Bharani 13, Krittika 22, Rohini 31, Mriga 40, Aridra 49 this is what the Longevity of the native. Aspect rashi of the Kanya Rashi is Meena, Meena rashi shows the month of February. Aspect rashi of Mithuna is Dhanu. Moola nakshatra is on 180° of Aridra, then the date must be of Moola nakshatra, that is on 19th of the February at his 49 years he died. Add 49 years in his birth year, 1866 plus 49=1915. i.e. on 19th February 1915 he died.

Shree **G. K. Gokhale**

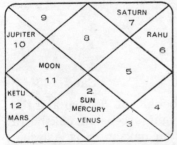

Birth date 9.5.1866
Date of Expiry 19.2.1915
Long. 54° East
Lat. 24°-1' North.

Example No. 9. Birth date 2.10.1869. We will find the birth day, 1800=4, 69=2, October=6, Birth date is 2=2 plus 6 plus 2 plus 4=14 divided by 7=Remainder is 0=Saturday is the Birth day. See the month 22nd of September to 21st of October in the

year 1869 the third part of the Southern hemisphere Saturday shows 14-30 hours and Makara rashi, but due to the spherical triangle Makara rashi is negative.   14-30 hours means Chitra nakshatra, it is negative. Dhanishtha nakshatra is the greater nakshatra. Dhanishtha nakshatra is in Makara rashi, it is negative, Aslesha nakshatra is on 180° of the Dhanishtha, then see fourth part of the northern hemisphere for Karka rashi. Saturday shows 24-30 hours, add 2 hours the difference of Southern hemisphere, 24-30 plus 2=26-30 hours, it s negative (26-30 means Uttarabhadrapada nakshatra) Pushya nakshatra is the greater nakshatra, it shows Karka rashi. Tuesday is on 180° of Saturday. Mars is the Lord of Vrischika and Mesha rashi. Then see the Vrischika rashi of Mars, in the first part of northern hemisphere. Tuesday shows 10-30 hours, add two hours the difference of the negative part, in Saturday hours, 14-30 plus 2=16-30 hours, deduct 10-30 hours of Tuesday from 16-30 hours=16-30—10-30=6 hours is the Longitude. See the Longitude chart for 6 hours, shows 90° East.

Dhanishtha nakshatra is No. 23, it means 23° solar degrees of makara rashi. See the Latitude chart for 23° on Tuesday, it shows 324°-21′ north, deduct 300° of the Makara rashi, 324°-21′—300°= 24°-21′ Latitude North. From 22nd of September to 21st of October Lunar horoscope works, then the opening month January of the year 1869 is in the eleventh house, 22nd of January to 21st of December eleventh house, 22nd of December to 21st of November twelfth house, 22nd of November to 21st of October first house, 22nd of October 21st of September second house, here is the opening rashi of the Mars Vrischika, it shows Thula Lagna, from 14th of September to 14th of October the Sun is in Kanya rashi. Birth day has shown 14-30 hours, that is Chitra nakshatra of the Mars. Birth date has shown Jupiter's aspect nakshatra or the nakshatra of the Venus. Tuesday shows Jupiter's nakshatra No. 7 or 7-30 hours, then put the Mar's nakshatra No. 5 on the birth date.

5	7	1	3
Sat	Mon	Wed	Fri
6	8	2	4
Sun	Tue	Thur	Sat

It shows that the Moon is working on behalf of Saturn and the Sun is working on behalf of Mars. The right ascension nakshatra of the Moon is Punarvasu and her declination nakshatra is Aslesha, the right ascension nakshatra of the Sun is Uttara and declination nakshatra is Chitra, his right ascension aspect nakshatra is Purvabhadrapada and declination nakshatra is Revati. Declination nakshatra of both the planets Sun and the Moon is No. 9. Then

218

count Moon's nakshatra Punarvasu upto No. 9, Aswini 7, Bharani 16, Krittika 25, Rohini 34, Mriga 43, Aridra 52, Punarvasu 61, Pushya 70, Aslesha 79, this is the Longevity of the native.

Opening rashi of the Moon is in the month of January or opening rashi of the Solar horoscope on 1900 years is fourth house, that is Makara rashi of this horoscope shows January month. Krittika the aspect nakshatra of Venus is in the eighth house, Krittika 3, Uttara 12, Uttarashadha 21, and Krittika 30, this is what the Last date of the native. Add 79 years in the birth year, 1869 plus 79=1948, that is on 30.1.1948 he died.

Mahatma Gandhi

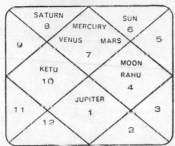

Birth date 2.10.1869
Date of expiry 30.1.1948
Long. 90° East
Lat. 24°-21' North
Birth time 7-30 hours.

Example No. 10. Birth date 24.8.1908. We will see the birth day. 1900=2, 8=3, August=1, Birth date is 24,=24 plus 1 plus 3 plus 2=30 divided by 7=Remainder is 2=Monday is the birth day. See the month 22nd of August to 21st of September in the year 1908. The second part of the northern hemisphere Monday shows 21-30 hours, but due to the spherical triangle it is negative part. The Moon is the Lord of Monday as well as she is the Lord of Karka rashi, then see Karka rashi of the Moon in the fourth part of the southern hemisphere. Monday shows 4-30 hours, it means Rohini nakshatra, it is of the Moon, it shows Karka rashi, add two hours in Rohini nakshatra, 4-30+2=6-30 hours in Longitude Friday is on 180° of the Monday. Venus is the Lord of Friday as well as he is the Lord of Vrishabha ·and Thula rashi. Then see Thula rashi in the second part of the southern hemisphere, Friday shows 8-30 hours, deduct 1-30 hours of Friday from Karka rashi, 8-30—1-30 hours=7 hours means Punarvasu nakshatra. That is Moon and Venus are in Punarvasu nakshatra, Karka rashi, 6 hours Longitude means 90° Deduct 5° of the Venus (Monday 1°, Tuesday 2°, Wednesday 3°, Thursday 4°, Friday 5°, 90°—5°=85° Longitude East.

The second part of the Northern hemisphere Monday shows 21-30 hours, deduct 20' of Ayanachalana, 21-30—20'=21-10' hours, it means 21 nakshatra or 21 solar degrees, then see Latitude chart for 21° on Monday of Mesha rashi, it shows 47°-59', deduct 30° of the Mesha 47°-59'—30°=17°-50' Latitude North. 22nd of the August to 21st of September is the period of Solar horoscope, but Mesha rashi is negative, then instead of the Solar horoscope, the Lunar horoscope works for the native. The opening month of the year 1908 is in the eleventh house, then 22nd of January to 21st of December eleventh house, 22nd of December to 21st of November twelfth house, 22nd of November to 21st of October first house, 22nd of October to 21st of September second house, 22nd of September to 21st of August third house, here is the aspect nakshatra of the Venus and Moon (Uttarashadha first part is on 180° of Punarvasu third part), then put the Dhanu rashi in the third house, it shows Thula rashi.

Birth date is 24, it means Shatataraka nakshatra, Purva nakshatra is aspect nakshatra of the Shatataraka, then put the 7th aspect nakshatra on the birth day.

2	4	6	8
Mon	Wed	Fri	Sun
1	3	5	7
Tue	Thur	Sat	Mon

It shows that the Moon is working for Venus and the Sun is working for the Moon. The right ascension nakshatra of the Moon is Punarvasu and her declination nakshatra is Aslesha. Shravana nakshatra is her seventh aspect nakshatra. The Sun is in Purva and his declination nakshatra is Hasta. Both the declination nakshatras are originally of the Moon, then count No. 4 nakshatra upto No. 3, the aspect nakshatra of the Venus eighth house nakshatra Krittika, Aswini 4, Bharani 13, Krittika 22, this is the Longevity of the native. Vrishabha rashi of Venus is in the month of March, Uttarashadha is right ascension nakshatra 7th aspect nakshatra of the Moon and Dhanishtha is her Declination nakshatra. Dhanishtha is No. 23 that is on 23rd of March at his 22 he died. Add 22 years in his birth year 1908, 1908 plus 22=1930, he died on 23rd March 1930.

Shree S. H. Rajguru

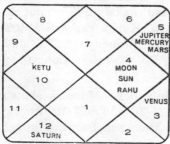

Birth date 24.8.1908
Date of expiry 23.3.1930
Long. 85° East.
Lat. 17°-59' North.

Example No. 11. Birth date 19.5.1910. We will see the birth day of the native. 1900=2, 10=5, May=7, Birth date is 19=19 plus 7 plus 5 plus 2=33 divided by 7=Remainder is 5=Thursday is the birth day. See the month 22nd April to 21st of May in the year 1910. The second part of the Southern hemisphere Thursday shows 1-30 hours, but due to the spherical triangle it is a negative rashi. Jupiter is the Lord of Thursday as well he is the Lord of Meena and Dhanu rashi. Meena rashi as well as Thursday is here, still it is negative part, then it is aspect nakshatra of the Moon, 1-30 hours means Aswini nakshatra, Chitra nakshatra is on 180° of the Aswini that is the Moon is in Chitra nakshatra. See the other rashi of Jupiter in the fourth part of the southern hemisphere. Thursday shows 18-30 hours. Monday is on 180° of the Thursday. Moon is the Lord of Monday as well as she is the Lord of Karka rashi, then see the third part of the northern hemisphere for Karka rashi. Monday shows 12-30 hours, deduct 12-30 hours of Monday from 18-30 hours, 18-30—12-30=6 hours is Longitude. See the Longitude chart for 6 hours it shows 90°, deduct 6° of the Monday from Thursday (Thursday 2, Friday 3, Saturday 4, Sunday 5, Monday 6°), 90°-6°=84° East. Now deduct the 1-30 hours of Meena rashi, Thursday from 18-30 of Dhanu rashi. Thursday 18-30—1-30=17 hours or 17 nakshatra or 17 solar degrees.

See 17° of the Dhanu rashi on Monday in the Latitude chart, it shows 288°-11', deduct 270° of Dhanu rashi 288°-11'—270=18°-11' Latitude North, 22nd of April to 21st of May is the period of Solar horoscope. Opening month of the year 1910 is in the fourth house. Then 22nd of January to 21st of December fourth house, 22nd of December to 21st November third house, 22nd November to 21st of October second house, 22nd of October to 21st of September first house, 22nd of September to 21st of August twelfth house, 22nd of August to 21st of July eleventh house, 22nd of July to 21st of June tenth house, 22nd of June to 21st of May nineth house, 22nd of May to 21st of April eighth house, here is Makara Rashi the seventh aspect rashi of the Karka. It shows Mithuna Lagna. The Moon is in Kanya rashi. 14th of May to 14 of June Sun is in Vrishabha rashi.

Put the birth date on the birth day.

1	3	5	7
Thurs	Sat	Mon	Wed
2	4	6	8
Fri	Sun	Tues	Thur

Saturn is the Lord of the eighth house, Moon is in triangle of the eighth house, it shows the Moon is working on behalf of Saturn and the Sun is working on behalf of Jupiter.

Right ascension of the Moon is Chitra nakshatra and her declination nakshatra is Vishakha, her right ascension aspect nakshatra is Aswini and declination nakshatra is Krittika, right ascension Nakshatra of the Sun is Krittika and his declination nakshatra is Mriga, then count Moon's aspect declination nakshatra Krittika 3 upto Sun's declination nakshatra, Mriga 5, Aswini 3, Bharani 12, Krittika 21, Rohini 30, Mriga 39. This is the Longevity of the native. Simha rashi is the 7th aspect rashi of the Saturn the Lord of the eighth and ninth house, Simha rashi month is November, Swati No. 6 first date Shatataraka, Second date of No. 6, that is 15 November at his 39 his last day will take place, add 39 years in his birth year, 1910 plus 39=1949 on 15th of November 1949 he died.

Shree N. V. Godse

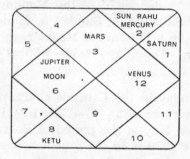

Birth date 19.5.1910
Date of expiry 15.11.1949
Long. 84° East
Lat. 18°-11' North.

Example No. 12. Birth date 27.11.1888. We will see the birth day of the native. 1800=4, 88=5, November is 2, Birth date is 27=27 plus 2 plus 5 plus 4=38 divided by 7=Remainder is 3=Tuesday is the birth day. See the month 22nd of November to 21st of December in the year 1888 the first part of the southern hemisphere Tuesday shows 6-30 hours, and Dhanu rashi due to the spherical triangle it is a negative part. Mars is the lord of Tuesday as well as he is the Lord of Vrischika and Mesha rashi. Vrischika rashi as well as Tuesday is here but due to the spherical triangle is a negative part. Friday is on 180° of the Tuesday, Friday shows 2-30 hours. Now see the other rashi of the Mars, in the second part of the northern hemisphere Tuesday shows 16-30 hours. Now Friday of Vrischika rashi shows 2-30 hours, it means Bharani nakshatra, it is a negative nakshatra, Purva is the greater nakshatra, it is in Simha rashi, that is, the Moon is in Simha rashi and the the Venus is in triangle of the Purva nakshatra. Bharani is negative, then the Venus is in Purvashadha. Tuesday of the northern hemiphere second part shows 16-30 hours, it means Vishakha nakshatra

222

of Guru which shows the aspect rashi of Venus, that is, Guru is in Vrischika rashi on 180° of the Vrishabha rashi.

The first part of the southern hemisphere Tuesday shows 6-30 hours, deduct 20' of the Ayanachalana, 6-30—20'=6-10' hours means Aridra nakshatra, it is a negative nakshatra, Shatataraka is the greater nakshatra. Shattataraka is No. 24, that is 24 solar degrees. See Latitude chart for 24° of Vrischika rashi on Tuesday, it shows 263°-36', deduct 240° of Vrischika 263°-36'—240°=23°-36' Latitude North, Aridra nakshatra that is the Longitude. See the Longitude chart for 6-10' hours. It shows 92°-30°, deduct 4° of the Venus (Tuesday 1°, Wednesday 2°, Thursday 3°, Friday 4°) 92°-30'—4°= 88°-30' Longitude East.

22nd of November to 21st of December is the period of the Lunar horoscope. The opening month of the year 1888 is in the eleventh house. Then 22nd of January to 21st of December eleventh house, 22nd of December to 21st of November twelfth house, here is Vrischika rashi of Mars, then put Vrischika rashi in the twelfth house, it shows Dhanu Lagna. The Moon is in Simha rashi, from 14th of November to 14th of December Sun is in Vrischika rashi.

The Moon is the Lord of the eighth house, her right ascension nakshatra is Purva and declination nakshatra is Hasta, her right ascension 7th aspect nakshatra is Purvabhadrapada and declination nakshatra is Revati No. 9. Right ascension nakshatra of the Sun is Vishakha and declination nakshatra is Jyestha No. 9. Both the planets Sun and the Moon show their declination aspect nakshatra No. 9. Moon is the Lord of the eighth house. Hasta and Shravana are her original nakshatras. Rohini is the aspect nakshatra of the Sun, then count No. 4 upto Aslesha No. 9, Aswini 4, Bharani 13, Krittika 22, Rohini 31, Mriga 40, Aridra 49, Punarvasu 58, Pushya 67, Aslesha 76. This is what the Longevity of the native. Declination nakshatra of the Moon is Hasta that is in Kanya rashi and Kanya rashi is in the month of February. Revati is her seventh aspect nakshatra. Revati is 27th nakshatra, it shows the date, add 76 years in the birth year 1888=1888 plus 76=1956 that is on 27th of the February 1956 he died. Put the birth date and 7th aspect nakshatra on the birth day.

8	2	4	6
Tue	Thur	Sat	Mon
3	5	7	9
Wed	Fri	Sun	Tue

It shows 2-4-6-8 years are bad for the native and in these years, 2-4-6-8 months are bad, in these months 3-5-7-9 dates as well as days of the date are bad, 3-5-7-9 years are good, in the years 3-5-7-9 months are good and in these months 2-4-6-8 days of the dates are good.

Shree G. V. Mavalankar

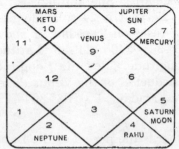

Birth date 27.11.1888

Date of expiry 27.2.1956

Long. 88° East.

Lat. 23°-36′ North

Example No. 13. Birth date 13.2.1809. We will see the birth day of native. 1800=4, 9=4, February=2, Birth date is 13=13 plus 2 plus 4 plus 4=23 divided by 7=Remainder is 2=Monday is the birth day. See the month 22nd of January to 21st of February in the year 1809. The second part of the Southern hemisphere Monday shows 1-30 hours, and Dhanu rashi. Thursday is on 180° of Monday. Moon is the Lord of Monday as well as she is the Lord of Karka rashi, then see Karka rashi of the Moon in the second part of the northern hemisphere, Monday shows 15-30 hours, deduct 1-30 hours of the negative Monday. 15-30—1-30=14 hours, is the aspect hours of Jupiter, 14 hours means Chitra nakshatra, it is the negative nakshatra of the Moon. The greater nakshatra is Dhanistha, that is the Moon is in Dhanistha nakshatra, it is the original nakshatra of Mars. Then Mars must be in the triangle of Dhanishtha. Jupiter is the Lord of Thursday as well as he is the Lord of Dhanu and Meena rashi. Then see Meena rashi. The fourth part of the northern hemisphere. Monday shows 8-30 hours, it is negative for Jupiter, 8-30 hours means Pushya nakshatra, Uttarabhadrapada is the greater nakshatra, it means Jupiter is in the Uttarabhadrapada nakshatra. Uttarabhadrapada nakshatra is the original of Saturn, it shows Saturn is in the triangle of Jupiter. The second part of the southern hemisphere Monday shows 1-30 hours, See the Longitude chart for 1-30 hours, It shows 22°-30′, add 8-30 hours of the Monday of Meena rashi, 22-30 plus 8-30=31°.

Now add 1-30 of the Monday of Dhanu rashi, 31 plus 1-30= 32-30 is the Longitude West. The second part of the northern hemisphere Karka rashi Monday shows 15-30 hours, deduct 1-30 hours of Southern hemisphere Monday, 15-30—1-30=14 hours. It means Chitra nakshatra, it is negative nakshatra. Dhanistha nakshatra is the greater nakshatra for the Moon, Dhanistha nakshatra is 23rd nakshatra or 23 solar degrees, then see 23° of Dhanu rashi on Thursday and deduct the degrees of Vrischika rashi, because Monday is on border of Vrischika. Dhanu rashi 23° Thursday Latitude shows 293°-58′, deduct 240° of Vrischika rashi, 293°-58′—240°=53°-58′ Latitude North.

22nd of January to 21st of February shows the period of the Moon. Opening month of the year 1809 is in the eleventh house, then 22nd of January to 21st of December eleventh house, 22nd of December to 21st of November twelfth house, 22nd of November to 21st of October first house, 22nd of October to 21st of September second house, 22nd of September to 21st of August third house, 22nd of August to 21st of July fourth house, 22nd of July to 21st of June fifth house, 22nd of June to 21st of May sixth house, 22nd of May to 21st of April seventh house, 22nd of April to 21st of March Eighth house, 22nd of March to 21st of February nineth house, 22nd of February to 21st of January tenth house, here is the seventh aspect rashi of Jupiter. Kanya is on 180° of Meena rashi, then put Kanya rashi in the tenth house, it shows Dhanu Lagna. From 14th of the January to 14th of February the Sun is in the Makara rashi. The Moon is in Makara rashi. It shows new-Moon day. Right ascension nakshatra of both planets is Dhanistha and declination nakshatra is Purvabhadrapada No. 7. The right ascension nakshatra of the Jupiter is Uttarabhadrapada and declination nakshatra is Aswini. Then count No. 1 upto No. 7, Aswini 1, Bharani 10, Krittika 19, Rohini 28, Mriga 37, Aridra 46, Punarvasu 55, this is the Longevity of the native. Moon is the Lord of the eight house, month of April is in the eighth house, put the birth date on the birth day.

6	8	1	3
Mon	Wed	Fri	Sun
7	9	2	4
Tue	Thur	Sat	Mon

It shows 1-3-6-8 years are bad, and in these years 7-9-2-4 months are bad and in these months 6-8-1-3 dates and days of the dates are bad.

Moon is the Lord of the eighth house nakshatra No. 6 of the Moon is bad upto Shatataraka that is Swati 6 and Shatataraka 15 date. Add 55 years in the birth year 1809 plus 55=1864 that is on 15th of April 1864 he died.

225

President Abraham Lincoln

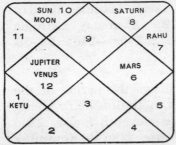

Birth date 13.2.1809

Date of expiry 15.4.1864

Long. 32°-30′ West

Lat. 53°-58′ North

Example No. 14. Birth date 1.9.1935. We will see the birth day of the native. 1900=2, 35=1, September=4 Birth date is 1=1 plus 4 plus 1 plus 2=8 divided by 7=Remainder is 1=Sunday is the birth day. See the month 22nd August to 21st of the September in the year 1935. The third part of the southern hemisphere for Sunday, but Sunday is not there in the part. Sun is the Lord of Sunday as well Simha rashi. Simha rashi is here. Wednesday is on 180° of Sunday. Wednesday shows 6-30 hours. Budha is the Lord of the Wednesday as well as he is the Lord of the Mithuna and Kanya rashi. Kanya rashi is here but it is negative due to the spherical triangle, then add 2 hours the difference of the negative part, 6-30 plus 2=8-30 hours means Pushya nakshatra, it is negative. Uttarabhadrapada is the greater nakshatra, it means Uttarabhadrapada is 7th aspect nakshatra of the Budha and Chandra, then see Meena rashi of the 7th aspect rashi in the Third part of the northern hemisphere, Sunday shows 20-30 hours and Wednesday shows 16-30 hours, deduct Wednesday hours from Sunday hours, 16-30—8-30=8 hours, deduct the difference of the southern hemisphere 2 hours, 8—2=6 hours, is the Longitude. See the Longitude chart for 6 hours=90°, deduct 6° of the Sun, 90°-6°=84° Longitude East. Meena rashi Sunday shows 20-30 hours, deduct 20′ of Ayanachalana, 20-30—20′=20-10′ hours, it means 20 nakshatra or 20 solar degrees. See the Latitude chart for Meena rashi 20° on Sunday, it shows 18°-4′ North.

22nd of August to 21st of September shows the period of the Sun. Opening month of the year 1935 is in the fourth house, then 22nd of January to 21st of December fourth house, 22nd of December to 21st of November third house, 22nd of November to 21st of October second house, 22nd of October to 21st of September first house, here is 7th aspect rashi of Budha. Meena rashi is on 180° of the Kanya, that is Meena Lagna. Moon is in Kanya rashi, from 14th of the August to 14th of September Sun is in the Simha rashi. Right ascension nakshatra of the Moon is Chitra and her declination nakshatra is Vishakha, her right ascension. 7th aspect nakshatra is Aswini and declination nakshatra is Krittika. The declination nakshatra of the Sun is Uttara and his right ascension nakshatra is Magha, his 7th aspect nakshatra of the Uttara is Uttarabhadrapada and his 7th aspect nakshatra of the Magha is Dhanistha. Dhanistha nakshatra is No. 5 and Krittika nakshatra of the Moon is No. 3, then count No. 5 of the Sun upto No. 3 of the Moon. Aswini 5, Bharani 14, Krittika 23rd, this is what the Longevity of the native. Dhanistha nakshatra is in Kumbha rashi, Kumbha rashi shows the month of August. Magha 1, Aswini 10, Moola 19 and Aswini 28. Add 23 years in the birth year, 1935 plus 23=1958, that is on 28 of August 1958 he died. Put the 7th aspect nakshatra on the birth day.

7	1	3	5
Sun	Tue	Thur	Sat
6	8	2	4
Mon	Wed	Fri	Sun

It shows 1-3-5-7 years are bad, in these years, 2-4-6-8 months are bad and in these months 1-3-5-7 dates and days of the dates are bad, 2-4-6-8 years are good and in these years 1-3-5-7 months are good, in these months 2-4-6-8 dates and days of the dates are good.

Shree V. M. Phathak

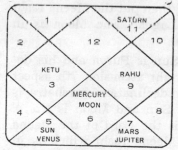

Birth date 1.9.1935
Date of expiry 28.8.1958
Long. 84° east
Lat. 18°-4' North

Example No. 15. Birth date 23.8.1936. We will see the birth day of the native. 1900=2, 36=3, August=1, Birth date is 23=23 plus 1 plus 2 plus 3=29 divided by 7=Remainder is 1=Sunday is the birth day. See the month from 22nd of August to 21st of September in the year 1936. The third part of the southern hemisphere, Sunday is not there in the third part. Sun is the Lord of Sunday as well as he is the Lord of Simha rashi. Simha rashi is here but no Sunday, it shows that the Sun is negative, that is he is in Simha rashi and his 7th aspect rashi is Meena and Kumbha because Thursday is on 180° of the Sunday. Then see Meena rashi in the third part of the northern hemisphere. Thursday shows 17-30 hours and Sunday shows 20-30 hours (it shows that Jupiter is in Anuradha nakshatra and his 7th aspect rashi is in triangle of the Saturn's rashi. Sun is in conjunction of Venus or Venus is in triangle of the Sun's rashi. 20-30 hours means Purvashadha nakshatra, it is a negative nakshatra for the Sun. Purva is the greater nakshatra and he is in Purva, Purvashadha is negative nakshatra for the Moon. Bharani is the greater nakshatra for the Moon, that is Bharani nakshatra is her 7th aspect nakshatra. That is the Moon is in Thula rashi. Thursday shows 17-30 hours, deduct 12 hours the difference of the southern hemisphere, Simha rashi day, 17-30—12=5-30 hours is the Longitude. See the Longitude chart for 5-30 hours, it shows 82°-30′ East, Now add 2° more of the Sunday (Thursday 0, Friday 1, Saturday 2) 82°-30′ plus 2°=84°-30′ Longitude East. Sunday shows 20-30 hours, deduct 20′ of Ayanachalana, 20-30—20=20-10′, it means 20 nakshatra or 20 solar degrees, then see the Latitude chart for Meena rashi 20° on Sunday it shows 18°-4′ Latitude North.

22nd of August to 21st of September is the period of the Sun but the Sun is negative, it shows the Moon's horoscope. The opening month of the year 1936 is in the tenth house, 22nd of January to 21st of December tenth house, 22nd of December to 21st of November eleventh house, 21st of November to 21st of October twelfth house, 22nd of October to 21st September first house, 22nd of September to 21st of August second house, here is the aspect rashi of the Sun, Meena and Triangle Rashi of the Guru, then put the Meena rashi in the second house, it shows Kumbha Lagna. The Moon is in Thula rashi, and the Sun is in Simha rashi.

The right ascension nakshatra of the Sun is Purva and his declination nakshatra is Hasta No. 4. The right ascension 7th aspect nakshatra of the Moon is Bharani and her declination nakshatra is Rohini. The declination nakshatra of the Sun and Moon is No. 4. Jupiter is in the Anuradha nakshatra, he is the Lord of the Meena Rashi, Uttarabhadrapada nakshatra is in Meena rashi which is in triangle of the Anuradha. Uttara No. 3 nakshatra is the 7th aspect nakshatra of Guru which is original nakshatra of the Sun. Jupiter is the Lord of Dhanu rashi, there is also his 7th aspect nakshatra Uttarashadha, Pushya nakshatra is on 180° of Uttarashadha, Pushya nakshatra is in Karka Rashi. Month of May is in Karka rashi, so month of May is the Last month of the native. Moon is the Lord of Karka rashi, her right ascension nakshatra is Punarvasu and her declination nakshatra is Aslesha, her seventh aspect nakshatra is Dhanistha, Dhanistha is No. 23, it shows 23rd of May is the last date of the native.

ILLUSTRATIONS TO FIND LONGEVITY

Now count declination nakshatra of the Sun and the Moon upto original nakshatra of the Sun No. 3, Aswini 4, Bharani 13, Krittika 22, this is what the Longevity of the native. Add 22 years in his birth year 1936, 1936 plus 22=1958 that is on 23rd of May 1958 he died. Put the seventh aspect nakshatra on the birth day

1	8	6	4
Sun	Tue	Thur	Sat
9	7	5	3
Mon	Wed	Fri	Sun

it shows 1-4-6-8 years are bad and in these years 3-5-7-9 months are bad, in these months 3-5-7-9 dates and days of the dates are bad and vice versa.

Shree S. G. Kulkarni

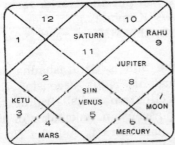

Birth date 23.8.1936
Date of expiry 23.5.1958
Long. 84°-30′ East
Lat. 18°-4′ North.

Example No. 16. Birth date 30.1.1882. We will see the birth day of the native. 1800=4, 82=4, January=6, Birth date is 30=30 plus 6 plus 4 plus 4=44 divided by 7=Remainder is 2=Monday is the birth day. See the month 22nd of January to 21st of February in the year 1882, the first part of the Northern hemisphere, Monday shows 15-30 hours, but due to the spherical triangle it is a negative part. Moon is the Lord of Karka rashi and she is the Lord of Monday, it shows 15.30 hours are negative, 15-30 hours means Swati nakshatra, it is negative. Aridra nakshatra is the greater nakshatra. Aridra nakshtra is in Mithuna rashi, then see Mithuna rashi in the second part of the northern hemisphere, Monday shows 15-30 hours. Thursday is on 180° of Monday. Thursday shows 11-30 hours. Jupiter is the Lord of Thursday as well as he is the Lord of Dhanu and Meena rashi. Dhanu rashi is on 180° of the Mithuna, then see Dhanu rashi in the first part of the Southern hemisphere. Thursday shows 4-30 hours (deduct 4-30 hours of this Thursday from the Thursday of Mithuna rashi, 11-30 —4-30=7 hours, 7 hours means Punarvasu nakshatra, it means the Moon is in Punarvasu nakshatra in Mithuna rashi). Thursday of Mithuna rashi shows 11-30 hours, add 2 hours the difference of the Southern hemisphere 11-30 plus 2 hours the difference of

229

the southern hemisphere. 11-30 hours plus 2=13-30 hours, deduct 20' of Ayanachalana, 13-30—20'=13-10' hours, it means 13 nakshatra or 13 solar degrees.

See 13° of the Mesha on Sunday in the Latitude chart, it shows 40°-13' north, Thursday shows 4-30 hours, see the Longitude chart for 4-30 hours, it shows 67°-30', add 4° the difference of Sunday (Thursday 1°, Friday 2°, Saturday 3°, Sunday 4°) 67°-30' plus 4°=71°-30' West, (the first part of the northern hemisphere Sunday shows Karka rashi and Thursday shows Simha rashi. 18-30 hours are negative for Jupiter, add 2 hours, 18-30 plus 2=20-30 means Purvashadha nakshatra, it is negative. Bharani nakshatra is greater for Jupiter, Bharani nakshatra is in Mesha rashi. So we have seen the Latitude of the Mesha rashi, 22nd of January to 21st of February is the period of the Moon. The opening month of the year 1882 is in the eleventh house, so put the Karka rashi of the Moon in the eleventh house, it shows Kanya Lagna, from 14th of January to 14th of February Sun is in the Makara rashi. Moon is in the Mithuna rashi.

The right ascension nakshatra of the Sun is Uttarashadha and his declination nakshatra is Dhanistha, his right ascension 7th aspect nakshatra is Punarvasu and declination nakshatra of the 7th aspect is Aslesha No. 9. The right ascension nakshatra of the Moon is Punarvasu and her declination nakshatra is Aslesha No. 9. Declination nakshatra of both the planets is No. 9, then count No. 9 upto 7 which is the original nakshatra of the Jupiter.

Aswini 9, Bharani 18, Krittika 27, Rohini 36, Mriga 45, Aridra 54, Punarvasu 63 this is the Longivety of the native. Jupiter is the Lord of the fourth house, as well as seventh, his fourth house shows the longevity, and his seventh house shows us the last month April, 7th aspect declination nakshatra of the Moon is shravana 4, count this number upto ascendent. Hasta nakshatra means 13th nakshatra, that shows the date of expiry, add 63 years in his birth year 1882, 1882 plus 63=1945, that is on 13th of April 1945 he died.

President D. Roosevelt

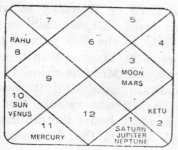

Birth date 30.1.1882

Date of expiry 13.4.1945

Long. 71°-30' West

Lat. 40°-13' North.

230

Example No. 17. Birth date 14.12.1895. We will see the birth-day of the native. 1800=4, 95=6, December=4 Birth date is 14=14 plus 4 plus 6 plus 4=28 divided by 7=Remainder is 0= Saturday is the Birth day. See the month 22nd of November to 21st of December in the year 1895. The fourth part of the northern hemisphere, Saturday shows 6-30 hours, but it is negative due to the spherical triangle. Tuesday is on 180° of Saturday. Tuesday shows 9-30 hours, it is also negative due to spherical triangle. Add 2 hours the difference of the negative part. 6-30 plus 2=8-30 hours, it is negative, 8-30 hours means Pushya nakshatra, Anuradha is the greater nakshatra. Sun is in Anuradha nakshatra, 9-30 hours are negative. 9-30 hours means Aslesha nakshatra, The Jyeshtha nakshatra is the greater nakshatra. The Moon is in Jyeshtha nakshatra. Mars is the Lord of Tuesday as well as he is the Lord of Vrischika and Mesha rashi. Then see the Vrischika rashi of Mars in the first part of the southern hemisphere. Saturday shows 3-30 hours. Tuesday shows 6-30 hours, and the fourth part of the northern hemisphere Saturday shows 6-30 hours, deduct Saturday hours from Tuesday hours, 6-30— 6-30=0 Longitude West.

The fourth part of the northern hemisphere Tuesday shows 9-30 hours, deduct 20' of Ayanachalana, 9-30—20'=9-10' hours. It means Aslesha nakshatra, Shravana nakshatra is on 180° of Aslesha. Shravana is No. 22, nakshatra or 22° solar degrees, then see the Latitude chart for 22° of Kumbha rashi on Tuesday, it shows 51°-28' Latitude North (357°-28'—300°=57°—28' North) here 9-30 hours are in both rashis, in Makara as well as in Kumbha, both the rashis are of the Saturn.

22nd of the January to 21st of December is the period of the Moon. Opening month of the year 1895 is in the eleventh house, then put the 7th aspect rashi of Saturn in the eleventh house. Simha rashi is the 7th aspect rashi, put it in the eleventh house, it shows Thula Lagna. Sun is Vrischika rashi. Moon is in Vrischika rashi.

Right ascension nakshatra of the Sun is Swati and his declintion nakshtra is Anuradha, his right ascension 7th aspect nakshatra is Aswini and his 7th aspect declination nakshatra is Krittika. The declination nakshatra of the Moon is Jyeshtha and her right ascension nakshatra is Vishakha, her 7th aspect right ascension nakshatra is Mriga and declination nakshatra is Krittika, declination nakshatra of both the planets is Krittika No. 3. Then count No. 3 nakshatra upto Punarvasu nakshatra which is in the Karka rashi the 7th aspect rashi of the Saturn, Aswini 3, Bharani 12,

Krittika 21, Rohini 30, Mriga 39, Aridra 48, Punarvasu 57 this is what the Longevity of the Native. Karka rashi shows the Month, 22nd of February to 21st of January. Right ascension nakshatra of the Moon is Jyeshtha, her declination nakshatra is Purvashadha. Aridra is her 7th aspect nakshatra (Aridra is on 180° of the Purvashadha) that is on 6th of February at his 57 he died, add 57 years in his birth year 1895, 1895 plus 57=1952 on 6th of February 1952, he died.

King Gorge VI

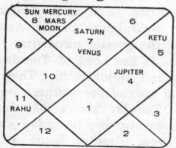

Birth date 14.12.1895
Date of expiry 6.2.1952
Long. 0° West
Lat. 51°-28′ North.

Example No. 18. Birth date 14.7.1856. We will see the birth day of the native. 1800=4, 56=7, July=5, birth date is 14=14 plus 5 plus 7 plus 4=30 divided by 7=Remainder is 2=Monday is the birth day. See the month 22nd of June to 21st of July in the year 1856. The fourth part of the southern hemisphere, Monday is not there. Friday is on 180° of Monday. Friday shows 23-30 hours, but it is a negative part due to spherical triangle. 23-30 means Dhanishtha nakshatra, it is negative. Mriga nakshatra is the greater nakshatra, it shows that Mriga nakshatra is 7th aspect nakshatra of the Moon. Venus is the Lord of Friday as well as he is the Lord of Vrishabha and Thula rashi. Moon is the Lord of Monday as well as she is the Lord of Karka rashi. Then see the Vrishabha rashi in the third part and Karka rashi in the second part of the southern hemisphere, Vrishabha rashi Monday shows 2-30 hours and Karka rashi Friday shows 6-30 hours. Deduct Monday hours from Friday hours, 6-30—2-30=4 hours, is the Longitude, add 6° of the Monday. 60° plus 6°=66° Longitude East. See the Friday 23-30 hours, deduct 20′ of Ayanachalana, 23-30 —20′=23-10′ hours, it means 23 nakshatra or 23 solar degrees. See the Latitude chart for 23° of Mesha rashi on Monday, it shows 20°-30′ Latitude north. 22nd of June to 21st of July is the period of the Sun. The opening month of the year 1856 is in the third house, then 22nd of January to 21st of December third house, 22nd of December to 21st of November second house, 22nd of November to 21st of October first house, 22nd of October to 21st of September

232

twelfth house, 22nd of September to 21st of August eleventh house, 22nd of August to 21st of July tenth house, here is the 7th aspect rashi of the Moon, Makara rashi is the 7th aspect rashi of the Moon's rashi Karka. Put the Makara rashi in the tenth house, it shows Mesha Lagna.

The Moon is in the Vrischika rashi, 14th of June to 14th of July Sun is in the Mithuna rashi. The right ascension nakshatra of the Moon is Jyeshtha and her declination nakshatra is Purvashadha, her right ascension 7th aspect nakshatra is Punarvasu and 7th aspect declination nakshatra is Mriga No. 5. The right ascension nakshatra of the Sun is Mriga and his declination nakshatra is Punarvasu, his right ascension 7th aspect nakshatra is Moola and 7th aspect declination nakshatra is Uttarashadha No. 3. Then count declination nakshatra No. 3 of the Sun upto declination nakshatra No. 5 of the Moon. Aswini 3, Bharani 12, Krittika 21, Rohini 30, Mriga 39, this is the Longevity of the native. Mars is the Lord of Mriga nakshatra and he is the Lord of the eighth house, it shows the month of 22nd of May to 21st of June. Moon is the Lord of Rohini nakshatra, her 7th aspect nakshatra is Anuradha No. 17 that is in the eighth house, it shows the last date. Put the declination nakshatra Mriga on Tuesday (because birth time of the native is in between, see the time of Monday in Mesha).

6	8	2	4
Mon	Wed	Fri	Sun
5	7	1	3
Tue	Thur	Sat	Mon

It shows 3-5-7-9 years are bad, and in these years, 2-4-6-8 months are bad, in these months 2-4-6-8 are the bad dates and days of the dates and vice versa. Add 39 years in the birth year, 1856 plus 39=1895, that is on 17th June 1895 he died.

Shree Gopalrao Agarkar

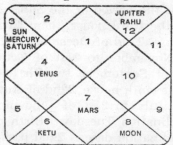

Birth date 14.7.1856

Date of expiry 17.6.1895

Long. 66° East

Lat. 20°-30′ North.

Example No. 19. Birth date 23.7.1856. We will see the birth day of the native. 1800=4, 56=7, July=5, Birth date is 23=23 plus 5 plus 7 plus 4=39 divided by 7=Remainder is 4=Wednesday is the birth day. See the month 22nd of July to 21st of August in the year 1856. The fourth part of the Southern hemisphere but there is no Wednesday in fourth part. Saturday is on 180° of Wednesday. Saturday shows 7-30 hours but due to the spherical triangle it is negative. Purvabhadrapada is the greater nakshatra, it shows that the Moon is in the Purvabhadrapada nakshatra in the Meena rashi. Budha is the Lord of Wednesday as well as he is the Lord of Mithuna and Kanya rashi. Saturn is the Lord of Saturday as well as he is the Lord of Makara and Kumbha rashi. Kanya rashi in negative i.e. the 7th aspect rashi of Moon who is in Meena. Then see the other rashi of Budha in the first part of the northern hemisphere. Wednesday shows 4-30 hours. See the Saturn rashi Kumbha in the fourth part of the northern hemisphere, Wednesday shows 21-30 hours, and Saturday shows 17-30 hours, deduct 4-30 hours of Wednesday from 21-30 of Wednesday of Kumbha rashi, 21-30—4-30=17 hours. Now deduct these hours from Saturday hours, 17-30—17=30', it shows declination. Then see Saturday of the Southern hemisphere and add 2 hours the difference of the northern hemisphere. 7-30 plus 2=9-30, deduct 20' of Ayanachalana, 9-30—20'=9-10', it means Aslesha nakshatra. Shravana is on 180° of the Aslesha. Shravana is No. 22, it means 22 solar degrees in declination chart on Wednesday, it shows 17°-56' Latitude North. Reader should understand these are the declination degrees and not the right ascension (See 22' of Karka or 7° of Mesha).

Now add 2 hours the difference of the Southern hemisphere in Wednesday 4-30 hours, 4-30 plus 2=6-30 hours. Deduct 20' of the Ayanachalana. 6-30—20'=6-10' hours. See the Longitude chart for 6-10 hours, it shows 92°-30', deduct 6° of Wednesday which was not in the fourth part of the southern hemisphere, 92°-30'—13°= 79°-30' Longitude east.

22nd of July to 21st of June shows the period of the Sun. The opening month of the year 1856 is in the third house, then 22nd of January to 21st of December third house, 22nd of December to 21st of November second house, 22nd of November to 21st of October first house, 22nd of October to 21st of September twelfth house, 22nd of September to 21st of August eleventh house, 22nd of August to 21st of July tenth house, 22nd of July to 21st of June nineth house, here is Mesha rashi of the declination Tuesday. Birth date is 23 which is right ascension date, declination date is 22nd it shows Tuesday. When declination rashi is Karka its opening declination rashi is Mesha. See the declination chart, it shows Simha Lagna.

14th of July to 14th of August the Sun is in Karaka, Moon is Meena rashi.

The declination nakshatra of the Moon is Purvabhadrapada and her right ascension nakshatra is Dhanishtha. Her 7th aspect declination nakshatra is Uttara and her 7th aspect right ascension nakshatra is Magha.

The right ascension nakshatra of the Sun is Pushya and his declination nakshatra is Magha. Declination nakshatra of both the planets is No. 1. Then count No. 1 upto to Saturn's nakshatra Pushya (because he is the Lord of the sixth house, and he is ruler that is why we have seen his day in the fourth part of the Southern hemisphere in his birth year 1856), Aswini 1, Bharani 10, Krittika 19, Rohini 28, Mriga 37, Aridra 46, Punarvasu 55, Pushya 64, Add 64 years in his birth year, 1856 plus 64=1920. The opening month of the year 1920 is in the fourth house, then 22nd of January to 21st December fourth house, 22nd of December to 21st November third house, 22nd of November to 21st of October second house, 22nd of October to 21st of September first house, 22nd of September to 21st of August twelfth house, here is the 7th aspect rashi of Saturn and his Pushya nakshatra. Aswini is the first 7th aspect nakshatra of the Moon, because Magha is on 180° of the right ascension nakshatra Dhanishtha. Moola nakshatra, she cannot pass because the Longevity of the native is upto 21st of August, then Chitra is only remainder nakshatra which shows the 7th aspect nakshatra Aswini.

Put the birth date on the birth day.

5	7	1	3
Wed	Fri	Sun	Tues
6	8	2	4
Turs	Sat	Mon	Wed

It shows 1-3-5-7 years are bad, and in these years 2-4-6-8 months are bad, in these months 1-3-5-7 dates and the days of the dates are bad and vice versa.

Lokmanya B. G. Tilak

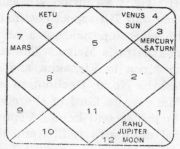

Birth date 23.7.1856

Date of Expiry 1.8.1920

Long. 79°-30′ East

Lat. 17°-56′ North Dec.

R.A. 17° North.

Example No. 20. Birth date 10.9.1887. We will see the birth day of the native. 1800=4, 87=3, September=4, Birth date is 10=10 plus 4 plus 3 plus 4=21 divided by 7=Remainder is 0=Saturday is the birth day. See the month 22nd of August to 21st of September in the year 1887 the first part of the southern hemisphere, but there is no Saturday, then Tuesday is on 180° of Saturday and it shows 12-30 hours, but due to the spherical triangle it is negative, 12-30 hours means Uttara nakshatra it is negative, Krittika nakshatra is the greater nakshatra, it means the Moon is in the Krittika nakshatra and her 7th aspect rashi is Vrischika, Saturn is the Lord of Saturday as well as he is the Lord of the Kumbha and Makara rashi. Then see the third and fourth part of the northern hemisphere for Saturday and his rashi. There is no Saturday in the fourth part, but there is Saturday in the third part Kumbha rashi. Saturday shows 19-30 hours, add 2 hours the difference of the Southern hemisphere, 19-30 plus 2=21-30 hours, this is his 7th aspect nakshatra, Uttarashadha of Saturn, 21-30 hours, deduct 20′ of the Ayanachalana, 21-30—20′=21-10′ hours or 21 nakshatra or 21 solar degrees, then see 21° of the Makara on Saturday for Latitude, it shows 323°-25′—300°-=23°-25′ Latitude North, add 9 hours the difference of the southern hemisphere day in Tuesday hours. 12-30 plus 9=21-30, now deduct it from Saturday hours, 21-30—21-30=0° is the Longitude East.

22nd of August to 21st of September is the period of Sun. The opening month of the year 1887 is in the third house, then 22nd of January to 21st of December third house, 22nd of December to 21st of November second house, 22nd of November to 21st of October first house, 22nd of October to 21st of September twelfth house, 22nd of September to 21st of August eleventh house, here is Saturn in Karka rashi and Makara his 7th aspect rashi. Then put Karka rashi in the eleventh house, it shows Kanya Lagna. The Moon is in Vrischika rashi, 14th of August to 14th of September Sun is in Simha rashi. Right ascension nakshatra of the Sun is Uttara and his declination nakshatra is Chitra. His right ascension 7th aspect declination nakshatra is Purvabhadrapada and 7th aspect declination nakshatra is Revati No. 9. The right ascension nakshatra of the Moon is Krittika and her declination nakshatra is Mriga. The right ascension 7th aspect nakshatra of the Moon is Vishakha and her 7th aspect declination nakshatra is Jyeshtha No. 9. Declination nakshatra of both the planets is No. 9. Mars is the Lord of the eighth house, his 7th aspect rashi is Thula in the second house, Venus is the Lord of the Thula rashi his original nakshatra is Bharani, then count No. 2 upto No. 9.

Aswini 2, Bharani 11, Krittika 20, Rohini 29, Mriga 38, Aridra 47, Punarvasu 56, Pushya 65, Aslesha 74, this is the Longevity of the nativity, add 74 years in the birth year 1887, 1887 plus 74=1961. The opening month of 1961 is in the fourth house, then sixth house shows month of March.

Put the birth date on birth day.

3	5	7	1
Sat	Mon	Wed	Fri
4	6	8	2
Sun	Tue	Thur	Sat

It shows 2-4-6-8 years are bad, in these years 1-3-5-7 months are bad, in these months 1-3-5-7 dates and the days of the dates are bad and vice versa. Aswini nakshatra in the eighth house and Magha nakshatra in the twelfth house, here the month March has his 7th aspect. It shows date 10, that is on 10th of March 1961 he died.

Shree G. V. Pant

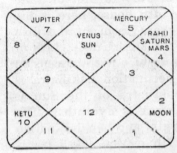

Birth date 10.9.1887

Date of expiry 10.3.1961

Long. 0° East

Lat. 23°-25' North.

Example No. 21. Birth date 28.5.1916. We will see the birth day of the native. 1900=2, 16=6, May=7, Birth date is 28=28 plus 7 plus 6 plus 2=43 divided by 7=Remainder is 1=Sunday is the birth day. See the month 22nd of August to 21st of September in the year 1916. The second part of the southern hemisphere, Sunday shows 23-30 hours, Wednesday is on 180° of Sunday, Wednesday shows 19-30 hours, but it is a negative part, due to the spherical triangle. 23-30 hours means Dhanishtha nakshatra, it is negative. Mriga nakshatra is the greater nakshatra for the Sun. Wednesday shows 19-30 hours, it means Moola nakshatra, it is negative due to the spherical triangle. Aswini nakshatra is the greater nakshatra for the Moon. The Sun is the Lord of Sunday as well as he is the Lord of Simha rashi. Mercury is the Lord of Wednesday as well as he is the Lord of Mithuna and Kanya rashi. Then see Simha rashi which is on 180° of Kumbha rashi in the first part of the southern hemisphere. Sunday shows 13-30 hours, deduct these hours from Wednesday's hours. 19-30—13-30 hours=6 hours. See the Longitude chart for six hours and deduct the Longitude of the Wednesday which is not in Simha and Kanya rashi. 6 hours= 90°-4°=86° Longitude East.

(Sunday 1°, Monday 2°, Tuesday 3°, Wednesday 4°). Second part of the southern hemisphere Sunday shows 23-30 hours, deduct two hours the difference of the northern hemisphere 23-30—2=21-30 hours, deduct 20′ of Ayanachalana 21-30—20′=21-10′ hours, it means 21 nakshatra or 21 solar degrees. See 21° of Makara on Wednesday in the Latitude chart, it shows 322°-6′—300°=22°-6′ North.

22nd of May to 21st of June is the period of the Moon. The Opening month of the year 1916 is in the tenth house, then 22nd of January to 21st of December tenth house, 22nd of December to 21st of November eleventh house, 22nd of November to 21st of October twelfth house, 22nd of October to 21st of September first house, 22nd of September to 21st of August second house, 22nd of August to 21st of July third house, 22nd of July to 21st of June fourth house, 22nd of June to 21st of May fifth house, here is the Makara rashi of Saturn, then put the Makara rashi in the fifth house, it shows Kanya Lagna. Moon is in the Mesha rashi, 14th of May to 14th of June Sun is in Vrishabha rashi. Right ascension nakshatra of the Sun is Krittika and his declination nakshatra is Mriga. The right ascension 7th aspect nakshatra of the Sun is Vishakha, his 7th aspect declination nakshatra is Jyeshtha. The right ascension nakshatra of the Moon is Aswini and her declination nakshatra is Krittka, her right ascension 7th aspect nakshatra is Chitra and 7th aspect declination nakshatra is Vishakha. Mars is the Lord of the eighth house as well as he is the Lord of the third house, his original nakshatra is Chitra which is the right ascension 7th aspect nakshatra of the Moon. Then count No. 9 upto No. 5 nakshatra, Aswini 9, Bharani 18, Krittika 27, Rohini 36, Mriga 45, this is the Longevity of the native. Vrischika rashi shows the Month of July. Moon's declination nakshatra Vishakha shows the date, add 45 years in the birth year, 1916 plus 45=1961. That is on 16th of July 1961 he died. Put the 7th aspect declination nakshatra of the Sun on Tuesday.

7	9	3	5
Sun	Tue	Thur	Sat

6	8	2	4
Mon	Wed	Fri	Sun

It shows 3-5-7-9 years, months and dates are bad, and vice versa.

King Jivajirao Shinde

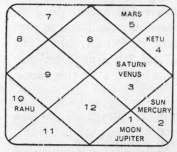

Birth date 28.5.1916
Date of Expiry 16.7.1961
Lon. 86° East
Lat. 22°-6′ North

Example No. 22. Birth date 14.8.1867. We will sec the birth day of the native. 1800—4, 67=6, August=1 Birth date is 14=14 plus 1 plus 6 plus 4=25 divided by 7=Remainder is 4=Wednesday is the birth day. See the month 22nd of June to 21st of July in the year 1867. The third part of the Southern hemisphere, Wednesday has 11-30 hours and Thula rashi. Sunday is on 180° of Wednesday. Sunday shows 8-30 hours and Kanya rashi, but due to the spherical triangle it is a negative part, add 2 hours the difference of the negative part. 11-30 hours plus 2=13-30 hours, it means Hasta nakshatra, it is negative. Shravana nakshatra is the greater nakshatra, it shows the Moon is in Shravana nakshatra. Add 2 hours in Sunday hours. 8-30 plus 2=10-30 it shows Sun is in Magha nakshatra. Budha is the Lord of Wednesday as well as he is the Lord of Mithuna and Kanya rashi. Kanya rashi is negative here, then see the other rashi Mithuna in the first part of the Northern hemisphere, Wednesday shows 4-30 hours. No Sunday is here, add 2 hours the difference of the southern hemisphere. 4-30 plus 2=6-30 hours. Deduct 20′ of Ayanachalana. 6-30—20′=6-10′ hours. See the Longitude chart for 6-10 hours and deduct the Longitude of the Sun, 6-10 hours shows 92°-30′—5°=87° East. Sunday shows 10-30 hours, deduct 20′ of Ayanachalana, 10-30—20′=10-10′ hours, it means Magha nakshatra or 10 solar degrees. See the Latitude chart for 10° of Simha rashi on Wednesday, it shows 163°-6′, deduct 150° of Simha rashi, it is 13°-36′ Latitude North.

22nd of July to 21st of August is the period of the Moon. The opening month of the 1867 is in the eleventh house, then 22nd of January to 21st of December eleventh house, 22nd of December to 21st of November twelfth house, 22nd of November to 21st of October first house, 22nd of October to 21st of September second house, 22nd of September to 21st of August third house, 22nd of August to 21st of July fourth house, here is the Kanya rashi of Budha. It shows Mithuna Lagna. The Moon is in Makara rashi, from 14th of August to 14th of September Sun is in Simha rashi.

Right ascension nakshatra of the Moon is Shravana, and her declination nakshatra is Shatataraka. The right ascension 7th aspect nakshatra of the Moon is Pushya and her 7th aspect declination nakshatra is Magha No. 1. Right ascension nakshatra of the Sun is Magha and his declination nakshatra is Uttara, his right ascension 7th aspect nakshatra is Dhanistha and 7th aspect declination nakshatra is Purvabhadrapada, then count No. 1 of the Moon upto No. 7 of the Sun.

Aswini 1, Bharani 10, Krittika 19, Rohini 28, Mriga 37, Aridra 46, Punarvasu 55, this is what the Longevity of the native. Sun's right ascension 7th aspect nakshatra is Dhanishtha. Dhanishtha nakshatra is in the eighth house Makara rashi. Makara rashi shows the month of March (22nd of April to 21st of March) right ascension nakshatra of Makara rashi is Uttarashadha and 7th aspect nakshatra is Punarvasu. Punarvasu is the date that is 7th of March, add 55 years in the birth year 1867, i.e. 1867 plus 55=1922, on 7th March 1922 he died.

Put the declination nakshatra of the Moon on Monday and 7th aspect nakshatra of the Sun on Sunday.

9	3	5	7
Wed	Fri	Sun	Tue
2	4	6	8
Thur	Sat	Mon	Wed

It shows 3-5-7-9 years, months and dates as well as days of the dates are bad and vice versa.

Shree Ganpatrao Joshi

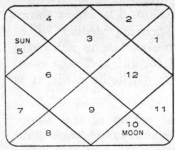

Birth date 14.8.1867
Date of expiry 7.3.1922
Long. 87° East
Lat. 13°-6′ North

Example No. 23. Birth date 29.3.1899. We will see the Birth day of the native. 1800=4, 99=3, March=2, Birth date is 29=29 plus 2 plus 3 plus 4=38 divided by 7=Remainder is 3=Tuesday is the birth day. See the month 22nd of March to 21st April in the year 1899. Third part of the southern hemisphere. Tuesday shows 16-30 hours and Kanya rashi. Friday is on 180° of the

Tuesday. Friday shows 12-30 hours. It shows the Moon is in Vishakha nakshatra and her seventh aspect nakshatra is of the Sun. 7th aspect nakshatra of Venus is Uttara. Mars is the Lord of Tuesday as well as he is the Lord of Mesha and Thula rashi. Tuesday shows 16-30 hours, it means Vishakha nakshatra, is a negative nakshatra for Mars due to the spherical triangle. Punarvasu is the greater nakshatra for the Mars, that is the Mars is in the Punarvasu nakshatra. Friday shows 12-30 hours, it means Uttara nakshatra, it is also negative due to the spherical triangle, its 7th aspect nakshatra Purvabhadrapada, it shows the Venus is in Purvabhadrapada nakshatra. Mars is the Lord of Mesha and Vrischika rashi and Venus is the Lord of Vrishabha Thula rashi. Then see Vrischika rashi of the Mars in the first part of the southern hemisphere, there is no Tuesday, then see Friday. Friday shows 19-30 hours, add 2 hours the difference of the negative part. 19-30 hours plus 2—21-30, deduct 20' of Ayanachalana, 21-30—20' =21-10' hours, it means 21 nakshatra, 21 solar degrees. Then see the Latitude chart for 21° on Friday Kumbha rashi, it shows 349°-22', deduct 300° of the Makara rashi, it shows 349°-22'—300°=49°-22' Latitude North. Friday of Vrischika rashi shows 19-30 hours, deduct 12-30 hours of Kanya rashi Friday, 19-30—12-30=7 hours. Now deduct the difference of 2 hours of the negative rashi Kanya, 7—2=5 hours. See the Longitude chart for 5 hours, it shows 75°, add 6° of the Mars, 75° plus 6°=81° West.

22nd of March to 21st of April is the period of the Moon. The opening month of the year 1899 is in the eleventh house, then 22nd of January to 21st of December eleventh house, 22nd of December to 21st of November twelfth house, 22nd of November to 21st October first house, 22nd of October to 21st of September second house, 22nd of September to 21st of August third house, 22nd of August to 21st of July fourth house, 22nd of July to 21st of June fifth house, 22nd of June to 21st of May sixth house, 22nd of May to 21st of April seventh house, 22nd of April to 21st of March eighth house, here is the 7th aspect rashi of the Moon as well as Mars-rashi Mesha. Then put the Mesha rashi in the eighth house, it shows Kanya Langna. The Moon is in Vishakha nakshatra of Thula rashi, 14th of March to 14th of April Sun is in the Meena rashi.

The right ascension nakshatra of the Moon is Vishakha and her declination nakshatra is Jyeshtha No. 9. The right ascension nakshatra of the Sun is Uttarabhadrapada and his declination nakshatra is Aswini. The right ascension 7th aspect nakshatra of the Sun is Hasta and his 7th aspect declination nakshatra is Swati No. 6.

241

Then count declination nakshatra of the Moon No. 9 upto 7th aspect declination nakshatra of the Sun No. 6. Aswini 9, Bharani 18, Krittika 27, Rohini 36, Mriga 45, Aridra 54, this the Longevity of the native. Mars is the Lord of the eighth house and third house, his eighth house shows us Longevity, his third house shows us the month December, Venus is the Lord of the nineth and second house, Mriga nakshatra is the first aspect nakshatra of the Moon and Dhanistha is her second aspect nakshatra. Dhanistha is No. 23, it shows the date, add 54 years in the birth year 1899, 1899 plus 54=1953, that is on 23rd December 1953 he died.

Put the 7th aspect-date on the birth day.

7	9	2	4
Tue	Thur	Sat	Mon
8	1	3	5
Wed	Fri	Sun	Tue

it shows 2-4-7-9 years are bad and in these years 1-3-5-8 months are bad and in these months 1-3-5-8 dates and days of the dates are bad and vice versa.

John Barria (U.S.S.R.)

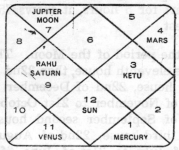

Birth date 29.3.1899
Date of expiry 23.12.1953
Lat. 49°-22′ North.
Long. 81° West

Example No. 24. Birth date 15.8.1872. We will see the birth day of the native. 1800=4, 72=6, August=1, Birth date is 15=15 plus 1 plus 6 plus 4=26 divided by 7=Remainder is 5=Thursday is the birth day. See the month 22nd of July to 21st of August in the year 1872. The second part of the southern hemisphere, Thursday shows 12-30 hours. Sunday is on 180° of the Thursday. Sunday shows 15-30 hours but due to the spherical triangle it is a negative part. 12-30 hours of Thursday means Uttara nakshatra, it is negative and Uttarashadha is the greater nakshatra for the Moon. 15-30 hours means Swati nakshatra, it is negative. Shatataraka is the greater nakshatra for the Sun. Jupiter is the Lord of Thursday as well as he is the Lord of Dhanu and Meena rashi. Sun is the Lord of Sunday and Simha rashi. Then see Simha rashi of the Sun in the fourth part of the southern hemisphere. Sunday shows 8-30 hours. Add 2 hours the difference of the negative part. 8-30 plus 2=10-30 hours, now deduct these hours from Sunday hours of the second part, 15-30—10-30=5 hours. See the Longitude chart for 5 hours, it shows 75° East, add 5° more for Thursday, 75° plus 5°=80° East. Southern hemisphere second part Sunday shows 15-30 hours, and fourth part Sunday shows 8-30 hours, deduct these hours from 15-30 hours of Sunday, 15-30—8-30=7 hours means Punarvasu nakshatra. Purvashadha is on 180° of Punarvasu. Purvashadha No. 20, or 20° solar degrees. See 20° of the Simha rashi on Thursday in Latitude chart, it shows 172°-49' deduct 150° of the Simha rashi, 172°-49'—150=22°-49' Latitude North.

22nd of July to 21st of August is the period of Moon. The opening month of the year 1872 is in the eleventh house. Then 22nd of January to 21st of December eleventh house, 22nd of December to 21st of November twelfth house, 22nd of November to 21st of October first house, 22nd of October to 21st of September second house, 22nd of September to 21st of August third house, 22nd of August to 21st of July fourth house, here is the Vrischika rashi of Thursday the second part of the southern hemisphere. Then put Vrischika rashi in the fourth house, it shows Simha Lagna. The Moon is in Uttarashadha nakshatra, that is the Moon is in Dhanu rashi, 14th of August to 14th of September, Sun is in the Simha rashi.

The right ascension nakshatra of the Sun is Aslesha and his declination nakshatra is Magha, his right ascension 7th aspect nakshatra is Shravana and his 7th aspect declination nakshatra is Shatataraka No. 6. The right ascension nakshatra of the Moon is Uttarashadha and her declination nakshatra is Dhanistha. The right ascension 7th aspect nakshatra is Punarvasu and her 7th aspect declination nakshatra is Aslesha No. 9. Then count declination nakshatra of the Sun No. 6 upto declination nakshatra of the Moon No. 9., Aswini 6, Bharani 15, Krittika 24, Rohini 33, Mriga 42, Aridra 51, Punarvasu 60, Pushya 69, Aslesha 78. This is the Longevity of the native.

Jupiter is the Lord of eighth and fifth house. Moon is in the fifth house, her 7th aspect rashi is Mithuna, it shows month of December. The opening rashi of the horoscope is Vrischika. Mars is the Lord of Vrischika, Jyeshtha nakshatra is there which is his own, the 7th aspect nakshatra of the Jyeshtha is Mriga No. 5, it shows the date. Then put the fifth nakshatra on Tuesday, add 78 years in the birth year, 1872 plus 78=1950, i.e. he died on 5-12-1950.

9	2	4	6
Thur	Sat	Mon	Wed
1	3	5	7
Fri	Sun	Tue	Thur

It shows 2-4-6-9 years are bad, in these years 1-3-5-7 dates and months are bad and vice versa.

Shree Arvind Ghosh I.C.S.

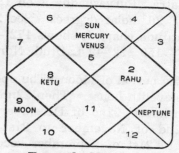

Birth date 15.8.1872

Date of expiry 5.12.1950

Long. 80° East

Lat. 22°-49′ North

Example No. 25. Birth date 18.5.1891. We will see the birth day of the native. 1800=4, 91=1, May=7, Birth date is 18=18 plus 7 plus 1 plus 4=30 divided by 7=Remainder is 2=Monday is birth day. See month 22nd of April to 21st of May in the year 1891 the fourth part of the southern hemisphere, no Monday is there, then Thursday is on 180° of the Monday. Thursday shows 18-30 hours and Vrischika rashi, but due to the spherical triangle it is negative part, 18-30 hours means Jyeshtha nakshatra, it is negative. Revati nakshatra is the greater nakshatra, it is 7th aspect nakshatra of the Moon. Jupiter is the Lord of Thursday as well as Meena and Dhanu rashi. Moon is the Lord of Monday as well as Karka rashi. The third part of the northern hemisphere Thursday shows 8-30 hours and Monday shows 12-30 hours, Deduct the hours of the Monday from Thursday hours of the fourth part. 18-30—12-30=6 hours is the Longitude, deduct Longitude of the Monday which is not in the fourth part of southern hemiphere. 6 hours means 90°—9°=81° (9° of negative Monday) Longitude East, add two hours the difference of southern hemisphere in the Thursday hours of Karka rashi 8-30 plus 2=10-30 hours, deduct 20′ of the Ayanachalana, 10-30—20=10-10′ hours. It means Magha nakshatra, Shatataraka is No. 24 which is on 180° of Magha. Shatataraka is No. 24 means 24 solar degrees. See the Latitude chart for 24° of Kumbha rashi on Thursday, it shows 352°-30′ deduct 330° of Kumbha rashi, 352°-30′—330=22°-30′ Latitude North.

22nd of the April to 21st of May is the period of Sun. The opening month of the year 1891 is in the third house. Then 22nd of January to 21st of December third house, 22nd December to 21st of November second house, 22nd of November to 21st of October first house, 22nd of October to 21st September twelfth house, 22nd of September to 21st of August eleventh house, 22nd of August to 21st of July tenth house, 22nd of July to 21st of June nineth house, 22nd of June to 21st of May eighth house, 22nd of May to 21st of April seventh house, here is the Karka rashi of the Moon, then put the Karka rashi of the Moon in the seventh house. It shows Makara Lagna. 14th of April to 14th of May the Sun is in Vrishabha rashi. The Moon is in Kanya rashi.

The right ascension nakshatra of the Moon is Hasta and her declination nakshatra is Swati No. 6. Right ascension nakshatra of the Sun is Krittika. Sun is the Lord of the eighth house. His original nakshatra is No. 3 and his 7th aspect nakshatra is Anuradha, original 7th aspect nakshatra is No. 8. Then count No. 6 of the Moon upto eighth nakshatra of the Sun, Aswini 6, Bharani 15, Krittika 24, Rohini 33, Mriga 42, Aridra 51, Punarvasu 60, Pushya 69. This is the Longevity of the native.

Sun is the Lord of the eighth house, his 7th aspect rashi is Kumbha, it shows the month of November, his original nakshatra is No. 3, and his 7th aspect nakshatra is No. 8, that is on eighth of November at his 69 he died; add 69 years in his birth year, 1891 plus 69=1960, i.e. on 8-11-1960 he died.

Put the declination nakshatra of the Moon No. 6 on the birth day.

1	3	5	7
Mon	Wed	Fri	Sun
8	2	4	6
Tue	Thur	Sat	Mon

It shows 2-4-6-8 years, months and dates bad and vice versa.

Shree Baburao Dandekar M.L.C.

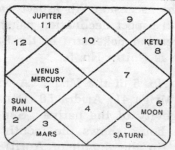

Birth date 18.5.1891
Date of expiry 8.11.1960
Long. 81° East
Lat. 22°-30′ North.

Example No. 26. Birth date 7.10.1853. We will see the birth day of the native. 1800=4, 53=3, October=6 Birth date is

7=7 plus 6 plus 3 plus 4=20 divided by 7=Remainder is 6=Friday is the birth day. See the month 22nd of September to 21st of October in the year 1853. The first part of the northern hemisphere, there is no Monday. Then Thursday is on 180° of Monday. Thursday shows 24-30 hours, it is negative due to the spherical triangle, 24-30 hours means Shatataraka nakshatra, it is negative. Swati nakshatra is the greater nakshatra, it is the 7th aspect nakshatra of the Moon, it shows the Moon in Mesha rashi.

Moon is the Lord of Karka rashi and Jupiter is the Lord of Meena and Dhanu rashi. Then see Meena rashi in the third part of the Northern hemisphere. Thursday shows 17-30 hours. Now see Karka rashi in the fourth part of the southern hemisphere. Monday shows 4-30 hours, add 2 hours the difference of the negative part in Thursday hours. 17-30 plus 2=19-30 hours, deduct 20' of Ayanachalana, 19-30—20'=19-10', it means 19 nakshatra or 19 solar degrees. Then see the Latitude chart for 19° degrees of Meena rashi on Thursday, it shows 15°-35' north, add 2 hours in 4-30 hours of Monday, 4-30 plus 2=6-30 hours, deduct 20' of Ayanachalana 6-30'—20'=6-10' hours. See Longitude chart for 6-10 hours and deduct the Monday Longitude, 92°-30'—12°=80°-30' (Monday first part of the Northern hemisphere 6° and Monday third part of Northern hemisphere 6° means 12° deduct it from 92°-30') Longitude 80°-30' east.

22nd of September to 21st of October is the period of Moon. Opening month of the year 1853 is in the eleventh house, then 22nd of January to 21st of December eleventh house, 22nd of December to 21st of November twelfth house, 22nd of November to 21st of October first house, here is the 7th aspect rashi Makara of the Moon's rashi Karka, it shows Makara Lagna, 14th September to 14th October Sun is in Kanya rashi. Moon is in Mesha rashi.

Right ascension nakshatra of the Moon is Aswini and her declination nakshatra is Krittika. The right ascension 7th aspect nakshatra of the Moon is Swati and her 7th aspect declination nakshatra is Anuradha No. 8. The right ascension nakshatra of the Sun is Uttara and his declination nakshatra is Chitra No. 5.

Then count No. 5 of the Sun upto No. 6 of the Moon. Aswini 5, Bharani 14, Krittika 23, Rohini 32, Mriga 41; Aridra 50, Punarvasu 59, Pushya 68. This is the Longevity of the native. Sun is the Lord of the eighth house, eighth house shows the month of April. The right ascension nakshatra (in the month of April) of the Moon will be Anuradha and her declination nakshatra will be Moola, her right declination 7th aspect nakshatra will be Aridra first and Swati second, it shows 15th day of April, add 68 years in the birth year, 1853 plus 68=1921, that is on 15th of April 1921 he died.

Put the birth date on Saturday instead of Friday because Friday shows 1-30 hours in Vrishabha declination rashi, that is why Monday and Thursday are taken into consideration instead of Friday and Wednesday. This is the reason to give up the idea of common day.

6	8	2	4
Fri	Sun	Tues	Thur
7	1	3	5
Sat	Mon	Wed	Fri

It shows 1-3-5-7 years are bad, in these 2-4-6-8 months are bad and in these months 2-4-6-8 dates and days of the dates are bad and vice versa.

Shree Anant Shivaji Desai

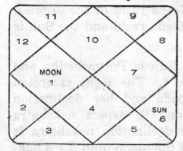

Birth date 7.10.1853
Date of expiry 15.4.1921
Long. 80°-30′ East
Lat. 15°-35′ North

Example No. 27. Birth date 22.12.1887. We will see the Birth day of the native. 1800=4, 87=3, December=4, Birth date is 22=22 plus 4 plus 3 plus 4=33 divided by 7=Remainder is 5=Thursday is birth day. See the month 22nd of December to 21st of January in the year 1887. The first part of the northern hemisphere but there is no Thursday, then Monday is on 180° of Thursday. Monday shows 8-30 hours, but it is a negative part due to the spherical triangle. 8-30 hours means Pushya nakshatra, it is negative. Uttarabhadrapada is the greater nakshatra for the Moon, it shows the Moon is in Meena rashi. Moon is the Lord of Karka rashi. Then see Karka rashi for the Moon in the second part of the southern hemisphere. Monday shows 18-30 hours, 18-30 hours means Jyeshtha nakshatra, it shows the Jupiter is in Jyeshtha nakshatra. Add 2 hours the difference of the northern hemisphere. 18-30 plus 2=20-30 hours, it shows the Sun is in Purvashadha nakshatra in Dhanu rashi. Jupiter is the Lord of Dhanu and Meena rashi. Then see Dhanu rashi in the second part of the northern hemisphere. Thursday shows 4-30 hours. The first part of the northern hemisphere Thursday shows 8-30 hours and Thursday of second part shows 4-30 hours, deduct these hours from 8-30 hours, 8-30—4-30=4 hours, this is the Longitude, add 3° of the Monday which is not in the Dhanu rashi. 4 hours=60° plus 3°=63° Longitude East. Monday of Karka rashi shows 18-30 hours, add 2 hours the difference of the northern hemisphere, 18-30 plus 2=20-30 hours. Now Monday of Meena rashi shows 8-30 hours, deduct Monday hours from 20-30 hours, 20-30—8-30=12 hours, it means 12th nakshatra or 12 solar degrees, then see 12° of Dhanu rashi on Thursday in the Latitude chart, it shows 282°-34' deduct 270° of Dhanu i.e. 282°-34'—270°=12°-34' Latitude North.

22nd of January to 21st of December is the period of Moon and 22nd of December to 21st of January is the period of the Sun, it means the equinox Monday is the birth day and Moon is in Meena rashi, then we must give first preference to the Moon, then 22nd of January to 21st of December eleventh house, 22nd of December to 21st to November twelfth house, here is Meena rashi of the Jupiter. It shows Mesha Lagna. The Moon is in Meena rashi and the Sun is in Dhanu rashi.

The right ascension nakshatra of the Sun is Purvashadha and his declination nakshatra is Shravana No. 4. The right ascension nakshatra of the Moon is Uttarabhadrapada and her declination nakshatra is Aswini. The right ascension 7th aspect nakshatra of the Moon is Hasta and her 7th aspect declination nakshatra is Swati No. 6. Then count No. 6 nakshatra of the Moon upto No. 4 nakshatra of the Sun. Aswini 6, Bharani 15, Krittika 24, Rohini 33, this is what the Longevity of the native. Mars is the Lord of eighth and first house, his eighth house shows us the month of April and right ascension nakshatra Uttarabhadrapada of the Moon shows the date (the declination nakshatra of the Sun is Shravana, Pushya nakshatra is his 7th aspect nakshatra No. 8, Uttarabhadrapada will be his second nakshatra and Anuradha will be third. That is when he will come in Vrishabha rashi his 7th aspect will be in Vrischika rashi). Put the birth date on the birth day.

4	6	8	1
Thur	Sat	Mon	Wed
5	7	9	2
Fri	Sun	Tue	Thur

It shows 1-4-6-8 years are bad and in these years 1-4-6-8 months are bad, and in these months 1-4-6-8 dates and days of the dates are bad. 33 years added to his birth year will give his Longevity. 1867 plus 33=1920, that is on 26th April 1920 he died.

Shree Ramanujam

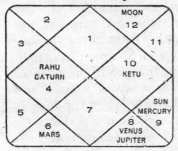

Birth date 22.12.1887
Date of expiry 26.4.1920
Long. 63° East
Lat. 12°-34' North.

Example No. 28. Birth date 31.8.1886. We will see the birth day of the native. 1800=4, 86=2, August=1, Birth date is 31=31 plus 1 plus 2 plus 4=38 divided by 7=Remainder is 3=Tuesday is the birth day. See the month 22nd of August to 21st of September in the year 1886, the first part of the southern hemisphere. Tuesday shows 12-30 hours. Friday is on 180° of Tuesday but there is no Friday. It is a negative part due to the spherical triangle. 12-30 hours means Uttara nakshatra, it is negative for Mars. Krittika nakshatra is the greater nakshatra for Mars, it is the 7th aspect nakshatra of the Mars and Moon is in his negative nakshatra, Uttara. Mars is the Lord of Vrischika and Mesha rashi. Venus is the Lord of Thula and Vrishabha rashi. Then see the Thula rashi in the second part. Friday shows 8-30 hours. Tuesday shows 12-30 hours, deduct Friday hours, 12-30—8-30=4 hours is Longitude, add 9° of the Venus which is not in the first part, 60° plus 9°=69° Longitude east. Now see Mesha rashi of Mars in the second part of the northern hemisphere. Tuesday shows 22-30 hours, deduct 12-30 hours of Tuesday of the southern hemisphere, 22-30—12-30=10 hours, means Magha nakshatra. Dhanistha is on 180° of the Magha. Dhanistha is No. 23 nakshatra or 23 solar degrees. Then see 23° of the Thula in the Latitude chart on Tuesday. It shows 262°-32', deduct 240° of Vrischika. 262°-32'—240°=22°-32' Latitude North. 22nd of August to 21st of September is the period of Sun. The opening month of the year 1886 is in the third house, then 22nd of January to 21st of December third house, 22nd of December to 21st of November second house, 22nd of November to 21st of October first house, 22nd of October to 21st of September twelfth house, 22nd of September to 21st of August eleventh house, here is the seventh aspect rashi Vrishabha of Vrischika. Then put Vrishabha rashi in the eleventh house, it shows Karka Lagna. The Moon is in the Uttara nakshatra and Kanya rashi. 14th of August to 14th of September Sun is in Simha rashi. The right ascension nakshatra of the Sun is Magha and his declination nakshatra is Uttara. The right ascension 7th aspect nakshatra of the Sun is Shatataraka and his 7th aspect declination nakshatra is Uttarabhadrapada No. 8. The right ascension 7th aspect nakshatra of the Moon is Uttara and her 7th aspect declination nakshatra is Magha (Dhanishtha is her declination nakshatra because we find Sun and Moon in one nakshatra Uttara that indicates New-Moon day, the ascension node of the Moon must be in Danishtha on New-Moon day of August and her descension node must be in Magha nakshatra). When the Moon's 7th aspect nakshatra is Uttara her right ascension nakshatra is Uttarabhadrapada. Both the planets show their declination nakshatra No. 8. Then count No. 8 of the Moon upto No. 8 of the Sun. Saturn is the Lord of the eighth house Kumbha rashi and Simha rashi is his 7th aspect rashi because his original nakshatra is No. 8 which vibrates to No. 3 means Uttarashadha nakshatra, it shows the month December. Mriga nakshatra in Vrishabha rashi is the opening nakshatra of the horoscope, it is of the Mars, it shows date. Then count No. 8 of the Moon upto No. 8 of the Sun. Aswini 8, Bharani 17, Krittika 26, Rohini 35, Mriga 44, Aridra 53, Punarvasu 62, Pushya 71. This is the Longevity of the native. Add 71 years in his birth year 1886, 1886 plus 71=1957 that is on 5th of December 1957 he died.

Shree Shripad Mahadeo Mate

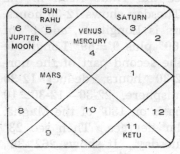

Birth date 31.8.1886

Date of expiry 5.12.1957

Long. 69° East

Lat. 22°-32′ North.

Example No. 29. Birth date 9.2.1856. We will see the birth day of the native. 1800=4, 56=7, February=2, Birth date is No. 9=9 plus 2 plus 7 plus 4=22 divided by 7=Remainder is 1=Sunday is the Birth day. See the month 22nd of January to 21st of February in the year 1856 the fourth part of the northern hemisphere. Sunday shows 7-30 hours and Kumbha rashi. Thursday is on 180° of Sunday but here is no Thursday. It is a negative part due to the spherical triangle. 7-30 hours means Punarvasu nakshatra, it is negative. Uttarashadha is on 180° of the Punarvasu, it is of the Sun. The Sun is the Lord of Sunday and Simha rashi, then see Simha rashi of the Sun in the fourth part of the Southern hemisphere. Sunday shows 17-30 hours and Thursday shows 21-30 hours.

17-30 hours means Anuradha nakshatra, it is negative for the Sun. Krittika nakshatra is on 180° of the Anuradha, it shows Krittika nakshatra of the Moon. 21-30 hours shows Uttarashadha nakshatra, it is of the Sun. Now see Dhanu rashi of Jupiter in the first part of the southern hemisphere. Thursday shows 4-30 hours. Add 2 hours the difference of the southern hemisphere in Sunday hours 7-30 of northern hemisphere 7-30 plus 2=9-30 hours, now deduct 4-30 hours of Dhanu rashi. Thursday 9-30—4-30=5 hours is the Longitude and deduct 5° of Jupiter day which is not in the fourth part of the northern hemisphere. 5 hours=75°—5° of Jupiter=70° Longitude cast. Fourth part of the northern hemisphere Sunday shows 7-30 hours and fourth part of Southern hemisphere Sunday shows 17-30, add these hours together 17-30 plus 7-30=25 hours means Purvabhadrapada nakshatra or 25 Solar degrees. Then see the Latitude chart for 25° of Dhanu rashi on Thursday. It shows 297°-58', deduct 270° of Dhanu rashi. 297°-58'—270°=27°-58' Latitude North.

22nd of January to 21st of February is the period of Moon. The opening month of the 1856 is in the eleventh house, then 22nd of January to 21st of December eleventh house, 22nd of December to 21st of November twelfth house, 22nd of November to 21st of October first house, 22nd of October to 21st of September second house, 22nd of September to 21st of August third house, 22nd of August to 21st of July fourth house, 22nd of July to 21st of June fifth house, 22nd of June to 21st of May sixth house, 22nd of May to 21st of April seventh house, 22nd of April to 21st of March eighth house, 22nd of March to 21st of February nineth house, 22nd of February to 21st of January Tenth house. Here is the 7th aspect rashi of the Dhanu. Then put Mithuna rashi in the Tenth house, it shows Kanya Lagna. The Sun is in Makara and Moon is in Mesha.

The right ascension nakshatra of the Sun is Moola and his declination nakshatra is Uttarashadha. The right ascension 7th aspect nakshatra is Aridra and his 7th aspect declination nakshatra is Pushya No. 8. The right ascension nakshatra of the Moon is Aswini and her declination nakshatra is Krittika. The right ascension 7th aspect nakshatra is Vishakha No. 7 (Mars is the Lord of Eighth house as well as he is the Lord of third house. The Sun is working on behalf of Mars, when the Sun will come in Dhanu rashi that is when his declination nakshatra will be Anuradha in Vrischika rashi the month indicates death of the native. Pushya is the first 7th aspect nakshatra, Uttarabhadrapada second and Anuradha third, i.e. on 26th date of December at his 70 he died). Then count

Moon's 7th aspect nakshatra No. 7 upto Sun's 7th aspect nakshatra No. 8, Aswini 7, Bharani 16, Krittika 25, Rohini 34, Mriga 43, Aridra 52, Punarvasu 61, Pushya 70, add 70 years in his Birth year 1856, 1856 plus 70=1926. Vrischika rashi of the Mars shows the month of December and Lord of Makara rashi shows his Uttarabhadrapada No. 26 nakshatra for the date, that is, on 26th of December 1926 he died.

Put the Saturn nakshatra No. 8 on birth day.

8	2	4	6
Sun	Tue	Thur	Sat
1	3	5	7
Mon	Wed	Fri	Sun

It shows 1-3-5-7 years, months are bad and vice versa.

Swami Shradhananda

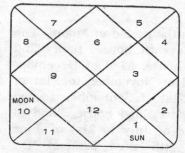

Birth date 9.2.1856
Date of expiry 26.12.1926
Long. 70° East
Lat. 27°-58′ North

Example No. 30. Birth date 30.6.1906. We will see the Birth day of the native. 1900=2, 6=7, June=3, Birth date is 30=30 plus 3 plus 7 plus 2=42 divided by 7=Remainder is 0=Saturday is the birth day. See the month 22nd of June to 21st of July in the year 1906 the third part of the northern hemisphere. No Saturday is there, then see Tuesday which is on 180° of Saturday. Tuesday shows 13-30 hours, but due to the spherical triangle it is a negative part. Then deduct 2 hours of the negative part and see the greater nakshatra. 13-30 hours—2=11-30 means Purva nakshatra, it is negative. Bharani nakshatra is the greater nakshatra. It is a seventh aspect nakshatra of the Moon, that is the Moon is in Thula rashi. Mars is the Lord of Tuesday as well as he is the Lord of Mesha and Vrischika rashi. Vrischika rashi is negative here, then see Mesha rashi of Mars in the third part of the Southern hemisphere. Saturday shows 24-30 hours and Tuesday shows 3-30 hours. Add 2 hours the difference of the Northern hemisphere. 3-30 plus 2=5-30 hours means Mriga nakshatra, it shows the Sun is in Mriga nakshatra, Mithuna rashi. Now see Kumbha rashi of Saturn in the first part of the northern hemisphere. Tuesday shows 20-30 hours. The third part of the southern hemisphere Saturday shows 24-30 hours, add 2 hours the difference of the northern hemisphere. 24-30 plus 2=26-30 hours, deduct 20-30 hours of Tuesday in Makara rashi. 26-30—20-30=6 hours is the Longitude, deduct 9° of Saturn which is not in the Vrischika and Makara, 90° —9°=81° Longitude East.

Tuesday shows 5-30 hours, deduct 20′ of Ayanachalana 5-30 —20′=5-10′ hours means 5 nakshatra or 5 Solar degrees. See latitude chart for 5° of Makara rashi on Tuesday, it shows 306°-36′, deduct 270° of Dhanu=36°-36′=Latitude North, deduct 6° of the Saturn 36°-36′ 6=30°-6′ North.

22nd of June to 21st of July is the period of Sun. The opening month of year 1906 is in fourth house; 22nd of January to 21st of December fourth house, 22nd of December to 21st of November third house, 22nd of November to 21st of October second house, 22nd of October to 21st of September first house, 22nd of September to 21st of August Twelfth house, 22nd of August to 21st of July eleventh house, 22nd of July to 21st of June tenth house. Here is Vrischika rashi of the third part of the northern hemisphere, then put Vrischika rashi in the tenth house, it shows Kumbha Lagna. The Moon is in Thula rashi and the Sun is in Mithuna rashi.

The right ascension nakshatra of the Moon is Swati and her 7th aspect nakshatra is Bharani, the declination nakshatra of the Moon is Anuradha, the 7th aspect nakshatra is Rohini No. 4. The right ascension nakshatra of the Sun is Rohini and his declination nakshatra is Aridra No. 6. Then count No. 4 of the Moon upto No. 6 of the Sun. Aswini 4, Bharani 13, Krittika 22, Rohini 31, Mriga 40, Aridra 49 this is the Longevity of the native.

Mercury is the Lord of the eighth house as well as fifth house. The Sun is in the fifth house, it shows the Lord of the eighth house is in conjunction. Mercury is neutral, the Sun is working on behalf of the Mercury. Sun is the Lord of seventh house. 7th house shows the month of March. Mars is the Lord of the opening house of the horoscope, his original nakshatra is Mriga which is in the 7th aspect rashi of Vrischika, his second nakshatra is Chitra which is in the eighth house, that is on 14th of March at his 49 he died. Add 49 years in his birth year, 1906 plus 49=1955, on 14th March 1955 he died. Put the birth date on his birth day.

7	5	3	1
Sat	Mon	Wed	Fri
8	2	4	6
Sun	Tues	Thur	Sat

It shows 1-3-5-7 years, months and dates are bad and vice versa.

Raja Tribhuwan(Nepal)

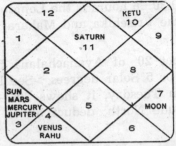

Birth date 30.6.1906
Date of expiry 14.3.1955
Long. 21° East
Lat. 30°-6′ North.

Example No. 31. Birth date 22.4.1870. We will see the birth
day of the native. 1800=4, 70=3, April=5 Birth date is 22=22
plus 5 plus 3 plus 4=divided by 7=Remainder is 6=Birth day is
Friday. See the month 22nd April to 21 of May in the year 1870
the third part of the Northern hemisphere. Friday shows 9-30
hours in Karka rashi, Monday is on 180° of Friday. Monday
shows 12-30 hours in Simha rashi but due to the spherical triangle
it is a negative part, add 2 hours the difference of the negative part
in Friday hours. 9-30 plus 2=11-30 hours means Purva nakshatra,
it is negative. Bharani nakshatra is a greater nakshatra, it shows
the Sun is in the Bharani nakshatra Mesha rashi. Monday shows
12-30 hours, it means Uttara nakshatra, it is negative, Uttarashadha
is a greater nakshatra for the Moon, it shows the Moon is in the
Uttarashadha nakshatra Makara rashi. Venus is the Lord of Friday
as well as he is the Lord of Vrishabha and Thula rashi. The Moon
is the Lord of Monday and Karka rashi. Then see Vrishabha rashi
of Venus in the northern hemisphere. Monday shows 5-30 hours and
Friday shows 9-30 hours. See the other rashi of Venus in the first
part. Friday shows 16-30 hours. Now deduct fourth part Friday
hours from the Friday hours, 16-30—9-30 hours=7 hours. Deduct
Monday hours from 7 hours, 7—5-30 hours=1-30 hours is the
Longitude. Add 9° of Monday which is not in the first part of the
northern hemisphere. 1-30 hours means 22°-30′ plus 9°=31°-30′
Longitude East, Sun is in the Bharani nakshatra. Bharani means 2
nakshatra or 2 solar degrees, then see 2° of Vrishibha rashi on
Monday in the Latitude chart, it shows 59°-27′ Latitude North.

22nd of April to 21st of May is the period of the Sun,
the opening month of the year 1870 is in the third house, then 22nd
of January to 21st of December third house, 22nd of December
to 21st November second house, 22nd of November to 21st of October
first house, 22nd of October to 21st of September twelfth house,

22nd of September to 21st of August eleventh house, 22nd of August to 21st of July tenth house, 22nd of July to 21st of June ninth house, 22nd of June to 21st of May eighth house, 22nd of May to 21st April seventh house, here is the 7th aspect rashi Makara of the Moon Karka. Then put Makara rashi in the 7th house, it shows Karka Lagna. The Moon is in Makara rashi and the Sun is in Mesha rashi.

The right ascension nakshatra of the Sun is Revati and his declination nakshatra is Bharani, his seventh aspect declination nakshatra is Swati No. 6.

The right ascension nakshatra of the Moon is Uttarashadha and her 7th aspect right ascension nakshatra is Punarvasu. The declination nakshatra of Moon is Dhanistha and her 7th aspect declination nakshatra is Aslesha No. 9. Swati nakshatra is in Thula rashi, Venus is the Lord of Thula rashi. Thula rashi shows the month of January. Now count Moon's nakshatra No. 9 upto Sun's nakshatra No. 6. Aswini 9, Bharani 18, Krittika 27, Rohini 36, Mriga 45, Aridra 54. This is the Longevity of the native. At his 54 the right ascension nakshatra of the Sun will be Bharani and his declination nakshatra will be Rohini No. 4. That is his right ascension rashi will be Makara. Then count No. 4 from Makara to Makara rashi. Shravana 4, Rohini 13, Hasta 22, and Shravana 31. That is on 31st of January at his 54 he died. Add 54 years in his birth year 1870; 1870 plus 54=1924, i.e. on 31st January 1924 he died.

Lenin (Russia)

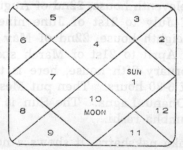

Birth date 22.4.1870
Date of expiry: 31.1.1924
Longitude 31°-30' East
Lat. 59°-27' North.

Put the birth day on the birth date.

Example No. 32. Birth date 7-3-1864. We will see birth day of the native. 1800=4, 64=3, March=2 Birth date is 7=7 plus 2 plus 3 plus 4=16 divided by 7=Remainder is 2=Monday is Birth day. See the month 22nd of February to 21st of March in the year 1864 the third part of the northern hemisphere, there is no Monday. Then Thursday is on 180° of Monday. Thursday shows

6-30 hours, but due to the spherical triangle it is a negative part. 6-30 hours means Aridra nakshatra, it is negative. Shatataraka is the greater nakshatra, it shows the Moon is in Shatataraka nakshatra Kumbha rashi. Moon is the Lord of Monday as well as she is the Lord of Karka rashi. Then see the Karka rashi of the Moon in the first part of the Northern hemisphere. Monday shows 10-30 hours and Thursday shows 13-30 hours. 10-30 hours means Magha nakshatra. Shatataraka is on 180° of the Magha, it shows the Sun is in Shatataraka nakshatra. Thursday shows 13-30 hours, it is negative for Jupiter, it means Jupiter is in the greater nakshatra Shravana that is his 7th aspect nakshatra is Shravana. It shows the Jupiter is in Karka rashi. See the other rashi Dhanu of the Jupiter in the first part of the southern hemisphere. Thursday shows 23-30 hours, deduct 2 hours the difference of the northern hemisphere. 23-30 hours—2=21-30 hours. Deduct 20' of Ayanachalana, 21-30—20'= 21-10 hours means 21 nakshatra or 21 solar degrees. Then see 21° of Meena rashi on Thursday in Latitude chart, it shows 17°-28' Latitude North. Thursday of Meena rashi shows 6-30 hours. 6-30 hours means 97°-30' Longitude, deduct Monday Longitude. Monday of Meena rashi 6° and Monday of Dhanu rashi 6° which is not in both rashis. 97°-30'—12°=85°-30' Longitude East. 6-30 hours of Jupiter is on the border of Mesha.

22nd of February to 21st of March is the period of Sun, the opening month of the year 1864 is in the third house, then 22nd of January to 21st of December third house, 22nd of December to 21st of November second house, 22nd of November to 21st of October first house, 22nd of October to 21st of September Twelfth house, 22nd of September to 21st of August eleventh house, 22nd of August to 21st of July tenth house, 22nd of July to 21st of June nineth house, 22nd of June to 21st of May eighth house, 22nd of May to 21st of April seventh house, 22nd of April to 21st of March sixth house, 22nd of March to 21st of February fifth house, here is the Mesha rashi which is on the border of 6-30 hours. Then put Mesha rashi in the fifth house. It shows Dhanu Lagna. The Sun is in Kumbha rashi and the Moon is in Kumbha rashi.

Both the planets are in Shatataraka nakshatra, it shows a new Moon day. Then the right ascension nakshatra of both the planets is Shravana and declination nakshatra is Shatataraka No. 6. The right ascension 7th aspect nakshatra of both the planets is Pushya and 7th aspect declination nakshatra is Magha No. 1. Magha nakshatra is original of Mars and Ketu, it shows the seventh aspect of Ketu or Mars is in the twelfth house or eighth house, but Mesha is the opening rashi of the horoscope, it shows the 7th aspect rashi of Ketu must be Vrischika because Jupiter himself is in Vrishabha. It means the opening month rashi is bad for the native and Jupiter's original nakshatra No. 7 is bad. Then count No. 1 the declination 7th aspect nakshatra of the Sun and Moon upto No. 7 nakshatra of the Jupiter.

Aswini 1, Bharani 10, Krittika 19, Rohini 28, Mriga 37, Aridra 46, Punarvasu 55, this is the Longevity of the native. Mesha rashi is of Mars and Mars is the Lord of Twelfth house. Mesha rashi shows the month of March. Krittika is the first 7th aspect nakshatra of the Jupiter and it is his original nakshatra, it shows the date of month, add 55 years in his birth year 1864, 1864 plus 55=1919, i.e. on 5th of March 1919 he died.

Put the 7th aspect date on the birth day.

3	5	7	1
Mon	Wed	Fri	Sun
4	6	8	2
Tue	Thur	Sat	Mon

It means 3-5-7-1 years are bad and in these years 1-3-5-7 months are bad and in these months 1-3-5-7 dates and days of the dates are bad and vice versa.

Shree Hari Narayan Apte

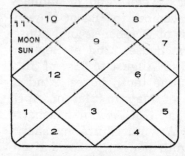

Birth date 7.3.1864
Date of expiry 3.3.1919
Long. 85°-30′ East
Lat. 17°-28′ North.

Example No. 33. Birth date 7.5.1901. We will see the birth day of the native. 1900=2, 1=1, May=7, Birth date is 7=7 plus 7 plus 1 plus 2=17 divided by 7=Remainder is 3=Tuesday is the birth day. See the month 22nd of April to 21st of May in the year 1901 the third part of the southern hemisphere. Tuesday shows 23-30 hours. Saturday is on 180° of Tuesday, Saturday shows 20-30 hours, but due to the spherical triangle it is a negative part. 23-30 hours means Dhanistha nakshatra, it is the nakshatra of Mars (he is the Lord of Tuesday still it is negative nakshatra, it shows Dhanistha nakshatra is his 7th aspect nakshatra and he himself is in Magha nakshatra), add 2 hours the difference of the negative part, 23-30 plus 2=25-30 hours means Purvabhadrapada nakshatra, it is negative. Vishakha is the greater nakshatra, Vishakha nakshatra is in Thula, it means it is 7th aspect nakshatra of the Sun. Saturday shows 20-30 hours in Dhanu rashi, it shows that the Moon herself is in Purvashadha and her 7th aspect nakshatra is Punarvasu.

Saturn is the lord of Saturday and he is the Lord of Makara and Kumbha rashi. Mars is the Lord of Mesha and Vrischika rashi as well as he is the Lord of Tuesday. Then see Mesha rashi of Mars in the first part of the southern hemisphere, Saturday shows 3-30 hours and Tuesday shows 6-30 hours. See the Vrischika rashi of Mars in the first part of the northern hemisphere. Saturday shows 17-30 hours. Deduct these hours from Saturday of southern hemisphere third part. 20-30—17-30=3 hours is the Longitude, add 4° more of Tuesday. 3 hours means 45° plus 4°=49° Longitude West. The third part of southern hemisphere Tuesday shows 23-30 hours and the first part of southern hemisphere Tuesday shows 6-30 hours. Add the hours together 23-30 plus 6-30=30 hours means 30 nakshatra or 30 solar degrees. See the Latitude chart for 30° of Makara rashi on Tuesday, it shows 333°-11', deduct 330° of Makara. 333°-11'—330°=3°-11' Latitude South.

22nd of April to 21st of May is the period of Sun, opening month of the year 1901 is in the seventh house. Then 22nd of January to 21st of December fourth house, 22nd December to 21st of November third house, 22nd of November to 21st of October second house, 22nd of October to 21st of September first house, 22nd of September to 21st of August twelfth house, 22nd of August to 21st of July eleventh house, 22nd of July to 21st of June tenth house, 22nd of June to 21st of May ninth house, 22nd of May to 21st of April eighth house, here is the seventh aspect rashi of Aswini nakshatra of Mars, Chitra nakshatra is on 180° of Aswini, Chitra nakshatra is in Kanya. Then put Kanya in the eighth house, it shows Kumbha Lagna. The sun is in Mesha rashi, the Moon is in Dhanu rashi. Right ascension nakshatra of the Sun is Aswini and his declination nakshatra is Krittika. His right ascension 7th aspect nakshatra is Chitra and his 7th aspect declination nakshatra is Vishakha 7. The right ascension nakshatra of the Moon is Purvashada and her 7th aspect right ascension nakshatra is Aridra No. 6. Then count No. 6 of the Moon upto No. 7 of the Sun.

Aswini 6, Bharani 15, Krittika 24, Rohini 33, Mriga 42; Aridra 57, Punarvasu 60. This is the Longevity of the native. The Moon is the Lord of the sixth house. The opening month of the Lunar horoscope is, in the tenth house, then Karka rashi shows the month of May. Rohini No. 4 is the original nakshatra of the Moon. Hasta nakshatra is her second nakshatra which shows the date 13. Add 60 years in his birth year, 1901 plus 60=1961, i.e. on 13th May 1961 he died.

Put the birth date on the birth day

8	2	4	6
Tue	Thur	Sat	Mon
1	3	5	7
Wed	Fri	Sun	Tue

It shows 1-3-5-7 years are bad, in these years 1-3-5-7 months are bad and in these months 2-4-6-8 dates and days of the dates are bad and vice versa.

Shree Gary Cooper

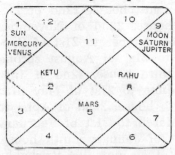

Birth date 7.5.1901

Date of expiry 13.5.1961

Long. 49° West

Lat. 3° 11' South.

Example No. 34. Birth date 1.2.1901. We will see the birth day of the native. 1900=2, 1=1, February = 2 Birth date is 1=1 plus 2 plus 1 plus 2=6=Friday is the birth day. See the month 22nd of January to 21st of February in the year 1901. The third part of the southern hemisphere, Friday shows 22-30 hours, Tuesday is on 180° of the Friday. No Tuesday is here. It is a negative part due to the spherical triangle. 22-30 hours means Shravana nakshatra, it is negative for Venus. Aslesha nakshatra is on 180° of Shravana, it shows the Moon is in the Shravana. There is no Tuesday, then Venus itself working for both the planets for the Sun and for the Moon. It means the Sun is in the Shravana nakshatra, the opposition of both the planets indicates full-moon day.

Venus is the Lord of Friday as well as Thula and Vrishabha rashi. Thula rashi is negative here, then see the Vrishabha rashi in the third part of the northern hemisphere. Friday shows 12-30 hours and Tuesday shows 9-30 hours. Now see the Vrischika rashi of the Mars in the second part of the northern hemisphere,

Tuesday shows 2-30 hours. The third part of the Northern Hemisphere Friday shows 12-30 and Tuesday shows 9-30 hours. Deduct 9-30 hours from 12-30 hours of Friday. 12-30—9-30=3 hours is the Longitude. Add 6° more of the Tuesday which is not in the third part of the southern hemisphere. 3 hours=45° plus 6°=51°.

Third part of the southern hemisphere Friday shows 22-30 hours add 2 hours the difference of the northern hemisphere. 22-30 plus 2=24-30 hours, deduct 20' of Ayanachalana 24-30—20'=24°-10' it means Shatataraka nakshatra. Magha nakshatra is on 180° of Shatataraka. Magha is tenth nakshatra or 10 solar degrees. Then see 10° of Karka rashi on Tuesday in south latitude chart, it shows 131°-37', deduct 120° of Karka rashi, 131°-37' —120°=11°-37' South Latitude.

22nd of January to 21st of February is the period of Moon. the opening month of the year 1901 is in the tenth house, then 22nd of January to 22nd of December tenth house, 22nd of December to 21st of November eleventh house, 22nd of November to 21st of October twelfth house, 22nd of October to 21st of September first house, 22nd of September to 21st of August second house, 22nd of August to 21st of July third house, 22nd of July to 21st of June fourth house, 22nd of June to 21st of May fifth house, 22nd of May to 21st of April sixth house, 22nd of April to 21st of March seventh house, 22nd of March to 21st of February eighth house, 22nd of February to 21st of January ninth house, here is the Vrishabha rashi of Venus, then put the Vrishabha rashi in the ninth house. It shows Kanya Lagna. The Moon is in the Karka rashi, and the Sun is in Makara rashi.

The right ascension nakshatra of the Sun is Dhanishtha and his declination nakshatra is Purvabhadrapada No. 7. The right ascension nakshatra of the Moon is Aslesha and her declination nakshatra is Purva. The right ascension 7th aspect nakshatra of the Moon is Dhanishtha and her 7th aspect declination nakshatra is Purvabhadrapada No. 7. The declination nakshatra of both the planets is Purvabhadrapada No. 7.

Mars is the Lord of eighth house as well as he is the Lord of third house. His original nakshatra is No. 5 and his 7th aspect nakshatra is No. 1, but here in the eighth house his nakshatra is No. 1 and his 7th aspect nakshatra is No. 5, then count No. 5 of the Mars upto No. 7.

Aswini 5, Bharani 14, Krittika 23, Rohini 32, Mriga 41, Aridra 50, Punarvasu 59, this is the Longevity of the native. The declination nakshatra of both the planets is Purvabhadrapada. It shows the Sun or the Moon changed his or her polarity. Add 59 years in the birth year, 1901 plus 59=1960. The opening month of the year 1960 is in the fourth house. Mars is the Lord of third house, it shows the month of November. Moon's original nakshatra is Rohini in Vrishabha rashi and Anuradha nakshatra is her 7th aspect nakshatra. Anuradha is No. 17, it indicates the date, that is on 17th of November 1960 he died. Put the seventh aspect nakshatra on the birth day

7	1	3	5
Fri	Sun	Tue	Thur
8	2	4	6
Sat	Mon	Wed	Fri

It shows 1-3-5-7 years are bad, in these years, 2-4-6-8 months are bad, in these months 2-4-6-8 dates are bad and vice versa.

Shree Clarke Gable

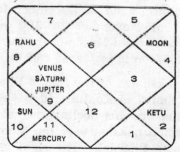

Birth date 1.2.1901
Date of expiry 17.11.1960.
Long. 51° West
Lat. 11°-37′ South.

Example No. 35. Birth date 30.10.1887. We will see the birth day of the native. 1800=4, 87=3, October=6, Birth date is 30=30 plus 6 plus 4 plus 3=43 divided by 7= Remainder is 1= Sunday is the birth day. See the month 22nd of October to 21st of November in the year 1887. The first part of the southern hemisphere, Sunday shows 22-30 hours. Wednesday is on 180° of Sunday, Wednesday shows 18-30 hours, it is a negative part due to spherical triangle; 22-30 hours means Shravana nakshatra, it is negative. Hasta nakshatra is the greater nakshatra for the Moon, it is a seventh aspect nakshatra of the Moon, that is the Moon is in Meena rashi. 18-30 hours means Jyeshtha nakshatra, it is negative. Add 2 hours the difference of the negative part. 18-30 hours plus 2= 20-30 hours, it means Purvashadha nakshatra, it is negative. Bharani nakshatra is the greater nakshtra for the Sun, it is 7th aspect nakshatra of the Sun, that is the Sun is in Thula rashi. The Sun is the Lord of Sunday and Simha rashi. Mercury is the Lord of Wednesday as well as Kanya and Mithuna rashis. Mithuna rashi is negative here. Then see Kanya rashi of Mercury in the third part of northern hemisphere. Sunday shows 1-30 hours and Wednesday shows 4-30 hours.

The first part of the southern hemisphere Sunday shows 22-30 hours and Third part of the northern hemisphere Sunday shows 1-30 hours. Add together the hours of both the days 22-30 plus 1-30=24 hours means Shatataraka or 24° Solar degrees. Then see 24° of Kumbha rashi on Wednesday in the Latitude chart, it shows 352°-24′, deduct 330° of Kumbha rashi, 352°-24′ minus 330°=22°-24′ North latitude. Third part of the northern hemisphere Wednesday shows 4-30 hours, add 2 hours the difference of the southern hemisphere 4-30 plus 2=6-30 hours. Deduct 20′ of Ayanachalana 6-30 —20=6-10 hours. See the Longitude chart for 6-10 hours and deduct 4° of the negative Wednesday 92°-30′—4°=88°-30′ Longitude East.

22nd of October to 21st of November is the period of the Sun. The opening month of the year 1887 is in the third house, then 22nd of January to 21st of December third house, 22nd of December to 21st of November second house, 22nd of November to 21st of October first house, here is the seventh aspect rashi Mesha of the Sun. Mesha Lagna. The Sun is in Thula, The Moon is in Meena rashi.

The right ascension seventh aspect nakshatra of the Sun is Bharani and his 7th aspect declination nakshatra is Rohini. Right ascension nakshatra of the Sun is Vishakha and his declination nakshatra is Jyestha No. 9. The right ascension nakshatra of the Moon is Revati and her declination nakshatra is Bharani. The right ascension seventh aspect nakshatra of the Moon is Chitra and her seventh aspect declination nakshatra is Vishakha No. 7. Then count declination nakshatra of the Sun No. 9 upto declination nakshatra of the Moon No. 7. Aswini 9, Bharani 18, Krittika 27, Rohini 36, Mriga 45, Aridra 54, Punarvasu 63, this is the Longevity of the native.

Mars is the Lord of 8th house, and his 7th aspect rashi is Vrishabha (which is the opening rashi of the southern hemisphere first part, Wednesday 18-30 hours and Sunday 22-30 hours). Sun is the ruler, it shows Mithuna rashi, it shows the month of December. Aridra is the first nakshatra No. 6 and Swati will be second because Purvashadha nakshatra was negative due to the spherical triangle, now it is positive that the Sun has changed his polarity. Aridra is the first 7th aspect nakshatra and Swati second. It indicates the date of the month. Add 63 years in his birth year, 1887 plus 63= 1950, that is on 15th of December 1950 he died.

Shree Sardar Patel

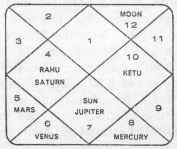

Birth date 30.10.1887

Date of expiry 15.12.1950

Long. 88°-30′ East

Lat. 22°-24′ North

Example No. 36. Birth date 23.2.1795. We will see the Birth date of the native. 1700=6, 95=6, February=2, Birth date is 23=23 plus 2 plus 6 plus 6=37 divided by 7=Remainder is 2=Monday is the birth day. See the month 22nd of February to 21st of March in the year 1795 the third part of the northern hemisphere. There is no Monday, then Thursday is on 180° of the Monday. Thursday shows 6-30 hours, but due to the spherical triangle it is a negative part. 6-30 hours means Aridra nakshatra, it is negative, Shatataraka is the greater nakshatra, it shows the Sun is in Shatataraka nakshatra. Jupiter is the Lord of Thursday as well as he is the Lord of Meena and Dhanu rashis. Moon is the lord of Karka rashi as well as she is the Lord of Monday.

See the Dhanu rashi of the Jupiter in the first part of the Southern hemisphere. Thursday shows 23-30 hours it shows the Moon is in Dhanishtha nakshatra, Makara rashi because no Monday is here.

See the Karka rashi of the Moon in the fourth part of the southern hemisphere. Monday shows 13-30 hours and Thursday shows 16-30 hours, deduct 13-30 hours of Monday from 16-30 hours of Thursday. 16-30—13-30=3 hours is the Longitude. Add 4° of negative Monday 3 hours=45° plus 4°=49° Longitude West.

First part of the southern hemisphere Thursday shows 23-30 hours, deduct 20′ of Ayanachalana, 23-30—20′=23-10′, it means 23 nakshatra or 23 solar degrees. See the Latitude chart for 23° of Kumbha rashi on Thursday, it shows 356°-29′, deduct 330° of Kumbha. 356°-29′—330°=26°-29′ South Latitude. (add 2 hours the difference of negative part). The first part of the southern hemisphere Thursday. 6-30 plus 2=8°-30′. See 8° of Mesha on Thursday, it is 37°-15′, deduct 30° of Mesha, 37°-15′—30°=7°-15′ South Latitude. The given Latitudes are of two horoscopes. One is tropical and the other is sidereal. See supplimentary chapter for details.

263

The fourth part of the southern hemisphere Thursday shows 16-30 hours. Add 2 hours the difference of the northern hemisphere. 16-30 hours plus 2=18-30 hours means 18°. See 18° of Sihma=167°-150° of Sihma=17° Latitude South. Now the first part of southern hemisphere Thursday shows 23-30 hours. See 23° of Dhanu 295°-47'-270° of Dhanu=25°-47' South Latitude. The third part of the northern hemisphere Thursday shows 6-30 hours. See 6° declination Meena on Thursday 6°-59' north for Meena and south for Kanya, in this way we can find Latitude of any rashi. See the poles of the house from the equator to 60° of Latitude for Male and Female in the appendix.

22nd of February to 21st of March is the period of Sun, opening month of the year 1795 is in the second house, then 22nd of January to 21st of December second house, 22nd of December to 21st of November first house, 22nd of November to 21st of October twelfth house, 22nd of October to 21st of September eleventh house, 22nd of September to 21st of August tenth house, 22nd of August to 21st of January third house, here is the 7th aspect rashi Thula house, 22nd of June to 21st of May seventh house, 22nd of May to 21st of April sixth house, 22nd of April to 21st of March fifth house, 22nd of March to 21st of February fourth house, 22nd of February to 21st of January third house, here is the 7th aspect rashi Thula of the Mesha, it shows Mesha Lagna. The Moon is in the Makara rashi and the Sun is in the Kumbha rashi.

The right declination nakshatra of the Sun is Uttarabhadrapada and his 7th aspect declination nakshatra is Uttara. The right ascension nakshatra is Shatataraka and his right ascension 7th aspect nakshatra is Magha. Mars is the Lord of eighth house as well as he is the Lord of Lagna, his rashi is in the triangle Simha rashi, it shows the Sun is working on his behalf. His original nakshatra is No. 5 and his 7th aspect nakshatra is No. 1. The right ascension nakshatra of the Moon is Dhanistha No. 5. Then count No. 5 of the Moon upto No. 1 Magha nakshatra.

Aswini 5, Bharani 14, Krittika 23, Rohini 32, Mriga 41, Aridra 50, Punarvasu 59, Pushya 68, Aslesha 77, Maga 86. This is the Longevity of the native. 7th aspect of the Lagna rashi shows the month of June. The right ascension nakshatra of the Moon is Dhanistha and her declination nakshatra is Purvabhadrapada No. 7. The opening rashi of the horoscope is Mithuna, Punarvasu nakshatra is there which is first and Vishakha is second in the month of June. Vishakha nakshatra indicates date, add 86 years in his birth year, 1795 plus 86=1881, that is on 16.6.1881 he died.

Sir John Meson

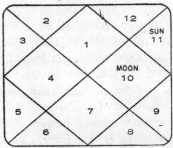

Birth date 23.2.1795
Date of expiry 16.6.1881
Long. 49° West
Lat. 26°-29′ South.

Example No. 37. Birth date 14.11.1889. We will see the birth day of the native. 1800=4, 89=6, November=2 Birth date is 14=14 plus 2 plus 6 plus 4=26 divided by 7=Remainder is 5= Thursday is the birth day. See the month 22nd of the October to 21st of November in the year 1889. The first part of the southern hemisphere, Thursday shows 22-30 hours and Simha rashi. Monday is on 180° of Thursday. Monday shows 2-30 hours, but due to the spherical triangle it is a negative part. 22-30 hours means Shravana nakshatra, it is negative. Rohini is the greater nakshatra, it is 7th aspect nakshatra of the Sun (Rohini is on 180° of the Anuradha). It shows the Sun is in Vrischika rashi. Monday shows 2-30 hours, 2-30 means Bharani nakshatra, it is also negative for the Moon. Purvashadha is the greater nakshatra, it shows Jupiter is in the Dhanu rashi. Jupiter is the Lord of Thursday as well as he is the Lord of Meena and Dhanu rashis. See the Karka rashi of the Moon in the second part of the southern hemisphere. Monday shows 9-30 hours and Thursday shows 22-30 hours, 9-30 hours shows the node of the Moon and 22-30 hours are 7th aspect nakshatra of the Moon. 22-30 hours means Shravana nakshatra, it is 7th aspect nakshatra of the Moon (Aslesha is on 180° of the Shravana). That is, the Moon is in Karka rashi.

Now see the Meena rashi and Dhanu rashi of the Jupiter. The first part of northern hemisphere Meena rashi Monday shows 12-30 hours and second part of the northern hemisphere Dhanu rashi Thursday shows 8-30 hours, add 2 hours the difference of the southern hemisphere. 8-30 plus 2 = 10-30. Deduct 20′ of Ayanachalana, 10-30—20′ 10-10′ hours means Magha nakshatra. Shatataraka is on 180° of Magha. Shatataraka is No. 24. 24 nakshatra means 24 solar degrees. See the Latitudes chart for 24° of Dhanu rashi on Thursday, it shows 294°-59′, deduct 270° of Dhanu rashi, 294°-59′— 270°=24°-59′ Latitude North.

The first part of the southern hemisphere, Thursday shows 22-30 hours, it is a negative part due to the spherical triangle. 4-30 hours are greater. See the Longitude chart for 4-30 hours and deduct the Monday Longitude which is not in the first part. 4-30=67°-30'—6° of Monday=61°-30' Longitude East. (The first part of the northern hemisphere Meena rashi Monday shows 12-30 hours, add 2 hours the difference of the southern hemisphere, 12-30 plus 2=14-30 hours, it is negative but it will be positive on his last day according to Indian Standard Time). 22nd of October to 21st of November is the period of Sun, opening month of the year 1889 is in the third house, then 22nd of January to 21st of December third house, 22nd of December to 21st of November second house, 22nd of November to 21st of October first house, here is the Simha rashi of Thursday first part of southern hemisphere. It shows Simha Lagna. The Moon is in Karka rashi. The sun is in Vrischika rashi. The right ascension nakshatra of the Sun is Swati and his declination nakshatra is Anuradha. Right ascension 7th aspect nakshatra of the Sun is Aswini and his 7th aspect declination nakshatra is Krittika No. 3.

The right ascesion nakshatra of the Moon is Punarvasu and her declination nakshatra is Aslesha No. 9. Then count declination nakshatra of the Sun No. 3 upto declination nakshatra of the Moon No. 9.

Aswini 3, Bharani 12, Krittika 21, Rohini 30, Mriga 39, Aridra 48, Punarvasu 57, Pushya 66, Aslesha 75.

Jupiter is the Lord of eighth house as well as fifth house, Jupiter is in the Purvashadha, that is, his right ascension nakshatra is Purvashadha which is the seventh aspect right ascension nakshatra of the Moon. Declination nakshatra of the Jupiter is Shravana which is the 7th aspect declination nakshatra of the Moon. Jupiter's eighth house shows the Month and his declination 7th aspect nakshatra shows the date. Makara 9, Kanya 18 and Vrishabha 27.

Add 75 years in his birth year 1889, plus 75=1964 that is on 27th May 1964 he died. Revati nakshatra is on 180° of the Chitra. Chitra nakshatra means 14 hours (it is negative nakshatra. Mriga

Shree Jawaharlal Nehru

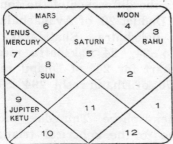

Birth date 14.11.1889
Date of expiry 27.5.1964
Lat. 24°-59' North.
Long. 61°-30' East

266

is the greater for the Moon, that is, the Moon is in Jyeshtha nakshatra).

We have seen nearly 37 horoscopes which we have studied only with the help of the birth day. I have proved that the week has astronomical significance. The ancient Rishis were not fools to make astronomical week divisions. I have tried to give the correct meaning of secret verses known to the Hindus long before the period of the so-called dawn of scientific knowledge.

सप्त युंजति रथमेकचक्रं एको अश्वां वहति सप्तनाम ।
त्रिनाभि चक्रं अजरं अनर्व्यं यत्रेगा विश्वाभुवनानि तस्थू: ॥

The Sun is working on behalf of each planet or each day. The cycle of 3 nakshatras Aswini, Magha and Moola never becomes old and is not loose. Thus the cycle of days or planets and nakshatras never become old, the chart of twelve months proves the universal truth to our readers. Now take the advantage of this chapter by studying it closely and the reader will understand the whole theory of the Rigveda and the rules of the Lord Vishnu, as well as his Law of determinism.

CHAPTER VII

ILLUSTRATIONS TO FIND THE MARRIAGE DAY OF THE NATIVES

It will be seen that all the rude shocks that determinism is supposed to have received were only in the realm of atom and the electrons. If we take a human being we find that some sort of determinism exists. We have seen the Law of determinism in the last chapter.

It must not be supposed that the Western modern scientists made a discovery of atoms, or electrons of the atoms—'That the electron of the atom does not travel uniformly in a continuous stream but by jumps', this is the fundamental law of the universe which was known to the ancient Hindus. The credit goes to the Hindus of having discovered electron of the atoms. The following verse reads the same:

'एकाचमे तिस्रश्चमे पंचचमे सप्तचमे नवचमे एकादशचमे त्रयोदशचमे पंचदशचमे सप्तदशचमे नवदशचमे एकर्विंशतिश्चमे त्रयोविंशतिश्चमे पंचर्विंशतिश्चमे सप्तर्विंशतिश्चमे नर्वविंशतिश्चमे एकर्त्रिंशच्चमे त्रयस्त्रिंशश्चमे चतस्रश्चमेष्टौचमे द्वादशचमे षोडशचमे विंशतिश्चमे चतुर्विंशतिश्चमेष्टार्विंशतिश्चमे द्वात्रिंशच्चमे षट्त्रिंशच्चमे चत्वारिंशच्चमे चतुश्चत्वारिंशच्च मेष्टाचत्वा।रिंशच्चमे वाजश्च प्रसवश्च पिजश्चऋतुश्च सुवश्च मृत्वीच व्याशिनयश्चांत्या यनश्चां- त्यश्च मौवनश्च भुवनश्चाधिपतिश्च ।' Rudra verse 11.

It clearly shows that the nakshatras and the planets are nothing but the generators of electrons. Rahu and Ketu are the ascending and descending nodes of the Moon, means the North and South poles of the magnetic field. Sun, Mars, Jupiter, Saturn and Ketu generate 1-3-5-7-9 electrons which we say positive electrons. Moon, Mercury, Venus and Rahu generate 2-4-6-8 electrons which we say negative electrons and the pressure of both the electrons is 19 ampere with 100 cycles.

1-3-5-7-9, 11-13-15-17, (=) 19, add it together 1 plus 3 plus 5 plus 7 plus 9 plus 11 plus 13 plus 15 plus 17 plus 19=100.

We know Eclipses recur every Nineteen years (18 years and 11.3 days) and we know 19th nakshatra is Moola which is of the Ketu. It is clear that the nineteen turns of the Sun returns the eclipses and polarity change is also at the same time, i.e. 1-3-5-7-9 numbers turn into 2-4-6-8.

Naturally electron of the atom does not travel uniformly in continuous stream but by jumps such as 1-3-5-7-9, 2-4-6-8, then it is clear that the ancient Maharshis discovered this grand truth, the fringe of which Einstein and Eddington have just now reached.

Now we have to see the other pole of the natives. Unless he ends the first astronomical electron cycle, it is impossible to get the other pole. So we must find out the ending moment of the first negative cycle of the native. We see some examples now.

Example No. 1. Birth date 15.5.1937. We will see the birth day of the native. 1900=2, 37=4, May=7, Birth date is 15=15 plus 7 plus 4 plus 2=28 divided by 7=Remainder is 0=Saturday is birth day. See the month 22nd of the April to 21st of May in the year 1937 the third part of the northern hemisphere. Saturday shows 10-30 hours and Karka rashi. Tuesday is on 180° of the Saturday but no Tuesday is here. It is a negative part due to the spherical triangle. Add 2 hours the difference of the negative part. 10-30 plus 2=12-30 hours means Uttara nakshatra, it is negative for the Saturn. (Uttarabhadrapada is on 180° of the Uttara, it means the Saturn is in the Uttarabhadrapada). Krittika nakshatra is the greater nakshatra, it shows the Sun is in Krittika nakshatra. Saturn is the Lord of Saturday as well as he is the Lord of Makara and Kumbha rashis. Then see the Makara rashi of the Saturn in the third part of the southern hemisphere. Saturday shows 20-30 hours and Tuesday shows 23-30 hours. Saturday shows 20-30 hours means Purvashadha nakshatra and Tuesday shows 23-30 hours means Dhanistha nakshatra, it means the right ascension 7th aspect nakshatra of the Moon is Dhanishta, that is the Moon is in the Aslesha (The right ascension nakshatra of the Jupiter is Purvashadha and his declination nakshatra is Shravana). First Saturday shows 10-30 hours and second Saturday shows 20-30 hours, add it together 20-30 plus 10-30=31 hours. Tuesday shows 23-30 hours. Add 2 hours the difference of the northern hemisphere. 23-30 plus 2= 25-30 hours, deduct these hours from 31 hours. 31—25-30=5-30 hours is the Longitude. Add 3° more of Tuesday. 5-30 means 82°-30′ plus 3°=85°-30′ Longitude East. Now see the Mesha rashi of the Mars in the first part of the southern hemisphere. Saturday shows 3-30 hours and Tuesday shows 7-30. Saturday of Dhanu rashi shows 20-30 hours and Saturday of Mesha rashi shows 3-30 hours. Deduct 3-30 hours from 20-30 hours. 20-30—3-30=17 hours means 17th nakshatra or 17 solar degrees of Simha rashi on Saturday, it shows 168°-30′. Deduct 150° of Simha rashi. 168°-30′ —150°=18°-30′ Latitude North.

22nd of April to 21st of May is the period of Sun. Opening month of the year 1937 is in the fourth house, then 22nd of January to 21st of December fourth house, 22nd of December to 21st of November third house, 22nd of November to 21st of October second house, 22nd of October to 21st of September first house, 22nd of September to 21st of August twelfth house, 22nd of August to 21st of July eleventh house, 22nd of July to 21st of June tenth house, 22nd of June to 21st of May nineth house, 22nd of May to 21st of April eighth house, here is Kumbha rashi of the Saturn. Then put the Kumbha rashi of the Saturn in the eighth house. It shows Karka Lagna, The Moon is in Karka rashi and the Sun is in Vrishabha rashi. We have to see the marriage day of the native, naturally we must see the Lord of seventh house as well as the Lord of the first house. The Lord of first house is Moon and she is in Aslesha nakshatra her 7th aspect nakshatra is Dhanishtha, that is in Makara, Dhanishtha nakshatra is No. 23, it shows native will get married at her 23. The Lord of the seventh house is in Uttarabhadrapada nakshatra that is in Meena rashi. Meena rashi shows the month 21st of the May to 22nd of the June, in other way Moon is working on behalf of the Mars. Mars is the Lord of Mesha and Vrischika rashis. His nakshatra is No. 5 which is in Vrishabha rashi, it is in the triangle of Makara rashi, Vrischika rashi shows the month of May. When Moon will come in Vrischika or in Meena her seventh aspect nakshatra will be Hasta or Rohini. Then count Rohini from Vrischika to Vrischika of the Sun, or count Hasta nashatra from Meena, to Meena of the Moon. Vrischika No. 4, Meena 13, Karka 22. (Meena 4, Karka 13, Vrischika 22). On both the ways we are getting the date 22nd May, add 23 years in her birth year, 1937 plus 23=1960. That is on 22nd of May 1960 she gets married. Put the birth date on the birth day.

6	2	4	8
Sat	Mon	Wed	Fri
7	3	9	5
Sun	Tue	Thur	Sat

It shows 3-5-7-9 years are good, in these years 3-5-7-9 months are good, in these months 2-4-6-8 dates and days of the dates are good and vice versa. (Meena rashi is of Jupiter when Saturn will come in the other rashi of the Jupiter native will get married. That is Saturn has to change the polarity not only this but she will get married with the person in whose horoscope Saturn will be in the third house of Dhanu rashi because the Saturn of the lady's horoscope is in the nineth house and Meena rashi).

Miss Kulkarni

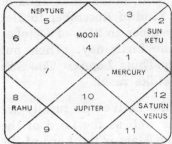

Birth date 15.5.1937

Date of marriage 22.5.1960

Long. 85°-30′ East

Lat. 18°-3′ North.

Example No. 2. Birth date 26.11.1935. We will see the birth day of the native. 1900=2, 35=1, November=2, Birth date is 26= 26 plus 2 plus 1 plus 2=31 divided by 7=Remainder is 3=Tuesday is the birth day. See the month 22nd of November to 21st of December in the year 1935. The third part of southern hemisphere, Tuesday shows 23-30 hours in Kanya rashi. Saturday is on 180° of Tuesday. Saturday shows 20-30 hours in Simha rashi, it is a negative part due to the spherical triangle. 23-30 means Dhanishtha nakshatra, it is negative. Mriga nakshatra is the greater nakshatra, it shows the 7th aspect nakshtra of the Sun. That is the Sun is in the Jyeshtha nakshatra. Saturday shows 20-30 hours. 20-30 hours means Purvashadha nakshatra. (It is the original nakshatra of Venus). It is negative. Purva is the greater nakshatra, it shows the 7th aspect nakshatra of Saturn. That is, the Saturn is in Kumbha rashi. Mars is the Lord of Tuesday as well as he is the Lord of Vrischika rashi and Mesha rashi. Then see the first part of the Southern hemisphere for Vrischika rashi. Saturday shows 3-30 hours. 3-30 hours means Krittika nakshatra. Anuradha is on 180° of the Krittika. It shows the Moon is in Anuradha nakshatra Vrischika rashi. Tuesday shows 6-30 hours in Dhanu rashi, 6-30 hours means Aridra nakshatra, Moola is on 180° of Aridra, it shows the ascending node of the Moon is in Aridra and descending node of the Moon is in Dhanu with Mars. Now third part of the southern hemisphere Tuesday shows 23-30 hours and Tuesday of first part shows 6-30 hours. Add the hours together: 23-30 plus 6-30=30 hours. Deduct 24 hours and 10° of the Mars, Ketu. 30—24=6 hours shows 90° Longitude. 90°—10°=80° Longitude East. See the Mesha rashi of the Mars in the second part of the northern hemisphere. Saturday shows 13-30 hours. The first part of the southern hemisphere Saturday shows 3-30 hours, add together both these hours, 13-30 plus 3-30=17 hours, it means 17th nakshatra or 17 solar degrees. Then see the Latitude chart for 17° of the Makara on Saturday, it shows 319°-29′ north, deduct 300° of Makara, 319°-29′ —300°=19°-29′ north.

22nd of November to 21st of December is the period of Moon. Opening month of the year 1935 is in the tenth house, then 22nd of January to 21st of December tenth house, 22nd of December to 21st of November eleventh house, 22nd of November to 21st of October twelfth house, here is Kanya rashi of the birth day. Then put Kanya rashi in the twelfth house, it shows Thula Lagna. The Sun is in Vrischika rashi, the Moon is in Vrischika rashi.

We have to see the marriage day of the native. Naturally we must see the Lord of the seventh house as well as the Lord of the first house. Venus is the Lord of Lagna and Mars is the Lord of the seventh house, Venus is the Lord of Lagna, his original nakshatra is No. 2, that is Bharani, Purva, Purvashadha. Purva is Saturn's 7th aspect nakshatra, it means the Venus is in triangle of Saturn; Purvabhadrapada nakshatra is the right ascension nakshatra of the Saturn. Saturn is working on behalf of the Venus. Purvabhadrapada is 25th nakshatra, it means native is getting married at her 25th year. Mesha rashi is in the seventh house, it shows the month of March. Mars is in Dhanu rashi. Mithuna is his 7th aspect rashi. Moon must come in Mithuna for her marriage. Shukra is in Vishakha nakshatra, it is the nakshatra of Jupiter, then Jupiter must come in Dhanu for her marriage, his seventh aspect nakshatra is Punarvasu, it indicates the date of marriage. Add 25 years in her birth year 1935, 1935 plus 25=1960 that is on 7th of March 1960 she got married. (Sun and Moon are in Vrischika rashi, it shows the New Moon day. Rahu is in the third house of Dhanu rashi. Saturn is in the fifth house and Venus is in Lagna. Now Saturn has to change his polarity. Rahu has to change his polarity. Saturn must come in Jupter's rashi because he is in the Jupiter's nakshatra. Rahu is in the Jupiter's rashi, he must come in Jupiter's other rashi Meena, not only this but she must get married with person in whose horoscope Jupiter will be of Meena rashi. Ketu will be of Dhanu rashi, Venus will be Thula).

Miss Dange P.K.

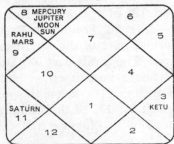

Birth date 26.11.1935
Date of marriage 7.3.1960
Long. 80° East
Lat. 19°-29′ North

272

Put the birth date on the birth day

9	3	5	7
Tues	Thur	Sat	Mon
6	4	2	8
Wed	Fri	Sun	Tues

It shows 3-5-7-9 years are good, in these years 3-5-7-9 months are good, in these months 3-5-7-9 dates are good and vice versa.

Example No. 3. Birth date 23.11.1930. We will see the birth day of the native. 1900=2, 30=2, November=2 Birth date is 23=23 plus 2 plus 2 plus 2=29 divided by 7=Remainder is 1=Sunday is the birth day. See the month 22nd of November to 21st of December in the year 1930. The fourth part of the southern hemisphere Sunday, shows 21-30 hours in Karka rashi. Wednesday is on 180° of Sunday. But due to the spherical triangle it is a negative part. Sunday shows 21-30 hours means Uttarashadha nakshatra, it is his own nakshatra still it is negative, it means the Sun is on 180° of the greater nakshatra, Uttarashadha is negative, Krittika is the greater nakshatra and Sun is on 180° of Krittika, that is the Sun is in Vrischika rashi, his negative nakshatra Uttarashadha is in Karka rashi. Moon is the Lord of Karka rashi, it means the Moon is in the negative nakshatra, Uttarashadha because Wednesday shows 17-30 hours, 17-30 hours means Anuradha nakshatra, it is negative, Pushya nakshatra is the greater nakshatra, it is 7th aspect nakshatra of the Moon. 17-30 hours are in Mithuna rashi, Dhanu rashi is on 180° of Mithuna, it means the Moon is in Uttarashadha nakshatra, Dhanu rashi. Sun is the Lord of Sunday and Simha rashi. Mercury is the lord of Mithuna and Kanya. Mithuna rashi is negative here, then see the other rashi Kanya in the second part of the southern hemisphere. Wednesday shows 24-30 hours. Add 2 hours the difference of the negative part 24-30 plus 2=26-30 hours, it means Uttarabhadrapada nakshatra, it shows the descending node of the Moon is in the Uttarabhadrapada nakshatra in Meena rashi. Wednesday of Kanya rashi 26-30, deduct 21-30 hours of Sunday Karka rashi, 26-30—21-30 =5 hours=90°-6°=84° Longitude East. The fourth part of the southern hemisphere Wednesday shows 17-30 hours, deduct 20' of Ayanachalana 17-30—20'=17-10' hours, it means 17th nakshatra or 17 solar degrees. Then see Latitude chart for 17° of Dhanu rashi on Wednesday, it shows 287°-55', deduct 270° of Dhanu rashi, 287°-55'-270°=17°-55' Latitude North.

22nd November to 21st of December is the period of Moon. Opening month of the year 1930 is in the tenth house, then 22nd

273

of January to 21st of December tenth house, 22nd of December to 21st of November eleventh house, 22nd of November to 21st of October 12th house, here is the Kanyarashi of Budha, then put the Kanya rashi in the twelfth house, it shows Thula Lagna, the Sun is in the Vrischika rashi, the Moon is in the Dhanu rashi.

We have to see the marriage day of the native. Naturally we must see the Lord of the seventh house as well as Lord of the Lagna. Lord of the Lagna is Venus and Lord of the seventh house is Mars. Moon is in the triangle of seventh house. Moon is in Uttarashadha nakshatra in Jupiter's rashi, Uttarashadha is on 180° of the Punarvasu, Punarvasu is the original nakshatra of the Jupiter, and Dhanu rashi is also of Jupiter, it shows that the Jupiter is in the triangle of Venus and his 7th aspect nakshatra is No. 3. Then count No. 3 nakshatra of the Moon is Uttarashadha. Uttarashadha is No. 21, add 9 more nakshatras of Mesha rashi. 21 plus 9=30 or count No. 3 nakshatra from Dhanu rashi to Dhanu rashi. Dhanu 3, Mesha 12, Simha 21, Dhanu 30, it shows at his 30 he is getting married. Meena rashi of Jupiter shows the month of marriage, that is 22nd of May to 21st of April is in the sixth house. The right ascension nakshatra of the Moon is Uttarashadha and her declination nakshatra is Dhanishtha. The right ascension 7th aspect nakshatra of the Moon is Punarvasu and her 7th aspect declination nakshatra is Aslesha, it shows the Mars is in Aslesha nakshatra and his 7th aspect nakshatra is original of the Moon No. 22 Shravana, it indicates the date of marriage, add 30 years in his birth year 1930, 1930 plus 30=1960, that is on 22nd of May 1960 he got married. (He will get married with the Lady who has Jupiter of Shravana nakshatra, Moon is of Karka rashi Aslesha nakshatra, Saturn is of Meena rashi and Sun is of Vrishabha rashi). Put the Sun's nakshatra No. 3 on Tuesday and 7th aspect nakshatra of Mars on birth day.

1	3	5	7
Sun	Tue	Thur	Sat
2	4	6	8
Mon	Wed	Fri	Sun

It shows 1-3-5-7 years are good to the native, in these years 2-4-6-8 months are good, in these months 2-4-6-8 dates and days of the dates are good and vice versa.

Shree Deo

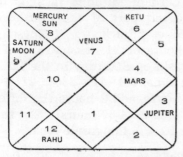

Birth date 23.11.1930
Date of marriage 22.5.1960
Long. 84° East
Lat. 17°-55' North

Example No. 4. Birth date 30.1.1934. We will see the birth day of the native. 1900=2, 34=7, January=6 Birth date is 30=30 plus 6 plus 7 plus 2=45 divided by 7=Remainder is 3=Birth day is Tuesday. See the month 22nd of January to 21st of February in the year 1934. The fourth part of the Southern hemisphere, Tuesday shows 9-30 hours in Meena rashi. Saturday is on 180° of Tuesday, Saturday shows 6-30 hours, but due to the spherical triangle it is a negative part. 9-30 hours means Aslesha nakshatra, it is negative. Shravana nakshatra is on 180° of the Aslesha It shows the Saturn is in Moon's nakshatra. Shravana and the Moon herself is in the Aslesha nakshatra. 6-30 hours means Aridra nakshatra, it is a negative nakshatra. Shatataraka is the greater nakshatra, it shows, the Mars is in Shatataraka nakshatra. Aridra nakshatra is original of Rahu, it is negative, then add two hours the difference of the negative part. 6-30 plus 2=8-30 hours. 8-30 hours means Pushya nakshatra, it shows the ascending node of the Moon is in the Pushya. Naturally descending node of the Moon is in Shravana, Makara rashi. Saturn is the Lord of Saturday as well as he is the Lord of Makara and Kumbha rashi. Kumbha rashi is negative here, then see the other rashi Makara in the first part of the Southern hemisphere. Saturday shows 6-30 hours in Makara rashi and Tuesday shows 2-30 hours in Dhanu rashi. 2-30 hours means Bharani nakshatra, it is in Mesha rashi. Jupiter is the Lord of Meena and Dhanu rashi, the first Tuesday shows us Meena rashi and second Tuesday shows us Dhanu rashi, it means the Lord of. Dhanu and Meena rashi is in triangle of the Mars and his 7th aspect nakshatra is Bharani in Mesha rashi, it shows the Jupiter is in the Thula rashi.

Now see the Vrischika rashi of the Mars in the second part of the Southern hemisphere. Saturday shows 23-30 hours means Dhanishtha nakshatra in Vrischika rashi, that is the Lord of Vrischika rashi is in Dhanishtha nakshatra Kumbha rashi and Saturday shows the Lord of Kumbha. Tuesday shows 2-30 hours in Dhanu

275

rashi, add 2 hours the difference of the negative aspect of Jupiter, 2-30 plus 2=4-30 hours, it shows the Lord of Mithuna rashi is in Shravana nakshatra Makara rashi. Second part of the Southern hemisphere Saturday shows 23-30. Deduct 2.30 hours of Tuesday from Saturday hours, 23-30—2-30=21 hours or 21 nakshatra or 21 solar degrees, then see 21° of Kumbha rashi on Saturday in the Latitude chart, it shows 351°-44'—330° of Kumbha, 351°-44'—330°=21°-44' north Latitude, Wednesday shows 2-30 hours, add 2 hours the difference of the northern hemisphere, 2-30 plus 2=4-30 hours. See the Longitude chart for 4-30 hours, it shows 62°-30' Longitude East.

22nd of January to 21st of February is the period of Moon. Opening month of the year 1934 is in the tenth house, then 22nd of January to 21st of December is in the tenth house. Naturally 22nd of February to 21st of January is in the ninth house, here is the 7th aspect rashi Simha of Kumbha, then put the Simha rashi in the ninth house, it shows Dhanu lagna. 14th of January to 14th of February the Sun is in Makara rashi. The Moon is in Karka rashi. We have to see the marriage day of the native. Naturally we must see the Lord of the seventh house and the Lord of Lagna. The right ascension 7th aspect nakshatra of the Jupiter is Bharani and his 7th aspect declination nakshatra is Rohini. The right ascension nakshatra of the Moon is Punarvasu and her declination nakshatra is Aslesha. The right ascension 7th aspect nakshatra of the Moon is Purvashadha and her declination nakshatra is Shravana. It shows the Moon is working on behalf of Jupiter. The Lord of seventh house is Mercury, he is in Shravana nakshatra, his 7th aspect nakshatra is Pushya No. 8. Then count Pushya nakshatra upto Meena rashi of the Jupiter, Pushya 8 Anuradha 17 and Uttarabhadrapada 26. This is the marriage year of the native. Add 26 years in his birth year, 1934, 1934-plus 26=1960. Meena rashi is the 7th aspect rashi of Kanya, Budha is the Lord of Kanya, he has shown the year, his second rashi is Mithuna which shows us the month of March, Shravana nakshatra No. 22 is on 180° of the Aslesha, it indicates the marriage day. (The ascending node of the Moon must come in Meena rashi, Jupiter must be in Dhanu rashi. Mars must be in Kumbha rashi and the Moon must be in Makara on his marriage day).

8	1	3	5
Tue	Thur	Sat	Mon
6	9	2	4
Wed	Fri	Sun	Tue

Put the Saturn's nakshatra and Moon's nakshatra on birth day. It shows 1-3-5-8 years are good to the native, in these years 1-3-5-8 months are good, in these months 2-4-6-9 dates and days of the dates are good and vice versa.

Shree Bhide

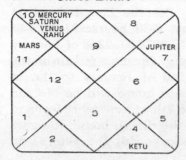

Birth date 30.1.1934
Date of marriage 23.3.1960
Long. 62°-30′ East
Lat. 21°-44′ North.

Example No. 5. Birth date 10.2.1923. We will see the birth day of the native. 1900=2, 23=7, February=2 birth date is 10=10 plus 2 plus 7 plus 2=21 divided by 7=Remainder is 0=Saturday is the birth day. See the month 22nd of January to 21st of February in the year 1923 the first part of the northern hemisphere Saturday shows 6-30 hours in Makara rashi, Tuesday is on 180° of Saturday, Tuesday shows 2-30 hours but due to spherical triangle it is a negative part, add 2 hours the difference of the negative part 0-30 plus 2 —0-00 hours means Pushya nakshatra, it is negative, Uttarabhadrapada is the greater nakshatra, it shows the Mars is in the Uttarabhadrapada nakshatra Meena Rashi, 2-30 plus 2=4-30 hours it is negative nakshatra. 4-30 means Rohini, it is negative. Hasta nakshatra is the greater nakshatra, it shows that the Saturn is in Hasta nakshatra Kanya rashi, it is the nakshatra of Venus, it shows Venus is in Dhanu rashi and Jupiter is in 7th aspect nakshatra. That is Jupiter is in Thula rashi and Bharani nakshatra is his 7th aspect nakshatra and Venus is in the triangle of Bharani nakshatra.

Mars is the Lord of Tuesday as well as he is the Lord of Vrischika and Mesha rashi, Saturn is the Lord of Saturday as well as he is the Lord of Makara and Kumbha rashi. See the Vrischika rashi of Mars in the second part of the southern hemisphere Saturday of Vrischika rashi shows 23-30 hours, it means Sun is in Dhanistha nakshatra in Kumbha rashi. Tuesday shows 2-30 hours in Dhanu rashi, deduct 2 hours the difference of the Dhanu rashi. 2-30 hours Bharani nakshatra, it is negative, Purvashadha is the greater nakshatra, Purvashadha means 20-30 hours, deduct 2-30=18 nakshatra is Jyeshtha nakshatra, it shows the Moon is in the Jyeshtha nakshatra and her descendent node is in Purva nakshatra Simha rashi. Saturday of Vrischika rashi shows 23-30 hours, deduct

Ayanachalana, 23-30—20′=23-10′ hours means Dhanistha nakshatra or 23 solar degrees. Then see Latitude chart for 23° of Kumbha rashi, on Saturday it shows 353°-35′, deduct 330° of Kumbha rashi, 353°-35′—330=23°-35′ Latitude North. Saturday first part of the Northern hemisphere shows 6-30 hours. See the Longitude chart for 6-30 hours and deduct 6° of Tuesday, 6-30 hours=97°-30′—6° =91°-30′ East (deduct 3° of Ketu 91°-30′—3°=88°-30′). 22nd of January to 21st of February is the period of Moon. Opening month of the year 1923 is in the tenth house, then 22nd of January to 21st of December is in the tenth house, then nineth house will be of 22nd of February to 21st of January, here is the 7th aspect rashi Meena of the Saturn, then put the Meena rashi in the nineth house, it shows Karka Lagna. The Moon is in Vrischika rashi, the Sun is in Kumbha rashi.

We have to see the marriage date of the native, then we must see the Lord of Lagna as well as Lord of seventh house. The Lord of Lagna is in the fifth house and she is in Jyeshtha nakshatra. Rohini is her seventh aspect nakshatra No. 4, Shravana nakshatra is also her seventh aspect nakshatra is in the seventh house. Shravana is No. 22, it shows that the native is getting married at his 22. Saturn is the Lord of seventh house as well as he is the Lord of eighth house means the month, 22nd of March to 21st of February. Saturn is in the Hasta nakshatra, his 7th aspect nakshatra is Uttarabhadrapada. Saturn nakshatra is Pushya, it indicates the date. Add 22 years in his birth year 1923 plus 22=1945. That is on 8th February he got married.

Shree Mehta

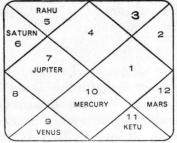

Birth date 10.2.1923
Date of marriage 8.2.1945
Long. 88°-30′ East
Lat. 23°-35′ North.

Put the birth date on the birth day.

4	7	9	2
Sat	Mon	Wed	Fri
3	6	8	1
Sun	Tue	Thur	Sat

It shows 2-4-7-9 years are good, in these years 2-4-7-9 months are good, in these months 3-6-8-1 dates and days of the dates are good and vice versa.

Example No. 6. Birth date 19.6.1936. We will see the birth day of the native. 1900=2, 36=3, June=3, Birth date is 19=19 plus 3 plus 3 plus 2=27 divided by 7=Remainder is 6=Friday is the birth day. See the month 22nd of May to 21st of June in the year 1936. The third part of the northern hemisphere Friday shows 4-30 hours. Tuesday is on 180° of Friday, but due to the spherical triangle it is negative. 4-30 hours means Rohini nakshatra, add 2 hours the difference of the negative part. 4-30 plus 2=6-30 hours means Aridra nakshatra, it shows the Moon is in Aridra nakshatra, Mithuna rashi. Tuesday shows 8-30 hours, add 2 hours the difference of the negative part, 8-30 plus 2=10-30 hours. 10-30 hours means Magha nakshatra, it is negative nakshatra. Moola nakshatra is the greater nakshatra, it is a 7th aspect nakshatra of the Mars, it means the Mars is in the Mriga nakshatra, Mithuna rashi. Venus is the Lord of Friday as well as Thula and Vrishabha rashi. Mars is the Lord of Tuesday as well as Mesha and Vrischika rashi. Then see Vrishabha rashi of the Venus in the fourth part of the northern hemisphere. Tuesday shows 1-30 hours and Friday shows 4-30 hours, add 2 hours in Friday, it shows 4-30 hours plus 2=6-30 hours, it is negative hours for the Venus, 6-30 hours means Aridra nakshatra, it shows the Venus is with Moon. Tuesday shows 1-30 hours, it is negative for the Mars, add 2 hours the difference of the negative part. 1-30 hours plus 2=3-30 hours, it is negative nakshatra of Jupiter that is 7th aspect nakshatra of Jupiter, it shows the Jupiter is in Vishakha nakshatra in Mars rashi Vrischika. Now see Vrischika rashi of Mars and Thula rashi of Venus in the third and fourth part of the southern hemisphere. Tuesday of Vrischika rashi shows Jyestha nakshatra 18-30 hours, it is the nakshatra of the Budha, it is in Vrischika that means the Budha is in Vrishabha i.e. the lord of Vrishabha is in Mithuna and Lord of Mithuna is in Vrishabha. 6-30 hours of Friday are negative and Shatataraka is greater nakshatra for Saturn, it means the Saturn is in Kumbha, 14th of June to 14th of July Sun is in the Mithuna, it shows a new Moon day. Then the ascending node of the moon must be in Mithuna rashi. Thula rashi Saturday shows 15-30 hours, add 2 hours the difference of the northern hemisphere, 15-30 plus 2=17-30 hours, deduct 20' of Ayanachalana. 17-30—20'=17-10' hours means 17 nakshatra or 17 solar degrees. Then see 17° of Dhanu rashi on Tuesday, it shows 288°-2', deduct 270° = 18°-2' North.

Friday of Vrishabha rashi shows 4-30 hours, add 2 hours the difference of negative part 4-30 plus 2=6-30 hours. See the Longitude chart for 6-30 hours, 97°-30′, deduct 6° of Tuesday and 6° of Ketu, 97°-30′—12°=85°-30′ Longitude East.

22nd of May to 21st of June is the period of Moon. Opening month of the year 1936 is in the tenth house, then 22nd of January to 21st of December tenth house, 22nd of December to 21st of November eleventh house, 22nd of November to 21st of October twelfth house, 22nd of October to 21st of September first house, 22nd of September to 22nd of August second house, 22nd of August to 21st of July third house, 22nd of July to 21st of June fourth house, 22nd of June to 21st of May fifth house, here is Mesha rashi of the Mars and 7th aspect rashi of Venus Thula, then put Mesha rashi in the fifth house, it shows Dhanu Lagna. The Sun and Moon are in Mithuna rashi.

We have to see the marriage day of the Lady, naturally we must see the Lord of Lagna and Lord of seventh house. The Lord of Lagna is Jupiter and he is in the twelfth house. Sixth house is his 7th aspect rashi, it shows the month of May. The Lord of seventh house is Budha, he is in Vrishabha rashi, he is neuter, he gives aspect of Venus, Venus is in the Mithuna rashi, Aridra nakshatra. Ketu is in conjunction of the Venus. Saturn is in triangle, when Saturn will come in Dhanu she will get married, that is the opening nakshatra of the Venus is Swati (because the ascending node of the Moon is in Aridra, Aridra is negative nakshatra). Then count No. 6 Aridra nakshatra first, Shatataraka second, Swati, third, that is Mithuna 6, Kumbha 15 and Thula 24, this is the year to get married. Budha is in the Vrishabha rashi, Rohini nakshatra. He is working on behalf of Venus, when he will come in conjunction of Venus and when Moon will come in her own rashi her seventh aspect nakshatra will be No. 4 (Shravana), then native will get married, add 24 years in her birth year, 1936 plus 24=1960, on 4th of May 1960 she got married.

Put the birth date on the birth day

1	3	5	7
Fri	Sun	Tue	Thur

9	2	4	6
Sat	Mon	Wed	Fri

It shows 2-4-6-9 years are good to the native and in these years 1-3-5-7 months are good, in these months 2-4-6-9 are the dates and the days of the dates good to her and vice versa.

280

Miss Lohokare

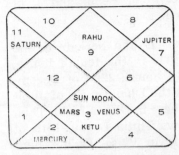

Lat. 18°-2′ North.

Long. 85°-30′ East

Date of marriage 4.5.1960

Birth date 19.6.1936

Example No. 7.   Birth date 15.11.1929.   We will see the birth day of the native. 1900=2, 29=1, November=2 Birth date is 15=15 plus 2 plus 1 plus 2=20 divided by 7=Remainder is 6= Friday is the Birth day. See the month 22nd of October to 21st of November in the year 1929. The fourth part of the southern hemisphere, Friday shows 16-30 hours of Vrishabha rashi. Tuesday is on 180° of the Friday. Tuesday shows 13-30 hours of Mesha rashi. Due to the spherical triangle it is a negative part. Friday shows 16-30 hours in his own rashi. 16-30 hours means Vishakha nakshatra, it is original of Jupiter, it shows that the Venus is in Vishakha nakshatra and Jupiter is on 180° of the Vishakha that is in Krittika nakshatra Vrishabha rashi, Tuesday shows 13-30 hours in Mesha rashi, add 2 hours the difference of Vrishabha 13-30 hours plus 2=15-30 hours, it means Swati nakshatra, it is originally of Venus that is the Venus is in Swati nakshatra and Moon is in the 7th aspect nakshatra Bharani—Mesha rashi.

Venus is the Lord of Vrishabha and Thula rashi, Mars is the Lord of Mesha and Vrischika rashi. Then see Thula rashi of the Venus in the fourth part of the northern hemisphere. Friday shows 2-30 hours means Bharani nakshatra, it shows the descending node of the Moon.

Now in Vrischika rashi of Mars in the third part of the northern hemisphere, Tuesday shows 6-30 hours on Dhanu rashi border, it shows Saturn's 7th aspect nakshatra Aridra, that is, Saturn is in Dhanu rashi, Purvashadha nakshatra. It is a negative nakshatra for Mars, add two hours the difference of Dhanu rashi, 6-30 plus 2—8-30 hours, it is negative, Anuradha is the greater nakshatra for Mars, that is, the Mars is in Vrischika rashi.

Anuradha nakshatra of Mars means 17 solar degrees. Then see the Latitude chart for 17° of Dhanu rashi on Tuesday, it shows 288°-2′ North, deduct 270° of Dhanu 288°-2′—270°=18°-2′ Latitude North.

Tuesday shows 6-30 hours, deduct 20′ of Ayanachalana 6-30 —20′=6°-10′ hours is the Longitude, deduct 6° of Venus and 3° of Ketu. 6-30 hours=92°-30′—9°=84°-30′ Long. East.

22nd of October to 21st of November is the period of the Sun, then opening month of the year 1929 is in the fourth house, 22nd of January to 21st of December fourth house, 22nd of December to 21st of November third house, here is the Dhanu rashi of Jupiter, he is the friend of Saturn and Saturn is there in Dhanu rashi. Then put Dhanu rashi in the third house, it shows Thula Lagna, 14th of November to 14th of December the Sun is in Vrischika but here is the descending node of the Moon in Mesha that shows the Sun is in Thula rashi. Sun is in Thula, Moon is in Mesha. We have to see the marriage day of the native. Naturally we must see the Lord of Lagna as well as the Lord of seventh house. Venus is the Lord of Lagna rashi. He is in Swati nakshatra and Bharani is his 7th aspect nakshatra. Rahu is there, so Bharani is negative nakshatra. Then count Bharani nakshatra upto Bharani; Bharani 2, Purva-shadha 11, Purva 20, Bharani 29, this is her age to get married (Saturn is in triangle of the Bharani nakshatra, Bharani nakshatra is 7th aspect nakshatra of the Jupiter, he is in the Vrishabha rashi when he will change the polarity the lady will get married, it means Jupiter must come in seventh house, Venus must come in conjunction of Saturn in Dhanu rashi of the Jupiter and Moon must come in place of Jupiter eighth house. The descending node of the Moon Rahu must come in Jupiter's rashi Meena and Sun must be in Dhanu rashi for her marriage). Saturn is working on behalf of the Venus, Saturn is the Lord of fourth and fifth and he himself is in Dhanu rashi. Dhanu rashi shows the month and Kumbha rashi shows the date. Purva nakshatra is on 180° of the Shatataraka, that is, the 7th aspect nakshatra of the Venus and Saturn, it indicates the date, Dhanu rashi shows the month December, add 29 years in her birth year, 1929 plus 29=1958, that is on 24th of December 1958 she got married. Put the 7th aspect nakshatra on the birth day.

| 1 | 3 | 5 | 7 |
| Fri | Sun | Tues | Thur |

| 2 | 4 | 6 | 8 |
| Sat | Mon | Wed | Fri |

It shows 2-4-6-8 years are good, in these years 1-3-5-7 months are good, in these months 2-4-6-8 days and dates of the days are good and vice versa.

Miss Rahurkar

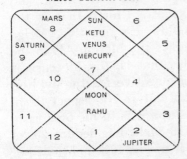

Birth date 15.11.1929
Date of marriage 24.12.1958
Long. 24°-30′ East
Lat. 18°-2′ North.

Example No. 8. Birth date 13.6.1939. We will see the Birth day of the native. 1900=2, 39=6, June=3, Birth date is 13=13 plus 3 plus 6 plus 2=24 divided by 7=Remainder is 3=Tuesday is the birth day. See the month 22nd of May to 21st of June in the year 1939. The third part of the northern hemisphere, Tuesday shows 8-30 hours in Karka rashi. Friday is on 180° of Tuesday. Friday shows 4-30 hours in Mithuna rashi, but due to a spherical triangle it is a negative part, 8-30 hours means Pushya nakshatra (it is of the Saturn it shows that it is the 7th aspect nakshatra of the Saturn), add two hours the difference of the negative part, 8-30 plus 2=10-30 hours means Magha nakshatra, it is negative. Aswini nakshatra is the greater nakshatra, it means Saturn is in the Aswini nakshatra. Dhanishtha nakshatra is on 180° of the Magha, it shows the Mars is in Dhanishtha nakshatra Makara rashi which is on 180° of the Karka rashi.

Friday shows 4-30 hours, add 2 hours the difference of the negative part, 4-30 plus 2=6-30, it means Aridra nakshatra which is of Rahu, it is negative, Swati nakshatra is greater nakshatra, it shows the descending node of the Moon is in the Swati nakshatra, Thula rashi, and the Venus is in the Rohini nakshatra in his own rashi, Venus is the Lord of Vrishabha and Thula rashi and Mars is the Lord of Mesha and Vrischika rashi. Then see the Vrishabha and Mesha rashi in the fourth part of the northern hemisphere. Friday shows 4-30 hours in his own rashi, it is the nakshatra of the Moon, it shows the Moon is in his nakshatra Bharani and he himself is in the Rohini of the Moon. Tuesday of Mesha rashi shows 1-30 hours, it is the nakshatra of the Ketu and Mars, it shows the Ketu is in the Aswini nakshatra Mesha rashi.

See the Vrischika rashi of the Mars and Thula rashi of the Venus. Vrischika rashi Tuesday shows 18-30 hours on the border of Dhanu rashi. (Then 18-30 hours means Jyeshtha nakshatra, it is in his rashi but it is original of Mercury, it is negative, Revati

283

is the greater nakshatra it shows the Jupiter Lord of Dhanu and Mesha rashi is on 180° of the Mars nakshatra Chitra that is the Jupiter is in the Meena rashi) 18-30 hours are negative, Mriga nakshatra is on 180° of the Jyeshtha, it shows the Mercury is in the Mriga nakshatra on 180° the Dhanu rashi, that is, the Mercury is in the Mithuna rashi. Mriga nakshatra is negative for the Jupiter, Chitra nakshatra is greater for him because it is 7th aspect Rashi of the Jupiter-rashi Meena. It shows the Jupiter is in his own rashi Meena. Tuesday of Dhanu rashi shows 18-30 hours, deduct 20′ of Ayanachalana 18°-30′—20′=18°-10′ hours, it means 18th nakshatra or 18 solar degrees, then see the Latitude chart for 18° of Dhanu rashi on Tuesday. It shows 289°-5′, deduct 270° of Dhanu 289°-5′ —270°=19°-5′ is the Latitude North. Friday of Mithuna rashi shows 4-30 hours, add 2 hours difference of the negative part. 4-30 plus 2=6-30 hours. See the Longitude chart for 6-30 hours and deduct 6° of Tuesday 3° of Ketu, 6-30 hours shows 97°-30′ deduct 9° of Mars and Ketu, 97°-30′—9°=88°-30′ Longitude east. 22nd of May to 21st of June is the period of Moon. Opening month of the year 1939 is in the tenth house, then 22nd of January to 21st of December tenth house, 22nd of December to 21st of November eleventh house, 22nd of November to 21st of October twelfth house, 22nd of October to 21st of September first house, 22nd of September to 21st of August second house, 22nd of August to 21st of July third house, 22nd of July to 21st of June fourth house, here is the 7th aspect rashi Makara of Karka rashi Tuesday. Then put Makara rashi in the fourth house, it shows Thula Lagna, 14th of June to 14th of July the Sun is in Mithuna rashi. The Moon is in Mesha rashi. We have to see the marriage day of the native. Naturally we must see the Lord of Lagna as well as Lord of the seventh house. Lord of the Lagna is in the 7th aspect rashi of the Mars Vrischika and Lord of the 7th house is in the 7th aspect rashi of the Moon Karka, it shows that the Venus is working on behalf of Mars and Mars is working on behalf of the Moon. Aswini is the right ascension 7th aspect nakshatra of the Mars and Krittika is 7th aspect declination nakshatra of the Mars. That is the right ascension nakshatra of the Mars is Dhanishsha and his declination nakshatra is Purvabhadrapada. His right ascension 7th aspect nakshatra is Magha and his 7th aspect declination nakshatra is Uttara, it shows when Mars will come in Jupiter's rashi Meena, she will get married, when Moon will come in Magha and her declination nakshatra will be Uttara, as well as Venus will come in Krittika and Jupiter will come in Uttarashadha she will get married. Then count Krittika the 7th aspect declination nakshatra of the Mars upto Uttarashadha,

Krittika 3, Uttara 12, Uttarashadha 21, this is her marriage year. 7th aspect rashi of Karka rashi shows the month of June and Krittika declination nakshatra of the Mars indicates the date, add 21 years in her birth year 1939 plus 21=1960, that is on 3rd of June 1960 she gets married.

Put the declination and right ascension nakshatra of the Mars on birth day.

9	2	4	6
Tue	Thur	Sat	Mon
1	3	5	7
Wed	Fri	Sun	Tue

It shows 1-3-5-7 years are good, in these years 2-4-6-8 months are good, in these months 1-3-5-7 dates and days of the dates are good and vice versa.

Miss Modak

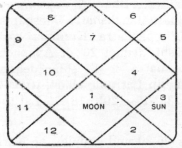

Birth date 13.6.1939
Date of marriage 3.6.1960
Long. 88°-30′ East
Latitude 19°-5′ North

Example No. 9. Birth date is 5.2.1941. We will see the birth date of the native. 1900=2, 41=2, February=2 Birth date is 5=5 plus 2 plus 2 plus 2=11 divided by 7=Remainder is 4=Wednesday is the birth day. See the month 22nd of January to 21st of February in the year 1941 the third part of the northern hemisphere. Wednesday shows 10-30 hours in Vrishabharashi, Sunday is on 180° of the Wednesday but no Sunday is here in Vrishabha rashi. 10-30 hours means Magha nakshatra, it is negative due to the spherical triangle, add 2 hours the difference of the negative part, 10-30 plus 2=12-30 hours, it is negative. Krittika nakshatra is the greater nakshatra, it is in the Vrishabha rashi, it shows the Moon in the Vrishabha rashi.

Mercury is the Lord of Wednesday as well he is the Lord of Kanya and Mithuna rashi. Sun is the Lord of Simha rashi and Sunday. Then see the Simha rashi of the Sun in the fourth part of the southern hemisphere. Sunday shows 17-30 hours in Simha and Wednesday shows 20-30 hours in Kanya. 17-30 hours means Anuradha nakshatra, it is the nakshatra of the Saturn and 7th aspect nakshatra Krittika is of Sun, it shows the Sun in the greater nakshatra, Uttarashadha in the Makara rashi of the Saturn and Saturn is in the 7th aspect nakshatra of the Anuradha, it shows the Saturn in the Krittika nakshatra. Mesha rashi. Wednesday of Kanya rashi shows 20-30 hours, it means Purvashadha nakshatra of Venus or descending node of the Moon. There is no nakshatra of No. 2 in Kanya rashi, then it is negative nakshatra, add 2 hours the difference of negative part, 20-30 plus 2=22-30, it shows the Venus in the Shravana nakshatra and Hasta is the greater nakshatra for descending node of the Moon. Rahu is in Kanya and Venus is in the Makara rashi. Now see the Mithuna rashi of the Mercury in the second part of the northern hemisphere. Sunday shows 15-30 hours in Karka rashi and no Wednesday is there, then deduct 2 hours of Mithuna from Karka rashi, 14-30—2=12-30. Thursday is there on 12-30 hours in Mithuna rashi, it means Mercury is on 180° of the Purva nakshatra, and in the nakshatra Purvabhadrapada of Jupiter, then it is negative nakshatra for Jupiter. Bharani nakshatra is greater, it shows the Jupiter is in Bharani nakshatra Mesharashi and Mercury is in Purvabhadrapada nakshatra Kumbha rashi. Sunday shows 14-30 hours in Karka rashi, deduct 20' of Ayanachalana. 14°-10' hours means Chitra nakshatra or 14 solar degrees, then see 14° of Karka rashi on Thursday in Latitude chart, it shows 138°-1', deduct 120° of Karka rashi, 138°-1'—120°=18°-1' Latitude North.

Wednesday of Kanya rashi shows 20-30 and Sunday of Karka rashi shows 14-30 hours, deduct Sunday hours from Wednesday hours, 20-30—14-30=6 hours is Longitude, deduct 6° of Sunday. 90°—6°=84° Longitude East.

22nd of January to 21st of February is the period of the moon, opening month of the year 1941 is in the tenth house. Naturally 22nd of January to 21st of February is in the nineth house, here is Mithuna rashi of Budha. It shows Thula Lagna. The Moon is in Vrishabha rashi and the Sun is in Makara rashi.

We have to see the marriage day of the native. Naturally we must see the Lord of Lagna and Lord of the seventh house. The Lord of Lagna rashi is Venus, his right ascension nakshatra is Shravana and his declination nakshatra is Shatatarka. The right ascension 7th aspect nakshatra of Venus is Pushya and his 7th aspect declination nakshatra is Magha 1. Then count Magha nakshatra No. 1 upto seventh house, Simha 1, Dhanu 10, Mesha 19, this is the year to get married. Mercury is the Lord of Mithuna and he is in triangle of Lagna, that shows Mars is working on behalf of Mercury. Mithuna rashi shows the month of February. Right ascension nakshatra is of the Moon Krittika and her declination nakshatra is Mriga. The right ascension 7th aspect nakshatra of the Moon is Vishakha and her 7th aspect declination nakshatra is Jyeshtha, it indicates the date of Marriage. Jyeshtha is 18th nakshatra (Then Venus, Jupiter and Saturn must be in Dhanu, the Sun and Mercury must be in Kumbha, Ketu must be in Meena and Moon in the Thula on her marriage day), add 19 years in her birth year 1941 plus 19=1960. That is on 18th of February 1960 she got married. Put the Rahu nakshatra on the birth day.

1	3	5	7
Wed	Fri	Sun	Tue
9	2	4	6
Thur	Sat	Mon	Wed

It shows 1-3-5-7 years are good, in these years 2-4-6-9 months are good, in these months 2-4-6-9 dates and days of the dates are good and vice versa.

Miss Gujar

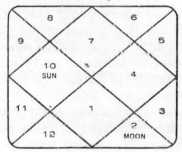

Birth date 5.2.1941
Date of marriage 18.2.1960
Long. 84° East
Lat. 18°-1′ North

Example No. 10. Birth date 27.9.1933. We will see the Birth day of the native, 1900=2, 33=6, September=4 Birth date is 27=27 plus 4 plus 6 plus 2=39 divided by 7=Remainder is 4=Wednesday is birth day. See the month 22nd of September to 21st of October in the year 1933. The fourth part of the Southern hemisphere Wednesday shows 11-30 hours in Dhanu rashi. Saturday is on 180° of the Wednesday, but no Saturday is here. 11-30 hours means Purva nakshatra, it is a negative nakshatra due to the spherical triangle, Purvashadha is the greater nakshatra for Moon, that is the Moon is in the Dhanu rashi, it is the original nakshatra of the Venus and Rahu, that is Rahu is on 180° of the Purva nakshatra, it means the Rahu is in the Kumbha and the Venus himself is on 180° of the Bharani nakshatra, it means Venus is in Thula and as the birth day is Wednesday the Lord of the Wednesday is with Venus.

Mercury is the Lord of Wednesday as well as he is the Lord of Mithuna and Kanya rashi. Then see Mithuna rashi of Mercury in the fourth part of the Northern hemisphere. Wednesday shows 21-30 hours in Mithuna and Saturday shows 24-30 hours in Karka rashi, 21-30 hours means Uttarashadha nakshatra. There is no Uttarashadha in Mithuna rashi, it is negative. Uttara is the greater nakshatra which is in the Kanya rashi of the Mercury, it means the Lord of the Uttarashadha nakshatra is in Uttara and Lord of Dhanu rashi is in 7th aspect nakshatra of the Lord of Dhanu is in Uttara, that is, the Sun and Jupiter are in Uttara nakshatra Kanya rashi, add 2 hours the difference of Mithuna rashi in 24-30 hours of Saturday, 24-30 plus 2=26-30 hours, it is negative for Karka. Pushya is the greater nakshatra for Karka rashi, it shows the 7th aspect nakshatra of the Saturn, that is the Saturn is in Makara rashi.

Now see the Kumbha rashi of Saturn in the third part of the northern hemisphere. Saturday shows 14-30 hours on the border of Makara. 14-30 hours means Chitra nakshatra, it is the original nakshatra of the Mars, but it is negative in Makara and Kumbha rashi. Mriga nakshatra is the greater nakshatra, it is 7th aspect nakshatra, it means Mars is in his own rashi Vrischika.

Saturday of Makara rashi shows 14-30 hours, add 2 hours the difference of the negative rashi Makara the fourth part of the northern hemisphere, 14-30 plus 2=16-30 hours, deduct 20' of Ayanachalana, 16-30—20'=16-10, hours, it means 16 nakshatra or 16 solar degrees. Then see the Latitude chart for 16° of Makara on Saturday, it shows 318°-29' deduct 300° of Makara, 318°-29'—300°=18°-29' is Latitude North. Saturday of Mithuna rashi shows 24-30 hours, add 2 hours the difference of Northern hemisphere. 24-30 plus 2=26-30 hours. Now deduct 21-30 hours of Wednesday from 26-30 hours of Saturday, 26-30—21-30=5 hours is the Longitude, add 6° of Mercury and 3° of Rahu, 5 hours=75° plus 9° of Rahu and Budha =84° Longitude East.

22nd of September to 21st of October is the period of Moon. The opening month of the year 1933 is in the 10th house, then 22nd of January to 21st of December is tenth house, 22nd of December to 21st of November eleventh house, 22nd of November to 21st of October twelfth house, 22nd of October to 21st of September first house, here is Kumbha rashi of Saturn. It is Kumbha Lagna. The Sun is in Kanya rashi, Moon is in Dhanu rashi.

We have to see the marriage day of the native. Naturally we must see the Lord of Lagna and the Lord of the seventh house. The Lord of the Lagna is Saturn, he is in the Shravana nakshatra Makara rashi, that is, his right ascension nakshatra is Shravana and his declination nakshatra is Shatataraka, his right ascension seventh aspect nakshatra is Pushya and his 7th aspect declination nakshatra is

288

Magha No. 1, the ascending node of the Moon is in Magha nakshatra, so Magha nakshatra is uncounted nakshatra. Then count Magha from 7th house to 7th house. Simha 1, Dhanu 10, Mesha 19, Simha 28. This is his marriage year. Pushya nakshatra is 7th aspect nakshatra of Saturn, Pushya is in Karka rashi, Karka rashi is in the month of April. Sun is the Lord of Uttara nakshatra, Purvabhadrapada is his 7th aspect nakshatra. Purvabhadrapada nakshatra indicates the date of marriage, add 28 years in his birth year, 1933 plus 28=1961. That is on 25th of April 1961 he got married.

(Saturn must be in Makara with Jupiter, Ketu must be in Simha, Mars must be in Karka, Sun must be in Mesha and Moon must be in Simha, Venus and Mercury must be in Meena on his marriage day.) Put the birth date on birth day

1	3	5	7
Wed	Fri	Sun	Tues
2	4	6	9
Thur	Sat	Mon	Wed

Shree Modak R.

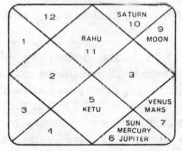

Birth date 27.9.1933,
Date of Marriage 25.4.1961
Long. 84° East
Lat. 18°-29′ North

Example No. 11. Birth date 21.8.1936. We will see the birth day of the native. 1900=2, 36=3, August=1 Birth date is 21=21 plus 1 plus 3 plus 2=27 divided by 7=Remainder is 6=Friday is the birth day. Monday is on 180° of Friday, but here is no Monday. Friday shows 6-30 hours means Aridra nakshatra, but due to spherical triangle it is a negative part. Aridra nakshatra is of Rahu, it shows that Rahu is on 180° of Aridra nakshatra and Aridra is his 7th aspect nakshatra, that is descending node of the Moon. Rahu is in the Dhanu and ascending node (Ketu) of the Moon is in the Mithuna, deduct 2 hours the difference of the negative part 6-30—2=4-30 hours means Rohini nakshatra, it is negative. Hasta nakshatra is the greater nakshatra, it shows the Moon is in Hasta nakshatra Kanya rashi, Mercury is the Lord of Kanya rashi. Revati is his original nakshatra and Hasta is his 7th aspect nakshatra, it shows the Mercury is in Kanya rashi. Venus is the Lord of Friday, he has shown Rohini nakshatra of the Moon although he is the Lord of Swati nakshatra, it is negative nakshatra for him due to the spherical triangle, it shows the Venus is also in Kanya rashi, Venus is the Lord of Friday as well as he is the Lord of Vrishabha and Thula rashi. Moon is the Lord of Monday and Karka rashi. See the Thula rashi of the Venus in the third part of the southern hemisphere. Monday shows 9-30 hours in Kanya rashi, 9-30 hours means Aslesha nakshatra, it is 7th aspect nakshatra of the Mars, that is the Mars aspects Makara rashi Shravana nakshatra. The Lord of Makara rashi must be opposite to the moon, that is, Saturn is in Meena rashi and Mars is in the 7th aspect rashi of the Makara, that is Mars is in Karka in the triangle of Saturn. Now see Karka rashi of the Moon in the first part of the Northern hemisphere. Monday shows 2-30 hours in Mithuna rashi, that is, 7th aspect nakshatra of the Punarvasu nakshatra in Mithuna rashi, Punarvasu nakshatra is of Guru, it is negative, then add 2 hours difference in Bharani, 2-30 plus 2=4-30 hours means Rohini, it is the nakshatra of the Moon and Jupiter is on 180° of the Rohini, that is Jupiter is in the Vrischika rashi. See the Vrishabha rashi of Venus, Friday shows 23-30 hours, it is the nakshatra of Mars, it shows the Mars is in the 7th aspect nakshatra of the Dhanistha, that is Mars is in Aslesha nakshatra.

Friday of Vrishabha rashi shows 23-30 hours, deduct 20' of Ayanachalana 23-30—20'=23-10' hours, it means 23 nakshatra or 23 solar degrees. Then see 23° of Kumbha rashi on Friday in Latitude chart, it shows 323°-22'—300° of Makara, that is 23°-22' Latitude North. Mithuna rashi Monday shows 2-30 hours, add 2 hours the difference of Southern hemisphere, 2-30 hours plus 2=4-30 hours. See the Longitude chart for 4-30 hours and deduct 6° of Monday and 3° of Ketu. 4-30 hours=67°-30'—9=58°-30' Longitude East 22nd of July to 21st of August is the period of Moon. Opening month of the year 1936 is in the tenth house, then 22nd of January to 21st of December tenth house, 22nd of December to 21st of November eleventh house, 22nd of November to 21st of October twelfth house, 22nd of October to 21st of September first house, 22nd of September to 21st of August second house, here is Karka rashi of the Monday which is on 180° of the Friday. Then put Karka rashi on the second house, it shows Mithuna Lagna, 14th of August to 14th of September, The Sun is in the Simha, The Moon is in the Kanya rashi. We have to see the marriage day of the native. Then we must see the Lord of Lagna as well as the Lord of seventh house. The lord of the seventh house is Jupiter and Lord of the Lagna is

Mercury. Mercury is in conjunction of Moon that is Mercury will show the date. The Lord of the seventh house is in the sixth house. It shows the month of April, Jupiter is the Lord of Punarvasu nakshatra. Then count Punarvasu nakshatra upto seventh aspect rashi of the Budha or upto Jupiter's own rashi Meena. Punarvasu 7, Vishakha 16, Purvabhadrapada 25, this is the year to get married. The Mercury is in Hasta nakshatra and Revati is his 7th aspect nakshatra, Jyeshtha is first and Revati is second, 18 indicates the 18th day of April, that is when the Moon will come in Vrishabha rashi in the month of April. Her Rohini nakshatra will show the date on 7th aspect nakshatra Jyeshtha (Mars will be in Punarvasu nakshatra Karka rashi, Jupiter and Saturn will be in Makara in Uttarashadha nakshatra, Venus and Mercury will be in Meena rashi and Rahu will be in Purva nakshatra, Simha rashi. Moon will be in Rohini nakshatra Vrishabha rashi).

Add 25 years in his birth year, 1936 plus 25=1961. That is on 18th of April 1961 he got married. Put the birth date on the birth day

4	6	9	2
Fri	Sun	Tue	Thu
5	7	1	3
Sat	Mon	Wed	Fri

It shows 1-3-5-7 years are good, in these years 2-4-6-9 months are good, in these months 2-4-6-9 dates and days of the dates are good.

Shree Sahastrabudhye

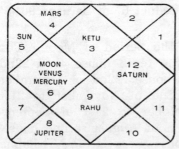

Birth date 21.8.1936
Date of marriage 18.4.1961
Long. 58°30′ East
Lat. 23°-22′ North

Example No. 12. Birth date 22.7.1941. We will see the birth day of the native. 1900=2, 41=2, July=5 Birth date is 22=22 plus 5 plus 2 plus 2=31 divided by 7=Remainder is 3=Tuesday is the Birth day. See the month 22nd of July to 21st of August in the year 1941. Third part of the southern hemisphere, Tuesday shows 10-30 hours in Thula rashi, Saturday is on 180° of the Tuesday, but no Saturday is here. 10-30 hours means Magha nakshatra, it shows the Lord of Thula rashi is in Magha nakshatra, it is ·negative nakshatra for Rahu. Aswini is the greater nak- shatra that is the 7th aspect nakshatra of the Rahu, it means Rahu is in Chitra nakshatra Kanya rashi. Moola nakshatra is the greater nakshatra for Moon, it means the Moon is in Mithuna rashi in the triangle of Thula or in triangle of Saturn's rashi Kumbha.

See the Vrischika rashi of the Mars in the second part of the southern hemisphere. Saturday shows 14-30 hours in Dhanu, it means the Lord of the Dhanu is in the Mriga nakshatra, deduct 2 hours the difference of Dhanu, 14-30—2=12-30 hours, that is Jupi- ter is in Krittika nakshatra Vrishabha rashi.

See the Makara rashi of Saturn in the first part of the southern hemisphere. Tuesday shows 17-30 hours, it is the nakshatra of Saturn and it is in the Makara, it means Saturn is on 180° of Anu- radha and in the triangle of Makara, that is Saturn is in Vrishabha Rashi. Krittika nakshatra. Saturday of Dhanu rashi shows 14-30 hours, 14-30 hours means Chitra nakshatra, it is of Mars, it means the Mars is in Jupiter's rashi on 180° of the Chitra, that is Mars is in the Meena rashi, Revati nakshatra. See Kumbha rashi of Saturn in the fourth part of the Northern hemisphere. Saturday shows 17-30 hours and Tuesday shows 20-30 hours. Saturday shows 17-30 hours, deduct 20′ of Ayanachalana. 17-30—20′=17-10′ hours means 17th nakshatra or 17 solar degrees, then see 17° of Kumbha on Saturday in the Latitude Chart. 17°=348°-3′, deduct 330° of Kumbha, 348°-3′—330°=18°-3′ Latitude North.

Saturday of Southern hemisphere first part shows 14-30 hours, deduct these hours from 20-30 hours of Tuesday in Meena rashi, 20-30—14-30=6 hours is the Longitude, deduct 6° of Saturn=90°-6° of Saturn=84° Longitude East.

22nd of July to 21st of August is the period of Moon. The opening month of the year 1941 is in the tenth house, then 22nd of January to 21st of December tenth house, 22nd of December to 21st of November eleventh house, 22nd of November to 21st of October twelfth house, 22nd of October to 21st of Septem- ber first house, 22nd of September of 21st of August second house, 22nd of August to 21st of July third house, here is the Vrishabha rashi of Venus and 7th aspect rashi of Mars, then put the Vrishabha rashi in the third house, it shows Meena Lagna, 14th of July to 14th of August the Sun is in Karka rashi. The Moon is in Mithuna rashi.

We want to see the marriage day of the native. Naturally we must see the Lord of Lagna and the Lord of seventh house. Jupiter is the Lord of Lagna and he is in the house of Venus. Mercury is the Lord of 7th house and he is in his own house with Moon, it means

Moon is working on behalf of the Mercury. Right ascension nakshatra of the Moon is Mriga and her declination nakshatra is Punarvasu. The right ascension 7th aspect nakshatra of the Moon is Jyeshtha and her 7th aspect declination nakshatra is Purvashadha. Purvashadha is No. 20, that is her year to get married. Jupiter is in the house of Venus and Venus is in the house of Sun, it shows that Jupiter is working on behalf of Venus. Simha rashi shows the month of April. Jupiter is in Mriga nakshatra. Jyeshtha nakshatra is his 7th aspect nakshatra, it indicates the date of marriage. Add 20 years in her birth year 1941 i.e. 1941 plus 20=1961. That is on 18th of April 1961 she got married (See the marriage day planets in example 11).

Birth date is 22nd, it means Shravana nakshatra, Pushya is on 180° of the Shravana, then put the Pushya No. 8 nakshatra on the birth day.

8	1	3	5
Tue	Thu	Sat	Mon
9	2	4	6
Wed	Fri	Sun	Tue

It shows 2-4-6-9 years, months and dates are good to her and vice versa.

Miss Damale

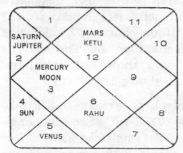

Birth date 22.7.1941
Date of marriage 18.4.1961
Long. 84° East
Lat. 18°-3′ North.

Example No. 13. Birth date 22.7.1921. We will see the birth day of the native. 1900=2, 21=5, July=5, Birth date is 22=22 plus 5 plus 5 plus 2=34 divided by 7=Remainder is 6=Friday is the birth day. See the month 22nd of July to 21st of August in the year 1921. The first part of the northern hemisphere, Friday shows 6-30 hours. Monday is on 180° of Friday. Monday shows 2-30 hours, but due to the spherical triangle it is a negative part. Friday shows 6-30 hours, it means Aridra nakshatra, it is the nakshatra of the Rahu, but it is negative, then add 2 hours the difference of the negative part. 6-30 plus 2=8-30 hours, it is negative. Anuradha is the greater nakshatra, it is the 7th aspect nakshatra of the Venus, it means the Venus is in the Vrishabha rashi. Monday shows 2-30 hours, it is also negative nakshatra. 2-30 hours means Bharani nakshatra, it is negative, Purva is greater nakshatra, it is 7th aspect nakshatra of the Moon, it means the Moon is in the Purvabhadrapada nakshatra Kumbha rashi, add 2 hours the difference of the negative part in Purvabhadrapada, that is Revati nakshatra in which the ascending node of the Moon is there (Ketu). Venus is the Lord of Friday as well as he is the Lord of Vrishabha and Thula rashi. Then see the Vrishabha rashi of Venus in the second part of the northern hemisphere, Friday shows 23-30 hours in Vrishabha rashi, 23-30 hours means Dhanistha nakshatra, it is original of Mars, it is not in Vrishabha rashi, it shows that Mars is in Mriga nakshatra in triangle of Moon, that is Mars is in Mithuna. Monday shows Bharani nakshatra in Mithuna, it is not in Mithuna, then purva-shadha is on 180° of Punarvasu and the Lord of Mithuna is in the Punarvasu, that is Mercury is in the Mithuna.

Now see the Thula rashi of the Venus in third part of the southern hemisphere. There is no Friday in Thula, Monday shows 9-30 hours in Kanya. 9-30 hours means Aslesha. There is no Aslesha in Kanya, it means Lord of the Kumbha is in the 7th aspect of the Revati, that is Saturn is in the Kanya rashi, Hasta nakshatra. As the declination nakshatra of the Moon is Revati in Meena rashi, it shows that the Jupiter's 7th aspect nakshatra is the right ascension nakshatra of Moon, that is the Jupiter is in Purva nakshatra Simha rashi. See the Moon's declination nakshatra Revati No. 27 in Meena Rashi on Thursday in the Latitude chart. 27 nakshatra means 27 solar degrees. See 27° of Meena rashi on Thursday, it shows 23°-11' Latitude North. Now Venus shows 18 nakshatra, then see 18° of Meena rashi on Monday, it shows 16° North.

The first part of the northern hemisphere Friday shows 6-30 hours, deduct 20' of Ayanachalana, 6-30—20'=6-10'. See the Longitude chart for 6-10' hours, it shows 92°-30' Longitude East. Now Friday shows 6-30 hours, and Monday shows 2-30 hours, add the Monday hours of Kanya rashi, 9-30 plus 2-30=12-30 hours now deduct 6-30 hours of Friday 12-30—6-30=6 hours. Now deduct 6° of Friday. 90°-6°=84° Longitude East. (I have given two different cities for Latitude and Longitude to show that both persons got married on same day and the horoscope of both the persons is the same).

22nd of July to 21st of August is the period of Moon. Opening month of the year 1921 is in the tenth house, then 22nd of January to 21st of December tenth house, 22nd of December to 21st of November eleventh house, 22nd of November to 21st of October twelfth house, 22nd of October to 21st of September first house, 22nd of September to 21st of August second house, 22nd of August to 21st of July third house, here is Thula rashi of Friday. Then put the Thula rashi in the third house, it shows Simha Lagna, 14th of July to 14th of August the Sun is in Karka. Then Moon is in Kumbha rashi.

We have to see the marriage day of the native. Naturally we must see the Lord of Lagna and the Lord of seventh house. The Lord of Lagna is the Sun and the Lord of seventh house is Saturn. The Lord of Lagna is the Sun and his nakshatra is Uttara, Purvabhadrapada nakshatra is on 180° of the Uttara. Purvabha-drapada is No. 25, that is his year to get married. Saturn is the Lord of Kumbha rashi, Kumbha rashi shows the month of March. When Moon will come in Purvabhadrapada, her 7th aspect nakshatra will be Uttara and (when Jupiter will come in the opening rashi Thula, his seventh aspect nakshatra will be Krittika and when Mercury will be in Meena his seventh aspect nakshatra will be Uttara). Jupiter is in the Lagna. Thursday is Jupiter's day. Sunday is on 180° of Thursday that is Sunday is marriage day, when the Sun will come in Kumbha and Purvabhadrapada nakshatra, his seventh aspect nakshatra will be Uttara and the day must be Sunday, that is 3rd of March is the only day on which Sunday is there, add 25 years in his birth year, 1921 plus 25=1946, that is on 3rd of March 1946 he got married. Put the seventh aspect nakshatra of the date on the birth day. Birth date is 22 means Shravana, Aslesha is on 180° of the Shravana. Put the Aslesha on the birth day.

9	3	5	7
Fri	Sun	Tues	Thur
1	4	6	8
Sat	Mon	Wed	Fri

It shows 3-5-7-9 years are good, in these years 3-5-7-9 months are good and in these months 3-5-7-9 dates and days of the dates are good and vice versa.

Shree Samant K. D.

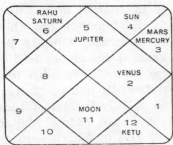

Birth date 22.7.1921

Date of Marriage 3.3.1946

Long. 84° East

Latitude 16° North.

Example No. 14. Birth date 11.3.1925. We will see the birth day of the native. 1900=2-, 25=3, March—2, Birth date is 11=11 plus 2 plus 3 plus 2=18 divided by 7=Remainder 4=Wednesday is the birth day. See the month 22nd of February to 21st of March in the year 1925. The first part of the southern hemisphere, Wednesday shows 22-30 hours, in Vrischika rashi. Saturday is on 180° of the Wednesday, it shows 1-30 hours in Dhanu rashi, 22-30 hours means Shravana nakshatra, it shows the ascending node of the Moon is in Shravana, it is negative nakshatra, greater nakshatra is Hasta, it shows the Moon is in the Hasta nakshatra. Mercury is the Lord of Wednesday, it shows that the Mercury is on 180° of the Hasta. That is Mercury is in the Meena rashi. Saturday shows 1-30 hours in Dhanu rashi, it means the Lord of Dhanu rashi is in the Dhanu rashi and Aswini is the greater nakshatra for Saturn, it is his 7th aspect nakshatra, that is the Saturn is in Thula rashi, add 2 hours the difference of the negative part, 1-30 plus 2=3-30 hours, it shows the Lord of the Vrischika rashi is in the Vrishabha rashi. Now see Mithuna rashi of the Mercury in the first part of the northern hemisphere, Wednesday shows 12-30 hours, 12-30 hours means Uttara nakshatra, it is of the Sun, it shows the 7th aspect nakshatra of the Mercury is Uttara and he is in Meena rashi with the Sun, because the second part of the northern hemisphere Mithuna rashi Sunday shows 9-30 hours, it means Revati nakshatra. Now see the Makara and Kumbha rashi of the Saturn. Saturday of Makara rashi shows 1-30 hours, it shows the nakshatra of Mars, that is Mars is in the triangle of Makara, 1-30 hours means the opening rashi of the triangle of Makara and that is Vrishabha and the Lord of Vrishabha is in Dhanistha in triangle of 7th aspect rashi of the Mars or in triangle of Saturn, that is the Venus is in the Kumbha. Wednesday shows 5-30 hours means the same, 5-30 hours means Mriga nakshatra, Jyeshtha is on 180° of the Mriga. Jyeshtha is No. 18. Then see 18° of Vrishabha on Wednesday in the Latitude chart, it shows 76°-33′ deduct 60° of Vrishabha, 76°-33′—60°=16°-33′ Latitude North. Wednesday shows 5-30 hours. See the Longitude chart for 5-30 hours and add 3° of Ketu, 5-30 hours=82°-30′ plus 3°=85°-33′ Longitude East.

22nd of February to 21st of March is the period of the Sun. The opening month of the year 1925 is in the fourth house, then 22nd of January to 21st of December fourth house, 22nd of December to 21st of November third house, 22nd of November to 21st of October second house, 22nd of October to 21st of september first house, 22nd September to 21st of August twelfth house, 22nd of August to 21st of July eleventh house, 22nd of July to 21st of June tenth house, 22nd of June to 21st of May nineth house, 22nd of May to 21st of April eighth house, 22nd of April to 21st of March seventh house, here is the seventh aspect rashi of Saturn Simha rashi. Then put Simha rashi in the seventh house, it shows Kumbha Lagna. The Sun is in Meena rashi and the Moon is in Kanya rashi.

We want to see the marriage day of the native. Naturally we must see the Lord of the Lagna as well as Lord of the seventh house. Saturn is the Lord of Lagna and he is in the nineth house Thula rashi. The right ascension nakshatra of the Saturn is Chitra and his declination nakshatra is Vishakha, his right ascension seventh aspect nakshatra is Aswini and his 7th aspect declination nakshatra is Krittika. Lord of the seventh house is Sun, Uttara is original nakshatra of the Sun. Then count Uttara nakshatra of the Sun from Mesha rashi Krittika nakshatra 0, Uttara 3, Uttarashadha 12, Krittika 21, Uttara 30, this is the year to get married.

Saturn is in Thula, Thula rashi shows the month of June, when Moon will come in Thula her nakshatra will be of Venus (Swati) and her seventh aspect nakshatra also will be of Venus (Bharani) that is Bharani indicates the date of month, add 30 years in his birth year, 1925 plus 30=1955, that is on 2nd of June 1955 he got married. Put the birth date 7th aspect nakshatra on the birth day.

7	1	3	5
Wed	Fri	Sun	Tue
2	4	0	8
Thur	Sat	Mon	Wed

It shows 1-3-5-7 years are good, in these years 2-4-6-8 months are good, in these months 2-4-6-8 dates and days of the dates are good and vice versa.

(When Mars will be in Mithuna, Venus will be in Mesha, Saturn will be in Thula and Jupiter will be in Karka, Moon will be in Thula, Sun will be in Vrishabha he will get married).

When 7th aspect nakshatra will be No. 3 of Mars, Mercury, Ketu, Jupiter, Saturn and right ascension nakshatra No. 3 will be of Sun, Venus, Rahu, he will get married on the day of above planets' position.

Shree Desai

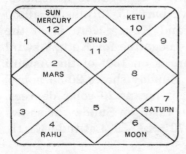

Birth date 11.3.1925

Date of marriage 2.6.1955

Long. 85°-30' East

Latitude 16°-33' North

Example No. 15. Birth date is 25.8.1935. We will see the birth day of the native, 1900=2, 35=1, August=1 Birth date is 25=25 plus 1 plus 1 plus 2=29 divided by 7=Remainder is 1=Birth day is Sunday. See the month 22nd of August to 21st of September in the year 1935, the third part of southern hemisphere. There is no Sunday, then see the Thursday which is on 180° of the Sunday. Thursday shows 7-30 hours in Kanya rashi, due to the spherical triangle it is negative part. Thursday shows 7-30 hours, it means Punarvasu nakshatra. There is no Punarvasu nakshatra in Kanya rashi, Mercury is the Lord of Kanya rashi as well as Mithuna rashi, it means Punarvasu nakshatra is of Moon and Lord of the Mithuna is in Kanya rashi and Purvabhadrapada is greater nakshatra which is the 7th aspect nakshatra of the Mercury.

Sun is the Lord of Sunday and Simha rashi. Then see Simha rashi in the fourth part of the southern hemisphere. Sunday shows 3-30 hours on the border of Simha. 3-30 hours means Krittika nakshatra. There is no Krittika nakshatra in Simha rashi, it means Krittika is negative and Uttara is the greater nakshatra for the Sun, that is the Sun is in Simha rashi. See Dhanu rashi of Jupiter in the fourth part of the northern hemisphere. Sunday shows 13-30 hours in Dhanu rashi, 13-30 hours means Hasta nakshatra. No Hasta nakshatra is in Dhanu, then it is a negative nakshatra. Deduct 2 hours of negative part 13-30—2=11-30 hours, 11-30 means Purva nakshatra, it is of the Venus, it means Venus is in Simha rashi Purva nakshatra and Purvashadha is the greater nakshatra for the descending node of the Moon, that is Rahu is in Dhanu rashi. Thursday shows 17-30 hours in Makara rashi, 17-30 means Anuradha nakshatra. There is no Anuradha nakshatra in Makara rashi, then it is a negative nakshatra, deduct 2 hours of the negative part, 17-30—2=15-30 hours, it means Swati nakshatra, it is in Thula rashi. It shows the Lord of Thursday is in Swati nakshatra and Lord of Makara is in the greater nakshatra Shatataraka in Kumbha rashi. See Meena rashi of Jupiter in the third part of the northern hemisphere. Thursday shows 17-30 hours in Kumbha rashi. 17-30 hours means Anuradha nakshatra. There is no Anuradha in Kumbha rashi, it is a negative nakshatra, add 2 hours the difference of the negative part, 17-30 plus 2=19-30 hours, it is the nakshatra of the Mars and Ketu. Ketu is in the Mriga nakshatra Mithuna rashi, then it is negative for Ketu, Aswini is the grater nakshatra, it means the Mars is on 180° of the Aswini that is in Thula rashi Chitra nakshatra. Sunday shows 20-30 hours, it means Purvashadha nakshatra No. 20, it means 20 solar degrees. Then see Latitude chart for 20° of Dhanu rashi on Sunday, it shows 291°-39', deduct 270° of Dhanu, 291°-39'-270°=21°-39' Latitude North.

Third part of the southern hemisphere Thursday shows 7-30 hours and Sunday of Simha rashi shows 3-30 hours, then deduct Sunday hours from 7-30 hours of Thursday, 7-30—3-30=4 hours, add 6° of Jupiter and 3° of Rahu in the Longitude of 4 hours. 4 hours means 60° plus 9°=69° Longitude East.

22nd of August to 21st of September is the period of Sun. The opening month of the year 1935 is in the fourth house, then 22nd of January to 21st of December fourth house, 22nd of December to 21st of November third house, 22nd of November to 21st of October second house, 22nd of October to 21st of September first house, 22nd of September to 21st of August twelfth house, here is the Dhanu rashi of the Thursday which is on 180° of the birth day, then put Dhanu rashi in the twelfth house, it shows Makara Lagna. The Sun is in Simha rashi and the Moon is in Mithuna rashi. We have to see the marriage day of the native. Naturally we must see the Lord of Lagna as well as the Lord of seventh house. Saturn is the Lord of Lagna and he is in the second house in Shatataraka nakshatra, his 7th aspect rashi Simha and 7th aspect nakshatra is Purva. Venus is the Lord of Purva nakshatra and his rashi Vrishabha is in triangle of Lagna, that is the Saturn is working on behalf of the Venus because Shatataraka and Purva are the nakshatras of Venus. Then Vrishabha rashi shows the month of January. Shatataraka is No. 24, it indicates the date of marriage. Moon is the Lord of Seventh house, she herself is in Mithuna in the Punarvasu nakshatra. Punarvasu nakshatra is of Jupiter and Mithuna rashi is of Mercury. Purvabhadrapada the third nakshatra of Jupiter is on 180° of the Kanya rashi of Mercury, it shows that the native is getting married at his 25th year, add 25 years in his birth year 1935, plus 25=1960, that is on 24th of January 1960 he got married.

(When Moon will come in Anuradha nakshatra and Jupiter Venus, Mars will be in Dhanu rashi, Mercury and Sun will be in Lagna and Ketu in Jupiter's rashi in Meena the native will get married). Put the seventh aspect nakshatra of the Venus on birth day.

7	5	3	1
Sun	Tue	Thur	Sat
9	2	4	6
Mon	Wed	Fri	Sun

It shows 1-3-5-7 years are good to him, and in these years 1-3-5-7 months are good, in these months 2-4-6-9 dates and days of the dates are good and vice versa.

Shree Vazirkar

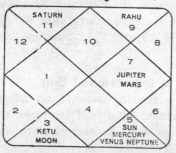

Birth date 25.8.1935
Date of marriage 24.1.1960
Long. 69° East
Lat. 21°-39′ North.

Example No. 16. Birth date 27.10.1931. We will see the birth day of the native. 1900=2, 31=3, October=6 Birth date is 27=27 plus 6 plus 3 plus 2=38 divided by 7=Remainder is 3=Tuesday is birth day. See the month 22nd of October to 21st of November in the year 1931. The fourth part of the southern hemisphere, Tuesday shows 13-30 hours. Saturday is on 180° of Tuesday. Saturday shows 17-30 hours in Vrishabha rashi, but due to spherical triangle it is genative part. 13-30 hours means Hasta nakshatra, it is original of the Moon, it means the ascending node of the Moon is in the Hasta nakshatra (Ketu), deduct 2 hours the difference of the negative part. 13-30—2=11-30 hours, it is the nakshatra of the Venus but it is not in Mesha rashi, it is negative, Bharani nakshatra is greater nakshatra, it shows the Moon is in the Bharani nakshatra and the Lord of Bharani is on 180° of the Moon, that is Venus is in Swati nakshatra Thula rashi. Saturday shows 17-30 hours in Vrishabha rashi. 17-30 hours means Anuradha nakshatra, it is the nakshatra of Saturn but there is no Anuradha nakshatra in Vrishabha rashi, Rohini nakshatra is in Vrishabha, it shows Rohini is the nakshatra of the Moon, is in Mesha that is the Mars aspect rashi is Vrishabha, then Mars is in Anuradha nakshatra Vrischika rashi, add 2 hours the difference of the negative part, 17-30 plus 2=19-30 hours, it shows the Saturn is in the Moola nakshatra, Dhanu rashi and his 7th aspect nakshatra is Mriga in Vrishabha rashi. Mars is the Lord of Mriga nakshatra and it is his 7th aspect nakshatra that clearly shows Mars position in Vrischika rashi. Mars is the Lord of Tuesday as well as he is Lord of Mesha and Vrischika rashi. Saturn is the Lord of Saturday as well as he is the Lord of Makara and Kumbha rashi. See Vrischika rashi of Mars in the third part of the northern hemisphere, Tuesday shows 6-30 hours on the border of Dhanu. Jupiter is the Lord of Dhanu rashi, 6-30 hours means Aridra nakshatra, it is not in Dhanu rashi. Then add 2 hours the difference of the Vrischika rashi, 6-30 hours plus 2=8-30 hours means Pushya nakshatra, it shows the Lord of Dhanu is in the triangle of Mars and in the seventh aspect of Saturn, that is Jupiter is in Pushya nakshatra Karka rashi. Now see Kumbha rashi of Saturn in the first part of the northern hemisphere. Saturday shows 10-30 hours and Tuesday shows 13-30 hours. 10-30 hours of Saturday means Magha nakshatra, it is in Simha rashi. Dhanishtha nakshatra is in Kumbha, it shows Magha nakshatra is negative. Aswini is the greater nakshatra which is in triangle of Saturn and lord of Simha is on 180°, of Aswini in triangle of Kumbha, it means the Sun is in Thula rashi. Thursday shows 13-30 hours means Hasta nakshatra, it is in the Kanya rashi, the Lord of Kanya rashi is Mercury. Hasta nakshatra is not in Meena rashi, it is negative, then add 2 hours the difference of negative part, 13-30 plus 2=15-30 hours, it means Swati, it shows the Lord of the Mithuna is in triangle. Jupiter is the Lord of Meena as well as Dhanu, it means the seventh aspect nakshatra of Mercury is in the triangle of Saturn and Mercury is in triangle of Mithuna that is the Mercury is in Swati nakshatra Thula rashi. Saturday of Vrischika rashi shows 17-30 hours, add 2 hours the difference of the Southern hemisphere, 17-30 plus 2=19-30 hours, deduct 20' of Ayanachalana, 19-30—20'=19-10' hours means Moola nakshatra or 19 solar degrees, then see the Latitude chart for 19° of Vrishabha rashi on Saturday, it shows 78°-2', deduct 60° of the Vrishabha rashi 78°-2'—60°=18°-2'=18°-2' Latitude North. The fourth part of the southern hemisphere Saturday shows 17-30 hours, add 2 hours the difference of the Mesha rashi. 17-30 plus 2=19-30 hours now deduct 13-30 hours of Tuesday from Saturday hours, 19-30—13-30=6 hours is the Longitude, deduct 6° of the Mars. 6 hours=90°-6°=84° Longitude East. 22nd of the October to 21st of the November is the period of Sun. The opening month of the year 1931 is in the fourth house, then 22nd of January to 21st of December fourth house, 22nd of December to 21st of November third house, 22nd of November to 21st of October second house, here is the Vrischika rashi of the Mars and the birth day. Then put the Vrischika rashi in the second house. It shows Thula Lagna, the Sun is in Thula and the Moon is in the Mesha rashi.

We want to see the marriage day of the native. Naturally we must see the Lord of Lagna as well as the Lord of seventh house. The Lord of Lagna is Venus and the Lord of the seventh house is Mars. The Lord of the seventh house is in the second house and Rohini nakshatra is his 7th aspect nakshatra. The lord of the Lagna is Venus and he is in the Vishakha nakshatra. The right ascension nakshatra of Venus is Vishakha and his declination nakshatra is Jyestha No. 9, it shows the Moon is working on behalf of the Venus, as well as on behalf of the Mars because Right ascension nakshatra of the Moon is Bharani and her declination nakshatra is Rohini.

The right ascension seventh aspect nakshatra of the Moon is Vishakha and her 7th aspect declination nakshatra is Jyeshtha No. 9. Then count Jyeshtha 9, nakshatra upto her own house. Vrischika 9, Meena 18, Karka 27 this is the marriage year of the native. Dhanistha nakshatra is on 180° of the Aslesha, Dhanishtha nakshatra indicates the date of marriage. Dhanishtha nakshatra is in the Makakra and Kumbha, Kumbha rashi is in triangle of the Lagna, it shows the month of marriage, then count the months from fourth house. Kumbha rashi shows the month of February, add 27 years in his birth year, 1931 plus 28=1958 that is on 23rd of February 1958 he got married. (The Venus must come in Makara in Shravana nakshatra for 7th aspect of nakshatra Aslesha, Saturn and Mars must come in Dhanu for 7th aspect to Mriga nakshatra of the Mars in the Mithuna rashi, Jupiter and Rahu must come in Thula for their 7th aspect to Aswini nakshatra in Mesha, Sun and Mercury must come in Kumbha to complete the triangle of Aswini, Magha and Moola. Moon must come in Aswini to start new cycle of the life).

Shree Godse

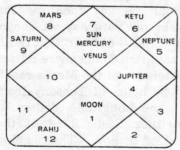

Birth date 27.10.1931
Date of marriage 23.2.1958
Long. 84° East
Lat. 18°-2′ North.

Example No. 17. Birth date 7.10.1922. We will see the birth day of the native. 1900=2, 22=6, October=6, Birth date is 7=7 plus 6 plus 6 plus 2=21 divided by 7=Remainder is 0=Saturday is the birth day. See the month 22nd of June to 21st of July in the year 1922. The first part of the northern hemisphere. There is no Saturday, then Tuesday is on 180° of Saturday. Tuesday shows 20-30 hours, 20-30 hours means Purvashadha nakshatra, it means Mars is in Purvashadha nakshatra Dhanu rashi and the Moon is in the greater nakshatra Bharani in the Mesha rashi, deduct 2 hours the difference of the negative part. 20-30—2=18-30 hours means Jyeshtha nakshatra. It shows the Venus is in Jyeshtha nakshatra because Tuesday shows us Purvashadha nakshatra of Venus which was negative for Mars and it is due to the spherical triangle Jyeshtha nakshatra is negative, Revati nakshatra is the greater, it shows the 7th aspect nakshatra of Rahu that is the Ketu is in Revati nakshatra Meena rashi, Tuesday has shown us

302

20-30 hours in Kumbha rashi, it means the Lord of the Kumbha rashi is in the 7th aspect of Ketu or in conjunction of Rahu. That is Saturn is also in Kanya rashi. Mars is in Dhanu rashi which is of Jupiter, then Saturn must be on 180° of Meena rashi because the Jupiter is the Lord of Meena and Dhanu. It shows Jupiter is in the aspect of both the planets Mars and Saturn. Mars is the Lord of Tuesday as well as he is the Lord of Mesha and Vrischika rashi, then see the Vrischika rashi of Mars in the third part of the northern hemisphere. Tuesday shows 13-30 hours, 13-30 hours means Hasta nakshatra, it is in Kanya rashi. Mercury is the Lord of Kanya rashi and not of Vrischika, then it shows the other rashi of the Mars Mesha, then add 2 hours the difference of the Mesha 13-30 plus 2=15-30 hours, it means the Lord of Kanya rashi is in Swati nakshatra Thula rashi. There is no Saturday in Vrischika rashi, see the other rashi of Mars. Mesha in the fourth part of the northern hemisphere, Saturday, shows 24-30 hours in Mesha rashi 24-30 hours means Shatataraka nakshatra in the Mesha rashi, it means it is negative nakshatra. Swati is the greater nakshatra, it shows the Jupiter is in the Swati nakshatra in triangle of Saturn's rashi, Meena rashi is the 7th aspect rashi of Saturn, then the Lord of Meena rashi must be in triangle of Saturn's rashi, Mars is in Dhanu rashi, it means Mars rashi must be in 7th aspect of Jupiter.

The first part of the northern hemisphere Tuesday shows 20-30' hours, deduct 20' of Ayanachalana. 20-30—20'=20-10' hours it means 20 nakshatra or 20 solar degrees, then see the Latitude chart for 20° of Kanya rashi on Saturday, it shows 198°-27', deduct 180° of the Kanya rashi. 198°-27'—180°=18°-27' North. The first part of the northern hemisphere Tuesday shows 20-30 hours and third part of the northern hemisphere Tuesday shows 13-30 hours, deduct 13-30 hours from 20-30 hours, 20-30—13-30=7 hours, deduct 2 hours the difference of third part, 7-2=5 hours is the Longitude of the Mars (Mars is in the Dhanu by deducting 2 hours we made him Lord of Vrischika) 5 hours means 75° and 6° of Saturn and 3° of Rahu, 75° plus 9°=84° Longitude East.

22nd of June to 21st of July is the period of Sun, the opening month of year 1922 is in the fourth house, 22nd of January to 21st of December fourth house, 22nd of December to 21st of November third house, 22nd of November to 21st of October second house, 22nd of October to 21st of September first house, 22nd of September to 21st of August twelfth house, 22nd of August to 21st of July eleventh house, 22nd of July to 21st of June tenth house, here is Kumbha rashi of Saturn or birth day. Then put Kumbha rashi in the tenth house, it shows Vrishabha Lagna. The Sun is in Kanya and the Moon is in Mesha rashi.

We want to see the marriage day of the native. Naturally we must see the Lord of Lagna and Lord of seventh house. Lord of the Lagna is in the seventh house and Lord of the seventh house is in the eighth house, it shows that the Lord of Lagna is working on behalf of the Lord of 7th house and Jupiter is working on behalf of the Lord of 7th house because Jupiter is in the house of Venus and Mars is in the house of Jupiter. Jupiter is in Swati nakshatra and his 7th aspect nakshatra is Aswini No. 1. Then count Aswini nakshatra upto Mesha that is Mesha 1, Dhanu 10, Simha 19, and Mesha 28, this is the year to get married. Now count the months upto Vrischika from the opening month of the horoscope, it shows March month. Mriga nakshatra is on 180° of Jyeshtha, it indicates the date, add 28 years in his birth year 1922, 1922 plus 28=1950, that is on 5th of March 1950 he got married.

(Mercury must be in Kumbha rahsi, Jupiter and Venus must be in Makara rashi, Mars and Ketu must be in Kanya with Moon. Saturn must be in Simha and Sun must be in Meena with Rahu on his marriage day).

Put the seventh aspect nakshatra of the date on the birthday.

6	9	2	4
Sat	Mon	Wed	Fri
5	7	1	3
Sun	Tue	Thur	Sat

It shows 1-3-5-7 years, months and dates are good and vice versa.

Shree Manohar Datar

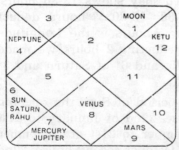

Birth date 7.10.1922.
Date of marriage 5.3.1950
Long. 84° East
Lat. 18°-27′ North.

Example No. 18. Birth date 25.9.1933. We will see the birth day of the native. 1900=2, 33=6, September=4. Birth date is 25=25 plus 4 plus 6 plus 2=37 divided by 7=Remainder is 2=Monday is the birth day. See the month 22nd of September to 21st of October in the year 1933. The fourth part of the southern hemisphere, Monday shows 4-30 hours, Friday is on 180° of the

Monday, Friday shows 4-30 hours but due to the spherical triangle it is a negative part. 4-30 hours means Rohini nakshatra, it is negative. It is the nakshatra of the Moon. It means the Moon is on 180° of Rohini that is the Moon is in Jyeshtha nakshatra Vrischika rashi, Rohini nakshatra shows Simha rashi, there is no Rohini nakshatra in Simha rashi, that means the Lord of Simha is in the greater nakshatra. Rohini is negative for the Sun, Hasta is the greater nakshatra, that is the Sun is in the Hasta nakshatra. Venus shows 1-30 hours in Karka rashi, 1-30 hours means Aswini nakshatra, there is no Aswini in Karka rashi, then add 2 hours of the negative part 1-30 plus 2=3-30 hours. It means Venus (Lord of Friday) is on 180° of the Krittika, that is Venus is in Vishakha nakshatra, Thula rashi, Makara rashi is on 180° of the Karka, it means the Lord of the Makara is on 180° of Punarvasu nakshatra, that is Saturn is in Uttarashadha nakshatra Makara rashi. The ascending node of the Moon is in Uttara and descending node of the Moon is in Purvabhadrapada, Kumbha rashi is in the triangle of Venus.

Venus is the Lord of Friday as well as he is the Lord of Thula and Vrishabha rashi. Then see the Thula rashi of Venus in the second part of the southern hemisphere, Friday shows 8-30 hours in Thula rashi. 8-30 hours means Pushya nakshatra, there is no Pushya in Thula rashi, then it is a negative nakshatra. Uttarabhadrapada is the greater nakshatra, it is in Meena rashi. The Lord of Meena rashi is Jupiter, it means Jupiter is on 180° of Uttarabhadrapada, that is Jupiter is in Hasta nakshatra in triangle of Saturn, Jupiter has shown the nakshatra of Saturn and Saturn has shown the nakshatra of Jupiter. Monday shows 11-30 hours in Vrischika rashi, 11-30 hours means Purva nakshatra, there is no Purva nakshatra in Vrischika rashi, then it is negative nakshatra. Add 2 hours the difference of the negative part. 11-30 plus 2=13-30 hours, it is negative. Rohini nakshatra is the greater nakshatra, it means the Lord of the Vrischika rashi is in the 7th aspect of Rohini that is the Mars is in Jyeshtha nakshatra Vrischika rashi (Purva nakshatra indicates the right ascension of Mars is Vishakha nakshatra because Right ascension of Rahu is Purvabhadrapada and right ascension of the Ketu is Purva). Now see Vrishabha rashi of Venus in the first part of the northern hemisphere. No Monday in Vrishabha rashi, Friday shows 1-30 hours in Mithuna rashi. 1-30 hours means Aswini nakshatra. Mithuna rashi shows the Lord of Mithuna is on 180° of the Aswini, that is Mercury is on 180° of Aswini Chitra nakshatra Thula rashi. Mriga nakshatra of Mithuna rashi means 5 hours. See the Longitude chart for 5 hours and deduct 6° of Monday and 3° of Ketu, 5 hours means 90°—9°=81° Longitude East. Mriga nakshatra is on 180° of the

Jyeshtha. Jyeshtha is No. 18, then see 18° of the Mithuna on Monday in the Latitude chart, it shows 109°-48′, deduct 90° of Mithuna=19°-48′ Latitude North.

22nd of September to 21st of October is the period of Moon, the opening month of the year 1933 is in the tenth house, then 22nd of January to 21st of December tenth house, 22nd of December to 21st of November eleventh house, 22nd of November to 21st of October twelfth house, 22nd of October to 21st of September first house, here is Karka rashi of the birth day, then put Karka rashi in the Lagna, that is Karka Lagna, The Moon is in Vrischika rashi, the Sun is in Kanya rashi.

We want to see the marriage day of the native. Then we must see the Lord of Lagna as well as the Lord of seventh house. The Lord of Lagna is Moon, she is in the fourth house, her right ascension nakshatra is Vishaka No. 7. The Lord of the seventh house is Saturn, his 7th aspect nakshatra is Punarvasu No. 7, then count No. 7 from Vishakha upto Punarvasu, Vrishabha 7, Kanya 16, Makara 25, this is her marriage year. Saturn is the Lord of seventh house and eighth house Purvabhadrapada nakshatra is in the eighth house, it shows the month of February. The right ascension nakshatra of the Saturn is Uttarashadha and his declination nakshatra is Dhanishtha No. 23, it indicates the date of marriage, add 25 years in her birth year, 1933 plus 25=1958, that is on 23rd February 1958 she got married.

(Venus must come in Shravana nakshatra for 7th aspect of Aslesha nakshatra, Saturn and Mars must come in Dhanu for 7th aspect to Mriga nakshatra of Mithuna, Jupiter and Rahu must be in Thula for 7th aspect to Aswini nakshatra, Sun and Mercury must be in Kumbha for 7th aspect to Magha and to complete the triangle of Aswini, Magha and Moola, and there 7th aspect to Chitra Dhanishtha, and Mriga, Moon must be in Aswini to start new cycle of Life).

Put the birth date on the birth day.

7	9	3	5
Mon	Wed	Fri	Sun
8	2	4	6
Tue	Thur	Sat	Mon

It shows 3-5-7-9 years are good, in these years 2-4-6-8 months are good, in these months 1-3-5-7 dates are good and vice versa.

Miss S. K. Dange

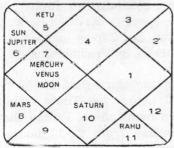

Birth date 25.9.1933
Date of marriage 23.2.1958
Long, 81° East
Lat. 19°-48′ North.

Example No. 19. Birth date 18.1.1918. We will see the birth day of the native. 1900=2, 18=1, January=6, birth date is 18=18 plus 6 plus 1 plus 2=27 divided by 7=Remainder is 6=Friday is the birth day. See the month 22nd of December to 21st of January in the year 1918. The first part of the southern hemisphere, Friday shows 22-30 hours in Kanya rashi. Tuesday is on 180° of Friday, Tuesday shows 19-30 hours in Simha rashi, it is a negative part due to spherical triangle Friday shows 22-30 hours means Shravana nakshatra, it shows Venus is in Shravana nakshatra, it is the nakshatra of the Moon but Venus has shown it, it means Shravana nakshatra is negative for the Moon and Hasta nakshatra is the greater nakshatra for the Moon, it means the Moon is on 180° of Hasta nakshatra in Meena rashi. Tuesday shows 19-30 hours, it means Moola nakshatra, it shows the ascending node of Moon is on 180° of Moola nakshatra, that is Ketu is in Mriga nakshatra Mithuna rashi, 19-30 hours means Moola nakshatra and Lord of Mithuna is with Rahu in Mithuna rashi, that is 19-30 hours are negative for Mars, then add 2 hours the difference of the negative part, 19-30 plus 2=21-30 hours, it is negative, it means the Sun is in Uttarashadha nakshatra and Uttara is the greater nakshatra for the Mars, that is, the Sun is in Uttarashadha nakshatra Makara rashi, Venus is the Lord of Friday as well as he is the Lord of Vrishabha and Thula rashi, Mars is the Lord of Mesha and Vrischika rashi. Then see Vrishabha rashi of Venus in the third part of the southern hemisphere. Friday shows 15-30 hours in Mithuna rashi, 15-30 hours means Swati nakshatra, there is no Swati nakshatra in Mithuna, it means it is a negative nakshatra. Aridra is the greater nakshatra, then add 2 hours in Aridra nakshatra 6-30 plus 2=8-30, it is Pushya nakshatra, it is the nakshatra of Saturn, it means Saturn is in his nakshatra and his 7th aspect is on his rashi, that is Saturn is in Karka rashi, See Mesha rashi of Mars in the fourth part. Tuesday shows 12-30 hours in Mesha rashi, 12-30 hours means Uttara nakshatra. There is no Uttara nakshatra in Mesha rashi, it means the Mesha rashi and Uttara nakshatra is negative. Vrischika rashi is greater and Krittika nakshatra is greater. Krittika nakshatra is 7th aspect nakshatra of Jupiter, but here is Vrischika rashi, it is in the 7th aspect of Krittika, it shows Jupiter is in Krittika nakshatra and his 7th aspect nakshatra is Vishakha which is his own, that is Jupiter is in Vrishabha rashi.

Now see Vrischika rashi of Mars in the third part of the northern hemisphere. Tuesday shows 2-30 hours, see Thula rashi of Venus in the fourth part of the northern hemisphere, Friday shows 22-30 hours, deduct 2-30 hours of Tuesday from 22-30 hours of Friday, 22-30—2-30=20 hours, it means 20 nakshatra or 20 solar degrees. Then see 20° of the Thula rashi on Friday in Latitude chart, it shows 229°-12′, deduct 270° of Thula 229°-12′—210°=19°-12′ Latitude North. First part of the southern hemisphere Friday shows 22-30 hours and third part of the southern hemisphere Friday shows 15-30 hours, add 2 hours the difference of the negative part in 15-30 hours, 15-30 plus 2=17-30 hours from Friday 22-30′ hours 22-30—17-30=5 hours is the Longitude, add 6° of Mars, 5 hours means 75° plus 6°=81° Longitude East.

22nd of the December to 21st of January is the period of Sun. The opening month of the year 1918 is in the fourth house, then 22nd of January to 21st of December fourth house, naturally 22nd of February to 21st of January will be in the fifth house and there is Vrischika rashi of the Mars and 7th aspect rashi of Venus Vrishabha, of the birth day. Then put Vrischika rashi in the fifth house, it shows Karka Lagna. The Sun is in Makara rashi and the Moon is in Meena rashi.

We want to see the marriage day of the native. Then we must see the Lord of Lagna and the Lord of seventh house. Saturn is the Lord of seventh house and he is in Karka rashi in Lagna. The lord of the Lagna is the Moon and she is in the Uttarabhadrapada nakshatra in the triangle of Saturn, it means Saturn is the only planet which is working himself as well as on behalf of the Moon. Right ascension nakshatra of the Saturn is Pushya and his declination nakshatra is Magha, then count Magha nakshatra of Saturn from start to end. Simha 1, Mesha 10, Dhanu 19, Simha 28, this is his year for marriage. Magha nakshatra is in Simha rashi which is on 180° of kumbha. kumbha rashi is of Saturn, it shows the month of marriage. Vrischika rashi is the opening rashi of the horoscope. Mars is the Lord of opening rashi, he is in Hasta nakshatra, his 7th aspect nakshatra is Revati and the Moon is there, then count Revati nakshatra of the Moon from Meena rashi to Vrischika rashi. Meena 9 Vrischika 18, Jyeshtha nakshatra indicates the date of marriage, add 28 years in his birth year 1918, 1918 plus 28=1946, that is on 18th of May 1946 he got married.

(Saturn must come in Mithuna rashi in the triangle of Kumbha rashi for his 7th aspect on Uttarashadha nakshatra to show the tithi and day of marriage. Moon must come in Jyeshtha nakshatra, Vrischika rashi for her 7th aspect on Mriga nakshatra, the Sun must come in Vrishabha rashi to show the month of May as well as to complete triangle of Makara, Jupiter must come in Kanya for his 7th aspect to Meena rashi and to complete the triangle of Makara rashi seventh house. Venus and Rahu must be in Mithuna. Mars must come in Karka rashi for his 7th aspect on the 7th house because he is the Lord of the opening house of the horoscope).

The Saturn is in Punarvasu nakshatra and his 7th aspect nakshatra is Uttarashadha, Venus is also in Punarvasu nakshatra, his 7th aspect nakshatra is Purvashadha, Rahu, is in Aridra nakshatra and his 7th aspect nakshatra is Moola, reader should see the third part of the southern hemisphere, Friday hours, shows 15-30 hours in Mithuna rashi that is Aridra nakshatra of Rahu. Now at the marriage time it must be in Aridra nakshatra and Saturn must be along with him. Now see the Vrischika rashi of the Mars in the third part of the northern hemisphere. Tuesday shows 2-30 hours, it means the second tithi of the Dark half or add 2 hours the difference of the northern hemisphere in the hours of Friday of southern hemisphere third part, 15-30 plus 2= 17-30 hours, 17-30 means 17°-30′, deduct 15° or 15 days of bright half, Remainder is 2-30, it shows the second day of the dark half and the Moon is in the Jyeshtha. Lord of the Jyeshtha is Mars, Saturday is on 180° of the Tuesday, that is on Saturday 18th of May 1946, 2nd tithi of the Dark half he got married. Now if you see the Ephemeris of 19° Ayanamsa you will find each planet is mistaken by 4° tithi is mistaken and Moon will show the ending moment of Jyeshtha nakshatra. Now we will see the other way, 1918 is an odd year, 1 plus 9 plus 1 plus 8=19, 1 plus 9=10 i.e. 1 plus 0=1. Third part of the Punarvasu vibrates to first part of Uttarashadha, it clearly shows that Saturn is in Mithuna rashi. Now first part of Aridra nakshatra vibrates to the third part of Moola nakshatra, first part of Punarvasu vibrates to third part of the Purvashadha. Thus Rahu shows Moola nakshatra, Venus shows Purvashadha nakshatra and the Saturn shows Uttarashadha nakshatra. Magha, Purva, Uttara are in Simha and Aswini, Bharani, Krittika are in Mesha, this triangle of Dhanu, then 7th aspect nakshatra must be of Mithuna, Thula and Kumbha, it clearly shows that Saturn is in Mithuna and not in Karka.

Put the 7th aspect date nakshatra on Wednesday.

7	1	3	5
Fri	Sun	Tue	Thur
9	2	4	6
Sat	Mon	Wed	Fri

It shows 1-3-5-7 years are good, in these years 1-3-5-7 months are good, in these months 2-4-6-9 dates and days of the dates are good and vice versa.

Shree Shirolkar

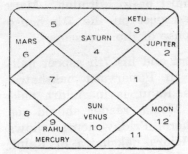

Birth date 18.1.1918
Date of Marriage 18.5.1946
Long. 81° East
Lat. 19°-12' North.

Example No. 20. Birth date 9.6.1915. We will see the Birth day of the native. 1900=2, 15=4, June=3, Birth date is 9=9 plus 3 plus 4 plus 2=18 divided by 7=Remainder is 4=Wednesday is the birth day. See the month 22nd of May to 21st of June in the year 1915 the second part of the southern hemisphere, Wednesday shows 19-30 hours in Makara rashi, Saturday is on 180° of the Wednesday, Saturday shows 22-30 hours, but due to the spherical triangle it is a negative part. Wednesday shows 19-30 hours means Moola nakshatra, there is no Moola nakshatra in the Makara, it means the Lord of the day as well as the Lord of Makara rashi is on 180° of Moola, that is Mercury and Saturn are in Aridra nakshatra Mithuna rashi. Add two hours the difference negative part. 19-30 plus 2=21-30 hours, it means the Lord of Moola nakshatra Ketu is on 180° of Uttarashadha, that is Ketu is in the Punarvasu nakshatra. Karka rashi and Lord of Moola nakshatra is Mars which must be in triangle of Moola, Moola nakshatra is negative and Aswini nakshatra is the greater nakshatra for Mars, it shows Mars is in Mesha rashi, Saturday shows 22-30 hours means Shravana nakshatra, it is of Moon. Rahu is in Makara, it means Shravana is a negative nakshatra, Rohini is the greater nakshatra, it shows the Sun is in Rohini nakshatra because Rashi of the Sun is on 180° of Kumbha and Saturday shows 22-30 hours in Kumbha. Mercury is the Lord of Wednesday as well as he is the Lord of Mithuna and Kanya rashi, then see Kanya rashi of Mercury in the fourth part of the northern hemisphere. There is no Wednesday in Kanya rashi, but Saturday shows 15-30 hours on the border of Thula, 15-30 hours means Swati nakshatra, it is of Venus, it shows the Moon is on 180° of Swati nakshatra, that is the Moon is in Bharani nakshatra Mesha rashi, now add 2 hours the difference of the border of Kanya 15-30 plus 2=17-30 hours, it means the Lord of Thula is in Vrishabha rashi in triangle of Kanya. See Kumbha rashi of Saturn in the first part of the southern hemisphere, Saturday shows 22-30 hours in Kumbha and Wednesday shows 2-30 hours in Meena rashi. 2-30 hours means Bharani nakshatra, there is no Bharani nakshatra in Meena rashi. Then Wednesday is the Lord of Mithuna. Punarvasu nakshatra is there and Purvashadha is on 180° of the Punarvasu that is in Dhanu rashi. Jupiter is Lord of Dhanu and Meena rashi, it means Mithuna rashi is negative. Purva nakshatra is the greater nakshatra, add 2 hours the difference of the negative rashi Mithuna. Purva Means 11-30 plus 2=13-30 hours, it means Hasta nakshatra, it is in Kanya and Wednesday is the Lord of Kanya, 'it shows the Lord of Dhanu rashi is on 180° of Kanya, that is Jupiter is in the Meena rashi, Saturday shows 22-30 hours in Kumbha, deduct 20' of Ayanachalana, 22-30'—20'=22-10' hours, it means 22nd nakshatra or 22 solar degrees. Then see the Latitude chart for 22° of Kumbha rashi on Wednesday, it shows 351°-4', deduct 330° of Kumbha rashi, 351°-4'—330°—21°-4' Latitude North.

Third part of the Northern hemisphere Saturday shows 5-30 hours in Mithuna. See the Longitude chart for 5-30 hours and deduct 3° of Rahu, 5-30 hours means 82°-30°—3°=79°-30' Longitude East.

22nd of May to 21st of June is the period of Moon. The opening month of the year 1915 is in the tenth house, then 22nd of January to 21st of December tenth house, 22nd of December to 21st of November eleventh house, 22nd November to 21st of October twelfth house, 22nd of October to 21st of September first house, 22nd of September to 21st of August second house, 22nd of August to 21st of July third house, 22nd of July to 21st of June fourth house, 22nd of June to 21st of May fifth house, here is Dhanu rashi the seventh aspect rashi of Mithuna. Then put Dhanu rashi in the fifth house, it shows Simha Lagna. The Moon is in Mesha rashi and the Sun is in Vrishabha rashi.

We want to see the marriage day of the native. Then we must see the Lord of the Lagna as well as the Lord of the seventh house. The Lord of Lagna is Sun and Lord of the seventh house is Saturn. The Lord of Lagna is in the tenth house, his right ascension nakshatra is Rohini and his 7th aspect nakshatra is Jyeshtha No. 9, then count No. 9 from Vrishabha to Makara rashi. Vrishabha 9, Kanya

18, Makara 27, this is the age of his marriage. Sun is the Lord of Simha rashi, his 7th aspect rashi is Kumbha, then count the months upto Kumbha. The opening month of the year is in tenth house, Kumbha rashi shows the month of March. Hasta nakshatra is the first nakshatra from the ascendant. Shravana is the second, that is Hasta 4, Shravan 13, indicates the date of marriage, add 27 years in his birth year 1915, 1915 plus 27=1942 that is on 13th of March 1942 he got married. Put the birth date on Thursday instead of Wednesday because Jupiter is working on behalf of the Mercury.

2	4	6	8
Wed	Fri	Sun	Tue
9	3	5	7
Thur	Sat	Mon	Wed

It shows 3-5-7-9 years are good, in these years 3-5-7-9 months are good, in these months 2-4-6-8 dates and days of the dates are good and vice versa.

Shree Shirolkar

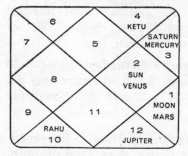

Birth date 9.6.1915
Date of marriage, 13.3.1942
Long. 79°-30′ East
Lati. 21°-4′ North.

Example No. 21. Birth date 28.12.1909. We will see the birth day of the native. 1900=2, 9=4, December=4, Birth date is 28=28+4+4+2=38 divided by 7=Remainder is 3=Tuesday is the birth day. See the month 22nd of the December to 21st of January in the year 1909. The second part of the northern hemisphere, Tuesday shows 19-30 hours in Karka rashi, Saturday is 180° of the Tuesday. Saturday shows 16-30 hours in Mithuna rashi, it is a negative part due to the spherical triangle. Tuesday shows 19-30 hours in Karka rashi, 19-30 hours means Moola nakshatra, there is no Moola nakshatra in Karka rashi. Moola nakshatra is of Ketu the ascending node of the Moon, Mars is the Lord of Tuesday and Mars is the Lord of Vrischika and Mesha rashi, then Moola nakshatra is negative for Mars, deduct 2 hours the difference of the negative part. 19-30—2=17-30 hours, it means the Lord of the Moola nakshatra Ketu is in the Anuradha nakshatra Vrischika rashi, then it is negative nakshatra for Mars, it means the Mars is in the greater nakshatra with the Lord of Anuradha nakshatra, that is the Mars and Saturn are in the Uttarabhadrapada nakshatra Meena rashi, ascending node of the Moon is in the Vrischika rashi and the Moon herself is in the Karka rashi Pushya nakkshatra, Saturday shows 16-30 hours in Mithuna rashi, 16-30 hours means Vishakha nakshatra, it is not in Mithuna, Punarvasu nakshatra is in Mithuna. Mercury is the Lord of Mithuna and Punarvasu is his 7th aspect nakshatra, it means Mercury is in Dhanu rashi Uttarashadha nakshatra.

Mercury is the Lord of Mithuna and Kanya. Mercury is in Uttarashadha nakshatra and the Lord of Uttarashadha nakshatra is the Sun whose rashi is on 180° of Saturn's rashi Kumbha, it means the Sun is in the Uttarashadha nakshatra Dhanu rashi. Punarvasu is on 180° of Uttarashadha. Jupiter is the Lord of Punarvasu nakshatra when Punarvasu nakshatra is 7th aspect nakshatra of the Sun, then it is a negative nakshatra for the Jupiter. Purvabhadrapada is greater nakshatra for him, it means Jupiter is on 180° of Purvabhadrapada in the second rashi of Mercury Kanya, that is Jupiter is in Uttara nakshatra Kanya rashi opposite to Saturn.

See Mesha rashi of Mars in the fourth part of the southern hemisphere, Saturday shows 9-30 hours, it means Saturn is in Revati nakshatra. Tuesday shows 12-30 hours, Purvabhadrapada is on 180° of the Uttara, it means the Lord Mesha is in Purvabhadrapada nakshatra, Meena rashi. See Kumbha rashi of the Saturn in the first part of the northern hemisphere, Saturday shows 6-30 hours in Kumbha rashi, 6-30 hours means Aridra nakshatra, it is the nakshatra of Venus, deduct 2 hours the difference of Kumbha, 6-30—2= 4-30 hours, it means Venus is in the Greater nakshatra Shravana. Tuesday shows 9-30 hours, it means Aslesha nakshatra, it is in Karka rashi, it means the Lord of Karka is in the triangle of Meena, that is the Moon is in Karka rashi.

See Vrischika rashi of the Mars in the third part of the northern hemisphere, Tuesday shows 2-30 hours. Now add 9-30 hours of Tuesday Meena rashi 9-30 plus 2-30=12 hours, deduct Saturday hours of Kumbha rashi, 12—6-30=5-30 hours is Longitude. Tuesday of Karka rashi shows 19-30 hours, deduct 20' of Ayanachalana 19-30—20=19-10' hours means 19 nakshatra or 19 solar degrees. See Latitude chart for 19° of Karka rashi on Saturday 141°—27', deduct 120° of Karka rashi, 141°-27'—120°=21°-27' Latitude North. 5-30 hours means 82°-30', deduct 3° of Ketu, 82°-30°=79°-30' Longitude East.

22nd of December to 21st of January is the period of Sun. The opening month of the year 1909 is in the fourth house, then 22nd of January to 21st of December fourth house, here is Vrischika rashi of Mars or Birth day. Then put Vrischika rashi in the fourth house, it shows Simha Lagna. The Sun is in Dhanu rashi, the Moon is in Karka rashi.

We want to see the marriage day of the native. Then we must see the Lord of Lagna as well as the Lord of seventh house. The lord of Lagna is in Dhanu rashi. The right ascension nakshatra of the Sun is Uttarashadha and his declination nakshatra is Dhanishtha No. 23, Lord of the seventh house is in the eighth house. Right ascension nakshatra of Saturn is Uttarabhadrapada and his declination nakshatra is Aswini. The right ascension 7th aspect nakshatra of Saturn is Uttara and his 7th aspect declination nakshatra is Chitra No. 5, then count Chitra No. 5 from Kanya to Makara, Kanya 5, Vrishabha 14, Makara 23, this is the year to get married. The Sun is in Dhanu rashi, it shows the month of marriage. February month is the marriage month. The opening rashi of the horoscope is Vrischika, Ketu is there in Anuradha nakskhatra, his 7th aspect nakshatra is Rohini, it indicates the date of marriage, add 23 years in his birth year, 1909 plus 23=1932 that is on 4th February 1932 he got married.

Put the birth date on his birth day

1	3	5	7
Tues	Thur	Sat	Mon
2	4	6	8
Wed	Fri	Sun	Tue

It shows 1-3-5-7 years are good, in these years 2-4-6-8 months are good, in these months 2-4-6-8 dates and days of the dates are good and vice versa.

Shree Shirolkar

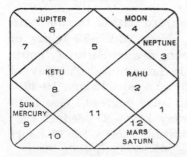

Birth date 28.12.1909
Date of marriage 4.2.1932
Long. 79°-30⁸ East
Lat. 21°-27′ North

Example No. 22. Birth date 3.6.1927. We will see the birth day of the native. 1900 = 2, 27=5, June=3, Birth date is 3=3 plus 5 plus 3 plus 2=13 divided by 7=Remainder is 6=Friday is the birth day.

See the month 22nd of May to 21st of June in the year 1927. The fourth part of the northern hemisphere, Friday shows 4-30 hours. Tuesday is on 180° of Friday. Tuesday shows 1-30 hours, due to spherical triangle it is a negative part. Friday shows 4-30 hours it means Rohini nakshatra, Venus is the Lord of Friday as well as he is the Lord of Vrishabha and Thula rashi. Moon is the Lord of Rohini nakshatra, it shows the Lord of Vrishabha rashi is with Moon but Rohini nakshatra is negative and Shravana nakshatra is greater, it means the Moon and Venus are on 180° of Shravana in Pushya nakshatra Karka rashi. Tuesday shows 1-30 hours in Mesha rashi. Mars is the Lord of Tuesday as well as he is the Lord of Mesha and Vrischika rashi, but due to the spherical triangle it is negative, 1-30 hours means Aswini nakshatra, it means Aswini nakshatra is negative, and Moola nakshatra is greater for Ketu, that is Ketu is in Dhanu rashi, deduct 2 hours the difference of the negative part 19-30 hours—2=17-30 hours, it is the nakshatra of Saturn, it means Saturn is in Anuradha nakshatra Vrischika rashi and Mars is in the triangle of Vrischika rashi, Ketu is in Moola nakshatra Dhanu rashi, that is Rahu is on 180° of the Ketu, it shows Rahu is in Aridra nakshatra Mithuna rashi, add 2 hours the difference of Mars, 6-30 plus 2=8-30, it means Mars is in Pushya nakshatra Karka rashi and it is the triangle of Saturn. See Thula rashi of Venus in the fourth part of the northern hemisphere. There is no Friday or Tuesday in Thula but Friday of Kanya rashi shows 14-30 hours, it means Chitra nakshatra, it is the nakshatra of Mars and Mercury is the Lord of Kanya and Mithuna rashi, it shows that Mercury is in the greater nakshatra, Mriga which is his own rashi, it means Mercury is in Mithuna rashi. See Vrischika rashi of Mars in the third part of the northern hemisphere, Tuesday shows 18-30 hours on the border of Dhanu, Jupiter is the Lord of Meena and Dhanu rashi, it means 18-30 hours are negative for Jupiter, 18-30 hours means Jyeshtha nakshatra, it is negative, Revati is the greater nakshatra for the Jupiter, it shows Jupiter is in Revati nakshatra Meena rashi which is his own rashi.

The third part of the southern hemisphere Tuesday shows 18-30—20'=18-10' hours means Jyeshtha nakshatra or 18 solar degrees, then see the Latitude chart for 18° of Dhanu rashi on Tuesday, it shows 289°-5', deduct 270°, of Dhanu rashi, 289°-5'—270°=19°-5' Latitude North. The fourth part of northern hemisphere Friday shows 4-30 hours and Tuesday shows 1-30 hours, add it together 4-30 plus 1-30=6 hours is the Longitude, Deduct 6° of Mars and 3° of Ketu, 6 hours means 90°—9°=81° Longitude East.

22nd of the May to 21st of June is the period of Moon, the opening month of the year 1927 is in the tenth house, then 22nd of January to 21st of December tenth house, 22nd of December to 21st of

315

November eleventh house, 22nd of November to 21st of October first house, 22nd of September to 21st of August second house, 22nd of August to 21st of July third house, 22nd of July to 21st of June fourth house, here is Makara rashi the 7th aspect rashi of Mars and Venus. Then put Makara in the fourth house, it shows Thula Lagna, 14th of May to 14th of June the Sun is in Vrishabha rashi, the Moon is in Karka rashi.

We want to see the marriage day of the native, then we must see the Lord of Lagna, and the Lord of the seventh house. The Lord of Lagna is Venus and he is in Karka rashi. The right ascension nakskhatra of Venus is Pushya and his declination nakshatra is Magha No. 1, Mars is the Lord of seventh house and he is in Karka rashi. The right ascension nakshatra of Mars is Pushya and his declination nakshatra is Magha No. 1, both the planets Mars and Venus show their declination nakshatra Magha, then count Magha nakshatra No. 1 from Simha rashi upto Mesha rashi (seventh house) Simha 1, Dhanu 10 and Mesha 19, this is her year to get married. The seventh aspect rashi of Magha nakshatra Simha rashi is Kumbha rashi. It shows the month of May when Moon will be in Vrishabha rashi of Venus, her seventh aspect nakshatra will be Jyeshtha, Jeshtha nakshatra indicates the date of marriage. Add 19 years to her birth year, 1927 plus 19=1946 that is on 18th of May 1946 she got married.

(Third part of the northern hemisphere Tuesday shows 18-30 hours. Now deduct Tuesday hours of birth year, that is the fourth part of northern hemisphere Tuesday shows 1-30 hours, 18-30—1-30 =17 hours, it means 17 nakshatra or 17° or 17 tithis, deduct 15 tithis of the bright half as her birth month shows the period of Moon 17-15=2, it shows the second tithi of the dark half. 17th nakshatra is Anuradha, it is of Saturn, the marriage month shows Kumbha rashi, it clearly shows that the Saturn must be in triangle of Kumbha rashi and as Mars has shown the opening rashi of the Dhanu of the horoscope, then the seventh aspect rashi must be Mithuna the marriage year 19, it clearly indicates the nakshatra Moola in the Dhanu rashi. Thus the Ephemeries of 19° Ayanamsa is absolutely wrong which has shown Saturn in Karka rashi. See the example 19 for planets on marriage day). Put the seventh aspect nakshatra of the date on her birth day or put the right ascension nakshatra of Venus on birth day

8	1	4	6
Fri	Sun	Tues	Thur
9	2	5	7
Sat	Mon	Wed	Fri

It shows 1-4-6-8 years are good, in these years 2-5-7-9 months are good, in these months 2-5-7-9 dates and the days of the dates are good and vice versa.

Miss XX

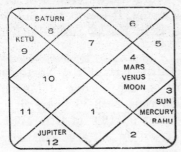

Birth date 3.6.1927
Date of marriage 18.5.1946
Long. 81° East
Lat. 19°-5′ North.

Example No. 23. Birth date 3.8.1924. We will see the birth day of the native. 1900=2, 24=2, August=1, Birth date is 3=3 plus 1 plus 2 plus 2=8 divided by 7=Remainder is 1=Sunday is the birth day. See the month 22nd of February to 21st of March in the year 1924. The first part of the southern hemisphere, Sunday shows 2-30 hours in Dhanu rashi. Thursday is on 180° of Sunday. Thursday shows 23-30 hours in Vrischika rashi, due to spherical triangle it is a negative part. Sunday shows 2-30 hours in Dhanu rashi, 2-30 hours means Bharani nakshatra, it is negative due to the spherical triangle, Jupiter, Ketu are the Lord of Dhanu rashi and Purvashadha is the greater nakshatra in Dhanu rashi, it is the nakshatra of Venus, it means the Venus is on 180° of Purvashadha in the nakshatra of Jupiter and Ketu is in Purvabhadrapada nakshatra, Venus is in Mithuna, it shows the Lord of Mithuna rashi is in the greater nakshatra of Bharani, the Lord of Mithuna is Rahu as well as Mercury, it means Mercury and Rahu are in Purva nakshatra Simha Rashi because Sunday has shown us Bharani nakshatra and Dhanu rashi, Thursday shows 23-30 hours in Vrischika rashi, 23-30 hours means Dhanishtha nakshatra, it is of Mars, it shows Mars is in Dhanishtha nakshatra, it is negative nakshatra for Jupiter, Mriga nakshatra is the greater nakshatra, it shows Jupiter is on 180° of Mriga nakshatra, that is Jupiter is in Vrischika rashi in Jyeshtha nakshatra.

Sun is the Lord of Sunday and Simha rashi, then see Simha rashi of the Sun in the third part of the southern hemisphere, Thursday shows 16-30 hours in Simha rashi, 16-30 hours means Vishakha nakshatra, it is the nakshatra of Jupiter, it shows Jupiter himself is in Vishakha nakshatra, Purvabhadrapada is the greater nakshatra, Purvabhadrapada nakshatra is in Kumbha rashi which is on 180° of the Simha, Saturn is the Lord of Kumbha, it means the Lord of Kum-

317

bha is in Vishakha nakshatra in triangle of Simha, that is Saturn is in Thula rashi. Sunday shows 19-30 hours in Kanya rashi, 19-30 means Moola nakshatra, it is not in Kanya, Mercury is the Lord of Kanya and Mithuna, it shows Kanya rashi is negative for the Sun and Mithuna is the greater rashi, add 2 hours the difference of the negative rashi Kanya 19-30 plus 2=21-30 hours, it means the Sun is on 180° of the Uttarashadha, that is he is in Karka rashi Pushya nakshatra.

See Meena rashi of Jupiter in the third part of the Northern hemisphere. Thursday shows 6-30 hours on the border of Meena, add 2 hours the difference of Meena, 6-30 plus 2=8-30 hours, it is the nakshatra of Saturn, it means the Moon is on 180° of Uttarabhadrapada, that is the Moon is in Simha rashi in Uttara nakshatra (Saturn's rashi is on 180° of the Moon's rashi).

Sunday shows 19-30 hours in Kanya rashi, deduct 20' of Ayanachalana, 19-30—20'=19-10' hours means 19 nakshatra or 19 solar degrees. See Latitude chart for 19° of Kanya rashi on Thursday, it shows 199°-25' deduct 180° of Kanya, 199°-25'—180°=19°-25' Latitude North. Thursday of Meena rashi shows 6-30 hours, it shows 97°-30', deduct 6° of Sunday and 3° of Rahu, 97°-30'—9°=88°-30' Longitude East.

22nd of July to 21st of August is the period of Moon the opening month of year 1924 is in the tenth house, then 22nd of January to 21st of December tenth house, 22nd of December to 21st of November eleventh house, 22nd of November to 21st of October twelfth house, 22nd of October to 21st of September first house, 22nd of September to 21st of August second house, 22nd of August to 21st of July third house, 22nd of July to 21st of June fourth house, here is Meena rashi of Jupiter which is on 180° of the birth day Sunday. Then put Meena rashi in the fourth house, it shows Dhanu Lagna, the Sun is in Karka, the Moon is in Simha rashi.

We want to see the marriage day of the native. Then we must see the Lord of Lagna and the Lord of seventh house, Jupiter is the Lord of Lagna and he is in Vrischika rashi. The right ascension nakshatra of Jupiter is Vishakha and his declination nakshatra is Jyeshtha No. 9, Mercury is the Lord of seventh house and he is in Simha rashi. The right ascension nakshatra of Mercury is Purva and his declination nakshatra is Hasta, his right ascension 7th aspect nakshatra is Purvabhadrapada and his 7th aspect declination nakshatra is Revati No. 9. The declination nakshatra of both the planets is No. 9. Then count No. 9 from Vrischika rashi upto Meena rashi. Vrischika 9, Meena 18, this is her marriage year.

Mithuna rashi of the seventh house shows the month of marriage, that is March is the month of Marriage. Rohini is the 7th aspect nakshatra of Jupiter, count it upto Kanya, Vrishabha 4, Kanya 13, add 18 years in her birth year 1924, 1924 plus 18=1942. That is on 13th of March 1942 she got married.

Venus and Moon must come in Makara. The Sun must be in Meena, Mars, Jupiter, Saturn must be in Vrishabha, Ketu and Mercury must be in Mesha on her marriage day.

Put the seventh aspect date nakshatra on the birth day.

7	1	3	5
Sun	Tues	Thur	Sat
9	2	4	6
Mon	Wed	Fri	Sun

It shows 2-4-6-9 years are good, in these years 1-3-5-7 months are good, in these months 9-2-4-6 dates and days of the dates are good and vice versa.

Miss XXX

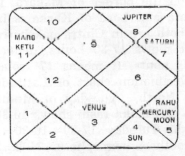

Birth date 3.8.1924
Date of marriage 13.3.1942
Long. 88°-30' East
Lat. 19°-25' North.

Example No. 24. Birth date 16.10.1917. We will see the birth day of the native. 1900=2, 17=7, October=6 Birth date 16=16 plus 6 plus 7 plus 2=31 divided by 7=Remainder is 3=Tuesday is the birth day. See the month 22nd of the September to 21st of October in the year 1917 the first part of the northern hemisphere. Tuesday is on 180° of Saturday. See Tuesday and Saturday. Tuesday shows 10-30 hours in Vrischika rashi and Saturday shows 7-30 hours in Thula rashi, but due to the spherical triangle it is a negative part. Tuesday shows 10-30 hours, 10-30 hours means Magha nakshatra, it is a nakshatra of Ketu, it means Mars is in the Magha nakshatra and Ketu is in the greater nakshatra, that is Ketu is in the 7th aspect of Moola nakshatra Dhanu rashi, that is Rahu is in Dhanu rashi and Ketu is in Mithuna rashi, Saturday shows 7-30 hours in Thula rashi, it means the Lord of Thula rashi is on 180° of the Punarvasu nakshatra, that is Venus is in Uttarashadha nakshatra Dhanu rashi and Saturn himself is in Karka rashi in Punar-vasu nakshatra. The Moon is in the greater nakshatra that is the Moon is in Vishakha nakshatra Thula rashi, Punarvasu or Vishakha is the nakshatra of Jupiter, it means Jupiter is in it which means Jupiter is in the house of Venus. Krittika nakshatra is on 180° of the Vrishabha, that is Jupiter is in Vrishabha rashi. See the Mesha rashi of Mars in the second part of the Southern hemisphere. Tuesday is on the border of Meena, it shows 17-30 hours, it means Anuradha nakshatra. There is no Anuradha nakshatra in Meena rashi, then Jupiter is the Lord of Meena rashi and Kanya rashi is 7th aspect rashi of Jupiter, it means the Lord of Meena rashi is on 180° of the Lord of Kanya, that is Mercury is on 180° of Jupiter, Jupiter is in Krittika nakshatra Vrishabha rashi and Mercury is in Anuradha nakshatra Vrischika rashi and Tuesday is on the border of Kanya. On the other way his 7th aspect rashi is on the border of Meena. Now see the Kumbha and Makara rashi of Saturn in the third part of the northern hemisphere, Saturday shows 14-30 hours in Kumbha rashi, 14-30 hours means Chitra nakshatra, Simha rashi is on 180° of Kumbha, it means the Lord of Simha rashi is in the Chitra nakshatra, 14-30 are on the border of Makara, it means Karka rashi is on 180° of Makara and Lord of Karka is in Chitra, that is the Sun and the Moon both are in Chitra nakshatra Thula rashi. Tuesday of Meena rashi shows 17-30 hours, deduct 20′ of Ayanachalana 17-30′—20′=17-10′ hours, it means 17° solar degrees. See 17° of Meena rashi in declination chart of Latitude on Tuesday, it shows 19°-48′ Latitude North. Tuesday of Mesha rashi shows 17-30 hours and Tuesday of Vrischika rashi shows 10-30 hours, deduct hours of Vrischika rashi Tuesday 17-30—10-30=7 hours, deduct 2 hours the difference of southern hemisphere. 7—2=5 hours is the Longitude. Add 6° of the Saturday. 5 hours means 75°, 75° plus 6°=81° Longitude East.

(The first part of the northern hemisphere Tuesday shows 10-30 hours and Saturday shows 7-30 hours, add them together, 10-30 plus 7-30=18 hours. Second part of the southern hemisphere Tuesday shows 17-30 hours, deduct these hours from 18 hours, 18—17-30 =30′ it shows the new Moon day on Tuesday 16,10.1917).

22nd of September to 21st of October is the period of Moon. The opening month of the year 1917 is in the tenth house, then 22nd of January to 21st of December tenth house, 22nd of December to 21st of November eleventh house, 22nd of November to 21st of October twelfth house, 22nd of October to 21st of September first house, here is the seventh aspect rashi Thula of Mesha rashi. Then it shows Thula Lagna, the Moon is in Thula and the Sun is in Thula rashi.

We want to see the marriage day of the native. Then we must see the Lord of Lagna and the Lord of 7th house. The Lord of Lagna is Venus and the Lord of 7th house is the Mars. The Lord of the Lagna is in Dhanu rashi, he is in conjunction of Rahu, it means Rahu is working on behalf of the Venus. Rahu is in Moola nakshatra and his 7th aspect nakshatra is Aridra No. 6, then count No. 6 from Mithuna upto Thula, Mithuna 6, Thula 15, this is her year to get married. Mithuna rashi shows the month of February. Jupiter is in Vrishabha rashi in the rashi of Venus and Venus is in the rashi of Jupiter, it means Jupiter is showing the date of marriage. The opening rashi of the horoscope is Vrischika rashi. Budha is there the Lord of Mithuna rashi, he is in Anuradha nakshatra, his 7th aspect nakshatra is Rohini, it indicates the date of marriage. Add 15 years in her birth year 1917, 1917 plus 15=1932 that is on 4th of February 1932 she got married.

Put the birth date on the birth day

3	5	7	9
Tue	Thur	Sat	Mon
2	4	6	8
Wed	Fri	Sun	Tue

It shows 2-4-6-8 years, months and dates are good to her and vice versa.

(All the major planets are in nakshatra No. 7 and Mercury is in 7th aspect of the right ascension nakshatra of the planets, it shows Anapatya yoga, the lady will have no issues).

Miss XXX

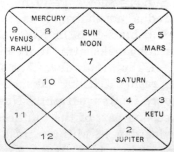

Birth date 16.10.1917
Date of Marriage 4.2.1932
Long. 81° East
Lat. 19°-48′ North.

Example No. 25. Birth date is 13.2.1912. We will see the birth day of the native. 1900=2, 12=1, February=2, birth date is 13=13 plus 2 plus 1 plus 2=18 divided by 7=Remainder is 4=Wednesday is the birth day. See the month 22nd of January to 21st of February in the year 1912. The second part of the southern hemisphere, Wednesday shows 3-30 hours in Dhanu rashi. Sunday is on 180° of Wednesday, Sunday shows 24-30 hours in

321

Vrischika rashi, it is negative part due to the spherical triangle. Wednesday shows 3-30 hours in Dhanu rashi, 3-30 hours means Krittika nakshatra, it means the Lord of Mithuna rashi is in Krittika nakshatra (3-30 hours shows Uttarashadha in Dhanu rashi, it is 7th aspect nakshatra of Mithuna rashi. Mercury and Rahu are the Lords of Mithuna. So we have taken the descending node of the Moon first). Punarvasu nakshatra is on 180° of the Uttarashadha. Punarvasu nakshatra is in Karka rashi, it is the nakshatra of Jupiter, and it is the Rashi of Moon, it means the Moon is in Uttarashadha nakshatra Dhanu rashi and Lord of the Mithuna is in Uttarashadha nakshatra Makara rashi, that is Mercury is in Makara rashi, Jupiter is the Lord of Dhanu rashi and Punarvasu nakshatra, but due to the spherical triangle it is a negative nakshatra, Jupiter must be in greater nakshatra Vishakha which is in triangle of Karka rashi, it shows Jupiter is in Vrischika rashi in Vishakha nakshatra. Sunday shows 24-30 hours in Vrischika rashi, 24-30 hours means Shatataraka nakshatra, there is no Shatataraka nakshatra in Vrischika rashi, Shatataraka nakshatra is in Kumbha rashi, then Vrischika rashi is negative here, Mars is the Lord of Vrischika and Mesha rashi, Vrischika rashi is negative here, then Mesha rashi of Mars is greater, Shatataraka nakshatra is negative, Swati nakshatra is greater, it means the Lord of Kumbha rashi is on 180° of Swati nakshatra, that is Saturn is in Aswini nakshatra Mesha rashi, and Lord of Sunday is in Shatataraka nakshatra Kumbha rashi, deduct 2 hours from Shatataraka nakshatra, it shows the Venus is in Shravana nakshatra Makara rashi. The Sun is the Lord of Sunday and Simha rashi, then see Simha rashi of Sunday in the fourth part of southern hemisphere, Sunday shows 17-30 hours in Simha rashi, 17-30 hours means Anuradha nakshatra, it is not in Simha rashi, it is in Vrischika rashi, Sun himself is in Kumbha and he has shown Simha rashi, and Anuradha nakshatra, it means the Lord of Vrischika rashi is on 180° of the Anuradha, that is Mars is in Krittika nakshatra Vrishabha rashi, Krittika nakshatra is of the Sun, Wednesday shows 20-30 hours in Kanya rashi. Now see the other rashi of the Mercury in the second part of the southern hemisphere. There is no Sunday or Wednesday in Mithuna rashi. Sunday of Karka rashi shows 14-30 hours, deduct 14-30 hours from 20-30 hours of Kanya rashi. 20-30—14-30=6 hours is the Longitude, deduct 6° of Wednesday and 3° of Rahu, 6 hours means 90°—9°=81° Longitude East. Sunday of Karka rashi shows 14-30 hours, deduct 20′ of Ayanachalana, 14-30—20=14-10′ hours, it means 14th nakshatra or 14 solar degrees, then see the Latitude chart for 14° of Karka rashi on Sunday, it shows 136°-47′, deduct 120° of the Karka, 136°-47′—120°=16°-47′ Latitude North.

22nd of January to 21st of February is the period of Moon. The opening month of the year 1912 is in the tenth house, then 22nd of January to 21st of December tenth house, 22nd of December to 21st of November eleventh house, 22nd of November to 21st of October twelfth house, 22nd of October to 21st of September first house, 22nd of September to 21st of August second house, 22nd of August to 21st of July third house, 22nd of July to 21st of June fourth house, 22nd of June to 21st of May fifth house, 22nd of May to 21st of April sixth house, 22nd of April to 21st of March seventh house, 22nd of March to 21st of February eighth house, 22nd of February to 21st of January nineth house, here is Mesha rashi of Mars, which is on 180° of the Sunday. Then put Mesha rashi in the nineth house, it shows Simha Lagna, the Sun is in Kumbha, the Moon is in Dhanu rashi.

We want to see the marriage day of the native. Then we must see the Lord of the Lagna as well as the Lord of seventh house, Sun is the Lord of Lagna and he is in the seventh house. The Saturn is the Lord of seventh house and he is in the nineth house, it shows the sun is working on behalf of Mars. Right ascension nakshatra of the Sun is Shatataraka and his declination nakshatra is Uttara-bhadrapada. The right ascension seventh aspect nakshatra of the Sun is Purva, and his 7th aspect declination nakshatra is Hasta No. 4. The right ascension nakshatra of the Saturn is Aswini and his 7th aspect nakshatra is Chitra No. 5. Then count 7th aspect nakshatra of the Saturn upto No. 4 of the Sun. Aswini 5, Bharani 14, Krittika 23, Rohini 32, this is his year to get married. Rohini nakshatra is in Vrishabha and Mars is there in Rohini nakshatra, his 7th aspect nakshatra is Anuradha which is of Saturn and Saturn is in Mesha. Then count the months of Vrischika rashi from the opening month of the year 1912, Vrischika rashi shows the month of July. Swati nakshatra is the first nakshatra No. 6 and Shatataraka is second. No. 15 indicates the date of marriage. Add 32 years in his birth year 1912, 1912 plus 32=1944, that is on 15th of July 1944 he got married.

Put the seventh aspect nakshatra of the Sun on Sunday and declination nakshatra Mercury on Wednesday.

5	7	1	3
Wed	Fri	Sun	Tue
4	6	9	2
Thurs.	Sat	Mon	Wed

It shows 1-3-5-7 years are good, in these years 1-3-5-7 months are good, in these months 2-4-6-9 dates and days of the dates are good and vice versa.

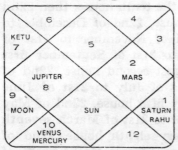

Shree Jog

Birth date 13.2.1912
Date of marriage 15.7.1944
Long. 81° East
Lat. 16°-47′ North

Example No. 26. Birth date 18.1.1925. We will see the birth day of the native. 1900=2, 25=3, January=6, Birth date is 18=18 plus 6 plus 3 plus 2=29 divided by 7=Remainder is 1=Sunday is the birth day. See the month 22nd of December to 21st of January in the year 1925 the first part of the southern hemisphere. There is no Sunday, then see Wednesday which is on 180° of Sunday. Wednesday shows 20-30 hours on the border of Simha rashi, 20-30 hours means Purvashadha. Purvashadha nakshatra is in the Dhanu rashi. Purvashadha nakshatra is of Venus, Wednesday has shown Purvashadha nakshatra on the border of Simha rashi, it means the Lord of Purvashadha is Venus, the Lord of Dhanu rashi is Jupiter and the Lord of Wednesday is Mercury, they are all in Purvashadha nakshatra and it is negative nakshatra to the Lord of Simha rashi, then add 2 hours the difference of the negative part. 20-30 hours plus 2=22-30 hours, it means Shravana nakshatra, that is the Sun is in the Shravana nakshatra Makara rashi. The Moon is the Lord of the Shravana nakshatra and the Lord of Mithuna is on 180° of the Shravana. That is the Rahu is in the Pushya nakshatra Karka rashi, the Ketu and Sun are in Makara rashi, Venus, Mercury and Jupiter are in Purvashadha nakshatra Dhanu rashi. Mercury is the Lord of Wednesday as well as he is the Lord of Kanya and Mithuna rashi. Then see Mithuna rashi of Mercury in the second part of the southern hemisphere, Sunday shows 17-30 hours on the border of Mithuna. 17-30 hours means Anuradha nakshatra. It is of the Saturn, there is no Anuradha nakshatra in Mithuna rashi, it is in Vrischika rashi. Saturn is the Lord of Anuradha nakshatra. Then deduct 2 hours the difference of the negative part. 17-30—2=15-30 hours, it means the Saturn is in the Swati nakshatra Thula rashi, it is on the border of Kanya rashi, it means the Lord of Kanya is in triangle, that is the Saturn and Moon are in Thula rashi.

Now 17-30 hours means Anuradha nakshatra, it is in the Vrischika rashi, but it is shown in Mithuna, there is no Anuradha nakshatra in Mithuna, it means it is negative rashi for Mars the Lord of Vrischika rashi. Kanya rashi of Mercury is greater for Mars because Mercury is the Lord of Mithuna and Kanya, Anuradha is negative for Mars, Uttarabhadrapada is greater, it shows Mars is in Uttarabhadrapada nakshatra Meena rashi. Uttarabhadrapada is No. 26 it means 26 solar degrees. Then see the declination latitude chart for 26° of Meena rashi on Wednesday, it shows 13°-46' Latitude, North.

Wednesday of Kanya rashi shows 20-30 hours. Deduct Sunday hours of Mithuna rashi 20-30—17-30=3 hours and add 9° of Sunday which was not in the first part of the southern hemisphere and 3° of Ketu. 3 hours means 45° plus 12°=57° Longitude East. 22nd of December to 21st of January is the period of the Sun. The opening month of the year 1925 is in the fourth house. Then 22nd of January to 21st of December is in the fourth house, naturally 22nd of February to 21st of January is in the fifth house, here is the 7th aspect rashi of the birth day Sunday, that is Kumbha rashi is in the fifth house and Simha rashi is in the eleventh house. Then put the Kumbha rashi in the fifth house, it shows Thula Lagna. The Sun is in Makara rashi and the Moon is in Thula rashi.

We want to see the marriage day of the Lady, we must see the Lord of Lagna and the Lord of seventh house, The Lord of Lagna is Venus and he is in the Dhanu rashi Purvashadha nakshatra Lord of the seventh house is Mars and he is in Meena rashi Uttarabhadrapada nakshatra, his right ascension nakshatra is Uttarabhadrapada and his declination nakshatra is Aswini. The 7th aspect right ascension nakshatra of the Mars is Hasta and his 7th aspect declination nakshatra is Swati, it clearly shows that Mars is working on behalf of Saturn whose right ascension nakshatra is Swati and his seventh aspect nakshatra is Bharani which is of Venus and Venus is in Purvashadha No. 20. That is she is getting married at her 20. The seventh aspect rashi of Venus is Mithuna, it shows the month of June. Mriga nakshatra of Mars is there, count it upto Kumbha rashi of Saturn because his Kumbha rashi is in triangle of Lagna. Dhanishtha nakshatra is in Kumbha rashi, it indicates the date of marriage, add 20 years in her birth year, 1925 plus 20=1945, that is on 23rd of June 1945 she got married.

Put the seventh aspect nakshatra of the day nakshatra on Tuesday or date nakshatra on Saturday because Thula rashi Sunday shows 24-30 hours which indicates the birth time of the Lady.

2	4	6	9
Sun	Tue	Thu	Sat
1	3	5	7
Mon	Wed	Fri	Sun

It shows 2-4-6-8 months are good, in these months 1-3-5-7 dates and days of the dates are good and vice versa.

(The Lord of the eighth house is in conjunction of Mercury. Mars is in triangle of Rahu the Lord of Mithuna. Sun is in 7th aspect of Rahu, it indicates Inflammatory Tuberculosis to her better half as Mars is Lord of seventh house. Hasta nakshatra the right ascension 7th aspect nakshatra of Mars indicates the death of her husband in the greater nakshatra Shravana, that is at her 22nd she will be a widow.

Miss Ayangar

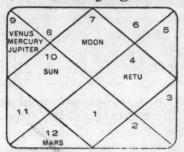

Birth date 18.1.1925
Date of marriage 23.6.1945
Long. 57° East
Lat. 13°-46' North.

Example No. 27. Birth date 11.3.1930. We will see the birth day of the native. 1900=2, 30=2, March=2, Birth date is 11=11 plus 2 plus 2 plus 2=17 divided by 7=Remainder is 3=Tuesday is the birth day. See the month 22nd of February to 21st of March in the year 1930 the fourth part of the northern hemisphere, Tuesday shows 4-30 hours in Kumbha rashi. Saturday is on 180° of Tuesday. Saturday shows 1-30 hours in Makara rashi, it is a negative part due to a spherical triangle. Tuesday shows 4-30 hours in Kumbha rashi, 4-30 hours means Rohini nakshatra. Moon is the Lord of Rohini nakshatra. Saturn is the Lord of Kumbha and Makara, it shows negative nakshatra for the Moon, it means Rohini nakshatra is negative. Shravana nakshatra is the greater nakshatra for the Moon, it shows the Moon is on 180° of Shravana, that is the Moon is in Pushya nakshatra Karka rashi. Mars is the Lord of Tuesday, it shows 4-30 hours which are negative for the Mars, then add 2 hours the difference of Mars in Pushya nakshatra hours, Pushya nakshatra means 8-30 hours plus 2=10-30 hours means Magha nakshatra, it shows the Mars is on 180° of the Magha nakshatra. Dhanishtha nakshatra is in Kumbha rashi, that is Mars is in Kumbha rashi, Dhanishtha nakhatra. Saturday shows 1-30 hours in Makara rashi. Saturn is the Lord of Saturday and Makara rashi, still it is a negative part. 1-30 hours means Aswini nakshatra, the Ketu is the Lord of Aswini, it shows Ketu is on 180° of Aswini, that is Ketu is in Chitra nakshatra Thula rashi. Aswini is negative nakshatra for

Saturn, it means Saturn is in greater nakshatra, Moola nakshatra is greater, that is Saturn is in Moola nakshatra Dhanu rashi.

See the Mesha rashi of Mars in the third part of the northern hemisphere. Saturday shows 8-30 hours in Mesha rashi, deduct 1-30 hours of Makara rashi, 8-30—1-30=7 hours means Punarvasu, it means the Moola nakshatra is declination nakshatra of Saturn and Purvashadha is right ascension nakshatra of Saturn. Tuesday shows 4-30 hours in Meena rashi. Jupiter is the Lord of Meena rashi, but Jupiter is not Lord of Rohini nakshatra and no Rohini nakshatra in Meena rashi, Rohini nakshatra is in Vrishabha rashi, it shows the Lord of Vrishabha is in Meena rashi and Lord of Meena rashi is in Rohini nakshatra Vrishabha rashi. Rohini nakshatra is negative for Venus. Hasta nakshatra is greater for him, it means Venus in Uttarabhadrapada nakshatra on 180° of Hasta nakshatra Meena rashi.

See Vrischika rashi of the Mars in the first part of the southern hemisphere, there is no Tuesday in Vrischika rashi. Saturday shows 1-30 hours in Dhanu rashi, it is negative for the Saturn. Aridra nakshatra is on 180° of the Moola. Aridra nakshatra is in Mithuna, Mercury is the Lord of Mithuna, it means Mercury is in Saturn's house. Aridra nakshatra is negative for the Mercury. Shatataraka is greater nakshatra, that is the Mercury is in Kumbha rashi Shatataraka nakshatra. Moola nakshatra is negative for the Saturn, then add 2 hours the difference of the negative part, 19-30 plus 2=21-30 hours, it is the nakshatra of the Sun, it is negative. Uttara is greater nakshatra, it means the Sun is on 180° of the Uttara, that is the Sun is in Purvabhadrapada nakshatra Kumbha rashi.

The fourth part of Northern hemisphere Saturday shows 1-30 hours, add 2 hours the difference of negative part, 1-30 plus 2=3-30. See the Longitude chart for 3-30 hours, it shows 52°-30', add 6° of Tuesday and 3° of Ketu=61°-30' Longitude East. Saturday 1-30 hours is negative, 19-30 hours are greater, deduct 20° of Ayanachalana 19-30—20'=19-10', it means 19 nakshatra or 19 solar degrees. See 19° of Makara rashi on Tuesday in Latitude chart. 320°-29', deduct 300° of Makara, 320°-29'-300°=20°-29' Latitude North. 22nd of February to 21st of March is the period of Sun, the opening month of the year 1930 is in the fourth house. Then 22nd of January to 21st of December is in the fourth house, 22nd of December to 21st of November is in the third house, 22nd of November to 21st of October is in the second house, 22nd of October to 21st of September is in first house, 22nd of September to 21st of August twelfth house, 22nd of August to 21st of July eleventh house, 22nd of July to 21st of June tenth house, 22nd of June to 21st of May is ninth house,

22nd of May to 21st of April eighth house, 22nd of April to 21st of March is in seventh house, here is the Vriśchika rashi of Mars, then put Vrischika rashi of Mars in the seventh house, it shows Vrishabha Lagna. The Sun is in Kumbha and the Moon is in Karka rashi.

We want to see the marriage day of the lady. Naturally we must see the Lord of seventh house and the Lord of Lagna. The Lord of Lagna is Venus and he is in Meena rashi. The Lord of seventh house is Mars and he is in Kumbha rashi. Mars has shown his own position in Kumbha rashi and he has shown the position of Venus, Moon and Jupiter, it means Mars is a double role player. That is Rahu is in Mesha, his right ascension nakshatra is Aswini and his declination nakshatra is Krittika No. 3. Then count No. 3 from Mesha upto Dhanu, Mesha 3, Simha 12, Dhanu 21 this is her year to get married. Jupiter is the Lord of Dhanu rashi, Dhanu rashi shows the month of April. Krittika is the first declination nakshatra of Rahu, it indicates the date of marriage. Add 21 years in her birth year, 1930 plus 21=1951. That is on 3rd of April 1951 she got married. Rahu the descending node of the Moon is in Mesha when he will be in Kumbha, and Mercury and Venus will come in Mesha the first marriage will take place. Now the right ascension nakshatra of Mars is Dhanishtha and his declination nakshatra is Purvabhadrapada. The right ascension 7th aspect nakshatra of Mars is Magha and his 7th aspect declination nakshatra is Uttara when his 7th aspect nakshatra will be his right ascension nakshatra with Rahu and when right ascension nakshatra of Venus will be Rohini and Jupiter with Saturn will come in triangle of Venus her second marriage will take place. That is, the cycle of Venus will start from Hasta nakshatra and will end in Rohini nakshatra. The right ascension nakshatra of Venus is Uttarabhadrapada and his right ascension 7th aspect nakshatra is Hasta. Then count Hasta nakshatra No. 4 from Kanya rashi to Kanya. Kanya 4, Vrishabha 13, Makara 22, Kanya 31, this is her year to get married. Mars is in Kumbha rashi, count the months upto Kumbha rashi, Kumbha rashi shows the month of July, Dhanishtha is the first nakshatra of Mars, it indicates the date of marriage, add 31 years in her birth year, 1930 plus 31=1951 1930+31=1961 i.e. that is on 5th July 1961 she got married.

Put the birth date of native on Monday.

3	6	8	1
Tues	Thur	Sat	Mon
5	7	9	4
Wed	Fri	Sun	Tue

It shows 3-6--8-1 years are good upto her 26 years and in these years 5-7-9-4 months are good, in these months 1-3-6-8 dates and the days of the dates are good and vice versa. After her 26 years 5-7-9-4 years are good, in these years 5-7-9-4 months are good, and in these months 5-7-9-4 dates and the days of the dates are good and vice versa.

Miss Kulkarni

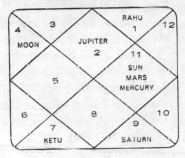

Birth date 11.3.1930

Date of Marriage:

(1) 3.4.1951

(2) 5.7.1961

Long. 61°-30′ East

Lat. 20°-29′ North.

Example No. 28. Birth date 20.5.1921. We will see the birth day of the native. 1900=2, 21=5, May=7, Birth date is 20=20 plus 7 plus 5 plus 2=34 divided by 7=Remainder is 6=Friday is the birth day. See the month 22nd of April to 21st of May in the year 1921. The first part of the southern hemisphere, Friday shows 2-30 hours in Mesha rashi. Tuesday is on 180° of the Friday. Tuesday shows 6-30 hours in Vrishabha rashi. Due to the spherical triangle it is a negative part. Friday shows 2-30 hours, 2-30 hours means Bharani nakshatra, it is the nakshatra of Venus and Rahu, it means Rahu is on 180° of Bharani nakshatra, that is Rahu is in Swati nakshatra Thula rashi. Ketu is in Aswini nakshatra Mesha rashi. Swati nakshatra is negative for Venus, he is in the greater nakshatra Shatataraka. That is Venus is in Kumbha rashi. Tuesday shows 6-30 hours in Vrishabha rashi. 6-30 hours means Aridra nakshatra, it is the nakshatra of Venus and Rahu, it is not in Vrishabha rashi, it is in Mithuna. Mercury is the Lord of Mithuna, it shows the Lord of Mithuna is on 180° of the greater nakshatra Swati, that is Mercury is in Mesha rashi. Swati nakshatra is negative for the Mars, then add 2 hours the difference of the negative part of the Mars. 15-30 plus 2=17-30, it shows Mars is on 180° of the Anuradha nakshatra, that is the Mars is in Rohini nakshatra Vrishabha rashi.

Mars is the Lord of Tuesday as well as he is the Lord of Mesha and Vrischika rashi. See the Vrischika rashi of Mars in the fourth part of the Southern hemisphere. Friday shows 19-30 hours. Venus is on the border of Vrischika and Dhanu rashi. Mars is the Lord

329

of Vrischika rashi, he is in Anuradha nakshatra which is the nakshatra of Saturn's own rashi, Moola nakshatra is in Dhanu, Jupiter
is the Lord of Dhanu rashi, it means Saturn and Jupiter both are in
the greater nakshatra Magha on 180° of Shatataraka nakshatra in
which Venus is positive now. That is Saturn and Jupiter are in
Magha nakshatra Simha rashi. See Thula rashi of Venus in the
first part of the northern hemisphere shows 16-30 hours in Thula
rashi, 16-30 hours means Vishakha nakshatra, it is the nakshatra of
Jupiter and 7th aspect nakshatra of the Sun, it shows the Sun is
in Krittika nakshatra Mesha rashi. Tuesday shows 23-30 hours in
Makara rashi, it is the nakshatra of the Mars, Makara rashi is on
180° of Karka, it shows the Lord of the Karka is in Dhanishtha,
add 2 hours the difference, 23-30 plus 2=25-30. The fourth part of
the southern hemisphere Friday shows 19-30 hours, deduct 20' of
Ayanachalana, 19-30—20'=19-10' hours, it means 19 nakshatra or
19 solar degrees; then see 19° of Dhanu rashi on Tuesday in the
Latitude chart. 19°=290°-8' deduct 270° of Dhanu rashi, 290°-8'—
270°=20°-8' Latitude North.

The first part of the southern hemisphere Friday shows 2-30
hours and Tuesday shows 6-30 hours, deduct Friday hours from
Tuesday hours. 6-30—2-30=4 hours is the Longitude, add 3° of
the Ketu, 4 hours=60° plus 3°=63° Longitude East.

22nd of April to 21st of May is the period of Sun, the opening
month of the year 1921 is in the fourth house, then 22nd of January
to 21st of December is in the fourth house, 22nd of December to 21st
of November is in third house, 22nd of November to 21st of October
is second house, 22nd of October to 21st of September is first house,
22nd of September to 21st of August is twelfth house, 22nd of
August to 21st of July eleventh house, 22nd of July to 21st of June
tenth house, 22nd of June to 21st of May nineth house, 22nd of May
to 21st of April is eighth house, here is Karka rashi of the Moon
which is on 180° of Dhanishtha. Then put Karka rashi in the eighth
house, it shows Dhanu Lagna. The Sun is in Mesha rashi Krittika
nakshatra. The Moon is in Kumbha rashi Purvabhadrapada nakshatra.

We want to see the marriage day of the native. Then we
must see the Lord of seventh house and the Lord of Lagna. The
Lord of the Lagna is Jupiter as well as the Ketu, Jupiter is in
Simha rashi and Ketu is in Mesha rashi. The right ascension nak-
shatra of Ketu is Aswini and his declination nakshatra is Krittika
No. 3. Then count No. 3 upto Simha rashi. Mesha 3,

Dhanu 12, Simha 21, this is the year to get married. Ketu is in the Mesha rashi, it shows the Month of February. Aridra is the first 7th aspect nakshatra of the Ketu, it indicates the date of marriage No. 6. Add 21 years in his birth year, 1921 plus 21=1942, that is on 6th of February 1942 he got married. At his 25th the Ketu has changed the polarity. His 7th aspect declination nakshatra is the right ascension nakshatra. Now, his right ascension nakshatra was Aswini and his declination nakshatra was Krittika. His 7th aspect right ascension nakshatra was Chitra and his 7th aspect declination nakshatra was Vishakha. At the same time right ascension nakshatra of the Moon was Purvabhadrapada and her declination nakshatra was Revati. Now the right ascension nakshatra of Ketu is Dhanistha and his declination nakshatra is Purvabhadrapada which was of the Moon at his birth time. Now the right ascension nakshatra of the Moon is Chitra and her declination nakshatra is Vishakha which was of Ketu at the time of birth. It clearly shows that Ketu has changed his polarity. Naturally Saturn was in Magha nakshatra, now he is in Aswini. Thus the planets changed their polarities. Now we see the Lord of seventh house. The Lord of Seventh house is Rahu, he is in Thula rashi. The right ascension nakshatra of Rahu is Swati and his declination is Hasta No. 4. Then count No. 4 of Rahu from Mesha to Mesha 31. This is his year to get married. Kanya rashi of Mercury and Hasta nakshatra is the opening nakshatra cycle of Rahu. It shows the month of marriage, July. Rohini nakshatra was the right ascension nakshatra of Mars, it is in triangle of Kanya rashi. Mriga nakshatra is the original nakshatra of Mars, that indicates the date of marriage. Mriga nakshatra is the first nakshatra of Mars in the seventh house, add 40 years in his birth year, 1921 plus 40=1961, that is on 5th of July 1961 he got married.

Put the seventh aspect nakshatra of Venus on the birth day.

6	8	1	3
Fri	Sun	Tue	Thur

5	7	9	2
Sat	Mon	Wed	Fri

It shows 6-8-1-3 years are good upto his 25th, in these years 5-7-9-2 months are good, in these months 6-8-1-3 dates and days of the dates are good; after 25th 5-7-9-4 years are good, in these years 5-7-9-4 months are good and in these months 5-7-9-4 dates and days of the dates are good and vice versa.

Shree Golwilkar

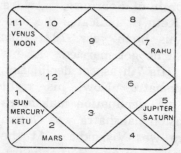

11 VENUS MOON	10	8	
	9	7 RAHU	
12		6	
1 SUN MERCURY KETU	3	5 JUPITER SATURN	
2 MARS		4	

Birth date 20.5.1921
Dates of Marriages:
   (1) 6.2.1942
   (2) 5.7.1961
Long. 63° East
Lat. 20°-8′ North

Example No. 29. Birth date 13-6-1921. We will see the birth day of the native. 1900=2, 21=5, June=3, Birth date is 13=13 plus 3 plus 5 plus 2=23 divided by 7=Reminder is 2=Monday is the birth day. See the month 22nd of May to 21st of June in the year 1921. The first part of the southern hemisphere, Monday shows 24-30 hours on the border of Kumbha and Meena rashi. Friday is on 180° of Monday but there is no Friday in the first part. It is negative part because of the spherical triangle. Monday shows 24-30 hours on the border of Meena rashi, add 2 hours the difference of the negative part. 24-30 plus 2=26-30 hours means Uttara-bhadrapada nakshatra, it is the nakshatra of the Saturn, it means Saturn is on 180° of Uttarabhadrapada that is Saturn is in Uttara nakshatra Simha rashi, because Monday has shown us the border of Kumbha and the Saturn is the Lord of Kumbha and his 7th aspect nakshatra is of his own, Monday shows it, it means the Lord of Monday is also in the Uttara nakshatra but she is on the border of Meena, that is she is in the Uttara nakshatra Kanya rashi. Saturn is the Lord of Kumbha rashi and Monday has shown 24-30 hours, it means Shatataraka nakshatra. Shatataraka nak-shatra is of Rahu and Venus, it means Shatataraka nakshatra is negative for Venus because Kumbha rashi is not of Venus. Swati is the greater nakshatra, it shows Venus is on 180° of Swati, that is Venus is in Aswini nakshatra Mesha rashi and Rahu the Lord of Swati nakshatra is in Swati nakshatra Thula rashi. Moon is the Lord of Monday as well as she is the Lord of Karka rashi. Venus is the Lord of Friday as well as he is the Lord of Vrishabha and Thula rashi. Then see the Thula rashi of Venus in the fourth part of the southern hemisphere.

Friday shows 14-30 hours, it means Chitra nakshatra, it is the nakshatra of Mars, it is in the Kanya rashi, it is not the nakshatra of Venus or Rahu, then why Friday has shown it? It means the Lord of the Kanya is in greater rashi of Rahu with Lord of Chitra nak-shatra, that is Chitra nakshatra is negative for Mars and Mercury.

Mriga nakshatra is greater for them in the Rashi of Rahu. It shows that Mars and Mercury are in the Mriga nakshatra Mithuna rashi. See Karka rashi of the Moon in the second part of the northern hemisphere. Monday shows 7-30 hours in Karka rashi and Friday shows 11-30 hours in Simha rashi, 7-30 hours means Punarvasu nakshatra, it is the nakshatra of the Jupiter, it is in Karka rashi and it is the 7th aspect nakshatra of the Sun, then it is negative nakshatra for the Sun. Vishakha is the greater nakshatra, it shows the Sun is on 180° of Vishakha nakshatra, that is the Sun is in Krittika nakshatra Vrishabha rashi in triangle of the Moon and that is why Monday has shown 7-30 hours, Friday shows 11-30 hours, it means Purva nakshatra, it is the nakshatra of Venus and 7th aspect nakshatra of Jupiter, it means Bharani nakshatra is greater nakshatra for Venus and Purva nakshatra is for Jupiter, that is Jupiter is in the Purva nakshatra Simha rashi and Venus is in Bharani nakshatra Mesha rashi, see the Vrishabha rashi of Venus in the fourth part of the northern hemisphere, Friday shows 4-30 hours, add 2 hours the difference of the southern hemisphere. 4-30 hours plus 2=6-30 hours, see the Longitude chart for 6-30 hours and deduct 6° of Monday and 3° of Ketu, 6-30 hours=97°-30'—9°=88°-30' Longitude East.

The first part of the Southern hemisphere Monday shows 24-30 hours in Kumbha rashi, deduct 20° of Ayanachalana 24-30—20'=24-10' hours means Shatataraka nakshatra or 24 solar degrees. Then see the Latitude chart for 24° of Kumbha on Monday, it shows 350°-42', deduct 330° of Kumbha, 353°-42'—330°=23°-42' Latitude North.

22nd of May to 21st of June is the period of Moon. The opening month of the year 1921 is in the tenth house, then 22nd of January to 21st of December tenth house, 22nd of December to 21st of Novmber eleventh house, 22nd of November to 21st of October twelfth house, 22nd of October to 21st of September first house, 22nd of September to 21st of August second house, 22nd of August to 21st of July third house, 22nd of July to 21st of June fourth house, 22nd of June to 21st of May fifth house, here is Dhanu rashi of Jupiter or Ketu, because birth day Monday has shown Shatataraka nakshatra of Rahu. The Rahu is in Swati nakshatra but his original rashi is Mithuna and his 7th aspect rashi is Dhanu. Then put Dhanu rashi in the fifth house, it shows Simha Lagna. The Moon is in Kanya rashi, the Sun is in Vrishabha rashi.

We want to see the marriage day of the native, then we must see the Lord of Lagna and the Lord of seventh house. The Lord of seventh house is Saturn and he is in Magha nakshatra Simha rashi. Magha nakshatra is of Ketu and he is the Lord of Dhanu rashi, it means Saturn is working on behalf of Ketu. Dhanishtha nakshatra is on 180° of Magha, it is in Kumbha, it shows the native is getting married at his 23. Then count the months upto Dhanu rashi from the opening month of the birth year. Dhanu rashi shows the month of May. Aslesha is on 180° of the Dhanistha which is the first nakshatra of the Ketu which indicates the date of marriage. Add 23 years in his birth year, 1921 plus 23=1944. That is on 9th of May 1944 he got married. Put the seventh aspect nakshatra of the Moon on the birth date.

8	1	3	5
Mon	Wed	Fri	Sun
9	2	4	7
Tue	Thur	Sat	Mon

Ketu will be in Makara. Jupiter will be in Simha, Saturn will be in Mithuna, Mars and Rahu will be in Karka, Sun and Venus will be in Vrishabha, Moon will be in Vrischika rashi on the day of marriage. It shows 1-3-5-8 years are good, in these years 1-3-5-7 months are good, in these months 2-4-7-9 dates and the days of the dates are good and vice versa.

Shree Janorikar T. D.

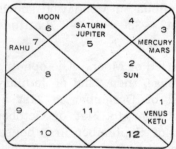

Birth date 13.6.1921

Long. 88°-30′ East

Date of marriage 9.5.1944

Lat. 23°-42′ North.

Example No. 30. Birth date 5.10.1929. We will see the birth day of the native. 1900=2, 29=1, October=6, Birth date is 5 (5)=5 plus 6 plus 1 plus 2=14 divided by 7=Remainder is 0=Saturday is the birth day. See the month 22nd of September to 21st of October in the year 1929. The fourth part of the southern hemisphere, there is no Saturday, then see Tuesday which is on 180° of Saturday. Tuesday shows 10-30 hours in Dhanu rashi. 10-30 hours means Magha nakshatra, it is the nakshatra of Ketu. It means Saturn is in Moola nakshatra. Magha nakshatra is negative for Ketu, it means Ketu is on 180° of the greater nakshatra

334

Aswini, that is Ketu is in the Chitra nakshatra Thula rashi. Mars is the Lord of Tuesday, he has shown Aswini nakshatra, it shows that the Mars is in the conjunction of Ketu and his nakshatra is Chitra in Thula rashi. See Makara and Kumbha rashi of Saturn in the third part of the southern hemisphere. Saturday shows 14-30 hours on the border of Makara and Kumbha. 14-30 hours means Chitra nakshatra, it is of Mars, it is in Thula and Kanya rashi, it is not in the Makara and Kumbha rashi, it shows that the Lord of the 7th aspect rashi of Makara and Kumbha are in Chitra nakshatra, 7th aspect rashi of Makara is Karka, and 7th aspect rashi of Kumbha is Simha, Moon is the Lord of Karka rashi and Sun is the Lord of Simha rashi. They both are in Chitra nakshatra Thula rashi. See Vrischika rashi of Mars in the first part of the northern hemisphere. Tuesday shows 10-30 hours in Vrischika rashi, 10-30 hours means Magha nakshatra, it is not in Vrischika rashi, then add 2 hours the difference of the negative rashi, 10-30 plus 2=12-30 hours, it means Uttara nakshatra, it is the 7th aspect nakshatra of the Jupiter, it is in Kanya rashi, it means the Lord of Kanya is in Uttara nakshatra Kanya rashi and Jupiter is in the greater nakshatra. Krittika is on 180° of the Vrischika rashi. That is, Jupiter is in the Krittika nakshatra Vrishabha rashi and Lord of the Vrishabha is in Uttara nakshatra Kanya rashi when Mars has shown the nakshatra of Jupiter, it means Jupiter is in the Mriga nakshatra or say right ascension nakshatra of Jupiter is Krittika and his declination nakshatra is Mriga in Vrishabha rashi. That is, Jupiter is in Mriga nakshatra Vrishabha rashi.

Tuesday shows 10-30 hours and Saturday shows 7-30 hours, deduct Saturday hours from Tuesday hours, it shows 3 hours, that is the birth day, it is the third day of the bright half, it shows there is no new Moon day although Sun and Moon are in Chitra nakshatra. It shows the Moon is in the seventh aspect of Rahu. The fourth part of the southern hemisphere Tuesday shows 10-30 hours, it is negative, 19-30 hours is greater, deduct 20′ or Ayanachalana, 19-30—20′=19-10′ hours, it means 19th nakshatra or 19 solar degrees, then see the Latitude chart for 19° of Dhanu rashi on Tuesday, it shows 290°-8′, deduct 270° of Dhanu rashi, 290°-8′—270°=20°-8′ Latitude North. The fourth part of the southern hemisphere Tuesday shows 10-30 hours, add 2 hours the difference of the northern hemisphere 10-30 plus 2=12-30 hours. Now see the first part of the northern hemisphere Saturday, it shows 7-30 hours, deduct it from Tuesday hours. 12-30 minus 7-30=5 hours is the Longitude. Deduct 6° of the Tuesday and 3° of Ketu. 5 hours means 90°—9°=81° Longitude East.

22nd of the September to 21st of October is the period of Moon. The opening month of year 1929 is in the tenth house. Then 22nd of January to 21st of December is tenth house, 22nd of December to 21st of November is eleventh house, 22nd of November to 21st of October twelfth house, 22nd of October to 21st of September first house, here is Thula rashi which is on 180° of Mesha rashi. Chitra nakshatra of Ketu is here, it shows Thula Lagna. The Sun is in Chitra nakshatra, the Moon is in Swati nakshatra Thula rashi.

We want to see the marriage day of the lady. Then we must see the Lord of seventh house as well as the Lord of Lagna. The Lord of the seventh house is Mars and he is in Lagna rashi. The Lord of Lagna is Venus and he is in Kanya rashi, it shows Rahu is working on behalf of Venus. Rahu is in Aswini nakshatra, his 7th aspect nakshatra is Swati which is of Venus, it shows the marriage year. The right ascension nakshatra of Venus is Uttara and his 7th aspect nakshatra is Purvabhadrapada which is in Kumbha rashi. Kumbha rashi shows the month of marriage. The right ascension nakshatra of Rahu is Aswini and his declination nakshatra is Revati which is the first nakshatra of Rahu, it indicates the date of marriage. Add 15 years in her birth year, 1929 plus 15=1944 that is on 9th of May 1944 she got married.

Put the birth date on her birth day

5	7	1	3
Sat	Mon	Wed	Fri
6	9	2	4
Sun	Tue	Thur	Sat

It shows 6-9-2-4 years are good, in these years 1-3-5-7 months are good and in these months 2-4-6-9 dates and days of the dates are good and vice versa.

Miss Mahajan

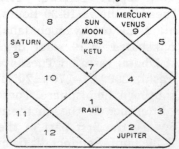

Birth date 5.10.1929

Date of marriage 9.5.1944

Long. 81° East

Lat. 20°-8′ North

Example No. 31. Birth date 10.4.1924. We will see the birth day of the native. 1900=2, 24=2, April=5, Birth date is 10=10 plus 25 plus 2 plus 2=19 divided by 7=Reminder is 5=Thursday is the birth day. See the month 22nd of March to 21st of April in the year 1924. The first part of the southern hemisphere, Thursday shows 18-30 hours in Vrischika rashi. Monday is on 180° of Thursday, Monday shows 22-30 hours in Dhanu rashi, but due to the spherical triangle it is a negative part. Thursday shows 18-30 hours in Vrischika rashi, it is the nakshatra of Mars and not of Jupiter, it shows it is negative nakshatra for Mars, then add 2 hours the difference of the negative part. 18-30 plus 2=20-30 hours, it shows Mars is in Purvashadha nakshatra Dhanu rashi and Jupiter is in Jyeshtha nakshatra Vrischika rashi. Mars is in Purvashadha nakshatra, it is the nakshatra of Venus. Venus is the Lord of Vrishabha rashi, it means Venus is on 180° of Jyeshtha nakshatra. That is on 180° of Mars-rashi Vrischika rashi. It means Venus is in Vrishabha rashi Mriga nakshatra. Purvashadha is the 7th aspect nakshatra of Rahu but Mars is there, then Purvashada is negative nakshatra for Rahu, it shows that Rahu is in the greater nakshatra Purva, Purva nakshatra is in Simha rashi, it shows Rahu is in Simha rashi. Naturally Ketu is in Kumbha rashi. Now Monday shows 22-30 hours in Dhanu rashi. 22-30 hours means Shravana nakshatra. There is no Shravana nakshatra in Dhanu rashi, it is in Makara, Karka rashi is on 180° of the Makara, Karka rashi is of the Moon, it shows Shravana nakshatra is negative for the Moon, then add 2 hours the difference of the negative part Dhanu rashi. 22-30 plus 2=24-30 hours, it means Shatataraka nakshatra, it is the nakshatra of the ascending node of the Moon, it shows the Moon is in the greater nakshatra Aridra in Mithuna rashi, which is on 180° of the Dhanu rashi. Monday has shown us 22-30 hours means Shravana nakshatra, it is in the Makara, it shows the Lord of Makara is in triangle of Moon and Ketu. Ketu is in Kumbha, Moon is in Mithuna, naturally Saturn is in Thula rashi, Swati nakshatra. Now see Karka rashi of the Moon in the fourth part of the southern hemisphere, Thursday shows 11-30 hours on the border of Mithuna, 11-30 hours means Purva nakshatra, it is in the Simha and not in the Mithuna rashi. Mercury is the Lord of Mithuna but there is no Purva nakshatra in Mithuna, then it is negative nakshatra for both the planets, it shows the Lord of Simha as well as Lord of Mithuna are in greater nakshatra Bharani in Mesha rashi because Jupiter has shown it and he himself is in Vrischika rashi of Mars and Mars is on 180° of Mithuna rashi, that is Jupiter has shown us the second rashi of Mars Mesha rashi, that is Mercury and the Sun are in Bharani nakshatra Mesha rashi.

See the Meena rashi of Jupiter in the second and third part of the northern hemisphere, Monday shows 5-30 hours in Meena rashi and Thursday shows 1-30 hours in Kumbha rashi.

337

See the Longitude chart for 5-30 hours and add 3° of Ketu, 5-30 hours means 82°-30′ plus 3°=85°-30′ Long. East. The first part of the southern hemisphere Thursday shows 18-30 hours, add 1-30 hours of Thursday of Kumbha rashi. 18-30 plus 1-30 hours=20 hours, it means 20 nakshatra or 20 solar degrees. See the Latitude chart for 20° of Vrischika rashi on Thursday, it shows 259°-31′, deduct 240° of Vrischika rashi, 259°-31′—240°=19°-31′ Latitude North.

22nd of March to 21st of April is the period of Moon. The opening month of the year 1924 is in the tenth house. Then 22nd of January to 21st of December tenth house, 22nd of December to 21st of November eleventh house, 22nd of November to 21st of October twelfth house, 22nd of October to 21st of September first house, 22nd of September to 21st of August second house, 22nd of August to 21st of July third house, 22nd of July to 21st of June fourth house, 22nd of June to 21st of May fifth house, 22nd of May to 21st of April sixth house, 22nd of April to 21st of March seventh house, here is Meena rashi of Jupiter who is the Lord of birth day. Put Meena rashi in the seventh house, it shows Kanya Lagna. The Sun is in Mesha rashi. The Moon is in Mithuna rashi.

We want to see the marriage day of the native. Naturally we must see the Lord of Lagna and the Lord of seventh house. The Lord of the Lagna is Mercury and he is in the eighth house Bharani nakshatra. It shows Mercury is working on behalf of Venus and Jupiter. The right ascension nakshatra of Venus is Mriga and his declination nakshatra is Punarvasu. The right ascension 7th aspect nakshatra of the Venus is Moola and his 7th aspect declination nakshatra is Uttarashadha No. 21. This is his year to get married. Uttarashadha nakshatra is in Makara rashi in triangle of Vrishabha rashi, it shows the month of June. Punarvasu is his declination nakshatra, count it upto Meena rashi. Karka 7, Vrischika 16 and Meena 25. Purvabhadrapada nakshatra of Meena rashi indicates the date of marriage. Add 21 years in his birth year 1924, 1924 plus 21, 1945. That is on 25th June 1945 he got married.

Put the birth date on the birth day

2	4	6	9
Thur	Sat	Mon	Wed
3	5	7	1
Fri	Sun	Tue	Thur

It shows 1-3-5-7 years are good, in these years 2-4-6-9 months are good, in these months 1-3-5-7 dates and the days of the dates are good and vice versa.

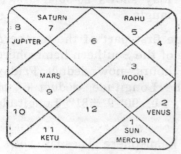

Shree Garud

Birth date 10.4.1924
Date of marriage 25.6.1945
Long. 85°-30′ East.
Lat. 19°-31′ North.

Example No. 32. Birth date 26.9.1930. We will see the birth day of the native. 1900=2, 30=2, September 4, Birth date is 26=26 plus 4 plus 2 plus 2=34 divided by 7=Remainder is 6=Friday is the birth day. See the month 22nd of September to 21st of October in the year 1930. The fourth part of the southern hemisphere, Friday shows 13-30 hours, Tuesday is on 180° of the Friday. Tuesday shows 10-30 hours in Dhanu rashi. It is a negative part due to the spherical triangle. Friday shows 13-30 hours in Makara rashi, 13-30 hours means Hasta nakshatra, it is in Kanya rashi and not in Makara rashi, Moon is the Lord of Hasta nakshatra, Venus is the Lord of Friday, Saturn is the Lord of Makara rashi and Hasta nakshatra is in Kanya. Mercury is the Lord of Kanya rashi, then it is negative nakshatra for Venus, Rohini is the greater nakshatra, it shows the Moon is on 180° of Rohini nakshatra, that is, the Moon is in Anuradha nakshatra Vrischika rashi, deduct 2 hours the difference of the negative nakshatra, Rohini, 4-30—2=2-30 hours, it means Bharani nakshatra, it is the nakshatra of Venus, it shows Venus is on 180° of Bharani in Swati nakshatra Thula rashi. The Lord of Kanya is in the greater nakshatra Purva, and the Lord of Makara is in the greater nakshatra of Mercury, that is Saturn is in Purvashadha nakshatra Dhanu rashi. Tuesday shows 10-30 hours in Dhanu rashi. 10-30 hours means Magha nakshatra, Ketu is the Lord of Magha nakshatra, Jupiter is the Lord of Dhanu rashi, Mars is the Lord of Tuesday. Magha nakshatra is in Simha rashi, Sun is the Lord of Simha rashi. It shows Magha nakshatra is negative for Mars. Moola nakshatra is greater, it shows the Lord of Dhanu and Mars are on 180° of Moola nakshatra, that is Mars and Jupiter are in Mriga nakshatra Mithuna rashi, Moola is negative nakshatra for Ketu, Aswini is the greater nakshatra for him, that is Ketu is on 180° of Aswini, Swati nakshatra in Thula rashi and the Sun is on 180° of Aswini, Chitra nakshatra Kanya rashi. See Mesha rashi of Mars. Tuesday shows 17-30 hours, it means the Moon is in Anuradha nakshatra in his second rashi Vrischika. See the Vrishabha rashi of Venus in the

339

first part of the northern hemisphere Friday shows 20-30 hours, it means the Lord of Dhanu rashi in his Triangle.

See Thula and Vrischika rashi in the first part of the northern hemisphere, add two hours the difference of the Southern hemisphere in Tuesday hours 10-30 plus 2=12-30 hours, now deduct Friday hours 12-30—6-30 hours=6 hours, is the Longitude, deduct 6° of Tuesday and 3° of Ke u, 6 hours=90°, i-e. 90°-9°=81° Longitude East.

The second part of the southern hemisphere Tuesday shows 17-30 hours, deduct 20' of Ayanachalana 17-30—20'=17-10' hours means 17th nakshatra or 17 solar degrees. See the Latitude chart for 17° of Mithuna rashi on Friday, it shows 109°-18', deduct 90° of Mithuna, 109°-18'—90°=19°-18' Latitude North.

22nd of September to 21st of October is the period of Moon. The opening month of the year 1930 is in the tenth house, then 22nd of January to 21st of December is the tenth house, 22nd of December to 21st of November is eleventh house, 22nd of November to 21st of October is twelfth house, 22nd of October to 21st of September first house, here is Mithuna rashi of Friday and 7th aspect rashi Dhanu of Tuesday. Then put Mithuna rashi in Lagna. The Sun is in Kanya, The Moon is in Vrischika rashi.

We want to see the marriage day of the Lady, then we must see the Lord of Seventh house and the Lord of Lagna. The Lord of seventh house is Jupiter and he is in Lagna. The right ascension nakshatra of the Jupiter is Mriga and his declination nakshatra is Punarvasu No. 7, the Lord of Lagna is Mercury, he is in Purva nakshatra Simha rashi, his 7th aspect nakshatra is Purvabhadrapada in Kumbha rashi, Purvabhadrapada is No. 25. Mercury is the Lord of Mithuna and Kanya rashi, his second rashi Kanya is on 180° of Meena rashi and Purvabhadrapada nakshatra which is the declination nakshatra of Jupiter. Kanya rashi shows the month of June and Jupiter's nakshatra Purvabhadrapada indicates the date of marriage. Mercury is in Purva nakshatra, it is the nakshatra of the Venus. Venus is in Thula rashi, his nakshatra is Swati No. 15, that is her year to get married, add 15 years in her birth year, 1930 plus 15=1945, that is on 25th of June 1945 she got married. Put the 7th aspect nakshatra of the day and the date nakshatra on the birth day

3	5	7	1
Fri	Sun	Tues	Thur
2	4	6	8
Sat	Mon	Wed	Fri

It shows 2-4-6-8 years are good, in these years 2-4-6-8 months are good, in these months 1-3-5-7 dates and days of the dates are good and vice versa.

Mrs. Garud

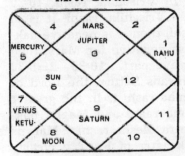

Birth date 26.9.1930
Date of marriage 25.6.1945
Long. 81° East
Lat. 19°18′ North.

Example No. 33. Birth date 22.9.1911. We will see the birth day of the native. 1900=2, 11=6, September=4, Birth date is 22=22 plus 4 plus 6 plus 2=34 divided by 7=Remainder is 6= Friday is the birth day. See the month 22nd of September to 21st of October in the year 1911. The second part of the northern hemisphere, Friday shows 6-30 hours in Thula rashi. Tuesday is on 180° of Friday. Tuesday shows 3-30 hours in Kanya rashi. It is a negative part due to the spherical triangle, Friday shows 6-30 hours, it means Aridra nakshatra, it is in Mithuna rashi and not in Thula, it is the nakshatra of Rahu and Venus. Thula rashi is of Venus and Mithuna rashi is of Rahu and Mercury, it means Aridra is negative nakshatra for Rahu and Swati is the greater nakshatra for Rahu, that is Rahu is on 180° of the Swati nakshatra, he is in Aswini nakshatra Mesha rashi, deduct 2 hours the difference of Rahu, 15-30 hours minus 2=13-30 hours, it is the nakshatra of the Moon, it means the Moon is in conjunction of Mercury, the Lord of Mithuna. That is the Moon and Mercury are in Hasta nakshatra Kanya rashi.

Swati is negative nakshatra for Venus. Shatataraka is the greater nakshatra that is Venus is on 180° of Shatataraka. Purva is his own nakshatra in Simha rashi, it shows Venus is in Purva nakshatra Simha rashi. Tuesday shows 3-30 hours in Kanya rashi. Mars is the Lord of Tuesday. Sun is the Lord of Krittika nakshatra, and Krittika is 7th aspect nakshatra of Jupiter, it shows the Mars is in the Krittika nakshatra on 180° of Vrischika his own rashi and Lord of Kanya is in the triangle of Mercury. Then it is negative nakshatra for the Sun, deduct 2 hours the difference of the negative nakshatra, 3-30—2=1-30 hours, it means Aswini nakshatra, it shows the Sun is on 180° of the Aswini nakshatra, Chitra is in Kanya rashi which is in triangle of Vrishabha rashi, add 2 hours the difference of the Sun, it snows Jupiter is in Vishakha nakshatra Thula rashi.

See Vrischika rashi of Mars in the first part of the northern hemisphere, Tuesday shows 10-30 hours in Vrischika rashi, 10-30 hours means Magha nakshatra, it is not in Vrischika rashi, it is in Simha rashi, Sun is the Lord of Simha rashi, then it is negative nakshatra for Mars and Vrischika rashi is also negative for Mars, then deduct 2 hours the difference of the negative part. 10-30—2=8-30 hours, it is the nakshatra of Saturn, it means Saturn the Lord of Kumbha rashi which is on 180° of the Simha rashi is in the greater nakshatra Aswini, in the triangle of Simha rashi and Magha nakshatra, that is Saturn is in Aswini nakshatra Mesha rashi. Mars is the Lord of Mesha, he has shown the nakshatra of Ketu, it clearly shows that Saturn is on 180° of Chitra nakshatra in the 7th aspect of Ketu. See Mesha rashi of Mars in the second part of the southern hemisphere. Tuesday shows 17-30 hours, it means it is the 7th aspect nakshatra of Mars. See Vrishabha rashi of Venus. Friday shows 20-30 hours, add 10-30 hours of Tuesday the first part of the northern hemisphere. 20-30 plus 10-30=31 hours, deduct 15 hours of the bright half, it shows the first tithi of the Dark half, and not the new Moon day. 17-30 hours of Mesha rashi means 17-30 hours deduct 20' of Ayanachalana, 17-30—20'=17-10' hours means Anuradha nakshatra or 17° solar degrees, then see 17° of Vrischika rashi on Tuesday in the Latitude chart, it shows 256°-11', deduct 240° of Vrischika rashi, 256°-11'—240°=16°-11' Latitude North. The first part of the northern hemisphere Tuesday shows 10-30 hours in Vrischika rashi, add 2 hours the difference of Mesha, 10-30 plus 2=12-30 hours. Now deduct 6-30 Friday hours of Vrischika rashi, 12-30 minus 6-30 hours=6 hours is the Longitude, deduct 6° of Tuesday of Mesha and 6° Rahu, 6 hours means 98°-12°=78° Longitude East.

22nd of September to 21st of October is the period of Moon, the opening month of the year 1911 is in the tenth house, then 22nd January to 21st December is the tenth house, 22nd of December to 21st of November eleventh house, 22nd of November to 21st of October twelfth house, 22nd of October to 21st of September first house, here is Vrishabha rashi of the birth day. Vrischika rashi is on 180° of Vrishabha of Tuesday, then put Vrishabha rashi in the first house Vrishabha Lagna. The Sun is in Kanya and the Moon is in Kanya.

We want to see the marriage day of the native. Then we must see the Lord of Lagna as well as the Lord of seventh house. The Lord of seventh house is Mars and he is in Vrishabha rashi. The Lord of Lagna is Venus and he is in Simha rashi. The right ascension nakshatra of the Mars is Krittika and his seventh aspect nakshatra is Vishakha. The right ascension nakshatra of Venus is Purva and his 7th aspect nakshatra is Purvabhadrapada, the seventh aspect nakshatra of both the planets is No. 7, it shows the Jupiter is working on behalf of both the planets. The right ascension nakshatra of Jupiter is Vishakha and his 7th aspect nakshatra is Bharani, then count Bharani nakshatra from Mesha rashi to Mesha rashi, Mesha 2, Dhanu 11, Simha 20, Mesha 29. This is his year to get married. Thula rashi is on 180° of the Mesha. Thula rashi shows the month of May. The 7th aspect nakshatra of Venus is Purvabhadrapada, it indicates the date of marriage, add 29 years in his birth year, 1911 plus 29=1940, that is on 25th of May 1940 he got married. Put the seventh aspect nakshatra of the birth date on the birth day

8	1	3	5
Fri	Sun	Tue	Thur
7	9	2	4
Sat	Mon	Wed	Fri

It shows 2-4-7-9 years are good, in these years 1-3-5-8 months are good, in these months 2-4-7-9 dates and days of the dates are good and vice versa.

Shree Hulyalkar

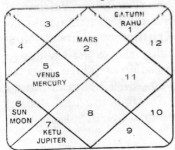

Birth date 22.9.1911
Date of Marriage 25.5.1940
Long. 78° East
Lat. 16°-11′ North.

Example No. 34. Birth date 26.6.1906. We will see the birth day of the native. 1900=2, 6=7, June=3 Birth date 26=26 plus 3 plus 7 plus 2=38 divided by 7=3 Remainder, it means Tuesday is the birth day. See the month 22nd of June to 21st of July in the year 1906. The third part of the northern hemisphere, Tuesday shows 13-30 hours, in Thula rashi. Friday is on 180° of Tuesday. Friday shows 16-30 hours in Vrischika rashi. It is a negative part due to the spherical triangle. Tuesday shows 13-30 hours in Thula rashi, 13-30 hours means Hasta Nakshatra, it is not in Thula rashi, it is in Kanya rashi. Mercury is the Lord of Kanya and Mithuna rashi. Then Hasta nakshatra is negative for Mars, 22-30 hours are greater for Ketu, it means the Ketu is in Shravana nak-

343

shatra in triangle of Kanya rashi and Mars himself is in Mithuna rashi of the Buddha. 4-30 hours are greater for the Mars, add 2 hours of the negative part. 4-30 plus 2=6-30, it means Mars is in Mithuna rashi Aridra nakshatra. 22-30 hours means Shravana nakshatra, it is the nakshatra of the Moon. It shows the Moon is in the conjunction of Rahu, that is the Moon and Rahu are in Aslesha nakshatra Karka rashi. The Lord of Kanya rashi is in Rohini nakshatra Vrishabha rashi. Friday shows 16-30 hours in Vrischika rashi. Venus is the Lord of Thula as well as Vrishabha rashi. 16-30 hours means Vishakha nakshatra. It is the nakshatra of Jupiter and 7th aspect nakshatra of the Sun, it shows the Sun and Jupiter is on 180° of Vishakha nakshatra Vrischika rashi, that is the Sun and Jupiter are in Krittika nakshatra Vrishabha rashi.

Venus is the Lord of Vrishabha and Thula rashi and Mars is the Lord of Mesha and Vrischika rashi. We have seen Thula and Vrischika rashi. Now see Vrishabha rashi of Venus and Mesha rashi of Mars in the third and fourth part of the southern hemisphere. Fourth part of the southern hemisphere Friday shows 23-30 hours. 23-30 hours means Dhanistha nakshatra, it is in the Kumbha rashi, it means the Saturn is in Kumbha rashi in Dhanistha nakshatra, Friday has shown us 23-30 hours, it means the Saturn is in the Triangle of Venus, Venus is in Mithuna. Thula rashi is on 180° of the Mesha which has shown us the centre of the Triangle. Vrishabha rashi Tuesday shows 3-30 hours, 3-30 hours means Krittika nakshatra, it is of the Sun and the Sun is in Krittika nakshatra. Now fourth part of the northern hemisphere, Friday shows 9-30 hours in Kanya rashi, Deduct 2-30 hours of the Tuesday of Third part of the southern hemisphere Vrishaba rashi, 9-30—3-30 hours=6 hours is the Longitude. See the Longitude chart for 6 hours and deduct 6° of Tuesday and 3° of Ketu, 6 hours=90°—9°=81° Longitude East.

Third part of the northern hemisphere, Friday shows 16-30 hours in Vrischika rashi, deduct 20' of Ayanachalana 16-30—20'= 16-10' hours, it means Vishakha nakshatra or 16 solar degrees. See the Latitude chart for 16° of Vrischika rashi on Friday. It shows 255°-27', deduct 240° of the Vrischika rashi, 255°-27'—240°=15°-27' Latitude North.

22nd of June to 21st of July is the period of Sun. The opening month of the year 1906 is in the fourth house. Then 22nd of January to 21st of December is the fourth house, 22nd of December to 21st of November third house, 22nd of November to 21st of October second house, 22nd of October to 21st of September first house, 22nd of September to 21st of August twelfth house, 22r.

of August to 21st of July eleventh house, 22nd of July to 21st of June tenth house, here is Thula rashi of the birth day and triangle centre rashi of Venus, then put the Thula rashi of Venus in the tenth house, it shows Makara Lagna, the Sun is in Vrishabha rashi, and the Moon is in Karka rashi.

We want to see the marriage day of the native. Then we must see the Lord of the seventh house as well as the Lord of the Lagna. The Lord of the Lagna is Saturn, he is in Kumbha rashi and in the Dhanishtha nakshatra, his seventh aspect nakshatra is Aslesha. The Lord of the seventh house is Moon and she is in her own rashi. The right ascension nakshatra of the Moon is Aslesha and her seventh aspect nakshatra is Shravana No. 4, it shows the Moon is working on behalf of Saturn. Then count Moon's nak-shatra No. 4 from Makara to Makara rashi. Makara 4, Vrishabha 13, Kanya 22 and Makara 31. This is his year to get married. Venus is the Lord of Friday and he is Lord of the opening rashi Thula of the horoscope, he is in the triangle of Saturn, it means he is showing the month of Marriage June. The Moon is in the Asle-sha nakshatra, her seventh aspect nakshatra is Shravana No. 22 indicates the date of marriage. Add 31 years in his birth year. 1906 plus 31=1937, that is on 22nd of June 1937 he got married.

Put the 7th aspect date of the birth date on his birth day.

4	6	8	2
Tue	Thur	Sat	Mon
5	7	9	3
Wed	Fri	Sun	Tue

It shows 4-6-8-2 years are good, in these years 4-6-8-2 months and days of the dates are good and vice versa.

Shree Shirolkar

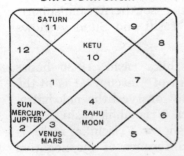

Birth date 26.6.1906
Date of marriage 22.6.1937
Long. 81° East
Lat. 15°-27′ North.

Example No. 35. Birth date 17.5.1940. We will see the birth day of the native. 1900=2, 40=1, May=7 Birth date is 19=19 plus 7 plus 1 plus 2=29 divided by 7=Remainder is 1=Sunday is the birth day. See the month 22nd of April to 21st May in the year 1940. The third part of the southern hemisphere, Sunday shows 11-30 hours in Simha rashi, Thursday is on 180° of the Sunday. Thursday shows 8-30 hours in Karka rashi, it is a negative part due to the spherical triangle, Sunday shows 11-30 hours in Simha rashi, 11-30 hours means Purva nakshatra, it is the nakshatra of Venus, it is in Simha rashi. The Sun is the Lord of Simha rashi. Still it is negative nakshatra, it means the Lord of Purva nakshatra is on 180° of the greater nakshatra Purvashadha, that is Venus is in Aridra nakshatra Mithuna rashi. Add 2 hours the difference of the negative part in Purva nakshatra 11-30 plus 2=13-30 hours, it means Rahu is in Hasta nakshatra Kanya rashi, and Sun the Lord of Sunday, it is in the greater nakshatra Rohini in Vrishabha rashi. Thursday shows 8-30 hours in Karka rashi. 8-30 hours means Pushya nakshatra, it is the nakshatra of Saturn, Jupiter is the Lord of Thursday and Moon is the Lord of Karka rashi. Pushya nakshatra is in Karka rashi but it is negative nakshatra due to the spherical triangle, it means Pushya nakshatra is negative for the Moon, Anuradha is greater nakshatra. Deduct 2 hours the difference of the negative part. 17-30 hours—2 hours=15-30 hours =Swati, it shows the Moon is in the Swati nakshatra Thula rashi. Pushya and Anuradha nakshatra are of the Saturn and Saturn's rashi Makara is on 180° of the Mars. Moon is the Lord of Karka rashi, it shows the Saturn is on 180° of the Swati. That is Saturn is in Mesha rashi, Aswini nakshatra. Thursday has shows us Karka rashi and Pushya nakshatra, it means the Lord of the Thursday is in conjunction of Saturn and he is also on 180° of Swati nakshatra, that is Jupiter is in Aswini nakshatra Mesha rashi. The Sun is the Lord of Simha rashi and Sunday. The Jupiter is the Lord of Thursday as well as he is the Lord of Dhanu and Meena rashi. We have seen Simha rashi of the Sun. Now see Dhanu rashi of Jupiter in the fourth part of the southern hemisphere, Thursday shows 18-30 hours in Vrischika rashi and Sunday shows 21-30 hours in Dhanu rashi.

Thursday shows 18-30 hours in Vrischika rashi, 18-30 hours means Jyestha nakshatra, it is the nakshatra of Mercury, it is in the Vrischika rashi, it shows Mercury is on 180° of Jyeshtha nakshatra, that is the Mercury is in Rohini nakshatra Vrishabha rashi. Now Mars is the Lord of Vrischika rashi, it shows Vrischika rashi is negative for Mars, then add 2 hours the difference of the negative part 18-30 plus 2=20-30 hours, Purvashadha nakshatra is in Dhanu rashi. Jupiter is the Lord of Dhanu rashi. It shows the Lord of Vrischika rashi is on 180° of Purvashadha nakshatra, that is the Mars is in Aridra nakshatra Mithuna rashi. Thursday has shown

Aridra nakshatra, it means the Lord of Vrischika is in the 7th aspect of Jupiter the Lord of Dhanu rashi. Now Sunday shows 21-30 hours in Dhanu rashi, add two hours the difference of the northern hemisphere, because Simha rashi is in the northern hemisphere. 21-30 plus 2=23-30 hours, deduct 20' of Ayanachalana, 23-30—20'=23-10' hours means Dhanishtha nakshatra or 23 solar degrees. Then see the latitude chart for 23° of Dhanu rashi on Tuesday, it shows 293°-58', deduct 270° of Dhanu rashi. 293°-58'—270°=23°-58' Latitude North. Now see the Meena rashi of Jupiter in the second part of the southern hemisphere Thursday shows 1-30 hours, deduct 2 hours the difference of the northern hemisphere, 2—1-30=30' hours. See the Longitude chart 30' and deduct 6° of the Sun and 3° of Rahu. 30°=8°-30', now 9°—8°-30'=30' that is 0 Longitude East.

22nd of April to 21st of May is the period of the Sun. The opening month of the year 1940 is in the fourth house, then 22nd of January to 21st of December fourth house, 22nd of December to 21st of November third house, 22nd of November to 21st of October second house, 22nd of October to 21st of September first house, 22nd of September to 21st of August twelfth house, 22nd of August to 21st of July Eleventh house, 22nd of July to 21st June tenth house, 22nd of June to 21st of May nineth house, here is 7th aspect rashi of Mesha rashi in which Jupiter and Saturn are there, then put Thula rashi in the nineth house, it shows Kumbha Lagna, the Sun is in Vrishabha and the Moon is in Thula rashi.

We want to see the marriage day of the lady. Naturally we must see the Lord of seventh house as well as the Lord of the Lagna. The Lord of Lagna is Saturn and he is in Aswini nakshatra Mesha rashi. The right ascension nakshatra of Saturn is Aswini and his declination nakshatra Krittika No. 3, which is of Sun. It shows the Saturn and Jupiter are working on behalf of the Sun. Then count No. 3, the declination nakshatra of the Saturn and Jupiter upto Dhanu rashi. Mesha 3, Simha 12, Dhanu 21. This is her year to get married. Mesha rashi the declination nakshatra of the Saturn and Jupiter shows the month of Marriage December. The right ascension nakshatra of the Sun is Rohini and his seventh aspect nakshatra is Jyestha No. 9, then count No. 9 from Vrishabha rashi to Makara rashi of the Saturn, Vrishabha 9, Kanya 18, Makara 27, it indicates the date of Marriage, add 21 years in her birth year 1940, 1940 plus 21=1961. That is on 27 of December 1961 she got married.

Put birth date on the birth day.

1	3	5	7
Sun	Tue	Thu	Sat
6	9	2	4
Mon	Wed	Fri	Sun

It shows 1-3-5-7 years are good, in these years 1-3-5-7 months are good, in these months 2-4-6-9 dates and days of the dates are good and vice versa.

Mrs. Shirolkar

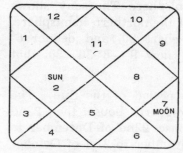

Birth date 19.5.1940
Date of marriage 27.12.1961
Long. 0° East
Lat. 23°-58′ North.

Example No. 36. Birth date 1.7.1937. We will see the Birth day of the native. 1900=2, 37=4, July=5, Birth date is 1=1 plus 5 plus 4 plus 2=12 divided by 7=Remainder is 5=Thursday is the birth day. See the month 22nd of June to 21st of July in the year 1937. The third part of the Southern hemisphere, Sunday shows 1-30 hours in Mesha rashi. Thursday is on 180° of Sunday, there is no Thursday in the third part, it is negative part due to the spherical triangle. Sunday shows 1-30 hours in Mesha rashi. 1-30 hours means Aswini nakshatra, it is the nakshatra of Mars and Ketu, it is negative for Ketu because his rashi is Dhanu, it means Mars is on 180° of Aswini nakshatra because Mesha rashi is of Mars. That is Mars in the Chitra nakshatra Thula rashi. It is negative nakshatra for Ketu, then add 2 hours the difference of the negative nakshatra Aswini, 1-30 plus 2=3-30, the 3rd nakshatra Krittika, it shows Rahu is on 180° of the Krittika, that is, Rahu is in Vishakha nakshatra Vrischika rashi. Aswini nakshatra is negative for the Sun. Moola nakshatra is greater nakshatra for the Sun, it means the Sun is on 180° of Moola nakshatra, that is, the Sun is in Mriga nakshatra in the triangle of Mars. That is why Sunday is in Mesha rashi, it means the Sun is in Mriga nakshatra, Mithuna rashi.

Now see Mesha rashi in fourth part. Thursday shows 22-30 hours in Meena rashi. 22-30 hours means Shravana nakshatra, it is the nakshatra of the Moon, it means the Moon is in Jupiter's rashi and Jupiter is in Shravana nakshatra Makara rashi or in other way

Jupiter is in Shravana nakshatra and it is negative for the Moon. Hasta nakshtra is greater nakshatra, it shows the Moon is on 180° of Hasta, that is the Moon is in the Revati nakshatra with Saturn in Meena rashi.

Sun is the Lord of birth day as well as he is the Lord of Simha rashi, then see the Simha rashi of the Sun in the first part of the southern hemisphere, Sunday shows 8-30 hours on the border of Kanya rashi and Simha rashi, 8-30 hours means Pushya nakshatra, it is the nakshatra of Saturn, it is not in Simha rashi, it means it is negative nakshatra for Saturn. Uttarabhadrapada is the greater nakshatra for him, it means Saturn is in the Uttarabhadrapada nakshatra Meena rashi and his 7th aspect nakshatra is Uttara which is on the border of Simha and Kanya rashi.

Now see Dhanu rashi of Jupiter in the second part of the northern hemisphere, Thursday shows 15-30 hours in Dhanu rashi. 15-30 hours means Swati nakshatra, it is not in Dhanu rashi, it is in Thula rashi. Venus is the Lord of Swati nakshatra, then deduct 2 hours the difference of the negative part, 15-30—2=13-30, it means Hasta nakshatra, it is in the Kanya, it means the Mercury is in the greater nakshatra, Aridra and Venus is also in greater nakshatra Rohini. Mercury is on 180° of Dhanu rashi and Venus is in triangle of Jupiter, that is Mercury is in Mithuna rashi and Venus is in Vrishabha rashi. Sunday shows 18-30 hours in Makara rashi, deduct 20' of Ayanachalana, 18-30—20'=18-10' hours, it means Jyeshtha nakshatra or 18 solar degrees. See 18° of Makara on Thursday in the Latitude chart. It shows 318°-53'—300° of Makara =18°-53' Latitude North. Mesha rashi Sunday shows 1-30 hours and Makara rashi Sunday shows 18-30 hours, and add it together 1-30 plus 18-30=20 hours means Purvashadha nakshatra. Aridra nakshatra is on 180° of the Purvashadha. Aridra means 6 hours. See the Longitude chart for 6 hours and deduct 6° of Thursday 6 hours=90°—6°=84° Longitude East.

22nd of June to 21st of July is the period of the Sun. The opening month of the year 1937 is in the fourth house. Then 22nd of January to 21st of December is in the fourth house, 22nd of December to 21st of November third house, 22nd of November to 21st of October second house, 22nd of October to 21st of September first house, 22nd of September to 21st of August twelfth house, 22nd of August to 21st of July eleventh house, 22nd of July to 21st of June tenth house, here is Mesha rashi which is the birth day, then put the Mesha rashi in the tenth house, it shows Karka Lagna. The Moon is in Meena rashi. The Sun is in Mithuna rashi.

349

We want to see the marriage day of the lady. Naturally we must see the Lord of Lagna and the Lord of the seventh house. The Lord of Lagna is Moon and the Lord of the seventh house is Saturn. The Lord of Lagna is in Revati nakshatra Meena rashi and her seventh aspect nakshatra is Hasta. The Lord of Lagna is in Meena rashi and his 7th aspect nakshatra is Hasta No. 4. Then count No. 4 from Kanya to Makara rashi. Kanya 4, Vrishabha 13, Makara 22; This is her year to get married. Kanya rashi shows the month of December, Uttarabhadrapada nakshatra of the Saturn is on 180° of the Hasta, it indicates the date of marriage, add 22 years in her birth year 1937. 1937 plus 22=1959, that is on 26th of December 1959 she got married.

Put the seventh aspect nakshatra of the birth date on the birth day

5	8	1	3
Thur	Sat	Mon	Wed
6	9	2	4
Fri	Sun	Tue	Thur

It shows 2-4-6-9 years are good, in these years 1-3-5-8 months are good, in these months 1-3-5-8 dates and days of the dates are good and vice versa.

Mrs. Shirolkar J. B.

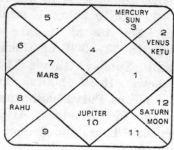

Birth date 1.7.1937
Date of marriage 26.12.1959
Long. 84° East
Lat. 18°-53′ North

CHAPTER VIII

SUPPLEMENTAL

The learned readers have seen 37 examples of Longevity and 36 examples of Marriages. How has this wonderful result been arrived at, and how do we feel certain that it is true? Those who wish thoroughly to understand it must study standard works on Astronomy, but it may be possible to give some clear idea of the processes by which it has been arrived at, and of the cogency of the reasoning by which we are compelled to accept facts so contrary to the first impressions of our natural senses.

The fundamental principle upon which all measurements of space depend, which are beyond the actual application of human standards, is this; that distant objects change their bearings for a given change of base (Birth-year by deducting the Saptarishikal) more or less in proportion as they are less or more distant. Suppose I am on board a steamer sailing down the Gateway of India, and I see two lighthouses on the Kolaba coast, directly opposite to me, or bearing due north, the first of (light house) which is one Kilometer and the other 10 kilometers distant. I sail one kilometer due east and again take the bearings. It is evident that the first light house will now bear northwest,

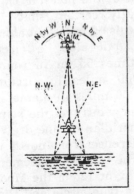

Figure according to R'gved 1-164-17

or have apparently moved through 45° i.e. one-eighth part of the circumference (see eight parts of the Pancha Samvatsara Yuga in each of the months) of a complete circle, assuming this circumference to be divided into 360 equal parts or degrees; while the more distant lighthouse will only have altered its bearing by a much less amount, easily determined by calculation, but which may be taken roughly 5° instead of 45°. (See the five days of the week given to each part of the Pancha Samvatsara Yuga).

The branch of mathematics known as Trignometry enables us in all cases, without exception, where we know the apparent displacement or change of bearing of a distant object produced by

351

taking it from the opposite ends of a known base. (See east Rashi for west years given in the Pancha Samvatsara Yuga form and west rashi for east years—vice versa) to calculate the distance of the object with as much ease and certainty as if we were working a simple sum of the rule of three. The first step is to know our base, (The calendar years given in the form of Pancha Samvatsara Yuga) and for this purpose it is essential to know the size and form of the earth on which we live. These are determined by very simple considerations.

If I walk a mile in straight line, an object at a vast distance like a star will not change its apparent place perceptibly. But I walk the same distance in semicircle, what was originally on my left hand will now be on my right hand or will have changed its apparent place by 180°. (See the commencement of the Sun and Moon in the Chapter second and third).

If I walk my mile on the circumference of a circle of twice the size, I shall have travelled a quardrant or one fourth part of it, and changed the bearing of the distant object exactly half as much or 90°, and so on, according to the size of the circle, which may, therefore, be readily calculated from the length that must be travelled along it shift the bearing of the remote object by a given amount, say of 1°.

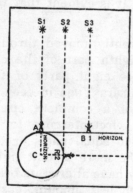

Figure according to R'gved 1-164-18

If, for instance by travelling 65 miles from north to south we lower the apparent height of the polestar 1°, it is mathematically certain that we have travelled this 65 miles not along a flat surface, but along a circle which is 360 times 65, or in round numbers, 24,000 miles in circumference and 8,000 miles in diameter, and if, whenever we travel the same distance on a meridian or line drawn on the circumference from north to south, we find the same displacement of 1°, or one tithi, or 12° of the Moon we may be sure that our journey has been in a true circle and that the form of the earth is a perfect sphere of these dimensions.

Now, this is very nearly what actually occurs when we apply methods of scientific accuracy to measure the earth. The true form of the earth is not exactly spherical but slightly oval or flatter at the poles, being almost precisely the form it would have assumed, if it had been fluid mass rotating about a north and south axis.

But is very nearly spherical, the true polar diameter being 7,899 miles, and the true equatorial diameter 7.925 miles. (Naturally true polar right ascension will be mesha, then the true equatorial right ascension will be Mithuna. Thus the following are the pairs which are Mesha-Mithuna, Vrishabha-Karka, Mithuna-Simha, Karka-Kanya, Simha-Thula, Kanya-Vrischika, Thula-Dhanu, Vrischika-Makara, Dhanu-Kumbha, Makara-Meena, Kumbha-Mesha), so that for practical purposes we may say roughly that the earth is spherical body, 24,000 miles round and 8,000 miles across.

Now we can find out the Lagna (Right ascension) by having part of the birth year and its Rashi. Put the same Rashi in the Birth month. If the birth date falls in the Solar influence month then opening month January will be in the fourth house in current century, and if the birth date falls in the Lunar influence month then the opening month of the year (January) will be in the tenth house. Put rashi in the birth month and you will find the Lagna. First you will find polar rashi. See the other rashi if needed. Now you know the pairs of Polar and Equatorial Rashis. On 180° of the above rashi you will find the female rashi. Suppose Mesha and Mithuna are male rashi, then Thula and Dhanu will be female rashi on that particular day. For the details we will see some examples. But before that we must see the Chamak Sutra of Rudra verse in Yajurveda (See page 323 Chapter VII) 1-3-5-7-9 are positive electrons or positive hormones and 11-13-15-17, that is 2-4-6-8 are negative electrons or negative hormones. Positive hormones mean male sex and negative hormones mean female sex. It clearly means odd numbers are for male and even numbers are for females. Now according to Rgveda verse 1-164-16 (See page 6) the Birth date is first nakshatra, Birth month is second nakshatra and Birth year is third nakshatra. Reduce the number of the date into single digit, reduce the number of the month into single digit, deduct the Saptarishikal from the birth year and reduce it into single digit. See that the number of the date is odd, the number of the month is odd as well as the number of Saptarishikal nakshatra is odd. If the three of them are odd, it is female sex, and if three of them are even it is female sex. One number is odd, and two are even it is male sex, one number is even and two are odd it is male sex.

For example birth date of the native is 28-11-1927. Deduct the Saptarishikal from the birth year 1927. 1927—1908=19, reduce it into single digit 1 plus 9=10=1. The birth month is 11, reduce it into single digit. 1 plus 1=2. See the birth date 28 and reduce it into single digit 2 plus 8=10=1. Now birth date number is one, birth month number is two, birth year number is one, here are two odd numbers and one is even number so it is a male sex. Again take birth date 24.12.1921 1921—1908=13=1 plus 3=4, date 24=2 plus 4=6, Month 12=1 plus 2=3, here are two even numbers and one number is odd. So it is male. According to Ṛgveda verse 1-164-1 "that the sum of the three angles of triangle is 180° degrees" no longer holds on a curved surface, it is always greater upto 4 degrees. Naturally any of the two or three numbers correspond to one another on 180° the male sex should be converted into female, and the female sex must be converted into male sex. The number of date corresponds to the number of month on 180°, or the number of the date corresponds to the Saptarishikal, on 180°, or the number of month corresponds to the number of Saptarishikal on 180°. The male sex is getting change into female and vice-versa.

The following are the corresponding numbers 1-5, 2-6, 3-7, 4-8, 5-9, 6-1, 7-2, 8-3, 9-4, 1-2-3, 2-3-4, 3-4-5, 4-5-6, 5-6-7; 6-7-8, 7-8-9, 8-9-1, 9-1-2, on above groups of the number male sex is getting changed into female sex, and vice-versa. But following groups of the numbers are constant for both the sexes 1-4-7, 2-5-8, 3-6-9 on which you will find twins or male and female sex on the same time. For example birth date is 22.9.1931; birth year 1931-1908=23=2 plus 3=5 is the Saptarishikal, Birth date is 22=2 plus 2=4, Birth month is No. 9, here are two odd numbers and one number is even. Naturally it shows male sex but due to corresponding number 4 and 9 it is female. In this way we can find out the male and female sex.

According to Ṛgveda verse 1-164-12 (see page 5) and the following Ṛgveda verse 1-164-48.

द्वादश प्रधयश्चक्रमेकं त्रीणि नभ्यानि क उ तच्चिकेत
तस्मिन्त्साकं त्रिशतां न शंकवोर्ऽपितो:षष्ठिनं चलाचलास:

Twelve arcs are divisions of the Zodiac. The group of Aswini, the group of Magha and the group of Moola nakshatras are the base of the spokes (360° days) these spokes are constantly moving on the base of three nakshatras, it changes the sex on movement of North and South hemisphere of the sky by a pentagon angle or pancha teja पंचतेज: (See Ṛgveda 1-164-13).

पंचारे चक्रे परिवर्तमाने तस्मिन्नातस्थु: भुवनानि विश्वा
तस्य नाक्ष: तप्यते मूरिभार: सनादेव न शीर्यंते सनाभि:

On that pentagon angle revolving wheel, lie all the worlds. Its heavily loaded axis is not heated nor does it give way from its hub, since it is eternal. Here pentagon angle is taken into consideration as Pancha teja. In this verse the only consideration of Tejotatwa. The axis is not heated nor does it give way from its hubs (due to expansion by the heat).

The following tabular form of the group of three nakshatras will show you the sex and the time of sex.

P = Prithvitatwa, J = Jaltatwa, T = Tejotatwa
V = Vayutatwa, A = Akashtatwa.

Week Day	Time from Sunrise = I.S.T.									
	From-to		From-to		From-to		From-to		From-to	
	H	M	H	M	H	H	H	M	H	M
Sunday and Tuesday	0 to 0	3 21	0 to 0	21 45	0 to 1	45 15	1 to 1	15 21	1 to 1	21 33
	T	male	V	female	A	male	P	male	J	female
Monday and Friday	0 to 0	3 15	0 to 0	15 33	0 to 0	33 57	0 to 1	57 27	1 to 1	27 33
	J	female	T	male	V	female	A	male	P	male
Wednesday	0 to 0	3 9	0 to 0	9 21	0 to 0	21 39	0 to 1	39 3	1 to 1	3 33
	P	male	J	female	T	male	V	female	A	male
Thursday	0 to 0	3 33	0 to 0	33 39	0 to 0	39 57	0 to 1	57 9	1 to 1	9 33
	A	male	P	male	J	female	T	male	V	female
Saturday	0 to 0	3 27	0 to 0	27 57	0 to 1	57 3	1 to 1	3 15	1 to 1	15 33
	V	female	A	female	P	male	J	female	T	male

Asterism Table
Rising Sign

Time from Sunrise Minutes		Moveable			Fixed			Common		
0	3	3	12	21	5	14	23	7	16	25
3	6	4	13	22	6	15	24	8	17	26
6	9	5	14	23	7	16	25	9	18	27
9	12	6	15	24	8	17	26	1	10	19
12	15	7	16	25	9	18	27	2	11	20
15	18	8	17	26	1	10	19	3	12	21
18	21	9	18	27	2	11	20	4	13	22
21	24	1	10	19	3	12	21	5	14	23
24	27	2	11	20	4	13	22	6	15	24

RULE: For the Longitude—add together the sine (given hours) of the body's right ascension, and deduct the hours of the day which is on 180° of the birth day (cosine) and the Sum will be Longitude when turned into degrees and minutes. For the Latitude: Add together the sine (given hours) of the body's declination and the Sum will be the sine of the planet's latitude. Or in simple way see birth year rashi which is in the negative part and see the given hours to the day, convert it into solar degrees and see the Latitude chart for given nakshatra or solar degree to the given day which is on 180°, or on the day of birth.

MEANING OF THE CRITICAL WORDS IN ṚGVEDA

Ṛgveda 1-164-1.

अस्य = ध्रुवस्य =Polar star= विष्णु

Ṛgveda 1-164-2.

त्रिनाभि: =base of trine, Aswini, Magha, Moola.

Ṛgveda 1-164-3.

सप्तचक्रं =wheel of seven days   सप्तवहन्त्यश्वा =seven planets

सप्तस्वसार: =seven tithis   गवां सप्तनाम =seven tithis known as seven cows.

Ṛgveda 1-164-4.

जायमानमस्थन्वन्तं यदनस्थ = अस्थीनि = नक्षत्राणि

This universe coming into existence through cosmic rays.

Ṛgveda 1-164-5.

बभ्रयेअधिसप्ततंतूनओतवाऽउ =who knows the Angles of seven threads (of seven planets) and how to weave पदानि =Angles.

Ṛgveda 1-164-6.

यस्तस्तम्भ =Equator, षळिग्मा =six days षळ+इत+यमा =Latitude 6 in pairs of the planet north or south from the equator.

रजांस्य जस्य =seven planets.

Ṛgveda 1-164-7

वेदास्य=ब्रह्महृदय =on the left hand.

Ṛgveda 1-164-8

बीमत्सु: गर्भरस: =wishing to concieve to carry water.

Ṛgveda 1-164-9.

स्त्रिषुयोजनेषु =Three Zones of Aswini, Magha, Moola.

Ṛgveda 1-164-10

तिस्त्रोमातृस्त्रीन् पितॄन्=Three nakshatras of the Northern hemisphere and three nakshatras of the Southern hemisphere.

Ṛgveda 1-164-11.

Twelve parts. द्वादशारम्

Ṛgveda 1-164-12.

पंचपादं =Pentagon Angle.

सप्तचक्रं =Wheel of seven planets.

षळर =Six Latitude.

Ṛgveda 1-164-13.

पंचारे =Five parts=Pentagon Angle.

Ṛgveda 1-164-14.

दशयुक्तावहन्ति =The Sun is centre of the universe; the wheel of time starts from Moola, that is the Adhana nakshatra and from there ten nakshatra back and fourth he moves.

Ṛgveda 1-164-15.

सप्तयमाहुँरेकजं =Wheel of seven days and Saptarishi born (together) are of one. यमा = द्वेशीर्षे =Northern and Southern hemisphere, See द्वे शिर्षे on page 159.

ॐ सहनाववतु । सहनौ भुनक्तु । सह वीर्यंकरवावहै ।
तेजस्विनावधीतमस्तु मा विद्विषावहै॥ । ॐ शांति: शांति: शांति: ।

इति शम्

SOME OPINIONS

श्री श्री श्रृंगेरी जगद्गुरु महासंस्थानम्, श्रृंगेरी मठ शारदापीठम्
पो. श्रृंगेरी – कड्रूः (मैसूर् स्टेट्)

Sri Sri Sringeri Jagadguru Mahasamsthanam,
Sringeri Math Sharada Peetham
P.O. SRINGERI-KADUR (Mysore State)

N. Lakshminarayana Sastry
Private Secretary

Office of the Private Secretary
to His Holiness the Jagadguru
Sri Shankaracharya of Sri Sringeri
Mutt.

Camp : Vijayawada

Ref. No. 8554/01/68

Date : 10-12-67

श्रीयुतेषु गोविन्द-विष्णु-चौधरीमहोदयेषु सादरा सनतिका च विज्ञप्तिः ।

भवद्भिः सङ्कलितो वेदिक-नुमेरोलॉजि नामको ग्रन्थः अस्मद्धस्ततलमलञ्चकार । श्री-
जगद्गुरुचरणारविन्दयोः निवेदितश्च । श्रीगुरुचरणाश्चेमं ग्रन्थं दृष्ट्वा अत्यन्तं समतुष्यन् । आशासते
चायं ग्रन्थः स्वोपज्ञेन फलावगममार्गेण समेतः । आर्चिकज्यौतिषानुसारी, ऋद्ङ्मन्त्रमूलकश्च ।
यथावत्-फलजिज्ञासूनामुपकारकश्च । सचायं ग्रन्थः श्रीशारदाचन्द्रमौलीश्वरयोः प्रसादमहिम्ना
फलमवजिगमिषूणां हस्ततलमलङ्करोतु । भवन्तश्च श्रेयोभिः चिरं समभिवर्धन्तामिति ।

निवेदयिता

(Sd.) N. Lakshminarayana Sastry
Private Secretary
to His Holiness the Jagadguru
Mahaswamigalavaru of
Sri Sringeri Mutt.

Phonetics Laboratory
Poona, 13.7.1965

I have been strongly impressed with the "Vedic Numerology" of Shri G. V. Chaudhary. Although i is a maiden work of his, it is holding much promise. I find his interpretations of some of the Rg-Vedic Mantras refreshingly original. He has taken great pains to do a stupendous work whether or not other scholars in both the fields of Astronomy and Astrology will agree with all his striking and novel interpretations. Personally speaking, I am very much struck with the attempt of Shri G. V Chaudhary towards synthesising astronomy with astrology. Such a unified outlook, as Shri G. V. Chaudhary possesses, is necessary for any fundamental work. It does credit to Shri G. V. Chaudhary that he has shown all the details in constructing horoscope giving correct dates of births of individuals.

I do hope that the subject of Astrology in the pioneering manner Shri G. V. Chaudhary deals with, will be introduced in all the Indian Universities and that Shri G. V Chaudhary will be given all the necessary facilities to pursue his favourite subject to still profounder levels with his critical acumen and extraordinary brilliance.

C. R. SANKARAN

Reader in Dravidian Philosophy and Experimental Phonetics, Deccan College Research Institute, Poona-6 and Richard-Merton Visiting Professor in the Institute for Phonetics and Communications Science at the University of Bonn, (West Germany) in 1960.

Dr. H. G. Narahari,
M.A., M.Litt., Ph.D.
Deccan College,
Poona 5. Dated 24.7.1965.

I have read with pleasure the manuscript of *Vedic Numerology* by Shri G. V. Chaudhary. There is no doubt of the fact that the Vedic Aryans had a fairly good knowledge of Astronomy. Constantly engaged in the performance of a variety of sacrifices, they had to be familiar with the movement of the stars and planets. As a result the science of Astronomy (Jyautisa) is an important ancillary text of the Vedas (Vedanga). The Vedic Samhitas also mention the names of a number of stars and planets. Astrology, which is the theory of the influence of the stars on human life, has long been associated with Astronomy. The earliest treatise known to represent this combination is the *Vriddha Garga Samhitā*, though the later writer Varāhamihira is better known in this context.

SOME OPINIONS

Shri Chaudhary finds Numerological data in the Veda and its associate texts and has built up a system of his own for prediction and casting of horoscopes. His ambition is to see that the subject receives attention in University circles.

I wish him every success in his efforts.

H. G. NARAHARI

Department of Linguistics, University of Poona; sometime C. Subba Rao Research Scholar, University of Mysore; Fellow in Sanskrit, University of Madras.

Dr. R. N. Vale,
M.A., B.T., Ph.D.

Poona, 27th July 1965.

This is to certify that Shri G. V. Chaudhary, a highly devoted student of the science of Astronomics or the Triskandha Jyotisa which consists of three parts of Horā, Ganita and Siddhānta. By applying the basic principles of Spherical Geometry which, it appears, must have been familiar to the Vedic Seer Dīrghatamas, by his use of terms like Sanku in R.V.I. 164-48, he has been able to explain the significance of the famous RgVedic hymn 'Asya Vāmasya'. His recent work 'Vedic Numerology' is a fresh approach to solve the riddle of the Universe by adopting the hints left by the Vedic Seers. It seeks to establish a definite connection between the astronomical facts and the astrological premises by citing a number of illustrations and cases. The threefold grouping of asterisms is the fulcrum of his thesis; it has made the entire predictive astrology simple, economic and mathematically sound. His interpretations of the Vedic expressions 'Pancapada' and 'Dvādassākrti' Rg. I 164-12 as the revolving pentagon with twelve such figures corresponding to twelve signs of Zodiac or twelve months forming as if the modern Planetarium Box, is simply revolutionary.

The subject of Astronomics, as worded above, touches life at all points. It deserves to be introduced at the University level in India, turning out every year worthy Sāvatsarikas like the Great Varāhamihirācarya, solving our historical, geographical, medical, meteorlogical, economical, political and psychological problems.

I wish Shri Chaudhary every encouragement and facilities for further studies in the science.

R. N. VALE

Ex-Educational Inspector, Class I
Bombay State
At present, Lecturer in Applied
Linguistics, Poona University, Poona.

N.J. Shende,
> M.A., Ph.D., D.Litt.

'Vedic Numerology' by Shri Chaudhary is a book of absorbing interest to a student of Indian Astrology. He has traced some of the ideas of the later Indian Astrology to the Rigveda 1.164, the *asya vāmasya* hymn of the seer, Dīrghatamas.

We find that Sāyaṇa explains the word *dvādasāra* occurring in the RV 1.64.12, as referring to the twelve signs of Zodiac such as *mesa* and others. It is thus possible to suppose that some systematic thought about the *kālacakra* was prevalent in the ancient Sanskrit tradition.

Apart from the Vedic source of the science of Astrology, the various topics having practical bearing will be found useful to a student of the science of Numerology.

Shri Chaudhari deserves every encouragement from the learned bodies interested in the pursuit of knowledge.

10.8.1965

N. J. SHENDE
Bhandarkar Oriental Research Institute, Poona-4.

Bangalore Venkata Raman   Sri Rajeswari,
Editor, *The Astrological Magazine*.   Bangalore-20.

I have perused the book "Vedanga Jyotisha Sankhya Sastra" written by Shri G. V. Chaudhary, with pleasure. I have also had the opportunity of a personal discussion with the author. My first impression is that Shri Chaudhary has shown considerable originality in evolving a certain method of finding the time of birth and important events in life by a combination of Vedic astronomy, astrology and numerology. Simple mathematical methods amenable to easy calculations are employed. I have no doubt the book will prove useful not only to those who wish to learn astrology, but also to astrologers and numerologists.

Shri Chaudhary appears to possess considerable insight into Vedic astronomy and his attempts to evolve a reliable system of prognostication based on ancient techniques are indeed laudable.

I wish the author every success and I hope the public and centres of learning will extend to him the encouragement he richly deserves.

.10th August 1964.

B. V. RAMAN

Dr. A. Sankaran, M.A., Ph.D.   Poona, 2nd Aug. 1965.

Shri G. V. Chaudhary has read out to me and explained portions of his book 'Vedic Numerology'. His book is based upon his interpretation and exposition of some Vedic Suktas and Vedang Jyotish. He has brought to bear on the interpretation and exposition of these texts and subjects of numerology his acute intelligence and superior imagination and the book appears to be a *masterly production* on the subject and I am happy to find that it is wholly based on original Sanskrit-texts.

I am sure his endeavour will be appreciated and will meet with signal success.

A. SANKARAN.

Retired Principal, Government College, Kumbakonam, now Asstt. Editor, Sanskrit Dictionary Department and Honorary Prof. of Sanskrit, Deccan College, Poona-6.

I have gone through Shri Chaudhary's treatise on 'Vedic Numerology' and am so much impressed and struck by the extraordinary method, based on Vedic pronouncements, which he has adopted therein for arriving at the exact time of Lagna and Rashi in astrology and of marriage and death of individuals that I am convinced that Shri Chaudhary is blessed by Providence with a special insight into these matters. His interpretation of the अस्य वामस्य Sukta and certain parts of the Brahmanas is so appropriate and convincing that one is constrained to feel that even the meanings put on them by Acharyas like Yaska and Sayana appear as if foisted on the Vedic *Psalm* on account of their ignorance of the correct interpretations as now put on them by Shri Chaudhary. The old seers have taken the word वाम as equivalent to वामनाय and this would probably be correct in most of the places, but the meaning which Shri Chaudhary has given to the word in the context of the Science of astrology, viz. 'left' which is the usual meaning of the word, strikes one as eminently natural. Shri Chaudhary's plan of publishing in book form, for the benefit of all devotees of the Science and other interested persons, the conclusions which he has reached and the methods of calculation based on the Vedic Numeral Science which he has evolved, with such important bearing on astrology, certainly deserves to be appreciated and supported since he could as well have kept it as his own secret possession. In conclusion, I express the hope that all astrologers will show the good sense and integrity to acknowledge the gratitude which they owe to Shri Chaudhary for his work.

KESHAV BHIKAJI BAPAT
Sanskrit Scholar and Grammarian

Chiplun,
25.2.1966.

JYOTIRVIDYA PARISANSTHA, POONA
Lok. Tilak Smarak Mandir, Poona 2.

I have critically gone through the manuscript of 'Vedic Numerology' by Shri G. V. Chaudhary. His book is based on the basic astronomical phenomena as understood by ancient Indian Scholars. It is revealing to find that the ancients had detected the Oscillation of the ecliptic about the celestial equator and determined its periodicity.

I have nothing to say, about the astrological prediction part of this work. However, one thing must be stressed that the simple numerical—arithmetical methods of working out the positions of the Sun, the Moon and the Planets, to a fair degree of accuracy—developed by Shri Chaudhary appear to be worth consideration.

I wish, he gets all encouragement and help in his work.

Dated: 8.10.1965

M. N. GOKHALE
Hon. Secretary.

M. Katakkar, Astro-Palmist,   Dated: 15.12.1966.
Erandawana, Karve Road,
Poona 4.

Dear Shri Chaudhary,

I have gone through your First Volume on Vedic Numerology. After going through it I feel that the task you have undertaken is huge and it requires great patience to pursue a very critical and abstruse subject such as this.

What pleases me most is that you have brought the hidden meaning of the Vedas on this subject into realisation, which proves the authenticity of our Vedas.

Your work also equals the different (संहिता) Samhitas, such as Surya Samhita, Brighu Samhita etc. in the sense that as these different Sanhitas are the works which depict the life of a person and delineate even the small shades of his life, your work is also equally useful in depicting the various aspects in one's life. The system you have evolved in finding out the dates of the marriages and of deaths is marvellous.

I have no doubt that your work will be a memorial one and will have its own place in history.

M. KATAKKAR
Astro-Palmist.